Stephen Decatur Carpenter

Logic of history

five hundred political texts ; being concentrated extracts of abolitionism

Stephen Decatur Carpenter

Logic of history

five hundred political texts ; being concentrated extracts of abolitionism

ISBN/EAN: 9783744741996

Printed in Europe, USA, Canada, Australia, Japan

Cover: Foto ©ninafisch / pixelio.de

More available books at **www.hansebooks.com**

COMMENDATIONS.

We are indebted to our brethern of the Press, and many friends, for the most flattering commendations of our compilation of the "Logic of History," &c., and we make room for the following, as samples of the general whole:

[From Gov. Seymour, of New York.]

STATE OF NEW YORK, EXECUTIVE DEPARTMENT, }
Albany, January 18th, 1864. }

SIR:—I have read with great interest that part of your book entitled, "Five Hundred Political Texts," which you sent me. I do not hesitate to say that it is a work which every friend of Constitutional Liberty should have in his possession. No one who cares for public events can be without it. It is not only of great importance at this time in its bearings upon the questions of the day, but it is also a valuable contribution to the history of evils which now afflict our country. I hope that it will be widely circulated, and that all classes of conservative men will aid in its sale.   Truly yours, &c.,
HORATIO SEYMOUR.
To S. D. Carpenter, Esq., Madison, Wisconsin.

From the Conservative Members of the Wisconsin Legislature.]

SENATE AND ASSEMBLY CHAMBERS, }
CAPITOL OF WISCONSIN, Feb. 13, 1863. }

S. D. CARPENTER:

The undersigned Democratic members of the Legislature of Wisconsin for the year 1864, having read your book so far as completed, entitled "Concentrated Extracts of Abolitionism" or "Logic of History," beg leave to assure you that your efforts in producing a book so much needed in a crisis like this, is duly appreciated by us. This book ought to be in the hands of every conservative man, for nothing can be so well calculated to open the eyes of the people to the long cherished aims and purposes of the radicals. Your book settles the question of "loyalty," and we trust you may succeed in placing it in the hands of all conservative men.

SENATORS.

John E. Thomas, 1st Dist.   H. P. Reynolds, 6th Dist.
Fred. S. Ellis, 2d Dist.   W. K. Wilson, 5th Dist.
G. L. Frost, 15th Dist.   Fred. O. Thorp, 4th Dist.
Sat. Clark, 33d Dist.   John R. Bohan, 3d Dist.
J. H. Earnest, 13th Dist.   J. D. Clapp, 23d Dist.
Joseph Vilas, Jr., 19th Dist.

REPRESENTATIVES.

O. F. Jones, Dodge County.   Geo. B. Smith, Dane.
A. S. Sanborn, Dane.   W. J. Abrams, Brown.
E. McGarry, Milwaukee.   Carl Zillier, Sheboygan.
David Smoke, Manitowoc.   Robt. Hase, Jefferson.
Max. Bachuber, Dodge.   Robt. Cochrane, Marquette.
J. W. Eviston, Milwaukee.   Thos. Thornton, Manitowoc.
Wm. Costigan, Waukesha.   David, Knab, Milwaukee.
Thomas McLean, Calumet.   T. Dunn, Lafayette.
Geo.[Kreis, Outagamie.   James Watts, Milwaukee.
John G. Daily, Dodge.   Anton Frey, Milwaukee.
H. Hildebrandt, Washington   W.T. Bonniwell, Jr., Ozaukee
B. Ringle, Marathon.   F. T. Zettlor, Miwankee.
N. Boutin, Kewaunee.

[From the Hon. L. B. Vilas, Chairman of the State Union Committee, of Wisconsin,]

MADISON, Feb. 1st, 1864.

S. D. CARPENTER, ESQ.

Sir: The facts contained in your "Logic of History," ought to be read and pondered by every American citizen. Fanaticism and extreme views both North and South, together with public corruption, are the fruitful sources of our national troubles.

The sooner we learn the true causes and correct them, the sooner we shall have national unity, and its consequent blessings. If the people desire peace and unity, they must cease to do those things which inevitably produces strife and disunion. The logic of all history proves that with nations as well as individuals, what they sow they will reap. Trusting that the people in both sections will see the folly of thrusting their extreme opinions upon the other, and that your work may tend to produce this result,

I am very truly Yours &c.
LEVI B.. VILAS.

[From the Waukesha Democrat.]

"LOGIC OF HISTORY" OR "SCRAPS FROM MY SCRAP BOOK."
—This is the the title of a work about to be published by S. D. Carpenter, Esq., editor of the *Wisconsin Patriot*.—This work will be an invaluable book of reference, of some 360 pages, neatly printed and bound, containing five hundred political texts. In this work the author goes back to slavery in ancient times, and lays bare the effects of slavery agitation and abolitionism to the present time; the desire of leading abolitionists to excite a war of the sections, and their encouragement of secession by acts and words, are all placed before the reader, properly indexed for convenience of speakers and others.

A copy of this work should be in the hands of every man.

[From the Milwaukee News.]

"THE LOGIC OF HISTORY."—Mr. Carpenter, of the Madison *Patriot*, has compiled in an attractive shape a series of political facts, bearing upon the principal public questions of the day. He proposes to publish them in a book of 350 pages, conveniently arranged in chapters and designed for reference in the approaching presidential campaign. It will be conveniently indexed for the use of editors, speakers and others, and be sold at the low price of $1 50 per copy.

A publication of this character cannot fail to exert a salutary influence and prove a valuable record for reference.

[From the Chicago Times.]

S. D. Carpenter, the editor of the Madison (Wisconsin) *Patriot*, is preparing for publication in book form a work called " Logic of History, or Scraps from my Scrap Book." The work includes political affairs from the beginning of the slavery agitation to the present time, and consists mainly of the utterances of prominent men and newspapers in the abolitio-republican party, showing that it inaugurated and nurtured the treason which finally ruptured the Union. The work will be a *vade mecum* for democratic editors, speakers, and all classes of conservative people.

[From the Ozaukee Advertiser.]

THE LOGIC OF HISTORY.—Being Concentrated Extracts from my Scrap Book, containing Five Hundred Political Texts. By S. D. Carpenter, Editor of the *Wioconsin Patriot*.   *   *   *   *   *
The foregoing sufficiently indicates the character of the work, and make it evident that it is just the best thing published for the purpose of carrying the campaign right into the camp of the enemy. It ought to be in the hands of every man who can talk, and if you are attacked by the abolition demagogues with their usual weapons, "secessionist," "traitor," "copperhead," just give them a shot from "The Logic of History," and our word for it they will *skedaddle*, or if they don't there won't be enough left of them politically to make a grease spot. The work will be properly indexed for the convenience of editors, speakers and others.

[From the Shullsburg Local.]

SOMETHING WHICH EVERY DEMOCRAT SHOULD HAVE.—S. D. Carpenter, of the Madison *Patriot*, has in process of publication a most valuable work, " Logic of History, or Scraps from my Scrap Book," which should be in the hands of every democrat. At this time it is of immense value, as it contains a complete expose of the efforts of the abolitionists to destroy the Union, going back over a period of more than forty years. We cannot recommend it too highly. It is particularly valuable at this time, when we must defend the position we occupy by facts, not idle declamation.

1

[From the Manitowoc Pilot.]

"THE LOGIC OF HISTORY."--Mr. Carpenter, of the Madison *Patriot*, has been publishing in his paper for several months past, extracts from republican papers, and speeches from republican orators for years, clearly showing that they are responsible for the commencement of the existing rebellion, and its continuance to the present time. He is now preparing to print them in book form under the above title, and the work will be published some time this month. A copy of it should be in the hands of *every man* who loves the Union.

[From the Jefferson Banner.]

This book is intended for the use of editors and public speakers, and it should be in the hands of every Democrat in the country. Whoever has a copy of this work in his possession, need not fear to be called "traitor," "copperhead," and the like, for all he has to do will be to pull the volume out of his pocket, and cram a few Abolition sentences down the throats of those who assail him, and they will soon learn to let him alone.

[From the Fond du Lac Press.]

"CONCENTRATED EXTRACTS OF ABOLITIONISM" is the title of a new book soon to be issued from the press of the Madison *Patriot*. We have had the benefit of its contents published in the *Patriot*, and do not hesitate to say that it will be of great value as a book of reference.

[From the Mineral Point Intelligencer.]

The work will be valuable, and should be in the hands of every man who desires to keep himself posted in political affairs. The cost is trifling compared with its value, and who desire it should send for it at once. Single copies $1 50.

[From the Monroe County Democrat.]

The title of the work is "Scraps from my Scrap Book," and from a look at the table of contents, it appears to us a work of extraordinary merit for purposes of reference, and one which should be in the hands of every editor, politician and public speaker in the country. It gives a succinct documentary history of political abolition, secession, nullification, etc. It will contain some 350 pages closely printed, with a complete index, so that any extract may be readily referred to.

[From the Beaver Dam Argus.]

LOGIC OF HISTORY.—S. D. Carpenter, of the Madison *Patriot*, is compiling a work for the use of politicians, under the above title, which will contain some 350 pages, composed of the sayings of leading politicians and newspapers, and is particularly intended for the use of speakers and editors in the campaign next summer. For that purpose it will be just the thing, being divided into chapters and properly indexed. Some fifteen chapters have already been published in the *Patriot*, and from an examination of them, we would advise every democrat to procure this volume. Then if he is attacked by an abolitionist with the usual cry of "secessionist," "traitor," "rebel sympathizer," &c., he can straightway give a "solid shot" from "The Logic of History," which will cause any abolitionist to "retreat in disorder." It is the first work of the kind ever published in this state, and should be largely circulated by the democrats of Wisconsin.

Terms—Single copies $1.50; five copies to one address, each $1.40; Ten $1.30. Postage and other charges extra.

[P. S.—It will be seen that different parties refer to our work under different titles, which will be readily explained by the plurality of titles to the work itself, but which did not accompany its newspaper publication.]

LOGIC OF HISTORY.

FIVE HUNDRED POLITICAL TEXTS:

BEING

CONCENTRATED EXTRACTS OF ABOLITIONISM;

ALSO, RESULTS OF

SLAVERY AGITATION AND EMANCIPATION;

TOGETHER WITH SUNDRY CHAPTERS ON

DESPOTISM, USURPATIONS AND FRAUDS.

By S. D. CARPENTER,
EDITOR OF THE "WISCONSIN PATRIOT."

SECOND EDITION.

MADISON, WIS., 1864:
S. D. CARPENTER, PUBLISHER

Entered according to Act of Congress, in the year
one thousand eight hundred and sixty-four,

BY S. D. CARPENTER,

in the Clerk's Office of the District Court of the
United States, for the State of Wisconsin.

A WORD FOR MYSELF.

A PREFACE to a book is often synonymous with *excuses*, and I will render mine as briefly as possible. I have compiled this work, not with a view to win literary fame, though perhaps few, who have acquired the knowledge by experience, will deny me at least a modest claim to considerable research and laborious application; for, in truth I could have produced a volume of more than double the proportions of this, with less labor and painstaking, had I reduced it to a commentary on the subjects which it embraces. But, for the purposes intended, it was necessary to present the language employed by those who are herein represented. This I have done as tersely as possible, without perverting the sentiments uttered. The task has been an herculean one. The difficulty has not been *what to insert*, but *what to leave out*, lest I should compile a volume of too ponderous proportions, for it would have been much easier to have compiled 2,000 pages, without diminishing the interest. My whole aim has been to present to the conservatives of the country a useful and convenient digest of the sayings and doings of the Northern Disunionists for the last sixty-five years, together with a synopsis of the slavery agitation and results of emancipation, from the halcyon days of Rome down to the present time—embracing a statistical, didactic and editorial compendium of that restless spirit of meddling agitation that has ruined the fairest governments on earth. I have presented the *evidence* of Northern disunion and treason, in a convenient and tangible form, that the same may be demonstrated to the people who now suffer in consequence of these causes:—
1st. By Editors through the press.
2d. By public speakers from the rostrum.
3d. By citizens, among the masses—in the school house and other gatherings, and in private discussions.

The conduct of this war, from the highest official to the lowest parasite of power, has been such as to be as personally offensive as possible to all conservatives, by the use approbious epithets, such as "Traitor"—"Copperhead," &c. With this work in his possession, no Democrat need fear these epithets, for if he will compel his assailant to endure the infliction to read or listen to a few choice paragraphs herein, the insult will hardly be repeated; for, the following pages constitute a bomb-proof battery—an "iron clad" torpedo—that will be dangerous to trifle with.

For fifteen years I have been selecting and preserving in scrap book form, the within evidences of republican guilt, until I had created quite a "library" of scrap books. I was aware years ago that these scraps would one day become valuable. I was offered, during the political canvass of 1863, a large sum for my first volume of Scraps, and it occurred to me that if one of my many volumes was prized so highly, there were few that would not esteem it a privilege to pay $1.50 for the *cream of them all*.

All the libraries in the "Union as it was," might be searched in vain for the contents of this book. The same might be found mostly in the newspaper files of the last seventy years, but it would require a practiced antiquarian years of research to hunt up and codify these extracts from original sources, at an expense wholly inadequate to any probable remuneration. Possessing these extraordinary facilities, I have compiled this work both from the dictates of duty and hope of reward. I do not warrant it free from errors; for, in addition to my other duties of publishing a Daily and Weekly Newspaper, &c., I have without assistance, copied, codified and arranged the work each evening, as needed for the printers the next day, nor have I been able to re-examine a single sheet of "copy," previous to its use at the case. Still, I am quite sure I have done no injustice to the authors of the extracts, except, perhaps, in some unimportant typographical errors, that readily suggest themselves.

While I have endeavored to link together the various extracts in argumentative arrangement, I have, with but few exceptional cases, employed no more of my own language and sentiments than were necessary to a proper application and introduction of the sentiment or fact quoted.

Another reason for presenting this work, is, that during the canvass of 1863, I printed the first edition of 10,000 copies in pamphlet form, which were soon disposed of in all parts of the North, with no effort on my part, save a notice that a work of that character was for sale, and even after the last copy was sent as per order, I continued to receive orders from Wisconsin, Pennsylvania, Illinois, Iowa, Minnesota, Indiana, New York and other States, until calls for more than 6,000 accumulated on my table, beyond my power to fill. I commenced this edition in November last, to meet this demand, and already, before the first copy is bound, I have orders for more than two-thirds of my entire edition. I am making arrangements for issuing a 2d edition to supply the general demand, which I am in hopes to issue some time in June or July next.

To the conservatives of the country this work is especially dedicated, as the aggregation of guilt and treason of seventy years accumulation—to be by them exhibited as a living panorama of "disloyal practices" by the opponents of Democracy—lest the treason of these marplots may be overlooked, amid the din of their pharisaical protestations of "we-are-holier-than-thou" loyalty. These martinets of power must not be permitted to deceive the people with their "stop thief" cry of "*we are loyal*"—"*you are disloyal*"—when the evidences of their own guilt are so overwhelming. A sure antidote to their poison is to be found in this volume, which will have the good effect to rid the truly loyal possessor of the insults of that reptile tribe of arrogant, self-righteous bores, who breed in the sunshine of power—fatten on the sweat of honest toil, and parrot-like chatter virtues they never possessed.

To those who have known me for years, it is unnecessary to offer assurances that I am, as I have been from the start, in favor of the most "vigorous" prosecution of the war to crush the rebellion. I believe this can be done under the Constitution, and in the mean time preserve personal and civil liberty. I am, as I ever have been, opposed to secession, disunion, and treason—especially Abolitionism, believing that the latter combines the trinity of the former. I have no apology to offer for the rebellion, and am in favor of punishing all traitors—am opposed to any peace purchased at the expense of the honor and inalienable rights of loyal people, and am in favor of any peace—the sooner it comes the better—that shall secure the Union of our fathers, and be honorable in its terms, and believe that any sensible, conservative man would be an improvement on Mr. LINCOLN for President.

The "Shakesperean Irrepressible Conflict," which follows the general order of this work, I offer *gratis*—not as a specimen of literary genius, but in accordance with a promise made at the repeated requests of many of my friends. I attach no particular importance to it, for it was all prepared during the three last evenings of 1862, as a "message" for the carriers of my paper. It was only intended as a humorous salmagundi, to represent the "rise, progress and decline of the one idea." I may, without arrogance, however, claim for it this merit—a truthful, even though crude, reflex of transpiring facts.

With the foregoing "explanations," I offer the work to all those who would study the *great cause* of all the evils that now afflict this sorely oppressed people.   S. D. CARPENTER.

MADISON, Wis., February, 1864.

CONTENTS.

CHAPTER I.

EFFECTS OF ANCIENT SLAVERY AGITATION, ETC.

Application of the "Logic of History"—Effect of Early Slavery Agitation—Slavery in Ancient Times—Slavery Agitation in Rome—Its Terrible Effects: Agitation the Cause of the Downfall of the Roman Empire—Greece and her Dependencies Destroyed by Slavery Agitation—The Agitation in France—Bloody Effects of, in St. Domingo—BRISSOT, and other French Abolitionists, stir up the "Irrepressible Conflict"—A Servile Insurrection Ensues—Napoleon Issues a "Proclamation of Freedom"—Terrible Disasters follow the same—A French Army Destroyed—Servile Insurrection in St. Domingo—GIBBON, the Historian, on the Character of the Negro: their Fall from Ancient Superiority—McKENZIE, the Historian, on the "Cause" in the West Indies—Statistics of St. Domingo—The Sublime Teachings of History.

CHAPTER II.

EFFECTS AND INCIDENTS OF AGITATION IN THE WEST INDIES.

Agitation of the Slavery Question in England...Abolition of the Slave Trade...English Philanthropists Define their Position against immediate Emancipation...Abolition of Slavery in the British West Indies: Effects of such Emancipation...Testimony of Anti-Slavery men...Decline of Commerce...Destruction of Agriculture...The Negroes Tending to Heathenism...Valuable Statistics respecting Hayti...Indolence and Destitution of the Negroes...Present Condition of Hayti...Abolition Testimony...The Results of Emancipation in Jamaica...Census and Statistics...Great Falling Off in Products...Estates Going to Decay...The Negro Receding into a Savage State....The Public Debt Increasing....The "London Times" Owns Up...Dr. CHANNING's Prophecy not Fulfilled...TROLLOP and the "London Times"....Negroes will not render Voluntary Labor...Testimony of numerous Abolitionists, showing the Effects of Emancipation in the West Indies...Effect in Mexico...Mr. LINCOLN's Opinion...Statistics Applicable to the Question in the West Indies and the United States...General Conclusions, etc.

CHAPTER III.

HISTORY OF CAUSES OF WAR.

Slavery not the *Cause* of the War...Illustrations showing the Absurdity of the Claim that it is...Henry Ward Beecher declares the Constitution to be the Cause...Senator Douglas' Testimony...Alex. Stevens' Views...The Rebel Iverson on the "Cause"...Gov. Rhett on ditto ...The Rebel Benjamin, with Republican aid, *creates* a "Cause"...The Constitution the "Cause"...Early Times ...The Three Parties in 1786...Alex. Hamilton's "Strong Government"...Early Opposition to the Constitution...Vote close in some of the State Conventions...The Four Rebellions...Shays' Rebellion...South Carolina Rebellion in 1832—The great Abolition Rebellion...The great Southern Rebellion of 1861...What the Cause of the War... Abolition Petitions for Dissolution...A Public Debt a Public Blessing...The object to Destroy the Government ...Know-Nothingism as an Element to Wreck the Government by placing Power in the hands of its Destroyers...Numerous Extracts in Proof...Treason of the Clergy in 1814..Treason of the Federals in 1814...Support of the Government "Reprobated" by Federal Reprobates, &c.

CHAPTER IV.

DISUNION OF EARLY GROWTH.

Early Clamors for a Northern Confederacy...the Pelham Publication...Crusade Against Slavery in 1796...Its Baseness and Untruthfulness exhibited by CAREY, in 1814...The Federal Argument to show that Dissolution was close at hand...Early Caricatures of the North to stimulate Sectional Hatred...Falsity of the Agitators' statements...Comparison of Northern and Southern support of Government...The odious comparisons continued...Republican papers and the President's Message ...Section arrayed against Section.

CHAPTER V.

THE GREAT NEW ENGLAND CONSPIRACY.

New England Money Kings endeavor to Bankrupt the Government...Testimony of a Cotemporary...The Clergy in the Conspiracy...Consequence of the Conspiracy...Depreciation of Bank and Government Stocks...Mr. CAREY'S Statement...The Secret Federal Leagues...Monied men banded against the Government...Reign of Terror...Citizens dare not subscribe for Government Loan openly... Threats and Intimidations by the Federals...Treason of the Federals in buying and selling English Bills...The Sedition Law...Its object to crush out Free Discussion... Difference between MADISON and LINCOLN...Leading Federals Gazetted...Object of the Sedition Law...We, the Government, in 1798...Damn the Government in 1814... The Pious Rev. Federals curse the Government...Views of JEFFERSON and WEBSTER, &c.

CHAPTER VI.

PROOFS OF FEDERAL TREASON.—CONTINUED.

Tone of the Federals when in Power...Similar to the Tone of Those now in Power...Congregational Ministers' Address to President ADAMS...Extract from Sermon of Rev. JEDIDAH MORSE...Extracts from Sermon by Rev. F. S. F. GARDNER, 1812...Extracts from Discourses of Rev. Dr. OSGOOD, 1810...The Clamors of New England for Separation and Dissolution..."Extracts of Treason"...From Boston Centinel, Dec. 10, 1814...From same Dec. 14, 1814...Sundry other extracts from same...Ipswich Memorial...Deerfield, (Mass.) Petition...From the Crisis, No. 3...From the Federal Republican, 1814...Extract from Address to the Hartford Convention, &c...From Boston Daily Advertiser, 1814...From Federal Republican, 1814...Extracts from proceedings of a Treasonable Meeting in Reading, Mass...Also from Memorial of citizens of Newburyport to the Legislature—From Federal Republican, Nov. 7, 1814...From Boston Gazette...From Sermon of Rev. DAVID OSGOOD...Also from his Address before the Legislature...Extracts from a treasonable letter from Federals to JAMES MADISON...From Boston Repertory...From New York Commercial Advertiser.

CHAPTER VII.

OPPOSITION TO THE MEXICAN WAR—LIKE FATHER, LIKE SON—LIKE FEDERAL, LIKE WHIG.

Treasonable opposition to the Mexican War...Mr. LINCOLN charges the "Government" with being in the "wrong" ...CALEB B. SMITH glories in voting to condemn the war ...GIDDINGS would "not vote a man or a dollar"...The Press of 1848 on the War...From the Warren Chronicle ...Xenia Torch Light...Lebanon Star...Cincinnati Gazette ...Kennebeck Journal...New Hampshire Statesman... Haverhill Gazette...Boston Sentinel...Boston Atlas... Boston Chronotype...New York Tribune...North American...Baltimore Patriot...Louisville Journal...Nashville Gazette...Mt. Carmel Register, &c.,...Also CORWIN'S "bloody hands" diatribe, &c.

CHAPTER VIII.

FURTHER SCHEMES IN THE PROGRESS OF DISSOLUTION EXPOSED.

The efforts to create a public debt to hasten the "Strong Government" ... Mr. KING'S $2,000,000 gift, as a "means"...RANDOLPH opposed...CALHOUN, as a means to an end, votes against his party...Purpose of the "Fragments of the Whig party"...Continued efforts to dissolve the Union...The Slavery issue used as a lever...The warnings of JEFFERSON...The Slavery Agitation "the death knell of the Union"...Warnings of WASHINGTON ...The voice of JACKSON...of HARRISON, &c.

CHAPTER IX.

EFFORTS AT COMPROMISE—WHO RESPONSIBLE.

The Statement of Douglas...His last Letter...Senator Pugh's Statement...Endorsed by Douglas...Chicago Tribune wouldn't Yield an Inch...The Peace Congress... Efforts of Republicans to Hush it Up...Senator Chandler's "Blood-letting" Epistle, &c.

CHAPTER X.

THE MOTIVE FOR PRECIPITATING A CONFLICT.

Who Responsible for bringing on a Clash of Arms...The Administration resort to a "Trick" to Force the Rebels to Commence the Attack...Letter from the Hon. Harlow S. Orton...His charges of a "Trick" proved by Extracts from...The New York Times...Charleston Mercury...New York Tribune, &c.,...The United States Armada take no part to Relieve Major Anderson...New York Post details the Trick...Radicals Prophesying an Easy and Early Victory...Seward's Promise to deliver up Sumter.

CHAPTER XI.

PROGRESS AND EVIDENCE OF THE NORTHERN CONSPIRACY.

The Radicals conspire to overthrow the Government long before the Rebellion of 1861...DOUGLAS' testimony on this point...JOHN BROWN Raid originated in Kansas... Col. Jamison's testimony...Col. F. P. Blair on the cause of the war...Abolitionists and Secessionists united...Mr. Seward's testimony...Parson Brownlow on the designs of the Abolitionists...Thurlow Weed on the "Chief Architects" of the Rebellion...Abolitionists of New York Invite Southern Secessionists to join them...Massachusetts for Dissolution in 1851...Also in 1856...Ben. Wade Declares there was no Union...Garrison's "Covenant with Hell"...Republicans of Green County, Wis., "Pledged to Revolutionize the Government"...Anson Burlingame for a New Deal all Round...David Wilmot on Dissolution ...Wendell Phillips again...Lowell Republicans for Dissolution...Massachusetts Petitions for Dissolution... James Watson Webb for using "Fire and Sword"...Boston Free Soilers, 1854...Charles Sumner bound to Disobey law...The True American pronounces a Negro "Worth all the Unions on God's Earth"—Another Massachusetts Petition for Dissolution...Dissolution Resolution by Anti-Slavery Society...Another from same source...Disunion again in Massachusetts...From Redmund's Speech...Wendell Phillips labors nineteen years to Break up the Union...Parker Pillsbury labored twenty years to destroy the Union...Stephen Foster dissuading young men from enlisting in this Unholy War, &c.

CHAPTER XII.

PROGRESS OF THE NORTHERN CONSPIRACY— (CONTINUED).

Charles Sumner Advises Nullification and Disobedience to the Laws...Claims the Republican Party as Sectional, and suited to his Purpose...Greeley's Insult to the Flag : The "Flaunting Lie"...Is this an Abolition War?...Testimony of Gov. Stone, of Iowa...Statement of M. B. Lowry...Phillips on Secession..."Chicago Tribune and the Tax Bill...Extracts from a Massachusetts Pamphlet...Abuse of the Framers of the Constitution... Similarity between Northern and Southern Disunionists.

CHAPTER XIII.

DISUNION OF NORTHERN GROWTH.

Disunion began in the North...Admission by Wendell Phillips...The War brought on by the North as a Means to an End...The Kansas Imbroglio...Stimulated by the Radicals to Aid Secession and Disunion—Helper's "Impending Crisis" as a Means to hasten Dissolution...Mr. Seward Endorses its "Logical Analogies"—Treasonable Kansas War Meeting in Buffalo—Gerrit Smith and Gov. Reeder Stimulate the "Cause"...Beecher on Shooting at Men...Charles Sumner admits the Northern Conspiracy.

CHAPTER XIV.

THE JOHN BROWN RAID ENDORSED BY THE REPUBLICANS.

Seward, Hale and Wilson Toasted by the Louisville "Journal" for not exposing the John Brown Raid...John Brown's operations a part of the Dissolution Scheme... Numerous Extracts to prove that Republicans endorsed the John Brown Raid...Republican Press, Clergy and Orators endorse it...From "La Crosse Republican"... Rev. De Los Love...Rev. E. D. Wheelock..."Milwaukee Sentinel"..."Elkhorn Independent"..."Janesville Gazette"...Telegraphic Despatches, 1859..."Winsted Herald"...Speech of J. W. Phillips...Laconic Letter and Reply, between Elder Spooner and an Editor...Massachusetts Resolution...Meeting in Rockford, Ill....100 Guns Fired in Albany, N. Y....Theodore Parker's Formula...Indignation Meeting in Milwaukee : their Resolutions, etc. ...Rev. Geo. W. Bassett, of Ill....Telegram from New York...Horace Greeley on John Brown— "Milwaukee Free Democrat"...Speech of Rev. Mr. Staples, Milwaukee...Emerson at Tremont Temple...Rev. M. P, Kinney..."Menasha Conservator "..."Milwaukee Atlas "..." New York Tribune "..." Wood County (Wis.) Reporter "...A Prophetic Article from the "New York Herald "...Brown's Character in Kansas, by the "Herald of Freedom "—General Conclusions, &c.

CHAPTER XV.

WISCONSIN NULLIFICATION AND SECESSION.

The Four Shocks of Secession : 1st, New England ; 2d, South Carolina ; 3d, Wisconsin ; 4th, The Confederate

CONTENTS.

States...Wisconsin Bids "Positive Defiance" to the General Government...Constitutional Provisions Relative to Judicial Decisions...A Premeditated Conspiracy to take Wisconsin Out of the Union...Complete Chronological History of the Booth Case, and Judicial Action thereon...The Federal Supreme Court declare that Wisconsin was the First to Set Up the Supremacy of the State over the Federal Court...Republicans Break Open Arsenal, and Seize Arms to Defy the Power of the Government...Judge Paine's "Eloquent Extract"...Opposition to Law Placed Judge P. on the Bench...The Rescue Leaguers...Republican Meeting to Denounce Law...Judge Crawford Opposed solely because he felt Bound by the Decision of the Federal Court...The Constitution Quoted...Lloyd Garrison declares Fugitive Law Constitutional, but Defies It..."Milwaukee Sentinel" on Habeas Corpus and Jury Trial for Negroes...Opposition to the General Government a Political Test...The "Wisconsin State Journal" on said Test...Various Republican Papers on the Test...Judge Smith's Opinion... No Precedent to Sustain It...What Senator Howe said... Judge Smith Scouts the Consequences of His Own Acts ...The Seven Points as Proof...The "State Journal" declares "Dissolution no Misfortune"...Republicans Resolve to "Revolutionize the Government"...Republican Papers for Dissolution...To Sustain the Decision of the Federal Court declared a Crime...Republicans claim that Judge Paine was elected expressly to Defy the Federal Court...Disunionists in Mass Convention...General Government again Defied...Republicans endorse Southern Nullification...Wisconsin Legislature "Positively Defies" the Federal Government...Substitute to Sustain the Government Voted Down...Doolittle's Views...Northern Nullification a Twin of Southern Nullification... Wisconsin endorses South Carolina and South Carolina endorses Wisconsin.

CHAPTER XVI.

REPUBLICANS TRUE TO OLD FEDERAL INSTINCTS.

Classification of parties, principles and arguments, from 1798 to 1863...Thurlow Weed on Greeley...New York Tribune favors Secession...Greeley advocating Peace with Rebels...Mr. Lincoln Advocates the right of Secession...The Republican Congress vote down a Resolution against a Dictatorship...The Ayes and Noes on that Subject...The Constitution again the "Cause of all our Troubles"...Complete overthrow of the Public Liberties ...From the New York World...Republicans Raise a "Higher Standard than the Stars and Stripes"...Prefer "Their principles to Fifty Unions"...Who Discourage Enlistments...Reference to Abolition Votes in Congress.

CHAPTER XVII.

ABOLITION DISLOYALTY AND TREASON.

Extracts from Speeches and Sayings: by John A. Bingham...A. O. Riddle...Owen Lovejoy...Wm. Davis...F. A. Pike...W. P. Cutler...J. M. Ashley...J. P. C. Shanks ...John Huchings...F. A. Conway...C. F. Sedgwick... Benj. Wade...J. R. Rice...G. W. Julian...Thad. Stevens ...J. P. Hale (Petitions for Disunion)...David Wilmot ...Horace Mann...Wendell Phillips...Lowell Republicans..."Boston Liberator"...J. Watson Webb...Boston Free Soilers...Charles Sumner..."True American '... ' Hampshire Gazette"...Programme of Revolution... Senator Wilson...R. P. Spaulding...Erastus Hopkins... H. M. Addison...Abolitionists of Massachusetts...R. W. Emerson...Horace Greeley...H. Ward Beecher...S. P. Chase...Fred Douglas...Redpath...Rev. Chas. E. Hodges ...Lloyd Garrison..."N. Y. Tribune "...Wm. O. Duvall ...Geo. Banks...Anson Burlingame...Rev. Dr. Bellows... Ingersoll, of Ill....Defeat of the Crittenden Compromise ...Vote in the Senate...Policy of Won't-Yield-an-Inch... Treasonable Correspondence between M. D. Conway and J. M. Mason...F. A. Conway's Treasonable Speech in Congress... Also, his Treasonable Letter to the "N. Y. Tribune"...Garrison's Speech in Philadelphia...Extract from "Wisconsin Puritan."

CHAPTER XVIII.

MORE REPUBLICAN VOMITINGS OF DISUNION AND TREASON

The True Object of the War [the Negro] Avowed by the "N. Y. Independent"...Beecher and the "Sheepskin Parchment"...Nest Eggs of Treason: Laid by Wendell Phillips, Lloyd Garrison, Abraham Lincoln, American Anti-Slavery Society, F. E. Spinner, J. S. Pike; another by Phillips and Garrison; and one by the "Chicago Tribune"...Ingersoll invests Lincoln with the Power of the Czar of Russia...J. W. Forney on silencing "Laws and Safeguards"...The Abolition Conspiracy in the New York Riots: Important Testimony...The Union Not Worth Preserving...Tricks of the Ohio Abolitionists...The Revolutionary Spirit at Work..."New York Tribune" advocating Mobs and Riots against Law... Sen. Howe would "Do in the Name of God what can't be done in the Name of the Constitution"...Phillips, Peace and Dissolution...This War a "Barbarian Conquest."

CHAPTER XIX.

THE ADMINISTRATION UNDER THE BAN OF /THE "BALANCE OF POWER."

Power and Influence of the Abolitionists over the Administration...The Leading Abolitionists Feted and Provided with Place and Power...Superstition and Intolerance... 1796, 1800, 1814 and 1864 Compared...The Bigotry and Intolerance of To-Day Borrowed from the Pilgrims—A Chapter from the Puritans...Blue Lights and Blue Laws ...The Act Suspending the Writ of Habeas Corpus, in full...Ayes and Noes on said Bill, Politically Classified... "New York Tribune" on Peace...Oh! Abe and the "Union as it was," &c.

CHAPTER XX.

DISLOYALTY OF REPUBLICANS—THE GREAT ROUND-HEAD CONSPIRACY.

Threats to Force Mr. Lincoln to Issue the Proclamation... From "New York Independent"..."Chicago Tribune" Against the "Union as It Was"; also, its Threat to use Bayonets in Defiance of the People...The Radical Conspiracy of 1862...Disclosures of the Round-Head Plot...Suggestions of the "Boston Courier"; also, from an Albany Paper...The "St. Louis Anzeiger" Reveals the Plot...The "N. Y. Observer" Gives a Clue to It... Gov. Ramsey, of Minnesota, on "Machinations of Home Governments," &c......" Legalized Treason "......From "Boston Courier"...The Second Hartford Convention Toasted...Chas. Sumner Teaches Revolution...Mr. Seward Boasts of More Despotic Power than the Queen of England dare Exercise...Thad. Stevens declares the Constitution an "Absurdity"...Republicans Cheering for Dissolution...Republicans for "Extermination and Damnation"...The "Boston Commonwealth" Denounces Restoration a Crime...The "South Not Worth a Copper"..." Boston Commonwealth" Curses the "Union as It Was"...Bingham Don't Want the Cotton States... The Constitution Committed to the Flames by Garrison ...Senator Henkle and Vallandigham...Destruction of the Constitution a Test of Loyalty...God and the Negro... Beecher Declares that the Negro is our "Forlorn Hope" ...Republican Bloodthirstiness...Jim Lane would send all the White Men to "Hell"..."Chicago Tribune" Down on the "Union as It Was"...Amalgamation and Negro Equality...Fred. Douglas and White Women...Wendell Phillips Thanks God for Defeat..."N. Y. Tribune" Defies the National Government—Den. Wade on Dissolution...The Seceding States follow Den.'s Advice...C. M. Clay "Spots the Union as It Was"...Beecher Ridicules the "Sheepskin Parchment"...Daniel Webster on the "Grasp of Executive Power"..."Democrats Must Not Clamor for the Union as It Was "...Moulding Public Opinion...Mr. Lincoln in 1854...Mr. Seward and Violence...Mr. Seward on the "Last Stage of Conflict"

...Mr. Seward's Justification for Disunion...The Prefix "National" Stricken from the Republican Cognomen...Banks Predicts a Military Government...Carl Schurz on Revolution...J. P. Hale on Dissolution...Gen. Butler on Reconstruction...Object and Consequences of Slavery Agitation...Prophesies of Eli Thayer...General Conclusions, &c.

CHAPTER XXI.

ABOLITIONISTS SHOW THEIR PURPOSE TO DESTROY THE UNION.

The Various Efforts at Compromise...Compromise the Basis of all Governments...General Principles of, Applied...The Compromises of the Constitution: What were They?...Messrs. Yates and Lansing Retire from the Convention of 1787...Compromise between Delaware, Maryland and Other States...The First Draft...Luther Martin on Compromise...The Large and Small Small States at War on Suffrage...Compromise on Slave Trade and Navigation Acts...An Original Plan of Constitution...The Great Suffrage Question...Mr. Martin's Explanations...Compromise between Slavery and Navigation...The New England States Favor the Slave Trade...Official Proof...Hypocrisy of Abolition States...Massachusetts Stealing Negroes...The Virginia and New Jersey Plan of Government...Predictions of Geo. Mason...The Missouri Compromise...General Propositions...Jackson and Clay on Compromise...Compromise of 1832-3...Compromise of 1850...Why the Radicals would not Compromise in 1861.

CHAPTER XXII.

THE RADICALS DETERMINED TO PREVENT A SETTLEMENT.

Could the Present War have been Avoided...Complete History of the Crittenden Compromise...Votes, Resolves, Propositions, &c.

CHAPTER XXIII.

REPUBLICANS OBSTINATE AND REFUSE TO COMPROMISE.

The Conduct of the Abolitionists in the Wisconsin Legislature...Radical Reasons for not Compromising...The Chicago Platform Good Enough for the Radicals...Tenacity of the Wouldn't-Yield-An-Inchers...Effort of Democrats to send Commissioners to the Compromise Congress...Republicans Claim to have "Struggled Manfully against the United Democracy"...Carl Schurz and "Our Side"...Republicans of Sauk City opposed to Compromise...A Candid Admission...Edward Everett on Compromise...Lord Brougham on Coercion...Plan of Adjustment by the Peace Congress...Franklin's Substitute..."New York Post" on Effect...Greeley against Compromise...General Conclusions, &c.

CHAPTER XXIV.

REPUBLICAN EFFORTS TO STIMULATE DISSOLUTION—THEIR DISLOYALTY AND TREASON.

The Morrill Tariff as a Means to Hasten Dissolution...Opinions of the "Cincinnati Commercial," "New York Times," and "New York World"...From the "London Times"...The Tables Turned on the Charge of "Disloyalty"...Rules of Testimony, and the Proof of Republican Disloyalty...Testimony of Andrew Johnson...Senator Wilson on "Setting up with the Union"...What Constitutes a "Traitor" and a "Copperhead"...Mr. Lincoln on the Stand: His Preaching contrasted with his Practice...Congress on the "Object" of the War..."Indianapolis Sentinel" ditto...Thad. Stevens against the Constitution as it is...Mr. Chase Declares the Union Not Worth Fighting For...Frank Blair on Chase...Thur-

low Weed on Mob Inciters...Being for the Union as it was Declared an "Offense"...The Present Programme Blocked Out Just After Lincoln's Nomination...Dawson's Letter to the "Albany Journal"...Giddings in the Chicago Convention; His Radical Doctrine Voted Down There; How Acted On...Lincoln's Letter of Acceptance...Lincoln and the Chicago Platform in Juxtaposition...Sumner Opens the Radical Ball..."New York Post" and Other Papers fear it was Premature...The Other Class of Disunionists...Treason of the "Chicago Tribune"...The Crittenden Resolutions...The Proclamation and Emancipation: Conclusions Thereon..."New York Tribune" and Other Sheets" Predict Good Things ...The "Pope's Bull Against the Comet"...The Object to Divide the North, &c....Gov. Andrew Before and After the Proclamation...Choice Inconsistencies, &c...Money and Not the Proclamation Required to Make the "Roads Swarm"...Greeley Down on Old Abe...Seward Pronounces the Proclamation Unconstitutional

CHAPTER XXV.

DISLOYALTY AND "TREASON" OF THE RADICALS.

How the Radicals "Opposed the Government" before the Proclamation...Parker Pillsbury..."New York Times" Before and After the Election..."New York Post" "Opposes the Government"..."New York Times" Again..."Chicago Tribune" Denounces the President...Wisconsin Home League on "Imbecility and Cowardice"...Predictions of "New York Tribune"...Democratic Predictions...Gov. Stone admits this an "Abolition War"...A Short Tack after the Gale of 1862..."New York Tribune" ...More Prophesies by False Prophets...Wendell Phillips as a Prophet..."New York Post" as a Prophet..."National Intelligencer" a True Prophet...Gov. Andrew's Prophesies..."New York Tribune's" Prophesies...The "000,-000," &c...Remarks of "National Intelligencer" on Same...The Proclamation in a Nut Shell...Belief in the Proclamation a Test of Loyalty...Forney Thereon...Senator Wilson's Address..."Disloyalty" of "Janesville, (Wis.) Gazette"..."Waukesha, (Wis.) Freeman"..."New York Tribune" on "Blunders"...Wendell Phillips on the "Lickspittle Administration"..."Milwaukee Sentinel" Disloyal to the "Government"..."Slate Journal" Ditto ...Phillips Again...Beecher on the "Government"...Testimony of Senator Browning..."Milwaukee Wisconsin" Throws a Javelin at Seward..."Chicago Tribune" Corrects Old Abe..."New York Independent" on the Administration..."New York Times" Scores the "Government"..."Chicago Tribune" Ditto..."Milwaukee Sentinel" Ditto..."Buffalo Express" Ditto..."Pittsburgh Chronicle" Ditto..."Anti-Slavery Standard" Ditto..."New York Post" on "Mistakes," &c...The Loyal Siamese Twins..."New York Tribune" on "Cabbage Head" Halleck.

CHAPTER XXVI.

THE PROCLAMATION...THE RADICAL WAR POLICY.

Mr. Lincoln's Letter to the Utica-Springfield Meetings Editor's Remarks on the Negro Policy..."New York Tribune" Pledges the President, &c ...John P. Hale's Bill to Abolish the Constitution...The Proclamation in England..."New York Tribune" on "Servile Insurrections"...Opinions of English Abolitionists...Mr. Wilberforce on the Folly of the Proclamation...Wendell Phillips on the Rampage...The Proclamation Confessed a Failure...Caleb B. Smith Pledges the Administration against the Proclamation...Mr. Madison on Emancipation...Lord Dunmore's Proclamation...Bancroft, the Historian on the Same...Thurlow Weed's Prediction...Mr. Lincoln on Federal Authority...The Chicago Platform...General Remarks...Post Master General Blair as a Witness...His Rockville Speech.

CHAPTER XXVII.

CONFISCATION—VIOLATION OF THE CONSTITUTION, &c.

The Confiscation Scheme...The Constitution Ignored...Testimony of Senator Cowan...Political Extremes Com

CONTENTS.

pared...Postmaster General Blair on Secessionists and Abolitionists...Comments of "National Intelligencer"...Senator Doolittle on Colonization and Emancipation...The Three "Solutions" : Of Calhoun, John Brown, (the same as Radicals), and Jefferson...Doolittle on Confiscation...Also, on Same and Abolition Denunciations of the "Government"...A Republican Journal on Senator Doolittle.

CHAPTER XXVIII.

INDIRECT MODE TO VIOLATE AND NULLIFY LAWS.

The Personal Liberty Bills of the Various States...Sundry Provisions to Nullify the Fugitive Law...A Radical Organ admits the Purpose...Schemes of the Plotters exposed.

CHAPTER XXIX.

ARBITRARY POWER—MILITARY ARRESTS, &c.

Introductory Remarks...Loyalty and Patriotism of the North...Arbitrary Power used to Destroy the Northern Unanimity...Senator Fessenden on Stopping Enlistments...Senator Wilson on same...General Conclusions...The Cause and the Effect...Mr. Lincoln's claim to Unlimited Power...Order No. 38...Trial of Vallandigham...Resolves of the Democratic Meeting at Albany...Their Protest to the President...The President's Reply...The Rejoinder...Protest of the Ohio Committee...President's Reply...Committee's Rejoinder...The Law of the Case, from the "National Intelligencer"...Personal and Legal Rights...Crittenden's Views...Abolitionist Feel Uneasy...Administration Condemned by its own Organs...Views of the N. Y. "Post" and "Tribune"...Judge Duer on Usurpations of the Administration...From the "N. Y. World."

CHAPTER XXX.

ARBITRARY POWER—MILITARY ARRESTS, &c., (CONTINUED.)

John Adams a Monarchist...What the Early Fathers thought of the Vallandigham Case...Great Speech of Edward Livingston on the Alien Bill, 1798...Terrible Scathing of Assumptions of Arbitrary Power...Who was Edward Livingston?...Republican Confessions of Gross Abuses of Arbitrary Power...Case of Messrs. Brinsmade and Mahoney...Damaging Admissions by "Milwaukee Sentinel"...General Remarks thereon.

CHAPTER XXXI.

DESPOTISM, USURPATIONS, INALIENABLE RIGHTS TRAMPLED UPON, Etc.

Despotism Seeks the Semblance of Loyalty...Solicitor Whiting perverts Judge Taney's Decision...Provost Marshal Fry Acts Thereon...Star Chamber...Laws by Proclamation in England...Kidnapping in New York...Gov. Hunt on Arbitrary Arrests...The Case of Gen. Stone...Beecher on Arbitrary Arrests...A Nice Point to Silence a Press...Geo. W. Jones vs. Wm. H. Seward...Judge Clerke's Decision...A Young Lady Fined $15 for Playing the "Bonnie Blue Flag"...Burnside Favors the Arrest of Males and Females that wear Butternut Badges...Opening the Prison Doors...Case of Gov. Tod and Others...Opinion of Judge Van Trump..."New York Journal of Commerce" on the Powers of the Provost Marshal...Case of Judge Constable...Liberated from the Bastile...Atrocious Sentiments by Senator Wilson...Cincinnati Prison Full...Other Acts of Despotism...General Conclusions...Vallandigham's Acts compared with Leading Republicans...Loyalty of Democrats...Disloyalty of Republicans...$500 Reward for a Disloyal Democrat Not Taken...The Writ of Habeas Corpus the Palladium of Our Liberties...Extracts of the Magna Charta—Wrung

from King John...Lord Campbell's Boast English Bill of Rights..." Body of Liberties" Brought in the Mayflower...The Bill in the Declaration...Virginia Bill of Rights...Massachusetts' "Declaration of Rights" in 1780...From Bill of Rights in Our Constitution...General Remarks on Suspension of the Writ of Habeas Corpus...Law of Suspected Persons...A Leaf from French History, by Allison...Our Parallels...Thiers on French Confiscation...Danton's Prediction...General Remarks...Blackstone on the English Habeas Corpus...Our Constitution Applied...The Ordinance of 1787 Applicable...What Our Fathers Thought of it...Pinckney, Rutledge, Morris and Millson on the Habeas Corpus...Judge Curtis on "Loyalty" and Habeas Corpus...A Scathing Speech...Mr. Chase's Opinion of Loyalty...The Roman Law and Personal Liberty...St. Paul on Arbitrary Violations of Law Judge Festus and King Agrippa Respected the Roman Law..." New York Independent" on Arbitrary Arrests...What a Conservative Republican Thinks of it...President's Suspension of the Writ of Habeas Corpus : His Proclamation...Congress on Arbitrary Arrests...Official Vote...Supreme Court of Wisconsin on Suspending the Writ.

CHAPTER XXXII.

MORE REVOLUTIONARY SYMPTOMS.

Mobbing of Democrats and Democratic Presses...Schenck's Order Suppressing Newspapers...Hascall's Despotic Note to the "New York Express"...How the Republicans Love Free Speech...Mobbing of Douglas in Chicago...Republican Mob in Green County, Wis....Federals, Whigs and Republicans in Juxtaposition...Their Line of Consanguinity...Senator Doolittle vs. Political Doolittle...President Lincoln vs. Political Lincoln...Republicans in Congress Suppress Inquiry into Illegal Acts...Their Preaching vs. Practice...The Negro Voted Out of Illinois and Wisconsin...Abolitionists Selling Negroes for Cotton.

CHAPTER XXXIII.

HAVE WE A MILITARY DESPOTISM?

General Remarks...Educating the Army to the New Role...Adjutant General Thomas Preaching Politics to the Soldiers...Punishes Soldiers for Political Opinions...How the Soldiers View it...Anti-Copperhead Letters and Resolves from the Army...How Manufactured...General Remarks...General Hallock on "Crushing the Sneaking Traitors of the North"...Seward, Chase, Blair, &c., at the Cooper Institute Meeting...Case of Lieut. Edgerly...Abolitionism a Test of a Soldier's Duty...The Conscription Act intended to Ignore the Constitution..."Boston Commonwealth" Admits that the Administration Employed Bayonets to Carry Elections...Difference between Orthodoxy and Heterodoxy...Atrocious Sentiments of Senator Wilson...A Leaf from French History...A Fact by Sallust...Gov. Seymour on the Rotten-Borough System His Message of Jan. 5, 1864...A Flexible Platform...Henry Clay's Opinion...Free Speech Abolished...Senator Howe on...Petty Despotism...Arrests for Wearing Badges...Several Instances in Point...The Evidences of Approaching Despotism...A Link from " New York Tribune"...To Doubt the Infallibility of the President is "Treason"...Declaration of Independence Revised, &c.

CHAPTER XXXIV.

MORE OF THE ROLE OF DESPOTISM.

Abolition Schemes to Control Elections...Army Voting...Julius Cæsar the Originator of...Dr. Lieber on...Louis Napoleon and Army Voting...Army Vote for...General Tuttle and Vallandigham...Mr. V. Ahead...N. Y. World thereon...Tricks of the Administration to Saddle their Electioneering Expenses on the People...Governor Salomon of Wisconsin in the role...The Army Weakened.

CONTENTS.

...Soldiers sent home to Vote...Proofs in Connecticut...Proofs in New York, &c...Stanton Boasts of sending more Soldiers than Curtin's majority...The Contractors perform their part...Martial Law in Kentucky to force the Election...How a "loyal" Paper Views it...From Louisville Journal...Statements of Clerk of the Election...How a Congressman was elected by an "overwhelming majority"...Further evidences...The Administration carries Maryland by the Bayonet...Gov. Bradford's Proclamation on the Subject...The Great Frauds Practiced on New York by the Enrollment and Quota process...New York Overdrawn as compared with other States...Frauds in the Pennsylvania and Ohio Elections...Punishing officers for Voting the Democratic Ticket...Case of Capt. Sells...Officers' Threats to control Elections...Bribery at Elections...War on the "Copperheads"...Republican Organ Justifies Military Interference in Elections...The Politics of this War...Discharging disabled and dying Soldiers from Office of Sutler for Voting the Democratic Ticket...Abolition claim of "Those who Vote must Fight"...Abolition Roorbacks to Effect Elections...The Union League Machinery...Forney on Their Purposes...Dr. Lieber on Soldiers Voting...Gen. Milroy on "Home Traitors"...John Brough's Appeal from the Ballot to the Bullet...More Threats...New York Independent Boasts of the Infamy, &c.

CHAPTER XXXV.

SYMPATHY BETWEEN RADICALS AND REBELS—THE DRAFT, &C.

The Rebels Hate the Democracy and Sympathize with the Radicals...General Remarks...Benjamin's Speech in 1860...Breckinridge Secesshers Toasted with Office, &c...Richmond Examiner on Vallandigham, Cox, &c...Mobile Register on Democrats and Abolitionists...The Draft vs. Volunteering a Success...Wilson's and Fessenden's Admissions...Thad Stevens on "Alarming Expenses"...Too many Troops to pay, but none to Spare McClellan...General Remarks, &c...The number of Men called for...Cameron's Eulogy on Volunteering...Cost of Conscription...Opinions of the Republican Press on the Draft...Albany Statesman...The Draft in Rhode Island...A candid Statement by a Republican paper...The Conscription in Massachusetts...A mysterious Draft in New York...Result of Draft in ninth District of Massachusetts and eighth District of New York...Thurlow Weed on "Sneaks"...Drafting in the time of the Revolution...Remarks Thereon.

CHAPER XXXVI.

LOYALTY AND PATRIOTISM OF DEMOCRATS.

General Remarks and Facts pertaining to...The Democracy of New York...The Iowa Democracy...Doctrine of the Kentucky Democracy...The Ohio Democracy...The Democracy of Wisconsin...The Minnesota Democracy...Democracy of Pennsylvania...Illinois Democracy...Connecticut Democracy...Democracy of Indiana...Of Columbus, Ohio...Of Madison, Wis....The National Democracy...Sayings and Doings of Leading Democrats...Governor Seymour's Proclamation...Gov. Seymour's Message...Gov. Parker's Proclamation...Remarks of Hon. H. L. Palmer...Et tu Vallandigham...Democrats Rejoice at our Victories...Testimony of our opponents...New York Times...Mr. Seward, Official...Judge Paine, of Wis....Administration Compliment Gov. Seymour for his Patriotism, &c.

CHAPTER XXXVII.

MISCELLANEOUS FACTS AND FIGURES.

Political sine qua non of Wisconsin Legislature...Still refuse to yield an inch...N. Y. Round Table on Lincoln's Amnesty Proclamation...Two Millions in Men...Three Millions in Money...Is a National Debt a National Blessing...A Negro Nobility...Effects of a High Tariff...Vicksburg Discipline...Will the Rebellion succeed...1,685,000 Democratic Votes in the Loyal States...Gross Outrage by Abolitionists at Boscobel, Wisconsin.

CHAPTER XXXVIII.

FRAUDS, PLUNDERING, SHODDY AND TAXES.

Poetical applications...General Remarks on...Scions of the old Puritanical stock...New York Custom House Frauds...Testimony and Facts...Conclusions of committee...Van Wyck's speech on the Development of Astounding Frauds...Collector Barney and his subs...John P. Hale on corruptions of the Departments...Cattle contracts...Cummings' Agency...Charter of the Catalina...General Mania for stealing...Horse contracts...Contract Brokerage...Treasury Department Frauds...Fire Arms Frauds...George D. Morgan's Operations...Army Transportation...Mr. Dawes on Frauds...A Refreshing Expose...A New York Paper on Van Wyck's Report...The "Record of Infamy" by the Ohio State Journal...Members of Congress take a hand in...Simmons, of Rhode Island, takes $50,000...Jack Hale takes a "fee"...The Horse Swindle...Frauds in the Navy Yard...The Book Swindle...The Grimes Committee...Frauds, Rascality, and Perjury...The Vessel Charter Frauds...The Committee's Conclusions...The Mileage Steal...Stupendous Frauds in New York...Swindling at Cairo...A Defaulter Caught...General Wilcox on Contractors...Mr. Dawes on Larcenies...Millions upon Millions Wasted...Beauties of Republican Retrenchment...Fremont's Frauds...Marshal Lamon Mr. Lincoln's Right Bower...Honest Old Abe and Simon help their Friends...Mrs. Grimsley, the President's Sister-in-Law, figures in Fraud Investigations...Letters from Old Abe and Cameron to Major McKinstry...Congress Censures...that's all...The Holt and Owen Investigation...The Splendor of Fremont's operations...Frauds! Frauds!! Frauds!!! on every hand...General Remarks...Holy Ministers and Stolen Pictures...Swiudling the Soldiers...Hundreds of Millions Swindled...We are all Mortgaged...Our National Debt...The Means to pay it...General Remarks...The Currency Question...Stand from Under...General Remarks on Republican Thieves and Plunderers.

CHAPTER XXXIX.

WARNINGS AND ADVICE OF AMERICAN STATESMEN, &C.

From Washington's Farewell Address...Jackson's Farewell Address...By Daniel Webster...By Henry Clay...By Patrick Henry...From Webster's Great Oration...Further from Jackson's Farewell Addresses...Madison on the Liberty of the Press...Mr. Seward on Free Speech...Jefferson on the Plea of Necessity...John Adams on Arbitrary Power...Ex-President Filmore on the Negro Question...Gov. Seymour's Patriotic Letter...Senator Harris of New York, on the Despotism of Conscriptions...Rob't J. Walker on State Suicide...Sen. Trumbull on the Tyrant's Plea...Gen. McClellan on Constitution and Christian Civilization...Sen. Crittenden on the cause of our Troubles...President Harrison on the Rights of the States...Montesquiou and Jefferson on Preservation of Liberty...James Madison on same...Gen. Harrison at Ft. Meigs...J. Q. Adams on the "Link of Union"...The Father of the Constitution on Confiscation...List of Members and Delegates in Congress, &c.

FIVE HUNDRED POLITICAL TEXTS.

SLAVERY AGITATION:
CONSPIRACIES AGAINST THE UNION

SCRAPS FROM MY SCRAP-BOOK.

CHAPTER I.

EFFECTS OF ANCIENT SLAVERY AGITATION, ETC.

Application of the "Logic of History"—Effect of Early Slavery Agitation—Slavery in Ancient Times—Slavery Agitation in Rome—Its Terrible Effects : Agitation the Cause of the Downfall of the Roman Empire—Greece and her Dependencies Destroyed by Slavery Agitation—The Agitation in France—Bloody Effects of, in St. Domingo—BRISSOT, and other French Abolitionists, stir up the "Irrepressible Conflict"—A Servile Insurrection Ensues—Napoleon Issues a "Proclamation of Freedom"—Terrible Disasters follow the same—A French Army Destroyed—Servile Insurrection in St. Domingo—GIBBON, the Historian, on the Character of the Negro: their Fall from Ancient Superiority—McKENZIE, the Historian, on the "Cause" in the West Indies—Statistics of St. Domingo—The Sublime Teachings of History.

APPLICATION OF THE LOGIC OF HISTORY.

"WE CANNOT ESCAPE HISTORY."—*Message of A. Lincoln.*

This I hold to be the chief office of history :—To rescue virtuous actions from the oblivion to which a want of records would consign them, and that men should feel a dread of being considered infamous in the opinions of posterity, for their *depraved expressions* and base actions.—*Tacitus.*

It is said that history is like a lantern placed at the stern of a ship to show the course it has pursued, whereas it should be placed at the bow to indicate the track it is pursuing, and to shed the light of its rays on the rocks on which others have been wrecked. And herein all nations of every age have failed to profit by the light of past history. They place that light at the wrong end of the ship of State. It will be the object of this publication to place the light of history where it should be, as a beacon of warning on our onward course, through the dangerous Archipelago of the living present, and by a proper analogy to guide our tempest-tossed barque so as to shun the dangers of the unknown future.

Happily, we are not confined to the immediate past for analogies to illustrate our present condition, as a nation, but we are permitted to read our most probable fate by the light which ancient Greece, Athens and Rome, have left burning on the ruins of their historical altars. The history of those nations—their rise, progress and melancholy downfall, is full of warning to us. The First, Second, Third, Fourth and Fifth, speak to the Nineteenth century in no dead or equivocal language. Rome, from her gory grave of national oblivion, speaks in thunder tones to America. The once proud, erudite and far famed, though now almost fossilized Athens, hails us through the loud trumpet of history, and bids us beware the breakers on which ambition wrecked her greatness and glory. Heroic, historic and legendary Greece, warns us from her grave of woe, to beware of Macedonian and Peloponessian strifes. The chivalrous CATO, from the suicide's sepulchre, will act our monitor against the insidious agitations of Abolition GRACCHUSES, CRASSUSES and EUNUSES. The arts and sciences, now locked in the secret hecatombs of early oriental greatness, all admonish us to study and profit by the teachings and logic of history.

The writer hereof, having devoted much time for many years to the culling out and filing away such scraps of history as prophetic calculation (so to speak) induced him to believe would sooner or later be useful in a crisis, that the least observing must have known years ago would inevitably overtake our people, will regard himself amply compensated for the time which the within historical collation has required, if the same shall in the least degree serve to direct popular attention to a long train of evils now threatening the life of this nation, and which are so ineffaceably chiselled in the milestones that mark the great highway of nations, that he who runs may read, and he who reads without criminal prejudice, may learn a lesson of more value than the gold of Eldorado.

THE SLAVERY AGITATION—ITS CONSEQUENCES

Mr. LINCOLN tells us that we cannot escape history. This shows that he has at least read

2

enough of the history of ancient and modern nations to learn one fact; that as no nation ever did escape its own history, ours will cling to us with equal tenacity. In this, and the subsequent chapters, it will not be so much our object to present original propositions as it will be to collate and spread out before our readers the logic and argument of history, and we shall endeavor to avoid all verbiage except so far as may be necessary to present the various facts, sayings, doings and historical reminiscences, in such manner as to present the aims and purposes of the vast array of witnesses we shall place on their *voir dire*.

It has of late been a stereotyped phrase that "slavery is the cause of this war," but such declarations are mostly confined to slavery agitators. So far as our observation and belief go, such is in no sense the truth of history.—The *agitation* of the slavery question is no doubt the principal pretext, and without question has furnished the main pabulum on which treason has fed and waxed strong, but as we proceed it will be seen that the *real cause* has more to feed it than slavery, or even its agitation; but before we proceed to that "count" let us take observation of the

EFFECT OF EARLY SLAVERY AGITATION.

It will be neither our purpose to show that slavery is, or ever was, right or wrong. but barely to present the light of historical facts, leaving the reader to form his own conclusions.

Slavery has existed, under various phases, from the remotest periods of sacred and profane history. In the 17th chap. of Genesis, v. 12, 13, 23 and 27, the fact that Abraham bought men with his money is four times recognized. Verse 12 is represented to be in the language of God, Himself, speaking to ABRAHAM, viz.:

And he that is eight days old shall be circumcised among you, every man child in your generations; he that is born in the house, or bought with money of any stranger, which is not of thy seed.

In the 24th chap. 35th v., man and maid servants are mentioned among the blessings which GOD had bestowed upon ABRAHAM:—

And the LORD hath blessed my master (ABRAHAM) greatly, and he is become great, and He has given him flocks and herds, and silver and gold, and man servants, and maid servants, and camels and asses.

From the 14th chap. and 14th verse it appears that ABRAHAM had three hundred and eighteen "trained servants, born in his house." The 21st chap. of Exodus, the 25th chap. of Leviticus and the 25th chap. of Deuteromony recognize slavery and the buying of slaves, &c. Slavery is also recognized by PAUL in 1st Corinthians, and in the 6th chap. of the Ephetians, the 6th chap. of PAUL's 1st Epistle to TIMOTHY, in the 3d and 4th chapters of his Epistles to the Collossians, in chap. 24 of his Epistle to TITUS, in the 1st Epistle of PETER, the Epistle of PAUL to PHILEMON, &c.

SLAVERY IN THE TIME OF CLAUDIUS.

The following table exhibits the great number of slaves held in an early period:

Rome,	20,000,000
France,	23,000,000
Germany,	22,000,000
Hungary,	4,000,000
Italy,	18,000,000
Spain and Portugal,	8,000,000
Great Britain,	8,000,000
European Russia	12,000,000
Poland,	6,000,000
Greece and Turkey,	1,600,000
Sweeden,	4,000,000
Denmark and Norway,	3,000,000
Low Countries,	4,000,000

[*See Voltaire de Histoire Generale.*]

In those days white men were held as slaves, and not till long after were Ethiopeans brought to Roman servitude. The Roman law regulating slavery was in a great measure borrowed from the Hebrew code, modified to suit the spirit of the age. It gave power to the master over the life and limb of his slaves, and the utmost rigor prevailed. The Romans and their neighbors were continually at war, nor did they agree to cartels for the exchange of prisoners. All prisoners became slaves by the inexorable laws of war, and were held either by the state under the system of Roman helotry, or by citizens who purchased from the state. Not unfrequently citizens, as under the old Levitical law, voluntarily surrendered themselves as slaves, to escape the consequences of want and destitution.

SLAVERY AGITATION IN ROME.

Slavery was no doubt a monster political evil in the Roman Commonwealth—a thousand fold more so than any system known to civilized nations of the present age. Romans, Grecians and Athenians enslaved their equals, and frequently their intellectual superiors; and at one time, history tells us, every twelfth person in the realm either was, or had been a slave.— The evil, great as it was, could no doubt have been borne, until GOD, in his own way, should have wrought its extinction or amelioration, far better than the dreadful consequences that followed in the wake of its political agitation.

In those days, philanthropy, whether properly or improperly directed, as it has been ever since, tried to *force* its growth by hot-bed stimulants, and while good men, no doubt, were prompted to assail the institution from just and pure motives, yet it requires a very little attention to the "logic of history" to see that the moment the agitation became popular, as it did under the insipient agitations of Gracchus, by which he was called to the Tribunate, it attracted the legions of political demagogues and vampyres, who, from no better motive than to obtain power and plunder, contrive to float upon the surface of any move that promises popular favor.

GRACCHUS was no doubt originally governed by philanthropic motives. He struck at the evil in its *national* capacity, and at first urged measures of a humane and national character. He neither denounced individual slave-holders as guilty of the "sum of all villainy," nor threatened to confiscate their property. Hence, although standing forth as the avowed enemy of the system, he became the favorite of the slaveholders, who elected him Chief of the Tribunes. But the moment he had a taste of power, he inaugurated a political agitation—threatened to "*force* emancipation, speedily and without recourse"—and called around him some of the best talent, yet most ambitious men of Rome. GRACCHUS was to Rome what CHARLES SUMNER is to America—an eloquent agitator of the slavery question. APPIUS CLAUDIUS, his father-in-law, MUTIUS SCÆVOLA, the most famous lawyer of Rome, and CRASSUS, the leader of the priesthood, and the wealthiest man in the Commonwealth, were associated with GRACCHUS. Those influential abolitionists agitated the slavery question, until it entered into all the petty political questions of the day, and until their proselytes were counted by legions, and on the scum of the excitement floated a large class of demagogues and political hucksters, who scrupled not at any means to obtain place and power. These selfish plebians and patricians organized for offensive raids on the public exchequer, and carried their vile purposes with them to such ill extent, that all classes were aroused to the highest degree of excitement. An "Irrepressible Conflict" ensued, which not only destroyed Rome, and blotted her out from the map of the world, as a nation of power and vitality, but forever blasted the hopes, the happiness and the liberties of slaves, helots and people.

The hot blood of party was aroused to a fearful temper, and from that moment Rome began to totter to her final fall. GRACCHUS was a candidate for re-election, on the platform of confiscation and emancipation. The excitement is represented as intense. Appeals were made to passions and fanatical prejudices, and on the day of the election, the phrenzied multitude beat GRACCHUS to death and threw his body into the Tiber. Three hundred of his followers perished on the same day.*

Many of the measures of GRACCHUS were no doubt wise and beneficent, and had he not committed the fatal error of linking them with political Abolitionism and Agrarianism, he would without question have not only saved Rome. but secured lasting fame as a man of good impulses and great genius.

After the death of GRACCHUS his followers canonized him as a "martyr to a glorious cause." EUNUS, one of his disciples, undertook the spread of political Abolitionism into Italy and the Island of Sicily. He collected what force he could from the Plebian ranks—distilled the vain hope of sudden freedom into the ears of the common slaves and the helots, and as BLAKE says, managed to raise a motly army of 200,000, armed with scythes, pitchforks, &c., and marched forth, proud in the belief that he was to occupy a high *niche* in the Pantheon, as the deliverer of the slaves of Italy and Sicily. Mr. BLAKE, who wrote the "History of Slavery," containing 832 pages, a work especially designed for abolition use in this country, informs us that a million of persons were butchered in this "worse than Carthagenian war." EUNUS failed in his abolition purposes, and the slaves, whom he had promised liberty they were not prepared to enjoy, in the language of the same author, "committed one universal suicide!"

The tragic sequel of this Sicilian insurrection did not deter others from embarking in the Abolition crusade. TIBERIUS, brother of the Tribunate GRACCHUS, organized the Abolition party anew, and carried on the contest, he and his successors, until all—masters, helots and slaves, perished in the general wreck of the Empire.

That the agitation of the slavery question, and the blending that issue with Roman politics for the benefit of Roman demagogues, and to the disparagement of Roman Statesmen,was the primeval cause of the downfall of that Government—that once stretched its power from the Tiber to the Adriatic, is a fact too well authenticated by history to require other accumulative evidence than the admission of Mr. BLAKE himself, who on page 59 of his work says:

The laws of GRACCHUS cut the Patricians with a double edge. Their fortunes consisted in lands and slaves; it questioned their title to the public land; and tended to *force emancipation* [See American parallel in Lincoln's Proclamation]. by making their slaves a burden. In taking away the soil [see the parallel of the radical idea of reducing the states to territories, &c.] it took away the power that kept their live machinery in motion. *The moment was a crisis in the affairs of Rome—such a crisis as hardly occurs to a nation in the progress of many centuries* [see parallel in the American crisis.] Men are in the habit of prescribing JULIUS CAESAR as the destroyer of the Commonwealth. The civil wars, the revolutions of CAESAR, the miserable vicissitudes of the Roman Emperors—the avarice of the Nobles and the rabble, the crimes of the forum and the palace—*all have their germ in the ill success* of the reform of GRACCHUS.

Here, then, is the admission of the principal abolition historian of this country, that Rome was destroyed by the "ill successes" of the slavery agitation. Have we no fear for a like result from the same cause on this continent ?

President HARRISON, in his inaugural address, in censuring the interference of the non-slaveholding states, said:

It was the ambition of the leading states of Greece, *to control the domestic concerns of others*, that the destruction of that celebrated confederacy, and subsequently of all its members, is mainly to be attributed.

SLAVERY AGITATION IN FRANCE.

France, also, had her abolition societies and agitators, and the result of the agitation of this ill omened subject is familiar to the student of history. We offer no apology for the following copious extracts from ALLISON'S History, which was written long before the advent of our present troubles, and with no possible view to aid political ideas or dogmas.—For the purpose of the better exhibition of the parallels with the chain of history] we are making, and which Mr. LINCOLN truly says we cannot escape, we present the facts and incidents in semi-dramatic order, in four acts.—The period lies between 1791 and 1802:

* See Blake's History of Slavery.

ACT I—THE ABOLITIONISTS AGITATE AND STIR UP DISCORD.

The Jacobin abolitionists, in 1791, began the agitation of the slavery question in the Constituent Assembly. This proved to be a firebrand as it has been in our Congress. We quote as follows: [*See Allison's Hist. of Europe, vol. i. pp. 120-1.*]

"The second catastrophe, more extensive in its operation, yet more terrible in its details, was the revolt of St. Domingo. The slaves in that flourishing colony, agitated by the intelligence which they received of the leveling principles of the Constituent Assembly, had early manifested symptoms of insubordination. The Assembly, divided between the desire of enfranchising so large a body of men, and the evident dangers of such a step, had long hesitated on the course they should adopt, and were inclined to support the rights of the planters. But the passions of the negroes were excited by the efforts of a society styled 'The Society of Friends of Blacks,' [same as our Abolitionists,] of which Brissot was the leading member; and the mullattoes were induced, by their injudicious advice, to organize an insurrection. They trusted that they would be able to control the ferocity of the slaves even during the heats of a revolt; they little knew the dissimulation and cruelty of the savage character. A universal revolt was planned and organized, without the slightest suspicion on the part of the planters, and the same night fixed on for its breaking out over the whole island.

"At length, at midnight, on the 30th October, the insurrection broke forth. In an instant twelve hundred coffee and two hundred sugar plantations were in flames; the buildings, the machinery, the farm offices, reduced to ashes; the unfortunate proprietors hunted down, murdered or thrown into the flames by the infuriated negroes.— The horrors of a servile war universally appeared. The unchained African signalized his ingenuity by the discovery of new and unheard-of modes of torture. An unhappy planter was sawed asunder between two boards; the horrors inflicted on the women exceeded anything known even in the annals of Christian ferocity. The indulgent master young and old, rich and poor, the wrongs of an oppressed race were indiscriminately wreaked. Crowds of slaves traversed the country with the heads of the white children affixed on their pikes; they served as the standards of these furious assemblages. [Our abolitionists have organized to incite similar outrages in the South.] In a few instances only, the humanity of the negro character resisted the savage contagion of the time; and some faithful slaves, at the hazard of their own lives, fed in caves their masters or their children, whom they had rescued from destruction.

"The intelligence of these disasters excited an angry discussion in the Assembly. Brissot, the most vehement opponent of slavery, averil[ed] them all to the refusal of the blessings of freedom to the negroes; [precisely as our abolitionists ascribe every evil—the war and all—to slavery;] the moderate members, to the inflammatory addresses circulated among them by the Anti-Slavery Society of Paris; [precisely as our abolitionists have ever done, and are now doing.] At length it was agreed to concede the political rights for which they contended to the men of color; and, in consequence of that resolution, St. Domingo obtained the nominal blessings of freedom. ["At length" came Lincoln's proclamation—a perfect historical parallel.] But it is not thus that the great changes of nature are conducted; a child does not acquire the strength of manhood in an hour, or a tree the consistency of the hardy denizens of the forest in a season. The *hasty philanthropists* who conferred upon an ignorant slave population the precipitate gift of freedom, did them a greater injury than their worst enemies. [And our "hasty philanthropists," who clamor for immediate abolition, will do the slaves here "more harm than their worst enemies."] The black population remain to this day, in St. Domingo, a memorable example of the ruinous effect of precipitate emancipation. Without the steady habits of civilized society; ignorant of the wants which reconcile to a life of labor; destitute of the support which to a regular government might have afforded, they have brought to the duties of cultivation the habits of savage life. To the indolence of the negro character they have joined the vices of European corruption; profligate, idle, and disorderly, they have declined both in numbers and in happiness; from eing the greatest sugar plantation in the world, the Island have been reduced to the necessity of importing that valuable produce; and the inhabitants, naked and voluptuous, are fast receding into the state of nature from which their ancestors were torn, two centuries ago, by the rapacity of Christian avarice."

ACT II.—MORE FREEDOM TO THE NIGGERS DEMANDED.

As we have seen what came of the effort to free the negroes from bondage, so let us look at the effect of the Abolition effort to enfranchise the ignorant blacks We quote from the same history, vol. II, p. 241:—

By a decree on March 8, 1790, the Constituent Assembly had empowered each colony belonging to the Republic to make known its wishes on the subject of a Constitution, and that these wishes should be expressed by colonial assemblies, freely elected and recognized by their citizens. This privilege excited the most ruinous divisions among the inhabitants of European descent, already sufficiently menaced by the ideas fermenting in the negro population. The whites claimed the exclusive right of voting for the election of members of this important assembly, while the mulattoes strenuously asserted their title to an equal share in the representation; and the blacks, intoxicated with the novel doctrines so keenly discussed by all classes of society, secretly formed the project of ridding themselves of both. This decree of the National Assembly was brought out to the island by Lieutenant Colonel Ogé, a mulatto officer in the service of France, who openly proclaimed the opinion of the parent Legislature, that the half-caste and free negroes were entitled to their full share in the election of the representatives. The jealousy of the planters was immediately excited. They refused to acknowledge the decree of the Assembly, constituted themselves into a separate Legislature, and having seized Ogé in the Spanish territory, put him to death by the torture of the wheel, under circumstances of atrocious cruelty.

"This unpardonable proceeding, as is usually the case with such acts of barbarity, aggravated instead of stifling the prevailing discontents, and the heats of the colony soon became so vehement that the Constituent Assembly felt the necessity of taking some steps to allay the ferment. The moderate and violent parties in that body took different sides, and all Europe looked on with anxiety upon a debate so novel in its kind, and fraught with such momentous consequences to a large portion of the human race. Barnave Malouet, Alexander Lameth, and Clermont Tonnerre strongly argued that men long accustomed to servitude could not receive the perilous gift of liberty with safety either to themselves or others, but by slow degrees, and that the effect of suddenly admitting that bright light upon a benighted population would be to throw them into inevitable and final convulsions. But Mirabeau, the master-spirit of the Assembly, and the only one of its leaders who combined popular principles with a just appreciation of the danger of pushing them to excess, was no more, and the declamations of Brissot and the Girondists prevailed over these statesman-like ideas. By a decree on the 15th of May, 1791, the privileges of equality were conferred indiscriminately on all persons of color, born of a free father and mother.

"Far from appreciating the hourly increasing dangers of their situation, and endeavoring to form with the new citizens an organized body to check the further progress of leveling principles, the planters openly endeavored to resist this rash decree. Civil war was preparing in this once peaceful and beautiful colony; arms were collecting; the soldiers, caressed and seduced by both parties, were wavering between their old feelings of regal allegiance and the modern influence of intoxicating principles, when a new and terrible enemy arose, which speedily extinguished in blood the discord of his oppressors. On the night of the 22d of August, the negro revolt, long and secretly organized, at once broke forth, and wrapped the whole Northern part of the colony in flames. JEAN FRANCOIS, a slave of vast, penetrative, firm character, and violent passions, not unmingled with generosity, was the leader of the conspiracy; his lieutenants were BIASSON and TOUSSAINT. The former, of gigantic stature, Herculean strength and indomitable ferocity, was well fitted to assert that superiority which such qualities seldom fail to command in savage times; the latter, gifted with rare intelligence, profound dissimulation, boundless ambition, and heroic firmness, was fitted to become at once the Numa and the Romulus of the sable Republic in the Southern Hemisphere.

"This vast conspiracy, productive in the end of calamities unparalleled even in the long catalogue of European atrocity, had for its objects the *total extirpation of the whites, and the establishment of an independent black government over the whole island*."

[Beware of liberty to the blacks, and "extirpation" of the whites]
We quote as follows from the same Act, though in a different scene, p. 243-3 (1801):

"Meanwhile the legislative assembly, which had succeeded the constituent, a step farther advanced in revolutionary violence, were preparing ulterior measures of the most frantic character. Irritated at the colonial legislature for not having followed out their intention, and instigated at the populace, whom the efforts of Brissot and the Society at Paris, *des Amis des Sorris* had roused to a perfect phrensy on the subject, they revoked the decree on the 24th of September preceding, which had conferred such ample powers on the colonial legislature, dissolved the assembly at Cape Town, and dispatched three new commissioners, Arthanx, Santionax, and Polverel, with unlimited powers to settle the affairs of the colony. In vain Barnaves and the remnant of the constitutional party in the assembly strove to moderate these extravagant proceedings; the violence of the Jacobins bore down all opposition. 'Don't talk to us of danger,' said Brissot; 'let the colonies perish rather than one principle be abandoned.' [Don't talk to us, say our Abolition Brissots—let the Union perish rather than abandon our platform.]

The proceedings of the new commissioners speedily brought matters to a crisis. They arrived first at Port au Prince, and in conformity with the secret instructions of the government, which were to dislodge the whites from that stronghold, they sent off to France the soldiers of the regiment of Arteis, established a Jacobin club, transported to France or America thirty of the leading planters, and issued a *proclamation* [aye, aye, a "proclamation"] in which they exhorted the colonists "to lay aside at last the prejudices of color." Having thus laid the revolutionary train at Port au Prince, they embarked for Cape Town, where they arrived in the middle of June. Matters had by this time reached such a height there as indicated the immediate approach of a crisis. The intelligence of the executive of the King, and proclamation of a Republic, had roused to the very highest pitch the Democratic passions of all the inferior classes. The planters, with too good reason, apprehended that the convention which had succeeded the legislative assembly would soon outstrip them in violence and put the finishing stroke to their manifold calamities, by at once proclaiming the liberty of the slaves, and so destroying the remnant of property which they still possessed. But their destruction was nearer at hand than they supposed. On the 20th of June a quarrel accidentally arose between a French naval captain and a mulatto officer in the service of the colonial government; the commissioners ordered them both into their presence, without regard to the distinction of color, and this excited the highest indignation in the officers of the marine, who landed with their crews to take vengeance for the indignity done to one of their members. The colonists loudly applauded their conduct, and invoked their aid as the savior of St. Domingo; the exiles brought from Port au Prince fomented the discord as the only means of effecting their liberation; a civil war speedily ensued in the blockaded capital, and for two days blood flowed in torents in these insane contests, between the sailors of the fleet and the mulatto population.

"The negro chiefs, secretly informed of all these disorders, resolved to profit by the opportunity of finally destroying the whites thus afforded to them. Three thousand insurgents penetrated through the works stripped of their defenders during the general tumult, and making straight for the prisons, delivered a large body of slaves who were there in chains. Instantly the liberated captives spread themselves over the town, set it on fire in every quarter, and massacred the unhappy whites when seeking to escape from the conflagration. A scene of matchless horror ensued: twenty thousand negroes broke into the city, and, with the torch in one hand and the sword in the other spread slaughter and devastation around. Hardly had the strife of the Europeans with each other subsided, when they found themselves overwhelmed by the vengeance which had been accumulating for centuries in the African breast. Neither age nor sex were spared; the young were cut down in striving to defend their houses, the aged in the churches where they had fled to implore protection; virgins were immolated on the altar; weeping infants hurled into the fires. Amid the shrieks of the sufferers and the shouts of the victor, the finest city in the West Indies was reduced to ashes; its splendid churches, its stately palaces, were wrapped in flames; thirty thousand human beings perished in the massacre, and the wretched fugitives who had escaped from this scene of horror on board the ships, were guided in their passage over the deep by the prodigious light which arose from their burning habitations. They almost all took refuge in the United States, where they were received with the most generous hospitality; but the frigate *La Pine* foundered on the passage, and five hundred of the survivors from the flames perished in the waves.

"Thus fell the Queen of the Antilles: the most stately monument of European opulence that had yet arisen in the New World. Nothing deterred, however, by this unparalleled calamity, the commissioners of the Republic pursued their frantic career, and, amid the smoking ruins of the Capital, published a decree, which proclaimed the freedom of all the blacks [what could more perfectly represent this case than the President's proclamation, while the rebel armies were thundering at our capital?] who should enroll themselves under the standards of the Republic; a measure which was equivalent to the instant abolition of slavery over the whole island. Farther resistance was now hopeless; the Republican authorisies became the most ardent persecutors of the planters; pursued alike by Jacobin phrensy and African vengeance, they fled in despair. Polverel proclaimed the liberty of the blacks in the West, and Montbrun gave free vent to his hatred of the colonists, by compelling them to leave Port au Prince, which had not yet fallen into the hands of the negroes. Everywhere the triumph of the slaves was complete, and the authority of the planters forever destroyed.

"But, although the liberation of the negroes was affected, the independence of the island was not established."

ACT III.—NAPOLEON ISSUES AN ABOLITION PROCLAMATION.

In 1801, NAPOLEON, urged on by the Abolitionists, issued his proclamation abolishing slavery in the Island of St. Domingo, in which he called on the "brave blacks to remember that France alone had recognized their freedom," and on November 22, 1801, having appointed LE CLERC, his brother-in-law, to the command of the army about to visit St. Domingo in order to reduce the recusant TOUSSAINT to obedience, he issued the following "proclamation" [See p. 245]:

At St. Domingo, systematic acts have disturbed the political horizon. Under *equivocal appearances*, the government has wished to see only the ignorance which confounds names and things, which usurps when it seeks to obey; but a fleet and an army, which are preparing in the harbours of Europe, will soon dissipate these clouds, and St. Domingo will be reduced, in whole, to the government of the Republic." In the proclamation addressed to the blacks, it was announced by the same author.ty, "Whatever may be your origin or your colour, you are Frenchmen, and all alike *free* and *equal* before God and the Republic. At St. Domingo and Guadaloupe slavery no longer exists—all are free—all shall remain free. At Martinique different principles must be observed."

Now here seems an almost exact identity between NAPOLEON's and Old ABE's proclamations, especially the liberating the slaves in some localities and not in others.

ACT IV.

Here we have the tragedy, with our parallel close on its heels.
To show from British abolition sources what

a great curse abolition has been to the French and negroes, we quote from p. 251, as follows:

"Since the expulsion of the French from the island, St. Domingo has been nominally independent; but slavery has been far indeed from being abolished, and the condition of the people anything but ameliorated by the change. Nominally free, the blacks have remained really enslaved. Compelled to labor, by the terrors of military discipline, for a small part of the produce of the soil, they have retained the severity, without the advantages of servitude; the industrious habits, the flourishing aspect of the island have disappeared; the surplus wealth, the agricultural opulence of the fields, have ceased; from being the greatest exporting island in the West Indies, it has ceased to raise any sugar; and the inhabitants, reduced to half their Republican task masters, have relapsed into the indolence and inactivity of savage life.

"The revolution of St. Domingo has demonstrated that the negroes can occasionally exert all the vigor and heroism which distinguish the European character: but there is, as yet, no reason to suppose that they are capable of the continued efforts, the sustained and persevering toil, requisite to erect the fabric of civilized freedom. An observation of Gibbon seems decisive on this subject: 'The inaction of the negroes does not seem to be the effect either of their virtue or of their pusillanimity. They indulge, like the rest of mankind, their passions and appetites, and the adjacent tribes are engaged in frequent acts of hostility. But this rude ignorance has never invented any effectual weapons of defense or destruction; they appear incapable of forming any extensive plans of government or conquest, and the obvious inferiority of their mental faculties has been discovered and abused by the nations of the temperate zone. Sixty thousand blacks are annually embarked from the coast of Guinea but they embark in chains, never to return to their native country; and this constant emigration, which, in the space of two centuries, might have furnished armies to overrun the globe, accuses the guilt of Europe and the weakness of Africa.'

"If the negroes are not inferior, either in vigor, courage, or intelligence to the European, how has it happened that for six thousand years, they have remained in the savage state? What has prevented mighty empires arising on the banks of the Niger, the Quarra, or the Congo, in the same way as on those of the Euphrates, the Ganges, and the Nile? Heat of climate, intricacy of forests, extent of desert, will not solve the difficulty, for they exist to as great an extent in the plains of Mesopotamia or Hindostan as in Central Africa. It is vain to say the Europeans have retained the Africans in that degraded condition, by their violence, injustice and the slave trade.

"How has it happened that the inhabitants of that vast and fruitful region have not risen to the government of the globe, and inflicted on the savages of Europe the evils now set forth as the cause of their depression? Did not all nations start alike in the career of infant improvement? and was not Egypt, the cradle of civilization, nearer the Central African than the shores of Britain? In the earliest representations of nations in existence the paintings on the walls of the tombs of the Kings of Egypt, the distinct races of the Asiatics, the Jews, the Hottentots, and Europeans are clearly marked; but the blue-eyed and white-haired sons of Japhet are represented in cowskins, with the hair turned outward, in the pristine state of pastoral life, while the Hottentots are already clothed in the garb of civilized existence. What since has given so mighty an impulse to European civilization, and detained in a stationary or declining state the immediate neighbors of Egyptian and Carthagenian greatness? It is impossible to arrive at any other conclusion but that, in the qualities requisite to create and perpetuate civilization, the African is decidedly inferior to the European race; and if any doubt could exist on this subject, it would be removed by the subsequent history and present state of the Haytian Republic."—See Mackenzie's St. Domingo, vol. ii, 260, 321.

The following table contains the comparative wealth, produce, and trade of St. Domingo, before 1789, and in 1832, after forty years of nominal freedom.

	St. Domingo.	1789.	1832.
Population		000,000	250,000
Sugar exported		672,0000,000 lbs.	None.
Coffee		80,789,000 lbs.	32,000,000 lbs
Ships employed in trade		1,680	1
Sailors		27,000	167
Exports to France		£0,720,000	None.
Imports from ditto		9,890,000	None.

This last act in this abolition tragedy now remains for us to perform. The other acts we have scrupulously imitated, and it only remains for us to finish up the "afterpiece." The tragedians, prompters, supes and all are on the stage, playing to crowded houses.

CHAPTER II.

EFFECTS AND INCIDENTS OF AGITATION IN THE WEST INDIES.

Agitation of the Slavery Question in England...Abolition of the Slave Trade...English Philanthropists Define their Position against immediate Emancipation...Abolition of Slavery in the British West Indies: Effects of such Emancipation...Testimony of Anti-Slavery men...Decline of Commerce...Destruction of Agriculture...The Negroes Tending to Heathenism...Valuable Statistics respecting Hayti...Indolence and Destitution of the Negroes...Present Condition of Hayti...Abolition Testimony...The Results of Emancipation in Jamaica...Census and Statistics...Great Falling Off in Products...Estates Going to Decay...The Negro Receding into a Savage State....The Public Debt Increasing....The "London Times" Owns Up...Dr. CHANNING's Prophecy not Fulfilled...TROLLOP and the "London Times"....Negroes will not render Voluntary Labor...Testimony of numerous Abolitionists, showing the Effects of Emancipation in the West Indies...Effect in Mexico...Mr. LINCOLN's Opinion...Statistics Applicable to the Question in the West Indies and the United States...General Conclusions, etc.

SLAVERY AGITATION IN ENGLAND.

In England, for more than two centuries, the question of abolition was agitated, CANNING, CLARKSON, WILBERFORCE, BURKE and other humanitarians devoted their lives to the subject, and the world has given them credit for unambitious and human impulses, and while these philanthropists scorned to make political merchandise of their prejudices against slavery, their agitation of the subject, as in Rome and France, brought to the surface a horde of demagogues, cheap philanthropists and political agitators, who of course jostled from the stage an equal number of Statesmen. These agitators are indigious to all civilized countries, and are ever ready to mount the most popular hobby on which to ride into place and power, and herein we have a melancholy parallel in this country.

In 1798 Mr PITT introduced his bill in the House of Commons for the abolition of the slave trade, which finally became a law, and that inhuman traffic was no longer patronized by the British flag. But the system of slavery introduced under the ægis of that flag in America and in the British West Indies, had so fastened its fangs on the body politic, and so interwoven itself among all relations of life, that to attempt its sudden extirpation was considered by the wisest and best philanthropists of the day as an evil even greater than the system itself. PALEY, the great emancipationist, after a long agitation exclaimed,

"The truth is, emancipation should be gradual, or the consequences may be terrible."

CANNING, the great English emancipationist, in his speech on the subject in Parliament, March 6th, 1824, said:

"If I am asked whether I am for the permanent existance of slavery in our colonies, I say no; but if I am asked whether I am favorable to its immediate abolition, I say no; and if I am asked which I would prefer, permanent slavery or immediate abolition, I do not know whether under all the perplexing circumstances of the case, I should not prefer things remaining as they are.—*Canning's Select Speeches*, p. 414.

Here, we see the well grounded fears of a real philanthropist, who looked to remote consequences rather than to immediate political advantage.

It was not until 1833, thirty-five years after Pitt introduced his measure for the abolition of the slave trade, that England abolished slavery in her eighteen West Indian colonies, at a cost of $100,000,000, and it should be remembered that the home Government had no slaves, and hence nothing to fear, except to the pockets of her West Indian merchants, nor had she any constitutional barriers in the way. But, although slavery has been abolished in the British West Indies for over thirty years, and the system of free labor and African freedom thoroughly tested, there is no historical dissent from the well known fact that both master and slave, in every material fact pertaining to their commercial prosperity, their physical, moral and religious condition, are immeasurably below the standard of their former condition. Let a few statistical and historical facts settle this point.

EFFECTS OF EMANCIPATION IN THE WEST INDIES.

The West India Islands contain about 150,000 square miles of the richest territory on the globe, and a climate that no latitude or longitude surpasses. A distinguished traveller says:

"It is extremely difficult to convey to one unacquainted with the richness and variety of the island scenery of the tropics, a correct impression of its gorgeous scenery.—Islands rising from a crystal sea, clothed with a vegetation of surpassing luxuriance and splendor, and of every variety, from the tall and graceful palm, the stately and spreading mahogany, to the bright flowers that seem to have stolen their tints from the glowing sun above them. Birds, with colors as varied and gorgeous as the hues of the rainbow, flit amid the dark green foliage of the forests, and flamingoes, with their scarlet plumage, flash along the shore. Fish, of the same varied hues, glide through waters so clear that for fathoms below the surface they can be distinctly seen. Turn the eye where it will, on sea or land, some bright color flashes before it. Nature is here a queen indeed, and dressed for a gala day."

To this gorgeous picture may be added the fact that all the lucious fruits of the tropics, oranges, lemons, citrons, mangoes, coffee, plantains, bananas, yams, maize, millet, pine apples, melons, grapes, &c., grow spontaneously. Such a paradise—such a garden of Eden—ought to secure wealth, prosperity and happiness to even the least deserving effort. A light 'draft' on Prof. HOLTON's work on *New Grenada** will pay:

"What more could nature do for this people, or what has

*NEW GRENADA: Twenty Months in the Andes. By Isaac F. Holton, M. A. Harper & Bros.

she withholden from them? What production of any zone would be unattainable by patient industry, *if they knew of such a virtue?* But this valley seems to be encircled with the greatest fertility and the finest climate in the world, only to show the *miraculous power of idleness and unthrift to keep land poor!* Here, the family have sometimes omitted their dinner *because there was nothing to eat in the house!* Maize, cocoa and rice, when out of season, can hardly be had for love or money; so this valley (Cauca) a very Eden by nature, *is filed with hunger and poverty!*"

A distinguished writer, commenting on the above, says:

"Now, there are over 2,000,000 of square miles essentially in the same position, degraded in morals, lazy in habits, and worthless in every respect. The improvements under the Spaniards are gone to decay and ruin, while the mongrel population do nothing, except insult the name of "God and Liberty" by indulging in pronunciamentos and revolutions."

When God had made all things save man, He found there was "no one to till the ground," so he made Adam. Thus, it seems that the Divine object in creating man was to "till the land"—to labor and earn his sustenance "by the sweat of his brow," and that people who will not labor, defy the purposes of God, and his curses must follow, as we shall see.

The result of French and British philanthropy has been *emancipation from labor*, and degradation. Misery and want is the result of that emancipation, because it is historically true that the Ethiopean will not labor unless compelled by the thrift of his Caucasian or Castilian superiors, and herein lies the secret of retrogression, pauperism and crime, under the fatal mistake of philanthropists that all men should be equal by human laws, when God by His laws peremptorily forbids it.

In 1800 there was imported from the West Indies cotton to the amount of 17,000,000 lbs., and from the United States 19,789,803 lbs. Thus, in 1800 they were about equally productive in that fabric. In 1840, under their freedom of from 10 to 45 years, the West Indies exported only 866,157 lbs. of cotton, while the United States exported 743,941,061 lbs. Garrison, Thompson, and other British agitators, had predicted that the West Indies, under the new system of freedom would outstrip the slavery accursed United States. But the above facts do not show it in this light.

THE HAYTIEN FREE REPUBLIC.

Hayti is divided into two grand divisions, the Western portion being the Haytien, or negro colony, and the Eastern the Dominican Republic. It is first in size to Cuba, is the most luxuriant and fertile of the Antilles, and contains 27,690 square miles, of which 17,599 are comprised in the Dominican Republic.—The entire length of the Island is 406 miles by 163 broad. The population is estimated at from 550,000 to 650,000. The climate and natual resources surpass any other locality on this planet. Gold, silver, platina, sulphur, copper, tin, iron, rock salt, jasper, marble &c. &c, exist in abundance, and under the old system the mines and quarries were made to yield abundance of wealth, but these have long since ceased to be worked, as has the soil, and every department requiring labor.

In 1790 Hayti was in the heyday of its prosperity. "At that time," says a distinguished writer, "it supplied half of Europe with sugar. It was a French colony and contained a population of 500,000, of which 38,360 were whites and 28,370 free negroes, mostly mulattos, the rest were slaves." This was the error of the great French revolution, when BRISSOT was agitating the abolition of slavery in the French colonies, on the basis of "liberty, equality and fraternity." In 1793 the freedom of Hayti was decreed, and the "grand experiment" was entered upon. Let us put in juxtaposition a few statistics that exhibit the result of this humane course. In 1790, three years before emancipation, the exports from Hayti were $27,828,000. The following being the principal productions that entered into the exporting manifests. We compare them below for three periods, ranging from 1790 to 1849, the latest dates which furnish any reliable statisics:

	1790.	1826.	1849.
Sugar, lbs,	163,405,220	32,864	none.
Coffee, lbs,	68,151,180	32,189,784	30,008,643
Cotton, lbs,	6,286,126	620,972	544.516
Indigo, lbs,	930,016	none.	none.

Here is the result of three periods, the first three years before emancipation, the second thirty-three years after, and the third fifty-six years after. It will be seen that the article of coffee is the only article that has kept up to even an approximation to the original standard, the reason is, though flourishing under good cultivation, yields moderately well under spontaneous growth, and can be procured without agricultural labor, while sugar, indigo, and cotton cannot. Here is a striking evidence of the worthless indolence of the negro when left to himself. The above statistics are taken from the *United States Commercial Relations*, vol. 1, pp. 561-2, officially reported to Congress and published by its order.

"In colloninal times, when the soil was cultivated by forced labor, this same country (Hayti) produced for export five or six times the amounts now exported."—*Appleton's New American Cyclopedia*.

"The public revenue is derived chiefly from customs, navigation dues, monopolies, &c, and averages about $1,000,-000 a year, The expenditures exceed this amount, and hence the public debt has been constantly increasing."—*Ibid.*

But we are not left wholly to statistics. A foreign resident at the Haytien capital writes:

"This country has made, since its emancipation, no progress whatever. The population principally live upon the produce of the grown wild coffee plantations; remnants of the French dominion. Properly speaking, plantations of the model of the English in Jamaica, or the Spanish in Cuba, do not exist here. Hayti is the most fertile and the most beautiful of the Antilles, it has more mountains than Cuba, and more space than Jamaica. No where the coffee tree could better thrive than here, as it especially likes a mountainous soil, *but the indolence of the negro has brought the once splendid plantations to decay.* They now gather coffee from the grown wild tree. The cultivation of the sugar cane has entirely disappeared, and the Island that once supplied the one half of Europe with sugar now supplies its own wants from Jamaica and the United States."

THE PRESENT CONDITION OF HAYTI.

The present condition of Hayti is more graphically depicted by Mr. E. B. UNDERHILL

in his work just published, entitled *The West Indies—their Moral and Social Condition*. Mr. U. was sent out by the Baptist Missionary Society of London, and is an Abolitionist of undoubted orthodoxy. In his description of his journey to Port au Prince, he says:

"We passed by many, or through many *abandoned plantations, the buildings in ruins, the sugar mills decayed, and the iron pans strewing the road side, cracked and broken.* But for the law that forbids, on pain of confiscation, the export of all metals, they would long ago been sold to foreign merchants. *Only once in this long ride did we come upon a mill in use.* It was grinding canes, in order to manufacture the syrup from which *tafia* is made, a kind of inferior rum, the intoxicating drink of the country. The mill was worked by a large overshot or water wheel, the water being brought by an aqueduct from a very considerable distance. With the exception of a few banana gardens, or small. patches of maize around the cottages, nowhere did this magnificent and fertile plain show signs of cultivation.

"In the time of the French occupation, before the Revolution of 1798, thousands of hogsheads of sugar were produced, *now not one! All is decay and desolation!* The pastures are deserted, and the prickly pear covers the land once laughing with the bright hues of the sugar cane.

"The hydraulic works erected at vast expense, for irrigation, *have crumbled to dust. The plow is an unknown implement of culture,* although so eminently adapted to the great plains and deep soil of Hayti.

"A country so capable of producing for export, and therefore for the enrichment of its people, besides coffee, sugar, cotton, tobacco, cacao, spices—every tropical fruit, and many of the fruits of Europe, *lies unoccupied, uncultivated and desolate!* Its rich mines are neither explored nor worked, and its beautiful woods rot in the soil where they grow. A little logwood is exported, but ebony, mahogeny and the finest building timber, rarely fall before the woodman's axe, and then only for local use. *The present inhabitants despise all servile labor, and are for the most part content with the spontaneous productions of the soil and forest.*"

NEGROES RELAPSING INTO BARBARISM.

As showing the tendency of the negro to relapse into the barbarism of his African progenitors, we copy Mr. UNDERHILL's description of what is known as the Vaudoux religion or serpent worship:

"It is a native African superstition, and proves beyond all question the rapid return of the Hayti negroes to the original savageism of their African ancestors."

Mr. UNDERHILL gives a full description of this disgusting, heathenish rite, from which we select the chorus. The object of which is a small green snake, to worship which the negro naturally has a predisposition, but is repressed by control of the whites. Of late it has been revived in Hayti, and we give the chorus of the heathenish exercises:

Eh! eh! Bomba, hen! hen!
Conga bafilla te
Conga mourne de le!
Conga de ki li
Conga li!

Mr. Underhill further describes this heathenish rite:

"The Vaudoux meet in a retired spot, designated at a primary meeting. On entering, they take off their shoes, and bind about their bodies handkerchiefs, in which a red color predominates. The king is known by the scarlet band around his head, worn like a crown, and a scarf of the same color distinguishes the queen. The object of adoration, the serpent, is placed on a stand.— It is then worshipped; after which the box is placed on the ground, the queen mounts upon it, is seized with violent tremblings, and gives utterances to oracles, in response to the prayers of the worshippers. A dance closes the ceremony. The king puts his hand on the box; a tremor seizes him, which is communicated to the circle. A delirious whirl or dance ensues, heightened by the free use of *tafia*. The weakest fall as dead, on the spot.— The bacchanalian revelers, always dancing and turning about, are borne away into a place close at hand, where sometimes, under the tripple excitement of *promiscuous intercourse*, drunkenness and darkness, scenes are enacted, enough to make the impassable gods of Africa itself gnash their teeth with horror."

Can it be possible that the advocates of emancipation find in such lamentable evidences of retrogression, encouragement for continued zeal in a cause that suffers debasement without a remedy? And yet we are told, "only give the negro a chance. and he will become equal to the whites!" Mr. Webley, a missionary, in writing to the London *Missionary Herald*, in 1850, says:

"These Vaudoux almost deluge the Haytien part of the island. They practice witchcraft and mysticism, to an almost indefinite extent. They are singular adepts at poisoning—a person rarely escapes them when he has been fixed upon as a victim."

Such are the sickening orgies of a race we are being called upon to make equally free, at the expense of millions of treasure and the best Caucasian blood in our nation History furnishes us no example on this planet where the negro race, with every advantage at their command, have shown their ability for colonization and self-government, even approximating that of the white race.

THE RESULT IN JAMAICA.

Jamaica is the most extensive of all the British West Indies It is longitudinally 150 miles in extent, and 50 miles broad, containing near 6,500 square miles. The census of 1844 showed the following population:

Whites... 15,779
Mulattoes... 68,529
Negroes..293,128

Total...377,436

The census of 1861, and the last one taken, shows the following:

Whites... 13,816
Mulattoes... 81,065
Negroes..346,374

Total...441,255

Of this number, after twenty-eight years of freedom, only 50,726 could read or write. It will be seen also, that the white population decreases, while the negro and mulatto portion rapidly increased, thus showing that in time the white race must be merged and lost in the black race—a not very flattering aspect for the pride of blood.

Jamaica, like the other West Indies, abounds in all the rich minerals, woods and tropical vegetation The Island has been under the paw of the British lion ever since the halcyon days of Cromwell, and flourished without stint till 1838, the expiration of the apprentice system, under the emancipation act. Since that time the progress of the Island, has been positively downward in all that constitutes a people great, happy and prosperous. Of the vast sum appropriated by England for the liberation of the slaves, $30,000,000 went to the Island of Jamaica. We find that according to the *Encyclopædia of Commerce*, the following as the results for two periods, of exportations:

Before Emancipation.
Year.   Val. of Products.
1809....................................£3,033,204

After Emancipation.
Year.   Val. of Products.
1853....................................£837,276

Leading Products of Jamaica in 1805.
Sugar, hhds... 150,352
Rum, punch... 40,837
Pimento, lbs.. 1,041,540
Coffee, lbs...17,901,923

In 1834, the year emancipation was affected, the products stood as follows:

Products of Jamaica in 1834.
Sugar, hhds... 84,750
Rum, punch... 32,111
Pimento, lbs.. 3,605,400
Coffee, lbs...17,125,731

The next year, and first under the "free" system, the amount of sugar fell off to 77,970 hhds; coffee to 10,593,018 lbs., &c.

Products of Jamaica in 1856.
Sugar, hhds... 25,920
Rum, punch... 14,470
Pimento, lbs.. 6,848,622
Coffee, lbs... 3,025,147

Upon which the author of *Results of Emancipation in the North and West India Islands*, remarks:

"The only crop that had increased was that of Pimento or 'all-spice,' the increase of which, instead of being an evidence of the industry of the negro, is the reverse. The Pimento tree grows wild in Jamaica, and rapidly spreads over land formerly under cultivation. As the plantations were abandoned, they were overrun with this tree, and the negro women and children pick the berries without the trouble of cultivation. The coffee tree to a certain extent is like the Pimento, and grows wild in many places, hence the production of coffee has not fallen off in the same proportion as that of sugar, which can only be produced by careful cultivation. The coffee crop of Jamaica, however, in 1812, before the overthrow of slave labor, was 34,045,585 lbs, but the average crop for the past ten years has not been over 5,000,000 lbs., while the sugar crop had fallen in 1853 as low as 20,000 hhds. These facts and statistics demonstrate the downhill progress of Jamaica, and show what may be expected wherever the experiment of free negroism is attempted.

"The rapidity with which estates have been abandoned in Jamaica, and the decrease in the taxable property of the Island, is also astounding. The movable and the immovable property of Jamaica was estimated at £50,000,000, or nearly $250,000,000. In 1850 the assessed valuation had fallen to £11,500,000. In 1857 it was reduced to £9,500,000, and Mr. WESTMORELAND in a speech in the Jamaica House of Assembly, stated it was believed that the falling off would be £2,000,000 more in 1852. From a report made to the House of Assembly, of the number and extent of the plantations abandoned, during the years 1848, '49, '50, '51 and '52, we gather the following facts:

Sugar estates abandoned,..........................128
 "   "   partially abandoned,................ 71
Coffee plantations abandoned,..................... 96
 "   "   partially abandoned,................ 66

The total number of acres thus thrown out of cultivation, in five years, were 391,187. This is only a sample, for the same process has been going on ever since emancipation.

"In the five years immediately succeeding emancipation the abandoned estates stood as follows:

"'Sugar estates............................140=108,032 acres.
"'Coffee plautations......................465=188,400 acres.
"'These plantations employed 39,383 laborers, whose industry was therefore at once lost to the world, and the articles they had raised were just so much extracted from consumption. The price of these articles—sugar and coffee, was increased, on account of diminished production, and that increased cost represented the tax which the world paid for the privilege of allowing Sambo to loll in idleness. *The Cyclopedia of Commerce* says:
"'*The negro is rapidly receding into a savage state, and that unless there is a large and immediate supply of emigrants, all society will come to a speedy end, and the Island become a second Hayti!*'"

PUBLIC DEBT OF JAMAICA INCREASING.

Appleton's New American Cyclopedia says that the public debt of Jamaica has increased from £529,856 in 1817, to £913,618 in 1857," or an increase of $191,880 per annum.

TESTIMONY OF THE LONDON TIMES.

The London *Times*, the court organ of the British government, is forced to acknowledge the bad results of emancipation. Such a candid admission from such a source is worth a thousand theoretical, sentimental and fanatical sermons and speeches, that seek to arouse the prejudices, without stopping to consider results or offer remedies. The *Times* says:

"There is *no blinking the truth.* Years of bitter experience—years of hope deferred, of self devotion unrequited, of prayers unanswered, of sufferings divided, of insults unresented, of contumely patiently endured, have convinced us of the truth. It must be spoken out boldly and energetically, despite the wild mockings of howling cant. *The freed West India slave will not till the soil for wages.* The free son of the ex-slave is as obstinate as his sire. He will not cultivate lands which he has not bought for his own. Ynms, mangoes and plantains—these satisfy his wants. He cares not for your cotton. Sugar, coffee and tobacco, he cares but little for, and what matters it to him that the Englishman has sunk his thousands and tens of thousands on mills, machinery and plantations, which now totter on the languishing estates that for years has only returned him to beggery and debt? He eats his yams and sniggers at 'Duckra.' We know not *why* this should be, *but so it is!* The negro has been bought with a price—the price of English *taxation* and English *toil.* He has been redeemed from bondage *by the sweat and travail of some millions of hard working Englishmen!* Twenty millions of pounds sterling—$100,000,000—have been *distilled from the brains and muscles of the free English laborer, of every degree, to fashion the West India negro into a "free, independent laborer.*' 'Free and independent' enough he has become, God knows, but *laborer, he is not,* and so far as we can see, never will be. He will sing hymns and quote texts, but honest, steady industry he not only detests, but despises!"

Such is the candid admission of the official organ of the British Government, uttered about the time—some two or three years ago—when a British Lord submitted a serious proposition in Parliament to return to slavery in the West Indies, under the name and guise of cooley indentures. We have forgotten the noble Lord's name, but recollect quite well the general comments it encountered, both in Great Britain and this country.

ABOLITION PROPHECIES THIRTY YEARS AGO.

Let emancipationists look on the above picture, and then on the following by that great champion of abolition, as a prophesy, in 1833—the Rev. Dr. CHANNING:

"The planters in general would suffer little, if at all, from emancipation. This change would make them *richer* rather than poorer. One would think, indeed, from the common language on the subject, that the negroes were to be annihilated by being set free; that the whole labor of the South was to be destroyed by a single blow. But the colored man, when freed, will not vanish from the soil; he will stand there with the same muscles as before, only strung anew by liberty; with the same limbs to toil, and with *stronger motives* to toil than before. He will work from *hope*, not fear; will work for himself, not others; and unless all the principles of human nature are reversed under a black skin, he will work *better than before.*
"We believe that agriculture will revive, our worn out soils will be renewed, and the whole country assume a brighter aspect under *free labor.*"

TROLLOP AND THE LONDON TIMES.

This has been the syren song of the abolitionists for centuries, but in no case does it tally with historical or physical facts. Mr. Anthony Trollop, an Englishman, who has written a book on Jamaica, seems to take the other view of the matter, from actual observation, and not from theory, and the London *Times* thus disposes of the case:

"A servile race, peculiarly fitted by nature for the hardest physical work in a burning climate. The negro has no desire for property strong enough to induce him to labor with sustained power. He lives from hand to mouth. In order that he may have his dinner and some small finery, he will work a little, but after that he is content to *lie in the sun.* This, in Jamaica, he can very easily do, for emancipation and free trade have combined to throw enormous tracts of land out of cultivation, and on these the negro squats, getting all that he wants, with very little trouble, and sinking in the most resolute fashion to the savage state. Lying under his cotton tree, he refuses to work after 10 o'clock in the morning. 'No, tank 'ee, massa, me tired, now; me no want more money.' Or by the way of variety, he may say: 'No, workee no more; money no nuff; workee no pay.' And so the planter must see his cane foul with weeds, because he cannot prevail on Sambo to earn a second shilling by going into the corn-fields. He calls him a lazy nigger, and threatens him with starvation. His answer is: 'No, massa; no starvee now; God send plenty yam.' These yams, be it observed, on which Sambo lives, and on the strength of which he declines to work, are grown on the planter's own ground, and probably planted at his own expense.
"There lies the shiny, oily, odorous negro under his mango-tree, eating the lucious fruit in the sun. He sends his black urchin up for a bread fruit, and behold, the family table is spread. He pierces a cocoanut, and lo! there is his beverage. He lies on the ground surrounded by oranges, bananas and pine apples. Why should he work? Let Sambo himself reply; 'No, Massa, me weak in me belly; me no workee to-day; me no like workee just um little moment.' This is a graphic description of the negro character where the climate gives him a chance to show out his real nature. The same author says that 'one-half of the sugar-estates, and more than one-half of the coffee-plantations have gone back *into a state of bush.*'"

FREE NEGROES WON'T WORK IN AFRICA.

Negroes seldom ever go voluntarily into the field to work. Of all the negros in the North how many do we see in the fields, the workshops or at the forge? Those who do labor, as a general rule, are to be found in the capacity of servants in the towns and cities, or retailing fruits and nuts at a corner stand MUNGO PARK, many years ago, writing of his travels in Africa, said:

"Paid servants—persons of free condition, voluntarily working for pay—are *unknown here.*"

Such is the universal testimony of all travellers who allude to the subject.

SCRAPS FROM MY SCRAP-BOOK. 19

CHARACTER OF FREE NEGROES.

We copy as follows from *Results of Emancipation*, before alluded to:

"In *Lewis' West Indies*, written seventeen years before emancipation, it is remarked:—'As to free blacks, they are unfortunately lazy and improvident; most of them half starved, and only anxious to live from hand to mouth. Even those who profess to be tailors, carpenters or coopers, are, for the most part, careless, drunken and dissipated, and never take pains sufficient to attain to any dexterity in their trades. *As for a free negro hiring himself out for plantation labor, no instance of such a thing was ever known in Jamaica!*' Earl GREY said in the House of Lords, June 18, 1852, 'That it was established by statistical facts that the negroes were idle, and *falling back in civilization*;—that relieved from the coercion to which they were freely subjected, and a couple of days labor giving them enough food for a fortnight, the climate rendering clothing and fuel not necessary to life, they had no earthly motive to give a greater amount of service than for mere subsistance.'

MORE TESTIMONY.

"Sir H. LIGHT and Gov. BARKLEY have both shown also, that the majority of the free negroes of the West Indies are living in idleness, and the French colonies, according to a work from M. VACHEROT, published a few years ago, at Paris, demonstrate the same ruinous result under the emancipation act.

CAPTAIN HAMILTON'S STATEMENT.

"Capt. HAMILTON, on his examination as a witness before a select committee of Parliament, stated that *'Jamaica, without any exaggeration had become a desert !!'*

MR. BIGELOW'S VIEWS.

"In 1850, Mr. JOHN BIGELOW, then one of the editors of the New York *Evening Post*, paid a visit to Jamaica, and wrote a book thereon. As the testimony of an anti-slavery man, his statements are given. Mr. BIGELOW says that the land of that island is as prolific as any in the world. It can be bought for $5 to $10 per acre, and five acres confer the right of voting, and eligibility to public offices. Planters offer $1,50 per day for labor; sixteen days labor will enable a man to buy land enough to make him a voter, and the market of Kingston offers a great demand for vegetables at all times. These facts, said Mr. BIGELOW, place indepence within the reach of every black. But what are the results? There have been no increase in voters in twenty years. Lands run wild. Kingston gets its vegetables from the United States!'

MR. BAIRD'S OPINION.

"But we will accumulate proof—pile it up, if necessary, Mr. Robert Baird, who is an enthusiastic advocate of 'the glorious act of British Emancipation,' on visiting the West Indies for his health, could not fail to be struck with the desolate appearance there.

"That the West Indies,' says Mr. Baird, 'are always grumbling, is an observation often heard, and no doubt it is very true that they are so. But let any one who thinks that the extent and clamor of the complaint exceeds the magnitude of the distress which has called it forth, go to the West Indies and judge for himself. Let him see with his own eyes *the neglected and abandoned estates, the uncultivated fields, fast hurrying back into a state of nature, with all the speed of tropical luxuriance—the dismantled and silent machinery, the crumbling walls and deserted mansions, which are familiar sights in most of the British West Indian colonies!* Let him then transport himself to the Spanish Islands of Porto Rico and Cuba, and witness the life and activity which prevail in these slave colonies. Let him observe for himself the the activity of the slaves—the improvements daily making in the cultivation of the fields, and in the process carried on at the ingonois, or sugar mills—and *the general, indescribable air of thriving and prosperity which surround the whole*—and then let him come back to England and say, if he honestly can, that the British West Indian planters and proprietors are grumblers, who complain without adequate cause!

GOV. WOOD'S EXPERIENCE.

"Ex-Gov. Wood, of Ohio, who paid a visit to Jamaica in 1858, and who is no friend to slavery, says:
"'Since the blacks have been liberated, they have become indolent, insolent, degraded, and dishonest. They are a rude, beastly set of vagabonds, lying naked about the streets, as filthy as the Hottentots, and I believe worse. On getting to the wharf of Kingston, the first thing the blacks of *both sexes, perfectly naked*, came swarming about the boat, and would dive for small pieces of coin, that were thrown by the passengers. On entering the city, the stranger is annoyed to death by black beggars, at every step, and you must often show them your pistol, or an uplifted cane, to rid yourself of their importunities.'

SEWELL'S VIEWS OF KINGSTON—A GOD-FORSAKEN PLACE.

"Sewell, in his work on the *Ordeal of Free Labor*, in which he defends emancipation, and pleads for still more extended privileges to the blacks, says of Kingston:
"'There is not a house in decent repair; not a wharf in good order; no pavement, no sidewalk, no drainage, and scanty water; no light. There is nothing like work done. Wreck and ruin, devastation and neglect. The inhabitants, taken *en masse*, are stooped to the eyelids in immorality. The population shows a natural decrease. Illegitimacy exceeds legitimacy. Nothing is replaced that time destroys. If a brick tumbles from a house to the street it remains there. If a spout is loosened by the wind, it hangs by a thread, till it falls. If furniture is accidently broken, the idea of having it mended is not entertained. A God-forsaken place, without life or energy. Old, dilapidated, sickly, filthy, cast away from the anchorage of sound morality, of reason and common sense. Yet this wretched hulk is the Capital of an Island—an Island, the most fertile in the world. It is blessed with a climate the most glorious; it lies rotting in a shadow of mountains that can be cultivated from summit to base with every product of the tropic and temperate regions. It is the mistress of a harbor wherein a thousand line-of-battle ships can ride safely at anchor.'

THE AMERICAN MISSIONARY ON JAMAICA MORALITY.

"We might fill a volume with such quotations, showing the steady decline of the Island, but it is well to note the moral condition of the negro. The *American Missionary Association*, is the strongest kind of Abolition testimony in regard to the moral condition of the negroes. The *American Missionary*, a monthly paper, and organ of the Association, for July, 1855, has the following quotation from the letters of one of the Missionaries:
"'A man here, may be a drunkard, a liar, a Sabbath-breaker, a profane man, a fornicator, an adulterer, and such like, and be known to be such, and go to chapel, and hold up his head there, and feel no disgrace for these things, because they are so common, as to create a public sentiment in his favor. No may go to the communion table, and cherish a hope of Heaven, and not have his hopes disturbed. [A perfect paradise for BEECHER and GREELEY.] I might tell of persons guilty of some, if not of all these things, ministering in holy things.'

FROM REPORT OF AMERICAN ANTI-SLAVERY SOCIETY.

"The report of the *American and Foreign Anti-Slavery Society* of 1853, page 170, says of the nego:
"'Their moral condition is very far from being what it ought to be. It is exceedingly dark and distressing.— Licentiousness prevails to a most alarming extent among the people. The almost universal prevalence of intemperance is another prolific source of moral darkness and degradation of the people. The masses, among all classes, from the Governor in his palace to the peasant in his hut —from the bishop in his gown to the beggar in his rags— are *all slaves to their cups*.'

THE MARRIAGE RELATION AMONG FREE BLACKS.

"So much for 'freedom' elevating the blacks. It is complained that the marriage relation is not always regarded where 'slavery' exists, but it would seem from this statement that slavery had done more for the moral improvement of the negro in this respect than he was at all disposed to do for himself.

"Mr. UNDERHILL endorses the stories of the 'crowds of bastard children' in the Island, and says it is 'too true.' 'Outside the non-conformist communities,' he says, 'neglect of marriage is almost universal. One clergyman informed me, that of seventeen infants brought to his church for baptism, fifteen at least would be of illegitimate origin.' In fact, from all the admissions made, it does not appear there is any more marriage in Jamaica than in Africa. The churches, Mr. UNDERHILL allows, are less attended than formerly, and there is evidently little of the religious training of the whites left among the people. The negro, however, has all the advantages of 'impartial freedom,' and 'the highest offices of the state are open to colored men—they are found (says Mr. U.) in the Assembly, in the Executive, on the bench and at the bar. All colors mix freely.' This would be the paradise of SEWARD, PHILLIPS and GREELEY.

LOSS OF LABOR AND DECAY OF ESTATES.

"Mr. UNDERHILL estimates the annual loss of wages to the people from the decay of estates, and plantations, cannot be less than three hundred thousand pounds, or $1,500,000. Negroes who work at all cannot be prevailed upon to do so generally more than four days in the week, and rarely five. Mr. U. also states that it has been officially ascertained that two-thirds of the persons employed on sugar estates are women and children; yet, notwithstanding all these facts, the anti-slaveryite still adheres to his hobby. He has excuses and palliations for his friend, the negro. True, Jamaica is ruined, but still emancipation is a success. The seasons were poor, the estates were mortgaged—the planters have not treated the blacks kindly, and they have bought patches of ground of their own, rather than labor for others. Such are some of the excuses of the friends of the negro, but the facts still stand out in bold relief, despite the assertions of 'negro missionaries,' who are interested in keeping up the delusion. The facts they do admit. They cannot deny or controvert them. This is all we ask. We need none of their excuses. In order to relieve themselves of the odium of having ruined the fairest Island of the Antilles, they will naturally look for reasons not chargeable to themselves, but figures do not lie. The exports of Jamaica have been gradually decreasing ever since "slavery" in the Island was interfered with, until they have dwindled down to insignificance, and as the London Times says, 'there is no blinking the truth—the negro will not work for wages,' and hence the tropics are going back to jungle and bush, while white men are taxed double the price they ought to be for all tropical products."

NEGROES ONLY DESIRE TO BE FREED FROM LABOR.

We have a vivid illustration of the fact that negroes will not work when they can avoid it, by those set "free in the rebel states, by the operation of our armies. A correspondent of a New York paper says:

'Their highest idea of freedom is to be freed from labor, and permitted to bask in the sunshine of idleness.'

MR. LINCOLN'S TESTIMONY.

Mr. LINCOLN in his reply to the Chicago Divines, said:

"And suppose they (the negroes) could be induced by a proclamation from me, to throw themselves upon us, what should we do with them? Gen. BUTLER wrote me a few days since that he was issuing more rations to the slaves who had rushed to him than to all the white troops under his command! They call! call! and that is all!!"

MR. UNDERHILL ON CUBA.

The facts we have given relative to several of the principal freedomized West India colonies are true of all, and to the end it may not be said that the islands where abolition agitation has had no foothold, are in as bad way as their neighbors, we will permit an Abolitionist to tell his own story in his own way. Mr. UNDERHILL makes this comparison between Jamaica and Cuba. Of Havana (Cuba) he says:

"It is the busiest and most prosperous of all the Antilles. It's harbor is one of the finest in the world, and is crowded with shipping. Its wharves and warehouses are piled with merchandise; and the general aspect is one of great commercial activity. Its exports nearly reach the annual value of nine millions sterling ($45,000,000) and the customers furnish an annual tribute to the mother country, over and above the cost of government and military occupation. Eight thousand ships annually resort to the harbor of Cuba."

CUBA AND JAMAICA COMPARED.

The following comparison between the exports of Cuba and Jamaica, at three periods—before and after emancipation in the latter—tells more against the evils of slavery agitation than whole chapters from the most ready pen:

Exports from Cuba and Jamaica Compared.

Jamaica in 1809		$15,166,000
Cuba in 1826		12,809,388
Jamaica in 1854		4,480,661
Cuba in 1854		31,683,731
Jamaica in 1859		3,679,403
Cuba* in 1859		57,455,185

West India Productions before Emancipation.

Years.	lbs. Sugar.	lbs. Coffee.	lbs. cotton
Brit. West Ind's 1807	636,025,943	31,610,704	17,000,000†
Hayti 1790	163,318,840	76,835,219	7,286,126
	809,344,453	108,245,983	24,286,126

West India Products after Emancipation.

Years.	lbs. Sugar.	lbs. coffee	lbs cotton
Brit. West Indies 1848	313,306,112	6,770,792	427,520‡
Hayti 1848	very little.	34,114,717	1,591,454§
	313,306,112	40,885,509	2,018,983

COMPARATIVE STATISTICS OF THE UNITED STATES

We close this part of our subject by a reference to the comparison between the exports from the Northern and Southern States of this Union, which may be found by consulting the census statistics published by act of Congress.

Exports from Free States Exclusively—1860.

Fisheries,	$4,156,480
Coal,	731,817
Ice,	183,134
Total free states,	$5,071,431

From Free and Slave States—1860.

Products of the forest,	$11,756,000
Products of agriculture,	21,206,263
Vegetable food,	25,658,404
Manufactures,	33,154,644
Raw produce,	1,355,805
Total free and slave states,	$96,826,209

*Balanza General Del Commercio de la Isla de Cuba, 1859. Habana 1861.
†1800.
‡1840.
§1847.

From Slave States Exclusively—1860.

Cotton,	$191,806,555
Tobacco,	15,906,547
Rosin and Turpentine,	3,734,527
Rice,	2,566,390
Tar and pitch,	151,095
Brown Sugar,	103,244
Molasses,	44,562
Hemp,	8,951
Total slave states	$214,322,880

RECAPITULATION.

Free states exclusively,	$5,071,431
Free and slave states,	96,826,299
Slave states exclusively,	214,322,880
Total,	$316,220,610

The most careful estimates that have been made give the slave states credit for one-third embraced in the articles under the head of "Free and Slave States." If this be correct, the result would stand as follows:

Exports from Southern States,	$246,598,313
do Northern States,	69,622,297
Difference.,	$176,976,016

This does not show the greater wealth in the South. It only shows that with one-third the entire population of the United States, that section exports nearly $200,000,000 more to foreign countries than the Northern States do, and that if we should be so unwise as to Jamaicaize the Southern States, our "balance sheet" with the rest of the world would be slim indeed.

Total U. S. Exports for Forty Years—1821 to 1861.

Cotton,	$2,574,834,091
Tobacco,	424,118,067
Rice,	87,854,511
Naval Stores,	110,981,296
Food,	1,006,961,335
Gold,	458,588,615
Crude articles, manufactures, &c.,	892,010,457
	$5,556,401,272

Exports from the South exclusively, for Forty Years.

Cotton,	$2,514,834,091
Tobacco,	425,118,067
Rice,	87,854,511
Naval stores,	110,981,296
One third of food,	335,650,411
Forty per cent. gold,*	183,588,615
	$3,718,026,991

The total amount of duty paid during this forty years on imports was $1,191,874,443, of which

The South paid,	$799,508,378
The North paid,	392,365,065
Difference,	$407,144,313

Thus, the financial question to be determined now, is, shall the North kill the goose that has laid such golden eggs? That these eggs are being broken by our "philanthropists," we have numerous instances of proof. We make

---

*It may be supposed, without reflection, that this estimate of one third gold for the South, is too high, but it must be remembered that California has only been supplying gold for a few years out of the forty, and that previous to that time, our gold was principally taken from the Southern states.

---

the following quotation from a letter of a delegate of the Christian Commission at St. Louis, to the New York *Tribune:*

"After the departure of Pemberton's army, on the 15th of July (1862) thousands of these miserable creatures (contrabands) filled the vacant houses, churches, sheds and caves. Here they crowded together, sometimes thirty or more in a single room, weary, weak and sick from their long march and abstinence, spiritless and sad, and *many of them longing to be once more on old Massa's plantation.*"

EMANCIPATION AND PEONAGE IN MEXICO.

We might fill our entire space with similar articles, but for want of room we must be content to refer the reader to the thousands of cases exhibiting the sad results of forced emancipation, to the overburdened columns of the public press. We have barely room for the following extract from a correspondence by M. LaMonte, from Mexico to a Paris journal, in 1843:

"Fourteen years ago Mexico abolished slavery in all her departments, and the Central American states followed her example. *A worse measure for the slave, as well as the Republic, could not possibly be imagined.* It was immediately discovered that the freed slaves would not work, and the Mexican Congress was forced to pass the act of peonage, a species of slavery the most atrocious that ever disgraced a civilized nation. Under the old system the master was compelled to provide for his slave in sickness, health and old age. In fact, the slave had all his temporal wants supplied by force of self-interest and law, and never troubled himself about a thought of the morrow. Under the present system, he is compelled to hire himself to some one for such length of time as the employer designates, who, with an eye to profits, surveys the laborer, makes calculation how long he will live as an able bodied man, and then hires him for that period, stipulating for wages barely sufficient to subsist the man's family in health. The law compels a *specific performance of this contract*, and when old age and sickness comes on the poor peon is turned loose to feed upon the scanty pittance of reticent charity, or spend the remnant of his days amid the squalid want and vermin of an almshouse. In all the essential conditions that guarantee case and happiness, the *peon's condition is as much below that of the former slave as a Paris mendicant is below a millionaire on the Boulevard.*"

Mexico abolished slavery in 1829, and had we room to display her commercial statistics, in comparison, the disparity would be equally as great as we have shown in regard to the West Indies—not that slavery is the best condition, or that as an original question it would be politic, but having been fastened on the body politic, it becomes dangerous to all classes to suddenly remove it.

We have thus shown from irrefutable history, the dreadful effects of the enfranchisement of the slaves of Rome, by promises from Roman demagogues and ambitious politicians. We have exhibited the terrible consequences of the liberation of the slaves of St. Domingo, in obedience to the clamors of the Parisian abolitionists. We have brought to public gaze the retrograde and embittered condition of the West Indian and the Mexican "freedmen." We have given facts and figures that too vividly exhibit the destructive influence of that Utopian Abolition system which Abolition historians admit was the primeval cause of Roman suicide, and which not only cost the French nation the Queen of the Antilles, but reduced that "gem of the Ocean"—both master and slave—to a condition of meniality for which there is no abolition. We have shown, from a long array of unimpeachable evidence, that this same system is fast reducing the French and British West Indies from their former proud position of opulance and power, to degradation, misery and want, without regard to caste, condition or color. Have we not then, a right to infer from the analysis of history, and the stern development of physical facts, that any principle or policy which beggars ourselves and destroys the happiness of all alike—master as well as slave—white as well as black—is radically wrong, especially since the devotees of this Utopian philanthropy can point to no living fact within the world's history where the political agitation of the slavery question, has been of the least practical good service? And have we not a right to suppose that the effort to bring all grades of human society to one common level, as common partakers of common rights and privileges—in short, to do by legislation what God Himself has never seen fit to do, is at least one step beyond our prerogatives?

M'KENSIE'S OPINION.

Nor is it our purpose to argue that slavery is right or politic. We have nothing to do with it as an original question. We must treat it as a fact fixed by causes long anterior to our day, and by analogy to consider the consequences of its sudden demolition, by means known to have failed in every instance."

"No matter," says McKensie, "how worthy the motive of philanthropists, historical facts stare us in the face, that it is misplaced philanthropy to endeavor to elevate the African to an equality with the Caucassian race. Either the inferior becomes more abject and miserable, or both, like mixing tar with water, deteriorate, and will finally go into irretrievable decline. An inferior and superir race cannot exist together on terms of equality."

Indeed, this was almost the identical language of President Lincoln to the negro delegation that called upon him in Washington.

GENERAL CONCLUSIONS.

Are we to read our fate by the light of past history that sheds its hideous glare around us? We are now in the midst of a most gigantic revolution, receiving its main source of nourishment, and basing its excuses for the oblation of blood that now crimsons the soil of half this continent, on the same portentious cloud of agitation, behind which the sun of Roman greatness sat to rise no more—the same species of agitation that for two centuries shook the British Empire from centre to circumference, and has resulted in a confirmed failure of its objects in her West India possessions—the same grade of agitation that not only lost to France the "Queen of the Antilles," but has, to all present appearances, blotted out St. Domingoian happiness — the same restless, meddling, fanatical agitation that forced Mexican slaves from one species of servitude into an infinitely more degrading one—an agitation, that no truthful pen of history has shown, or can show, has ever wrought any permanent, lasting good to either the enslaved or the enslavers—an agitation, marked in every stage of its animus or progress, from Romish agrarianism, and French Jacobism, down to American political Puritanism, by selfishness and ambition, having no parallels, and but few exceptions.

As before stated, we offer no defense of slavery. That is far from our purpose or design. As an original question, it has, in our estimation, absolutely nothing to recommend it, save, perhaps, some passages of Holy Writ, to which we by no means appeal—nor do we fall back on a common,yet ingenious argument, that any species of servitude is slavery—that the weak and ignorant ever were, and ever will be subservient to, and consequently the slaves, in an essential degree, of the wise, the wealthy and powerful. We ask no such aids as these, however well grounded in the logic of philosophy. We freely grant, without equivocation or mental reservation, that to our view, legalized slavery is an evil, and while from our stand point of education, moral and religious training, we revolt when asked to defend the system, as of right, it is our duty, nevertheless, to treat it in all its phases, as a fixed fact, as we would any other great evil which the highest wisdom and holiest purposes of the world have failed to overthrow. We must treat it as a *de facto* system, having its germ in causes beyond the control of the people of this era. The present generation is not responsible for the existence of slavery. Mr. LINCOLN in his first annual message insists that the North is as much responsible as the South for the existence and continuance of slavery.

None but the merest criminal quack would cut the throat of his patient to cure a tumor on his neck, and the world would decide it criminal mal practice to eviscerate one afflicted with a cancer in his stomach, or to amputate a limb to remeve insipient ereasipelas.

Good and wise statesmen from the earliest period of our history saw this tumor, this cancer and this malady on the body politic. They grappled with the disease, and treated the patient according to the best skill and science of the age. They dared not apply the cauterizing lancet, lest its sudden severance from the system, and society to which it had been immemorially attached, should expire under the operation. Among all the illustrious statesmen and philosophers that have adorned the history of our common country, not one has ever been able to draw from the logic of past or present events, or from the theories of the future, a satisfactory solution to this vexed problem. Not one has been able to practically dispose of the question, with safety to the Caucasian and humanity to the African races on this continent.

To suddenly transport four millions of bondsmen from a long, immemorial servitude, under the besetting improvidence, want of care for themselves, ignorance, low vices and indolence, to a condition of freemen, with all the untutored responsibilities of providing against want, surrounded by the snares of temptation and vice to which the negro character too freely yields, without those checks of family police regulations that have for centuries restrained an inferior race, would inevitably propogate miseries untold for both classes, that ages could not efface; and, the great question is, as it ever has been, Which is the greater evil, to suddenly *force emancipation*, or permit God, in His administration of human affairs to solve a problem that many nations have, for centuries, been in vain endeavoring to determine by edicts, codes and Proclamations, and if it be asked, "Why not *try* it, as retributive punishment on the 'cause of the war?'" the answer has already been furnished by the tears and blood of nations that have been poisoned by quaffing from the same chalice. We have more to fear from punishing ourselves than others, in th's matter.

If history has any significance, can we afford to repeat the experiment? That is a question now before the nation. The people must be responsible for their answer. Our duty ends when we have placed the panorama of veritable history before them.

Gov. DENNISON (Rep.) in his message to the Ohio Legislature, in 1861, says:

"An act of immediate general emancipation, throwing four millions of the colored caste loose on society, North and South, would leave them more enslaved than they are now. Without the intelligence, power, and means of a *master* of the superior race, to support them in the competition of that race, in the business of life, *they would perish*. The North rejecting them, as it has done in many states, and might do in others, the four millions let loose in the South, would encounter *a war of castes*—A WAR OF EXTERMINATION!"

Gov. DENISON had probably been reading the history of the West Indies.

CHAPTER III.

HISTORY OF CAUSES OF WAR.

Slavery not the *Cause* of the War...Illustrations showing the Absurdity of the Claim that it is...Henry Ward Beecher declares the Constitution to be the Cause...Senator Douglas' Testimony...Alex. Stevens' Views...The Rebel Iverson on the "Cause"...Gov. Rhett on ditto ...The Rebel Benjamin, with Republican aid, *creates* a "Cause"...The Constitution the "Cause"...Early Times ...The Three Parties in 1786...Alex. Hamilton's "Strong Government"...Early Opposition to the Constitution... Vote close in some of the State Conventions...The Four Rebellions...Shays' Rebellion...South Carolina Rebellion in 1832—The great Abolition Rebellion...The great Southern Rebellion of 1861...What the Cause of the War... Abolition Petitions for Dissolution...A Public Debt a Public Blessing...The object to Destroy the Government ...Know-Nothingism as an Element to Wreck the Government, by placing Power in the hands of its Destroyers...Numerous Extracts in Proof...Treason of the Clergy in 1814...Treason of the Federals in 1814...Support of the Government "Reprobated" by Federal Reprobates, &c.

IS SLAVERY THE CAUSE OF THE WAR?

"Mad, let us grant him then, and now remains
That we find out the *cause* of this defect;
Or rather say the cause of this *defect*,
For this effect defective comes by cause.
               [*Shakespeare.*

So far as this question can be determined, history and facts must sit as umpires. That slavery was even the pretext for the present rebellion, may be safely denied, for it cannot be supposed any people would rebel against their own chosen institutions, but that the *agitation* of the slavery question gave to the *pretext* for war, its present momentum and its incipient *status* no one can in truth deny. The argument, based on the assumption that 'slavery is the cause of the war'"—that to put a stop to the *effect* we must remove the *cause*, is fallacious both in fact and theory. As we proceed, we shall endeavor to show it is not true in fact, and will endeavor here to exhibit the absurdity of the theory.

CAUSE AND EFFECT ILLUSTRATED.

It is asserted, and we believe no one has ever questioned the fact, that religion has been the cause of more wars and bloodshed than all other causes combined since the advent of man on this planet. Shall we argue that therefore religion should be abolished, to prevent the clashing of religious antagonisms? Bread was the "cause" of the great bread riot in London, in the 16th century. Should bread be abolished to remove the "cause" of bread riots? Banks have been the "cause" of numerous bank riots. Will bankers consent to the abolition of that "cause?" The conscription act was the "cause" of the great anti-conscription riot in New York, in 1863. Will the radicals be sufficiently consistent to admit, that to prevent such recurring evils in the future, the conscription act should be abolished?

These illustrations might be almost indefinitely multiplied, but we have given enough to show that an antecedent is not necessarily a "cause," or if it be a cause, the removal of it will not necessarily cure the evil. A cask of powder placed beneath a dwelling is perfectly harmless, until some "agitator" applies the torch, that developes its destructive powers, and so it is with the slavery question. So long as agitators permitted it to remain where our fathers placed it, all was prosperity and peace, but the moment fanatical agitators applied the spark, the magazine exploded, and the whole nation is now writhing in the agony developed by the incendiary's torch.

MR. BEECHER HITS THE "CAUSE."

We are more than half inclined to believe that HENRY WARD BEECHER was nearer right than that divine usually is, in political matters, when he declared—

"The truth is that it is the Constitution itself that is the cause of every division. * * *
It has been the fountain and father of all our troubles."

Not that this *should* be, but that demagogues who have hated our government from the start, have made it so. It is no doubt too true that the constitution has been made the "cause of every division," but had it not been for the slavery agitation, that "cause" could never have developed itself.

The Republican press have been in the habit of quoting the following to show that the South had nothing real to complain of. It will answer our end quite as well for another purpose, and that is to show, just what we are considering, that there has long existed a party in this country bent on the dissolution of the Union. The abolitionists furnished them with the slavery agitation, which answered their purpose as a *pretext*, and that was all they wanted.

DOUGLAS ON THE "CAUSE."

Said Senator DOUGLAS in the last speech he ever made:

"*I ask you to reflect, and then point out any act that has been done, any duty that has been omitted to be done of which any of these disunionists can justly complain.* Yet we are told simply because one party has succeeded in a Presidential election, therefore they choose to consider that their liberties are not safe, and therefore they break up the Government.*"

ALEXANDER STEPHENS SPURNS THE SLAVERY "CAUSE."

ALEXANDER H. STEPHENS, the Vice President over the Southern Confederacy, said, when the question of Secession was pending before the people of Georgia:

"What right has the North assailed? What justice has been demanded? and what claim founded in justice and right has been withheld? Can either of you name to-day one single act of wrong, deliberately and purposely done by the *Government* at *Washington,* of which the South can complain. *I challenge the answer.*"

THE REBEL IVERSON ON THE "CAUSE."

During the debates in the last Congress before the several states, except South Carolina, had seceded, Mr. IVERSON, a distinguished Senator from Georgia, in the Senate Chamber, said:

"Sir, before the 4th of March, before you inaugurate your President, there will be certainly five states, if not eight of them, that will be out of the Union and have formed a constitution and form of Government for themselves. * * * * *You talk about repealing the personal liberty bills as a concession to the South! Repeal them all to-morrow, sir, and it would not stop this revolution. * * * * Nor do we suppose there will be any overt acts on the part of Mr. Lincoln. For one, I do not dread these overt acts. I do not propose to wait for them. * * * * Now, sir, we intend to go out of this Union. I speak what I believe upon this floor, that before the 4th of March, five of the Southern states, at least, will have declared their independence; and I am satisfied that three others of the cotton states that are now moving in this matter are not doing it without due consideration. We have looked over the field.*

THE ELECTION OF LINCOLN NO "CAUSE"

Gov. RHETT, in the South Carolina secession convention, in December, 1860—just after the Presidential election—said:

"The election of Lincoln was not *the cause of secession. Disunion has been a cherished project for the last thirty years.*"

Senator TOOMBS, in his Georgia speech, brought up the old original grievance about Northern commercial advantages.

THE REBEL BENJAMIN TRIED TO CREATE A "CAUSE."

Early in 1860 Senator BENJAMIN made a speech denouncing DOUGLAS, and eulogizing LINCOLN. This was circulated all over the North under the franks of Republican members of Congress, and when BENJAMIN had succeeded in electing LINCOLN he seized the event as a warrantable *pretext* to dissolve the Union.— He knew that with DOUGLAS as President he could not use the slavery question as a pretext, hence the effort to create a *causus beli*, and then take advantage of it.

THE "CAUSE" DATES FROM THE BEGINNING.

From the beginning there has been a powerful party opposed to our form of government. If the reader will consult Elliott's Debates, and the "Madison Papers," and make himself familiar with the tone of opinion that prevailed in the National and State Conventions that formed and adopted our present Constitution, he will perceive that a powerful minority existed in those days against the principles declared by our Constitution. Mr. MASON was in favor of "a President for life, his successor being chosen at the same time—a Senate for life," &c. Various were the objections to the Constitution, but most of them arose from local prejudices and interests. Some members of the South Carolina Convention objected to a Union under the Constitution. because it gave too much commercial advantage to the Northern States, while members of the New England Conventions were equally opposed because of certain Southern advantages, among which was the Fugitive clause, and the three-fifths representation, &c., and in all the debates of those times the student of history will find a marked coincidence between the reasons advanced against adopting the Constitution, and those of latter-day politicians against its enforcement. It was predicted at the time, by those in favor of a "strong government," that it would be, just what Beecher says it is, the "father of troubles."

THE THREE PARTIES THAT FORMED THE CONSTITUTION.

Mr. CAREY, in his *Olive Branch*, a work of some 450 pages, published in 1815, says there were three classes in the National Convention that formed our Constitution—the purely Democratic, who had a constant dread of Federal encroachments, and were for gaguing the power of the General Government to the lowest scale; a Democratic Republican party, that desired to invest the Federal Government with just enough power to make it efficient, and no more; and the Monarchists, "a small but active division," who utterly repudiated a Republican form of government. This faction ultimately attached themselves to the Federal party.

HAMILTON'S "STRONG GOVERNMENT."

ALEXANDER HAMILTON, a leading Federalist of that day, under date of New York, September 16, 1803, in a letter to TIMOTHY PICKERING, Esq., defined his idea of government, from which we select the following:

"The highest toned propositions which I made in the

Convention were for a President, Senate and Judges during good behaviour, though I would have enlarged the legislative power of the General Government," which Mr. CAREY pronounces equivalent to "a President for life.—*Olive Branch*, p. 88.

EARLY OPPOSITION TO THE CONSTITUTION.

Unfortunately. we have not the full proceedings of all the conventions that adopted the Constitution, yet we have sufficient to show, by speech and vote, that it encountered a gigantic opposition, and, as Mr. MADISON often remarked, in his voluminous correspondence on the subject, its fate was shrouded in doubt until the last moment.

Rhode Island was ever attached to the monarchial form of government, and refused to accredit delegates to the national convention. North Carolina held back for a long while, and in every State a most determined opposition was manifest, but at last the Democratic spirit prevailed, and for a time the factious "Charterists" yielded assent. Then, as now, the opponents of the constitution opposed it for diverse reasons, according to location, but they acted together as one man, for the same purpose, each granting to the other the right to use pretexts the most popular in the several sections to which they belonged. The opponents in New England sought the pretext of slavery, and other localized popular ideas, while those equally opposed in the South, used the commercial pretext for their opposition. and this parallel of mutual opposition for different and local reasons, has been kept up to this hour.

THE VOTE A CLOSE THING.

The following shows the test votes on adopting the constitution in the several States named. We have not the record of the other States:

	Yeas.	Nays.	Ab.
South Carolina,	149	73	14
Massachusetts,	187	168	...
New York,	31	29	...
Virginia,	90	78	...

Maryland resolved not to take a vote, and voted to suppress the records of ayes and noes, and then immediately adjourned. RANDOLPH and MASON, of Virginia, and GERRY, of Massachusetts, refused to sign the constitution, as members of the National Convention; the former, however, finally favored it, and was charged by PATRICK HENRY with what was akin to bribery.

This opposition to our government has never ceased from that day to this, and to weld all the links of our historical chain, we will consider—

THE FOUR REBELLIONS.

These, we can but briefly notice, as it is essential to a proper appreciation of the details that are in various ways their cotemporaries and causes, as we shall show in the progress of this work.

Shays' Rebellion.

1st. The SHAY's Rebellion, which broke forth with armed resistance to the Government, in Massachusetts, in 1786-7, at the very time our fathers were deliberating on bringing forth (as Mr. LINCOLN said at Gettysburg) the new Government. The *pretext* for this rebellion was alledged to be the "oppressions of Government." (All rebellions have their pretexts.)

The Rebellion of 1832.

2d. The South Carolina Rebellion of 1832, when the "oppressive tariff laws" (called by South Carolina, before the constitution, Northern commercial advantages) were made to figure as the *pretext*. This Rebellion, though formidable, and enlisting the bitterest passions of that portion of the South, was principally confined to the hot-spurs of South Carolina, whose ancestors had opposed the constitution, and hated our form of government, and who longed for an opportunity to put in operation their cherished system of Aristocracy, similar to that of England, and who held, with the same class hailing from New England, that "a national debt was a national blessing." But, failing to use this *pretext* with sufficient success to arouse armed resistance, the excitement was finally quelled, partly by Old Hickory's firmness. and partly by Mr. CLAY's compromise tariff of 1833, and partly from the want of a disloyal peasantry to back up the malcontents.

The Great Abolition Rebellion.

3d The great Northern rebellion, which particularly manifested itself in public laws, (personal liberty bills) inflammatory declamations and resolves by leading men, which appealed to the people on the *pretexts* of "slavery aggression," to *resist* the laws of Congress and the mandates of the Supreme Court of the U. S. [*See Charles Sumner's speech at Worcester. Aug. 7*, 1854, *and Wisconsin conspiracy.*] This rebellion was formidable and threatening to the worst degree. The wealth of the North was poured out, free as water, to set in motion a train of circumstances that should "fire the Northern heart" to resistance, *vi et armis*, as was the case in many instances, particularly in Wisconsin, where armed mobs, unrebuked but encouraged by their partizans in office and out of office, forcibly, and for a long time successfully resisted the laws of Congress and the decisions of the Court of last resort. [The proofs of these outrages will appear under the head of "Revolutionary spirit of Republicanism."] This rebellion partially developed itself between the periods of 1854 and 1860. in which the Sharp's Rifle raid in Kansas, the HELPER "crisis" and the JOHN BROWN raid formed no inconsiderable parts of the general conspiracy. All these and their kindred plots had their germ in revolutionary guilt, occasionally "cropping out" in the *role* of monster petitions to Congress from the New England states, praying for a dissolution of the government. The *pretext* for this, not altogether bloodless revolution, was the slavery question, but the gist of the indictment goes back of the Constitution.

The Great Rebellion of 1861.

4th. The great Southern rebellion of 1861,

the disasters of which are too fresh and painful to be recited here. The *pretext* for this rebellion was the slavery question, and he who reads may learn, without a tutor, that this pretext was used only because it was the most *convenient* to arouse the Southern fears and prejudices and to "fire the Southern heart" to the pitch of armed resistance to what Southern demagogues had educated the people to believe, was danger and destruction to their domestic happiness. Thus did Prœtonean cunning inaugurate Macedonian strife, and the result is a worse than Carthagenian war.

Having thus briefly and historically sketched antecedent events down to the advent of our present troubles, let us enquire,

WHAT IS THE CAUSE OF THIS WAR?

As we have seen, the real, long slumbering *cause* or *motive* for this war existed not so much in hatred of slavery as in the hatred for the Constitution, which manifested itself long before the adoption of that instrument, and was confined to no section. The Northern Abolitionists and the Southern nullifiers, while they used antipodeal means, were banded together to accomplish the overthrow of the government, for the proof of which "let facts be submitted to a candid world."

J. Q. ADAMS PRESENTS A PETITION FOR DISSOLUTION.

On the 24th of February, 1842, John Quincy Adams presented a petition in the House of Representatives, signed by a large number of citizens of Haverhill, Mass., for a peaceable dissolution of the Union, "assigning as one of the reasons, the inequality of benefits conferred upon the different sections. [*See Blake's History of Slavery, p.* 524.

MR. ADAMS DEFENDED BY SOUTHERNERS.

This caused great excitement in Congress, and although ostensibly aimed at slavery, Mr. Adams found many of its warmest defenders among slaveholders at the South. In the course of the debate, Mr. Botts of Va. warmly defended Mr. Adams, and considered the presentation of this petition a bagatelle, compared with the open advocacy for dissolution by Mr. Upsher, the then Secretary of the Navy.— [*See p.* 527.

GIDDINGS PRESENTS A PETITION FOR DISSOLUTION.

On the 28th of February, 1842, Mr. GIDDINGS presented a petition from a large number of abolitionists ot Austinburg, in his district, praying for a dissolution of the Union, and a separation of the slave from the free states. Mr. TRIPLETT, of Kentucky, considering the petition disrespectful to both houses, moved that it be not received. Ayes, 24; (for reception) noes, 116.—[*See Ibid, p.* 529.

FACTIONS ON BOTH SECTIONS DESIRED DISSOLUTION.

These two simple facts show that the feeling existed, North as well as South, in favor of a dissolution of the Union, as the feeling existed at the close of the 18th century against the system of Government we did adopt. The old embers of dissolution were still alive, and only required an excitement to fan them into a blaze. Two things, *motive* and *opportunity* are necessary for the perpetration of any wrong.— The *motive* for dissolution consisted in the original desire, patented for heirs and successors, to have what HAMILTON and his friends termed a "strong government," generally understood to mean an aristocracy, similar to that of England, with such modifications as might be adapted to the occasion. Among the objects to be attained was a large standing army and a heavy public debt, owned by the favored few, to whom the masses should pay tribute, under the guise of interest—that the main public offices should be held by the rich and noble for long periods, or for life, &c. These, among other things, were the *motives* for dissolution, and a separation between the Northern and Southern states. The aristocrats of each section desired a monopoly in these and sundry other franchises, but the original weakness of the colonies, and the fear of foreign powers, together with the will of the Democratic masses, prevented dissolution in 1787-9. Still, the motive existed, and the only thing wanting was the *occasion*. The argument was often and vigorously advanced, that "a great national debt would be a national blessing"—even as late as 1840 this was a leading argument, and the various propositions to distribute the proceeds of the sales of the public lands, and to engage in a general system National Improvements—the establishment of a monster National Bank, &c.—all had their germ in the desire to create a great national debt. Prohibitory tariffs, under the specious guise of "protection to American industry," were also to play their part in clipping the amount received from customs, and thus to swell the national debt, but the laboring masses saw in all these efforts to create a heavy national debt, the foundation for their enslavement, to sweat out taxes to pay the interest. The West saw that Wall street, State street, and the monetary marts of the East would act as sponges for all time to suck up the entire revenue of its industry, and they put a veto on all those measures.

OBJECT OF THE KNOW NOTHING ORGANIZATION.

Though the *motive* still existed in its original power, the *occasion* had not yet arrived, and it was feared never would so long as the Democratic legions, who thronged our shores, as refugees from aristocratic and pauperized Europe, were permitted to vote, and the *occasion* was sought in the abridgment of the elective franchise, so as to exclude this powerful influx of voters from the polls, through the mystic operations of the Know Nothing order. This object, although successful in most of the New England States, utterly failed in the Middle and Western States. The Cleveland *Her-*

SCRAPS FROM MY SCRAP-BOOK 27

ald, a sheet that has always opposed the Democratic party, said:

"*We unhesitatingly aver that seven-tenths of the foreigners in our land, who bow in obedience to the Pope of Rome, are not as intelligent as the full blooded Africans of our state—we will not include the part bloods.*"

CHICAGO TRIBUNE ON "VOTING CATTLE."

The following, from the Chicago *Tribune*, though out of chronological order, will equally illustrate our point, that the opponents of Democracy have deemed it necessary to their purpose to browbeat the foreign voters into silence. In alluding to the monster torch light procession that turned out to welcome Douglas to Chicago, October 5, 1860, the *Tribune* said:

"Taken altogether, the squatter reception, last evening, fell below what had been promised, but furnished an instance of what a few determined wire pullers can do with a few hundred *voting cattle*"—(alluding to the Irish and Germans.)

KNOW NOTHINGISM ILLUSTRATED.

In a Republican meeting in Putnam county, Illinois, in 1860, Mr. ELIJAH W. GREEN delivered himself as follows:

"Mr. CHAIRMAN:—It is claimed by some here to-day, that it is not policy to nominate a full ticket, on account of the Dutch. Some suppose we should not nominate a man against ROTHEMAN. I say, Mr. Chairman, we don't want to favor the Dutch; we don't want to borrow any Dutch votes, nor trade them any *white* votes. If they don't want to vote our ticket, let them go to hell!! We have *white* votes enough, and can do without them.— Neither do we want the Irish Catholics in our party. We have *white* men in our party, and don't want the Irish or Dutch."

MORE KNOW NOTHINGISM.

A Republican candidate for the Senate, in Rock Island county. Ill., in 1860, said:

"Suppose I were to tell you that I despise the Pope and hate the Papists, and detest the Irish Catholic voting cattle, who swarm around our polls at election times!— * * * The Douglasites depend upon the faithfulness and ignorance of their Irish Catholic allies. We expect nothing from the Catholic element in the next election. All that was worth having of New York Americanism and Know Nothingism joined the Republican party weeks ago."

FEDERAL KNOWNOTHINGISM.

"The real cause of the war must be traced to the influence of *worthless foreigners* over the press and the deliberations of the Government in all its branches.—*Response to the Message of Gov. Strong, of Mass., by the Assembly, June,* 1814.

GEN. SCOTT'S VIEWS.

"I now hesitate between extending the period of residence before naturalization, and a total repeal of all acts of Congress on the subject—my mind inclines to the latter."—*General Scott in his celebrated Native American Letter.*

And, at another time he continued

"Concurring fully in the principles of the Philadelphia movement."

Which "movement" was started for his benefit by the Native American party, in 1852.

"If I had the power, I would erect a gallows at every landing place in the city of New York, and suspend every cursed Irishman as soon as the steps upon our shore."— *Remarks of Mathew L. Davis on receiving the news of the Democratic triumph in New York, in* 1852.

"It is our opinion, as our readers well know, that no man of foreign birth should be admitted to the exercise of the political rights of an American citizen."—*Albany Daily Advertiser.*

"We could not find any other remedy against the threatning danger, than a repeal of *all naturalization laws.*"—*Col. Webb, of New York.*

"*All* naturalization laws should be instantly repealed, and the term preceding the enjoyment of civil rights extended twenty-five years."—*Mr. Clark, Whig Mayor of New York.*

All the leading Know-Nothings of the country, who have not seriously relented their heresies against foreigners, are to-day members ef the Republican or "Union" party. We could fill volumes with similar extracts, but the foregoing must suffice.

Still, the *occasion* had not ripened. The spirit was willing, but the flesh was weak.— The "strong government" party could not get all the machinery of our Government into their hands. They came very near it under the Elder ADAMS and attempted to circumscribe the elective franchise, or rather to mould it more to their purposes, by the Alien law, and to hush up the Democratic sentiment of the country, by the Sedition law, but the spirit of the people was too strong, and the effort was abandoned.

TREASON OF THE FEDERAL CLERGY.

The next effort was to weaken this Government in its struggles with Great Britain in 1812-15, to the end that the world might see Democracy in America was a failure, and then would come the millenium of the "strong government." Then, as ever since, many of the leading clergy were with them. The Rev. Mr. GARDNER preached an anti-war sermon in Trinity Church, Boston, (1814) in which he said:

"The Union has been long since virtually dissolved, and it is full time that this part of the United States should take care of itself."

The Rev. Dr. PARISH said:

"How will the supporters of this anti-Christian war endure the sentence—endure their own reflection—endure the fire that forever burns— the worm which never dies— the hozannas of heaven, while the smoke of their torments ascends forever and ever."

Said the Rev. DAVID OSGOOD:

"Each man who volunteers his services in such a cause, or loans his money for its support, or by his conversation, his writings, or in any other mode of influence, encourages its prosecution, that man is an accomplice in the wickedness, loads his conscience with the blackest crimes, brings the guilt of blood upon his soul, and in the sight of God and His law is a murderer."

The *Olive Branch*, a work of that day, said:

"To sum up the whole, Massachusetts was energetic, bold, firm, daring and decisive in a contest with the General Government, she would not abate an inch. She dared it to the conflict. She seized it by the throat and determined to strangle it."

TREASON OF THE FEDERAL PRESS.

The Boston *Gazette*, the New England organ of the Federalists, said:

"Any Federalist who lends money to the Government, must go and shake hands with JAMES MADISON, and claim fellowship with FELIX GRUNDY. Let him no more call himself a Federalist, and friend to his country! He will be called by others infamous."

SUPPORT OF THE GOVERNMENT "REPROBATED."

In the Boston *Centinel*, Feb. 14, 1817, we find a long Federal address, which was written (probably by JOSIAH QUINCY) in reply to a Democratic Address of a previous date, and in answering a certain paragraph, this Federal Address proceeds to declare

"There is, however, one feature in this address at once so unprincipled, and so mischievous that it seems impossible for any man of the most common honesty or patriotism to notice it without reprobation. We allude to that part of it in which *Massachusetts is called upon to relinquish her opposition to the General Government.* * * Fellow citizens, it continues the Federal Address) in whatever point of view we consider this appeal (that is to desist in opposition to the General Government) whether as intended to influence the electors in Massachusetts, or as a faithful representation of the principles which govern our rulers, in the General Government, *nothing can be more shameless or degrading!*"

In 1817, the Boston *Centinel's* main objection to General DEARBORN, Democratic candidate for Governor of Massachusetts was, that he was "a friend of THOMAS JEFFERSON."—*Boston Centinel, March 8, 1817.*

THE FIRST PROPOSITION IN CONGRESS TO DISSOLVE THE UNION.

JOSIAH QUINCY, who was then on the Federal ticket for State Senator, and has never changed his politics to the present hour, but has of late been an ardent "Republican," made a speech in Congress, on the 14th of January, 1811, in which he declared that the purchase of Louisiana and admission of the State into the Union, would be a

"Virtual dissolution of the bonds of the Union * * rendering it the right of all, as it would become the duty of some, to prepare definitely for *separation—amicably*, if they might—*forcibly* if they must."—*Hildreth's History U. S., Vol. 4, p. 226.*

And to be more explicit Mr. Quincy reduced his threat to writing and sent it to the Clerk, whereupon Mr. POINDEXTER rose to his feet and declared it as the

"First time that on this floor a threat had been made to dissolve the Union,"

WHAT RHODE ISLAND DID FOR THE WAR.

"Rhode Island did actually order out and put upon duty an army of *fifteen* men, after having duly consulted on the matter with the 'Council of War'—Gov. MARTIN and CHRISTOPHER FOWLEN, Esq. It was not, however, thought, (in the language of the Governor) that this guard was 'capable of resisting an invading foe of any considerable magnitude.'"—*See his Message, vol. 14, p. 109. Niles' Register,* 1815, vol. 8, p. 30.

QUALIFICATIONS AND DISQUALIFICATIONS FOR MEMBERS OF MASS. LEGISLATURE.

During the last War with Great Britain, Massachusetts took the following action:

1st. That a member of that body was *not disqualified* to hold his seat on account of having taken an oath *not to bear arms, &c.,* against the enemy!

2d. The House of Representatives resolved that a Reverend member of this body *was disqualified* to hold his seat therein, because he had been appointed a Chaplain in the Army of the United States."—*Niles' Register,* 1815, vol. 8, p. 13.

A NEW ENGLAND CONFEDERACY.

On the 8th of October, 1814, a committee of the Massachusetts Legislature submitted a report by Mr. OTIS, chairman, in favor of calling a convention of the New England States with the end and object of forming a New England Confederacy. This measure passed and the Hartford Convention was its progeny.

THE DEMOCRATS PROTEST.

On the 15th of the same month a protest was entered by thirteen Senators and by seventy-five members against this treason and insipient secession.

"Ambition has destroyed every other Republic on earth," say the Senate protestants. The House protest concludes as follows:

"The reasoning of the report is supported by the alarming assumption that the *Constitution has failed in its objects,* and the people of Massachusetts are *absolved in their allegiance,* and adopt another. In debate it has been reiterated *that the Constitution is no longer to be respected* [just what is reiterated through the radical press and speeches to-day] and the *resolution is not to be deprecated.* The bond of our political union is *thus attempted to be severed,* and in a state of war and common danger, we are advised to the mad experiment of abandoning the combined energies of the nation might afford, for the selfish enjoyment of our present, though partial resources,— The resolutions of the Legislature, it is to be feared, will be viewed by other States as productive of this consequence, *that Massachusetts shall govern* the Administration, or the Government shall not be administered in Massachusetts. [Precisely what South Carolina done in 1832 and 1861.] Jealousy and contention will ensue.— The Constitution, hitherto respected as the character of national liberty and consecrated as the ark of our political safety, will be *violated and destroyed,* and in civil dissentions and convulsions, our independence will be annihilated, our country reduced to the condition of vanquished and tributary colonies, to a haughty and implacable foreign foe.—[LEVI LINCOLN, JR., *and seventy-five others,*" —*Niles Register, vol.* 7, p. 155.

MASSACHUSETTS "SET UP" FOR HERSELF.

The same legislature that passed these resolves voted to raise an army for "state defence" of 10,000 strong, &c., and actually made all the necessary preparations to go out of the Union, as much so as South Carolina did in 1861, except the *going*. Massachusetts also appointed a "Board of War," and was thus preparing to become an independent nation.—*Niles' Register, vol.* 7, *p.* 147.

GOV. STRONG ON THE BOARD OF WAR.

In Gov. STRONG's message to the legislature, dated the 16th of January, 1816, he refers to the resolve of the year previous, which required the "Board of War" to close accounts "of this commonwealth with the United States, and file the same in the Secretary's office," which was done.—*Niles' Register, v.* 9, *p.* 416.

FEDERALS TOAST THE HARTFORD CONVENTION

At a dinner in honor of Washington's birthday, in Philadelphia, Feb. 18, 1815, the following toast was drank:

"*The Hartford Convention, the dignified apostles of the true political faith.*"—*Niles Register, v.* 8, *p.* 14.

NEW JERSEY SPURNS THE TREASON.

The Legislature of New Jersey rejected the Federal Hartford Convention propositions as

"the master principle * * * to reduce within a narrow sphere the power and influence of the General Government. * * * The obvious tendency also is to throw among the states of the Union the apple of discord * * and nurture the seeds of dissention an I disunion, * * * by persons *professing* them to promote the general good," &c.

THE FEDERALS AGITATE SLAVERY.

This "Federal Divine" Hartford Convention also lugged in the slavery question, and sought to create prejudice in its favor by the agitation of that subject—just as the radicals do at the present day. [*See report of Committee of Pa. Legislature, April, 1815.*]

NEW YORK ON FEDERAL DISUNION.

Mr. EDWARDS, Chairman of the Committee in the Legislature of New York, harshly yet justly excoriated the "treason of Massachusetts" and charged on the Federals of that and other states that

"in the opinion of your committee (they mean) to make peace with the enemy, and forcibly to separate themselves from the Union."

MASSACHUSETTS TRIES TO KICK LOUISIANA OUT OF THE UNION.

In the Massachusetts Legislature, June 4, 1813, JOSIAH QUINCY submitted a lengthy report, as Chairman of the committee raised for that purpose, against permitting Louisiana to remain in the Union, and closed with a series of resolutions, which were adopted by the Federal majority, from which we copy the 3d,

"*Resolved*, That the act passed the 8th day of April, 1812, entitled "an act for the admission of the State of Louisiana into the Union, and to extend the Laws of the United States to said State," is a violation of the constitution of the United States; and that the Senators of this State in Congress, be instructed, and the representatives thereof requested, to use their utmost endeavors to obtain a repeal of the same."—[*Niles' Register, vol. 4, p. 287.*

TO REJOICE OVER OUR VICTORIES UNBECOMING A RELIGIOUS AND MORAL PEOPLE.

On the 15th of the same month there was a proposition before the same legislature for a vote of thanks to JAMES LAWRENCE, commander of the United States ship *Hornet*, and the officers and crew of that ship, for their gallantry and bravery in the destruction of the British ship *Peacock*—that as similar resolutions have been passed "on similar occasions" for "like service" "have given great discontent to many of the good people of this commonwealth," &c., therefore

"*Resolved*, As the sense of the Senate of Massachusetts, that in a war *like the present*, waged without justifiable cause, and prosecuted in a manner which indicates that conquest and ambition are its real motives, *it is not becoming a moral and religious people to express any approbation of military or naval exploits!!*" [*See Niles Register, v. 4, p. 287.*

The party that passed the foregoing resolution was called *Federal* then, *Federal Republican* in 1824; *Whig* in 1833; *Republican* in 1854; *Union* (?) in 1863! An unenviable consanguinity.

CHAPTER IV.

DISUNION OF EARLY GROWTH.

Early Clamors for a Northern Confederacy...the Pelham Publication...Crusade Against Slavery in 1795...Its Baseness and Untruthfulness exhibited by CAREY, in 1814...The Federal Argument to show that Dissolution was close at hand...Early Caricatures of the North to stimulate Sectional Hatred...Falsity of the Agitators' statements...Comparison of Northern and Southern support of Government...The odious comparisons continued...Republican papers and the President's Message ...Section arrayed against Section.

CLAMORS FOR A NORTHERN CONFEDERACY.

To show that the work of dissolution began, and the cry of a "Northern Confederacy" raised even under the Administration of WASHINGTON, we copy the following from Mr. CAREY'S *Olive Branch*, published in 1814, and the extracts he brings forward from a treasonable secession work of that day, to prove his statements, to which work we refer the reader, pages 270-1-2-3, &c.

One fact will strike the reader with peculiar unction, at first sight—to-wit: the same species of appeal to local prejudices, and against slavery that has for years stirred up the fountains of our whole society to its dregs. It will prove that the present generation of Abolition agitators come honestly by their hatred of the South—that they inherited it from the old Federals, and even now, while the result of this factious spirit has reached, and now sits on the throne of power, the leading orators, presses and pulpits in that interest, breathe out their scoffs, their jeers and their hatred of the Constitution, the only bond of our Union. All who maintain that the "Union as it was and the Constitution as it is" should be respected by the powers that be, are stigmatized as "traitors," "copperheads," &c. So far as the writer hereof is concerned, he is willing to send down to remote posterity his honest purpose to sustain the Constitution, as the only means of saving the Union, to be read in future history as we now read the following to-day:

THE PELHAM CONSPIRACY.

"A Northern Confederacy has been the object for a number of years. They (New England) have repeatedly advocated in public prints a seperation of the states, on account of a pretended discordance of views and interests of the different sections.

"This project of separation was formed shortly after the adoption of the Federal Constitution. Whether it was ventured before the public earlier than 1796, I know not. But of its promulgation in that year, there is the most indubitable evidence. A most elaborate set of papers under the signature of PELHAM, was then published in the city of Hartford, in Connecticut, the joint production of men of the first talents and influence in the state. They appear in the Connecticut *Courant*, published by HUDSON & GOODWIN, two eminent printers, of, I believe, considerable revolutionary standing. There were then none of the long catalogue of grievances, which since that period have been fabricated to justify the recent attempts to dissolve the Union. General WASHINGTON was President; JOHN ADAMS, an Eastern citizen, Vice President. There was no French influence—no Virginia dynasty—no embargo—no intercourse—no terrapin policy—no Democratic madness—no war. In fine, every feature in the affairs of the country was precisely according to their fondest wishes.

"To sow discord, jealousy and hostility between the different sections of the Union, was the first and grand step in their career, in order to accomplish the favorite object of a separation of the states.

"In fact, without this efficient instrument, all their efforts would have been utterly unavailing. It would have been impossible had the honest yeomanry of the Eastern States continued to regard their Southern fellow citizens as friends and brethren, having one common interest in the promotion of the general welfare, to make them instruments in the hands of those who intended to employ them to operate the unholy work of destroying the noble, the august, the splendid fabric of our Union, and unparalleled form of government.

"For eighteen years, therefore, the most unceasing endeavors have been used to poison the minds of the people of the Eastern States towards, and to alienate them from, their fellow citizens of the Southern States. The people of the latter section have been portrayed as demons incarnate, destitute of all the good qualities that dignify or adorn human nature—that acquire esteem or regard—that entitle to respect and veneration. Nothing can exceed the virulence of these caricatures, some of which would have suited the ferocious inhabitants of New Zealand, rather than a civilized or polished nation. To illustrate and remove all doubt on this subject, I subjoin an extract from Pelham's Essays, No. 1."

THE NEGRO AS A PRETEXT.

"Negroes are in all respects except in regard to life and death, the cattle of the citizens of the Southern States. If they were good for food the probability is that even the power of destroying their lives would be enjoyed by their owners as fully as it is over the lives of their cattle. It cannot be that their laws prohibit their owners from killing their slaves, because those slaves are human beings, or because it is a moral evil to destroy them. If that were the case how can they justify their being treated in all other respects *like brutes?* for it is in this point of view alone that negroes in the Southern States are considered in fact *as different from cattle.* They are bought and sold. They are fed or kept hungry. They are clothed or reduced to nakedness. They are beaten, turned out to the fury of the elements, and torn from their dearest connections, with as little remorse as if they were beasts of the field."

On the above, Mr. CAREY remarked in 1814:

"Never was there a more infamous or unfounded charicature than this. Never one more disgraceful to its author. It may not be amiss to state, and it greatly enhances the turpitude of the writer, that at the period when it was written, there were many slaves in Connecticut, who were subject to all the disadvantages that attended the Southern slaves."

Its vile character is further greatly aggravated by the consideration that a large portion of these very negroes and their ancestors had been purchased and sent from their homes, and families, by citizens of the Eastern States, who were actually, at that moment, and long afterwards, *engaged in the slave trade.* I add a few more extracts from PELHAM:

NO ONE BUT THE "THOROUGHLY DEMOCRATIC" CAN HESITATE.

"We have reached a critical period in our political existence. The question must soon be decided whether we will continue a nation at the expense even of our Union, or sink with the present wars of difficulty with confusion and slavery. Many advantages were supposed to be secured, and many evils avoided, by an union of the States. I shall not deny that the supposition was well founded, but at the time these advantages, and these evils were magnified to a far greater size than either would be if the question was at this moment to be settled.

"The Northern States can subsist as a nation—a republic, without any connection with the Southern. It cannot be contested that if the Southern States were possessed of the same *political ideas,* our Union would be more close than separation, but when it becomes a serious question whether we shall give up our government or part with the States south of the Potomac, no man *North* of that river, whose heart is not *thoroughly Democratic,* can hesitate what decision to make.

"I shall, in the future papers, consider some of the great events, which will *lead to a separation of the United States*—show the importance of retaining their present Constitution, even at the expense of a separation—endeavor to prove the impossibility of a Union for any long period in future, both from the *moral* and *political* habits of the citizens of the Southern States, and finally examine carefully to see whether we have not already approached to the era when they *must be divided.*"

And, Mr. CAREY comments:

"It is impossible for a man of intelligence and candor to read these extracts without feeling a decided conviction, that the writer and his friends were determined to use all their endeavors to *dissolve the Union,* and endanger civil war and its horrors, in order to promote their sectional views. This affords a complete clue to all the seditious proceedings that have occurred since that period. [Yea, and up to the present time—1863.] The increasing efforts to excite the public mind (continued ever since, in the slavery agitation) to that feverish state of discord, jealousy and exasperation, which was necessary to prepare it for consummation. The parties interested would, on a stage of a separate confederacy, perform the liveliest parts of kings and princes, Generals and Generalissimos, whereas on the grand scope of a general Union, embracing all the states, they are obliged to sustain characters of perhaps a second or third rate. *Better to rule in hell than obey in heaven.*"

"The unholy spirit that inspired the writer of this dissolution sentiment, has been from that hour to the present, incessantly employed to excite hostility between the different sections of the Union. [And we may add, has kept it up without abatement to this hour.] To such horrible lengths has this spirit been carried, that many paragraphs have occasionally appeared in the Boston papers, intended and well calculated to excite the negroes of the Southern States to rise and massacre their masters. This will undoubtedly appear incredible to the reader. It is nevertheless sacredly true. It is a species of turpitude and baseness of which the world has produced few examples.

"Thus, some progress was made, but it was inconsiderable, while the yeomanry of the Eastern States were enriched by a beneficial commerce with the Southern, they did not feel disposed to quarrel with them, for their supposed want of a due degree of piety or morality.

THE PRESS AIDED DISSOLUTION.

"A deeper game was requisite to be played, or all the pains taken so far would have been wholly fruitless, and this was sedeously undertaken. The Press literally groaned with efforts [as it has in our day] to prove five points wholly destitute of foundation;

"1st. That the Eastern States were supereminently commercial.

"2d. That the States south of the Susquehanna were wholly agricultural.

"3d. That there is a natural and inevitable hostility between commercial and agricultural States.

"4th. That this hostility has uniformly pervaded the whole Southern section of the Union; and

"That all the measures of Congress were dictated by this hostility, and were actually intended to ruin the commercial, meaning the Eastern States.

"I do not assert that these miserable—these contemptible—these deceptious positions—were ever laid down in regular form *as theses* to argue upon; but I do aver that they formed the basis of three-fourths of all the essays, paragraphs, squibs and croakers that have appeared in the Boston papers against the administration for many years past. "The Road to Ruin," ascribed to JOHN LOWELL, now before me, is remarkable for its virulence, its acrimony, its intemperence, and for the talent of the writer. He undoubtedly places his subject in the strongest point of light possible for such a subject. But if you extract from his essays the assumption of these positions, all the rest is a mere *caput mortuum*—all "sad and funny."—On these topics, the charges are many in endless succestion. The same observation will apply, and with equal force to hundreds and thousands of essays and paragraphs within the same topic.

"Never was the *gutta non vi, sed saepe, cadendo* more completely verified. These positions, however absurd, however extravagant, however ridiculous they appear in their naked form, have, by dint of incessant repetition made such an impression upon the minds of a large portion of the people of the Eastern States, that they are as thoroughly convinced of their truth, as of any problem in Euclid."

ABOLITION CHARICATURES.

To show that the charicatures by our Northern politicians, calculated to belittle and inflame the South, were not without their ancestral examples, we copy from the above named work, p. 274:

"The Rev. JEDEDIAH MORSE has in some degree devoted his geography to, and disgraced it by, the perpetuation of this vile prejudice. Almost every page that represents *his own section* of the Union is highly encomiastic. He colors with the flattering tints of a partial and enamored friend, but when once he passes the Susquehannah, what a hideous reverse. Almost everything is there a frightful charicature. Society is at a low and melancholy ebb, and all the sombre tints are employed in the description in order to elevate by the contrast, his favorite elysium, the Eastern States. He dips his pen in gall, when he has to portray the manners, or habits, or religion of Virginia or Maryland, either of the Carolinas or Georgia, or the Western country."

To the student of forty years ago the above might be pronounced a frightful and just criticism on the old Morse Geography. How perfectly in consonance with the maps of the Union that were circulated in 1856, one half printed black, to caricature the people of that section, and to breed hostile rejoinders. How consistent, also, much that we have quoted in the foregoing voluminous extracts, stand forth as the same species of beligerant menace, and typical of desire for disunion, were the carrying of flags and banners in 1856, with only fifteen stars thereon. Further comment on this point is unnecessary.

SECTIONAL PREJUDICES AROUSED.

It will be seen by the foregoing, that as of late, the Eastern states (the Federal, Republican, Abolition portions thereof) sought early to create prejudice and disunion—not on account of any adequate existing fact, but merely to array section against section, in order to stimulate hatred and discord, and accelerate their darling object—dissolution. As we have seen, the disunionists of the Eastern states were continually harping on their exclusive commercial interests—that they paid more than the Southern states for the support of Government, &c. As the Government was supported by revenue derived from customs, and to show how ill founded these early complaints were, and that disunion was the only motive that put them forth, we exhibit the following. Mr. Carey, in 1814, said:

"The Southern section of the Union, which has been so cruelly, so wickedly, so unjustly villified and calumniated for its hostility to commerce, is actually more interested in its preservation than the Eastern states, in the proportion of *five to three!*"

FALSITY OF THE STATEMENTS EXHIBITED.

The writer then goes on to show that at that date (1813) the city of Baltimore had as much tonnage afloat as the whole New England states, being:

New England, tons,.. 108,000
Baltimore, tons,... 103,000

The exports from the Southern states from 1791 to 1813, according to Mr NOURSE's report to Congress, shows that the Southern states exported nearly double that of the New England states:

Southern states, exports 22 years,............... $514,598,000
New England states, exports 23 years.......... 299,197,000

Difference,... $215,401,000

HOW THE NORTH AND SOUTH SUPPORT THE GOVERNMENT.

In fact, Virginia, Maryland, and the District of Columbia, exported more than the whole Eastern States. Mr. NOURSE, Register of the Treasury, prepared a table, which he reported to Congress, showing the amount of duties paid by each State from 1791 to 1812, inclusive, from which it appears that the

Southern, or slave States, paid duties,............$55,600,000
New England States paid duties,..................... 57,033,000

THE ODIOUS COMPARISONS CONTINUED.

Since that time, as we have shown elsewhere in this work, the Southern States have paid immensely more duties than all the Northern or free States combined. We only allude to these facts to show that the complaints of the Northern Abolitionists were unfounded and frivalous, and only put forth as one of the "irritations" mentioned by WASHINGTON in his Farewell Address, to "widen the breach," and consummate dissolution. Indeed, this system of unjust comparisons has been continued by that class of politicians from the earliest days to the present. Even the President's late Message to Congress, though not ostensibly of this order of complaints, nevertheless, so presented the figures relative to the postal affairs, as to enable his partizans to renew the old "irritation," which they have generally improved. We have one instance before us. It is from the Milwaukee *Sentinel* of December 12, 1863:

"WHAT IT COST THE NORTH TO CARRY THE MAILS FOR THE SLAVE STATES.

"There is one statement contained in the President's Message so significant that it is worthy of brief comment. Speaking of the condition of the Post Office Department, he says:

"'During the past fiscal year the financial condition of the Post Office Department has been of increasing prosperity, and I am gratified in being able to state the receipts at the postal revenue have nearly equalled the entire expenditures, the latter amounting to $11,314,000,84 and the former to $11,160,169,08, leaving a deficiency of $150,417,25. In the year immediately preceeding the rebellion the deficiency amounted to $5,656,705,49, the postal receipts of that year being $2,645,722.10 less than those of 1863. The decrease since 1860 in the annual amount of transportation has been only about 25 per cent.; but the annual expenditure on account of the same has been reduced 35 per cent. It is manifest, that the Post Office Department may become self-sustaining in a few years, even with the restoration of the whole service.'"

"This quite clearly demonstrates what it has cost the *free North* to carry the mails for the *slaveholding South*. Before the rebellion, when mail arrangements were uninterrupted throughout the South, the deficiency in the Department's finances was $5,686,705.49, whereas now, when the mail facilities of the Slave States have been withdrawn, the Department pays its expenses into $150,-417,23 ; or, in other words, it has cost the North annually five and a half million dollars to carry the mails for the *negroes-holding lords of the South.* There may be many reasons and incentives that will induce men to sigh for the "*Union as it was,*" but the above exhibit is not one of them."

Now, compare this with its "twin sisters" of fifty years ago, and see if you cannot discover a marked family resemblance—particularly the sneer at the "*Union as it was!!*"— We have nothing to do with the merits of the arithmetical statements, which have no doubt been influenced greatly by the fact that the army has vastly accelerated correspondence, and military operations require vast mail facilities, and consequently enhanced receipts, but it is the *animus* of such articles—their invidious comparisons, that "tend to alienate one section from the other," and, as Jefferson said, "to make Union impossible."

CHAPTER V.

THE GREAT NEW ENGLAND CONSPIRACY.

New England Money Kings endeavor to Bankrupt the Government...Testimony of a Cotemporary...The Clergy in the Conspiracy...Consequence of the Conspiracy...Depreciation of Bank and Government Stocks....Mr. CAREY's Statement...The Secret Federal Leagues....Monied men banded against the Government...Reign of Terror...Citizens dare not subscribe for Government Loan openly... Threats and Intimidations by the Federals...Treason of the Federals in buying and selling English Bills...The Sedition Law...Its object to crush out Free Discussion... Difference between MADISON and LINCOLN....Leading Federals Gazetted...Object of the Sedition Law...We, the Government, in 1798...Damn the Government in 1814... The Pious Rev. Federals curse the Government...Views of JEFFERSON and WEBSTER, &c.

CONSPIRACY OF NEW ENGLAND TO BANKRUPT THE GOVERNMENT.

The New England money kings knowing that money furnished the "sinews of war," and having control of a great share of the monetary interests of the country, during the last war with England, entered into a conspiracy to break down the credit of the Government, and to discredit Government bills. They were continually crying peace, yet doing all they could to prevent peace, well knowing that a prolongation of hostilities would only secure to them dissolution.

The Government under Mr. MADISON, needed money to prosecute the war, and issued eight per cent. bonds for that purpose. No sooner were those bonds in Market than New England money sharks set up a howl that they were worthless, never could be redeemed, &c. Elsewhere in this work, will be found numerous extracts, showing the vile purposes to defeat the obtaining money by the Government, but we will produce a few facts in this connection, as more clearly establishing the truth of that wicked conspiracy in New England, to break down the Government, in the darkest hour of its peril, and to show what peculiar claim that section has now to cry traitor to all those who believe in the "Union as it was and the Constitution as it is." We quote from the *Olive Branch,* p. 303:

"In consequence, every possible exertion was made, particularly in Boston, to deter the citizens from subscribing to the loans, in order to disable the Government from carrying on the war, and of course to compel it to make peace. Associations were entered into, in the most solemn and public manner for this purpose, and those who could not be induced by mild means, were deterred by denunciations. A folio volume might be filled with the lucubrations that appeared on this subject.

"The pulpit, as usual, in Boston, afforded its utmost aid to the press, to insure success. Those who subscribed were in direct terms declared participators, in and accessories to, all the murders, as they were termed, that might take place in the unholy, unrighteous, wicked, abominable, and accursed war." [See *Sermon by Rev. Osgood and others, elsewhere.*]

The consequence of these efforts was soon plainly visible. The currency of various banks out of New England began to depreciate, because they were not in the plot. The Boston *Price Current* makes the following extract from the *United States Gazette,* of Feb. 7, 1815:

	Below par.
All New York Banks	15 to 20 p. c.
Hudson Bank	2)
Orange Bank	2)
Philadelphia City Banks	20
Treasury Notes	24 to 25
United States six per cents	40

Says Mr. CAREY, in speaking of this conspiracy:

"The success of the Eastern States was considerable. Few men have the courage to stem the tide of popular delusion, when it sets in very strong. There were some, however, who subscribed (to the Government loan) openly, in defiance of denunciations and threats. Others, of less fine texture, loaned their money (to the Government) by stealth, and as clandestinely as if it were treasonable. What, alas! must be the awful state of society when a free citizen is afraid of lending his money publicly to support the government that protects him."

In support of this damaging accusation, we extract the following paragraph from a work by JOHN LOWELL, a most inveterate Federal, who charged the "Federal secret Leagues" (have we not their progeny in "Union secret Leagues"?) with violating their secret pledges, not to loan money to the Government. In denouncing the violation of the "professions and promises" of his secret League associates, he exposes their vile conspiracy. He says:

"Money is such a drug (the surest sign of the *former* prosperity and *present* insecurity of trade) that men, against their consciences, their honor, their duty, their *professions* and

PROMISES, are willing to lend it *secretly*, to support the very measures [that is, the war,] which are both intended and calculated for their ruin."

Thus, the men, who to get rid of their "drug" would lend it *secretly* (they dared not openly) to the Government, had violated the *secret* pledges and *promises* they had made in the *secret* club rooms of their *secret* Leagues.

Puritanital superstition was appealed to, to prevent loans to the Government. Just previous to the Fast day in Boston, while the Government was advertising for loans, the following paragraph appeared in the Boston Federal papers:

"Let no man who wishes to continue the war by active measures, by voting or *lending money*, dare *to prostrate himself at the altar on the Fast day*, for they are actually as much partakers in the war, as the soldier who thrusts his bayonet, and the *judgment of God will await them!!*"

"Will Federalists subscribe to the loan? Will they lend money to our national rulers? It is impossible! First, because of the principal, and secondly, of principal and interest. If they lend money now, they make themselves parties to the violations of the Constitution, the cruelly oppressive measures in relation to commerce, and to all the crimes which have occurred in the field and in the Cabinet. To what purpose have Federalists exerted themselves to show the wickedness of this war—*to rouse the public sentiment against it*, and to show the authors of it not only to be unworthy of public confidence, but *highly criminal*, if now they contribute the sums of money *without which these rulers must be compelled to stop*."

"By the very ruinous cause pointed out by Gov. STRONG, that is by *witholding all voluntary aid*, in prosecuting the war, and manfully expressing our opinion as to its injustice and ruinous tendency, *we have arrested its progress, and driven back its authors to abandon their nefarious schemes*, and to look anxiously for peace. * * But some say will you let the country become bankrupt? No, the country will never become bankrupt, *but pray do not prevent their trustees becoming bankrupt!* Do not prevent them from becoming *odious* to the public, and replaced by better men. Any Federalist who lends his money to government, must go and shake hands with JAMES MADISON and claim fellowship with FELIX GRUNDY. Let him no more call himself a Federalist, and friend to his country.—He will be called by others, *infamous*. But, secondly, Federalists will not lend money, because they will never get it again. Now, where and when are the Government to get money to pay interest, and who can tell whether future members of Congress may think the debt contracted under such circumstances, and by men who lend money to help out measures what they have loudly and constantly condemned, ought to be paid? On the whole, then, there are two very strong reasons, why Federalists will not lend money; first, because it would be an abandonment of *political and personal principles*, and secondly, because it is pretty certain they will never be paid again.—*Boston Gazette, April* 14, 1814.

"Our merchants constitute an honorable, high-minded, independent and intelligent class of citizens. [That faction always boasted of their intelligence.] They feel the oppression, injury and mockery, with which they are treated by the government. They will lend them money *to retrace their steps, but none to persevere in their present course. Let every highwayman find his own pistols.*"—*Boston Gazette.*

"We have only room this evening to say that we trust no *true friend to his country will be found among the subscribers to the Gallatin loan.*"—*New York Evening Post.*

"No peace will ever be made till the people say there shall be no war. If the *rich* men continue to furnish money, war will continue till the mountains are melted with blood; till every field in America is white with the bones of the people."—*Discourse at Byfield,* (*Mass.*) *April 7, 1814, by Rev. Dr. Parish.*

"So unjust is this offensive war, in which our rulers have plunged us, in the sober consideration of millions, that they cannot conscientiously approach the God of Armies for His blessing upon it."—*Boston Centinel, Jan.* 13, 1813.

"It is very grateful to find that the universal sentiment is, that any man who lends his money to the Government, at the present time, will forfeit all claim to common honesty and common courtesy, among all true friends to the country. God forbid that any Federalist should ever hold up his head and pay Federalists for money lent to the present rulers, and Federalists can judge whether Democrats will tax their constituents to pay interest to Federalists."—*Boston Gazette, April* 14, 1814.

The following announcement by Boston brokers show that the *terror* inspired by New England Federalists, through their *secret Leagues*, made it dangerous for any one to subscribe to the Government loan openly. It is a sad commentary on the extreme terrorism raised by the monied and "intelligent" aristocracy of New England.

PROOF OF TERRORISM IN BOSTON.

Advertisement which appeared in the Boston *Chronicle,* April 14, 1814:

"THE NEW LOAN.

" From the *advice* of several respected friends, we are *induced* to announce to the public that subscriptions to the new loan will be received by us, as agents, until the 25th inst, from individuals, or incorporated bodies, in sums of $500 and upwards. The subscriptions to conform to the regulations announced by the Secretary of the Treasury, dated the 4th of April. Payments may be made in Boston money, or in any other of the United States, the subscriber paying the customary rate of discount. Applications will be received from any persons who wish to receive their interest in Boston, by letters post paid, or by *written applications, from individuals in Boston, and the names of all subscribers shall be known ONLY TO THE UNDERSIGNED* according to the proposals of the Secretary of the Treasury- [For more particulars see his advertisement.] Each applicant must name the highest rate he will give, and if the loan is granted, lower than his proposal, it will of course be for his benefit, but on the other hand, if higher, he will lose the benefit of being a subscriber. The certificates and all the business relating to it will be delivered free of charge.

"GILBERT & DEAN, Brokers.
"EXCHANGE COFFEE HOUSE, Boston, April 12."

The following advertisement appeared in the Boston *Gazette*, Aril 14, 1814:

"THE LOAN.

"Subscriptions will be received through the the agency of the subscriber till the 25th inst., inclusive.

"To avoid the *inconvenience of personal appearance* to subscribe, applications in writing will be received from any part of the state. Each applicant will name the highest rate he will give, and if the loan shall be granted, lower than his proposal, he will reap the benefit, but if higher than his offer, he will have no share in it. The amount, rate and *name of any applicant, shall, at his request, be known only to the subscriber.* All the business shall be transacted, and certificates delivered to the subscribers, without expense.

"JESSE PUTNAM."

Upon which the Boston *Gazette* of the same date remarked as follows:

"How degraded must our Government be, even in their own eyes, *when they resort to such tricks to obtain money, which a common Jew broker would be ashamed of!* They must be well acquainted with the fabric of the men who are to loan them money, when they, offer, that if they will have the goodness to do it, *their names shall not be exposed to the world!* * * * Perhaps monied men may be bribed by the high interest that is offered, but if they withhold their aid, and so *force the Government into a peace,* will not their capital be better employed, if engaged in trade?

"On the whole, we think it no way to get out of war, *to give money to the Government when the very thing that prevents them from carrying it on is the want of money!*"

AID AND COMFORT TO THE ENEMY.

We regret that we have not ample room for the statistics before us, all going to show that the Federals of Boston, not only combined to make a run on the banks of New York, Pennsylvania, and the Southern states, and draw out the specie from their vaults, with a view to create a panic, and destroy the value of their currency, but they actually engaged openly in the smuggling trade, bought and sold British stocks and bills openly in State street—hoarded the specie drawn from loyal banks and sent it off to England, via. Canada, to purchase contraband goods and bills. So bold had these traitors become in their treasonable and illicit conduct, that on the 16th of December, 1814, the following advertisement appeared in the Boston Daily *Advertiser:*

"BRITISH GOVERNMENT BILLS FOR SALE.
1 Bill for 800*l*
1 do 250*l*
1 do 503*l*
                                                                            1,253*l*
"By CHA'S W. GREEN, No. 14, India Wharf."

This illicit intercourse with the public enemy was strictly prohibited by Acts of Congress of 1781 and 1782.

These bills were constantly bought and sold in the Boston market. The Federalists kept up a line of communication with Quebec, to which place they exported specie, and from which place they brought back British bills, which they forwarded to England to purchase contraband goods with, and so universal was the sentiment of resistance to the General Government, in Massachusetts, and so little respect was there existing for the Union, that this illicit and treasonable intercourse was kept up with the public enemy, all through the war, and the sentiment adverse to it was too weak to risk complaint and exposure. The moment our government gunboats were out of Boston harbor, the Federalists would hoist their signal *Blue Lights,* and the British merchantmen that continually hovered about the Massachusetts coast, would come in, deliver their contraband cargo, receive specie and British bills in exchange, and return for another cargo. Says Mr. CAREY:

"There is no country in the world, but the United States, wherein such crimes could be perpetrated with impunity. Even by our mildest of all mild constitutions, it is *treason!*"

These acts were not only treasonable, but they were the essence of treason, itself, and if

Mr. MADISON and caused the arrest of the leaders in the guilt, and confined them in some Government Fort, and transported them "beyond the lines," he would have been sustained by the just verdict of the nation. But he did not do it. He knew perhaps that all New England was so bent on the destruction of the Government, that it would make matters worse to have aroused a worse hostility than he had already met with. O, that Mr. LINCOLN, for his sake, could have been justified by a tithe of provocation and excuse in his arrest and banishment of Mr. VALLANDIGHAM and others. But in his reply to the Ohio and Albany committees, he is bound to say that Mr. V. had committed no crime, that he was arrested and banished because it was feard he *might* do something criminal! and Mr. LINCOLN lays down the general rule of "disloyalty," according to the reigning nomenclature, to be the use of a "but," or "and" or "if" or "saying nothing," when one is standing by, listening to criticism on the conduct of governmental affairs. This is the difference between Mr. MADISON and Mr. LINCOLN in this regard. But to proceed. On all occasions, the Federalists, who were dissatisfied with our Government, sought to enlist sectional animosities. From a joint report to the two Houses of the Massachusetts Legislature, Feb. 18, 1814, we extract the following:

"They (the South) have seen, at first an ill concealed, but at last an open and undisguised jealousy of the wealth and power of the *commercial states*, operating in continued efforts to embarrass and destroy that commerce, which is their life and support."

APPEALING TO SECTIONAL JEALOUSIES.

This report sets up the propriety, justice and necessity of *forcible resistance* to the General Government, and then adds:

"The question is not a question of *power or right*, with this Legislature, but of *time or expediency*."

And the committee proceed:

"There exists in all parts of this Commonwealth, a fear, and in many, a settled belief, that the cause of foreign and domestic policy, pursued by the government of the United States for several years past, has its foundation in a *deliberate intention to impair, if not to destroy that free spirit and exercise of commerce*, which, aided by the habits, manners and institutions of our ancestors, and the blessings of Divine Providence, have been the principal source of the freedom, wealth and general prosperity of this recently happy and flourishing people," &c.

And continue the Committee:

"The memorialists see in this deploriable descent from national greatness, a determination to harrass and annihilate that spirit of commerce," &c.

A WAIF FROM THE HARTFORD CONVENTION.

And this key note of false alarm to the people was taken up by the Hartford Convention from the Address of which we copy:

"Events may prove that the causes of our calamities are *deep and permanent*. They may be found to proceed, not merely from the blindness of prejudice, pride of opinion, violence of party spirit, or the confusion of the times, but they may be traced to implacable combinations of individuals or *states*, to monopolize power and office, and to trample without remorse upon the rights and interests of the *commercial sections of the Union*.

"The Administration, after a long perseverance in plans to baffle every effort of commercial enterprise, had fatally succeeded in their attempts at the epoch of the war."

In concluding this part of our subject, we refer the reader to the following notable Federalists, who in various ways have had a hand in fulminating the foregoing treasonable extracts, with hundreds of others, "too numerous to mention": the Brookses, the Strongs, the Otises, and the Quincys, of Boston; the Clarksons, Rays, Ludlows, Remsons, Ogdens, Pearsalls, Lenoxes, Harrisons, Lawrences, McCormicks, Colemans, and Webbs, of New York; the Willings, Francises, Norrises, Biddles, Latimers, Filghmans, Waluses, Ralstones, and Lewises, of Philadelphia; and the Gilmans, the Olivers, the Stewarts, the Howards, the Smiths, the Briggses, the Grahams, and the Coopers, of Baltimore.

The Federals were in power in Congress during the Administration of Gen. WASHINGTON, and completely in power during the Administration of the elder ADAMS. Then was their time to put in motion their machinery for a "strong government." The occasion was ripe, says CAREY, and they passed an alien law, calculated, under pretext of military necessity, to eventually keep all foreign born people from participating in our Government affairs. They knew that the "foreign element" when one settled in this country, went with the Democratic party, hence the alien law, under a plausible pretext, to cruse out that element, and to enable them to hold the reigns of power.

In the series of measures for their "strong government" was also the sedition law.

Having determined to force the Government into radical extremes, the Federals, knowing their conduct would be criticised, and through criticism and free discussion their purposes thwarted, they set about the means to prevent such discussion, and the following law was intended for that purpose.

THE SEDITION LAW.

"Sec. 1. *Be it enacted, &c.*, If any persons shall unlawfully combine or conspire together with *intent to oppose any measure or measures* of the Government of the United States [then as now the Government was the *party*] which are, or shall be directed by the proper authority, or to impede the operation of any law of the United States, or to intimidate or prevent any person from holding a place or office in or under the Government of the United States, from undertaking, performing or executing his trust, or duty, and if any person or persons with intent as aforesaid, shall counsel, advise or attempt to procure any insurrection, riot, unlawful assembly or combination, whether such conspiracy, threatening, counsel, advice, or attempt, shall have the *proposed effect ar not*, he or they shall be deemed guilty of a high misdemeanor and on conviction before any Court *of the United States* having jurisdiction thereof, shall be punished by a fine not exceeding *five thousand dollars*, and by imprisonment, during a term *not less than six months nor exceeding five years*, and further, at the discretion of the Court, may be holden to find sureties for his or their good behavior in such sum and for such time as the said Court may direct.

"Sec. 2. *And be it further enacted*, That if any person shall write, print, utter or publish, or shall cause or procure to be written, printed, uttered or published, or shall knowingly or willingly aid in writing, printing, uttering or publishing any false, scandalous and malicious writing or writings against the Government (the party in power) of the United States, or either House of the Congress of the United States, or the President of the United States, with intent to defame the said Government, or either House of the Congress, or the said President, or to bring them or either of them into *contempt or disrepute* [see Gen. Hascall's order for a copy from this] or to excite against them, or either, or any of them, the hatred of the good people of the United States, or to stir up sedition within the United States, or to excite any unlawful combination therein for opposing or resisting any law of the United States, or *any act of the President of the United States*, done in pursuance of any such law [this is much milder than the law of indemnity of 1862] or of the powers in him vested by the Constitution of the United States, or to resist, *oppose* or defeat any such *law* or *act*, or to aid, engage or abet any hostile designs of any foreign nation against the United States, their people or Government, then such person being thereof convicted before the Court of the United States having jurisdiction thereof, shall be punished by a fine, not exceeding $2,000, and by imprisonment not exceeding two years.

"Sec. 3. *And be it further enacted and declared*, That if any person shall be prosecuted under this act for writing or publishing any libel as aforesaid, it shall be lawful for the defendent upon the trial of the cause to give in evidence in his defense the truth of the matter contained in the publication charged as a libel, [this is milder than the action against VALLANDIGHAM and others] and the jury, who shall try the cause, shall have a right to determine the law and the fact, under the direction of the court, as in other cases.

"Sec 4. *And be it further enacted*, That this act shall continue and be in force until the 3d day of March, 1801, and no longer, *provided*, that the expiration of the act shall not prevent or defeat a prosecution and punishment of any offence against the law during the time it shall be in force.

"JULY 17, 1798."

OBJECTS OF THE SEDITION LAW.

Thus, this law was to continue to the very day the then Federal Administration was to go out of power, and no longer, and if they should succeed in prolonging their power, it could be re-enacted. The reader will see from this its real object, which was to silence all opposition to the Federal Administration, while they proceeded to mould their "strong government."

Under this act, MATHEW LYON, of Vermont was put in prison for speaking disrespectful of the President. A "culprit"

"Was found guilty and punished in New Jersey for the simple wish that the wadding of a gun, discharged on a festive day, had made an inroad into, or pierced the posterior of Mr. ADAMS, the President," &c.—[*Olive Branch*, *p*. 89.

WE, THE GOVERNMENT IN 1798.

Many other similar cases are recorded, but this will suffice. The Federals of that day, were great sticklers for "sustaining the Government." Everything the "Government" chose to propose or do, must be acquiesced in by the people without a murmur, as it is at the present day. *They* were in power *then*. We will give a few samples.

"I believe that some of the old French leaven remains against us, and that some vile and degenerate wretches, whom I shall call

French partizans, or American Jacobines will not join any military association or patriotic loan. These men should be watched.—[*Baltimore Federal Gazette, July* 5, 1798.

The following is pitched in the same key, ang runs in the same vein, of the demands of the *ins* to-day, and did we not assure the reader, was the preamble to a set of resolutions got up by the Federal majority of the New York Senate, and passed March 5, 1799, would be taken for granted as the "loyal" efferescence of some "Loyal League" of the present day:

"*And whereas*, Our peace, prosperity and happiness, eminently depend on the preservation of the Union, in order to which a reasonable confidence in the constituted authorities is indispensible, and

Whereas, Every measure calculated to weaken that confidence has a tendency to destroy the usefulness of our public functionaries," &c.

This was the Federal response to the murmurings of the people against the infamous Sedition and Alien laws.

And be it remembered, these same Federals just thirteen years afterward, joined in the crusade against MADISON's administration (as we have shown) without so much as pretending to a tangible excuse. They went below the hard pan of infamy to "excite jealousies," &c.

The clergymen of that day, of the leading orders, were mostly Federalists. Their sermons were full of devotion to "the Government."

"It is a time of day that requires cautious jealousy; not jealousy of your magistrates, for you have given them your confidence. * * Cursed be he that keepeth back his sword from blood. Let him that hath none, sell his coat and buy one.—*Sermon of Rev. Dr. Parish, of Boston, July* 4, 1799.

In this connection we give the views of JEFFERSON on a fair and candid discussion of public affairs, written probably in answer to the claim of the New York Federals, and we give the credit to Jefferson, lest the "loyal" men may read the sentiment as pure "copperheadism."

"It would be a dangerous delusion were a confidence in the men of our choice to silence our fears for the safety of our rights. Confidence is everywhere the parent of despotism. Free government is founded in jealousy, and not in confidence. It is jealousy and not confidence which prescribes limited constitutions to bind down those whom we are obliged to trust with power. Our constitution has accordingly fixed the limits to which and no further, our confidence may go, and let the honest advocate of confidence read the Alien and Sedition acts, and say if the constitution has not been wise in fixing limits for the government it created, and whether we should be wise in destroying those limits Let him say what the government is, if it be not a tyranny, which the men of our choice have conferred on the President, and the President of our choice has assented to and accepted over the friendly strangers to whom the united spirit of our country and its laws had pledged hospitality and protection. The men of our choice have more respected the bare suspicions of the President than the solid rights of innocence, the claims of justification, the sacred force of truth, and the forms and substance of law and justice."

Then read the following, and see if it comes within the limits of JEFFERSON's ideas of fair and candid discussion under a proper "jealousy" to guard and respect constitutional rights, and also let the reader determine in his heart whether the following extracts from Federal malcontents come within the just rule laid down by WEBSTER, as follows:

"The spirit of liberty is jealous of encroachments, jealous of power, jealous of men. It demands checks; it seeks for guarantees, it insists on securities; it entrenches itself behind strong defences, and fortifies itself with all possible care against the assaults of ambition and passion. It does not trust the amiable weaknesses of human nature, and therefore will not permit power to overstep its prescribed limits, though benevolence, good intent, and patriotic purposes come along with it."

DAMN THE GOVERNMENT IN 1814.

This was when *his party* were in *power*, and talked of war. This same Reverend preached a sermond at Byfield, April 7, 1814, when his party was out of power, and the country was actually at war with another country, in which he said, p. 18:

"The Israelites became weary of yielding the fruit of their labor to pamper their splendid tyrants. They left their political Moses. They separated. Where is our Moses? Where is the rod of his miracles? Where is our Aaron? Alas, no voice from the burning bush has directed the house."

On page 18 he says:

"There is a point, there is an hour, beyond which you will not bear."

"Such is the temper of American Republicans [the Democratic Republicans that supported the war and Mr. MADISON] so called. A new language must be invented before we attempt to express the baseness of their conduct, or dscribe the rottenness of their hearts."—p. 21.

"New England, if invaded, would be obliged to defend herself. Do you not then owe it to your children, and owe it to your God, *to make peace for yourselves?*"—p. 23.

"You may as well expect the cataract of Niagara to turn its currant to the head of Superior, as a *wicked Congress to make a pause in the work of destroying their country,* while the people will furnish the means."—p. 8

"A thousand times as many sons of America have probably fallen victims of this ungodly war, as perished in Israel by the edict of Pharaoh! Still, the war is only beginning. If ten thousand have fallen, ten thousand times ten thousand may fall."—p. 7.

This, says CAREY, would require 100,000,000 victims, when there were but 8,000,000 to select from.

"Tyrants are the same on the banks of the Nile and the Potomac, at Memphis and at Washington, *in a monarchy and a Republic.*"—p. 9.

"Like the worshippers of MOLOCH, the supporters of a vile administration sacrifice their children and families on the altar of Democracy. Like the widows of Hindoostan they consume themselves."—p. 11.

"The full vials of despotism are poured out on your heads, and yet you may challenge the ploddding Israelite, the stupid African, the feeble Chinese, the drowsy Turk, or the frozen exile of Siberia, to *equal you in tame submission to the powers that be.*—p. 12.

"Here we must trample on the *mandates of despotism,* or here *we must remain slaves forever.*"—p. 13.

"Has not New England as much to apprehend as the sons of JACOB had? but no child has been taken from the river to lead us through the sea."—p. 20.

"If judgments are coming on the nation;—if the sea does not open thee a path, where, how, and in what manner will you seek relief"—p. 20.

"GOD will bring good from every evil—the famishers of Egypt lighted Israel to the land of Cannan."—p. 22

"Which sooty slave in all the ancient dominion has more obsequiously watched the eye of his master or flew to the indulgence of his desires, more servilly than the same masters have waited and watched, and obeyed the orders of the great NAPOLEON.—[*Discourse delivered at Byfield, April* 8, 1813, *p.* 21.

"Let every man who sanctions this war by his suffrage or influence, remember that he is laboring to cover himself and his country with blood—the blood of the slain will cry from the ground against him."—p. 23.

"How will the supporters of *this anti-christian warfare* endure their sentence—endure their own reflections—endure the *fire that forever burns*—the worm which never dies—the hozannas of heaven, while the *smoke of their torments ascends forever and ever.*"—p. 24.

"The legislaters who yielded to this war, when assailed by the manifesto of their own party chief, established inequality and *murder by law.*"—p. 9.

"In the first onset [of the war] moral principle was set at defiance. The laws of God and hopes of man were utterly disdained.— Vice threw off her veil, and crimes were decked with highest honors. *This war not only tolerrtes crimes, but calls for them—demands them. Crimes are the food of its life—the arms of its strength.* This war is a *monster,* which every hour gormandizes a thousand crimes, and yet cries give! give! In its birth, it demanded the violation of all good faith, perjury of office, the sacrifice of neutral impartiality. The first moment in which the dragon moved, piracy and murder *were legalized.*— Havoc, death and conflagration were the viands of her first repast."—p. 11.

"Those western states which have been violent for this *abominable war of murder*—those states which have thirsted for blood, God has given them blood to drink. Their men have fallen. Their lamentations are deep and loud." —p. 16.

"Our Government—if they may be called the Government—and not the destroyers—of the country, bear these things as patiently as a colony of convicts sail into Botany Bay."— p. 5.

CHAPTER VI.

PROOFS OF FEDERAL TREASON.—CONTINUED.

Tone of the Federals when in Power...similar to the Tone of Those now in Power...Congregational Ministers' Address to President ADAMS...Extract from Sermon of Rev. JEDIDAH MORSE...Extracts from Sermon by Rev. F. S. F. GARDNER, 1812...Extracts from Discourses of Rev. Dr. OSGOOD, 1810...The Clamors of New England for Separation and Dissolution..."Extracts of Treason"...From Boston Centinel, Dec. 10, 1814...From same Dec. 14, 1814...Sundry other extracts from same...Ipswich Memorial...Deerfield, (Mass.) Petition...From the Crisis, No. 3...From the Federal Republican, 1814...Extract from Address to the Hartford Convention, &c...From Boston Daily Advertiser, 1814...From Federal Republican, 1814...Extracts from proceedings of a Treasonable Meeting in Reading, Mass....Also from Memorial of citizens of Newburyport to the Legislature—From Federal Republican, Nov. 7, 1814...From Boston Gazette...From Sermon of Rev. DAVID OSGOOD...Also from his Address before the Legislature...Extracts from a treasonable letter from Federals to JAMES MADISON...From Boston Repertory...From New York Commercial Advertiser.

THE TONE OF FEDERALS WHEN IN POWER.

In 1798, a Convention of Congregational ministers issued an address to President ADAMS, from which we take a short extract:

"The intimate connection between our civil and Christian blessings is alone sufficient to justify the *decided part which the clergy of America have uniformly taken in supporting the constituted authorities and political interests of their country*" Their political party was then in power.

On the 9th of May, 1798, the Rev. JEDEDIAH MORSE preached a sermon, in which he urged everybody to yield strict obedience to the powers that be, which were of his political faith. He said:

"To the unfriendly disposition and conduct of a foreign power, we may ascribe the unhappy dissensions that have existed among us, which have so permanently disturbed our peace, and threatened the overthrow of our government. Their maxim to which they have strictly and steadily adhered has been "divide and govern." Their too great influence among us has been exerted vigorously and in conformity to a deep laid plan in cherishing party spirit, in villifying the man we have by our free suffrages elected to administer our Constitution, and have thus endeavored to destroy the confidence of the people in the constituted authorities, and divide them from the Government."

Of the same tenor was Gov. GILLMORE's message to the Legislature of New Hampshire in 1798, the legislative response to the same—the Massachusetts Legislature and the Address of the Federalists of Elizabethtown, in 1798.

EXTRACTS FROM A SERMON DELIVERED BY THE REV. F. S. F. GARDINER, RECTOR OF TRINTY CHURCH. BOSTON, April 9, 1812.

"The British, after all, save for us by their convoys infinitely more property than they deprive us of, *where they take one ship they protect twenty;* where they commit one outrage they do many acts of kindness."—p. 15.

"England is willing to sacrifice everything to conciliate us except her honour and independence."—p. 10.

"It is a war unexampled in the history of the world; wantonly proclaimed on the most frivolous and groundless pretences against a nation from whose friendship we might derive the most signal advantages."—*Discourse delivered July 23d*, 1813, *p.* 3.

"Let no consideration, my brethren, deter your at all times, and in all places, from execrating the present war. It is a war unjust, foolish and ruinous."—p. 15.

"As Mr. MADISON has declared war, let Mr. MADISON carry it on."—p. 17.

"*The Union has long since been virtually dissolved, and it is full time that this part of the United States should take care of itself.*"—*p.* 19.

TREASON OF THE REV. DR. OSGOOD, PASTOR OF THE MEDFORD CHURCH.

"The strong prepossessions of so great a proportion of my fellow-citizens in favor of a race of demons, and against a nation of more religion, virtue, good faith, generosity, and beneficence, than any that now is, or ever has been, upon the face of the earth, wring my soul with anguish and fill my soul with apprehension and terror of the judgments of heaven upon this sinful people."—*Discourse of April 8th*, 1810, *p.* 40.

"If at the command of weak or wicked rulers, they undertake an unjust war, each man who volunteers his services in such a cause, or loans his money for its support, or by his conversation, his writings, or any other mode of influence, encourages its prosecution, that man is an accomplice in wickedness, loads his conscience with the blackest crimes, brings the guilt of blood upon his soul, and in the sight of God and His law, is a murderer."—*Discourse of June 27th*, 1812, *p.* 9.

"One hope only remains, that this last stroke of perfidy (the war) may open the eyes of a besotted people. that they may awake, like a giant from his slumbers, and *wreak their vengeance on their betrayers by DRIVING them from their stations,* and placing at the helm more skillful and faithful hands."—p. 12.

NEW ENGLAND CLAMORS FOR SEPARATION AND DISSOLUTION.

It gives us no pleasure to reproduce the following extracts, as the touch-stone of the *prevailing* public sentiment of the Puritans forty-nine years ago. These extracts furnish a sad commentary on the clamoring cry of "treason" by the same party and the same men against all whom, while willing to aid our Government in every essential way to reduce this rebellion, and preserve the Constitution, claim and exercise the right to criticise in a manly spirit what they believe to be measures destructive of constitutional rights and civil liberty.—The world has been taught that there is a vast difference between such articles as the following and a manly protest against the blow that strikes down civil rights arbitrarily, without any of those means of redress or modes of trial known to civil jurisprudence.

JAMES MADISON was often severely censured by many of his most ardent political friends for not imprisoning the utterers of the following sentiments of treason, and although the danger from these influences were imminent, and at the time threatened to finally destroy the Government, Mr. MADISON trusted to the good sense of the *people* to maintain this Government, nor did he arbitrarily arrest a man, nor proclaim the suspension of the writ of *habeas corpus* against all the people. The sequel proved the wisdom of MADISON'S course, for while the authors of that seditious treason that threatened to take New England out of the Union, soon found themselves buried in disgrace, he was spared the charge of even the attempt at oppression. All will agree that he would have been justified in arresting the authors of the following:

EXTRACTS OF TREASON.

"Those who startle at the danger of separation tell us that the soil of New England is hard and sterile—that deprived of the productions of the South, we should soon become a wretched race of cowherds and fishermen; that our narrow territory and diminished population would make us an easy prey to foreign powers. Do these men forget what national energy can do for a people? Have they not read of Holland? Do they not remember that it grew in wealth and power amidst combat and alarm! That it threw off the yoke of Spain (our Virginia) and its chapels became churches and its poor man's cottages prince's palaces?"—*Boston Centinel, Dec. 10, 1814.*

"It is said, that to make a treaty of commerce with the enemy is to violate the constitution, and to sever the Union. *Are they not both already virtually destroyed?* Or in what stage of existance would they be should we declare a neutrality, or even withhold taxes and men."—*Boston Centinel, Dec. 14, 1814.*

"By a commercial treaty with England which shall provide for the admission of such States as may wish to come into it, and which shall *prohibit England from making a treaty with the South and West*—which does not give us at least equal privileges with herself—our commerce will be secured to us; our standing in the nation raised to its proper level, and New England feelings will no longer be sported with, or her interest violated.—*Boston Centinel, 1814.*

"If we submit quietly our destruction is certain. If we oppose them with a highminded and steady conduct, who will say that we shall not *beat them all?* No one can suppose that a *conflict* with a tyranny at home, would be as easy as with an enemy from abroad, but firmness will anticipate and prevent it. Cowardice dreads it, and will surely bring it on at last. Why this delay? Why leave that to chance which our firmness should command? Will our wavering frighten Government into compliance?"—*Ibid.*

"We must do it deliberately, and not from irritation at our wrongs and sufferings, and when we have once entered on the high course of honor, and independence, let no difficulties stay our course, nor dangers drive us back."—*Ibid.*

"We are convinced that the time is arrived when Massachusetts must make a resolute stand, and recurring to *first principles,* view men and things as they are. The sophisticated Government which these States have witnessed for thirteen years past, has almost completed their ruin, and every day still adds to their distracted condition."—[*Ipswich Memorial, Sept. 18, 1813.*

"The sentiment is hourly extending, and in these *Northern States will soon be universal,* that we are in no better condition with respect to the *South* than that of a conquered people."—*Boston Centinel, Jan. 13, 1813.*

"We have no more interest in waging this sort of war at present, at the command of Virginia, than Holland in accelerating her ruin, by uniting her destiny with France."—*Ibid.*

"The land is literally taken from its old possessions and given to strangers."—*Ibid.* [This is just what New England is now clamoring for in the South.]

"Either the Southern States must drag us further into the war, or we must drag them out of it, *or the chain will break.—Ibid.*

"We must be no longer deafened by *senseless clamors* about a separation of the States."—*Ibid.*

"Should the present Administration, with the adherence in the Southern States still persist in the prosecution of this ruinous and *wicked war,* in unconstitutionally creating new States in the mud of Louisiana [just what we are fighting to keep in] (the inhabitants of which country are as ignorant of Republicanism as the alligators of their swamps,) and in opposition to the commercial rights and privileges of *New England,* much as we deprecate a separation of the Union, we deem it an evil much less to be dreaded than a co-operation with them in their nefarious projects."—*Deerfield (Mass.) Petition, Jan. 10, 1814.*

"We must put away all childish fears of resistance."—*Crisis No. 3.*

"What shall we do to be saved? One thing only: The people must rise in their majesty—protect themselves, and *compel* their unworthy servants to obey their will."—*Boston Centinel, Sept. 10, 1814.*

"The *Union is already dissolved, practically.*"—*Ibid.*

"You ask my opinion on a subject which is much talked of, a dissolution of the Union. On this subject I differ from my fellow-citizens generally, and therefore I ought to speak and write with diffidence. I have for many years considered the Union of the Northern and Southern states as *not essential to the safety, and very much opposed to the interest of both sections.* The extent of the territory is too large to be harmoniously governed by the same representative body. A despotic prince, like the Emperor of Russia may govern a wide extent of territory, and numerous distinct nations, for his will controls their jealousies and discordent interests; but when states, having different interests are permitted to decide on those interests themselves, no harmony can be expected. The commercial and non commercial states have views so different that I conceive it to be impossible that they ever can be satisfied with the same laws and the same system of measures. I firmly believe that each section would be better satisfied to govern itself, and each is large and populous enough for its own protection, especially as we have no powerful nations in our neighborhood. These observations are equally applicable to the Western States, a large body and a distinct portion of the country, which would govern themselves better than the Atlantic states can govern them. [This was in accordance with the old Federal notion that some states should be controlled and governed by others—and New England has ever acted on that doctrine.] That the Atlantic States do not want the aid of the strength, nor the counsels of the Western States is certain, and I believe the public welfare would be better consulted and more promoted in a *separate than in a Federal Constitution.* The mountains form a natural line of division, and moral and commercial habits would unite the Western people. In like manner the moral and commercial habits of the Northern and Middle states would link them together, as would the like habits of the slave holding states- Indeed, the attempt to unite this vast territory under one head, has long appeared to me *absurd*! I believe a peaceable separation would be for the happiness of all sections, but as the citizens of this country have generally been of a different opinion, it is best not to urge for a separation, till they are convinced of their error."—*Com. in Boston Centinel, July* 18, 1818.

"We will ask the infatuated man of property, beguiled by the arts of ALBERT GALLATIN, by what fund, and by whom, they will be repaid the advances made on exchequer bills and the loans, in the event of a *dissolution of the Union?* We ask them further, whether from present appearances, and under existing circumstances, there is the least foundation to build a hope *that the Union will last twelve months?* We look to Russia to save us from the horrors of anarchy. If a reverse of fortune is in reserve for ALEXANDER, and the war continues, *the Union is evidently gone*"—*Federal Republican,* 1814.

EXTRACT FROM AN ADDRESS TO THE HARTFORD CONVENTION.

"The once venerable Constitution HAS EXPIRED BY DISSOLUTION in the hands of those wicked men who were sworn to protect it. Its spirit, with the precious souls of its first founders, *has fled forever.* Its remains, with theirs, *rest in the silent tomb!* At your hands, therefore, *we demand deliverance. New England is unanimous,* and we announce our *irrevocable decree,* that the tyrannical oppression of those who at present usurp the powers of the Constitution, *is beyond endurance AND WE WILL RESIST IT.*"—*Boston Centinel Dec.* 28*th,* 1814.

"Long enough have we grasped at shadows and illusions, and been compelled to recoil upon ourselves, and feel the stings of real, substantial, hopeless woe, sharpened by disappointment. Long enough have we paid the taxes and fought the battles of the *Southern states!* Long enough have been scouted, abused and oppressed by men who claim a right to rule and to despise us! Long enough have we been submissive slaves of the senseless representatives ot the equally senseless *natives of Africa,* and of the semi-barbarous huntsmen of the western wilderness. Realities alone can work our deliverance, and deliverance we deliberately, solemnly, and *irrevocably decree to be our right, and WE WILL OBTAIN IT!*"—*Ibid, Dec.* 24*th,* 1814.

"The sufferings which have multiplied so thick about us have at length aroused New England. She will now meet every danger, and go through every difficulty, until her rights are restored to the full, and settled too strongly to be shaken. She will put aside all *half way measures.* She will look with an eye of doubt on those who oppose them. She will tell such men, that if they hope to lead in the *cause of* ' *New England* INDEPENDENCE, they must do it in the spirit of New England men."—*Ibid, Dec.* 7, 1814.

"Throwing off all connection with this wasteful war—making peace with the enemy, and opening once more our commerce, would be a wise and manly course."—*Ibid, Dec.* 17, 1814.

"My plan is to withhold our money and make a *separate peace with England.*"—*Boston Daily Advertiser,* 1814.

"That there will be a revolution if the war continues many months, no man can doubt, who is acquainted with human nature, and is accustomed to study cause and effect. The Eastern States are marching stealthily and straight forward up to the object. In times past there was much *talk* and loud *menaces,* but little action among the *friends of reform* in New England. Now, we shall hear little said, and much done. The new constitution [of the Hartford Convention] is to go into operation as soon as two or three states shall have adopted it."—*Federal Republican,* 1814.

On the 5th of January, 1815, a treasonable meeting was held by the Federals at Reading, which passed a long string of incendiary resolutions, from which we select the following:

" *Resolved,* That we place the fullest confidence in the Governor and Legislature of Massachusetts, and in the State authorities of New England, and that to them, under God, the Chief Governor of the Universe, we look for aid and direction, and that for the present, until the public opinion shall be known, we will not enter our earnings, pay our continental taxes, or aid, inform, or assist any officer in their collection."

"In this alarming state of things we can no longer be silent. When our unquestionable rights are invaded, we will not sit down and coolly calculate what it may cost to defend them. We will not barter the liberties of our children for slavish repose, or surrender our birthright, but with our lives.

"We remember the resistance of our fathers to oppressions which dwindle into insignificance when compared with those we are called upon to endure. The rights which we have received from God we will never yield to man. We call upon our State Legislature to protect us in the enjoyment of those privileges, to assert which our fathers died, and to defend which, we profess, ourselves, ready to *resist unto blood!* We pray your honorable body to adopt measures immediately to secure to us especially our undoubted right to trade [with Great Britain] within our own State.

"We are ourselves ready to aid you in securing it to us, to the utmost of our power, *peaceably if we can*—FORCEIBLY *if we must*, and we pledge to you the sacrifice of ourselves and property in support of whatever measures the dignity and liberties of this free, sovereign and INDEPENDENT STATE, *may seem to your wisdom to demand!*"—*Extract from a Memorial of the citizens of Newburyport, (Mass.,) Jan. 31, 1814, to the Legislature of Massachusetts.*

"On or before the 4th of July, if JAMES MADISON is not out of office, *a new form of government will be in operation in the Eastern section of the Union, instantly after, the contest in many of the States will be, whether to adhere to the old, or join the new government!* Like everything else, which was foretold years ago, and which is verified every day, this warning will also be vilified as visionary. Be it so. But, Mr. MADISON cannot *complete his term of service if the war continues!* It is not possible! and if he knew human nature, he would see it.—*Federal Republican, Nov.* 7, 1814.

"Is there a Federalist, a patriot, in America, who concedes it his duty to shed his blood for Bonaparte, for Madison, for Jefferson, and the *host of ruffians in Congress*, who have set their faces against *us* for years, and spirited up the *brutal part of the populace* to destroy us? Not one! Shall we then, any longer, be held in slavery, and driven to desperate poverty by *such a graceless faction?* Heaven forbid!"—*Boston Gazette.*

"If, at the present moment, no symptoms of *civil war* appear *they certainly will soon* unless the courage of the war party fails them."—*Sermon by David Osgood, D. D., Pastor of the Church at Medford, delivered June 26th, 1812, p. 9.*

"A civil war becomes as certain as the events that happen, according to the known laws and established course of nature."—*Ibid,* p. 15.

"If we would preserve the liberties of that struggle, (the American Revolution,) so dearly purchased, the call for RESISTANCE *against the usurpations of our own Government is as urgent as it was formerly against the mother country.*"—*Rev. Osgood's discourse before the Lieut. Governor and Legislature of Massachusetts, May* 31, 1809, *p.* 25.

"If the impending negociation with Great Britain is defeated by insidious artifice—if the friendly and conciliatory proposals of the enemy should not, from French subserviency, for views of sectional ambition, be met throughout with a spirit of moderation and sincerity, so as to terminate the *infamous war*, which is scattering its terrors around us, and arrest the calamities and distress of a disgraced country, it is necessary to apprise you that such conduct will be no longer borne with. The injured States will be compelled by every motive of duty, interest, and honor, by one manly exertion of their strength, to *dash into atoms the bonds of tyranny!* It will then be too late to retreat! The die will be cast—freedom purchased."—*Extract from a letter to James Madison, entitled "Northern Grievances" and extensively circulated through New York and New England, dated May,* 1814, *p.* 4.

"A separation of the States will be an inevitable result. *Motives* numerous and urgent will *demand that measure.* As they originate in oppression, the oppressors must be responsible for the momentous and contingent events arising from the *dissolution of the present Confederacy, and the erection of separate Governments!* It will be their work. While posterity will admire the independent spirit of the *Eastern section* of our country, and with sentiments of gratitude enjoy the *fruits of their firmness and wisdom*, the descendants of the *South and West* will have reason to curse the infatuation and folly of your councils."—*Ibid,* p. 9.

"Bold and resolute, when they step forth in the *sacred cause of freedom* [how much this sounds like latter day Abolition talk] *and independence,* the *Northern* people will *secure their object*. No obstacle can impede them! No force can withstand their powerful arm. The most numerous armies will melt before their manly strength! Does not the page of history instruct you that the feeble debility of the *South* never could face the vigorous activity of the *North?* Do not the events of past ages remind you of the valuable truth, that a single spark of *Northern* liberty, especially when enlightened by congenial commerce, will explode a whole atmosphere of sultry *Southern* despotism. [How like late Abolition talk.] *Ibid p.* 12.

"When such are the effects of oppression upon men *resolved not to submit*, as displayed in the north and south of Europe, and in all ages of the world, do you flatter yourself with its producing a different operation in this country? Do you think the energies of *Northern freemen* [very like late abolition boasts] are to be tamely smothered? Do you imagine they will allow themselves to be trampled upon with impunity, and by whom? The *Southern and Western* states? By men whose united efforts are not sufficient to keep in order their own *enslaved* population, and defend their own frontiers? [How familiar this sounds with latter day boastings!] By warriors, whose repeated attempts at invasion of a neighboring province have been disgracefully foiled by a handful of disciplined troops? By generals, monuments of arrogance and folly? By counsels, the essence of corruption, imbecility and madness?

" The aggregate strength of the *South* and *West*, if brought against the *North*, would be driven into the ocean, or back to their own Southern wilds. [How valiant Massachusetts was, *then*!] And they might think themselves fortunate if they escaped other punishment than a defeat which their temerity would merit. While the one would strive to enslave, the other would *fight for freedom*. [How familiar that phrase.] While the counsels of the one would be distracted with discordant interests, the decisions of the other would be directed by one soul! Beware! Pause!! before you take the fatal plunge."—*Ibid, p.* 13.

"You have carried your oppressions to the utmost stretch! We will *no longer submit!* Restore the Constitution to its purity. Give us security for the future—indemnity for the past! Abolish every tyrannical law! *Make an immediate and honorable peace!* Revive our commerce! Increase our navy! Protect our seamen! [That was what Mr. MADISON was fighting for.] Unless you comply with these just demands, without delay, WE WILL WITHDRAW FROM THE UNION—*scatter to the winds the bonds of tyranny*, and trasmit to posterity that liberty purchased by the Revolution."—*Ibid p.* 15.

"Americans, *prepare your arms!* You will soon be called to use them. We must use them for the Emperor of France or for *ourselves*. It is but an individual who now points to this ambiguous alternative; but, Mr. MADISON and his cabal may rest assured there is in the hearts of many thousands in this abused and almost ruined country, a sentiment and energy to illustrate the distinction when his madness shall call it into action."—*Boston Repertory*.

" Old Massachusetts is as terrible to the American now as she was to the British Cabinet in 1775. For America, too, has her BUTE'S and her NORTH'S. Let them, the *commercial states breast themselves to the shock*, and know, that to *themselves* they must look for safety. All *party* bickerings must be sacrificed [That sounds like the cant of Union Leaguers] on the altar of patriotism. Then,

and not till then, shall they humble the pride and ambition of Virginia, whose strength lives in their weakness, and chastise the insolence of those mad men of Kentucky and Tennessee who aspire to the government of these states, and threaten to involve the country in all the horrors of war"—*N. Y. Commercial Advertiser.*

This sheet has kept regular pace with its party in all its phases. It was a *Federal* sheet in 1812–14, &c.; *Federal Republican* in 1824; *Whig* in 1833; *Republican* in 1854; *Union* in 1863. Has any one a doubt of the geneology of its principles or name?

Mr. CAREY, in his *Olive Branch*, p. 132, says:

"It is a most singular fact, that the cause of England [during the war] has been far more ably supported in our debates and in our political speculations and essays, than in London itself."

CHAPTER VII.

OPPOSITION TO THE MEXICAN WAR — LIKE FATHER, LIKE SON — LIKE FEDERAL, LIKE WHIG.

Treasonable opposition to the Mexican War...Mr. LINCOLN charges the "Government" with being in the "wrong" ...CALEB B. SMITH glories in voting to condemn the war ...GIDDINGS would "not vote a man or a dollar"...The Press of 1848 on the War...From the Warren Chronicle ...Xenia Torch Light...Lebanon Star...Cincinnati Gazette ...Kennebeck Journal...New Hampshire Statesman... Haverhill Gazette...Boston Sentinel...Boston Atlas... Boston Chronotype...New York Tribune...North American...Baltimore Patriot...Louisville Journal...Nashville Gazette...Mt. Carmel Register, &c.,...Also CORWIN'S " bloody hands" diatribe, &c.

TREASONABLE OPPOSITION TO THE MEXICAN WAR.

To the same end, and showing a like animus, we collate sundry extracts from speeches and editorials relative to the Mexican war, uttered by those who were then, as now, hostile to the Democratic party, and as is believed, for the reasons already given.

Mr. ABRAHAM LINCOLN, in a speech in opposition to the Mexican war, said:

"That he, the President, (Mr. POLK) is deeply conscious of being in the wrong; that he feels the blood of this war, like the blood of ABEL, is crying to heaven against him," &c.

He then goes into a summing up of the cost of the war, &c. See p. p. 93, 94, *Ap. Cong. Globe*, 1st Sess. 30th Cong.

Mr. CALEB B. SMITH, at the same session,

in referring to the vote declaring the war unnecessary and unconstitutional, said:

"I had the good fortune—and I deem it extreme good fortune—to have the opportunity to record my vote in favor of this sentence of condemnation. In giving that vote my heart concurred with my judgment."—[p. 321.

Mr. GIDDINGS said in reference to the same war:

"But they (his friends) would permit him to say that he never had and never would, vote for a dollar or a man in a war which he had so long denounced as wicked and barbarous."

The following are extracts taken from the leading presses of that day which opposed and do now oppose the Democracy:

"The voice of lamentation and war, heard all over the country, from homes and firesides made desolate by the slaughter of fathers, and husbands, and brothers, is sweet music to the ears of the President and his friends, and they seem ambitious to swell the chorus *by increasing the victims.* * * * We rejoice to see a large and respectable number of Whig papers in this and other states taking ground against further appropriations by Congress of men and money for the Mexican cut-throating business. This is as it should be."—*Warren (O.) Chronicle.*

"They (the Mexicans) *are in the right—we in the wrong.* They may appeal in confidence to the God of battles, but if we look for aid to any other than human power, it must be *to the infernal machinations of hell,* for thus far it would seem, the devil has governed and guided all our actions in the premises."—*Xenia (O.) Torch Light.*

"If Congress is opposed to the war—if that body is of opinion that it is unjust, impolitic and of a dangerous tendency, *no duty can be more binding than that of refusing the means to prosecute it.*"—*Lebanon, (O.) Star.*

"No man, no people, looking upon the contest, *can help sympathizing with Mexico, and uniting in uttering a bitter denunciation against our own Government.*—*Cincinnati, (O.) Gazette.*

"None of the aggressors of Europe or Asia ever resorted to justificatory reasons which were so false and hypocritical as those alleged for our aggressions on Mexico."—*Kennebeck, (Me.,) Journal.*

"Let every one keep aloof from this *unrighteous, infamous, God-abhorred war,* and it will soon come to an end. The prospect is, that the Administration can get neither men nor money to carry on the war. *Thank the Lord for all that.*"—*N. H. Statesman.*

"To volunteer or vote a dollar to carry on the war, is *moral treason against the God of reason and the rights of mankind.*"—*Haverhill, (Mass.) Gazette.*

[This is the locality from which emanated the petition presented by Mr. ADAMS for a dissolution of the Union.]

"Talk of this war as we may, about, rejoice, illuminate your cities, *it is still a war of injustice, of conquest and of unmitigated evil,* and it is high time that the virtuous and patriotic should speak out in condemnation of it."—*Boston Sentinel,* 1848.

"The Mexican war appears to be fast settling down to a mere matter of plunder and murder. * * * We think the war disreputable to the age we live in, and the country of which it is our boast to be called her children."—*Boston Atlas.*

"If there is in the United States a breast worthy of American liberty, *its impulses to join the Mexicans, and hurl down upon the base, slavish, mercenary invaders, who, born in a Republic, go to play over the accursed game of the Hessians on the tops of those Mexican volcanoes, it would be a sad and woful JOY, nevertheless, to hear that the hordes under Scott and Taylor were every man of them swept into the next world!*—What business has an invading army in this?"—*Boston Daily Chronotype.*

"The whole world knows that it is Mexico which has been imposed upon, and that *our people are the robbers!* So far as our Government can affect it, the laws of heaven are suspended, and those of hell established in their stead. To the people of the United States. Your rulers are precipitating you into a fathomless abyss of crime and calumny!"—*N. Y. Tribune.*

"It is the President's war. Mexico is the Poland of America. If there were excuse for the war, there is none for the measure which opened it. But what excuse is found for the war itself?"—*North American.*

"What is it, then, that makes or allows Mr. Polk to sanction this war, and all the outrages of which it is the consequence? It is this: Mr. Polk is a weak man. He was selected to be the loco foco candidate for President because he was weak. It was this which recommended him to his party. It was this that elected him. It has been said, correctly, that it is a curse upon any nation to have weak minded rulers. We are under the judgment of that curse."—*Baltimore Patriot.*

"If there is any conduct which constitutes moral treason, it is an attempt to embark or encourage the country in a war against God, as is the case in a war like that in which we are now engaged."—*Louisville Journal.*

"To volunteer, or vote a dollar to carry on the war, is moral treason against the God of Heaven and the rights of mankind."—*Nashville (Tenn.) Gazette.*

"We cannot possibly look favorably upon this war. Its first act was a gross outrage upon

Mexico, and can it be supposed by Mr. POLK and his advisers, that an error so glaring—a crime so unpardonable, as this Mexican war, can be white-washed?"—*Mt. Carmel Register.*

Mr. CORWIN, in a bitter speech denouncing the war, said:

"Were I a Mexican, I would welcome these invaders with bloody hands to hospitable graves."

These quotations might be seemingly in a more appropriate place under some other head, but as showing the *motives* of those who ever favored a "strong Government" to strike whenever the iron of discord was hot, with a view to weld together opposing elements, to ultimately demonstrate a seeming *necessity* for their system of Government, they are here inserted.

We freely admit that many of the masses who were influenced to adopt these extreme views were not actuated by the *motives* that evidently governed the authors, but such is human nature, that when the pride of opinion is once fixed, it can be easily controlled by arch, designing men, to further their views.

CHAPTER VIII.

FURTHER SCHEMES IN THE PROGRESS OF DISSOLUTION EXPOSED.

The efforts to create a public debt to hasten the "Strong Government"... Mr. KING's $2,000,000 gift, as a "means"...RANDOLPH opposed...CALHOUN, as a means to an end, votes against his party..."Purpose of the "Fragments of the Whig party"...Continued efforts to dissolve the Union...The Slavery issue used as a lever...The warnings of JEFFERSON...The Slavery Agitation "the death knell of the Union"...Warnings of WASHINGTON ...The voice of JACKSON...of HARRISON, &c.

THE EFFORTS TO CREATE A PUBLIC DEBT.

Many have been the projects to create a National debt. As long ago as February 7th, 1817, Mr. KING, Federalist, offered in Congress "a proposition to appropriate $2,000,000, to be divided among the states in proportion to their free population, in aid of the funds of charitable and humane institutions, bible and missionary societies, &c."—[*See Niles Register, vol. 11, p.* 408.

On the same day the bill to "set apart and pledge as a fund for Internal Improvements, the *bonus* and United States share of the dividends in the National Bank," was passed by *two* majority in the House of Representatives. While some good men favored this scheme, it was generally supported by the Federals and ecessionists. Mr. RANDOLPH opposed and CALHOUN favored, contrary to his pretended school of politics.—[See same authority.

This was just after an expensive war.

Failing to inaugurate that change of Government for which aristocratic aspirations had so long struggled by popular commotions stirred up on the basis of wars, banks, tariffs, distributions, &c., the malcontents naturally turned their attention to measures and acts more promising and auspicious.

In an old, soiled and torn pamphlet, which survived the wreck of sundry newspaper files we had laid away years ago, occurs this prophetic language. [As the title page is entirely gone, we have neither the date or name of the author, but should judge it to have been written about the time the old Whig party gave way to the "Republican party."]

CONTINUED EFFORTS TO DISSOLVE THE UNION.

"The fragments of the Whig party having joined their fortunes with the abolition party, we may safely predict they will now yield nothing until they can bring about a dissolution of the Union. This seems to be their only purpose, for they see they can never control the *whole* Government as a unit."

Mr. SAMUEL J. TILDEN thus forcibly gives us a clue to the provocations of war, through the columns of the New York *Evening Post:*

"How long could an organized *pauper agitation* in England against France, or in France against England, continue without actual hostilities, especially if embracing a majority of the people, and the Governments' wars have as often been produced by popular passions as by the policy of rulers; but I venture to say, that in the *causes* of all such wars, during a century past, there has not been so much material for offense as could be found every year in the fulminations of a party swaying the governments of many Northern States against the entire social and industrial systems of fifteen of our sister states; so much to repel the opinions, to alienate the sentiments, and to wound the pride."

JEFFERSON'S OPINIONS AND WARNINGS.

JEFFERSON was a long-sighted statesman. He could see as far into real party aims and purposes as any other man. He was perfectly acquainted with the party and its ultimate designs, that opposed the formation of our Government, and when in later times the "Missouri question" was seized as a disturbing element, he comprehended at a glance the object of "throwing the tub to the whale," and in a series of letters he reminded the people of his forebodings of portending dissolution. On the 12th of March, 1820, he wrote to H. NELSON:

"I thank you, dear sir, for the information in your favor of the 4th inst., of the settlement for the present of the Missouri question. I am so completely withdrawn from all attention to public matters, *that nothing less could arouse me than the definition of a geographical line, which on an abstract principle,* IS TO BECOME THE LINE OF SEPARATION OF THESE STATES, *and to render desperate the hope that man can ever enjoy the two bl.ssings of peace and self-government. The question sleeps for the* PRESENT, *but is not dead!"*

On the 5th of April, 1820, he wrote to MARK LANGDON HILL:

"I congratulate you on the sleep of the Missouri question—I wish I could say on its *death;* but of this *I despair!* The idea of a geographical line once suggested, will brood in the minds of all those who prefer the gratification of their ungovernable passions to the peace and Union of the country!"

On the 13th of the same month, he wrote to WILLIAM SHORT.

"The Missouri question aroused and filled me with alarm. The old schism of Federal and Republican, threatened nothing, because it existed in every State, and united them together by the fraternism of party. But the coincidence of a marked principle, moral and political, with a geographical line, once conceived, I feared would never more be obliterated from the mind; that it would be recurring on *every* OCCASION, and renewing irritations until it would kindle such *mutual and mortal hatred,* as to render *separation preferable to eternal discord!* I have been among the most sanguine that our Union would be of long duration. *I now doubt it much, and see the event at no great distance, and the direct CONSEQUENCE of this question!*—not by the line which has been so *confidently counted* on ; the laws of nature control this ; but by the Potomac, Ohio, Missouri or more probably the Mississippi upward, to our northern boundary.— My only comfort and confidence is, that I shall not live to see this, and I envy not the present generation the glory of throwing away the fruits of their father's sacrifices of life and fortune, and of rendering *desparate* the experiment which was to decide ultimately, whether man is capable of self-government. This *treason* against human hope will signalize their epoch in future history as the counterpart of the model of their predecessors !"

He wrote to JOHN HOLMES, of Maine, April 22d, 1820, as follows:

"I had for a long time ceased to read newspapers, or to pay any attention to public affairs, confident they were in good hands, and content to be a passenger in our bark to the shore, from which I am not distant. But *this momen-tous question, like a fire bell in the night, awakened, and filled me with terror. I considered it at once as the* DEATH KNELL OF THE UNION! It is hushed, indeed, for the moment, *but this is a reprieve only, not a* FINAL *sentence. A geographical line, coinciding with a marked principle moral and political, once conceived and held up to the angry passions of men* WILL NEVER BE OBLITERATED, *and every new irritation will make it deeper and deeper!* I can say with conscious truth that there is not a man on earth who would sacrifice more than I would, to relieve us from this heavy reproach in any *practicable* way. The cession of that kind of property, (for so it is misnamed) is a bagatelle, which would not cost me a second thought. A general emancipation and *expatriation* could be effected, and gradually, and with due sacrifices, I think it might be. But, as it is, *we have the wolf by the ears, and we can neither hold him nor safely let him go! Justice* is in one scale *and self preservation* in the other. * * * * *

"I regret that I am now to die in the belief that the *useless* sacrifice of thousands, by the generation of 1776, *to acquire self government* and happiness to their country is to be thrown away by the unwise and unworthy passions of their sons, and that my only consolation is to be *that I live not to weep over it!* If they would but dispassionately weigh the blessings they will throw away, against an abstract principle, more likely to be Union than by secession, they would pause before they would perpetrate this act of *suicide* on themselves, and of *treason against the hopes of the world."*

Up to the hour of Mr. JEFFERSON's death this subject worked upon his mind, and caused him much uneasiness. It was the theme of his correspondence and of his conversation, for he saw in this agitation of the slavery question the seeds of early and certain dissolution. On the 20th of September, 1820, he wrote to Wm. Pinckney:

"The Missouri question is a mere party trick. The leaders of Federalism. [the same leaders now] defeated in the schemes of obtaining power, by rallying partizans to the principle of monarchism [as we have already charged]—a principle of personal, not if local division, have changed their tack, and thrown out another barrel to the whale. They are taking advantage of the virtuous people, to affect a division of parties, by a geographical line. They expect that this will insure them on local principles, the majority they could never obtain on principles of federalism; but they are still putting their shoulder to the wrong wheel—they are wasting jeremaids on the evils of slavery, as if we were advocates for it."

What better proof could be needed to prove the position we have taken, as to the ultimate designs of the party, whose lineage we trace by the blood dripping from their feet?

On the 29th of December, 1820, he wrote to Gen. LAFAYETTE:

"The boisterous sea of liberty, indeed, is never without a wave. and that from Missouri is now rolling toward us, but we shall ride over it as we have all others. It is not a moral question, but one merely of power. It's object is to raise a geographical principle for the choice of a President, and the noise will be kept up till that is effected. All know that permitting the slaves of the South to spread into the West will not add one being to that unfortunate condition—that it will increase the happiness of those existing, and by spreading them over a larger surface, will dilute the evil everywhere, and facilitate the means of getting finally rid of it—an event more anxiously wished by those on whom it presses, than by the noisy pretenders to exclusive humanity. In the mean time, it is a ladder for rivals to climb into power."

On the 21st of January, 1821, and but shortly before his death, he wrote to JOHN ADAMS:

"Our anxieties in this quarter are all concentrated in the question:

"'What does the holy alliance, in and out of Congress, mean to do with us on the Missouri question?'

"And this, by the by, is but the name of the case—it is the John Doe, or Richard Roe of the ejectment. The question, as seen in the states afflicted with this unfortunate population, is, Are our slaves to be presented with freedom and a dagger? For if Congress has the power to regulate the conditions of the inhabitants of the states within the states, it will be but another exercise of that power that *all shall* be free. Are we then to see again Athenian and Lacedemonian confederacies to wage another Peloponessian war, to settle the ascendancy between them, or is this the tocsin of merely a servile war? That remains to be seen; but not, I hope, by you or me. Surely, they will parley awhile, and give *us* a chance to get out of the way. What a bedlamite is man."

On the 15th of February, 1821, he wrote to Gov. BRECKINRIDGE:

"All, I fear, do not see the speck in our horizon [That "speck" was a heavy cloud *now*] which is to burst on us as a tornado, sooner or later. [That cloud *has* burst.] The line of division lately marked out between different portions of our confederacy is such as will never, I fear, be obliterated, and we are now trusting to those who are against us in position and principle, to fashion to their own form the minds and affections of our youth. If, as has been estimated, we send $300,000 a year to the Northern seminaries for the instruction of our own sons, then we must have there five hundred of our sons imbibing opinions and principles in discord with those of their own country. This canker is eating on the vitals of our existence, and if not arrested at once will be beyond remedy. We are now certainly furnishing recruits to their school."

On the 9th of March, 1821, he wrote to Judge ROANE:

"'Last and most portentious of all is the Missouri question. It is smeared over for the present, but its geographical demarkation is indelible. What is to become of it I see not, and leave to those who will live to see it. The University will give employment to my remaining years, and quite enough for my senile faculties."

On the 17th of August, 1821, he wrote to Gen. DEARBORN:

"I rejoice with you that the State of Missouri is at length a member of our Union. Whether the question it excited is dead, or only sleepeth, I do not know. I see only that it has given resurrection to the Hartford Convention men. They have had the address by playing on the honest feelings of our former friends to seduce them from their kindred spirits, and to borrow their weight into the Federal scale. Desperate of regaining power under political distinctions [that is their former political names] they have adroitly wriggled into its seat under the auspices of morality, and are again in the ascendency, from which their sins had hurled them."

Thus has JEFFERSON left on record the political consanguinity of the present party in power, by which we can easily trace their lineage to the old Hartford Convention, and the disunion purposes and aims of the old Federalists. They started out in 1819-20, under a change of name, to work their way into power on the crest of slavery agitation, and as JEFFERSON expresses it, have "wriggled" around, under various phases of political cognomens, with varied success, until they have at length been successful on the sectional or geographical issue that rang in JEFFERSON's ears as a "fire bell in the night"—and as the "death knell of the Union." No matter *who* the individuals, the present ruling party obtained the ascendency on the same *principle*, that brought the Hartford Conventionists into power in 1820, through the final triumph of which the immortal author of the Declaration of Independence saw in advance, through the lens of prophetic wisdom, the Union expire.

General WASHINGTON was President of the Convention that framed our Constitution. As he sat presiding over the deliberations of that body, day by day, he could not fail to have become acquainted with the peculiar views, aims and purposes of those who opposed the form of government he and his compatriots were endeavoring to establish. He knew those men. He knew there was a powerful party at that early day opposed to the government established for he saw the evidence in the Convention, that sooner or later this faction who were opposed to the kind of government adopted, would seek to overthrow the Union, using the sectional slavery question as their Archimedean lever. He knew these things, and he felt he could not retire from office and go down to his grave without leaving the weight of his advice to check the mad passions of those who would be seeking every occasion to overthrow this government, in hopes to build up one more to their liking. In his Farewell Address he said:

"My countrymen, frown indignantly upon every attempt to alienate any portion of our country from the rest. BEWARE OF SECTIONAL ORGANIZATIONS!—of arraying the North against the South, or the South against the North. In the end it will prove fatal to our liberties."

General JACKSON had the reputation of "seeing through a man at a glance." He knew there were a large class of malcontents who desired the overthrow of the Union, and like WASHINGTON and JEFFERSON, he readily discovered the lever they would use. He knew the struggle when it came would assume a sectional phase, for by such pretext only, could the Union be overthrown. He has left his warning voice for us to ponder over. In his farewell address he says:

"What have you to gain by divisions and dissentions? Delude not yourselves with the hope that the breach once made would be afterwards easily repaired. If the Union is once severed, the separation will grow wider and wider, and the controversies which are now debated, and settled in the Halls of Legislation, will be tried in the field of battle, and determined by the sword. Neither should you deceive yourselves with the hope that the first line of separation would be the permanent one. * * * * * Local interests would still be found there, and unchastened ambition.— If the recollection of common dangers, in which the people of the United States have stood side by side against the common foe, the prosperity and happiness they have enjoyed under the present Constitution—if all these recollections and proofs of common interests, are not strong enough to bind us together, as one people, what tie will hold united the warring divisions of empire, when those bonds have been broken, and the Union dissolved. The first line of separation would not last long—new fragments would be torn off—new leaders would spring up, and this glorious Republic would soon be broken into a multitude of petty States, armed for mutual aggressions—loaded with taxes to pay armies and leaders, seeking aid against each other from foreign powers—insulted and trampled upon by the nations of Europe, until harrassed with conflicts, and humbled and debased in spirit, they would be willing to submit to a domination of any military adventurer, and surrender their liberty for the sake of repose."

Gen. HARRISON also early saw the disunion purposes of the Hartford Convention-Slavery-Agitators, and he warns us of the danger in a letter to Mr. MONROE, in 1820:

"I am, and have been, for many years, so much opposed to slavery, that I will never live in a slave state. But I believe the Constitution has given no power to the General Government to interfere in this matter, and that to have slaves or no slaves, depends upon the people in each state alone. But besides the constitutional objection, I am persuaded that the obvious tendency of each interference on the part of the States which have no slaves with the property of their fellow-citizens of the others, is to produce a state of discord and jealousy, that will, in the end, prove fatal to the Union. I believe that in no other state are such wild and dangerous sentiments entertained on this subject, as in Ohio."

HENRY CLAY, the cotemporary of HARRISON and JACKSON, and the political opponent of the latter, knew the haters of the Union would, on the first favorable *opportunity* seize upon the slavery question to further their schemes, and in a speech in Congress in 1839, he said:

"Abolitionism should no longer be regarded as an imaginary danger. The Abolitionists, let me suppose, succeeded in their present aim of uniting the inhabitants of the free States as one man against the inhabitants of the slave States. Union upon one side will beget union on the other, and this process of reciprocal consolidation will be attended with all the violent prejudices, embittered passions and implacable animosities, which ever degraded or deformed human nature. * * * One section will stand in menacing and hostile array against the other. The collissions of opinion will be quickly followed by the clash of arms. I will not attempt to describe scenes which now happily lie concealed from our view. Abolitionists themselves would shrink back in dismay and horror at the contemplation of desolated fields, conflagrated cities, murdered inhabitants, and the overthrow of the fairest fabric of human government that ever rose to animate the hopes of civilized man."

CHAPTER IX.

EFFORTS AT COMPROMISE—WHO RESPONSIBLE.

The Statement of Douglas...His last Letter...Senator Pugh's Statement...Endorsed by Douglas...Chicago Tribune wouldn't Yield an Inch...The Peace Congress...Efforts of Republicans to Hush it Up...Senator Chandler's "Blood-letting" Epistle, &c.

And when the crash predicted by JEFFERSON, JACKSON, HARRISON and CLAY had come—when the "tornado" of the "geographical question" which so much annoyed JEFFERSON, had burst over the heads of the people, to show that those who had caused it were bent on consummating their plans at the expense of the Union, we quote the last letter written by Senator DOUGLAS:

"WASHINGTON, Dec. 20, 1860.

"MY DEAR SIR: * * * You will have received my proposed amendments to the constitution before you receive this. The South would take my proposition if the Republicans would agree to it. But the extremes, North and South, hold off, and are precipitating the country into revolution and civil war.

"While I can do no act which recognizes or countenances the doctrine of secession, my policy is peace, and I will not consider the question of war until every effort has been made for peace, and all hope shall have vanished. When that time comes, if unfortunately it shall come, I will then do what it becomes an American Senator to do on the then state of facts. Many of the Republican leaders desire a dissolution of the Union, and urge war as a means of accomplishing disunion; while others are Union men in good faith. We have now reached a point where a compromise on the basis of mutual concession, disunion and war, are inevitable. I prefer a fair and just compromise. I shall make a speech in a few days.

"Yours, truly, S. A. DOUGLAS."

Thus, by this testimony it will be seen that the "extreme" men of both North and South held back, and refused terms of accommodation, not—as we may reasonably suppose, from a long line of antecedents—that the northern extremists hated slavery more than they loved the Union, or the Southern "extremists" loved slavery more than they hated the Union—but in reality, because both factions saw in the then existing facts, the occasion for getting rid of the old Union. The Northern "extremists" declared they would "not yield an inch" and the Southern "extremists" would "not yield an inch" well knowing that the least mutual yielding would produce just what neither "extreme" wanted—a continued Union.

During the pendency of the deliberations of the Peace Congress, the Chicago *Tribune* thus defined its "position" against any compromise. It was one of the "won't-yield-an-inchers:"

"Others may do as they please, but this journal stands where it has always stood. It concedes nothing that would weaken the North in her great triumph over that infernal despotic institution which has debauched the National conscience, and now strives to emasculate the National courage. We surrender no inch of ground that has been won. Standing solidly on the Constitution and the laws; intending evil to none, but exact justice, under the National compact to all; animated by a pervading conviction of the sacredness of the cause in which we are engaged, we shall be content to do that which duty to GOD our country and ourselves demands, and trust the consequences to that Power which shapes all things for the best; and this is the position in which the genuine Republicans of Illinois should stand, and these are the words which they should use. But whether they falter or keep on, our course is marked out."

Senator PUGH, of Ohio, has put on record the following testimony as to what could have been done under a proper desire to save the Union:

"The CRITTENDEN proposition has been indorsed by the almost unanimous vote of the Legislature of Kentucky. It has been indorsed by the Legislature of the noble old commonwealth of Virginia. It has been petitioned for by a larger number of electors of the United States than any proposition that was ever before Congress. I believe in my heart to-day, that it would carry an overwhelming majority of the people of my state; aye, sir, and of nearly every state in the Union. Before the Senators from the state of Mississippi left this Chamber I heard one of them, who assumes at least to be President of the Southern Confederacy, propose to accept it and maintain the Union if that proposition, could receive the vote it ought to receive from the other side of the Chamber. Therefore, all of your propositions, of all your amendments, knowing as I do, and knowing that the historian will write it down, at any time before the first of January, a two-thirds vote for the Crittenden resolutions in this Chamber would have saved every state in the Union but South Carolina.—Georgia would be here by her representatives, and Louisiana, those two great states which at least would have broken the whole column of secession."—p. 1480, *Globe*.

To show that yielding would have saved us, we quote the lamented DOUGLAS at an earlier period, while in his official robes:

"The Senator (Mr. Pugh) has said that if the Crittenden proposition could have passed early in the session, it would have saved all the states except South Carolina. I firmly believe it would. While the Crittenden proposition was not in accordance with my cherished views, I avowed my readiness and eagerness to accept it, in order to save the Union, if we could unite upon it. I can confirm the Senator's declaration, that Senator Davis himself, when on that committee of thirteen, was ready, at all times, to compromise on the Crittenden proposition. I will go further, and say that Mr. Toombs was also.—*p.* 1381 *Globe.*

Judge DOUGLAS said in a speech in the Senate, January 3, 1861:

"I address the inquiry to the Republicans alone, for the reason, that in the committee of thirteen, a few days ago, every member of the South, including those from the cotton states, (Messrs. TOOMBS and DAVIS,) expressed their readiness to accept the proposition of my venerable friend from Kentucky, (Mr. CRITTENDEN,) as a final settlement of the controversy, if tendered and sustained by Republican members. Hence, the sole responsibility of our disagreement. The only difficulty in the way of amicable adjustment is with the Republican party.

At one time it was likely the Peace Congress would effect some amicable arrangement to *compromise* and save the Union. Prior to this several Northern States had refused to send delegates to that Congress, but as some of the Administration States had, and their action was likely to compromise the Administration in a compromise for peace, the politicians who *now* declare they don't believe in the Constitution, took immediate steps to break up, or defeat the purposes of that Peace Congress.

CARL SCHURZ, then being East, telegraphed to Gov. RANDALL, of Wisconsin, to favor the move and to appoint him as one of the delegates (SCHURZ boasted of his opposition to Peace compromises) as it "will strengthen *our* side."

For the same reason Senator CHANDLER wrote to Gov. BLAIR, of Michigan, as follows:

"WASHINGTON, Feb. 11, 1861.

"MY DEAR GOVERNOR:—Gov. BINHAM and myself telegraphed you on Saturday, at the request of Massachusetts and New York, to send delegates to the Peace or Compromise Congress. They admit that we are right and they are wrong—that no Republican State should have sent delegates; but they are here and can't get away. Ohio, Indiana and Rhode Island are coming in, and there is danger of Illinois, and they beg us for God's sake to come to their rescue, and save the Republican party from a rupture! I hope you will send stiff-backed men or none! The whole thing was got up against my judgment and advice, and will end in thick smoke. Still, I hope as a matter of courtesy to some of our erring brethren that you will send the delegates.
"Truly your friend, Z. CHANDLER.
"His Excellency, Gov. BLAIR.

"P. S.—Some of the Manufacturing States think that a fight would be awful. Without a little blood-letting, this Union, in my estimation, will not be worth a rush."

These politicians cared nothing for saving the Union, but to "*save the Republican party*" was their great desire.

CHAPTER X.

THE MOTIVE FOR PRECIPITATING A CONFLICT.

Who Responsible for bringing on a Clash of Arms...The Administration resort to a "Trick" to Force the Rebels to Commence the Attack...Letter from the Hon. Harlow S. Orton...His charges of a "Trick" proved by Extracts from...The New York Times...Charleston Mercury...New York Tribune, &c,...The United States Armada take no part to Relieve Major Anderson...New York Post details the Trick...Radicals Prophesying an Easy and Early Victory...Seward's Promise to deliver up Sumter.

It is not of so much moment now to ascertain the *cause* of the war as it is the *motive.*—The former cannot now be remedied, so as to effect present results, while by duly exposing the latter we may avoid its repetition for some time to come, as the expose of Federal designs prevented a disruption of the Union in 1814–16.

LETTER FROM JUDGE ORTON.

We cannot better illustrate the *animus* of the party in power to provoke *actual hostilities*, with a view of throwing the *onus* of war's inception on the rebels, than by copying entire the letter and "accompanying documents" by the Hon. HARLOW S. ORTON, Judge of the 9th Wisconsin Circuit, to the Wisconsin *Patriot*, as follows:

"TO THE EDITORS OF THE PATRIOT:

"The *Journal*, in its generally correct report of what I said in the recent Democratic Convention, says:

"'He charged that this war was brought upon the country by the present administration in accordance with an infamous plot—a disgraceful political trick! That the sending of a vessel to Fort Sumter with the avowed object of sending provisions to the men in the Fort, was only a pretense, gotten up to provoke South Carolina to make an attack! to form an excuse for the administration to declare war! The party in power would not hear to any terms of compromise," &c.

"The general sense of what I said on that point, is perhaps sufficiently conveyed by the above report, yet much of the language used I respectfully disown. I said, in effect, that the inception of the war, (by which I meant the firing on Fort Sumter,) was the result of a trick of the administration. That the fleet with provisions and men was sent to lie off Charleston harbor, *ostensibly* for the purpose of reinforcing the Fort, but in fact with no such *real* design, but to provoke and induce the enemy to make their threatened attack in order to arouse and unite the North for the war. That the attempt to so reinforce the Fort at that time was in violation of a pledge given to the Southern Commissioners, that such an attempt would not then be made,

"I pledged myself able to prove this charge, if it was denied. It has been denied, and I have been made the subject of much personal abuse for having made it. Two years is not a very long time to remember the important facts which make up the history of the present war, and it is remarkable, that a fact so well known and discussed at the time, and especially in Washington, and never then contradicted by by anybody, should now be denounced as worse than a falsehood.

"Now for some of the proof.

"The New York *Times* of March 11th, 1861, said:

"The question of reinforcing Fort Sumter has been under consideration in the Cabinet, and it is understood that the question, whether or no, it is not desirable to withdraw all the troops except two or three men, rather than incur the bloodshed which will probably occur, before troops and supplies are put into it, is now to be decided. The question has been under discussion in high military circles for some days. Gen. SCOTT advises that reinforcements cannot now be put in without an enormous sacrifice of life. He is understood to say, that we have neither military or naval force at hand sufficient to supply the Fort against the threatened opposition, which it would require *twenty thousand* men to overcome. Besides, if it should *initiate civil war*, in addition to *uniting the South, and overwhelming the Union sentiment there,* in the waves of passion, it would require *two hundred and fifty thousand Government soldiers* to carry on the struggle, and a *hundred millions* of money to begin with."

"It is a fact of the current history of the time, that this discussion and under the advice of Gen. SCOTT, resulted in the unanimous decision of the Cabinet, that the fort should be evacuated, and the President's order for that purpose was anxiously awaited and expected by the public for several days, and the people had generally acquiesced in the wisdom and conciliation of the measure. It was at this juncture that Mr. SEWARD, or some other person having authority, pledged the Southern Commissioners that the fort would not be reinforced, and this was communicated to the Southern rebel authorities. In consequence of this understanding, the Charleston *Mercury* proclaimed—

"Sumter is to be ours without a fight! All will rejoice that the blood of our people is not to be shed in our harbor either in small or great degree."

"The fact that this pledge was given by Mr. SEWARD or some other member of the Cabinet, is charged in the last communication of the Southern Commissioners to the Secretary of State, and has never been denied officially or otherwise.

"So matters remained until the 5th of April. The New York *Tribune* of that date says:

"Many rumors are in circulation to-day. They appear to have originated from movements on the part of the United States troops, the reasons for which have not been communicated to the reporters at Washington as freely as the late Administration was in the habit of imparting Cabinet secrets. There can be no doubt that serious movements are on foot."

"These *mysterious* movements were the dispatching of eight vessels of war; with twenty-six guns and thirteen hundred and eighty men, between the 6th and 8th of April, with sealed orders for the south. On the 8th, information was communicated by the Government to the authorities at Charleston that they desired to send supplies to Fort Sumter by an unarmed vessel. They were informed that the vessel would be fired upon and not permitted to enter the port. On the same day official notification was given by the government that supplies would be sent to Major Anderson, *peaceably* if possible, otherwise by *force*. On the 9th the Southern Commissioners were dismissed from Washington, by the Secretary of State declining to receive them officially, but expressing great deference for them personally. On the 10th United States vessels were reported off Charleston, apparently standing in for the harbor.

"On the 11th, preparations were made by the military of Charleston for an attack on the Fort, in anticipation of a forcible attempt on the part of the Federal fleet to supply it. On the 12th, after a demand for its surrender, the Fort is fired into, and the war is commenced! During this infamous and cowardly attack upon the small and starved garrison of Sumter, the United States fleet is in sight, making no attempt to enter the harbor, or cooperate with the Fort, lying idly by, and witnessing the desperate and heroic yet useless struggle of the gallant ANDERSON and his men, to defend his Fort and his flag against an overwhelming force of rebels, unaided and alone. The deed is done, and the bloody struggle of a relentless civil war has commenced! The Fort has fallen into the hands of the rebel states, and its guns turned against the Government; and behold the effect. All party lines are obliterated, and the people of the Northern States, with one mind, and with the most patriotic impulses, rush to arms, to avenge the insult by fierce and bloody war. As Gen. Scott predicted would be the consequence of an attempt to reinforce the Fort, 'Civil war is initiated, the South is united, and the Union sentiment there is overwhelmed in the waves of passion.'

"The Border States, hitherto reluctant, now make haste to rush into the whirlpool of secession, and join the Southern Confederacy. All pending efforts and measures for compromise are scouted and contemned; and a peaceful solution of the sectional controversy is now rendered impossible.

Since that time, I have never once questioned the right and the imperative duty of the Administration to use all possible and adequate means to conquer and subdue a rebellion so causeless and wicked—only insisting that all the efforts of the Government to that end should be to restore the Union and maintain the obligations of the Constitution over all the states, and that when this is accomplished, the war ought to cease, and this, I understand, was the unquestioned and universally conceded policy of the Administration when the war commenced, and by the unanimous action of Congress in the adoption of the CRITTENDEN resolutions. But while using the highest degree of military force to coerce submission to the Government, and obedience to the Constitution, I have thought it not inconsistent with our high national character and the true dignity of the Government, to propose and constantly tender to the rebel states such just and proper terms of compromise of the sectional controversies out of which this terrible war has arisen, as might result in the speedy restoration of the Union, conscientiously believing that war alone, without mutual conciliation could never restore it. With these views, I still insist that the inception of the war was the result of a trick of the Administration, and with the evident design on the part of those whose policy has since been adopted in the conduct of the war, to sieze upon this terrible national calamity as their long waited opportunity to abolish slavery, regardless of the fate of the Government.

"I have already briefly stated the facts connected with the event—facts of history which none will deny, and it only remains to prove what were the real motives and designs, or what was the strategy or plan of the administration in sending a fleet to Charleston under the pretence or feint of reinforcing Fort Sumter. To prove that it was a mere feint or pretence, and that the designs were such as I have stated, I shall, for the present, adduce only the cotemporaneous statements of the then most prominent and credible witnesses, then and now in the secrets, confidence and interest of the administration, and leave the controversy upon these points between them and my accusers.

The New York *Times*, of the 15th of April, said:

"The curtain has fallen upon the first act of the great tragedy of the age.' Fort Sumter has been surrendered, and the Stars and Stripes of the American Republic give place to the felon flag of the Southern Confederates.

"The defence of the fort did honor to the gallant commander by whom it was held, and vindicated the government under which he served. *Judging from the result, it does not seem to have been the purpose of the government to do anything more.* The armed ships which accompanied the supplies took no part in the contest. Whatever may have been the reason for it, their silence was probably fortunate."

"The New York *Tribune* of the same date, said:

"The announcement that Fort Sumter was on fire, sounded like a knell as well as an impossibility. It caused forebodings. ' *Where is the fleet?*' was on all lips. That there had been some unlucky miscarriage of the public mind had conceived its objects, was quite plain. Finally came the report that the Stars and Stripes would soon come down, and later, that they had actually given place to the flag of rebellion, in spite of doubts, and the strong inclination to disbelief, particularly of the statement that, notwithstanding the bombardment had continued nearly thirty-six hours, 'nobody was hurt' on either side, the feeling reached its climax. *No compromise now with rebellion, is the universal sentiment. If there were differences before, there cannot be said to be any now.*"

"The following article, of the same date, from the New York *Post*, I commend to those who care to know the full magnitude and particulars of the strategy, plan, or trick, which resulted in the first blow of the war. I quote largely from this article, for it is all pertinent to the issue.

The *Post* said:

"It is evident that Gen. SCOTT has once more beaten the enemies of his country, by the mere force of his admirable strategetical genius. To do so, he has, as was necessary *suffered not only traitors, but loyal men to rest under a misapprehension.* He who reads and compares carefully the dispatches from Charleston, Montgomery, and Washington in this morning journals cannot avoid the gratifying conclusion, *that that which looks at first blush like a disaster to the Government, is in reality, but the successful carrying out of an admirable military plan. Before this, the traitors see themselves caught in the iron toils.* In fact it seems to have sickened the Chief Traitor, DAVIS, already. For Montgomery dispatches relate, that when the news from Charleston came, and the mob serenaded DAVIS and WALKER, "the former was not well and did not appear."

"The facts which tend to the conclusion we have pointed out may be summed up as follows :

"Gen. SCOTT has been averse to the attempt to reinforce Fort Sumter. He saw that it would cost men and vessels which the Government could not spare just now. As an able General, he saw that Charleston and Sumter were points of no military importance, and would only need valuable men to hold if we took them—with no adequate advantage gained. He saw that the two keys of the position were Fort Pickens, in the Gulf, and Washington, the Capital. His plans, based on these facts, were at once laid. By every means in his power he concentrated the attention of traitors and loyal men on Sumter. He must have seen with infinite satisfaction the daily increasing force gathered at Charleston, while the Government lost no time in strengthening the capital. Every hour the traitors spent before Sumter gave them more surely into the hands of their master To make assurance doubly sure, he pretended to leave Fort Pickens in the lurch. It was said to be in danger, when SCOTT knew that a formidable force was investing it. At last Washington was reasonably safe. Forces now gathered. Once more our brave old General saw himself with means in his hands.

"Then came the armament *popularly believed to be destined for Sumter*.

"The Government said not a word—only asked of the traitors the opportunity to send its own garrison a needed supply of food. They refused, fearing the arrival of the Federal fleet—drunk and besotted with treason, and impatient to shed the blood of loyal soldiers, they made the attack. Scarce had they begun, when they saw with evident terror, ships hovering about the harbor's mouth; they plied their cannon in desperate haste; *but no ship came in to* ANDERSON'S *help. What was the matter?*

"Made bold by the furious thirst for blood, they dared the ships to come in, *but no ship offered its assistance to Anderson.* More, the guns of Sumter were only directed to the works of the traitors, and Major Anderson evidently tried to fire in such a manner as not to kill men. He did not even try a few bombs on the city, though it is certain, from a letter from one of his own officers, that his guns would reach beyond the centre of Charleston. What was the matter? Beauregard must have thought the Government officers both fools and cowards. When his own boats were sailing unharmed about the harbor between Sumter and Moultrie, bearing his orders, was it possible that the forces outside could stand apathotic while a brave garrison was being done to death? When the battle was to the death, would a shrewd officer neglect to divert his enemies' attention by firing his city?— *If it seems mysterious to us, waiting on Saturday with breathless suspense, it must have seemed incomprehensible to any cool head in the traitor camp.*

"Still no ships came in—and, in fact, the reports state that only three or four small vessels remained in the offing.

"After forty hours,' cannonade, in which not one man is killed, Major Anderson, an officer of undoubted courage and honor, runs up a white flag, surrendered the fort, and becomes the guest of Gen. Beauregard. *Let no man hastily cry traitor! He only obeyed orders.* He made an honorable defence. He took care to shed no blood. He gave orders not to sight men, but to silence batteries."

SCRAPS FROM MY SCRAP-BOOK. 53

"Mean,time, while the rebels are ignorantly glorifying the victory of five thousand men over eighty, what news comes from Montgomery? The telegraph in the hands of the rebels says, Fort Pickens was reinforced last night.'— 'It is understood that Charleston harbor is blockaded.' No wonder the rebel chief was sick and went to bed. "The position of affairs is this—Charleston is blockaded —Fort Pickens is reinforced by troops. *which the traitors foolishly believed were destined for Sumter.* Washington is secure beyond peradventure. *The traitors have, without the slightest cause, opened the war* they have so long threatened. The country is roused to defend its assailed liberties, and gathers enthusiastically about the Government, and treason has been checkmated at the first blow it has struck. Let them keep Sumter a few weeks."

"The above article is copied into the "Rebellion Record," as a part of the reliable history of the war.

"It will be seen that this article more than bears out the statement I made, and I trust those who have charged my statement with being false, will be fair and candid enough to read and republish the above article, that both parties may see some of the evidence upon which it was based. I regret the necessity of taking so much of your valuable space to present the evidence of a fact that I did not suppose would be questioned by any one. The fact itself is only important in throwing light upon the designs of the party in power, which at first were disguised, but now openly avowed, viz: the ultimate destruction of the Union, hostility to all compromises, the violation of the constitution, a war of conquest, and the abolition of slavery, regardless of consequences.
"H. S. ORTON."

Meanwhile, the radical press were belittling the magnitude of the Southern discontent, and under the Syren song of a "nine days bubble," assured the people that this treason could be "crushed out in thirty days." The New York *Tribune* said:

"The nations of Europe may rest assured that JEFF. DAVIS & CO. will be swinging from the battlements at Washington at least by the 4th of July. We spit upon a later and longer deferred justice."

The New York *Times* said:

"Let us make quick work. The 'rebellion,' as some people designate it, is an unborn tadpole. Let us not fall into the delusion, noted by HALLAM, of instituting a 'local commotion,' for a revolution. A strong active 'pull together,' will close our work in thirty days."

The Philadelphia *Press* said, that:

"No man of sense could, for a moment, doubt that this 'much-ado-about-nothing' would end in a revolt."

The Chicago *Tribune* was for undertaking the job itself. It said:

"Let the East get out of the way. This is a war of the West. We can fight the battle, and successfully, within two or three months, at farthest. Illinois can whip the South herself. We insist on the matter being turned over to us."

The Cincinnati *Commercial* said:

"The West ought to be made the vanguard of the war. * * * The rebellion will be crushed out before the assemblage of Congress—no doubt of it."

It is charged by POLLARD, in his work on the Southern rebellion, and not denied, that Mr. SEWARD promised Judge CAMPBELL, of the Supreme Court, that Fort Sumter should be evacuated to prevent war, but that faith was never kept in that regard. [See p. 47.]

CHAPTER XI.

PROGRESS AND EVIDENCE OF THE NORTHERN CONSPIRACY.

The Radicals conspire to overthrow the Government long before the Rebellion of 1861...DOUGLAS' testimony on this point...JOHN BROWN Raid originated in Kansas., Col. Jamison's testimony...Col. F. P. Blair on the cause of the war...Abolitionists and Secessionists united...Mr. Seward's testimony...Parson Brownlow on the designs of the Abolitionists...Thurlow Weed on the "Chief Architects" of the Rebellion...Abolitionists of New York Invite Southern Secessionists to join them...Massachusetts for Dissolution in 1851...Also in 1856...Ben. Wade Declares there was no Union...Garrison's "Covenant with Hell"...Republicans of Green County, Wis., Pledged to "Revolutionize the Government"...Anson Furlingame for a New Deal all Round...David Wilmot on Dissolution ...Wendell Phillipsagain...Lowell Republicans for Dissolution...Massachusetts Petitions for Dissolution... James Watson Webb for using "Fire and Sword"...Boston Free Soilers, 1854...Charles Sumner bound to Disobey law...The True American pronounces a Negro "Worth all the Unions on God's Earth"—Another Massachusetts Petition for Dissolution...Dissolution Resolution by Anti-Slavery Society...Another from same source...Disunion again in Massachusetts...From Redmund's Speech...Wendell Phillips labors nineteen years to Break up the Union...Parker Pillsbury labored twenty years to destroy the Union...Stephen Foster dissuading young men from enlisting in this Unholy War, &c.

STEPHEN A. DOUGLAS understood the secret designs of the leading Republicans, as well as any other living man, and he thus gave utterance to his honest convictions, in the U. S. Senate, Dec. 25, 1860:

"The fact can no longer be disguised that many of the Republican Senators desire war and disunion,under pretext of saving the Union. They wish to get rid of the Southern states, in order to have a majority in the Senate to confirm the appointments, and many of them think they can hold a permanent Republican majority in the Northern States, but not in the whole Union; for partisan reasons they are anxious to dissolve the Union, if it can be done without holding them responsible before the people."

"DATES BACK OF SUMTER."

Gen. JAMISON, one of the Abolition marplots of Kansas, made a speech to his soldiers on the 22d of January, 1862, which appeared in the Leavenworth *Conservative*, in which he shows that the firing on Sumter was not the beginning of the war:

"For six long years we have fought as guerrillas, what we are now fighting as a regiment. This war is a war which dates away back of Fort Sumter! On the cold hill side, in swamps and ferns, behind rocks and trees, ever since '54, we have made the long campaign. Away off there we have led the IDEAS of this age, always battling at home, and sometimes sending forth from among us a stern old missionary like JOHN BROWN, to show Virginia that the world does move."

COL. BLAIR ON THE "CAUSE OF THE WAR."

Col. FRANK P. BLAIR made a speech in Congress, on the 11th of April, 1862, and denied that slavery is the "cause" of the war. He says:

"Every man acquainted with the facts knows that it is fallacious to call this 'a slaveholder's rebellion.' If such was the fact, two divisions of our army would have supported it without difficulty; the negroes themselves could have easily put down 250,000 slaveholders; but it is a matter of history that the slaveholders, as a body, were the last and most reluctant to join the rebellion."

He thus states his theory of the rebellion:

"It was the negro question, and not the slavery question, which made the rebellion—questions entirely different, and requiring entirely different treatment, and it is as necessary to understand the distinction, to enable us to deal with it successfully, as it is that the physician should know the disease which he is called on to treat and cure. If the rebellion was made by 250,000 slaveholders, for the sake of perpetuating slavery, then it might be a complete remedy to extirpate the institution; but if the rebellion has grown out of the abhorrence of the *non*-slaveholders for emancipation and amalgamation, and their dread of negro equality, how will their discontent be cured by the very measure, the mere apprehension of which has driven them into rebellion?"

MR. SEWARD'S TESTIMONY.

We have high cotemporaneous authority for the belief that there has existed a class in both sections of our Union, anxious to destroy it, who have ever been experts in using the most convenient *pretexts* to favor their ends. Mr. SEWARD, in his dispatch "No. 287, confidential," to Minister ADAMS, thus offers his high testimony:

"DEPARTMENT OF STATE,
Washington, July 5, 1861.

"SIR:—Your dispatch of June 28, (No. 176,) has been received and read by Earl RUSSELL. The subject it presents is one of momentous import. It seems as if the extreme advocates of African slavery, and its most vehement opponents, were acting in concert, TOGETHER, to precipitate a servile war—the former by making the most desperate attempt to overthrow the Federal Union, the latter by demanding an edict of universal emancipation, as a lawful, if not, as they say, the only legitimate way of saving the Union!

"I reserve remarks on the military situation for a day nearer to the departure of the mails.
"I am Sir, your ob't serv't,
"WILLIAM H. SEWARD.
"CHARLES FRANCIS ADAMS, Esq.," &c.

This expose of the designs of the "extreme" radicals was the cause of the Senatorial raid which demanded the removal of Mr. SEWARD from the Cabinet. But Mr. SEWARD had exposed nothing more than WASHINGTON, MADISON, JEFFERSON, JACKSON, DOUGLAS, and other great and good men had predicted.

PARSON BROWNLOW ON THE ABOLITIONISTS.

Parson BROWNLOW, in his debate with Parson PRYNE, in Philadelphia, in 1858, said:

"A dissolution of the Union is what a large portion of the Northern Abolitionists are aiming at."—*See Brownlow and Pryne's debates.*

THURLOW WEED'S EVIDENCE.

THURLOW WEED, for penning the following truth, was, as he avers, driven from the editorial chair of the Albany *Journal :*

"The chief architects of the rebellion, before it broke out, avowed that they were aided in their infernal designs by the ultra Abolitionists of the North. This was too true, for without said aid the South could never have been united against the Union. But for the incendiary recommendations, which rendered the otherwise useful Helper Book, a fire brand, North Carolina could not have been forced out of the Union. And even now, the ultra Abolition Press, and speech makers are aggravating the horrors they helped to create, and thus by playing into the hands of the leaders of the rebellion, are keeping down the Union men of the South, and rendering reunion difficult, if not impossible !"

ABOLITIONISTS UNITE WITH THE SECESSIONISTS.

We are not left to the charge of Mr. WEED alone. We have the positive testimony of the Abolitionists themselves that they were in league with the Southern secessionists. In 1859, the Abolitionists of New York met in convention and passed the following resolutions:

"*Whereas*, The dissolution of the present inglorious Union between the free and slave

States, would result in the overthrow of slavery, and the consequent formation of another Government, without the incubus of slavery, therefore

"*Resolved*, That we invite a free correspondence with the disunionists of the South, in order to agree upon the most suitable measures to bring about so desirable a result."

Now, a simple reflection will thoroughly strip this pretended pretext of hatred of slavery, as the foundation of a desire to dissolve the Union, of its treasonable gauze. If hatred of slavery induced the New York Abolitionists to believe a dissolution of the Union would "result in the overthrow of slavery," they could not be such fools as to believe they could make willing allies of those who insisted on slavery as the "corner stone of their edifice." Indeed, these Abolitionists had furnished the very best reason to the slaveholders for a continuance of the Union, as the only means to save their "system." But hatred of slavery was not the moving cause of these Abolitionists. They were secessionists, *per se*, and only used the slavery ghost to frighten unsuspecting and otherwise well disposed persons into their schemes. The "secessionists of the South" knew this, and hence they could agree to act together, not that they cared a straw about the slavery question, but only using that as the most convenient pretext for breaking up the Union. And so it was in 1814, when the secessionists of the Hartford Convention made opposition to slavery one of the corner stones of their disunion edifice. A large number of slaveholders went with them, well knowing that disunion, as the *motive*, was in the background, and slavery, as the shibboleth or pretext, in the foreground.

THE LATE GREAT NORTHERN CONSPIRACY.

Having shown the wicked motive and the guilty occasion for war and secession, which not only "dates back of Sumter," but dates back of our constitution, and have been developing themselves for more than sixty years, we will now exhibit to the world the *modus operandi* by which the motive was to be gratified, and the occasion fully developed. It will hardly be practicable in all cases to place the sayings, doings and resolves of the conspirators in chronological order, nor shall we endeavor to set down aught in malice or aught extenuate. The object of the authors of the following extract was no doubt to stir up and hasten that "Irrepressible Conflict," which Mr. SEWARD predicted in his Rochester speech, and which is now upon us.

MASSACHUSETTS FOR DISSOLUTION IN 1851.

In their State convention of 1851, the radicals of Massachusetts, on whom the mantle of the Hartford Convention had fallen, and animated by the same purposes

"*Resolved*. That the constitution which provides for a slave representation and a slave oligarchy in Congress, which legalizes slave catching on every inch of American soil, which pledges the military and naval power of the country to keep four millions of chattle slaves in their chains, is to be trodden under foot, and pronounced accursed, however unexceptionable or valuable, it may be in its other provisions."

"That the one great issue before the country is the dissolution of the Union, in comparison with which all other issues with the slave power are as dust in the balance; therefore, we have given ourselves to the work of 'annulling this covenant with death,' as esential to our own innocency, and the speedy and everlasting overthrow of the slave power."

MASSACHUSETTS FOR DISSOLUTION IN 1856.

In 1856 the same party passed the following in convention:

"*Resolved*, 1st, That the necessity of disunion is written in the whole existing character and condition of the two sections of the country in their social organization, education, habits and laws; in the dangers of our white citizens in Kansas, and our colored men in Boston; in the wounds of CHARLES SUMNER, and the laurels of his assailants, and no Government on earth was ever strong enough to hold together such opposing forces."

"*Resolved*, 2d, That this movement does not merely seek disunion, but the more perfect union of free States by the expulsion of the slave States from the Confederation, in which they have ever been an element of discord, danger, and disgrace.

"*Resolved*, 3d, That it is not probable that the ultimate severance of the Union will be an act of deliberation or discussion; but that a long period of deliberation and discussion must precede it, and here we meet to begin the work.

"*Resolved*, 4th, That henceforward, instead of regarding it as an objection to any system of policy, that it will lead to the separation of the States, we will proclaim that to be the highest of all recommendations, and the greatest proof of statesmanship; and will support politically, such men and measures as appear to tend most to this result."

BEN. WADE ON DISSOLUTION.

In 1855 Senator WADE, of Ohio, made a speech in Portland Maine, in which he declared:

"There is really no Union now between the North and the South. I believe no two nations on earth entertain feelings of more bitter rancor towards each other than these two portions of the Republic."

"THE UNION IS A LIE."

Mr. GARRISON made a speech in 1856, in which he declared:

"I have said, and I say again, that in proportion to the growth of disunionism, will be the growth of Republicanism. * * * * * The Union is a lie. The American Union is an imposture, and a covenant with death, and an agreement with hell. * * * * I am for its overthrow. * * * Up with the flag of disunion, that we may have a free and glorious Union of our own."

GREEN COUNTY, WISCONSIN, FOR REVOLUTION

At a Republican convention held at Monroe, Green county, Wis., in 1856, the following resolution was passed:

"*Resolved*, That it is the *duty of the North* in case they fail in electing a President and Congress that will *restore* freedom to Kansas, *to revolutionize the government!*"

A NEW DEAL ALL ROUND.

ANSON BURLINGAME made a speech in 1856 in which he blasphemously said:

"The time is coming and soon will be that we must have an anti-slavery constitution, an anti-slavery bible and an anti-slavery God."

DAVID WILMOT ON DISSOLUTION.

The Montrose *Democrat* of May 10th, 1856, says:

"We recollect a little over a year ago, that we heard Mr. WILMOT make the following declaration:

"'I am determined to arouse the people to the importance of the slavery issue, and get up an organization through which they can get control of the Government in 1856. And if I become satisfied that these efforts will fail, and that the people will not assert their rights, then I'll be d—d if I dont join the party that I think will send the country to h—l the quickest!'"

MORE TREASONABLE EXTRACTS.

"In conclusion I have only to add that such is my solemn and abiding conviction of the character of slavery, and under a full sense of my responsibility to my country and my God, I deliberately say, better disunion—better a civil or servile war—better anything that God in his providence shall send—than an extension of the bonds of slavery."—*Hon Horace Mann*

"No man has a right to be surprised at this state of things. It is just what we abilitionists and disunionists have attempted to bring about. There is merit in the Republican party. It is the first *sectional party* ever organized in this country. It does not know its own face, but calls itself national; but it is not *national*—it it sectional. The Republican party is a party of the North pledged against the South."—*Wendell Phillips.*

"*Resolved*, That the Union was established to secure the liberties of American citizens. When it fails to do that, our only voice can be, let the Union be dissolved."—*Lowell Republican Resolution.*

The Boston *Liberator*, in an article headed in large type—"But one issue—the dissolution of the Union"—recommends signatures to a petition for that purpose, of which the following is the spirit:

"We therefore believe that the time has come for a new arrangement of elements so hostile; of interests so irreconcilable, of institutions; so incongruous; and we earnestly request Congress, at its present session, to take initiatory measures for the speedy, peaceful and quiet dissolution of the existing Union, as the exigencies of the case require."

"If the Republicans fail at the ballot-box, we shall be forced to drive back the slaveocrats with fire and sword."—*James Watson Webb in* 1856.

" *Resolved*, That Constitution, or no Constitution, law, or no law, we will not allow a fugitive slave to be taken from Massachusetts."—*Boston Free Soilers of* 1854.

"I have before declared that the path of duty was clear as to the fugitive slave act, and that I am bound to disobey it!"—*Chas. Sumner, Sept.* 1854.

The *True American*, a Republican organ in Erie county, Pa., in commenting upon a speech delivered at a Democratic meeting, said:

"This twaddle about the Union and its preservation is too silly and sickening for any good effect. We think the liberty of a single slave is worth more than all the Unions God's universe can hold."

The Hampshire (Mass.) *Gazette* of August 23d, 1856, a Republican paper, published a letter from a citizen of Northampton, who was engaged in circulating there the petition for a dissolution of the Union, wherein he stated that— .

" more than one hundred and fifty legal voters of that town have signed this petition."

Resolution adopted on motion of WENDELL PHILLIPS, by the American Anti-Slavery Society, New York, May, 1848.

"*Resolved*, That recognizing as we do, with profound gratitude, the wonderful progress our cause has made during the last eighteen years, and yet considering the effort now making to impress the community with the idea that the church and the land will abolish slavery by its own virtue, and that the parties are able and willing to grapple with the evil this society deems it a duty to reiterate its convictions that the only exodus for the slave out of his present house of bondage is over the ruins of the present American Church, and the present American Union."

Resolution adopted by the American Anti-Slavery Society, New York, December, 1858.

"*Whereas*, The dissolution of the present imperfect and inglorious Union between the free and slave States would result in the overthrow of slavery and the consequent foundation of a more perfect and glorious Union, without the incubus of slavery, therefore

"*Resolved*, That we invite a free correspondence with the disunionists of the South, in order to devise the most suitable way and means to secure the consummation so devoutly to be wished,

Resolution adopted by the Essex County (Mass.,) Anti-Slavery Society, May 10, 1862.

"*Resolved*, That the war as hitherto, prosecuted, is but a wanton waste of property, a dreadful sacrifice of life, and worse than all, of conscience and of character, to preserve and perpetuate a Union and Constitution which should never have existed, and which, by all the laws of justice and humanity, should in their present form, be at once and forever overthrown."

From Redmond's Speech, Boston.

"Remembering that he was a slaveholder, he could spit upon Washington. * * So near to Faneuil Hall and Bunker Hill, was he not to be permitted to say that scoundrel GEORGE WASHINGTON had enslaved his fellow men?"

From Phillips' Speech, same occasion.

"Washington was a sinner. It became an American to cover his face when he placed his bust among the great men of the world."

And again another time:

"I have labored nineteen years to take fifteen States out of the Union; and if I have spent any nineteen years to the satisfaction of my Puritan conscience, it was those nineteen years."

From Parker Pillsbury's Speech, April, 1862,

"I do not wish to see this government prolonged another day in the present form. I have been for twenty years attempting to overthrow the present dynasty. The constitution never was so much an engine of cruelty and crime as at the present hour. I am not rejoiced at the tidings of victory to the northern arms; I would far rather see defeat, etc."

From Stephen F. Forters's Speech, Boston, 1862.

"I have endeavored to dissuade every young man I could from enlisting, telling them that they were going to fight for slavery."

CHAPTER XII.
PROGRESS OF THE NORTHERN CONSPIRACY—
(CONTINUED).

Charles Sumner Advises Nullification and Disobedience to the Laws...Claims the Republican Party as Sectional, and suited to his Purpose...Greeley's Insult to the Flag: The "Flaunting Lie"...Is this an Abolition War?...Testimony of Gov. Stone, of Iowa...Statement of M. B. Lowry...Phillips on Secession....."Chicago Tribune and the Tax Bill...Extracts from a Massachusetts Pamphlet...Abuse of the Framers of the Constitution... Similarity between Northern and Southern Disunionists.

CHARLES SUMNER ON NULLIFICATION.

To show that CHARLES SUMNER came honestly by his nullification and resistance-to-law doctrine, we present the following extract from his speech delivered at Worcester, Massachusetts, Sept. 7, 1854, just after the slave ANTHONY BURNS had been rescued from the Boston mob, at which poor BACHELDER was killed by said mob, while in the discharge of his duty, in guarding the prisoner. Mr. SUMNER, among other things said:

"But it is sometimes gravely urged that since the Supreme Court of the United States has affirmed the constitutionality of the Fugitive act, there only remains to us in all places, whether in public station or as private citizens, the duty of absolute submission. Now, without stopping to consider the soundness of their judgment, affirming the constitutionality of this act, let me say that the Constitution of the United States, as I understand it, exacts no such passive obedience, * * and no man, who is not lost to self respect, and ready to abandon the manhood which is shown in the heaven directed countenance, will voluntarily aid in enforcing a "judgment" which in his conscience he solemnly believes to be against the fundamental law, whether of the Constitution or of God! * * * The whole dogma of passive obedience must be rejected—in whatever guise it may assume, and under whatever alias it may skulk; whether in the tyranical usurpations of king parliament or judicial tribunal."

He thus sets off the aims and objects of the Republican party just then organized:

"To the true-hearted, magnanimous men who are ready to place Freedom above Party, and their party above Politicians, I appeal.— (Immense cheering.) Let them leave the old parties, and blend in an organization, which, without compromise, will maintain the good cause surely to the end. Here, in Massachusetts a large majority of the people concur in sentiment on slavery; a large majority desire the overthrow of the slave power. It becomes them not to scatter their votes, but to unite in one firm consistent phalanx, (applause) whose triumph shall constitute an epoch of Freedom, not only in this commonwealth, but throughout the land. Such an organization is now presented by this Republican Convention, which according to the resolutions by which it is convoked is to co-operate with the friends of freedom in other States."

And this is the way he undertook to educate the public mind to the pitch of resisting the decisions of the Supreme Court:

"But let me ask gentlemen who are disposed to abandon their own understanding of the Constitution, to submit their conscience to the standard of other men, by whose understanding do they swear? Surely not by that of the President. This is not alleged. But by the understanding of the Supreme Court. In other words, to this Court, consisting at present of nine persons, is committed a power of fastening such interpretation as they see fit upon any part of the Constitution—adding to it or sub tracting from it—or positively varying its requirements—actually making and unmaking the Constitution; and all good citizens must bow to their work as of equal authority with the original instrument, ratified by solemn votes of the whole people. [Great applause.] If this be so, then the oath to support the Constitution of the United States is hardly less offensive than the famous "et cetera" oath devised by Archbishop Laud, in which the subject swore to certain specified things, with an "&c." added. Such an oath I have not taken. [Good, good.]

For myself, let me say that I hold judges, and especially the Supreme Court of the country, in much respect; but I am too familiar with the history of judicial proceedings to regard them with any superstitious reverence.—[Sensation.]

He thus clinches the subject, by boldly setting up the purpose of the Republican organization, to "overthrow the slave power" and "to open the gates of emancipation in the slave states:"

"To the overthrow of the slave power we are thus summoned by a double call, one political and the other philanthropic; first, to remove an oppressive tyranny from the National Government, and secondly, to open the gates of Emancipation in the Slave states. [Loud applause.]

"But while keeping this great purpose in view, we must not forget details. The existence of slavery anywhere within the national jurisdiction—in the territories, in the District of Columbia, or on the high seas beneath the national flag, is an unconstitutional usurpation, which must be opposed. The Fugitive Slave Bill, monstrous in cruelty, as in unconstitutionality, is a usurpation which must be opposed."

With what huge delight must CHARLES SUMNER have heard the tocsin of war—as the natural and inevitable consequence of his partizan raid on the South. With what avidity must he devoured the fruits (the war) of his pious labors.

As an original proposition, with no constitution to bind us, we should never have been in favor of the Fugitive Slave Law. But it was passed in 1793, by our fathers, in pursuance of a solemn, constitutional agreement they had entered into. WASHINGTON, the Father of his Country, President of the Constitutional Convention, and as President of the United States, signed that law, and gave it vitality. The Supreme Court in many instances declared it to be enacted in accordance with the constitution; and all good citizens were bound to yield to its requirements, whether they personally liked it or not. But, as we have seen, there was from the beginning, a powerful faction in our country, opposed to our Government, who were ready to seize the most favorable pretext to consummate their destroying object. As we have already seen this pretext assumed various shapes and forms—anything to cater to the prevailing whims of the day. The thing or idea that could produce the greatest "irritation" was always in the vanguard. In 1798, it was slavery and commerce. In 1812, &c., it was the array of the Agricultural against the Commercial States—Peace vs. War, &c. In 1833, the "oppressive tariff of 1828" was held up, as the initiating pretext, and from that time till 1860 the most prolific of all "irritations"—the slavery question—furnished the pretext.

In all these quotations we have made from old, and latter-day Federals, and from their progeny, the Republicans and Abolitionists, we request the reader to particularly notice the great similarity in the *animus* and "style" of denunciation.

When, in 1854, the slave Burns had been delivered at Boston, and put on board of a United States vessel, in charge of his claimant, in pursuance of that law which Mr. SUMNER advised his followers to resist, though the supreme tribunal of the land had decided it constitutional, the New York *Tribune*, true to the instincts and purposes of the old haters of our Government, garnished its columns with the following poetical rhodomontade:

THE AMERICAN FLAG.
[From the New York Tribune, 1854.]

All hail the *flaunting lie!*
The stars look pale and dim;
The stripes are bloody scars—
A lie the vaunting hymn!

It shields a *pirate's* deck!
It binds a man in chains!
It yokes the captive's neck,
And wipes the bloody stains!

Tear down the flaunting lie;
Half-mast the starry flag;
Insult no sunny sky
With *hate's polluted rag!*

Destroy it, ye who can;
Deep sink it in the waves!
It bears a fellow man,
To groan with fellow slaves!

Furl, furl the boasted *lie!*
Till Freedom lives again,
To rule once more in truth,
Among untrammeled men!

Roll up the starry sheen,
Conceal its bloody stains,
For in its folds are seen
The stamp of rustling chains!

IS THE WAR PROSECUTED TO ABOLISH SLAVERY?

Mr. SUMNER sounded the key note of revolt in 1854. The Abolitionists caught it up, and demanded dissolution, as we have already seen. The war followed, as naturally as that any any effect follows a cause Whether this war is being prosecuted with sole reference to abolishing slavery, regardless of what may become of the Union, shall not rest on our charge. We will introduce Abolition testimony.

Col. WM. STONE, the Governor of Iowa, in canvassing that state in the summer of 1863, in his speech at Keokuk, on the 3d of August, said:

"Fellow citizens—I was not formerly an abolitionist, nor did I formerly suppose I would ever become one; but I am now, I have been for the last nine months, an unadulterated abolitionist. [At this the abolition portion of his audience shouted loudly and cried out, 'That's it,' 'That's the way to talk it out,' 'Hurrah, hurrah!'] As a matter of policy, perhaps, it would have been more prudent not to have so publicly declared that I have become an abolitionist; but, since I have said it, I will not take it back, and let those who don't like it make the most of it. [Again the old Whig-hating Abolition faction of his audience shouted most lustily, while a number of Republicans, in an under tone, were heard to express dissatisfaction.]

"Fellow-citizens — The opposition charge that this is an abolition war. Well, I admit that it is an abolition war. It was not such in the start ; but the administration has discovered that they could not subdue the South else than making it an abolition war, and they have done so ; and it will be continued as an abolition war so long as there is one slave at the South to be made free. Never, never can there be peace made, nor is peace desirable, until the last link of slavery is abolished.— [Loud and prolonged cheers from the abolitionists, while the republican Unionists muttered much dissent.]

"Butler, Stanton, Burnside, and men of that stamp, I regard as true patriots ; but as for the copperhead democracy, I hold for them the utmost contempt, and I would rather eat with a nigger, drink with a nigger, live with a nigger, and sleep with a nigger, than with a copperhead. [At this declaration in favor of sleeping, etc., with niggers rather than with the copperhead democracy, as he termed it all true democrats, the shouts of the advocates of negro amalgamation were loud and defiant.]"

MORROW. B. LOWRY, an abolition State Senator in Pennsylvania, at a League meeting in Philadelphia, in 1863, said :

"This war is for the African and his race.— The six hundred colored men who have recently fallen, have elevated the race. For all I know, the Napoleon of this war may be done up in a black package. (Laughter.) We have no evidence of his being done up in a white one, as yet. When this war was no bigger than my hand, I said that if any negro would bring me his disloyal master's head, I would give him one hundred and sixty acres of his master's plantation. (Laughter and applause.) The man who talks of elevating the negro would not have to elevate him very much to make him equal to himself."

We might crowd a small octavo volume with similar declamations and admissions, but these must suffice until some one shall impeach the veracity of these revolutionists.

In a speech by WENDELL PHILLIPS in 1862, he said:

"Slavery had suggested secession, and it had a right to do so, for he, (Mr. PHILLIPS,) being a secessionist, believed that those people were the sole judges of what causes they had for revolution."

While the tax bill was pending in Congress, a Washington correspondent of the Chicago *Tribune* said through that sheet:

" The Tax Bill is slowly grinding through the House, in committee of the whole, and is one of the most telling anti-slavery documents ever devised by the wit of man. If there had been no slavery, there would have been no rebellion, and of course no tax bill. Every man, woman and child in the loyal states must now commence paying for the luxury of having neighbors who own and flog negroes. There are none so poor that they can escape this slavery tax—none so dull they cannot see what has caused it."

This is the same species of argument as that of the man who shot his neighbor, and charged the fault to the man who invented gunpowder. Had there been no powder the man would not have been shot. As slavery caused no war previous to the agitation by those who had nothing to do with it, would it not be quite as charitable to suppose that *slavery agitation* was the cause of the war tax?

For years, the disunionists of the North have manifested the boldness of a CROMWELL, the assiduity of beavers, the cunning of foxes, the malignancy of ISCARIOTS. Their money has been poured out free as water, in publishing and circulating Abolition tracts, speeches, inflammatory and incendiary appeals—not to national honor and pride, but to the passions and hot bed sentimentalities that fester in the breasts of malcontents. In 1852, a series of pamphlets were issued for Massachusetts, entitled, "The United States Constitution and its pro slavery compromises." From the "Third edition, enlarged," of this treasonable publication we take the following:

"If, then, the people and the courts of a country are to be allowed to determine what their own laws mean, it follows that at this time, and for the last half century, the Constitution of the United States has been, and still is a pro-slavery instrument, and that any one who swears to support it, swears to do pro-slavery acts, and violates his duty both as a man and an Abolitionist.

"If, then, the Constitution be what these debates (the Madison papers) show that our fathers intended to make it, and what, too, their descendants, this nation, say they did make it, and agreed to uphold, then we affirm that it is 'a covenant with death, and an agreement with hell,' and ought to be immediately annulled! No Abolitionist can consistently take office under it, *or swear to support it.*

"To continue this *disastrous* alliance (the Federal Union) longer, is *madness!* We dare not prolong the experiment, and with double earnestness, we repeat our demand upon every honest man to join in the outcry of the American Anti-Slavery Society—*No union with slaveholders!*"

Speaking of the framers of the Constitution, it says:

"Now, these pages prove the melancholy fact, that willingly, with deliberate purpose, our fathers bartered honesty for gain, and *became partners with tyrants!* that they might share in the profits of their tyranny."

On page 145, the following occurs:

"Fidelity to the cause of human freedom, and allegiance to God [the Higher law which Mr. SEWARD borrowed from the Puritanical fathers] require that the existing National compact *should be instantly dissolved; that secession from the Government is a religious and political duty.*"

What more did the South Carolina Nullifiers and Secessionists ever declare? What more have they ever done than to act upon this pious hint, and yet the authors of the foregoing have never been arrested by the powers that be, nor have they ever been denounced by those powers or their backers.

But while those fanatical disunionists were denouncing our fathers, for becoming partners with tyrants, and showing their proof for this charge from the MADISON papers, they ought not to have neglected the important fact that it was mainly owing to the vote of Massachusetts and Rhode Island that the report of the committee of thirteen, and the voice of slaveholding Virginia and Delaware were overruled, and the slave trade, now pronounced piracy by the greatest Powers on the globe, was prolonged from 1800 to 1808. Yes, Massachusetts done this to "protect" her sordid shipping interest, on a plea of gain, and to have been consistent those Massachusetts Abolitionists, who now shout for the war, only because "it is an instrument in the hands of God" to confiscate the slave property at the South, purchased from the guilty slave importers of Boston—under that constitutional license, prolonged for eight years at the special request, and by the solid vote of Massachusetts and Connecticut, against the earnest protest of old Virginia and Delaware. Now comes Massachusetts and declares the consequences of her own crimes a cause for dissolving the Union, after she has *gone out of the trade!*

CHAPTER XIII.

DISUNION OF NORTHERN GROWTH.

Disunion began in the North...Admission by Wendell Phillips...The War brought on by the North as a Means to an End...The Kansas Imbroglio...Stimulated by the Radicals to Aid Secession and Disunion—Helper's "Impending Crisis" as a Means to hasten Dissolution....Mr. Seward Endorses its "Logical Analogies"—Treasonable Kansas War Meeting in Buffalo—Gerrit Smith and Gov. Reeder Stimulate the "Cause"...Beecher on Shooting at Men...Charles Sumner admits the Northern Conspiracy.

DISUNION BEGUN AT THE NORTH.

WENDELL PHILLIPS is the most honest and outspoken of all the Northern Disunionists. He does not hesitate to claim that this revolution *began* at the North, and that it had a *purpose* in view, and that *purpose* was dissolution—the *means* being the slavery agitation. In a letter to the Boston *Liberator*, July 21, 1863, he makes the following remarkably candid declarations:

"The disunion we sought was one which

should be *begun by the North on principle.* * *. The *agitation* for such disunion, based on the idea that slavery is a sin, to be immediately repudiated at every cost, was the most *direct* and *effective* way of *educating the public to a stern anti-slavery principle.* * * Abolition of slavery was our object, disunion our weapon. [This reversed, would accord more nearly with the general purpose of Abolitionists.] * * The North had the *right of revolution*—the *right to break the Union,* and that such disunion would sooner end slavery than continuing under a Constitution that forbade the North *during peace* to interfere with the slave systems of the Southern states."

Here is a bold declaration that this war was of "right" brought on by the North, by the slavery agitation, so that slavery could be abolished, which could not be done in a state of peace. This admission covers the whole ground, as to who is responsible for the war. It admits as plain as language can that the slavery agitators drove the South into it with the avowed purpose of accomplishing in a state of war what they admit they could not in a state of peace.

But, Mr. PHILLIPS leaves us nothing to guess, and in the following paragraph he gives us the Abolition reasons for stimulating war, as simple as a child would narrate a May-day exploit:

"In these circumstances, the Abolitionists, who were not peace men, and had never asserted the sinfulness of war, perceived that the war itself would produce an overwhelming national opinion adverse to slavery, sooner than any *other* agency. The manifestation war must make of the nature and designs of the slave power, would inevitably make every Unionist an Abolitionist. The need of the negro in the conflict would destroy prejudice against color more speedily than any other means could, and his presence in the army would be the *first step* to civil equality. We saw that the preservation of the Union would efficiently protect the negro in his transition to *perfect* freedom, and that the nation he helped to *create, owed him this aid,* which is of vast importance.

"As things stand, therefore, *since* the war: "1. The Union means liberty, and to save itself, must free the blacks. To uphold it in this struggle for existence, is the readiest way to convert the nation into Abolitionists. One year of such war is worth, for *this* purpose, twenty years of peaceful agitation."

This plan of inciting all the horrors of a civil war as the best means to liberate the African and make him in all respects our equal, is certainly more ingenious than reputable. It is worthy the sinister purposes of the agitating authors of this war. Mr. P. continues:

"The sharp sword of war kills or cures at once, and as God has linked success with justice, we must be whipped into a people hating slavery, as their conqueror, or we must be successful, with justice for our ally—*the negro our acknowledged equal and brother!* We see nevertheless, the *use* of our disunion agitation. If we did not fully convert the community by our cry, 'Liberty and justice are *letter than Union,*' we so far leavened their minds, and wakened their consciences, that when the war came, the hour found them ready to accept the issue. When the question was put—the *old Union,* with slavery, or a *new one* without it, the people have been found far more ready than any man supposed, to answer, give us, at any cost, Union and freedom," &c.

Thus, we have the admission that the Abolitionists brought on the war to put down slavery, and then we have the Proclamation as a "military necessity" to put down the war. How easy and simple the proposition.

We have ever regarded MR. PHILLIPS as a talented, truthful, bold, fanatical, bad man.— When he tells us that he and his class have been endeavoring to bring on war and dissolution we believe him, not because we want to believe him, but because his admission comes from one of that class—yea, its principal leader, who are now on trial before the great tribunal of history as inciters, aiders and abetors of treason against the best human government ever established on this globe.

THE KANSAS IMBROGLIO.

We are to read the Kansas imbroglio in the light of Mr. PHILLIP's admission. That th unhappy state of affairs in Kansas was made to play into the hands, and aid the designs of the Northern disunionists and the Southern disunionists, we have not a doubt.

It was unquestionably the purpose of Southern "propagandists" to make a show of establishing slavery in Kansas, not that advocates ot the "peculiar system" ever believed slavery would be either profitable or permanent, if established in that territory. But it furnished a coveted point to both sides for a "conflict," and while those politicians in the interest of the South played *their role* to the best ad vantage, and committed many criminal acts, that ought to "make the dogs blush," their counterparts in treasonable opposition, "jumped at the chance" to stimulate their long cherished "idea," by precipitating the "irrepressible conflict." Had even the agitators of the North been dictated by purely patriotic motives, there would have been no serious conflict, for the North having the means to furnish five to one of the emigration, could have voted down the Southern influx, and the North could have afforded to rely on its strength and wait for time to settle the matter.

But the contest originated, as we have seen in the progress of our compilation thus far, over forty years before Kansas was organized as a territory. The contest began in 1798, and raging with unremitting violence up to that time, could not be abandoned by the haters of the "league with hell, the covenant with death," in 1857-8. The abolition agitators have often "thanked God for the *occasion* which the Kansas imbroglio afforded to stimulate the cause." It was hoped by the secessionists, North and South, that Kansas would prove to be the rock on which the Union would split.— Each party of factionists and disunionists bent every nerve to this end. Traitors in the South, under the guise of Democrats, and traitors in the North, as members of the Republican organization, furnished their "quota" of men and arms. Each party, anxious for the fray— both factions praying with impious fervency, that the "hour had come" that should rend asunder the ligaments of Union. Christian men (?) and pastors of Christian churches (?) bundled off their frenzied partizans with the bible in one hand and a Sharpe's rifle in the other, and bid them God speed in the holy crusade. O, that was a rich and exhilerating carnival, when the fires of civil discord were lighted by vandal torches—when the proud Romans went forth with a shout of brotherly hate (!) to prick the barbarian Persians with the javelin of holy revenge, that the empire might perish between them!

The embittered feelings engendered by the Kansas imbroglio, was but the dawn of that abolition millenium which the agitators had prayed for for years. It gave them new life and hope, and they threw up their caps and shouted God curse the Republic. The fires of secession had been kindled, and it was determined that no shower of patriotism should quench the flames. New and inflamable material must be added, and the breath of denunciation, with ten thousand bellows power, was employed to fan the flames of discord to an inextinguishable conflagration. Inflamatory speeches were made, denunciatory newspaper articles, and incendiary sermons and threats were sent broadcast over the land, to keep the fires of discord to a "welding heat." The HELPER. book, the most incendiary and exasperating of all, was issued, not in the name of its real Northern author, but in the name of a purchased stool pigeon, who hailed from a slave state, so as to give point. piquancy and *sting* to. its pages. We select some specimens from this book, which was endorsed and recommended as a work calculated to have "great influence on the public mind," by seventy-eight members of Congress, belonging wholly to the Republican party. We quote as follows:

THE "IMPENDING CRISIS."

"It is against slavery on the whole, and against slave-holders as a body that we wage an exterminating war.'—p. 129.

"Do not reserve the strength of your arms until you have been rendered powerless to strike.

"We contend, moreover, that slave-holders are more criminal than common murderers.'— p. 140.

"But it is a fact, nevertheless, that all slave holders are under the shield of a perpetual license to murder.'—p. 144.

"Against this army for the defence and propagation of slavery, we think it will be an easy matter—*independent of the negroes, who in nine cases out of ten would be delighted at the opportunity to cut their master's throats*, and without accepting a single recruit from either of the free States, England, France or Germany—to muster one at least three times as large, and far more respectable, for its extinction.'—p. 147.

"But we are wedded to one purpose, from which no earthly power can divorce us We are determined to abolish slavery at all hazards.'—p. 149.

"Now is the time for them to assert their right and liberties; never before was there such an appropriate period to strike for freedom in the South.'—p. 153.

"Not to be an abolitionist is to be a wilful and diabolical instrument of the devil.'—p. 368.

"No man can be a true paoriot without first becoming an abolitionist.'—p. 116.

"Small pox is a nuisance; strychnine is a nuisance; mad dogs are a nuisance; slavery is a nuisance; and so are slave breeders; it is our business, nay it is our imperative duty to abate nuisances; we propose therefore, with the exception of strychnine, to exterminate this catalogue from beginning to end.'—p. 130.

"Foam, sirs, fret, foam' prepare your weapons, threaten, strike, shoot, stab, bring on civil war, dissolve the Union; nay, annihilate the solar system if you will—do all this, more, less, better, worse, anything—do what you will sirs, you neither foil nor intimidate us; our purpose is as firmly fixed as the eternal pillars of heaven; we have determined to abolish slavery, and so help us God, abolish it we will!—

Take this to bed with you to-night. [S]irs, and think about it, and let us know how you feel to-morrow morning."'

Mr. Seward, the author, in this country, of the "irrepressible conflict" doctrine gave it the weight of his great influence as follows:

"AUBURN, N. Y., June 28. 1857.

"GENTLEMEN:—I have received from you a copy of the recent publications, entitled the "Impending Crisis of the South," and have read it with deepest attention—it seems to me a work of great merit; rich, yet accurate in statistical information, and logical in analogies; and I do not doubt that it will exert a great influence on the public mind, in favor of truth and justice.

"I am gentlemen, very respectfully,
"W. H. SEWARD."

THE KANSAS IMBROGLIO A PART OF THE SCHEME.

Can any one doubt the truth and sincerity of Mr. PHILLIPS, after reading this, and knowing the fact that it was publicly endorsed by nearly every Republican member of Congress, that war and disunion was from that day to be the "weapon" to accomplish what Mr. P. says could not be consummated in peace?

The Republican partizans were holding meetings in all parts of the country to organize for a civil war in Kansas. Many of their leaders were reticent and cautious about admissions that should give a clue to their real purposes, but there were others who made no secret of their intentions and objects. Among this class we select the following from the proceedings of a public meeting held in Buffalo, N. Y., wherein Gov. REEDER (then late of Kansas) and GARRIT SMITH acted as colporteurs of the Republican party in raising funds to carry on a civil war in Kansas:

"Mr. SMITH continued to speak of the aggressions of the South, and said he only hoped to hear of a collision at the South, and said he only hoped to hear of a collision at Topeka; that he only desired to hear of a collision with the Federal troops, and that northern men had fallen; and then he would hear of Northern states arraying themselves against the Federal Government. And would that be the end? No; Missouri would be the next battle field, and then slavery would be driven to the wall. Her strength is only apparent; it consists half in Northern cowards and doughfaces. It has been brave and rampant only because the North has fled before it. It will run when the North faces it. He believed the time had come to use physical force."

"Gov. REEDER read to the convention the report from Kansas, of the dispersion of the Territorial Legislature by Colonel SUMNER, and remarked, at the close that he was sorry that the Legislature had not waited till driven out at the point of the bayonet." (Cheers.)

"Mr. L. R. NOBLE asked how many troops there were belonging to the United States in Kansas?

"Gov. REEDER said about 600.

"Mr. NOBLE—And how many in the entire army of the United States?

"Governor REEDER—I believe 15,000.

"Mr. NOBLE—I learn from a friend near me, that they can't send more than 10,000 men into Kansas; and so I say let us go on.

"GERRIT SMITH desired to see the contributions continued.

"A delegate said he would give 100 men who did not fear the devil, and who, like CROMWELL, would praise God and keep their powder dry.

"GERRIT SMITH thought funds were wanted first, and hoped to see the subscription go on. He urged in several speeches that the time had come when it was necessary to use physical force.

"To this Governor REEDER replied that he was not in favor of waiting *because they had not received wrongs enough*, but thought it right to wait until they *could strike an effective blow*. If it remained with him to use the power of the Government, he would not have waited thus long, but the oppressors before this would have been converted into heaps of dead men on the fields of Missouri. But he was willing to wait until to-morrow, or two to-morrows. When on the trail of the enemy, against whom he had a deadly hate, he would follow him with cat-like tread, and would not strike until he could strike him surely dead. He was, therefore, willing to wait until they had the power he would thus have used. He did not wish to give the South notice of their intentions by marching armed men into the Territory. The dragoons could go in as voters, or to cultivate the soil, and strike when the right time arrived. When the time came to strike, he wanted the South to have the first notice of the blow in the blow itself."

About this time MR. GIDDINGS is reported to have said :

"I look forward to the day when I shall see a servile insurrection at the South. When the black man supplied with British bayonets, and commanded by British officers, shall wage a war of extermination against the whites—when the master shall see his dwelling in flames, and his hearth polluted, and though I may not mock at their calamity, and laugh when their fear cometh, yet I shall hail it as the dawn of a political millenium."

HENRY WARD BEECHER, in presenting a Sharpe's rifle to one of his Kansas *proteges*, said :

"It is a crime to shoot at a man and not hit him."

CHAPTER XIV.

THE JOHN BROWN RAID -ENDORSED BY THE REPUBLICANS.

Seward, Hale and Wilson Toasted by the Louisville "Journal" for not exposing the John Brown Raid...John Brown's operations a part of the Dissolution Scheme... Numerous Extracts to prove that Republicans endorsed the John Brown Raid...Republican Press, Clergy and Orators endorse it...From "La Crosse Republican"... Rev. De Los Love...Rev. E. D. Wheelock..." Milwaukee Sentinel"..."Elkhorn Independent"..."Janesville Gazette"...Telegraphic Despatches, 1859..."Winsted Herald"...Speech of J. W. Phillips...Laconic Letter and Reply, between Elder Spooner and an Editor...Massachusetts Resolution...Meeting in Rockford, Ill....100 Guns Fired in Albany, N. Y....Theodore Parker's Formula...Indignation Meeting in Milwaukee : their Resolutions, etc. ...Rev. Geo. W. Bassett, of Ill....Telegram from New York...Horace Greeley on John Brown— " Milwaukee Free Democrat"...Speech of Rev. Mr. Staples, Milwaukee... Emerson at Tremont Temple...Rev. M. P. Kinney..."Menasha Conservator"..."Milwaukee Atlas "..." New York Tribune"..." Wood County (Wis.) Reporter"...A Prophetic Article from the " New York Herald "...Brown's Character in Kansas, by the " Herald of Freedom "—General Conclusions, &c.

THE JOHN BROWN RAID—A PART OF THE PROGRAMME.

We have the statement of Col JAMISON, (Abolitionist), that Kansas was employed as a nursery for disunion, for he tells us (see extract from his speech on page —) that JOHN BROWN had been sent from Kansas to Harper's Ferry.

The Northern sccsessionist, MR. PHILLIPS tells us, finding it impossible to abolish slavery in peace, sought to inaugurate a war, *as the only means to secure this object*. Take their conduct in this, step by step, from beginning to the end—from first to last,—and it all looks like *business*. They went to work as though they intended to accomplish their purpose.— They knew that to make hornets "fighting mad," they must be violently disturbed. The Kansas imbroglio had not sufficiently maddened Achilles to make a counter attack on Hector, and something else was necessary to *provoke* hostilities. Yes, this is the word under Mr. PHILLIP's and Colonel JAMISON's declarations, none other will answer.

CHARLES SUMNER, in a speech delivered before the Young Men's Republican Union of New York, Nov. 27, 1861, says:

"Alas, it is *ourselves* that have encourged the conspiracy, and made it strong. * * While professing to uphold the Union we have betrayed it. It seems now beyond question that the concessionists of the North have from the beginning, played into the hands of the Secessionists of the South."—p. 9.

That JOHN BROWN was equipped and *sent* to Virginia by the Abolitionists to stir up civil war, with a view to hasten the *crisis*, we have abundant evidence from the treasonable mutterings of those who rang bells on the day he expiated his crimes, and canonized him as a martyr, whose "soul is marching on." That leading and influential Abolitionists were made acquainted with his designs at Harper's Ferry before the shameful *emeute* took place, is abundantly in proof. FORBES, a compatriot of JOHN BROWN, and who from some spleen of disappointment "blowed" on his bloody preceptor, was a witness before the Senatorial Committee that investigated the Harper's Ferry affair. This FORBES testified that he had forewarned Senator WILSON, of Massachusetts, and others of BROWN's nefarious purposes, and still WILSON kept the matter from the public.—[*See Report of Senate Investigating Committee.*

THE LOUISVILLE JOURNAL'S EXPOSITION.

The following article from the Louisville *Journal*, at the time of the Congressional exposure, shows that not only Messrs. WILSON, HALE, SEWARD and other leading Republicans foreknew the purposes of BROWN, but that they kept the knowledge from the public, for reasons which all may readily divine. Many of the *Journal*'s suggestions have since been reduced to history:

"We are now prepared to comprehend the general character and extent of the disclosures which FORBES made to Mr. SEWARD in the interview before mentioned FORBES, it will be observed, had two separate and distinct grounds of complaint against the 'humanitarians,' as he somewhat loosely terms the Abolitionists, seeing that he is a man of culture and intelligence:—namely, first, the necessities of his family, consequent, as he alleged on the failure of the 'humanitarians' to redeem their engagements to him, [FORBES, be it remembered, was one of the JOHN BROWN guard, and 'blowed' on that band of assassins he had been associated with, because they neglected sundry money obligations] and secondly, the rejection of his plan by the perfidious 'humanitarians,' and their adoption of 'JOHN BROWN's project,' including 'the cotton speculation.' These are grievances for the redress of which FORBES desired to enlist the favor and influence of SEWARD and HALE. These are the crooked things which he wanted them to 'put straight.' The scope and force of the language in which he describes his respective interviews with them is now not only obvious, but unmistakable. 'Having made several ineffectual attempts,' he says, 'to get a quiet conversation with Senator JOHN P. HALE, of New Hampshire, I met him accidentally on Sunday morning. I could not then enter into the details of JOHN BROWN's project, therefore I confined myself to explaining the urgency of sending my family relief.' He could touch upon only a part of his grievances. Not so in his more deliberate interview with Mr. SEWARD. In that he touched fully upon the entire burden of his complaint. '*I went*' he says '*into the whole matter, in all its bearings.*' What now is left to inference or doubt? Assuming the genuineness of these developments, which we believe is not impeached, even by those most nearly concerned, it is an offense to reason, an insult to common sense, a gross violence to the constitution of the human mind, to ask one to believe *that Mr.* SEWARD *was not thoroughly cognizant of the bloody and demoniacal scheme which old* JOHN BROWN *and his fellow conspirators were meditating.* He did know it all. The conclusion is inevitable!"

REPUBLICAN ENDORSEMENT OF THE JOHN BROWN RAID.

As accumulative proof that the Republican party generally, if they did not plan or connive at the JOHN BROWN raid, for the purprse of bringing on a civil war—if they were not accessories before the fact, they were certainly and clearly after—we present the following testimony. Our witnesses are principally from Wisconsin, as the most convenient at hand, but their evidence is similar to the general mass of Republicans throughout the North.

In 1859, the Rev. W. DE LOSS LOVE, an orthodox Abolitionist of Milwaukee, preached a thanksgiving sermon in the Spring street Congregational Church, "on the death of JOHN BROWN, in which occurs these sentences:

"In Kansas *was sown the seed of the outbreak at Harper's Ferry!* * * If, indeed, you had power to *revolutionize* a nation, or *all* nations, and extinguish slavery at a blow, and plant society afterwards on a peaceable and sure foundation, doubtless you, as a people, *should do it!* * * JOHN BROWN may die on a gallows, *but his name will be embalmed in millions of hearts.* * *

"'The good he has done Will live after him.' * *

"The world will attribute the blood of JOHN BROWN, *not to justice*, but to those who shed the blood of his children. The blood of both father and sons will cry out against them from the ground."

"But thanks to God, several thousand are yet left in this Israel that have not bowed their knees to Baal nor prostituted their lips to kiss the rod of slavery. From these let your *hopes* arise, that our land will *yet* be redeemed from her insolvency," &c.

The Fort Atchison (Wis.) *Standard*, in its first issue after the execution of BROWN, thus blended its grief with its treason:

"JOHN BROWN DEAD.—The first act in the tragedy has been performed. The great State of Virginia has played the hangman's part, and is crowned with its bloody honors. A telegraphic message was received at Janesville yesterday afternoon, stating that BROWN was hung at Charleston, at a quarter past 11, A. M. For an hour previous to the arrival of the intelligence at this place, the *bell was tolled sadly in anticipation of the event!* No mercy was expected for the victim of southern vengeance. *But the end* is not yet. Troops cannot check the flow of *sympathy* that surges over the land. A wall of bayonets may guard the hideous bastile of *cruelty and wrong*, *but cannot obstruct the march of the free legions that will spring forth from their slumber, and make the earth tremble beneath their tread!*

"Now, may God help the right! and give us tongues of fire, and hands that shall never weary, to *wage an eternal crusade* against the diabolical sin of slavery.

"Peaceful be the sleep of the murdered BROWN, and glorious his awakening."

The above was draped in mourning to show the deep sorrow of the editor for the death of the diabolical murderer.

"If the decree of the court is fulfilled, Virginia will commit a crime in the murder of John Brown to-day, which will result in another step towards bringing to the light the dark blot upon the American Republic."—*LaCrosse* (Wis.) *Republican, Dec.* 2, 1859.

"One such man makes total depravity impossible, and proves that American greatness *died not with Washington!* The gallows from which he ascends into Heaven, *will be in our politics*, what the cross is in our religion—the sign and symbol of supreme self-devotedness, —and from his sacrificial blood, *the temporal salvation of four millions of our people shall yet spring!* On the second day of December he is to be strangled in a Southern prison, *for obeying the Sermon on the Mount.* But, to be hanged in Virginia, is like being crucified in Jerusalem—it is the last tribute which she pays to *Virtue!*"—*Extract from Sermon of Rev. E. D. Wheelock, of Dover, N. H., on the execution of John Brown.*

"THE HANGMAN'S DAY.—To-morrow, the 2d day of December, 1859, is to become memorable in history for the *martyrdom* of John Brown! The State of Virginia, represented by Gov. WISE, and the United States of America, 'the home of the free and the land of the brave,' represented by President BUCHANAN, are to see the effectual *hanging* of 'Ossawatamie.' Some twenty-five hundred State and Federal troops will assist in the ceremony. No one is to come within earshot of the dying *martyr*. No 'Northerner' will be permitted to record his parting words. But, in spite of all precautions, they will be heard, read and remembered by *millions of* FREEMEN, whose hatred of oppression, injustice and tyranny, in every form, will be *intensified* by the events of this black Friday. The bell that tolls for the departing spirit of JOHN BROWN, *will ring the knell of American Slavery!"—Milwaukee* (Wis.) *Sentinel, Dec. 1st* 1859.

"The moral effect of the hanging of BROWN will be to bring the hideousness of slavery home to thousands who were indifferent before. A thousand abolitionists will spring up for every one that is hung, and the 'irrepressible conflict' will *go on until the institution of slavery is rooted out of the Union.* The Union *may be dissolved,* but *slavery must die!* and if it can only die or be restricted to its present limits, *through a dissolution of the Union,* then in the name of the framers of the Union, who made it to secure the blessings of liberty, *let the Union be dissolved!"—Elkhorn* (Wis.) *Independent,* 1859.

"Even if BROWN is guilty of all that is charged against him, his bravery, magnanimity, and fortitude wins the *respect* of the generous. everywhere."—*Janesville* (Wis.) *Gazette,* 1859.

A telegraphic dispatch, dated Manchester, N. H., Dec. 2, 1859, said:

"An attempt was made to toll the City Hall bell to-day, in commemoration of JOHN BROWN. The bell was only struck a few times, when Mayor HARRINGTON appeared in the belfry, and ordered BROWN's sympathisers to desist. One of them refused, when the Mayor dropped him down through the scuttle, as the most convenient mode of enforcing his exit."

Another telegraphic dispatch read:

"Cleveland, Dec. 2.—A meeting was held here to-night, commemoratory of the execution of BROWN. Over 1,500 people were present. Able addresses were made by D. R. TILDEN, R. S. SPAULDING, C. H. LANGSTON, A. G. RIDDLE, Rev. J. C. WHITE, and others. Resolutions were adopted. *The hall was draped in mourning"*

There were a few Republican presses in various localities, fearing no doubt the bad political *effect* of mourning the loss of BROWN, chose rather to fish up excuses that he was insane, &c., and they pretended not to sympathize with his movements and murderous conduct, but in all their editorials, they would somehow or other contrive to weave in a word of excuse and palliation. To this class of Republican papers the Winsted (Conn.) *Herald* a rabid Republican sheet, thus discoursed:

"And here we may as well say, we have no admiration for that class of Republican newspapers which are so eager to disclaim and disown all fellowship and sympathy for old JOHN BROWN. Did they stop here, we could be patient with them, but when they go further, and pelt him with titles of madman, crazy, muddled and insane, we say out upon them, for *hypocrites and traitors*—'little villains,' unworthy to lick or feel the foot of old JOHN BROWN. * * * At all events he is so unsuccessful, and so Republican presses, fearful that their party will somehow lose a vote, and themselves an office, fell to mouthing old JOHN BROWN, as heartily as twelve months since they praised, and vie with each other in denouncing and abusing him. For shame! Old BROWN had more nobleness in his soul, more honesty in his heart, more principal in his action, more courage in a single finger, than all such politicians, from Maine to Oregon."

"We have almost brought the American people to that decision, which says '*Government or no Government—law or no law, but slavery come down!* Whether he broke law or violated Government, *God bless John Brown!!*' So says the American heart in the Northern states. The American head will *soon follow!* The American hand *will soon begin its work!* in obedience to that heart and head, and we shall see slavery, the *victim of its agitation*—the victim of pure politics and a Christian church."—*Extract from a speech of John W. Phillips before the Anti-Slavery Society of Mass,* 1859.

The Wisconsin *Chief,* a paper devoted temperance, took occasion to rebuke the mad spirit of fanaticism that was rushing the country to ruin on JOHN BROWN breakers, whereupon Elder SPOONER, one of the subscribers of that paper wrote the following note:

WAUKESHA, Dec. 2, 1859.

Mr. T. W. BROWN:—Discontinue my paper. I won't let my children read any paper that says JOHN BROWN was a fool. Send your bill. It will be paid.

N. A. SPOONER."

To which the editor of the *Chief* replied:

"JOHN BROWN had heroism to redeem his folly. Elder SPOONER is not so fortunate. He *is* fortunate, however, in living in a land where folly is not a capital offense."

A JOHN BROWN meeting was held at Natick, Mass., which was attended by U. S. Senator WILSON, at which the following resolution was passed:

"*Whereas,* Resistance to tyrants is obedience to GOD,

Resolved, That it is the right and duty of slaves to resist their masters, and the *right and duty of the people of the North to* INCITE THEM TO RESISTANCE, *and to aid them in it!"*

A JOHN BROWN meeting was held in Rockford, Ill., Dec. 2, 1859, attended by such leading men as Ex-Senator TALCOTT, who presided, and Dr. LYMAN, Mr. HULIN, Mr. LOOP, Judge CHURCH, Mr. BLINN, Rev. Mr. CANAUT, and others, who made speeches. The following is among the resolutions they passed, offered by Mr. HULIN, and adopted unanimously:

Resolved, That the memory of JOHN BROWN is now consigned to impartial history, which will vindicate his motives, and that his integrity, truthfulness, courage, fidelity and fortitude, stand as conspicuous examples for the veneration of all who love freedom and applaud true courage.

"*Resolved*, That the city bells be tolled one hour in commemoration of JOHN BROWN."

The following appeared among the telegraphic dispatches of the day:

"ONE HUNDRED GUNS IN HONOR OF THE EXECUTION OF JOHN BROWN.

ALBANY, N. Y., Dec. 2, 1859.

"To-day, between twelve and one o'clock, one hundred guns were fired, comemmorative of the execution of JOHN BROWN. It was previously hinted in some of the papers, that some of the more impulsive and enthusiastic portion of the Republicans intended thus to celebrate the event. A member of the common council of this city, at the last sitting, drew up a resolution, desiring that body to authorize that demonstration, but he was dissuaded from it. To-day, a cannon was taken from the State Arsenal by the keeper thereof, and planted upon the State Street Bridge, from which a hundred catridges were fired by the Deputy of the Commissionary General. * * During the day the white fanatics posted placards through the streets.

"Give us liberty or give us death—execution of Capt. JOHN BROWN."

THE POSTULA AND FORMULA OF THEODORE PARKER AND HORACE GREELY.

Shortly after the execution of JOHN BROWN a card appeared in the New York *Tribune*, from THEODORE PARKER of Boston, in which the following postulates are laid down as a formula for future action :

"1st. A man held against his will, as a slave, has a natural right to kill any one who seeks to prevent his enjoyment of liberty.

"2d. It may be a natural duty of a slave to develope this natural right in a practical manner, and actually kill those who seek to prevent his enjoyment of liberty.

"3d. The freeman has a natural right to help the slaves to recover their liberty, and in that enterprise to do for them all which they have a right to do for themselves.

"4th. It may be a natural charity for the freeman to help the slaves to the enjoyment of their liberty, and as a means to that end, to aid them in *killing* all such as oppose their natural freedom.

"5th. The performance of this duty is to be controlled by the freeman's *power* to help."

On the 2d day of Dec., 1859, an indignation meeting was held in the Chamber of Commerce in Milwaukee. A committee was appointed on resolutions, consisting of EDWARD D. HOLTON, (afterwards elected by the Republicans to the Legislature,) J. H. PAINE, a prominent lawyer of Milwaukee, GEO. TRACY, CLARENCE SHEPHERD and B. DOMSCHKE, a Republican editor, who reported among others the following resolutions:

"*Whereas,* The fundamental principle of the United States Government is, that all men are created equal, and are entitled to the protection of life, [except the white men murdered by JOHN BROWN,] liberty and property as an inalienable birthright, and,

"*Whereas,* There can be no allegiance due to a Government from those to whom it refuses such protection, and,

"*Whereas,* To enslave innocent human beings is the highest crime against humanity, therefore,

"*Resolved,* That the enslaved of this country owe no allegiance to the Government, either of the United States, or of the state in which they live, and have a right to regard and treat their enslavers as their enemies [Was not this a declaration of war?] and that a resort to force to obtain their freedom, is not only the right of the enslaved, but may be a duty which they owe to themselves and to their children, if they can use no other means, by which they can escape from the House of Bondage. [One fact should not be lost sight of in reading these vaporings, and that is, JOHN BROWN, though he often tried, could not induce the slaves to join him in effecting their "freedom," so that this criminal sympathy was a forced exotic.]

"*Whereas,* The State of Virginia, *under the forms of law*, has this day put to an ignominious death JOHN BROWN, for an attempt to deliver his fellow men from slavery, and,

"*Whereas*—All the evidence in relation to this attempt proves that they did not intend to destroy life, except in self defense, but were animated solely by the desire to relieve the oppressed, therefore

Resolved, That JOHN BROWN and his fellow sufferers, who have followed his example, have but obeyed the *Divine Command,* 'remember those that are in bonds as bound with them,' have but acted in the faith of the Declaration drafted by Virginia's greatest statesman, that all men are endowed by their Creator with an inalienable right to liberty, and placing the souls in the slave's souls stead, have translated into an immortal deed, the glorious motto, "give me liberty or give me death."

"*Resolved*—That those who justify the Revolution of '76, cannot condemn the attempt of JOHN BROWN," &c.

That is, if the revolution of the British control over this country was right, the attempt to revolutionize the government which was the result of such first revolution is right, and ought not to be condemned, and so on, *ad in finitum*, keeping society in constant revolution. Can it be possible that such monstrous doctrines were honestly entertained by honest men and good citizens? The resolutions also declare

"*Resolved*, That the spectacle of a great state, trembling with affright at the solitary voice of JOHN BROWN [when backed by the entire "voice" of the abolition party of the North] alone in prison, surrounded by thousands of armed soldiers, yet preaching repentance to oppressors, and ready to cheerfully seal his doctrine with his blood, is convincing proof of the weakness, cowardice and guilt of the slaveholders to an earnest that BROWN is the *John the Baptist of the new dispensation of freedom* [What solemn mockery] and that nothing but the united and earnest protest of the people of the North, to break every slaveholding yoke in the Union and let the oppressed go free.

"*Resolved*, That as the pusillanimity of the North, and its *want of fealty* to the principles of freedom, have encouraged the growth and spread of slavery, and the arrogance of the slave power, it is time that the North should awake to its responsibilities and duties, and that *as the Union is a mockery and a cheat to all who hold to the sentiments of the Declaration of Independence, and to the principles of Free Government*, we should not be deterred from speaking the truth in regard to slavery, and the rights and duties of both the oppressors and the oppressed, by the *silly and cowardly threats of dissolving the Union*," &c.

The Rev. GEO. W. BASSETT, of Ottawa, Ill., was one of the speakers at the John Brown meeting in Chicago, and being severely criticised by the *Times* of that city, wrote a note to the editor, of which the following is an extract:

"When you tell your readers that I eulogized Capt. BROWN, of Ossawatamie. I thank you for it, and I regard it as the shame of a pusillanimous and servile age, that the heroism of that most remarkable and heroic man, is not appreciated. His epitaph, like that of the noble, but equally unfortunate EMMET, shall be written by a subsequent and disenthralled age.

"Sirs, I prefer your outspoken, fearless and terribly consistent advocacy of despotism; or, as you will say, slavery as it is, to a truckling and time serving spirit, that while seeking to use the anti-slavery sentiment of the country *for a political result*, tries to cast odium upon the very unpopular development of it."

This was said of those Republican sheets that professed to dislike the JOHN BROWN raid, for fear of its probable *political* consequences, which might be adverse to their political prospects: •

The following appeared among the telegraph items of

"NEW YORK, Nov. 2, 1859.—WENDELL PHILLIPS, of Boston, delivered a lecture last night, in Brooklyn. in which he argued that JOHN BROWN was the only American who had acted boldly up to the *true* American *idea*, and cast aside all those false and fatal warpings of an effete conservative, and refused to regard anything as government, or any statute as law, except those which conformed to his own sense of justice and right. [This is the Higher Law doctrine on the point of a pike] Virginia was not a state. Mr. WISE was not a Governor. The Union was not a nation. All these so-called governments were *organized piracies*, and JOHN BROWN was to-day the only real and true government on the soil of Virginia, and had an infinitely better right to hang Governor WISE than Gov. WISE had to hang him."

Of course, having declared that it was the purpose of himself and his aiders and abettors to dissolve the Union, it only remained for him to second the means he and his secession compatriots had set in motion.

As that clause in the Constitution which recognizes the right to hold slaves, and also to secure their return if they escaped, was not forced upon the people of the North by the South, nor upon any State by the General Government, but was the free act of all the people combined, the utterance of such fulminations and the hundreds of others quoted in our "collection" of Abolition "curiosities," no language we can command can sufficiently express the abhorance all good people must entertain of such fanatical and treasonable diatribes. We quote again:

"JOHN BROWN, dead, will live in millions of hearts. It will be easier to die in a good cause even on the gallows, since JOHN BROWN has hallowed that mode of exit from the troubles and temptations of this mortal existance. Then, as to the 'irrepressible conflict,' who does not see that this sacrifice must inevitably intensify its progress, and *hasten* its end? [Why, PHILLIPS contends that was just what the JOHN BROWN raid was got up for.] Yes, JOHN BROWN dead, is verily a power—like SAMPSON in the falling temple of Dagon—like ZISKA, dead, with his skin stretched on a drum head, still routing the foes he bravely fought while he lived, so let us be reverently grateful for the privilege of living in a world rendered noble by the daring of heroes, the suffering of martyrs—among whom let none doubt that history will accord an *honorable* niche to old JOHN BROWN."—*Horace Greeley.*

Large handbills were posted in Philadelphia calling the citizens of the Republican "persuasion" together, Dec. 2, 1859, for the pur-

SCRAPS FROM MY SCRAP-BOOK.

pose of expressing sympathy for JOHN BROWN. Dr. FURNESS and LUCRETIA MOTT were announced as the speakers.

"EXECUTION OF JOHN BROWN.— Before this article reaches the eye of those for whom it was intended, Virginia will have wreaked her purposes on the body of JOHN BROWN, and he will be dead. * * * It is not disputed that John Brown had violated the statutes—rendered himself liable to the fate which has overtaken him. Why this universal feeling, attention and excitement, with reference to this case? It is simply this, through all the mist which obscures it, and all the laws referred to as justifying it, the grand fact is patent, that JOHN BROWN is CRUCIFIED as the representative of an idea—of a principle of importance to humanity, and dear to the instincts of every human heart."—Milwaukee Free Democrat, Dec. 2, 1859.

"The gallows of JOHN BROWN, said EMERSON, will be glorified, not as the cross, but like the cross, [a distinction without a difference,] and so it will, because the gallows of JOHN BROWN, as the cross, is used to persecute ideas, or great principles of enduring benefit and necessity to humanity, and as the ideas of christianity received from the cross their most potent and enduring impulses, so will liberty leap from the scaffold, when John Brown's spirit is dismissed, with an impulse which shall hereafter know no check, until its mission is accomplished."—Ibid.

"Man proposes and God disposes. Politicians may wrangle and split hairs, and dispute over the nice shades of legal and moral guilt involved in this matter, [JOHN BROWN'S] but it passes at once, so far as popular heart and judgment are concerned, out from under all subtleties, into the broad field—into the "irrepressible conflict," waging between barbarism [that is, opposition to murder] as represented by slavery on one hand, and christianity [that is, murder and rapine] as represented by freedom on the other."—Ibid.

"So far as they express sympathy for the honest, brave, but misguided and infatuated individual, who to-day falls a victim to his own indiscretion, and defiance of law, we accord assent and approval."—Wisconsin State Journal.

"I will apply the sentiment before I close, once applied to GEORGE HILLIARD to GARRISON; he said the time will come when Massachusetts will not find the marble white enough on which to write the name of Garrison, and I will say that the day is not far distant when Virginia will not be able to find the slab pure enough to bear the carved name of John Brown. (Applause.)—Speech of the Rev. Mr. Staples at the John Brown Meeting, Mil., Dec. 2, 1859.

"Virginia, herself, has crowned the very spirit of agitation that she ought to allay, and the blood of Old Brown will become the seed of that very conflict hitherto mentioned only by word of mouth."—Mil. Sentinel

', The saint whose fate yet hangs in suspense, but whose martyrdom, if it shall be perfected, will make the gallows as glorious as the cross."—Ralph Waldo Emerson, at the Tremont Temple, Boston.

"Brown has done for liberty in our country what few of our citizens have done, since the day of patriotic devotion on the great battlefields of the Revolution."—Rev. M. P. Kinney, Janesville, Wis.

"We disclaim sympathy with Brown's scheme of emancipation, but we regret that so brave a man should fall a victim to the generous impulses of his patriotic heart." — Menasha (Wis.) Conservator.

"A man will suffer death to-day because he fought for the liberty of a subject race, and for the honor of the Republic."—Mil. Atlas, (German Rep.)

"John Brown's body may not be, but his principles are imperishable."—Milwaukee Free Democrat.

"While the responsive heart of the North has been substantially sympathizing with the one whom they admire and venerate, and love, the great soul itself has passed away into eternal heavens. During the eighteen centuries which have passed, no such character has appeared anywhere. The galleries of the resounding ages echo with no footfall mightier than the martyr of to-day. He has gone. Efforts to save him were fruitless. Prayers were unavailing. He stood before his murderers defiantly, asking no mercy. * * *

"Bewildered not and daunted not, the shifting scenes of his life's drama, at the last, brought to him neither regrets nor forebodings. Having finished the work which God had given him to do, this apostle of a new dispensation, in imitation of the Divine, received with fortitude his baptism of blood! And this beholding, the heavens opened, and Jesus standing at the right hand of the throne of God this last of Christian martyrs stepped proudly and calmly upon the scaffold, and thence upward into the embrace of angels, and into the General Assembly and Church of the First Born, whose names are written in heaven."—New York Tribune, Dec. 2, 1859.

"Old Brown, Esq., is supposed to have been strangled to-day, for obeying the Golden Rule."—Wood County (Wis.) Reporter.

We have thus devoted considerable space to the foregoing treasonable vaporings, partly to exhibit the history of the times—partly to show the general sympathy of the leading Republicans with the avowed aims of John Brown, to bring on civil war and dissolve the Union—partly to show the holy and pious reverence in which both murderers and traitors were held by those who not only hate the Government of their fathers, but canonize its destroyers as worthy of all honor—that power and spoils may come.

Let us enquire why all this holy horror at the execution of John Brown. Who and what was he, that he should be assigned the highest niche in the Abolition Pantheon, as the "equal of Jesus Christ," and "not to be mentioned the same day with George Washington." John Brown was a Kansas horse thief and murderer. He devoted his time in that territory to making incursions into Missouri, in stealing, robbing and killing innocent persons, who had never harmed him in the least, for proof of which we refer to the Kansas Investigating report, made by a Republican committee, and published by order of the Republican House of Representatives. His gross and brutal murder of the Doyles, the Wilkinsons, and the robberies he committed, are set out in that report under oath. He then went to the Egyptian department of Canada, opened a line of communication with Abolitionists in Boston, who furnished him men and money to carry out his (no, not his, but their) infamous schemes to dissolve the Union.

The Abolitionists of Boston, the descendants in a regular line of those who resolved it "unbecoming in a *religious* and *moral* people to rejoice at the victories, obtained by our arms over the enemy"—knew too well the aims and purposes of Brown, for they had assisted in his plans, and had replenished his exchequer, and when the telegraph announced the failure of his *emeute*, there was a fluttering among the marplots of Boston. They feared that on the trial some damning testimony would expose their share of the plot, and hence they resolved that "no man shall be forced by law or otherwise, to leave Massachusetts, to attend the trial."

The prospect at one time seemed clear that the whole bubble would explode, and all the guilty be brought to punishment. Gerrit Smith became suddenly excited and was sent to the lunatic asylum as a "raving maniac," but as soon as the main witness "leaped the scaffold," he recovered.

Had the entire North, as one man, denounced the apparently fool-hardy foray of John Brown, the whole thing would have passed off as any other crime of equal magnitude would; but the general and almost universal endorsement which this development received from the ruling majority of the North—their laudations of the Godlike qualities of this old reprobate, horse thief and murderer, filled the South with just alarm, and horrified the friends of the Union everywhere. From that moment it was considered the "death knell of the Union," as JEFFERSON had predicted. No Government on earth could stand such a shock and survive.— We don't mean the shock of the handful of men under Brown, and their 2,500 pikes, but the "rear support" of that mighty "reserve" that filled the entire North with impious "*bravos*" for the actors in the first skirmish, which was so certain to usher in the "Impending Crisis" so vividly foretold by Hilton, the abolition *Helper*. Under such a pressure of open, undisguised sympathy as existed everywhere at the North, he that can acquit the abolition party of being *particeps criminis*, both before and after the fact, must carry more pounds of charity than the largest iron clad can of steam.— This ebullition of Northern riot plainly told the South to prepare for war, after the first *blow* had been struck. It was the beat of the "long roll"—the *reveille* of battle. And still, we are told that slavery is the *cause* of the war.

True, a few men at the South calmly folded their arms, and with a grim smile welcomed the shock as the harbinger of that conflict which was to destroy the Union *they* had so long hated. Says Yancy, the head devil of Southern secessionists:

"The blow is a severe one. We can well *afford* the blow—the pain is sweet, for it will accomplish more in aid of disunion than all the platforms, resolves and agitations of a lifetime."

In the published report of the proceedings of the Milwaukee District Convention, composed of thirty-one churches—six Presbyterian and twenty-five Congregational—held at Hartford, Washington county, Wisconsin, in 1859, we find the following:

"*Resolved*, That we mourn over the degeneration and guilt of our country, in having brought any of her citizens to the *necessity of disobedience* to human law, in order to render loyalty to the laws of heaven!"

The following graphic article from the New York *Herald* of December, 1859, when read by the light of subsequent events, is in some respects prophetic—yet that kind of phrophesy which comes by knowledge that *cause* is certain to produce its *effect:*

"The meeting at Tremont Temple, in Boston, on Saturday, for the benefit of 'the family of John Brown,' a report of which appeared in our issue of yesterday, is a significant fact, a sign of the times, whose import cannot be mistaken. Following up the letters and lectures, the editorial articles, speeches and sermons, which have been already laid before our readers, and which all look in the same direction, that meeting is well calculated to cause alarm throughout the land. If it stood alone, or if the rabid anti-slavery sentiment to which it gave such violent and war-like expression, were confined to a few fanatics at the North, the thing might be treated as simply ridiculous, but when we regard this demonstration as a symptom or outburst at one point of an inflammation which has seized the whole Republican party, and when we see the virulent poison of which that party is full, bursting forth at all points, then, indeed, there is cause for the most gloomy apprehension, especially when the conservative element, the salt of the body politic, designed to preserve it from putrifcation and from being resolved into its original elements, stands back apathetic and inactive, waiting we suppose, for God to interpose by some special Providence, and forgetting the grand old maxim that, 'Heaven always helps those who help themselves.'

"The meeting at Tremont Temple was numerously attended, and a large number of ladies were present. The assemblage was called to order by Hon. John A. Andrew, (now Governor of Massachusetts,) and cheek by jowl with Wendell Phillips were Rev. J. M. Manning and Rev. Dr. Neal, the latter of whom 'invoked the Divine blessing,' and offered up prayer, thus throwing a religious ingredient into the boiling cauldron of 'hellbroth,' in order to make it overflow into the fire, and set the house in flames.

"When the clergy encourage insurrection and civil war, and that with the approbation of the people, and even of the gentler sex, we are come upon dangerous times. Such was the fanaticism that prevailed at the meeting that a letter from a clergyman of milder counsels, who declined to attend, and took the opportunity of stating his reasons, while contradicting a public announcement that he was to be present, was hissed because he said he at first understood that both sides of the question were to be discussed—an idea the Hon. Mr. Andrews pronounced ridiculous, as it was hardly likely that at such a meeting there was any one present who thought there were two sides to the question as to whether 'John Brown's family' should be left to starve. No doubt they were all of the numerous family of John Brown, who, we are assured by Rev. Mr. Wheelock, count a million in the North.

"Rev. Mr. Manning rejected with scorn the notion that John Brown was insane. On the contrary he was 'the sword in the hand of a high power, the finger of God writing upon the wall of Belshazzar's palace the doom of tyrants.' The reverend fire-brand then goes on to institute a comparison between the case of John Brown and that of Crispus Attucks, the colored man who was the first Boston victim of the American Revolution, and whose remains the people of Boston followed to the grave in long processions, and years after celebrated the anniversary of the massacre, till at last the celebration was changed to the Forth of July. Daniel Webster had said that from the day of the Boston massacre was dated the disruption of the British empire. So might it be with the death of John Brown and some others.

"Daniel Webster might say hereafter that from the moment when John Brown swung between heaven and earth, might be dated the beginning of the end of American slavery and the disruption of the American Union. Thus is the parallel rendered complete. The first revolution began in the death of Crispus Attucks, the colored man. The second will begin in the death of John Brown. The first was a sanguinary struggle of seven long years. The second is to be of the same character, taking its hue and complexion¦ from the events at Harper's Ferry, and according to the Rev. Mr. Wheelock, inaugurating the "new era of the anti-slavery cause," in which "to moral agitation will be added physical, to argument action¦ for other devoted men will follow in the wake of John Brown, and carry on to its full results the work he has begun." It is the logic of bayonets, and rifles and pikes that is henceforth to convince the slave holders of the South. This, says Mr. Andrew, 'is the eternal and heaven sustained nature of the irrepressible conflict.' The same gentleman invokes 'the holy memories' of the Old South Church, and then turns to 'the battle ground of Concord.'

"Ralph Waldo Emmerson follows up these revolutionary parallels by tracing the genealogy of John Brown back to one of the pilgrims in the *Mayflower*, and showing that his grandfather was a Revolutionary captain, and

"'Our Captain Brown,' says Mr. Emmerson, 'is happily a representative of the American Republic. He did not believe in *moral* suasion, but in *putting things through!*'

"No doubt in the next edition of Emmerson's 'Representative Man,' the name of John Brown will have a most conspicuous place.

"'What a favorite will he be in history,' continues the abolition leader. 'Nothing can resist it. No man dare believe that there exists in their generation another man as worthy to live, as deserving of public and private honors.'

"The extremists in the French Revolution set up a naked courtesan for public worship as the 'Goddess of Liberty.' The orators of the second American Revolution propose the apotheosis of John Brown, after he dies the death of a murderer on the gallows—a man of whom the leading journalists of his own party in Kansas has admitted, that he took five respectable men —heads of families—out of their beds at dead hour of night, and mutillated and murdered them in cold blood. This, no doubt, Garrison, Rev. Messrs. Manning and Neal, and the rest, would call "doing God's service," and the brigand and the assassin, stained with the blood of his fellow-men, will be worshipped after death. His gallows will be the emblem and symbol of nigger redemption, and bits of the rope with which he will be hanged, will be sold at enormous prices, and be venerated, like pieces of the true cross. He will be regarded as a second Saviour, whose sacrificial blood has ransomed the black race His words and acts will become a new gospel, and the evangelists of revolution will present it from Maine to Virginia.

"Mr. Emerson gave the true interpretation to the object of the meeting and of the collection of the "sinews of war," when he said :

"I hope then, that in addition to our relief to the family of John Brown, we shall endeavor to relieve all those in whose behalf he suffers, and all *those who are in sympathy with him*, and not forget to aid him also, in the best way, by securing freedom and independence in Massachusetts itself."

"What Mr. Emerson means by the latter, he replies :

"He says that if any citizens of that State is summoned as a witness to Virginia, the *process of law must be resisted by force, if habeas corpus will not do*, that becomes a nuisance, and the citizens must rely upon the *substance*, instead of the *empty form*—in other words, we must go back to the *original right of resistance and revolution, and nullify the constitution, and the laws?* For such an object Mr. Emerson intimates that pecuniary and other aid will be wanted.

"Thus is the Republican party hurried along on the dark stream of its destiny by a power which its moderate leaders cannot resist. The party consists of two elements—one the political, the other the fanatical. The political wants merely spoils and power, and to that end keeps up the anti-slavery agitation, in which it has no faith. The other element— the fanatical, or abolition, pure and simple— is perfectly sincere, like John Brown, and is rapidly leavening the whole party. Already the Republicans are more than half Abolitionized, and the process is still going on, at a fearful speed. The moderate men will be carried away by the resistless current, and when the politicians, who always go with the strongest side, find out the strength of the revolutionary element, they will yield themselves up to its sweeping energy, preferring to be borne on the crest of the wave rather than to be overwhelmed beneath its weight."

In a speech in Philadelphia, 1863, Colonel FORNEY delivered himself as follows:

"A year ago this night, when an assemblage not so enthusiastic as this did me the honor to pay me a visit, I took a liberty with them; and for that I have since that time been slandered by all the copperheads, from Wm. H. Reed, to Chas. J. Biddle, ("up" or "down" as you may please to make it.) I asked the band to play a national hymn, the hymn of John Brown (Cheers.) I asked them to play the great poem or great epic which told to the world that the soul of that martyr, who fell because of his hostility to slavery, was still marching on, and I tell you gentlemen, it is marching on. (Cries of "that's so," and tremendous cheering) John Brown's knapsack is not only strapped to his back, but his soul is marching on: aye, his soul is commingling with yours. Now, gentlemen, in conclusion let me ask the band (a year ago the band that came here scarcely knew the tune) to play John Brown; for I suspect it has become as familiar to you as the "Star Spangled Banner" or "Hail Columbia." (Applause)

Do not such insane things prove the prophecy of the *Herald*.

(From the Kansas Herald of Freedom.)

"Old John Brown came to Kansas late in the summer or fall of 1855—that he came armed and in a peculiar manner—that these arms were furnished him in the State of New York —that their supply was made the condition of his coming here—that he showed a bloodthirstiness peculiarly his own, during the Waukarusa War, in December of that year, and that nowhere in his whole Kansas history do we find a particle of evidence that he desired to cultivate the principles of peace.

"We sincerely hope that the future historians of Kansas will take pains to post themselves on these subjects, that they may not do injustice to innocent parties. 'Old John Brown has figured as a hero in Kansas.' The time will come when history will be *ventilated*, and instead of a hero, he will stand before the country in his *true* character. Under cover of night, in the name of religion, *he committed crimes too base for common sinners to meddle with*."

Thus ends our quotations on this subject. We have shown that there was nothing in the life or character of this old horse thief and murderer, John Brown, calculated to draw after him the prayers, the good wishes, or even the sympathies of the wise or virtuous. We therefore, have the right to infer that all those who affected sympathy with John Brown, but manifested their own diabolical guilt, not merely as partakers in his crime at Harper's Ferry; but that higher crime of purposely and treasonably aiding a rebellion to break up the Union. A stretch of unbounded charity may possibly snatch a few "misguided fanatics" from the category of wilful treason, but history will not—cannot—exhonorate them from consequential guilt.

To the guilty Southern disunionists, the general Northern endorsement of John Brown was a God send. They saw in it the means to *develope* to the full a Southern disunion party,

SCRAPS FROM MY SCRAP-BOOK. 73

and the most fervent appeals were made by Yancey, Toombs, Rhett, Davis and other Southern traitors, to arouse the spirit of alarm in the Southern mind, and they met with a success which no other events had enabled them to gloat over.

It gives us no pleasure to record these disgraceful facts, but when our Gibbon shall take up his unbiased pen to write out the impartial history of our Greece and our Rome, he will thank us for collecting these facts, so convenient for his purpose, and when the crimes of this age shall be foliced, not by the penny-a-liner or cheap pamphleteer, but by the historian, who shall look through the telescope of truth, without bias, and scanning the designs of faction through the long vista of the then past, shall present the "logic of our history" to our children's children, as we now read that of our father's fathers.

That the Kansas conflict was stimulated, and the Harper's Ferry affair consummated, and afterwards so boldly endorsed, for the express purpose of so exciting the Northern mind as to cast the entire Northern electoral vote for an exclusively Northern candidate in 1860—that this great leading fact will appear in the unbiased history of the future, together with a full expose of its criminal aims and purposes, we have not the slightest doubt.

On looking back upon the events of the short past, our only wonder is that civil war had not actually broken out in 1859. The fact that it did not, will astonish all who can appreciate the explosive materials of which the American character is composed.

CHAPTER XV.
WISCONSIN NULLIFICATION AND SECESSION.

The Four Shocks of Secession : 1st, New England ; 2d, South Carolina ; 3d, Wisconsin ; 4th, The Confederate States...Wisconsin Bids "Positive Defiance" to the General Government...Constitutional Provisions Relative to Judicial Dicisions...A Premeditated Conspiracy to take Wisconsin Out of the Union...Complete Chronological History of the Booth Case, and Judicial Action thereon...The Federal Supreme Court declare that Wisconsin was the First to Set Up the Supremacy of the State over the Federal Court...Republicans Break Open Arsenal, and Seize Arms to Defy the Power of the Government...Judge Paine's "Eloquent Extract"...Opposition to Law Placed Judge P. on the Bench...The Rescue Leaguers...Republican Meeting to Denounce Law...Judge Crawford Opposed solely because he felt Bound by the Decision of the Federal Court...The Constitution Quoted...Lloyd Garrison declares Fugitive Law Constitutional, but Defies It..."Milwaukee Sentinel" on Habeas Corpus and Jury Trial for Negroes...Opposition to the General Government a Political Test...The "Wisconsin State Journal" on said Test...Various Republican Papers on the Test...Judge Smith's Opinion... No Precedent to Sustain It...What Senator Howe said...

Judge Smith Scouts the Consequences of His Own Acts ...The Seven Points as Proof...The "State Journal" declares "Dissolution no Misfortune"...Republicans Resolve to "Revolutionize the Government"...Republican Papers for Dissolution...To sustain the Decision of the Federal Court declared a Crime...Republicans claim that Judge Paine was elected expressly to Defy the Federal Court...Disunionists in Mass Convention...General Government again Defied...Republicans endorse Southern Nullification...Wisconsin Legislature "Positively Defies" the Federal Government...Substitute to Sustain the Government Voted Down...Doolittle's Views...Northern Nullification a Twin of Southern Nullification... Wisconsin endorses South Carolina and South Carolina endorses Wisconsin.

THE WISCONSIN CONSPIRACY.

" O, pity, God, this miserable age !—
What stratagems ! how fell ! how butcherly,
Erroneous, mutinous, unnatural,
This deadly quarrel daily doth beset ! "
[*King Henry* VI.

" Between the acting of a dreadful thing
And the first motion, all the interim is
Like a phantasma, or a hideous dream ;
The genius and the mortal instruments
Are there in council, and the state of a man,
Like a little kingdom, suffers then
The nature of an insurrection."
[*Shakspeare's Julius Cæsar.*

During the life of this Government, it has experienced four shocks of sesession. Startle not, for such is the truth of history. Sesossion does not necessarily consist in actually taking up arms and mustering hostile forces against the General Government, but it consists in treasonable resolves, defiant denunciations and authoritative declarations by the people by legislative bodies, and by Supreme Court decisions, *positively defying* the General Government. As we have already seen, Massachusetts, Connecticut and Rhode Island seceded from the Union in 1814. They were the pioneers in the criminal work of sesession, and by the blue light of the Hartford Convention, we read their treasonable anathemas, their criminal hatred of our Common Country, and their threats of "positive defiance," hurled boldly against the General Government.

In 1833 South Carolina seceded from the Union, as far as that treasonable State could, without successful revolution. She bid positive defiance to the General Government, and threatened to, and did resist its laws.

In 1854 and to 1859 Wisconsin followed in the wake of old treasonable Massachusetts, and traitorous South Carolina. Yes, Wisconsin seceded from the Union ! So far as it was possible for the reigning majority to take her out of the Union, they did it. The Supreme Court, composed of members who were elected expressly on the *issue of defiance* to the General Government, took the broad ground of Calhoun nullification, and seceded from the authority of the Federal Government. The Executive followed, in 1858, recommended resistance to the General Government—repeated it in 1859, when the legislative department endorsed the recommendation, and passed resolves, which the Governor signed, bidding *"positive defiance"* to the power of the Federal Union. Thus, by the conjoint action of her Judiciary, her Executive and Legislative Departments, Wisconsin seceded from the Union, by placing herself in open and undisguised hostility to the Government.

The constitution of the United States provides that—

"This constitution and the laws of Congress passed in pursuance thereof, shall be the supreme law of the land, and obligatory upon the judges in every State."

And the same constitution declares:

"The judicial power [of the United States] shall extend to all cases in law and equity, arising under this constitution, the laws of States," &c.—*Art. III, Sec. II.*

This is plain, unequivocal language, and defined by the highest court in the nation to mean just what it says—giving exclusive, final jurisdiction to the Federal Court over all laws passed by Congress, &c.

In 1793 Congress passed a Fugitive Slave Law, which the Supreme Court of the United States had decided in accordance with the provisions of the constitution of the United States. This ought to have settled the matter, and did settle it so far as judicial, or any official action could. Nothing short of *revolution* and disunion could overrule the decision and the law, unless the same power that enacted and adjudicated it. Any opposition, *vict armis*, or by legally constituted subordinate tribunals, was nothing short of *rebellion and revolution*, to the extent such opposition was carried.

We shall show, and we blush to record the fact, as a disgrace to our adopted State, that the party in power entered into a conspiracy to place Wisconsin in antagonism to the General Government, and by such antagonism, to retire it out of the Union.

We shall show that it was no child's play—no "lapsus judico"—no mistake of judgment—but a premeditated conspiracy, formidable in numbers, and dangerous from its association of power.

These politicians, knowing their obligations to the Federal Government to peaceably abide by all decisions of the superior Federal tribunal, until legally reversed, boldly set up the standard of revolt, and set an example which the traitors of the South were too willing to follow, for the truth of which let facts and history be summoned as witnesses.

On the 11th day of March, 1854, Sherman M. Booth, one of the most active, influential Republicans of Wisconsin, headed a mob in Milwaukee to forcibly rescue Joshua Glover, a refugee slave, who was then in the custody of the law, "on claim" of the one to whom his "servicess" had been adjudged as "due," under the Constitution of his country. It was a violent mob, that broke into the jail and forcibly took therefrom the object of their violence.

For this act of mob violence, Booth, with others, was arrested and brought before United States Commissioner Winfield Smith, who decided that Booth should be held to bail, to appear and answer before the United States District Court of Wisconsin, on the first Monday of July next ensuing. But on the 26th of May, (interim,) his bail, for some cause, delivered him up to the United States Marshal, in presence of the Commissioner, and requested that Booth be committed. Booth failed to again recognize, and was delivered to the keeper of the Milwaukee jail, to await the course of law.

On the 27th of May, Booth made application to Hon. A. D. Smith, one of the Justices of the Supreme Court of Wisconsin, for a writ of *habeas corpus*, stating that Stephen V. R. Ableman, United States Marshal, had unjustly restrained him of his liberty, and alleged that his detention was illegal, because the Fugitive Act, under which he was committed, was unconstitutional, though he knew the highest court in the land had decided it constitutional.

On the same day, Judge Smith allowed the writ, and directed the Marshal to bring the prisoner before him, which was complied with.

To the Marshal's return Booth *demurred*, as not sufficient in law to justify his detention.

Upon the hearing, Judge Smith ordered the Marshal to release the prisoner, which was done.

On the 9th of June following, the Marshal applied to the Supreme Court for a *certiorari*, and praying to have the proceedings brought to the Supreme Court for revision. This was allowed the same day, and was issued on the 12th of the same month. On the 20th Justice Smith

SCRAPS FROM MY SCRAP-BOOK. 75

made return, stating the proceedings before him:

On the 19th of July the case was argued before the Supreme Court of that state, and judgment was announced, affirming the decision of the Associate Justice.

On the 26th of October the Marshal sued out a writ of error to the Federal Supreme Court, returnable on the first Monday of December, 1854, in order to bring the judgment there for revision, and the defendant in error, (Booth) was cited to appear on that day. L. F. Kellogg, Esq., Clerk of the Supreme Court of Wisconsin, was directed to and did certify the record to the Federal Court—thus showing that the Wisconsin Court acknowledged the superior jurisdiction of the Federal Court on the 4th of December, 1854. Booth filed a memorandum in the Federal Court, and submitted a printed argument which was used before the Wisconsin Court.

Before this writ of error was sued out, the Supreme Court of Wisconsin entered on the record that they had decided the law of 1793 and 1850 unconstitutional, respectively.

Be it remembered, that at this time the Supreme Court of Wisconsin did not deny their obligation to obey the writ of error, and it went so far as to state minutely what the points were that they had decided—the non validity of the fugitive law, so that the Federal Court could have no difficulty in determining what to act on (?) and pronouncing its judgment thereon.

This matter rested in the Superior Court till the December term of 1858, so as to act upon the second Booth case, at the same time—both involving the same principle. And *be it remembered that while this case was pending* most of the following revolutionary history occurred—some of it even after it had been decided.

The second Booth case may be thus stated:

On the 4th of January, 1855, the Grand Jury of Milwaukee county found a bill of indictment against Booth for the part he took in the rescue mob, and on the 9th his counsel moved to quash the indictment, which the court over-ruled, and he plead not guilty. On the 10th a jury was empanelled to try the case. Byron Paine, now one of the Justices of the Supreme Court of the state, was his counsel.— On the 13th he was found guilty. On the 16th he moved for a new trial, which was argued on the 20th, and on the 23d the Court over-ruled the motion, and sentenced the prisoner to prison one month, and to pay a fine of $1,000 and costs, and to remain in custody till the sentence should be complied with. No one pretends he did not have a fair and impartial trial.

On the 26th of the same month the prisoner filed a petition in the Supreme Court of the state, that he was illegally convicted, because the law under which he was convicted was unconstitutional, &c., and asked for a writ of *habeas corpus*, with a view to his release. On the 27th the Court issued two *habeas corpus* writs, one directed to Sheriff Conover, of Milwaukee, and the other to Marshal Ableman.

On the 30th, the Marshal made his return, denying the jurisdiction of the Court, and citing the sentence and conviction of the District Court as his authority for holding the prisoner—that he had delivered the prisoner to the sheriff of Milwaukee county, &c. On the same day Sheriff Conover produced Booth in Court, when the constitutionality of the Fugitive Law was again drawn in question.

On the 2d of February following, the case was heard, and on the 3d the court decided the imprisonment illegal, and ordered Booth's discharge, and he was set at liberty.

On the 21st of April following, the Attorney General of the United States presented a petition to the Chief Justice of the Federal Court, accompanied with all the papers in the original case, duly certified by the Clerk of the Wisconsin Court, and praying that a Writ of Error might be issued to bring the action of the State Court up for revision. The writ was accordingly issued, and returnable on the first Monday of December, 1855, and the Defendant in Error cited to appear on that day.

No return having been made to this writ, the Attorney General of the United States, on the 1st of February, 1856, filed affidavits, showing that the writ of error had been duly served on the Clerk of the Supreme Court of Wisconsin, on the 20th of May, 1855, and the citation served on the defendant on the 28th of June following. An affidavit was also filed, from the United States District Attorney of Wisconsin, stating further that the clerk and one of justices of the Wisconsin Court had informed him

"that the court had directed the clerk to make no return to the writ of error, and to enter no

order upon the journal or records of the court containing the same."

Upon these proofs, the Attorney General of the United States moved the court for an order upon said clerk, to make return on or before the first day of the next ensuing term of the Federal court. The rule or order was accordingly laid, and the 22d of July, 1856, the said Attorney General filed with the clerk of the Federal court the affidavit of the United States Marshal of Wisconsin, that he had served the rule on the clerk, and no return having been made, the Attorney General, on the 27th of February, 1857, moved for leave to file a certified copy of the record of the Supreme Court of Wisconsin, and to docket the case in that form, and on the 6th of March, 1857, the case in that form was docketed, but the case was not reached for argument till the following term—1858.

Chief Justice Taney, in uttering his decision, remarked:

"And it further appears that the State Court have not only claimed and exercised this jurisdiction, but have also determined *that their decision is final and conclusive* UPON ALL THE COURTS OF THE UNITED STATES! and ordered their Clerk to disregard and refuse obedience to the writ of error issued by this Court, pursuant to the act of Congress of 1789, to bring here for examination and revision the judgment of the State Court.

"*These propositions are new in the jurisprudence of the United States, as well as of the states, and the supremacy of the state courts over the courts of the United States,* in cases arising under the Constitution and laws of the United States, *is now for the first time* asserted and acted upon in the Supreme Court of a state!!*"*

It seems that the Federal Court was unanimous in the decision they made, and although they say "we think it unnecessary to discuss this question" (that court having on several occasions decided it) still, as

"We [the Judges] are not willing to be misunderstood, it is proper to say, that in the judgment of this court, the Act of Congress, commonly called the Fugitive Slave Law, is, *in all its provisions*, fully authorized by the constitution of the United States."—21 *Howard*, pp. 514-26.

The judgment of the State court was therefore *reversed.*

After this decision was announced, Booth was re-arrested, and the Republican Legislature having in the meantime passed a law forbidding the use of jails in the State for such purposes, he was confined in an apartment of the Milwaukee United States Custom House, to serve out his sentence.

After he had thus been in durance vile for some time, a Republican mob, headed by one Edward Daniels, [who was afterwards appointed by Gov Randall as Colonel of the 1st Wisconsin Cavalry] forcibly rescued him from his confinement, when Booth took refuge among his disunion friends at Ripon, an intensely abolition district in the interior of the State. To this place he was followed by the Deputy United States marshal who sought, in the discharge of his official duty to arrest him, but the said marshal was set upon by an armed mob of Abolitionists, was roughly handled, and on one occasion, barely escaped with his life.

For a long while the officers of the law were baffled in their efforts to retake the prisoner. The Abolitionists had broken open the Arsenal at Fond du Lac and seized the arms therein, which enabled them to keep at bay the Federal officers, and intimidate all opposition.

Finally, by mere strategy Booth was captured and replaced in the Custom House at Milwaukee, where he was thoroughly guarded and kept till near the close of Mr. Buchanan's administration, when he was finally pardoned by that functionary.

Such in brief is the history of the Booth war, wherein the whole Republican party of the state acted the most vindictive and treasonable part. We have been thus particular to note the dates and progress of the revolution, that the reader may be the better able to appreciate contemporaneous events; all tending to the same general end—resistance to law and defiance to constitutional authorities—which we shall proceed to delineate.

The Hon. BYRON PAINE, now one of the Justices of the Supreme Court of Wisconsin, as we have seen, was BOOTH'S counsel. The closing of his speech on the occasion was published in nearly all the Republican papers as an "eloquent extract." We copy the following portion of it from the Wisconsin *State Journal*, the central organ of the party in the state, of January 31, 1855. In denouncing the fugitive law, while that law, in all its ports, was then before the highest tribunal of the land for adjudication, he assured the jury,

"No, gentlemen, the people of this country *never will obey this law*—and on the spirit which prompts to this disobedience, I hang all my hopes for the perpetuation of our liberties. * * * Our country is passing through a fiery ordeal. Men may weakly shut their eyes to the truth, but it cannot be disguised. They may cry *peace! peace!* but that *will not* still the raging waves of the ocean. * * If we are to have a government of force, that executes is laws with bristling bayonets, and bellowing cannon, and troops red with the blood of the people, it will be to the institution of slavery we shall owe it."

It is unfortunate that Mr. PAINE did not tell the jury that there need be no execution of the laws by "bristling bayonets," if his partizans would obey the laws, and not follow in the wake of South Carolina nullification. But again:

"You may commit this defendant to prison, but think you there is a man within the jurisdiction of this court, *that for this, would sooner obey the fugitive act?*"

Thus was the threat thrown out, that if the jury did convict BOOTH, he and his partizans would continue to resist the fugitive law.

That speech was the lever that placed Mr. PAINE on the supreme bench. He had had no such legal experience and reputation as would entitle him to such a responsible position. No tongue had lisped his name—no pen had chronicled his fitness for such high honors, till the denouement of that "maiden speech," which was attuned to the revolutionary spirit that had possesion of his party. Gen. RUFUS KING, editor of the Milwaukee *Sentinel*, and HORACE RUBLEE, editor of the *State Journal*, with others of the State Central Committee, issued an address to the people, calling on them to sustain Mr. PAINE for Judge, and basing his qualifications on his opposition to the Fugitive Law; and the press of that party throughout the state urged his "claims" on that ground exclusively. Indeed, the only real issue between the two parties was support of law and order on the part of the Democrats, and opposition to particular laws on the part of the Republicans.

The Republicans organized "*Rescue Leagues*" in different portions of the state, and amassed a "*Rescue Fund*," for the purpose of aiding and abetting the violators of law. RUFUS KING was chairman of the *Rescue Fund League* in Milwaukee, and on the 13th of February, 1855, issued an address, or circular, to the faithful from which we select the following:

"The committee have only to recommend, in conclusion, to their fellow-citizens of Wisconsin, that an organization be effected in *each school district in the state*, and a sub-committee appointed to collect and forward without delay to the address of Mr. E. D. Holton, whatever sums the lovers of justice and liberty may be disposed to give in aid of the "Rescue Friends Fund." They leave it to friends and *sympathisers* out of the state to determine in what time and manner their contributions shall be made, with the single remark, that whatever is given will be thankfully received and faithfully applied.

"By order of Committee,   RUFUS KING, Ch'n.
'EDWARD D. HOLTON, Treasurer.
"Milwaukee, Feb. 12, 1855."

The following was the committee:—RUFUS KING, JOHN H. TWEEDY, EDWARD D. HOLTON, EDWARD WUNDERLY, EDWIN PALMER, (now collector at Milwaukee,) of Milwaukee, F. W. D. BERNARD of Racine, and DAVID TAYLOR of Sheboygan, (now circuit judge)--all leading *Repulicans*.

The Republicans of Racine county held a meeting at Ives' Grove, on the 5th of January, 1856, to organize "a *County League* and unite for the *overthrow of the slave oligarchy of the country.*" The following is the 7th resolution unanimously adopted:

"*Resolved*, That we will stand by the *Rescuers of Glover*, with our influence, our purse, and *our right arms*, and *no court shall crush them—no prison walls or bars shall ever confine them,*" &c.

This was announced in the Racine Republican paper, with a flourish of trumpets, and the editor set forth that "a great number of delegates were in attendance."

On the 25th of January, 1855, immediately on the conviction of BOOTH and RYCRAFT, the *State Journal*, the court organ of the party, said:

"Here are two citizens of our State imprisoned and fined *for what ninety-nine one hundredths of the people will declare a* NOBLE ACT. * * The whole people [meaning the Republicans, of course,] *rejoiced at the escape of Glover*, and almost unanimously applauded the *conduct of the rescuers.* Should another similar outrage [that is should a Southern man claim a run away slave, under the constitution] upon humanity occur in Milwaukee to-day, a similar course would be pursued."

On the 26th of July, 1855, a mass meeting of Republicans was held in Milwaukee, to encourage resistance to law, which was announced in flaming letters by the *State Journal* on the 31st, and in other leading Republican papers, who endorsed the meeting in all its acts. The first resolution of the meeting declares it to be an outrage to empanel a jury to try such cases, &c.

"*Resolved*, That we desire to record an earnest and emphatic protest against the manner as well as results of the recent rescue trials in this city—that we regard the course pursued by the officers of the United States Court, in empanneling the grand and petit jurors as a gross and inexcusable *outrage upon law and right;* * * * that we *sympathise deeply* with the *victims of judicial tyranny*, official wrong and oppression, and unconstitutional legislation; that *our hearts are with them in the prison* in which they have been confined, and our hands are ready to liquidate the penalties imposed upon them."

If Booth's fine could have been paid by resolutions, it would have been instantly "liquidated," but these selfish politicians could write declamatory and treasonable resolutions easier than they could "shell out" the means. Although they often resolved, and made a great ado for political effect, they failed to pay Booth's fine. Their patriotism never extended so deep as their pockets.

Judge CRAWFORD, the only Democrat on the Supreme bench, refused to go with his brother judges, and declare the Fugitive Act unconstitutional. The *State Journal*, in alluding to the decision at the time, in speaking of Judge C.'s separate opinion, said:

"He considered the decision of the Supreme Court of the United States on *this* and all other matters as *binding on the State Courts*."

The *Journal* continued:

"Justice Smith's opinion was lengthy and covered the whole ground. He reiterates his former views relative to the unconstitutionality of the Fugitive Act. He took a *very decided* position with regard to *State Rights*, and held that the United States Courts had *no jurisdiction*, except in matters where jurisdiction was clearly granted them by the constitution [but Acts of Congress gave them no jurisdiction, if Republican judges did not like those acts!] The State courts must protect the rights and liberties of their citizens, and if in the prosecution of their duty, they were brought in *collision* with the *United States Courts*, no dangerous consequences would ensue."

That is, no dangerous consequences would ensue, if the Republican party of Wisconsin were not interfered with in nullifying laws. The same article concludes:

"The man Glover was borne [by Republican law breakers] beyond the reach of his hunters; the popular heart was stirred [by politicians and nobody else] to its *lowest* depths; and after this display of the quality of Southern chivalry, no slave hunter need *hereafter* pursue his fugitive human chattels across the Southern boundary of Wisconsin with any hope of success."

In this connection, we copy the following from a document not respected by the Republicans of Wisconsin:

"No person held to service or labor in one State, under the *laws thereof*, escaping into another; shall in consequence of any law or regulation therein, be discharged from such service or labor, but *but shall be delivered up upon claim of the party* to whom such service or labor may be due."—*Art. IV, Sec. II, Constitution United States.*

In this connection, we present the honest opinions and declaration of an honest, though dangerous abolitionist. Mr. LLOYD GARRISON was summoned before the committee of Federal Relations of the Massachusetts Legislature, to give his views on the pending bills to nullify the Fugitive Act. They had worked up this, that and the other excuse, indigenous to abolition climates, as reasons why the Fugitive Act was unconstitutional, &c. Mr. GARRISON answered them in the following manner:

"I cannot, gentlemen, place the same construction upon the constitution, respecting the rendition of fugitive slaves, which my respected friend, Mr. Sewall, has done. I cannot plead that it is not in the bond to give up the fugitive slave. It is for those who can to do so— for myself, I cannot *out-face* this nation, and say that for seventy years, it has never understood its own constitution, in this particular. *I believe that Massachusetts consented, with her eyes open, and for the sake of making a Union with the South possible, to allow the slave hunter to come here and take his property; and I would not spend one moment in attempting to argue, on the words of the Constitution, that we have never agreed to do any such thing.* I believe that the *intent* of the bargain, *whatever may be the language used*, and I would not try to get rid of an obligation, however unjust, by false interpretation of the instrument.

"I believe Washington, Franklin, Hamilton, Jefferson, Jay and Marshall, and all those who made the Constitution, and the people who adopted it, understood what they were about. They knew that they agreed to allow a slave representation in Congress, yet the *words* are not to be found in the Constitution. They intelligently agreed and deliberately agreed that the foreign slave trade should be prosecuted for the term of twenty years [but it would not for more than twelve years, but for the vote and influence of Massachusetts] without Congressional intervention; yet, they did not allow the term 'slave trade' to be inserted in the Constitution. *They also understandingly agreed*

SCRAPS FROM MY SCRAP-BOOK. 79

that slaves who should escape from their masters into other states, should be given up. Why, gentlemen, the Fugitive Slave law itself, which creates such universal disgust and horror [only by the politicians for political effect] does not contain the words 'runaway slave,' or 'slave holder,' or 'slave catcher;" in its language it is entirely unexceptionable. *It is the language of the Constitution of the United States!*

"What a waste of time and effort it would be to argue, from the phraseology of that nefarious law, that it was never designed by Congress to refer to fugitive slaves! *Enough, that for seventy years, all the courts, all the legislatures, all the congresses, and all the people, have unerstood these compromises of the Constitution in precisely the same way, and pronounced them obligatory!* It is too late, therefore, to get up a new and unwarrantable construction of the Constitution, in order to *justify* us in doing right and obliging God!— All I have to say is, as one holding loyalty to God, to be paramount in all cases, I care not, though every word in the Constitution be for slavery, or every sentence an argument on our part to stand by it; in that case it is all null and void, and a crime of the deepest dye for us to carry it out, and so I stand here on the ground of eternal justice, and appeal to the law of the living God, and ask you to do likewise."

Give us honesty before hypocracy. We therefore prefer GARRISON, as a consistent, outspoken, bold, bad man, to all those who hypocritically strike down the Constitution on pretext of saving it.

THE HABEAS CORPUS AND JURY TRIAL FOR NEGROES.

The Milwaukee *Sentinel*, the leading Republican organ in the State, in speaking of the decision of our Supreme Court in the rescue cases, said:

"Wisconsin is, and will remain a *free State*, and while she claims no right, and cherishes no desire to intermeddle in the domestic affairs of her sister sovereignties, she will at least assert and exercise at all times, and *at every hazard* the power to protect her own citizens, and to maintain and defend, in all their integrity, the writ of *habeas corpus* and right of trial by jury."

This was said in reference to the trial of black men, in 1854, but in 1863, the same paper gloried in the arrest and imprisonment of *white* men, without charge, judge, jury, or trial. As we cannot believe the Republicans *really* esteem black men higher than they do white men, we are led to take their vaporings in 1854-5, as nothing but so much fuel to fan the flame of popular excitement and dissolution.

OPPOSITION TO THE GENERAL GOVERNMENT —A POLITICAL TEST.

As proof that faith in the decision of the Supreme Court, and consequently organized political opposition to the General Government, in the execution of its laws, was made the *test* of political orthodoxy, we quote from the Wisconsin *State Journal*, the central Republican organ of the State, of February 15, 1855.

It must be noted, that Judge CRAWFORD, a Democrat, whose term of office was about to expire, had been called upon by the conservatives of all parties to become a candidate for re-election. As a man of ability and uprightness of character, he was pre-eminent. Even the "court organ," the *Journal*, was compelled to thus speak of him:

"It is of very great importance that a worthy man, and one competent to discharge the high responsibilities of the station, should be chosen. Judge Crawford is a man of fair abilities, of good address, possessing the elements of personal popularity in a high degree. When we have once got a good man upon the Supreme bench, good policy dictates that *he should be kept there*, until there is some good reason for filling his place with another. There is *one* objection, however, to Mr. Crawford—*his position with regard to the Fugitive Slave Act*.— [That is, he had decided that he, as a judge of an inferior tribunal was bound by the decisions of the Federal Supreme Court. *That* was his *only* offense.] A very great majority of the people of the State, sustain most cordially the opinions of the Chief Justice (Whiton) and Justice Smith. They will be aware that the election of Judge Crawford will go abroad, and will be received at Washington by the present dough-face Administration. [The "government" in modern nomenclature,] as an endorsement of the people of Wisconsin of the opinion, in which Judge Crawford dissented, from the decision of the court, as to the unconstitutionality of that act. We should by no means concede that it was such an endorsement, in case Judge Crawford were elected, but that it will be *declared so abroad*, every man who knows anything will acknowledge.

"Under *these circumstances*, there will be opposition to his (Judge C's) election. *There should be opposition*. If the people of Wisconsin desire to sustain the manly, fearless and *just position* of the Supreme Court, they should elect some man whose *past course* will be deemed a guarantee by them, that he will *sustain the decision* of a majority of the court! If they desire that Wisconsin should continue to occupy, as she *now occupies* an open uncompromising position of *hostility* to the further extensisn of slavery, and to the spread of that institution throughout the northern and free states as a national institution [a common child may understand the drift of this hypocritical rhodomontade] which is the effect of the fugitive act *if it be constitutional*—they will feel themselves bound to oppose the re-election of Judge Crawford. We regret to be obliged to take this ground. [Here we see the power of party drill.] Personally we should gladly see him (Judge C.) re-elected, but having endorsed the *decision* of the Judges, and *rejoiced over it as a great triumph of freedom*—a decision of which the state *may well feel proud*, consistency and a due regard to principle, compel us to believe this course the only proper one."

Now, to say nothing of the bad policy of making judicial decisions in the political caucus room, and selecting candidates cut and dried to announce them, the reader will not fail to see in the foregoing a preconcerted political move to so shape the judiciary of the state as to play into the hands of the political majority, in its treasonable *role* of "defiance" to the powers of the General Government.

FURTHER EVIDENCE OF THE POLITICAL CONSPIRACY.

The Republican papers of the state generally, during the judicial elections, have made the Supreme Court decision the *alpha* and *omega* of their political creed. We select a few specimens:

The Platteville *American*, rep., opposed Judge CRAWFORD and favored Judge COLE:—

"Whose *opinions in regard to the Fugitive Slave Act* are more nearly in accordance with the views of the majority of the voters of the state than Mr. Crawford, who conflicts with the other Judges of the Supreme Court, in deeming the Fugitive Slave Act, with all its obnoxious provisions, its denial of the writ of *habeas corpus*, and trial by jury, perfectly constitutional."

The Columbus *Journal* (Rep.) said:

"Exert that faculty which God has given you, sound common sense, and we have no fears of the result. Come up to the polls manfully on the 3d of April next, and show the world that you are not bound hands and feet to the slave-holders', slave-hunters', and slave-catchers' car, to be dragged, Hector-like, not around the walls of Troy, but the crumbling walls of your temple of liberty."

The Monroe *Sentinel* (Rep.) seemed to have an impression that the Supreme Court had at that time decided the fugitive act constitutional, for it said:

"Recollect that the Supreme Court of the United States, and all its branches, is placed beyond the reach of the will of the people.—The Court, in its pride of place and irresponsible power, has little sympathy with the cause of human freedom. All laws which tend to aggrandize the power of the General Government meet with the sympathy of that Court, for it is a part of that General Government; and here one of the frailties of human nature, selfishness, has a strong position from which to argue the aggrandizement of the whole—

"To make the worse appear the better side."

"The duty, as well as the interest of this generation, the interests of posterity, all combine to create a necessity for bringing back the judicial tribunals of the country, as rapidly as possible, to the standard of the Constitution as it reads and is construed by its authors and framers."

The *State Journal* of March 31st, said:

"When Messrs. Cole and Crawford were first called out, we supposed the real question was mainly, whether the people of this State *were in favor of the enforcement of the Fugitive Slave Act in our State or not;* whether the decision of a majority of the Supreme Court, by which a protecting ægis was interposed between the liberties of her citizens and a tyrannical and unconstitutional statute, were to be sustained."

The Appleton *Crescent*, a Democratic paper, though speaking well of Judge COLE, gave us to understand it understood the "issue," as follows:

"No objection can be urged against him, unless it is that Judge CRAWFORD has a decided advantage over him on account of two years' experience as a member of the Supreme Court, and that Mr. COLE is a staunch believer in the unconstitutionality of the Fugitive Slave Act."

This was thoroughly understood by all classes to be the issue—the Democrats taking ground in favor of *law* because it was law, as interpreted by the highest judicial tribunal —the Republicans taking ground against law, because they could make political capital by "positively bidding *defiance*" to the General Government.

NOTHING TO SUSTAIN JUDGE SMITH'S OPINION.

Judge SMITH, in reading his decision, which thus placed Wisconsin in open hostility to the General Government, seemed to ignore the legal maxim of *stare de cisis*, and also seemed to scout the idea of *res adjudicata*. His "opinion" stands alone, with not a prop to sustain it, save the fiat of the political club room. The *State Journal*, in alluding to his decision at the time, said:

"It is to be regretted *that the haste* with which the opinion was prepared, rendered it *impossible* to fortify the position taken by Judge Smith with reference to the authorities upon which they are founded, and which should accompany an opinion of so much importance."

The Hon. TIMOTHY O. HOWE, (now U. S. Senator) who was then considered conservative, was a member of the Republican State Convention to appoint delegates to the National Convention at Chicago, and also when the case of Judge Dixon came up, wherein the Judge had rendered a decision contrary to Judge SMITH. In reply to CARL SCHURZ, who went the whole Red Republican figure for the SMITH-state-rights doctrine, Senator HOWE said:

"I have seen a pamphlet here which gave more than *two hundred cases*, quoted from all the states of the Union, that sustain the position of Judge Dixon, and not one could be found in opposition."

JUDGE SMITH SCOUTS THE CONSEQUENCES OF HIS DECISION.

The Democracy feared the dreadful consequences of this revolutionary spirit, and they predicted that it would be the parent of collision between the State and the General Government, of civil discord, revolution and dissolution, which predictions were scoffed at by the Abolitionists at the time, and Judge Smith, in a note to his published opinion in the Booth case, takes occasion to treat these fears as ill grounded, &c. He says:

"It is the practice, of late, to hold up before the mind such frightful pictures of 'collision,' 'resistance,' 'civil discord,' 'revolution,' 'anarchy,' and 'dissolution,' that it would seem, that any effort of resistance to the exercise of unauthorized power, and every attempt to faithfully execute official duty, imposed by the constitution and laws, is to be dreaded as an approach to treason—that any diversity of opinion or action between the functionaries of the two governments must necessarily terminate in a dissolution of the Union * * * * But the real danger to the Union consists. not so much in resistance to laws constitutionally enacted, as in acquiescence in measures which violate the constitution."

And after reciting sundry former "collisions" between the General and the State Governments, the Judge comes to the conclusion that those "collisions" are just the thing to keep the Union together. He says:

"But I adduce these facts to show, that these 'collisions,' as they are now called, but which are *merely the healthful operation of the checks and balances which the Constitution has wisely provided*, are not the frightful things which they *are* represented to be."

And he congratulates certain "functionaries" that "the Union still survives."

Wonder what the Judge thinks now of the "check and balances" which he inaugurated to prevent dissolution?

From the great array of facts before us, we have not a particle of doubt that from 1854 to 1859, the leading Republicans of this state were in conspiracy to break up the Union.

1st. Look at their initiation of mobs against the officers of the law

2d. The Supreme Court discharging those mobocrats in defiance of law declared constitutional in all its points, by the highest court known to our laws.

3d. The making this action the test for office by the Republicans.

4th. The recommendation by Gov. RANDALL in his message, of *resistance* to the General Government

5th. The repetition of that recommendation.

6th. The resolutions of the Legislature of 1859, which bid "positive defiance" to the General Government, Supreme Court and all.

7th. The subsequent mobs that took the law into their own hands to enforce the revolutionary decrees of the court, the legislature and the secession politicians.

THE RADICALS WANT A DISSOLUTION.

At a Republican Convention held at Munroe, Green county, Wisconsin, in August, 1856, the following resolution was passed:

"*Resolved*, That it is the *duty of the North*, in case they fail in electing a President and Congress that whill *restore* freedom to Kansas, *to revolutionize the Government!*"

The author of this treasonable resolution was subsequently placed in several responsible positions by the Republican party. Green county has been intensely Republican since the organization of that party.

"DISSOLUTION NO MISFORTUNE"

The Wisconsin *State Journal*, of July 8, 1854, said:

"Now, we believe that if slavery is allowed to broaden and fortify itself without restriction, to grow insolent, intolerant and proscriptive, through the timid acquiescence of the free states, to increase in boldness and greed, for the next quarter of a century in the same ratio that it has for the past, that the ends sought to be accomplished in the formation of the Union will no longer be attained. *Disunion then would certainly be no misfortune!*"

If disunion was not in the heart, it would not escape from the lips.

"We repeat the assertion, that the Union *is not worth a copper to the North in any point of view*, but is a perpetual sacrifice of both money and morals, an assertion we can make good."—*Mil. Free Democrat*, 1859.

MORE TREASON CROPPING OUT.

The Elkhorn, (Wis.) *Independent*, a violent Republican sheet, in 1859, said:

"The Union may be dissolved, *but slavery must die*, and if it can only die or be restricted to its present limits, *through a dissolution of the Union*, then *in the name of the Framers of the Union*, who made it to secure the blessings of liberty. *let the Union be dissolved!*"

A CRIME TO SUSTAIN THE LAW AS EXPOUNDED BY THE FEDERAL COURT.

Just after the Supreme Court of the United States had decided the DRED SCOTT case, the Republicans of Racine county held a grand council, and

Resolved, That the decision of the Supreme Court in the Dred Scott case, and the endorsement thereof by the Democratic party, *is an insult to the memory of the founders of our country*—a violation of the plainest principles of natural and constitutional law—a perversion of history and an encroachment upon the rights of the States, and a blow struck at the inalienble rights of man."

So much for the arrogance of a political party that failed to inform the world from whence they derived their authority, to sit in judgment to revise the "natural laws" of God, and the decisions of the Supreme Court of the United States.

JUDGE PAINE "ELECTED WITH SPECIAL REFERENCE TO HIS VIEWS.

We have before stated that Judge PAINE was elected to the Supreme Bench, not so much on account of his judicial lore, as because he was pre-committed against the validity of the Fugitive law, or because his supporters awarded him that position. When the second BOOTH case came before the Court, Judge P. from a professional and judicial sense of the impropriety, refused to sit in the case, having been counsel for the defendant. For this the State Rights disunionists soundly berated him, as it left the Court without a majority to get up an actual conflict with the General Government.

The next morning after Judge PAINE refused to sit in the case, the Milwaukee *Free Democrat*, a most violent Republican sheet, issued the following bull of excommunication:

"The news from Madison informs us that Judge Paine refuses to sit in the *habeas corpus* with reference to Booth, leaving the decision of the case to Cole and Dickson. The result of this will probably be, the ultimate failure of the application [which was true, and the only thing that saved the State from the terrors of civil war.] The State Rights men of the State have got themselves into a peculiar position. With a majority of from seven to twelve thousand in the State, they are, nevertheless, paralyzed and powerless. [This shows that they relied on the caucus-room to govern the bench.] They, themselves, appear to have made a *mistake* in electing a man to the bench, who finds himself unable to be of any *service in the matter, for which almost exclusively he was preferred to many others;* while the Governor finds he made a mistake with reference to his appointee (Dickson.) Doubtless the delicacy of Judge Paine will be appreciated by the profession, but we fear the great mass of the people [the politicians] will fail to understand it. He is not ruled off by any statute or positive prohibition. He was once counsel for Booth in connection with this matter, though not upon this particular point, if we understand it, and retires in obedience to custom or common law. *He was elected, however, with special reference to his views on this point.* His views are no better known than those of Cole, who has once decided the case."

THE DISUNIONISTS IN MASS CONVENTION.

Several years ago the Republicans held a Mass State Convention, and closed their resolutions by declaring that the decision of the Supreme Court in the DRED SCOTT case:

"Has absolved the state from all obligation to regard them [fugitives from labor] as belonging to that class of "persons" who are to be delivered up as owing service or labor."

Capt. BROWN, of Kansas, and GERRIT SMITH aderessed the Convention. BOOTH was Chairman of the Committee on Resolutions. Several collections were taken up to aid the spread of the "cause" in Kansas and Kentucky.

THE GENERAL GOVERNMENT AGAIN DEFIED.

January 1857 the Republicans put forth a "platform," from which we take the following "plank." The heading or preamble sets out that

"The *people* of Wisconsin in Mass Convention assembled, in view of the alarming encroachments of the slave power, manifested through the Legislative, Executive and *Judi-*

cial *Departments* of the Federal Government," &c.

One of the planks is the following:

"That we cling to the sovereignty and rights of the *states* and to the protecting power of the *state courts* against the *encroachments* and *usurpations of the Federal Government*, as the sheet anchor of our liberties, and that we pledge ourselves to sustain the *state* courts and the *state* government in protecting the liberties of the people [that is the liberty of the politicians to violate law] *at all hazards and in all emergencies!*"

REPUBLICANS QUOTE SOUTHERN NULLIFIERS AS PROPER EXEMPLARS.

The following article appeared in the Milwaukee *Free Democrat*. It shows from what source the Republicans drew their nullification sustenance:

"SUPREME COURT OF GEORGIA.—We perceive from our Georgia exchanges that Judge Benning decided that the Supreme Court of Georgia is co-equal and co-ordinate with the Supreme Court of the United States, and not inferior and subordinate to that Court; that as to the reserved powers, the *State Court* is *supreme;* that as to the delegate powers, the United States Court is supreme; that as to the powers both delegated and reserved—*concurrent powers*—both Courts, in the language of Hamilton, are 'equally supreme,' and as a consequence, the Supreme Court of the United States has *no jurisdiction* over the Supreme Court of Georgia, and cannot therefore give it an order, or make it a *precedent.*"—*Charleston (S. C.) paper.*

"The above is the precise doctrine laid down by Mr. Justice Smith, of our Supreme Court, in his opinion announced verbally from written notes, in the case of S. M. Booth's petition for *habeas corpus*, carried to Supreme Court by Ableman on writ of error. And it is undoubtedly the *true doctrine*. For if the Supreme Court—the highest judicial tribunal of the state—is inferior to that of the United States, the *sovereignty* of the state represented by that tribunal must be an *inferior* sovereignty, which would be *no* sovereignty.

"The doctrine announced by the Georgia Judge, (and by Judge Smith, is to the effect that the opinions and decisions of the Supreme Court of the United States were of *no more binding force on the Supreme Courts of the states* than are the opinions and decisions of the latter on the former, and that neither have any more binding force on the other than the decisions of the highest court of England would have to control the action of the highest court of France. Each within its own sphere is the creation of a distinct sovereignty, between whom there is neither superiority nor inferiority, but *exact equality*. But the sphere of the action of these sovereignties is restricted, or limited by the provisions of the compact between the states, granting to the United States certain powers or attributes of sovereignty, and to that extent the states severally divested themselves of those powers and attributes, but all powers not so granted are withheld by the states severally. * * * * * * * * "Such have been the uniform doctrines of the most brilliant statesmen and party leaders *of the South*, and *such are the only doctrines by which this Federal Government can be maintained.*

"The positions taken by Judge SMITH are eminently in the right."

GOV. RANDALL RECOMMENDS "RESISTANCE."

Governor RANDALL, in his message to the Wisconsin Legislature of 1858, said :

"The tendency of the action of the Federal Government has been for many years, *aided by the Federal Courts*, to centralization, and to an absorption of a large share of the sovereignty of the States. *It has trespassed upon the reserved rights of the States and the people —assuming a jurisdiction over them* in their exercise of power undelegated. The Federal Government, so far as there is any sovereignty under our form of Government, is sovereign and independent in the exercise of its delegated powers, and the States are sovereign and independent in the exercise of their reserved powers. The safety of the States in the exercise of these powers, in defense of the lives and properties and liberties of the people, *demands a fair, deliberate opposition and resistance to any attempt* at usurpation or aggression [of which let the Republicans be the sole judges] by the *Federal Government*, its *Courts*, its *officers*, or *agents* upon the reserved rights of the States or the people."

And in his message to the Legislature of 1859, he thus reiterates his views:

"My views, as expressed in my last annual Message, in regard to the relative powers and duties of the State and Federal Governments," &c., "remain unchanged."

HOW THESE DISUNION RECOMMENDATIONS WERE RESPONDED TO.

After having pressed this matter close upon the Legislature for two sessions, that body, being "full in the belief," moved in the matter, during its session of 1859. Mr. N. S. Murphy, Chairman of the Judiciary Committee, introduced a series of "backbone" resolutions, on the 12th of March, which were thus noticed by the *State Journal* of that day:

"REFRESHING—A ROUSER.

"Mr. N. S. Murphy introduced a resolution brim full of genuine Republican doctrine upon the subject of the illegality and unconstitutionality of the proceding of the U. S. Court in relation to the case of S. M. Booth. which resolution assured the Assembly that the gallant young Virginian still lives, and is sound on the 'goose question.'"

Wen these resolutions came up in the afternoon, they were referred to the Committee on Federal Relations, of which Mr. A. E. BOVAY was Chairman, and on the 16th of March Mr. B. reported by substitute, which was the following, and which were passed by a strict party vote—47 to 37. *See p. 892, Assembly Journal* 1859.

"POSITIVE DEFIANCE" TO THE GENERAL GOVERNMENT.

Here are the resolutions as finally passed:

"*Joint Resolution relative to the decision of the United States Supreme Court, regarding the Supreme Court of Wisconsin.*

"*Whereas*, The Supreme Court of the United States has *assumed* appellate jurisdiction, in the matter of the application of Sherman M. Booth, for a writ of *habeas corpus*, presented and prosecuted to final judgment in the Supreme Court of this State, and has, without process, [see before, why they could not get "process"] or any of the forms recognized by law, assumed the power to reverse this judgment, in a matter involving the personal liberty of the citizen, asserted by, and adjudged to him by the regular course of judicial proceedings upon the great writ of liberty, secured to the people of each State by the constitution of the United States.

"*And Whereas*, Such assumption of power and authority by the Supreme Court of the United States to become the final arbiter of the liberty of the citizen, and to override and nullify the the judgments of the State Courts' declaration thereof, is in direct conflict with that provision of the constitution of the United States which secures to the people the benefits of the writ of *habeas corpus*, therefore

"*Resolved, the Senate concurring*, That we regard the action of the Supreme Court of the United States in assuming jurisdiction in the case before mentioned, as an arbitrary act of power unauthorized by the Constitution and virtually superceding the benefit of the writ of *habeas corpus*, and prostrating the rights and liberties of the people, at the foot of unlimited power.

"*Resolved*. That this usurpation of jurisdiction by the Federal Judiciary, in the said case, and without process, is an act of undelegated power, and therefore, without *authority*, *void and of no force*.

"*Resolved*. That the Government framed by the Constitution of the United States, was not made the exclusive or final judge of the extent of the powers delegated to itself [but that Wisconsin was] but that, as in all other cases, of compact among parties, having no common judge, each party has an equal right to judge for itself as well of *infractions*, as of the *mode and measure of redress*.

"*Resolved*, That the principle and construction contended for, by the party which now rules in the counsels of the nation—that the General Government is the exclusive judge of the extent of the powers delegated to it, stop nothing short of despotism, since the discretion of those who administer the Government, and not the Constitution, would be the measure of their powers—that the several states which formed that instrument, being sovereign and independent, have the unquestionable right to judge of its *infraction*, and that a POSITIVE DEFIANCE of those sovereignties, of all unauthorized acts, done, or attempted to be done, under color of that instrument, is the *rightful remedy!*

"Approved March 19, 1859.
(Signed,) "ALX. W. RANDALL, *Governor.*"

MR. HORN'S SUBSTITUTE VOTED DOWN.

While these resolutions were pending, F. W. HORN, (Dem.) offered the following as a substitute, which was rejected by ayes 36, noes 49—a strict party vote. *See p. 863 Assembly Journal*, 1859.

"*Whereas*, The Supreme Court of the United States has totally reversed the decision of the Supreme Court of this State in the case of the United States against Sherman M. Booth; and

"*Whereas*, Every law abiding citizen, no matter what his private views and feelings may be, should acquiesce in the decisions of the highest tribunals known by the Constitution of the United States, to whom the interpretation of the sacred document is especially confided; and

Whereas, It would lead to anarchy and a *dissolution of the Union*, (how prophetic) if the interpretation of that instrument should be usurped by the different State Courts, in *opposition* to the Supreme Court of the United States [this was the Democratic doctrine then, and not as the *Journal* asserted that our Supreme Court could make no original decision of the kind] where it has been placed by those who mutually pledged to each other their "lives, their fortunes and their sacred honor;" therefore

Resolved, by the Assembly, the Senate concurring, That we *will abide by the decisions of the Supreme Court of the United States declared by said Court to be constitutional*, without regard to our own private views and feelings. —*See p.* 778, *Assembly Journal*, 1859.

This shows the determination of the Republicans of Wisconsin to "*positively defy*" the whole power of the General Government, which they proceeded to execute, as we have seen, by sundry armed mobs, &c.

SENATOR DOOLITTLE'S VIEWS.

In a speech by Senator DOOLITTLE in the U. S. Senate February 24th, 1860, he said:

"The great question, in the science of American government is, when the jurisdiction of the state and federal governments came in conflict, who is to decide? It will never do to say that the decisions of the federal court should be received as conclusive. When it usurps power its decisions must not be respected, and are binding upon nobody."

Again: speaking of the writ of *habeas corpus* by state courts to persons arrested and held by virtue of U. S. process, he said:

"Add this doctrine of the Senator from Georgia, and there would be no constitutional limit upon his (a U. S. district judge's) power—whether constitutional or unconstitutional—whether with or without authority of the United States; whether within or outside of his constitutional jurisdiction, with or without cause, by his warrant alone he could arrest any citizen of Wisconsin, try him, sentence him, even to death, and there is no appeal. No *habeas corpus* could reach the prisoner, whether in the state prison or at the foot of the gallows! Where are we? In the United States of America, or at St. Petersburg, under the power of an autocrat, whose will is law, or under the Constitution of the United States, which declares that no person shall be deprived of his liberty but by the process of law, which law must itself be subject always to the constitution of the United States?"

Mr. DOOLITTLE don't talk thus now; *then* it was "*your* ox," &c.—*now* a different rule is urged.

By such arguments were the people of the state educated up to the standard of open resistance to the Federal power, and we have not the least doubt that had the Republicans failed in electing their candidate in 1860, they would, provided they had the same courage, have done precisely what South Carolina did in 1860— and precisely what the Republicans of Green county pledged themselves to do in 1856.

This chapter is a sad one—it galls our state pride to record it, but we should be false to truth and unjust to history, did we omit it. We trust that hereafter, the Republicans of Wisconsin will not have the face to claim *all* the loyalty and all the patrotism. May God forgive them for the wrongs they have done their country.

"LIKE FATHER, LIKE SON"— THE HARTFORD CONVENTION AND WISCONSIN REPUBLICANS.

To show that the Republicans are chips from the old Federal and Nullification blocks, we select a paragraph from the report of the Hartford Convention. This Tory Convention of New England traitors assembled in the city of Hartford, on the 15th of December, 1815. It put forth a disunion report, accompanied by a series of resolutions; from the former we select the following, seasoned with this apropos spice from HENRY IV:

" Treason is but trusted like the fox,
 Who, ne'er so tame, so cherish'd, and lock'd up,
 Will have a wild trick of his ancestors."

"In cases of deliberate, dangerous and palpable 'infractions' of the Constitution, affecting the 'sovereignty' of a 'state' and the 'liberties' of the people, *it is not only the right but the duty of each state to interpose its authority for their protection, in the manner best calculated to secure that end. When emergencies occur which are either beyond the reach of judicial tribunals, or too pressing to admit of the delay incident to their forms, states, which have no common umpire, must be their own judges, and execute their own decisions.*"

JUST WHAT THE SOUTH IS FIGHTING FOR.

Upon which POLLARD, author of the *Southern side of the Rebellion*, remarks:

"This is the doctrine *which the South had always held from the beginning, and for which the South is now pouring out her blood and treasure!*"

SOUTH CAROLINA ENDORSES JUDGE SMITH'S OPINION.

It will be observed that the substance of the Hartford Convention report, and the Republican resolutions of 1859, quoted above, are identical, while many of the words employed are the same, as well as certain phrases, leaving no doubt that their authors must have selected garbled sentences from the treasonable report of the Hartford Convention, as a foundation for their resolutions of "positive defiance." The only real difference is that the Wisconsin resolutions go deeper into resistance and positive defiance than their Federal fathers.

SOUTH CAROLINA QUOTES JUDGE SMITH.

Mr. RHETT, of South Carolina, on the day that treasonable State seceded from the Union, thus endorsed the decision of Judge SMITH, as good enough doctrine for South Carolina to go out of the Union on:

"Sir, the North threaten to fight us back into the Union, after we shall have taken our stand for Southern Independence. They now deny the right of a State to judge of its own grievances and to apply its own remedies, notwithstanding for years, many of the Northern States, Wisconsin in particular, have asserted this right for themselves. I want no better license for our action to-day than the decision of Judge SMITH in the Rescue cases of Wisconsin."

CHAPTER XVI.

REPUBLICANS TRUE TO OLD FEDERAL INSTINCTS.

Classification of parties, principles and arguments, from 1798 to 1863...Thurlow Weed on Greeley...New York Tribune favors Secession...Greeley advocating Peace with Rebels...Mr. Lincoln Advocates the right of Secession...The Republican Congress vote down a Resolution against a Dictatorship...The Ayes and Noes on that Subject...The Constitution again the "Cause of all our Troubles"...Complete overthrow of the Public Liberties...From the New York World...Republicans Raise a "Higher Standard than the Stars and Stripes"...Prefer "Their principles to Fifty Unions"...Who Discourage Enlistments...Reference to Abolition Votes in Congress.

DISLOYALTY AND REVOLUTIONARY SPIRIT OF REPUBLICANS.

[The crowd of other duties, and the necessary haste in which these extracts have been collected—involving the perusal of hundreds of books and newspapers—render it quite impossible to place them in chronological order, but by proper headings it is believed they will be convenient for reference.—COMPILER.]

We have already published enough to show that the leaders of the great party opposed to the Democracy desire the dissolution of the Government, by any means, and have been laboring to that end for seventy-five years.— Under all the dodges and guises of a change of name—shifting of ostensible purposes and objects, they have steadily pursued their destructive course—using the same class of arguments, and resorting to the same class of means to accomplish their purpose. The Federalists of 1812, though professing a different line of policy, used the same class of arguments, and hurled the same species of denunciation against the Government and the principles on which it was founded, as the Federals of 1798—always *professing* to be for the Constitution—yet insisting that Congress, the Executive and the courts had placed a wrong construction on its meaning. The Federal Republican of 1824 used the same class of arguments as the Federals of 1812. The Whig of 1833 was true to the reasoning of his Federal Republican progenitors of 1824, while the Republican or "Union" of the present era goes back to the Hartford Convention for the inspiration of his political history, and while this class of men (the leaders—we do not mean all) profess, as did their Federal progenitors, to revere the Constitution, they scout the idea of ever again enforcing it—laud those who wantonly violate it, and denounce as "traitors" and "copperheads" all who are sincerely devoted to it "as it is," or desire to maintain the "Union as it was." Future generations, that may chance to read the pages of this book, shall not have it to say we slandered the leaders of the Republican or "Union" party, for we shall let them speak for themselves, as AGRIPPA permitted PAUL to plead his own case. If the well studied words and phrases of the leaders of the present party in power do not sustain our charge that they desire a dissolution of this Union, and have been using the slavery question as but a *means* to accomplish the *end*, then let the present and future readers sentence us to the ignominy due to a slanderer.

THURLOW WEED'S TESTIMONY.

THURLOW WEED, late editor of the Albany *Journal*, is good Republican authority. He denounces HORACE GREELEY, the principal leader of the Republican party, with whom the President condescends and delights to correspond with, as the "architect of ruin," and proceeds, "first, while SLIDELL, TOOMBS, MASON, DAVIS, etc., etc., were maturing their schemes for rebellion, and the Gulf States, under their instructions, were seceding, Mr. GREELEY *approved, justified, and invited them to go forward with their treasonable designs*," and—

HERE IS THE EVIDENCE.

"If the cotton states shall become satisfied that they can do better out of the Union than in it, *we insist on letting them go in peace.* The *right* to *secede* may be a revolutionary one, but it *exists* nevertheless. * * * We must ever *resist the right of any state to remain in the Union* and nullify or defy the laws thereof. To *withdraw from the Union is quite another matter. Whenever a considerable section of our Union shall deliberately resolve to go out we shall resist all coercive measures designed to keep them in.* We hope never to live in a Republic whereof one section is pinned to another by bayonets."—*New York Tribune, Nov.* 9, 1860.

"If the cotton states unitedly and earnestly wish to withdraw peacefully from the Union, *we think they should and would be allowed to do so. Any attempt to compel them by force to remain, would be contrary to the principles enunciated in the immortal Declaration of Independence*—contrary to the fundamental ideas on which human liberty is based."—*New York Tribune, Nov.* 26, 1860.

How easy it is for heretics to summon the Bible to their aid, or political disunion lunatics, to summon the "immortal Declaration" or the "fundamental ideas of humanity" as evidence that Dissolution is according to the true *Union* faith! Again:

"If it (the Declaration of Independence) justified the secession from the British Empire, of three millions of Colonists in 1776, *we do not see why it should not* JUSTIFY *the secession of five millions of Southerners, from the Union, in* 1861."—*New York Tribune, Dec.* 17, 1860.

"*Whenever it shall be clear that the great body of the Southern people have become conclusively alienated from the Union and anxious to escape from it,* WE WILL DO OUR BEST TO FORWARD THEIR VIEWS!"—*New York Tribune, Feb.* 23, 1861.

Here, then, during the insipient stages of the Rebellion, we find the great leading organ of the Republican party, pleading for the right of secession, and pledging itself not only to *resist* any coercive measures but to *forward* the *views* of the traitors. No Republican press —no Republican orator—has from that day to this, denounced GREELEY, the author of these disunion sentiments; and why? Because GREELEY always *votes against the Democracy and supports the Republican ticket!!*

GREELEY ADVOCATING PEACE WITH THE REBELS.

To show still further the treasonable *animus* of the *Tribune,* we quote from its reply to Mr. WEED:

"We believe that should *they* (the rebels) be successful and *we* defeated, in the general results of the campaign *now opening,* impartial third parties will say, *that we ought to consent to peace, an the best attainable terms!* Whether we shall take that counsel, or *renew* the struggle [which actually did go against us at Fredericksburg and several other places] as a united people, who have come to understand, and to accept its real character, the *cost* and *suffering* involved, even will determine.

"But we believe the time *will* come—we do not say how soon, as that must depend on the results of the conflicts yet future, when the great powers of Europe will *mediate*—not by blows nor menaces, but by representations— against a *continuance of the struggle, as fruitless, wasteful butchery, and urge a settlement* in the interest of *humanity* and *commerce.*"

These are precisely the grounds on which the Federals of 1814 urged a "settlement."

To this last extract, Mr. WEED replies:

"In simple, direct, unequivocal language, Mr. Greeley says that if we are not successful in the campaign *now* opening, [the campaign of Fredericksburg] our cause and country are lost, and that we must have *peace* upon the 'best attainable terms.'

"This is saying openly and publicly, to the enemy, that they have only to hold out two or three months longer, to secure the triumph of rebellion and slavery. *Had an opposition journal or member of Congress uttered these sentiments, the Tribune would have demanded their removal to Fort Lafayette.*

"Mr. Greeley evades, though he does not deny, that he has communicated with the French Minister and Mr. Vallandigham, suggesting *mediation* to the former and *peace* to the *latter*. In entering upon the question of mediation with a foreign Minister, he *takes issue in violation of law against the* GOVERNMENT! And in opening a correspondence with a representative, whom he is constantly denouncing as a traitor, he commits an offense, I leave others to name and characterize it.

"And now I leave Mr. Greeley. The columns of his own *Tribune* being the exponent and witness, as first *inviting* the withdrawal from the Union, and then, after a hundred thousand lives had been sacrificed, and twelve hundred millions of treasure squandered, demanding the intervention of the Great Powers of Europe, in favor of, "*peace upon the best attainable terms!* 'for the sake of *humanity* and *commerce!*' ".

MR. LINCOLN ON THE RIGHT OF SECESSION.

Mr. GREELEY was not the first to advocate the right of secession and dissolution, nor was Mr. LINCOLN, but Mr. LINCOLN did advocate it as early as the 12th of January, 1848, on a question of reference of a portion of the President's message —*See Ap. Con. Globe,* 1*st Session,* 30*th Congress, p.* 94.

"Any people, any where, being inclined and having the power, have the right to rise up and *shake off the existing government* and form a *new one* that suits *them* better. * * * * Nor is this right confined to cases in which the people of an existing government may choose to exercise it.

Any portion of such people that can, may revolutionize, and may make their own of so much territory *as they inhabit.* More than this, a majority of any portion of such people may revolutionize, putting down a minority, intermingled with or near about them, who may oppose their movements."

THE RADICALS IN CONGRESS SHOW THEIR PURPOSE TO DESTROY THE UNION.

Mr. VALLANDIGHAM, who has been denounced as the "prince of copperheads," introduced a series of resolutions in Congress, testifying to the integrity of the Union, on the 5th of January, 1862, from which we select the following:

"*Resolved,* That the Union as it was must be restored, and maintained, one and indivisible, forever, under the constitution as it is, the 5th Article, providing for amendments, included.

"*Resolved,* That this Government can never permit the intervention of any foreign nation in regard to the present civil war.

"*Resolved,* That no two Governments can ever be permitted to exercise jurisdiction within the territory now belonging to the United States, and which ackowledged their jurisdiction at the beginning of this civil war.

"*Resolved,* That whoever shall propose, by Federal authority to *extinguish* any of the States of this Union, or to declare any of them *extinguished,* and to establish territorial governments within the same, will be guilty of a high crime against the constitution and the Union.

"*Resolved,* That whoever shall affirm that it is competent for this House, or any other authority, *to establish a Dictatorship in the United States, thereby superceding, or suspending the constitutional authorities of the Union,* and shall proceed to *make any move* towards the *declaring of a Dictator,* will be guilty of a *high crime against the constitution and the Union, and Public Liberty.*"

Mr. LOVEJOY (radical) immediately moved to table the resolutions, which would be equivlet to their final rejection.

The yeas and nays were demanded by Mr. VALLANDIGHAM, and resulted:

YEAS.

Aldrich, S. C. Fessenden, Porter,
Arnold, T. A. D. Fessenden, Potter,
Ashley, Fisher, J. H. Rice,
Babbitt, Franchott, E. H. Rollins,
Baker, Frank, Sargeant,
Baxter, Goodwin, Sedgwick,
Beaman, Gurley, Shank,
Bingham, Hale, Shellabarger,
Samuel S. Blair, Harrison, Sherman,
Blake, Hickman, Sloan,
Buffington, Hooper, Spaulding,
Chamberlain, Horton, Stevens,
Clark, Hutchins, Stratton,
Colfax, Julian, B. F. Thomas,
F. A. Conkling, Kelley, Train,
Roscoe Conkling, W. F. Kellogg, Trowbridge,
Covode, Loomis, Van Horn,
Cutler, Lovejoy, Van Valkenburg,
Davis, Low, Van Wyck,
Dawes, McPherson, Walker,
Delano, Mitchell, Wall,
Duell, Moorehead, Wallace,
Edgerton, Justin S. Morril, Washburne,
Elliott, Nixon, Wilson,
Ely, Pike, Windham,
Fenton, Pomeroy, Worcester.
75 Republicans.

NAYS.

W. J. Allen, Hall, Price,
Ancona, Hardy, Richardson,
Bailey, Holman, Robinson,
Biddle, Johnson, Sheffield,
W. G. Brown, Knapp, Shiel,
Clements, Law, Smith,
Cobb, LaZear, John B. Steele,
Conway, Leary, Wm. G. Steele,
Corning, Mallory, Stiles,
Cox, Maynard, Vallandigham,
Cravens, Menzies, Vibbard,
Crisfield, Noble, Voorhees,
Dunlap, Norton, C. A. White,
English, Nugen, Wickliffe,
Fourke, Pendleton, Woodruff,
Granger, Perry, Wright,
Grider, Yateman—50.

If this does not exhibit the true intent and purpose of the radicals in power to change our Union, establish a despotism or some new kind of government in its stead, then there is no meaning to be attached to the actions of men.

THE CONSTITUTION AGAIN THE "CAUSE OF ALL OUR TROUBLES."

During the summer of 1863, the Anti-Slavery Society of New York, passed the following resolution, WENDELL PHILLIPS being present and aiding in the same:

"*Resolved,* That while the Society has rendered this verdict with the deepest emphasis, it has not failed to remind the people of the North, that ever since the adoption of the constitution of the United States, 'their feet have run to evil, and they have made haste to shed innocent blood,' in the way of slaveholding complicity; that by consenting to a slave representation in Congress, to the arrest and rendition of fugitive slaves on their own soil, and to the suppression of slave insurrections by the iron heel of the General Government, they have made a covenant with death, and with hell they have been at agreement, till at last, judgment is laid to the line and righteousness to the plummet, and the hail sweeps away the refuge of lies, the waters overflow the hiding place, the covenant with death (the constitution) is annulled, and the agreement with hell no longer stands."

THE PURPOSE OF VOTING DOWN THE PLEDGE NOT TO ESTABLISH A DESPOTISM.

The following brief views of the act authorizing the President to suspend the writ of freedom, and to indemnify the President and all acting under him for any act they may commit, is from that able paper, the New York *World*. It should be read in the same connection with the sedition law of old, which was virtue, compared with this law. It gives a clue to the *real motives that governed* the majority in Congress in voting down Mr. VALLANDIGHAM's resolutions against a Dictatorship, noted above:

From the New York World.

THE COMPLETE OVERTHROW OF THE PUBLIC LIBERTIES.

"This is the darkest hour since the outbreak of the rebellion. Congress, by the act passed yesterday authorizing the President to suspend the writ of *habeas corpus* throughout the whole extent of the country, has consummated its series of measures for laying the country prostrate and helpless at the feet of one man. It was not enough that Mr. Lincoln has been intrusted with the purse and the sword; that, with an immense power to raise or manufacture money he has unrestricted command of the services of every able-bodied man of the country, Congress has thought it necessary to give the finishing stroke to its establishment of a military despotism, by removing all checks on the abuse of the enormous monetary and military power with which they have clothed the President.—What assurance has the country that we shall ever have another Presidential election? None whatever, except what may be found in the confidence, reasonable or unreasonable, reposed in the rectitude and patriotism of Mr. Lincoln. If any person, in any part of the country, shall think it his duty to resist unconstitutional encroachments on the rights of citizens, Mr. Lincoln is authorized, by what purports to be a law, to snatch up that individual and immure him in one of the government bastiles as long as he shall see fit, and there is no power in the nation to call him to account. He can send one of his countless provost marshals into the house of a governor of a State, or any other citizen, in the dead of night, drag him from his bed, hustle him away under the cover of darkness, plunge him in a distant and unknown dungeon and allow his friends to know no more of the whereabouts of his body, than they would of the habitation of his soul,if, instead of imprisoning the provost marshal had murdered him. With this tremendous power over the liberty of every citizen whom he may suspect, or whom he may choose to imprison without suspecting, the President is as absolute a despot as the Sultan of Turkey. All the guarantees of liberty are broken down; we all lie at the feet of one man, dependent on his caprice for every hour's exemption from a bastile. If he wills it, the State governments may continue in the discharge of their functions; but if he will it, every one of them that does not become his submissive and subservient tool can be at once suspended by the imprisonment of its officers. Considering the enormous power conferred on the Presinent by the finance and sonscription bills, a reasonable jealousy would have erected additional safeguards against its abuse. Instead of that, Congress has thrown down all the old barriers and left us absolutely without shelter in the greatest violence of the tempest.

"So far as the detestable act passed yesterday is an act of indemnity to shield the President from the legal consequences of past exertions of arbitrary power, it is a confession that he, his secretaries, provost marshals, and other minions, have been acting in violation of law. It annuls all laws passed by the state legislatures for the protection of their citizens against kidnapping; it provides for taking all suits for damages out of the state courts and transferring them to the Federal tribunals, and before those tribunals the fact that the injury complained of was done under color of executive authority is declared to be a full and complete defense. It even inflicts penalties on persons coming before the courts for redress of injuries, by declaring that if they are not successful, the defendant shall recover double costs. So that the aggrived party must take the risk of this penalty for venturing to ascertain, in a court of justice, whether his oppressor was or was not acting under the authority of the President. To this alarming pass have matters come, that not only does every citizen hold his liberty at the mercy of one man, but he is liable to be punished for inquiring whether the man arresting him really possessed; or only falsely pretended to possess, that man's authority!

"The attempt to disguise the odious charater f this detestable act by a sham provision to its second section is an insult to the intelligence of the people. "The Secretary of State and the Secretary of War," so it reads, "are directed, *as soon as it may be practicable,*" to furnish to the judges of the courts lists of the names of the persons arrested, that they may be presented to a grand jury for indictment.— And who is to judge of this *practicability?* Why the secretaries themselves, or the President for them. They will furnish such lists whenever it suits their pleasure, and not before. There is not only *no penalty* for neglecting to do this altogether, but the main purpose of the act is to protect these officers, and all persons acting under their directions, against all legal penalties for all arrests wherever made, and all detentions in prison however long protracted.

"The ninety days during which Congress has now been in session are the last ninety days of American freedom. Our liberties had previously been curtailed and abridged by executive encroachments, but the courts remained open for redress of wrongs. But this Congress has rendered their overthrow complete, by first putting the purse and sword in the hands of the President and then assuring him of complete impunity in all abuses of this enormous, this dangerous, this tremendous power."

A HIGHER STANDARD THAN THE STARS AND STRIPES.

Soon after FREMONT's removal from the Army of the West, his admirers held a meeting in Cincinnati, the Rev. Mr. CONWAY was the principal speaker, in the course of whose remarks we find the following:

"Now that the standard of liberty has been unfurled by Fremont over the contending parties—*a higher standard than the stars and stripes* or stars or bars—how wretched and *despicable* appear the *standards* raised by the pigmy generals who have gone out warm from the wings of the *Administration.*"

REPUBLICANS "PREFER THEIR PRINCIPLES TO FIFTY UNIONS."

Soon after Mr. SEWARD made his great speech, declaring that if need be all platforms must be sacrificed to save the Union, the New York *Tribune* became indignant, and thus rapped the Senator over the knuckles:

"Senator Seward, in his speech of Thursday last, declares his readiness to renounce Republican principles for the sake of the Union. In this readiness the Senator differs totally from the almost incomparable majority of the Republican party, and from the President elect. They regard these principles as sacred. They will not forswear them at the bidding of a world of seceding and treasonable slaveholders. They see no necessity to choose between them, but if such a choice must be made, they prefer their principles to fifty Unions."

ABOLITIONISTS DISCOURAGE ENLISTMENTS.

So long as the Boston *Liberator* supposed the war was being prosecuted to save the Union, it was bitter against all who enlisted. Here is an extract from its columns of 1862:

"Hasten back to a recognition of your own manhood—of your divine origin and destiny. Believe yourselves too sacred to be shot down like dogs by Jeff. Davis and his negro mymidons, and all in the cause of slavery! Die, rather, at home in the arms of loving mothers and affectionate sisters. Nay, be shot down, if you must, at home, and die like a Christian, and have a decent burial, rather than go and die in the cause of a Union and a government based on slavery, which should never have been formed, and which are blistered all over with the curses of God for wrongs, outrages and cruelties it has inflicted on millions of His poor children. Speak in tones of thunder to the Government until it hears, and declares a policy and purpose of such a character as that if you must die in battle it shall at least be in the cause of justice and liberty."

VOTES ON ABOLITION IN CONGRESS.

Not having room in this work for even extracts, we refer the reader for the votes on the various negro policies of the party in power to the *Congressional Globe* of 1861, pp. 5 and 159. Also to same of 1862, pp. 1179, 1653, 1548, 2359, 2363, 1408, 2793, 3107, 3267, 2536, 3397, &c.

CHAPTER XVII.

ABOLITION DISLOYALTY AND TREASON.

Extracts from Speeches and Sayings: by John A. Bingham...A. G. Riddle...Owen Lovejoy...Wm. Davis...F. A. Pike...W. P. Cutler...J. M. Ashley...J. P. C. Shanks ...John Hutchings...F. A. Conway...C. F. Sedgwick... Benj. Wade...J. H. Rice...G. W. Julian...Thad. Stevens ...J. P. Hale Petitions for Dissolution)...David Wilmot ...Horace Mann...Wendell Phillips...Lowell Republicans..." Boston Liberator"...J. Watson Webb...Boston Free Soilers...Charles Sumner..."True American '... 'Hampshire Gazette"...Programme of Revolution... Senator Wilson...R. P. Spaulding...Erastus Hopkins... H. M. Addison...Abolitionists of Massachusetts...R. W. Emerson...Horace Greeley...H. Ward Beecher...S. P. Chase...Fred Douglas...Redpath...Rev, Chas. E. Hodges ...Lloyd Garrison..." N. Y. Tribune"...Wm. O. Duvall ...Gen. Banks...Anson Burlingame...Rev. Dr. Bellows... Ingersoll, of Ill....Defeat of the Crittenden Compromise ...Vote in the Senate...Policy of Won't-Yield-an-Inch... Treasonable Correspondence between M. D. Conway and J. M. Mason...F. A. Conway's Treasonable Speech in Congress...Also, his Treasonable Letter to the "N. Y. Tribune"...Garrison's Speech in Philadelphia...Extract from "Wisconsin Puritan."

SLAVERY THE "CAUSE" OF AGITATION.

The following extracts, taken promiscuously from a large class, exhibit the true aims and purposes of the radicals to agitate the slavery question as the shortest route to a dissolution of the Union. Nothing can be plainer than this. It is the same old stereotyped lingo, used by PELHAM in 1796, when he boasted of his object to dissolve the Union. Most of these characters are the direct descendents of those who voted down Virginia and Delaware, then and now slave states, and succeeded in keeping open that execrable commerce, the slave trade, eight years longer than most of the South wanted it, that they might enrich their commerce, and sell its fruits to the very men and communities they now denounce. The picture is as true as it is sad.

"We believe that in the initiation of emancipation, of full and complete emancipation, will put an end to this civil war. After slavery is abolished, or put in process of ultimate extinction, there will be nothing left for traitors to fight for."—*Hon John A. Bingham, of Ohio, March* 18, 1862.

"The forces now moving the profound depths of our political compact, will themselves, ere they are spent, work its [slavery's] demolition."—*Hon. A. G. Riddle, of Ohio, January* 27, 1862.

"This war, without compromise or cessation will go forward till its beneficent end [the end of slavery] is accomplished through its own appointed means."—*Hon. A. G Riddle, April* 11, 1862.

"There can be no Union till slavery is destroyed. * * I say you cannot put down the rebellion and restore the Union without destroying slavery."—*Hon. Owen Lovejoy, of Illinois, April* 24, 1862.

"Slavery is at war with us, and slavery must die."—*Hon. Wm. Davis, of Penn., March* 6, 1862.

"And these three—tax, fight, and emancipate—shall be the trinity of our salvation. In this sign we shall conquer."—*Hon. F. A. Pike, of Maine, Feb.* 5, 1862.

"Slavery is a public enemy, and ought, therefore, to be destroyed; it is a nuisance, that must be abated. * * I reiterate the words used by the honorable gentleman from Pennsylvania (Mr. Stevens) in the preamble to his bill now under consideration: 'slavery has caused this present rebellion, and there can be no permanent peace and union in this republic so long as that institution exists.'

Everybody knows this to be true. * * * Shall we occupy the ridiculous position of having well nigh exhausted the blood and treasure of a nation to suppress a rebellion, and leave the admitted cause of it untouched?"—*Hon W. P. Cutler, of Ohio, April 23, 1862.*

"In my judgment, an enduring peace can be secured only by conquering the rebels, confiscating their property, and emancipating their slaves."—*Hon. J. M. Ashley, of Ohio, May 23, 1862.*

"This is the time, of all others, to release the slaves of rebels. Such law could only be enforced by the army. Hence, the army would be on the spot to quell any possible outbreak. —*Hon. J. P. C. Shanks, of Indiana, May 24, 1862.*

"All slaveholders, and those who sympathize with the institution of slavery more or less sympathize with this rebellion. I say that this is the cause of the whole difficulty now, and I think that this nation is false to its own interests, false to humanity, false to the claims of justice, if it does not destroy the institution on the occasion now presented.—*Hon. John Hutchings, of Ohio, May 24, 1862.*

"This is the immense sacrifice we are making for freemen and Union; and yet it is all to be squandered on a subterfuge and cheat! For one, I shall not vote another dollar or a man for the war until it assumes a different standing, and tends directly to an anti-slavery result.—*Hon. F. A. Conway, of Kansas, Dec. 12, 1862.*

"We will break it (slavery) down, destroy it, and overthrow the institution, if the laws of war, under the Constitution of the country, give us the authority, as I most solemnly believe they do. I will have no disguise of my opinions or intentions. My stand upon the subject is open to all observation. *I* am for destroying this hostile institution in every state that has made war upon the Government; and if we have military strength enough to reduce them to possession, I propose to leave not one slave in the wake of our advancing armies—not one"—*Hon. C. F. Sedgwick, of New York, May 23, 1862.*

"I would reduce the aristocratic slaveholders to utter poverty. I know they are conceited; I know they are essentially aristocratic. I am fully persuaded that their minds and their feelings are so in antagonism to Republican Democratic doctrines that it is impossible to reconcile them, and we shall never have peace until we have reduced the leaders to utter poverty, and taken thereby their influence away. I am for doing it. It ought to be done."—*Senator Wade, of Ohio, June 25, 1862.*

"I hope and believe that before this war is ended the sun will not shine upon a slave upon all this continent. I hope that the end of slavery and this war will be written together upon the same page of the history of the country."—*Hon. C. F. Sedgwick, June 25, 1862.*

"By the laws of peace it [slavery] was entitled to protection, and had it. By the laws of war, it is entitled to annihilation. In God's name, let it still have its rights."—*Hon. John H. Rice, of Maine, May 25, 1862.*

"The rebels have demanded a 're-construction' on the basis of slavery, let us give them a 'reconstruction' on the basis of freedom. Let us convert the rebel States into conquered provinces, remanding them to the status of mere territories, and governing them as such in our discretion."—*Hon. G. W. Julian, of Indiana, January 13, 1862.*

"Sir, I can no longer agree that this Administration is pursuing a wise policy." * * * "I cannot agree to the policy which is forbidding the employment and liberation of these men. Its policy ought to be to order our army, wherever they go, to free the slaves, to enlist them, to arm them, to discipline them as they have been enlisted, armed and disciplined everywhere else, and as they can be here, and set them shooting their masters, if they will not submit to this Government. Call that savage, if you please."—*Hon. Thad. Stevens, of Pa., July 5, 1862.*

"On the 7th day of February, 1850, John P. Hale insisted upon, and along with Chase and Seward alone, voted to receive, refer and consider a petition demanding of Congress 'an immediate dissolution of the Union,' because a union with slave-holders is violative of divine law and human rights."

"John P. Hale, on the 23d of March, 1848, presented a batch of eight petitions at once, demanding the dissolution of the Union."

The Montrose *Democrat* of May 10th, 1856, says:

"We recollect a little over a year ago, that we heard Mr. Wilmot make the following declaration:

"'I am determined to arouse the people to the importance of the slavery issue, and get up an organization through which they can get control of the Government in 1856. And if I become satisfied that these efforts will fail, and that the people will not assert their rights, then I'll be d—d if I don't join the party that I think will send the country to h—l the quickest!'"

"In conclusion I have only to add that such is my solemn and abiding conviction of the character of slavery, and under a full sense of my responsibility to my country and my God, I deliberately say, better disunion—better a civil or servile war—better anything that God in his providence shall send—than an extension of the bonds of slavery.' —*Hon. Horace Mann.*

"No man has a right to be surprised at this state of things. It is just what we abolitionists and disunionists have attempted to bring about. There is merit in the Republican party. It is the first *sectional party* ever organized in this country. It does not know its own face, but calls itself national; but it is not *national—it is sectional*. The Republican party is a party of the North pledged against the South."—*Wendell Phillips.*

"*Resolved,* That the Union was established to secure the liberties of American citizens.— When it fails to do that, our only voice can be, let the Union be dissolved."—*Lowell Republican Resolution.*

The Boston *Liberator*, in an article headed, in large type—"But one issue—the dissolution of the Union"—recommends signatures to a petition for that purpose, of which the following is a spirit:

"We therefore believe that the time has come for a new arrangement of elements so hostile; of interests so irreconcilable; of institutions so incongruous; and we earnestly request Congress, at its present session, to take initiatory measures for the speedy, peaceful and equitable dissolution of the existing Union, as the exigencies of the case require."

"If the Republicans fail at the ballot-box, we shall be forced to drive back the slaveocrats with fire and sword!"—*James Watson Webb.*

"*Resolved,* That 'Constitution, or no Constitution, law or no law, we will not allow a fugitive slave to be taken from Massachusetts.'"—*Boston Free Soilers of* 1850.

"I have before declared that the path of duty was clear as to the fugitive slave act, and that I am bound to disobey it!"—*Chas. Sumner, October,* 1850.

The *True American*, a Republican organ in Erie county, Pa., in commenting upon a speech delivered at a Democratic meeting says:

"This twaddle about the Union and its preservation is too silly and sickening for any good effect. We think the liberty of a single slave is worth more than all the Unions God's universe can hold."

The Hampshire (Mass.) *Gazette* of August 23d, 1856, a Republican organ, published a letter from a citizen of Northampton, who has been engaged in circulating there the petition for a dissolution of the Union, wherein he stated that

"More than one hundred and fifty legal voters of that town have signed this petition."

Says Senator WILSON, of Massachusetts:

"Freemen of the North have a right to govern this country. I tell you here, to-night, that the agitation of this question of human slavery will continue while the foot of a slave presses the soil of the American Republic."

Says CHARLES SUMNER:

"The good citizen, as he reads the requirements of this act,—the fugitive slave law—is filled with horror. * * * Here the path of duty is clear. I am proud to disobey this act. Sir, I will not dishonor the home of the pilgrims, and of the revolution, by admitting—nay, I cannot believe this will be executed here."

Said RUFUS P. SPAULDING, a member of the Convention that nominated FREMONT:

"In the case of the alternative being presented of the continuance of slavery, or a dissolution of the Union, I am for dissolusion, and I care not how quick it comes."

Said ERASTUS HOPKINS, a member of the Convention that nominated FREMONT:

"If peaceful measures fail us, and we are driven to the last extremity, where ballots are useless, then we'll make bullets effective."— [Tremendous applause.]

H. M. ADDISON, of the *American Advertiser*, says:

"I detest slavery, and say unhesitatingly, that I am in favor of abolition by some means, if it should send all the party organizations in the Union, and the Union itself, to the devil. It can only exist by holding millions of human beings in the most abject and cruel system of slavery that ever cursed the earth; it was a pity it was ever formed, and the sooner it is dissolved the better."

In 1854, the abolitionists of Massachusetts and other states sent petitions to Congress, from which the following is an extract:

"We earnestly request Congress, at its present session to take such initiatory measures for the speedy, peaceful and equitable dissolution of the existing Union as the exigencies of the case may require."

Said RALPH WALDO EMMERSON:

"We can no longer live in a Union with a barbarous community."

Says Senator WADE, of Ohio:

"I say there is another thing—and I put it as a question of *casuistry*—if the condition on which the Union is to be permanent can consist alone in trampling down nearly four millions of your inhabitants, (i. e. the existence of slavery,) I ask honest and honorable men, dare you wish that the Union should be continued upon even these nefarious conditions? No, sir; nor I, for it would be the most miserable selfishness that ought to *damn* any man wishing to benefit himself from such a sacrifice of all the rights belonging to human nature as this. (Applause.)

"And after all this to talk of a Union! Sir, I have said you have no Union. I say you have no Union to-day worthy of the name.

"Sir, I am here a conservative man, knowing as I do that the only salvation to your

Union is that you divest it entirely from all the taints of slavery.

"If we can't have that, then I go for no Union at all, but I go for FIGHT. (Great applause.) If there is any man here possessing a weaker spirit, let him show himself, for I want to see his meek face."

Says HORACE GREELEY:

"*All* nations have their superstitions, and that of our people is the Constitution."

HENRY WARD BEECHER says:

"A great many people raise a cry about the Union and the Constitution, as if the two were perfectly identical; but the truth is, *it is the Constitution itself* that is the cause of every division with this vexed question of slavery has ever occasioned in this country. It has been the *foundation of our troubles, by attempting to hold together, as reconciled, two opposing principles which will not harmonize nor agree.*"

JAMES WATSON WEBB remarked in a speech in the convention that nominated FREMONT:

"On the action of the convention depends the fate of the country; *if the Republicans fail at the ballot box, we will be forced to drive back slavocracy with* FIRE AND SWORD."

Says SAL. P. CHASE:

"Slavery in the States would not continue a year after the accession of the anti-slavery party to power, and it ought to be abolished by the constitutional *power of Congress.*"

Says FRED. DOUDLAS:

"From this time forth I consecrate the labors of my life to the dissolution of the Union; and I care not whether the bolt that rends it shall come from Heaven or from Hell!"

REDPATH, the English abolitionist, who has done the engineering for the Republicans in the Kansas matter, has published a book, in which his purpose is frankly avowed. He says:

"I believe that civil war between the North and South would ultimate in insurrection, and that the Kansas troubles would probably create a military conflict of the two sections. Hence I left the South and went to Kansas, and endeavored, personally and with my pen, to precipitate a revolution."

Now, the aforenamed traitors are not denounced as "copperheads," because they vote the Republican ticket.

In 1855 Senator WADE, of Ohio, made a speech in Portland, Maine, in which he declared:

"There is really no Union now between the North and the South. I believe no two nations on earth entertain feelings of more bitter rancor towards each other than these two portions of the Republic."

In a tract, by the Rev. CHAS. E. HODGES, and published by the Anti-Slavery Tract Society, occurs this passage:

"That Constitution is pro-slavery. Viewed, then, in the light of all that is urged, (and can logic or inspiration point to any other conclusion?) he is not a traitor to his country, but the only true patriot, as well as christian, who labors for the peaceful dissolution of the Union." * * *

"We do not expect to dissolve the Union alone. With the truest and most disinterested love of justice, humanity, and our country, we simply ask co-operation, and, for this, appeal to the conscience and understanding of the people. There is no necessity, therefore, for any definite answer to the question: How do you propose to do this thing? It is not the time to lay out a plan of a campaign, to open trenches, dispose forces, and besiege the citadel, while we have yet no forces, save only a few recruiting officers. The thing to be done now is, to urge upon every man this question: Are you ready?

Now, has this Rev. ever been denounced by any Republican press or orator? Never!—Why? Because the Rev. CHARLES E. HODGES votes the Republican ticket!

Mr. GARRISON made a speech in 1856, in which he declared:

"I have said, and I say again, that in proportion to the growth of disunionism, will be the growth of Republicanism. * * * The Union is a lie. The American Union is an imposture, and a covenant with death, and an agreement with hell. * * * I am for its overthrow. * * * Up with the flag of disunion, that we may have a free and glorious Union of our own."

No Republican was ever known to denounce GARRISON for this blasphemy, *because he never voted the Democratic ticket!*

We quote as follows from the New York *Tribune*, which was laid upon the members' desks just before the passage of the Kansas-Nebraska act:

"We urge, therefore, unbending determination on the part of Northern members hostile to this intolerable outrage, and demand of them, in behalf of peace, in behalf of freedom, in behalf of justice and humanity, resistance to the last. Better that confusion should ensue—better that discord should reign in the national councils—better that Congress should break up in wild disorder—nay, better that the Capitol itself should blaze by the torch of the incendiary, or fall and bury all its inmates beneath its crumbling ruins, than that this perfidy and wrong should be finally accomplished."

The next is an extract from a letter of WM. O. DUVALL, to a convention which he had been invited to address in New York:

"Were not the nominal free states of this Republic completely 'subdued?' Within forty-eight hours from the time Charles Sumner was murderously and cowardly assaulted in the Senate, every custom-house, arsenal and fortification of the North should have been in the possession of citizen soldiers, and long before this an army of twenty thousand men should have expelled from Washington the Goths and Vandals of the administration. And give me leave to say to you, the people are ready to do this work, and are only kept from it by the 'cool headed' management of political leaders. Only let the capitalists of the North furnish the means, and the men are ready to fight this propagandizing Government at once upon its good behavior. Let the capitalists generally take pattern from the noble Gerrit Smith, who proposes the raising at once of a million of dollars, and pledged himself for ten thousand of it. That is the ring of the true metal.—Where shall we find one more such? That there are more such I know, for my neighbor, Nathan Marble, told me yesterday, that if Mr. Smith's plan should be carried out he would give a thousand dollars towards it."

"I sincerely hope that a civil war may soon burst upon the country. I want to see American Slavery abolished in my day—it is a legacy I have no wish to leave my children; then my most fervent prayer is, that England, France and Spain may speedily take this slavery-accursed Nation into their special consideration; and when the time arrives for the streets and cities of this 'land of the free and home of the brave' to run with blood to the horses' bridles, if the writer of this be living, there will be one heart to rejoice at the retributive justice of heaven."

No Republican ever saw any "treason" in this, because Mr. DUVALL votes the Republican ticket!

Gen. BANKS said:

"I am willing in a certain contingency to let the Union slide,"

and no Republican has ever declaimed against the sentiment, *because Banks votes the Republican ticket.*

BURLINGAME, present minister to the Celestial Empire, said in a speech in Indiana, that

"the time will come when we must have an anti-slavery constitution—an anti-slavery Bible and an anti-slavery God,"

nor have we ever heard a Republican dissent from this blasphemy, *because Burlingame votes the Republican ticket.*

THAD. STEVENS, the chairman of the committee of Ways and Means in the House, made a speech in Congress, in which he declared:

"If we are to have a Union again, I would not have one with one part free—the other part slave. I would not, if I could, agree to such a Union!"

THAD. STEVENS has not been rebuked by his followers, because THAD. STEVENS votes the Republican ticket!

The Rev. Dr. BELLOWS, in one of his public discourses in the city of New York, disgraced the pulpit by uttering the following:

"It is no longer a war in defence of the Union, the Constitution, and the enforcement of the laws. It is a war to be carried on no longer with the aim of re-establishing the Union and the Constitution with all their old compromises. God means not to let us off with any half-way work. I am now convinced, and I consider it the most humane, the most economical, and the most statesmanlike now, to take the most radical ground possible—TO ASSUME THAT THIS IS A WAR FOR THE SUBJUGATION OR EXTERMINATION OF ALL PERSONS WHO WISH TO MAINTAIN THE SLAVE POWER:—*a war to get rid of slavery and slaveholders:* WHETHER IT BE CONSTITUTIONAL OR NOT!!!"

Dr. BELLOWS votes the Republican ticket and hence he is not denounced for such sentiments by that party!

Mr. INGERSOLL, the Abolition candidate for Congress at large in Illinois, during a late canvass, in a speech at Chicago, said:

"I say we must adopt whatever measures are necessary to crush this rebellion and save the country. I am not the judge of what is necessary, nor is any man here the judge. The President is the appointed judge, and when his mandate has gone forth, every man is bound to obey. Abraham Lincoln is Commander-in-Chief of the armies of the states. As such he possesses the power necessary to crush the rebellion. I care not what you name the measure; if it becomes necessary, that is the only question, and the man who does not respect the mandates of his supreme General when the country is in a death grapple with rebellion, is a traitor and deserves a traitor's doom. The President in such a time, I believe, is clothed with the power as full as that of the Czar of Russia over this question, and the question of its exercise is for him and his constitutional advisers to determine. The Chicago *Times* is not the judge. If it is necessary perhaps it is just as well for the people to become familiar with this power and the right to its exercise now as at any other time. If the President should determine that in order to crush this rebellion the constitution itself should be suspended during the rebellion, I believe he has the right to do it."

INGERSOLL was not denounced as a traitor, because INGERSOLL votes the Republican ticket.

PEACE AND THE CRITTENDEN PROPOSITION.

That the passage by Congress of the CRITTENDEN proposition would have brought peace to the country, and saved us millions of treasure, a million of precious lives, and rivers of blood, we have the best of evidence. Every Republican in the United States Senate voted against that proposition, and here is the vote:

AYES.

Bayard,   Johnson, of Tenn.,   Polk,
Bigler,   Kennedy,   Pugh,
Bright,   Lowe,   Rice,
Crittenden,   Latham,   Sebastian,
Douglas,   Mason,   Thompson,
Gwinn,   Nicholson,   Wigfall—18.
Hunter,

NAYS.

Anthony,   Durkee,   Morrill,
Bingham,   Fessenden,   Sumner,
Chandler (blood let- Foote,   Ten Eyck,
  ting),   Foster,   Trumbull,
Clark,   Grimes,   Wade,
Dixon,   Harlan,   Wilkinson,
Doolittle,   King,   Wilson—20.

If two, of those who voted in the negative, had voted in the affirmative, as DOUGLAS declared, on the floor of the Senate, it would have saved us the horrors of this war. The reader can form his own conclusion, as to whether that negative vote was the result of a desire to plunge us into a war and thus throw the onus of dissolving the Union upon the South.

THE WOULDN'T-YIELD-AN-INCH POLICY.

During the pending of the peace negotiations, the Chicago *Tribune* said:

"Others may do as they please, but this journal stands where it has always stood. It concedes nothing that would weaken the North in her great triumph over that infernal, despotic institution which has debauched the National conscience, and now strives to emasculate the National courage. We surrender no inch of ground that has been won. Standing solidly on the Constitution and the laws; intending evil to none, but exact justice, under the National compact, to all; animated by a pervading conviction of the sacredness of the cause in which we are engaged, we shall be content to do that which duty to God, our country and ourselves demands, and trust the consequences to that Power which shapes all things for the best; and this is the position in which the genuine Republicans of Illinois should stand, and these are the words which they should use. But whether they falter or keep on, our course is marked out."

OPEN TREASON OF THE ABOLITIONISTS.

The Rev. M. D. CONWAY went to England, as he himself admits, for the purpose of entering into negociations with the Rebel Envoy, J. M. MASON, and with a view to stipulate that on certain conditions the Abolitionists of America would oppose the further prosecution of the war. By the laws of war, and by our Constitution, this was rank, unmitigated treason—"adhering to the enemy—giving him aid and comfort," &c. And yet no Republican press or orator has denounced Mr. CONWAY as a traitor, because Mr. CONWAY *votes the Republican ticket*. Our "Government" has taken no steps towards having him brought to justice, but has winked at his treason—paying no attention to it, while it hunted down by the spy system, a citizen of Ohio, and sent him beyond our lines, as a felon, at the same time the President declaring he had committed no crime. A parallel for this conduct cannot be found in any civilized Government, and the real patriot is left to fall back on the vote against VALLANDIGHAM's resolutions, declaring against a Despotism, (see previous page) for a solution of the problem.

Here is the proof of CONWAY's treason:

Mr. Conway's Letter to Mason.

"AUBREY HOUSE, NOTTING HILL, }
  LONDON, W., June 16, 1863. }

"SIR:—I have authority to make the following proposition on behalf of the leading anti-slavery men of America, who have sent me to this country:

"If the states calling themselves 'The Confederate States of America' will consent to emancipate the negro slaves in those states, such emancipation to be guaranteed by a liberal European commission, the emancipation to be inaugurated at once, and such time to be allowed for its completion as the commission shall adjudge to be necessary and just, and such emancipation once made to be irrevocable—then the Abolitionists and anti-slavery leaders of the Northern states shall immediately oppose the prosecution of the war on the part of the United States Government, and since they hold the balance of power, will certainly cause the war to cease, by the immediate withdrawal of every kind of support from it.

"I know that the ultimate decision upon so grave a proposition may require some time; but meanwhile I beg to be informed at your early convenience whether you will personally lend your influence in favor of a restoration of peace and the independence of the South upon the simple basis of emancipation of slaves.

"Any guarantee of my own responsibility and my right to make this offer shall be forthcoming.
                          "MONCURE D. CONWAY.

"J. M. MASON, ESQ."

Mr. Mason's Reply.

"No. 24 UPPER SEYMOUR STREET,
Portman Square, June 11, 1863.

"SIR:—I have your note of yesterday. The proposition it contains is certainly worthy of the gravest consideration, provided it is made under a proper responsibility. Yet you must be aware that while you know fully the representative position I occupy, I have not the like assurance as regards yourself. If you think proper, therefore, to communicate to me who those are on whose behalf and authority you make the proposition referred to, with evidence of your 'right to make this offer,' I will at once give you my reply, the character of which, however, must depend on what I may learn of your authority in the premises.

J. M. MASON.
"MONCURE D. CONWAY."

Mr. Conway's Answer.

"AUBREY HOUSE, NOTTING HILL, W.,
"June 16, 1863.

"SIR:—Your note of the 11th, has been received. I could easily give you the evidence that I represent the views of the leading Abolitionists of America, but with regard to the special offer I have made. I have concluded that it was best to write out to America and obtain the evidence of my right to make it in a form which will preclude any doubt as to its sufficiency. I shall then address you again on the subject.
"MONCURE D. CONWAY."
"J. M. MASON, Esq."

Mr. Mason Closes the Correspondence.

"No. 24, UPPER SEYMOUR STREET,
"Portman Square, June 17, 1863.

"SIR:—I have received your note of yesterday. You need not write to America to 'obtain the evidence' of your right to treat on the matter it imports. Our correspondence closes with this reply.

"It was your pleasure to commence it, it is mine to terminate it.

"I desired to know who they were who were responsible for your mission to England as you present it, and who were to confirm the treaty you proposed to make for arresting the war in America, on the basis of a separation of the States with or without the sanction of their government. But such information is of the less value now as I find from an advertisement in the journals of the day that you have brought to England letters of sufficient credit from those who sent you, to invite a public meeting in London under the sanction of a member of Parliament who was to preside, to hear an address from you on the subject of your mission, with the promise of a like address from him.

"The correspondence shall go to the public and will find its way to the country, a class of the citizens which you claim to represent.— It will perhaps interest the government and the *soi disant* "loyal men," there to know under the sanction of your name, that the "leading anti-slavery men in America" are willing to negotiate with the authorities of the Confederate States for a "restoration of peace and independence of the South on a pledge that the abolitionists and anti-slavery leaders of the northern states, shall immediately oppose the further prosecution of the war on the part of the United States Government, and since they hold the balance of power, will certainly cause the war to cease by the immediate withdrawal of every kind of support from it.

"As some reward, however, for the interesting disclosure, your inquiry whether the Confederate States will consent to emancipation on the terms stated, shall not go wholly unanswered, you may be assured then, and perhaps it may be of value to your constituents to assure them that the Northern states will never be in a position to put this question to the south, nor will the Sothern states ever be in a position requiring them to give an answer.

"J. M. MASON.
"MONCURE D. CONWAY."

ANOTHER CONWAY IN THE ROLE OF TREASON.

The Kansas namesake of the Abolition Envoy Extraordinary to Secessia*ria* England, deserves a *niche* in our pantheon of the Abolition gods.

F. A. CONWAY, an Abolition member of the last Congress from Kansas, delivered a speech just before the close of the session of that illustrious body, in which he did what no Democrat North of the Potomac ever has done—advocated direct, the dissolution of the Union. We garnish our pages with enough to show its intent and purpose.

EXTRACT FROM CONWAY'S SPEECH.

"Sir, I am not in favor of restoring the Constitutional relations of the slaveholders to the Union, nor of the war to that end. On the contrary, I am utterly, and forever opposed to both. I am not in favor of the Union as it exists to-day. I am in favor of recognizing the loyal states as the American nation, based as they are on the principle of freedom for all, without distinction of race, color or condition. I believe it to be the manifest destiny of the American nation to ultimately control the American continent on this principle. I conceive, therefore, that the true object of this war is to revolutionize the national Government, by resolving the North into the nation, and the South into a distinct public body, leaving us in a position to recognize the latter as a separate state. I believe the direction of the war to any other end is a perversion of it, calculated to subvert the very object it was designed to effect.

"I have never allowed myself to indulge in that superstitious idolatry of the Union so prevalent among simple but honest people, nor that political cant about the Union so prevalent among the dishonest ones. I have simply regarded it as a form of government, to be valued in proportion to its merits as an instrument of national prosperity and power.

"The war which has come in between the North and the South for the past two years has made a revolution. This is the fact; and the fact in such a matter is the important thing. It settles the law. No technicality in a question of this kind can stand. The war has utterly dissolved the connection between the North and the South, and rendered them separate and independent powers in the world. This is the necessary effect of civil war anywhere. It makes the belligerent powers independent for the time being, and, unless the one succumbs to the other, they continue independent of each other forever. The principle is laid down by Vattel, as follows:

'When a nation becomes divided into two parties, absolutely independent, and no longer acknowledging a common superior, the state is dissolved, and the war between the two factions stands upon the same ground, in every respect, as a war between two different nations.'—*Book* 111, *chap.* 17, p. 428.

"It is not to be wondered at, therefore, that so learned and profound a jurist as the honorable member from Pennsylvania (Mr. Stevens) should express the same opinion.

* * * * * *

"The Democrats will not, of course, listen to separation for an instant. Such a suggestion, in their eyes, is treason—a proposition to dissolve the Union—for which any one ought to be hanged. They expect the question whether the Union shall be restored by force or by compromise, to be submitted to the people in the next election; and upon that to carry the country. Their plan is to oppose the Administration simply in its anti-slavery policy.— They put in issue the Confiscation Act, the Missouri Emancipation Act, and the President's Proclamation of Emancipation. These measures they pronounce unconstitutional, deny their validity, and every thing done, or to be done, in pursuance of them. In addition to this, they attack the Administration on account of its suspension of the writ of *habeas corpus*, false imprisonment, corruption, imbecility, &c., and a thousand other incidents.— But on the war and the integrity of the Union they are like adamant itself. They claim to favor the war, for the sake of the Union, but to be for peace rather than war. They say, very truthfully, that the Republicans have tried force for two years, and exhausted the country, and upon this claim the adoption of their method as all that is left to be done.— This is the manner in which the politicians of the country propose to terminate this great conflict. * * * * *

"The Senator from Massachusetts, (Mr. Sumner,) who has lately been re-elected to serve another term of six years in the body he has so long adorned, should, in this crisis, point to us the proper action. His purely Northern character, his great abilities, his lofty aspirations, his sacrifices for freedom, the entire confidence of his state so spontaneously bestowed upon him—and that state the noblest in America—all single him out as one authorized and required to speak with a decisive voice on this great occasion.

"There are also in this House, gentlemen whose words on this momentous theme, the country will listen to with intense interest. The honorable member from Pennsylvania, (Thad. Stevens,) one of the truly great men of America—full of learning and wisdom —tried by long years of arduous service in this cause, who has never faltered, and is now re-elected in his district by overwhelming numbers, stands foremost among those of whom the nation will expect deliverance from the dangers which encompass it. Let these men, and such as these speak, and tell the country what to do in this hour of transcendent peril.

"Nevertheless, I cannot refrain from expressing my individual opinion that the true policy of the North is to terminate this war at once. The longer it continues the worse our situation becomes. Let the two Houses of Congress adopt the following resolutions:

"*Resolved by the Senate and House of Representatives, &c.,* That the Executive be, and he is hereby requested to issue a general order to all commanders of forces in the several military departments of the United States to discontinue offensive operations against the enemy, and to act in the future entirely on the defensive.

"*Resolved,* That the Executive be and he is further requested to enter into negotiations with the authorities of the Confederate States with reference to a cessation of hostilities, based on the following propositions:—1, Recognition of the independence of the Confederate States. 2, A uniform system of duties upon imports. 3, Free trade between the two states. 4, Free navigation of the Mississippi river. 5, Mutual adoption of the Monroe doctrine.

"I entirely disagree with those who assert that it is impossible that the North and South could live peaceably side by side, because there are no natural boundaries between the two, such as Rocky Mountains or the Atlantic Ocean. This is a bug-bear with which we impose upon ourselves. The people of the North and South can never become foreign nations to each other in the sense in which the French and English or Russians are. They are sprung from the same origin, speak the same language, possess a common literature, inherit similar politics and religious views, and inhabit regions closely connected by natural and artificial ties. They will, therefore, both be always *American*. The only great difference between them is of a social and political nature, namely, that which arises from the existence of African slavery in one, and the absence of it in the other.

"This fact, however, presents no obstacle whatever to such a separation as is involved in independent political jurisdiction; on the contrary, it greatly facilitates it.

"Before the Federal Union was established, all the States were independent, and associated under the Articles of Confederation in the nature of a treaty.

"The articles are now adduced to show the impracticability of present separation between the North and South, with equal good force to prove the impossibility of what then actually existed and was accepted in the case of the thirteen original states of the Union. The latter stood toward each other precisely as the North and South in the Confederate States, resuming, as to them, the old basis of the Confederation. This would be the whole of it. It is, therefore, a very simple operation.

"I do not suggest this, however, on the idea that should it ever be adopted, the separation it implies would be permanent. I believe that it would insure an ultimate re-union on an anti-slavery basis.

"I have confidence in the inherent vitality of Northern civilization. I have no fear to set in competition with that of the South. Let them proceed side by side in the race of empire, and we shall see which will triumph."

Now, no Republican denounces Mr. CONWAY for thus offering to give up the ghost, and dissolve the Union, but they all denounce every Democrat who talks or thinks in favor of negotiations for peace on a basis of preserving the Union. The difference is just this: Democrats don't vote the Republican ticket, and Mr. CONWAY does!

When the conscription bill was before Congress, Mr. VALLANDIGHAM (Dem.) moved to so amend, that arrests in the *loyal states* should only be made by warrant, on oath, citing the particular offense committed, &c.— This the Republicans voted down by 101 to 57.

No Republican ever talked of arresting Mr. CONWAY for his ebullition of treason, and sending him over the lines, because he votes the Republican ticket. He became so bold, by sufferance, that he even issued his disunion bulls from the threshhold of the President's mansion, as it were, and still the President neither caused his arrest, or censured him. The following letter, written from Washington to the N. Y. *Tribune*, the grand receptacle for disunion offals, shows that his speech in Congress was not to be repented of:

CONWAY'S LETTER TO THE TRIBUNE—DISUNION A "FIXED FACT."

"A WORD

"TO THE EDITOR OF THE N. Y. TRIBUNE:

"SIR:—The recent avowal of Mr. Gerrit Smith, that he is in favor of a restoration of the Union, even if such restoration should involve renewed power to slavery, is a slight indication of that counter revolution in public sentiment, on this subject, which the war is calculated to effect, and which political leaders seem determined, through it, to bring about.

"The only period in which there was a ghost of a chance of giving this war an anti-slavery result, was the first two years of its existence. If it had been taken hold of at the outset, as an instrument of revolution, to dissolve the Union, and constitute the North a nation, thus liberating the Government from all constitutional obligations to slave holders, and had been rushed through with skill and energy, under wise ministers and competent generals, in a manner to give full effect to the power of the North, slavery would have been swept out of existence, and the seceding states conquered to the authority of the Union, and held as subject provinces.

"But this was not done. On the contrary, the war was employed as a means to prevent revolution, and to maintain the Union. The object was to enforce upon slaveholders the rights guaranteed to them by the Constitution they discarded. For nearly two years, the most zealous regard was paid to the "rights," and military operations conducted in a manner to induce the Southern people to return voluntarily to their Federal allegiance. In consequence of this policy the golden opportunity slipped away. The South became a settled and determined power—the North lost the prestige of victory, and its morale was broken.

"Thus the war became a failure, and utterly ceased to bear upon the question of the subjugation of the South, in any manner, whatsoever, and now whatever may be said to the contrary, there are few reflecting minds which have not come to the conclusion that ☞ the Independence of the South is an established fact, whether recognized or not.

"The war for the future, therefore, becomes simply an instrument in the hands of political managers to effect results favorable to their own personal ends, and unfavorable to the cause of freedom.

"What matters it that a few regiments of negroes—more or less—under white officers, are sent into the field? What matters it that the President's edict of Emancipation is printed in Little & Brown's edition of the United States Statutes at large? Is Richmond ours, or even Vicksburg? Does not the Confederacy still stand firm and defiant? And does it not promise to stand so in the future? And above all, is not the Presidential election approaching?

"It is now *assumed* that the Union is an object paramount over all other considerations, and we are told that it must never be relinquished. We are told to adhere to the war, not because it gives us successful achievements in the field, but for the reasons, simply, that otherwise, we give up the Union. We are told, also, that the institution of slavery, like all other institutions, (see the New York *Times* of to-day), is of minor importance, one way or the other, compared with the Union—that it must give way, or not give way—be destroyed, or granted a new lease of life, with increased power, just as the exigencies of the Union may require, and to this doctrine, that life-long Abolitionist, Gerrit Smith, and that zealous Republican, Mr. Raymond, and that eminent Democrat, Mr. Van Buren, all alike assert since the deportation of Vallandigham, it is supposed that this is to be the mongrel Democratic platform for the next Presidential race. "Now, Mr. editor, I desire thus publicly, and from the beginning, to announce my emphatic wish to be *counted out* of any such arrangement. I went into this anti-slavery business earnestly, and on the presumption that I was acting with honest men—men who hated slavery, and were determined to cast it out, come what might. I find that as to many of them I have been deceived. I find that men want power, and care for nothing else, and that for the sake of power they would kill all the white people of the South, or take them to their arms—that they would free all the slaves, or make their bondage still more hopeless, or do any other inconsistent wicked thing. I have no sympathy whatever for such an unhallowed lust of dominion.

"As to the Union, I would not *give a cent* for it, unless it stood as a guarantee for *freedom to every man, woman and child* within its entire jurisdiction. I consider the idea that everything must be sacrificed to the Union, as utterly preposterous. What was the Union made for? That we should sacrifice ourselves to it? I, for one, would beg to be excused.— As things stand, I would *sacrifice the Union to freedom any morning before breakfast!*
"Very truly yours, M. F. CONWAY.
"Washington, May 29, 1863."

"GOD OPPOSED TO THE UNION AS IT WAS."

WM. LLOYD GARRISON, in a speech in Philadelphia, in the fall of 1863, said:

"Since the war broke out there has been no Union. How did it happen that the Union was broken in the twinkling of an eye? The God of the oppressed has done it. The laws of justice and right are vindicating the commands of God. 'Woe to the rebellious children,' saith the Lord, 'that taketh not their counsel of me.' In spite of our experience, there are thousands of men yet in favor of the policy of restoring the Union as it was. As well might a man blown up by a bombshell propose, in the other land, to come back again and have the experiment tried over again with the bombshell as it was. [Laughter.]"

There are many who profess to ignore the idiosyncracies of Mr. GARRISON, and yet, by their acts acknowledge him as their co-laborer and leader. He is a veteran agitator, and hesitates not to boldly avow his treasonable aims, while others are vile enough to conceal theirs. GARRISON'S "Union" was always a bombshell, and he always managed to explode it to the damage of the Union.

GOD RESPONSIBLE FOR EMANCIPATION.

The Wisconsin *Puritan*, November. 1863, said:

"When in years past we prayed and talked in behalf of the bondmen of our land, we had no conception of the way by which those in bonds were to be made free. * * * God has chosen this process because he sees it the best, because in justice the circumstances demand it."

The Abolitionists declared that GOD had decreed emancipation in the West Indies, but after much experience, few will admit that GOD had any hand in it. It is nothing short of impious blasphemy for abolitionists to charge the Deity with their acts, in hopes to escape the just odium which comes after them.

CHAPTER XVIII.

MORE REPUBLICAN VOMITINGS OF DISUNION AND TREASON.

The True Object of the War [the Negro] Avowed by the "N. Y. Independent"...Beecher and the "sheepskin Parchment"...Nest Eggs of Treason : Laid by Wendell Phillips, Lloyd Garrison, Abraham Lincoln, American Anti-Slavery Society, F. E. Spinner, J. S. Pike; another by Phillips and Garrison; and one by the "Chicago Tribune"...Ingersoll invests Lincoln with the Power of the Czar of Russia...J. W. Forney on silencing "Laws and Safeguards"...The Abolition Conspiracy in the New York Riots : Important Testimony...The Union Not Worth Preserving...Tricks of the Ohio Abolitionists...The Revolutionary Spirit at Work..."New York Tribune" advocating Mobs and Riots against Law.... Sen. Howe would "Do in the Name of God what can't be done in the Name of the Constitution"...Phillips, Peace and Dissolution...This War a "Barbarian Conquest."

THE OBJECT OF THE WAR AVOWED.

The N. Y. *Independent*, more honest than most of its co-members, just after the proclamation was issued, thus let the cat out of the bag as to the object it and its friends had in bringing on the war, and refusing all means to suppress it:

"It has been our peculiar misfortune to be so tied up by civil restrictions, that the Government could not perform any act of justice, in consonance with the spirit of our age and the spirit of our constitution, without stepping over into the dangerous ground of revolution. Only war could give to the President liberty to emancipate. And now, he advances to an act of supreme justice and humanity by ways sound and constitutional, opened by the madness of the South. The sword has cut the knot that statesmen and economists could not untie. The war which at first seemed an awful disaster, a stupendous folly, has, indeed, proved to be a folly, but a Divine folly: 'Because the foolishness of God is wiser than men: and the weakness of God is stronger than men.' * *

"The nation is committed. Either there must be revolution in the North, or else all dissentients must submit, and the North stand as a mighty unit with the President! * *

"This proclamation is like Ithurial's rod.— It will turn every toad to his true infernal form. A distinction between supporting the war, and opposing the war policy. They are routed without a battle. They must go over to the South or take sides with the Administration. Public sentiment will compel the latter course. It will be impossible, then, to persuade the South, hereafter, that the North did not mean to injure her institutions. 'I, Abraham Lincoln, President of the United States of America, and commander-in-Chief of the army and navy thereof, do hereby proclaim and declare.' This is the authorized voice of the nation It is the hand-writing on the wall. That proclamation cannot be suppressed. Its edict cannot be rubbed out. The Southern eye reads, '*mene, teckel, upharsin.*'

"No more guises and vails. No more side issues. No more deceiptful compromises. The Government has taken ground, and every man in the nation must take ground. You are for or against this Government, and this Government is declared to mean Liberty to the Slave! There is no neutral ground for traitors to hide in, playing wolf by night and sheep by day. The President's Proclamation will sift the North, give unity to its people, simplicity to its policy, liberty to its army! That whole army is no longer a mongrel something between a police force and a political caucus. It is an army organized to strike where blows will be most felt."

It will be seen that this agitating organ, scouts the idea that the North in the beginning did not "mean to injure Southern institutions." All know that was the means to gain an end, and BEECHER is unsophisticated enough to admit it.

This same BEECHER, in Plymouth Church, in 1863, said:

"I know it is said that the President is not the government; that the Constitution is the government. What! a sheepskin parchment a government? I should think it was a very fit one for some men that I hear and see sometimes. What is a government in our country? It is a body of living men ordained by the people to administer public affairs according to laws that are written in a constitution and in the statute books, and the government is the living men that are administering in a certain method the affairs of the nation. It is not a dry writing or a book. President Lincoln, his Cabinet, the heads of the executive departments, are the government, and men have got to take their choice whether they will go against their government or go with them."

Upon which a Connecticut paper justly remarks as follows:

"Is this not another foreshadowing of despotism? The 'sheepskin parchment' as Beecher terms it, is to give place to Mr. Lincoln and his cabinet, who are the government, and men have got to take sides. Such assertions could only be made at this time, with the freedom of the press palsied, and the freedom of speech stifled in government dungeons."

NEST EGGS OF TREASON.

It is a favorite term of reproach by the abolition newspapers against Charleston that it was the "nest of the rebellion." If it be true that it was the nest where the eggs of rebellion were hatched, it is not true that it was the nest where the eggs of rebellion were laid. That nest was situated considerably to the Northeast of Charleston, in the region popularly known as New England, and eggs of rebellion were laid in it as long ago as 1815, by men assembled at Hartford, in the state of Connecticut, whose conclave is historical by the name of the "Hartford Convention." Other eggs were laid in it in 1844, when the Legislature of Massachusetts resolved that the annexation of Texas would be the cause of the dissolution of the Union. A great many other eggs have since been laid in it, by a great many men and a great many public meetings, both in and out of New England. Here is one laid by WENDELL PHILLIPS:

"The Constitution of our fathers was a mistake. *Tear it in pieces and make a better.*— Don't say the machine is out of order; it is in order; it does what its framers intended—protect slavery. Our aim is disunion, breaking up of the states! I have shown you that our work cannot be done under our institutions."

Here is one laid by WM. LLOYD GARRISON:

"This Union is a lie! The American Union is an imposition—a covenant with death, and an agreement with hell! * * * I am for its overthrow! * * * Up with the flag of disunion, that we may have a free and glorious Republic of our own; and when the hour shall come, the hour will have arrived that shall witness the overthrow of slavery."

Here is another laid by GARRISON:

"No act of ours do we regard with more conscientious approval or higher satisfaction—none do we submit more confidently to the tribunal of Heaven and the moral verdict of mankind, than when, several years ago, on the 4th of July, in the presence of a great assembly, we committed to the flames the Constitution of the United States."

SCRAPS FROM MY SCRAP-BOOK. 101.

Here is another laid by LINCOLN:

"I believe this government cannot endure permanently half slave and half free."

Here are three laid by the American Anti-Slavery Society at one of its anniversary meetings:

"*Resolved,* That SECESSION from the United States government is the duty of every ABOLITIONIST, since no one can take office, or deposit his vote under its constitution without violating his anti-slavery principles, and rendering himself an abettor to the slaveholder in his sin.

"*Resolved,* That years of warfare against the slave power have convinced us that every act done in support of the AMERICAN UNION rivits the chain of the slave—that the only exodus of the slave to freedom, unless it be one of blood, must be over the remains of the present American Church, and the grave of the present Union.

"*Resolved,* That the abolitionists of this country should make it one of the primary objects of this agitation, to DISSOLVE THE AMERICAN UNION.

Here is one laid by the present Assistant Secretary of the Treasury—FRANCIS E. SPINNER—during the FREMONT campaign:

"Should this (the election of Fremont) fail, no true man would be any longer safe here from the assaults of the arrogant slave oligarchy, who then would rule with an iron hand. For the free North would be left the choice of a peaceful dissolution of the Union, a civil war which would end in the same, or an unconditional surrender of every principle held dear by freemen."

Here is one laid by JAMES S. PIKE, long editorially connected with the New York *Tribune,* and new Minister to the Netherlands:

"I have no doubt that the free and slave states ought to separate. The Union is not worth supporting in connection with the South."

Here is one laid by WENDELL PHILLIPS shortly after the organization of the Republican party. He was speaking of that party:

"No man has a right to be surprised at this state of things. It is just what we abolitionists and disunionists have attempted to bring about. It is the first sectional party ever organized in this country. It does not know its own face, and calls itself national; but it is not national—it is sectional. The Republican party is a party of the North pledged against the South."

Here is one laid by WM. LLOYD GARRISON at about the same time:

"The Republican party is moulding public sentiment in the right direction for the specific work the Abolitionists are striving to accomplish, viz.: The dissolution of the Union, and the abolition of slavery throughout the land."

Here is one laid by the Chicago *Tribune* in December, 1860:

"Not a few of the republican journals of the interior are working themselves up to the belief, which they are endeavoring to impress upon their readers, that the seceded States, be they few or many, will be whipped back into the Union. We caution all such that in language of that sort they are adding new fuel to the flame which is already blazing too fiercely; and that the probabilities now are that the result will prove them to be false prophets. No man knows what public policy may demand of the incoming administration; but the drift of opinion seems to be that, if peaceable secession is possible, the retiring States will be assisted to go, that this needless and bitter controversy may be brought to an end. If the Union is to be dissolved, a bloodless separation is by all means to be coveted. Do not let us make that impossible."

These were the eggs of treason which were hatched out in the Charleston nest.

THE RIGHT TO SUSPEND THE CONSTITUTION CLAIMED.

E. C. INGERSOLL, Republican candidate for Congress at large, in Illinois, at Bryan Hall, in Chicago, in 1862, said:

"The President, in such a time, I believe, is clothed with power as full as that of the Czar of Russia over the question.

"If it be necessary, perhaps it is just as well for the people to become familiar with this power, and the right to its exercise, now as at any other time.

"If the President should determine that in order to crush the rebellion the Constitution itself should be suspended during the rebellion, I believe he has the right to do it."

If such teaching as this is not calculated to impress one with the idea of approaching despotism, then nothing can.

LAWS AND SAFEGUARDS TO BE SILENCED.

JOHN W. FORNEY, editor of the Philadelphia *Press,* over the *nom de plume* of "Occasional," writes to his paper:

"Let us unite the North by any means.— When men no longer volunteer let there be conscription. Silence every tongue that does not speak with respect of the cause and the flag. Do away with politics, with luxuries, with comforts. Let us cease for the present to speak of laws and restrictions, and what are called safeguards."

All know the intimate connection of Mr. FORNEY with the Administration, and hence such declarations, like double shotted guns, carry "long range," and promise heavy execution.

AN ABOLITION CONSPIRACY.

The official reports of Gen. WOOL and Gen. SANFORD threw much light on the dark subject of the New York riots. It is alleged by both the *Herald* (Lincoln paper) and the *World*, that the riots were prolonged three days by the operations of the Abolition authorities, who were determined to place New York under martial law, and not permit Gov. SEYMOUR to carry off the honor of putting down the riot. In short, the Abolition authorities threw every obstacle they could in Gov. SEYMOUR's way, with a view to use the riot for political purposes. The following, from the *World*, shows up the Abolition interference, without mincing the matter:

"In the light of these considerations, it will be easy to understand the remarkable facts which are stated with the naked simplicity of an annalist, by General Wool. The Mayor is a Republican; the police are under Republican control; so long, therefore, as the disturbances were slight, Provost Marshal Nugent depended on the police to arrest them. When they became formidable, the Mayor requested the assistance of General Wool, assigning the absence of the militia regiments as a reason for doing so; thus making a fresh Republican recognition of the principle that the suppression of the riot was the proper business of the local authorities. General Wool promptly acceded to the Mayor's request. The troops under his command in the forts being insufficient, he made application to Governor Seymour, who promptly furnished such militia as was within reach, and placed it under the command of General Sandford.

"Thus far, everything had been done without any interference from Washington, all the authorities and officers acting in perfect harmony. General Wool, who seems to have had no other motive than an honest desire to preserve that harmony and make short work of it with the rioters, directed that Major General Sandford, of the militia, should command the force of mixed militia and regulars assembled for the restoration of order, and that Brigadier General Brown, of the United States service, should act under his orders. What messages were interchanged between parties here and the authorities at Washington, during that and the two following days, the public have no means of knowing; it is certain that the telegraph was busy, and that the Administration felt a keen interest in all that was transpiring. It immediately became evident that the harmony between the state and Federal authorities, which General Wool was so wisely attempting to promote, was distasteful to the Administration, and was by some means to be broken.

"We know not by whose inspiration General Brown first volunteered his services to General Wool, and, to make sure of their acceptance, offered to serve in any capacity. But by whomsoever inspired, he immediately refused to obey Gen. Sandford's orders. This led to the issue by Gen. Wool of an order formally installing Gen. Sandford as commander of all the troops for the defence of the city, and requiring implicit obedience to his orders. The consequence was that the same evening Gen. Browe came to Gen. Wool, complaining of Gen. Sandford, and asking to be excused from the operations of the order. As he still persisted, after Gen. Wool's explanations, he was relieved from duty, and an order was immediately issued putting Col. Nugent in charge of the regular troops.

"This was Monday night. What messages passed between New York and Washington during the night must be left to conjecture.— Early the next morning, General Brown presented himself again to General Wool, confessed that he had been wrong, and asked to be restored to the position he had too hastily abandoned. Was this prompt repentance the consequence of a reprimand from Washington? Had General Brown been taken to task for his want of skill or want of perseverance in the attempt to nullify the authority of General Sanford? That he would *unprompted* have made this humiliating profession of penitence is incredible, especially as his subsequent course showed it to be a piece of pure dissimulation

"It was a mere trick to get back; once back, he made it his business to disobey and thwart General Sanford, even going so far as to issue orders to troops stationed at the latter's headquarters, and treating him with as little consideration as if a Major General's commission given by State authority were no better than a piece of blank parchment. He did not succeed in nullifying General Sanford's authority, and was therefore dismissed; but he did succeed in seriously obstructing and postponing the suppression of the riot. General Sanford states that the peace of the city would have been entirely restored as early as Tuesday, the second day of the riot, had it not been for the obstructive proceedings of General Brown. Thus we are indebted for the two worst days and the most fearful scenes of the riot to the Republican conspiracy against state sovereignty."

We copy copiously from the *Herald* as follows:

"THE REAL CONSPIRACY IN THE LATE RIOT.— The mystery that enveloped the events of the week of terror in this city is fast being cleared away. The nest of the conspirators has been probed, and they now stand before the public in their hideous forms. When we saw the *Tribune*, *Times* and *Post*, day after day, amidst the tumultuous and trying scenes in this city, filled with bitter, acrimonious and bloodthirsty articles, we concluded that there was some secret under and behind all the disturbances, which was purposely hidden from the general public. Time has verified our suspicions. Facts that have come to light within the last few days conclusively prove that the incendiary course of the radical journals was prompted solely by a fixed determination to increase the extent of the riot and to force a collision between the State and national authorities.

"The latter point accomplished, it was to be followed with the declaration of martial law, a military Governor, and all the appliances that this Satanic radical committee, with Greeley, Raymond, Godwin & Co. at its head, with its dozen or fifteen tails, could bring to bear to control future elections in this city. They were foiled in their evil and bloody work by the tact and skill of Generals Wool and Sandford, with the co-operation of Governor Seymour. The riot and suffering and the reign of terror were, however, extended by them at least three days by their nefarious work.

"How these radical conspirators tampered with the military is shown by the reports of Generals Wool and Sanford. The letter of the former states that on Monday afternoon (13th) General Harvey Brown tendered his services. His offer was accepted, and he was directed to report to Major General Sanford. It was soon found that General Brown did not act in harmony with General Sandford. General Wool thereupon issued an order; but this Brown did not obey, but presented himself in the evening, asking to be excused from the operations of the order. This Gen. Wool refused to grant him, declaring:

"That for efficient operations, a hearty co-operation of the State and United States troops with the police was necessary to put down the mob."

"General Brown persisting, he was excused from further service. Mark the sequel. The next morning the radical papers denounced the military authorities in unmeasured terms and howled for martial law. General Brown also appeared about eight o'clock in the morning at General Wool's headquarters and asked to be re-instated, "saying, in substance, that he was in the wrong." He was reinstated. What then? The same authority states that he acted without any reference to General Sandford.

"Right here comes in the important testimony of General Sanford. The latter, in his official report, asserts

"That the rioters were dispersed on Monday night and Tuesday morning, and the peace of the city would have been restored in a few hours but for the interference of Brevet Brigadier General Brown, who, in disobedience of the orders of General Wool, withdrew the detachments belonging to the general government."

"This act so weakened the small military force in the city that it was again placed at the mercy of the rioters, and the bloody scenes were continued two or three days longer. The *Tribune* clamored the next morning for the removal of Gen. Wool.

"Thus we have the official testimony that Gen. Brown was used by the radicals. It is a well known fact, that General Wool and Sandford were in frequent consultation with Governor Seymour, and that these three officials worked together in harmony. Brown, on the other hand, was no doubt urged to ask to be reinstated by the little satanic committees composed of Greeley, Raymond and Godwin, they fearing that unless he was there to interfere with the plans of Seymour, Wool and Sandford the riots would be put down and their plans of martial law and conflict between the state and national authorities defeated.

"Brown's reinstatement was essentially necessary for the success of their schemes.— Hence the pretended confession that he was wrong. General Brown is no doubt a member of a church in good standing and a good military officer. He has done good service for his country at Fort Pickens and other points, and like Phelps and Hunter, is a good fighter, when the negro is not about. But hold up the negro to such men and they forget all their military knowledge. The radicals hold up the nigger and nigger party to Brown, and all military ability departed except for mischief."

If the above facts, which are corroborated in every particular by the official reports of Generals WOOL and SANFORD, do not show that the New York riot was fanned and fed by the Abolitionists, if not by the Administration itself, for the purpose of aiding the Republican party, then the sun does not shine.

"SUCH A UNION NOT WORTH PERPETUATING."

During the excitement of the Oberlin riots, Mr. LANGDON, an Ohio Abolitionist, said:

"But why preserve the Union, when its only object is to eternize slavery? Such a Union is not worth perpetuating. With all my heart I should say, let it be abolished! I hate the Union of these states as I hate the devil! for by it I am denied all protection for my personal liberty"

A delegation from Lorain county, Ohio, turned out to resist the law, and to commit treason to their Government, by engaging in the Oberlin riots in 1859. [*See Ohio State Journal*, (*Rep.*) *May* 26, 1859.] The band that accompanied the delegation, played the revolutionary "Marseillaise hymn,"—the characters "1776" were inscribed upon their banners. One banner was inscribed on one side "Lorain," and on the other

"Here is the Government.
Let tyrants beware."

The "Government" was not then located in the White Palace—the mob was then "the Government."

A speaker at this mobocratic gathering said:

"Steady, trust in God and keep your powder dry, and look for the things that shall be."

Another said:

"Let the Federal authority make the issue and test the fact whether we will execute OUR LAWS. They know not how soon the smouldering volcano will burst under their rotten carcases."

One of the resolutions passed by that mob declared:

"That the enforcement of such laws (the Fugitive law) against an unwilling people, is productive only of evils threatening the public order and stability of governmental institutions."

This reminds us of the ancient maiden, when stoves were first put up in buildings and churches. She had heard that stoves were unhealthy, and insisted on fainting in church one day because the majority of the Society would insist on putting up "one of them pesky stoves." It turned out that there was no fire in the stove at the time of fainting, but nevertheless, the anti-stove party insisted that the stove was the cause of the church difficulty, and the church was actually split up and divided because the stubborn majority would insist on patronizing the stove. But the seceders would never own that the rebellion that broke hearts and religious ties, was in any degree attributable to them, when if *they* had not created dissensions *without cause*, all would have been well.

THE REVOLUTIONARY SPIRIT AT WORK.

The following short paragraph, from the Leavenworth *Bulletin*, concerning the state of affairs along the Missouri and Kansas state line, tells more than whole volumes, the nature of that revolutionary spirit we are considering:

"The General Order, requiring all to leave the border counties, has been carried out. All persons found without proper papers are shot at sight."

JIM LANE, a "Border Ruffian" United States Senator, is the reported author of that "order." And yet to complain of these things subjects the complainant to the charge of "sympathizers with the rebellion."

"EVANGELISTS, REBELS AND RIOTERS."

In 1854, when ANTHONY BURNS, a fugitive, was in the custody of the law, at Boston,—when a mob, of the rabble, backed by the pious and virtuous (?) undertook to "resist" the execution of the law, and by violence prevent its execution—when poor BACHELDER, a white man, was murdered in cold blood, for standing at his place of duty, as an officer of the law—when treason run riot in Massachusetts, the New York *Tribune* thus came to the "rescue" of the rescuers:

"The Rev. T. W. Higginson, of Worcester, Massachusetts, is on bail for $3,000 to respond to the charge of inciting a riot in Boston, at the time of the attempted rescue of Antony Burns. We don't know that Mr. H. did anything toward effecting the rescue of Burns, but he doubtless would have done it if he could, and now regrets that he did not succeed.— When U. S. marshals find it necessary to surround themselves with armed cohorts of jail birds, blacklegs, and brothel bullies, in order to prevent a rescue by the honest yeomanry who crowd the streets, it is pretty safe to presume that every real minister of the gospel stands opposed to the blacklegs and bullies.— When kidnappers are the chief saviors of the Union, of course evangelists will be rebels and riotors."

Thus, when the courts were protecting the authority of the Government, and endeavoring to prevent rebellion from usurping the throne of law, this leading organ of the exclusively "loyal" party was endeavoring to overthrow the constitutional powers by the "gospel of riot," and to evangelize the *heathens* of legal power with "thirty thousand bayonets" in the hands of an "honest yeomanry," and by displacing provost marshals with pious ministers of the "gospel of riot," to bring on the millennium, when "evangelists will be rebels and rioters." And when the "Government" was invoked to show its power for law and order, against the organized "Anti-Fugitive-Law League," in Wisconsin, the programme of said Leaguers was quoted by the New York *Tribune*, with fiendish delight, as follows:

"As Freemen, we can and will stand it no longer.

"We will stand by the rescuers of Glover, with our influence, our purses, and our right arms. No court shall crush them; no prison bars and walls shall ever confine them."

From the courts to the league in 1854; from the courts to the army in 1863. The appeal is the same; the last resort of the fanatic is still the last resort of the despot; self-will supreme over law; passion supreme over reason; force, and force alone, the final arbiter of states and men. Such is the disposition of the evangelist, of those who exclaim, "away with him"—"down with the Government," when they are out of power—and—"If you oppose *us* you oppose the Government"—when in power.

WHAT THE CONSTITUTION WILL NOT PERMIT DO "IN THE NAME OF GOD."

When the bill was before the U. S. Senate amending the act of 1790, relative to the calling out the militia, so as to call out slaves, &c., Mr. BROWNING, (rep.) of Illinois, moved to so amend that the wives and children of soldier slaves belonging to *rebels* should be set free instead of freeing all, including those belonging to loyal union men.

Mr. COWAN, (rep.) of Pennsylvania, was in favor of the amendment. He said:

"The country had prospered under the Constitution, and we are bound by it."

Mr. HOWE, (rep.) of Wisconsin, said there seemed to be some difficulty as to how we should support our Generals. There were too many controversies.

Mr. COWAN asked:

"Does not the Constitution exist? Are we not bound by it?

Mr. HOWE—"We are bound by it. Yes, we are bound by it, and bound to battle for it, and not stand here higgling about the force we are to send into the field. I would bring all the force into the field I could, not caring what the color of it might be. *Bring the negroes into the field in the name of God if we cannot do it in the name of the Constitution!"*

WENDELL PHILLIPS AT BEECHER'S TABERNACLE.

WENDELL PHILLIPS, the great war horse of the radical party in power, made a speech in BEECHER'S Political Synagogue, in 1862, in which he declared:

"This is not a war of sections—it is a war of ideas—ending only when one idea strangles another, and not before. Peace comes when freedom holds the helm, and not before. Now, I would accept anything on the anti-slavery basis. I would accept separation. I would accept compromise. I would accept Union [the last and least with PHILLIPS]. I would accept peace, and pay the whole Confederate debt, at par, on the anti-slavery basis."

"ABSOLUTE BARBARIAN CONQUEST."

In the same speech this Abolition-martinet advocated the killing of the whites at the South and giving their estates to the negroes, and strange to say his hearers cheered the sentiment. He declared that the Richmond of the South lay in two millions of blacks, and continued:

"If this be true of the two extremes of the Confederacy, what remains? Why, only the solid centre, the great Gibralter, the rich plantations, and the accumulated blacks, tha-

make a girdle round the Gulf, should be approached by the news that wherever it plants its flag, it should declare 'there is nothing here but people and land.' The land is ours—confiscated, guaranteed; its title given to the soldier who has finished his service. Give it to the black man, who is willing to take it, and plant a state, under the guarantee of the Union—employ free labor upon that fertile soil, and commence again the civil mahcinery, the organization of a state.

"I do not believe in battles ending this war. This is a war of ideas. You may plant a fort in every district of the South—you may take possession of her capitals, and hold them with armies, but you have not begun to subdue her. You don't annihilate a thing simply by abolishing it. The most successful superintendent of contrabands at Fortress Monroe, is begging of this timid, dilatory, indecisive government, to allow him to take possession of the abandoned plantations, and put the vagrant contraband, who is not allowed to work upon those acres, and make him self-supporting. A government has to be besieged and entreated before it can be brought to see that the conquest of Virginia is not to be had on the Rappahannock, but it is to be affected at Fortress Monroe, when the negro puts his foot upon the soil and owns it. I know this seems extreme doctrine. I know that it seems something like absolute barbarian conquest. I allow it. I don't believe there will be any peace until 347,000 slave holders are either hung or exiled. [Cheers.] History shows no precedent of getting rid of an aristocracy like this, except by the death of the generation."

This same WENDELL PHILLIPS, in a speech at Cincinnati, since the war commenced, boasted that

"I have labored nineteen years to take sixteen States out of this Union."

CHAPTER XIX.

THE ADMINISTRATION UNDER THE BAN OF THE "BALANCE OF POWER."

Power and Influence of the Abolitionists over the Administration...The Leading Abolitionists Feted and Provided with Place and Power...Superstition and Intolerance... 1790, 1800, 1814 and 1864 Compared...The Bigotry and Intolerance of To-Day Borrowed from the Pilgrims—A Chapter from the Puritans...Blue Lights and Blue Laws ...The Act Suspending the Writ of Habeas Corpus, in full...Ayes and Noes on said Bill, Politically Classified... "New York Tribune" on Peace...Old Abe and the "Union as it was," &c.

THE POWER AND INFLUENCE OF ABOLITIONISTS.

We are aware that the Republicans seek to parry the effect of the extreme abolition declarations, by assuring us that those who utter them have little or no influence, and consequently can do no harm. Indeed, it's just the reply of the Wisconsin *State Journal* to the Wisconsin *Patriot*, when it quoted a brace of PHILLIPS' treasonable paragraphs, but it was not long before PHILLIPS was invited by a Republican to lecture in the city where those two papers are published. Mr. HASTINGS, the Republican State Treasurer waited upon the great disunionist and traitor—received him at the depot in high livery—escorted him through the city as Canadian cockneys would a "Lion from London."

We assert, without fear of contradiction, that the class of Radicals from whose speeches and resolves we have so liberally quoted, and shall yet quote, have more influence over the Administration to-day, and the shaping its policy, than all those who style themselves "Conservative Republicans," combined. It was the clamors of the Radicals that forced from the President the Proclamation, but a few days after he refused to issue it.

Let us inquire the whereabouts and *status* of some of the leading Abolitionists.

Where is Senator WADE, who declared there was no Union?

In the United States Senate, as one of the President's constitutional advisers.

Where is Senator HALE, who in 1850, introduced petitions for a dissolution of the Union?

In the United States Senate, as one of the President's constitutional advisers.

Where is CHARLES SUMNER, who said at Worcester, the 7th of September, 1854, that it was the duty of the people to resist a law, even after it was decided constitutional by the highest Federal Court?

In the United States Senate, re-elected as one of the President's constitutional advisers.

Where is Mr. SEWARD, the author of the "Irrepressible Conflict," and who voted to receive a petition for Dissolution of the Union, in 1848?

In Mr. LINCOLN's Cabinet.

Where, to-day, do you find the man who declared that any people had the right to revolutionize their Government, and establish another—who pronounced the Mexican war a wicked war, and declared that this Union could "not exist half free and half slave," and bestows the blessings of his power on those who have for over a quarter of a century denounced the Government of our fathers?

Acting as President of the United States!

Where, to-day, is OWEN LOVEJOY, the man who moved to table a resolution which ignored the establishment of a despotism on the ruins of this Government?

A member of the American Congress.

Where are the seventy-eight Republicans who voted with OWEN LOVEJOY to table said resolution?

High in the Republican synagogue.

Where, to-day, is THADEUS STEVENS, who scouted the idea that he obeyed his oath to support the Constitution, in voting to dismember Virginia?

Chairman of the most important committee in the American House of Representatives.

Where, to-day, is BINGHAM, the man who declared that slavery or the Union must perish?

In Congress, a leader among the "loyal."

Where, to-day, is N. P. BANKS, whose easy loyalty would "let the Union slide?"

A Major General in the loyal army.

Where to-day is CASSIUS M. CLAY, who refused to fight for his country, unless he could have his way about slavery?

First appointed Minister to Russia, then honored with the commission and salary of a Major General, with plenty to eat and nothing to do.

Where have you found ANSON BURLINGAME, the Abolitionist who declared for a new Constitution, a new bible—a new GOD—in short, a new deal all round?

Appointed by Mr. LINCOLN to drink tea and eat ornamental mince pies in the Celestial Empire.

Where to-day do you find JOSHUA R. GIDDINGS, who in 1848 introduced a petition for the dissolution of the Union?

As Mr. LINCOLN's Consul to the Canadas.

Where do you find HANNIBAL HAMLIN, the Vice President of the United States?

Leaving the presiding officer's chair to welcome WENDELL PHILLIPS upon the floor of the Senate, a courtesy rarely accorded to any civilian.

Where to-day do you find HORACE GREELEY, the man who stigmatized the American flag as a "flaunting lie," and cried, "tear it down?"

As the editor of *the* leading Republican paper in America.

Where now is WM. LLOYD GARRISON, who pronounced our Constitution a "covenant with death, an agreement with hell?"

You will find him feted by Republicans, and addressing "loyal Union" meetings!

Thus, we might go on *ad infinitum*, and show that each and every one from whom we have quoted "disloyal," "disunion," and "treasonable" sentiments, are now high in the confidence and employ of the party in power. Why, as WENDELL PHILLIPS said, the Republicans "don't know their own faces." They are now even ahead of the abolitionists of old. One cannot find a leading Republican of to-day who will acknowledge he would be in favor of the old Union which GARRISON declared to be a "covenant with death, an agreement with hell!" —they and GARRISON believe the same thing now, and the reason that GARRISON has not some pet office, is, that he is honest in his denunciations of our Union, and will not take an oath to support the Constitution, while his Republican co-workers will, with a mental reservation to destroy it.

SUPERSTITION AND INTOLERANCE.

A man's peculiar natural characteristics are not guaged by his belief, but his belief, whim or caprice, are often the offsprings of his natural, or national characteristics. What a vast difference have we always observed between the two great leading parties of this country, even from its earliest period. The Federals, in power from 1796 to 1800, were arrogant, conceited and intolerant. They could not bear to tolerate the least opposition to, or criticism upon their measures. No matter how wild or destructive those measures, all must tamely acquiesce, without complaint. The sedition law was the offspring of this partizan reticence. Opposition was sure to call down on the victim, persecution.

Nor did the Federals waive this intolerance when they went out of power, but they kept it up, insisting on their prerogative to force obedience to their behests, and more than tolerance of their dogmas.

Nor has this particular characteristic forsaken that classification of men to the present hour. Witness their inflamatory denunciations of all those who do not endorse their every extreme idiosyncracy. You must believe that slavery ought to be abolished, constitution or no constitution, or you are a "traitor." You must believe that it is right, and a "military necessity," to put down and silence all criticism on public measures, by suppressing and mobbing persons; by the arrest and imprisonment of dissentients, under the law of "suspected persons." You must believe that the constitution is a "covenant with death" and the Union a "league with hell," or you are a "secessionist." If you believe in the "Union as it was, and the constitution as it is," including the article providing for amendments, you are a "copperhead." In short, if you do not endorse every act of the Administration, as just and proper, you "oppose the war," and ought to be sent "over the lines."

Such is the spirit of intolerance of that class of persons who have always opposed the Democracy—with a few honorable exceptions. Not so with the Democracy, for no recording pen of history has shown or can show that during the Democratic administration of Mr. JEFFERSON, when we were threatened with a war with France, that any opponent was arrested, and punished without "due process of law"— and under the Democratic administration of Mr. MADISON, when the nation was in a death-like grapple with the most powerful nation on the globe—no arbitrary arrests were made—no newspapers suppressed—no printing offices mobbed—no system of provost marshals to intimidate, annoy and arrest people, without charge or accusation—no indemnifying acts to shield officers guilty of striking down civil and personal liberty without cause—no deportation beyond our lines. In short, none of those intolerant, *revolutionary* means were resorted to, although, as we have shown in these pages, there was abundant *cause* for the most energetic and summary measures, Mr. MADISON might have arrested *thousands* of leading, wealthy and influential citizens of the Eastern States, with specific charges of treason and misprison of treason, and been content to have rested the prosecution in open court on their own published acts, resolves and speeches.

But Mr. MADISON did not do it. And herein consists the great difference between the characteristics of the two great parties of this country. The present party in power—intolerant and proscriptive as their Federal sires, have made thousands of arrests—most of which had not the merit of being based on *charges*, even, and none of which, so far as we have ever been able to learn, have ever been followed by proof that treason was either committed or intended. Newspapers have been suppressed (as we shall show hereafter) for no greater crime than a manly protest against such outrages, and fair criticism on the conduct of those in authority, with a view solely of preserving—not destroying—the Government of our fathers.

THE BIGOTRY AND INTOLERANCE OF TO-DAY—BORROWED FROM THE PILGRIMS.

To show that the leaders of the present reigning dynasty came honestly by their bigotry, intolerance and spirit of persecution, we will in this connection introduce

A CHAPTER FROM THE PURITANS.

And before we introduce our "ancient testimony," we wish to enter our protest against that indiscriminate denunciation against our Puritan fathers, which many indulge. The *Mayflower* brought many good, liberal and generous spirits as well as bad, illiberal, arrogant and intolerant ones. That early lump of emigration was leavened with a fair proportion of Democracy, from which sprang many of the leading, liberal Democratic ideas of our age. They were the pioneers of those free and liberal ideas that have for the most part governed our people for nearly two centuries.

But a large majority of the early Puritans were bigoted and intolerant, and to trace the genealogy of the illiberal and intolerant ideas of the present age to their proper source, we copy from an old work written in the latter part of the 17th century:

"The Quakers were whipped, branded, had their ears cut off, their tongues bored with hot irons, and were banished upon pain of death, in case of their return, and actually executed upon the gallows."

At a subsequent date, says another work:

"The Quakers prosecuted the Protestants with all manner of cruel atrocities," &c.

And continues this antiquarian work:

"The practice of selling the natives of North America into foreign bondage continued for two centuries. The articles of the early New England Confederacy classed persons among the spoils of war. A scanty remnant of the Pequod tribe in Connecticut, the captives treacherously made by Waldron in New Hampshire, the homeless remnants of the tribe of Annamon, the orphan offspring of King Phillip himself, were all doomed to the same hard destiny of perpetual bondage."

And again:

"The Pokanokets were the first tribe which sheltered the Pilgrims after their landing on Plymouth Rock, and they were the first to fall victims to their insidious and ungrateful policy."

And it is further recorded in the same history:

"At the two sessions of the court in September, 1769, fourteen women and one man were sentenced to death on charges of witchcraft. One old man of eighty refused to plead, and by that horrible decree of the then common law, was tortured to death. Although it was evident that confession was the only safety, in most cases, some few had courage to retract their confessions—some eighty of them were sent to execution. Twenty persons had already been put to death—eight more were under sentence; the jails were full of prisoners; and new accusations were made every day."

BLUE LIGHTS AND BLUE LAWS.

As the Puritans passed blue laws, the better to silence opposition to their illiberal ideas and dogmas, so their progeny burned blue lights to signal the enemy in war, and thus at times in our history, have rendered the cause of personal rights and civil liberty, to say nothing of National existence, *blue* indeed.

Among the laws alluded to in this early history, were the following:

"No one shall travel, cook victuals, make beds, sweep house, cut hair, or shave on the Sabbath day.

"If any man shall kiss his wife, or wife her husband, on the Lord's day, the party in fault shall be punished at the discretion of the court, or magistrate.

"No woman shall kiss her child on the Sabbath or fasting day."

To these provisions of law, the historian appends the following note:

"A gentleman, after an absence of some months, reached home on the Sabbath, and meeting his wife at the door, kissed her with an appetite, and for his temerity in violating the law, the next day was arraigned before the court, and fined, for so palpable a breach of the law on the Lord's day."

We by no means charge our opponents with the guilt or foibles of their early ancestors.—Our purpose is only to trace a proper genealogy of that illiberal, intolerant and bigoted spirit that to-day would consign to the dungeon all dissentients against their political dogmas, so that it may not be said our Abolition bigots came dishonestly by their intolerance.

SEDITION LAW NUMBER TWO—THE ACT TO STRIKE DOWN THE HABEAS CORPUS.

We have deemed it important, in the progress of this work, as showing the revolutionary spirit of those in power to place on record in these pages the

"*Act Relating to Habeas Corpus, and Regulating Judicial Proceedings in Certain Cases,*"

so that the reader may compare it with the aims and purposes of the Sedition Act of old, and to properly appreciate this Sedition Law No. 2, it should be read by the light of the vote in Congress, by which the resolution ignoring a despotism on the ruins of our Government was tabled.

"Sec. 1. *Be it enacted, &c.*, That during the present rebellion, the President of the United States, whenever in his judgment the public safety may require it, is authorized to suspend the privilege of the writ of *habeas corpus* in any case throughout the United States, or any part thereof, and whenever and wherever the said privilege shall be suspended, as aforesaid, no military or other officer shall be compelled, in answer to any writ of *habeas corpus*, to return the body of any person or persons detained by him, by authority of the President, but upon a certificate, under oath of the officer having charge of any one so detained, that such a person is detained by him as a prisoner, under authority of the President, further proceedings under the writ of *habeas corpus* shall be suspended by the Judge or court having issued the said writ, so long as said suspension by the President shall remain in force, and the said rebellion continue.

"Sec. 2. *And be it further enacted, &c.*, That the Secretary of State and the Secretary of War be, and they are hereby directed, as soon as may be practicable, to furnish to the Judges of the Circuit and District Courts of the United States, and of the District of Columbia, a list of the names of all the persons, citizens of the States in which the administration of the laws has continued unimpaired, in the said Federal Courts, who are now, or may hereafter be held as prisoners of the United States, or order or authority of the President of the United States, or either of said Secretaries, in any fort, arsenal, or other place, as State or *political prisoners*, or otherwise, than as prisoners of war, the said list to contain the names of all hose who reside in the respective jurisdictions of said Judges, or who may be deemed by the said Secretaries, or either of them, to have violated any law of the United States, in any of said jurisdictions, and also the date of each arrest; the Secretary of State to furnish a list of such persons as are imprisoned by the order or authority of the President, acting through the State Department, and the Secretary of War a list of such as are imprisoned by the order or authority of the President, acting through the Department of War. And in all cases where a grand jury having attended any of said courts, having jurisdiction in the premises, after the passage of this act, and after the furnishing of said list, as aforesaid, has terminated its session, without finding an indictment, or presentment, or other proceeding against such person, it shall be the duty of the judge of said court forthwith to make an order that any such prisoner desiring a discharge from such imprisonment, be brought before him to be discharged, and every officer of the United States having custody of such prisoner, is hereby directed immediately to obey and execute said judge's order. In case he shall delay or refuse so to do, he shall be subject to indictment for a misdemeanor, and be punished by a fine of not less than $500, and imprisonment in the common jail for a period not less than six months, in the discretion of the court; *Provided*, however, that no person shall be discharged by virtue of the provisions of this act, until after he or she shall have taken an oath of allegiance to the government of the United States, and to support the constitution thereof, and that he or she will not hereafter, in any way encourage or give aid and comfort to the present rebellion, or to the supporters thereof; and, *provided, also*, that the judge, or court, before whom such person may be brought, before discharging him or her from imprisonment, shall have power, on examination of the case, and if public safety shall require it, shall be required to cause him or her to enter into recognisance, with or without security, in a sum to be fixed by said judge or court, to keep the peace and be of good behavior towards the United States and its citizens, and from time to time, and at such times as such judge or court may direct, appear before such judge or court, to be further dealt with, according to law, as the circumstances may require, and it shall be the duty of the District Attorney of the United States to attend such examination before the judge.

"Sec. 3. *And be it further enacted*, That in case any of such prisoners shall be under indictment or prosecutions, for any offense against the laws of the United States, and by existing laws, bail or recognizance may be taken for the appearance, for trial of such person it shall be the duty of said judge at once to discharge such person, upon bail or recognizance, for trial, as aforesaid, and case the said Secretaries of State and War shall for any reason, refuse or omit to furnish the said list of persons held as prisoners, as aforesaid, at the time of the passage of this act, within twenty days thereafter, and of such persons as hereafter may be arrested within twenty days from the time of the arrest, any citizen may after a Grand Jury shall have terminated its session without finding an indictment or presentment, as provided in the second section of this act, by a petition, alleging the facts aforesaid, touching any of the persons, so as aforesaid imprisoned, supported by the oath of such petitioner, or any other credible person, obtain and be entitled to have the said judge order to discharge such prisoner on the same terms and conditions prescribed in the second section of this act, *provided*, however, that the said judge shall be satisfied, such allegations are true.

"Sec. 4. *And be it further enacted*, That any order of the President or under his authority, made at any time during the existence of the present rebellion, shall be a defense in all courts to any action or prosecution, civil or criminal, pending or to be commenced, for any search, seizure, arrest or imprisonment made, done or committed, or acts omitted to be done, under, and by virtue of such order, or under color of any law of Congress, and such defense may be made by special plea, or under the general issue.

"Sec. 5. *And be it further enacted*, That if any suit or prosecution, civil or criminal, has been or shall be commenced in any state court against any officer, civil or military, or against any other person, for any arrest or imprisonment, made, or other trespasses, or wrongs done or committed, or any act omitted to be done, at any time during the present rebellion, by virtue or under color of any authority derived from, or exercised by, under the President of the United States, or any act of Congress, and the defendant shall at the time of entering his appearance in such court, or if such appearance shall have been entered, before the passage of this act, then at the next session of the court, in which such suit or prosecution is pending, file a petition, stating the facts, and verified by affidavit for the removal of the cause for trial at the next Circuit Court of the United States to be holden in the district where the suit is pending, and offer good and sufficient surety for his filing in such court, on the first day of its session, copies of such process and other proceedings against him, and also for his appearing in such court, in entering special bail in the cause, if special bail was originally required therein, it shall then be the duty of the state court to accept the surety, and proceed no further in the cause or prosecution, and the bail that shall have been originally taken, shall be discharged, and such copies being filed, as aforesaid in such court of the United States, the cause shall proceed therein, in the same manner as if it had been brought in said court by original process, whatever may be the amount in dispute, or the damages claimed, or whatever the citizenship of the parties, any former law to the contrary notwithstanding. And any attachment of the goods or estate of the defendant, by the original process, shall hold the goods or estate of the defendant, so attached, to answer the final judgment, in the same manner as by the laws of such state they would have been holden to answer final judgment, had it been rendered in the court in which the suit or prosecution was commenced. And it shall be lawful in any such action or prosecution which may be now pending or hereafter commenced, before any state court whatever, for any cause aforesaid, after final judgment, for either party to remove and transfer, by appeal, such case during the session or term of said court, at which the same shall have taken place, from such court to the next Circuit Court of the United States, to be held in the district in which such appeal shall be taken, in manner aforesaid. And it shall be the duty of the person taking such appeal, to produce and file in the said Circuit Court attested copies of the process, proceedings and judgment in such cause, and it shall also be competent, for either party, within six months after the rendition of a judgment in any such cause, by writ of error or other process, to remove the same to the Circuit Court of the United States of that district in which such judgment shall have been rendered, and the said Circuit Court shall thereupon proceed to try and determine the facts and the law in such action, in the same manner as if the same had been there originally commenced, the judgment in such case notwithstanding. And any bail which may have been taken, or property attached, shall be holden on the final judgment of the said Circuit Court in such action, in the same manner as if no such removal and transfer had been made as aforesaid. And the state court from which any such action, civil, or criminal, may be removed and transferred as aforesaid, upon the parties giving good and sufficient security for the prosecution thereof, shall allow the same to be removed and transferred, and proceed no further in the case: *Provided*, however that if the party aforesaid shall fail duly to enter the removal and transfer, as aforesaid, in the Circuit Court of the United States, agreeably to this act, the state court by which judgment shall have been rendered, and from which the transfer and removal shall have been made, as aforesaid, shall be authorized, on motion for that purpose, to issue execution, and to carry into effect any such judgment, the same as if no such removal and transfer had been made: *And Provided also*, that no such appeal or writ of error shall be allowed in any criminal action or prosecution where final judgment shall have been rendered in favor of the defendant or respondent, in the state court. And if in any suit hereafter commenced, the plaintiff is nonsuited or judgment pass against him, the defendant shall recover double costs.

"Sec. 6, *And be it further enacted*, That any suit or prosecution described in this act in which final judgment may be rendered in the Circuit Court, may be carried by writ of error to the Supreme Court, whatever may be the amount of said judgment.

"Sec. 7. *And be it further enacted*, That no suit or prosecution, civil or criminal, shall be maintained for any arrest or imprisonment made, or other trespasses or wrongs done or committed, or act omitted to be done, at any time during the present rebellion, by virtue or under color of any authority derived from, or exercised by, or under the President of the United States, or by or under any act of Congress, unless the same shall have been commenced within two years next after such arrest, imprisonment, trespass, or wrong may have been done or committed, or act may have been omitted to be done! *Provided*, That in no case shall the limitation herein provided commence to run until the passage of this act, so that no party shall, by virtue of this act, be debarred of his remedy by suit or prosecution, until two years from and after the passage of this act."

VOTE ON THE PASSAGE OF SAID BILL.

The above act passed the House of Representatives, March 3d, 1863. We annex the list of yeas and nays so that the reader may see who "did this thing," and to what political faith they belong.

YEAS.

Aldrich, R.
Arnold, R.
Ashley, R.
Babbitt, R.
Baker, R.
Baxter, R.
Beaman, R.
Biglow, R.
Blair, (Va.) U.
Blair, (Pa.) R.
Blake, R.
Browne, (Va.) U.
Buffington, R.
Campbell, R.
Casey, U.
Chamberlain, R.
Clark, R.
Colfax, R.
Conkling, F. A., R.
Conklin, R., R.
Conway, R.
Cutler, R.
Davis, R.
Dawes, R.
Delano. R.
Dunn, R.
Edgerton, R.
Elliott, R.
Ely, R.
Fenton, R.
Fessenden, S. C., R.
Fessenden, T A F. R.
Flanders, U.

Fisher, R.
Frauchet, R.
Frank, R.
Gordin, R.
Gurley, R.
Hahn, U.
Hale, U.
Harrison, R.
Hooper, R.
Horton, R.
Hutchins, R.
Julian, R.
Kelley, R.
Kellogg, (Mich.)
Kellogg, (Ill.) R.
Killings, R.
Lansing, R.
Lary, U.
Lehman, D.
Loomis, R.
Low, R.
McIndoe, R.
McKean, R.
McKnight, R.
McPherson, R.
Marston, R.
Maynard, U.
Mitchell, R.
Moorehead, R.
Morill, (Me.) R.
Nixon, R.
Patton, R.
Phelps, (Cal.) R.

Pike, R.
Pomeroy, R.
Porter, R.
Rice, (Me.) R.
Riddle, R.
Rollins, (N. H.) R.
Sargeant, R.
Sedgwick, R.
Segar, R,
Shanks, R.
Shellabarger, R.
Sherman, R.
Sloan, R.
R.Spaulding, R.
Stevens, R.
Stratton, R.
Thomas, (Md.) U.
Trimble, R.
Trowbridge, R.
Vau Horn, R.
Van Valkenburg, R
Van Wyck, R.
Verree, R.
Walker, R.
Wall, R.
Walace, R.
Washburne, R.
Wheeler, R.
White, (Ind.) R.
Wilmer, R.
Windham, R.
Worcester, R.

Ayes 100; all anti-Democratic but one.

NAYS.

Allen, (O.) D.
Allen, (Ill.) D.
Anacona, D.
Biddle, D.
Calvert, D.
Cravens, D.
Crisfield, D.
Delaplaine, D.
Dunlap, U.
English, D.
Granger, D.
Grider, U.
Hall, D.
Harding, D.
Holman, D.

Johnson, D.
Karrigan, D.
Knapp, D.
Law, D.
Mallory, U.
May, D.
Menzies, U.
Morris, D.
Noble, D.
Norton, D.
Nugin, D.
Pendleton, D.
Perry, D.
Price, D.
Robinson, D.

Shiel, D.
Smith, D.
Steele, D. N. D.
Steele, (N. J.) D.
Stiles, D.
Thomas, (Mass.) U.
Vallandigham, D.
Voorhees, D.
Wadsworth, D.
Ward, D.
White, (O.) D.
Wickliffe, U.
Wood, D.
Woodruff, D.
Yeaman, D.

Nays 45—only one Republican.

As the foregoing act established a Dictatorship over the people so far as it was possible for Congress to do it, we are anxious the men of the future shall see who is responsible.

"ANYTHING BUT THAT."

The New York *Tribune* having been taken to task by a "conservative" Republican paper for its treasonable purposes, that sheet retorts as follows, which shows that its politics outweighs its "love" for the Union.

"A journal which seeks occasion to differ with the *Tribune*, asserts that after having been willing to 'let the cotton states go,' we have opposed every proposition looking to peace. This is astonishingly wide of the truth. The one thing that we *have* steadfastly opposed —that we have deemed too dear a price, even for peace—is new concessions—new guarantees to human slavery. Take any form but that. * * * Let us have a Union of peace as soon as possible, but never by new concessions to, new compromises with, slavery."

WITHOUT NEGRO EQUALITY THE UNION OF NO ACCOUNT.

The Chicago *Journal* uses the following ingenious argument to prove that the President is not in favor of the "Union as it was:"

"ALL A MISTAKE.—The Chicago *Tribune* complains with some bitterness of an expression in the President's letter to Horace Greeley, which quotes as follows: 'The sooner the National authority is restored the sooner the Union will be the Union *as it was*.' [The italics are not ours.] The *Tribune's* ground of complaint is, that the President seems to look to restoring the *old order of things*, just as it existed immediately preceding the rebellion. Such would be the inference if the President had used the language imputed to him, but the *Tribune* has misquoted. The language of the President, as we find it published in the *National Intelligencer*, the unquestionably correct version is as follows: 'The sooner the National authority can be restored, the nearer the Union will be the Union as it was.' This contains a different idea from that contained in the sentence quoted by the *Tribune*. It shows the President does not expect the old order of things will be restored," &c.

And we may add, his subsequent action proves that the *Journal* was correct:

A "LOYAL" APPEAL FOR DISSOLUTION.

From a speech by WENDELL PHILLIPS, at an Emancipation Anniversary meeting, in Abington, Mass., Aug. 1, 1862, we select the following, which was applauded to the echo by the large crowd of Republicans present:

"We shall never have peace until slavery is destroyed. As long as you keep the present *turtle* [Lincoln] at the head of the Government you make a pit with one hand and fill it with the other. * * * If any man present believes he has light enough to allow him, let him pray that Davis may be permitted to make an attack on Washington City within a week. * * * The speaker knew Mr. Lincoln. He had, while in Washington, taken his measure. He is a first rate *second rate* man. That is all. A mere convenience, and he is honestly waiting, like any other broom stick, for the people to take hold of him and sweep slavery out of the nation. Democracy is lifting up its fangs, and another Congress will not have the same amount of Republican and honest sentiment in it that the last had. Nothing less than a baptism of blood, to cry in anguish for a corporate idea, that the head of the army can save us.— Lincoln is as good as the people of the North want him. In years gone by, in yonder grove the Whigs fired cannons to smother the voices from the stand then occupied by the speaker, [Phillips,] and what is the result? The sons of those Whigs now fill graves in Chickahominy swamps. Let this Union be dissolved, in God's name, and the corner stone of a new one be laid, in which shall be organized forever equality in a political sense for every man who is born into the world!"

CHAPTER XX.

DISLOYALTY OF REPUBLICANS—THE GREAT ROUND-HEAD CONSPIRACY.

Threats to Force Mr. Lincoln to Issue the Proclamation... From "New York Independent"...."Chicago Tribune" Against the "Union as It Was"; also, its Threat to use Bayonets in Defiance of the People...The Radical Conspiracy of 1862...Disclosures of the Round-Head Plot...Suggestions of the "Boston Courier"; also, from an Albany Paper...The "St. Louis Anzeiger" Reveals the Plot...The "N. Y. Observer" Gives a Clue to It... Gov. Ramsey, of Minnesota, on "Machinations of Home Governments," &c......"Legalized Treason"......From "Boston Courier"...The Second Hartford Convention Toasted...Chas, Sumner Teaches Revolution...Mr. Seward Boasts of More Despotic Power than the Queen of England dare Exercise...Thad. Stevens declares the Constitution an "Absurdity"...Republicans Cheering for Dissolution......Republicans for "Extermination and Damnation"...The "Boston Commonwealth" Denounces Restoration a Crime...The "South Not Worth a Copper"..."Boston Commonwealth" Curses the "Union as It Was"...Bingham Don't Want the Cotton States... The Constitution Committed to the Flames by Garrison... Senator Honkle and Vallandigham...Destruction of the Constitution a Test of Loyalty...God and the Negro... Beecher Declares that the Negro is our "Forlorn Hope" Republican Bloodthirstiness...Jim Lane would send all the White Men to "Hell"..."Chicago Tribune" Down on the "Union as It Was"...Amalgamation and Negro Equality...Fred. Douglas and White Women...Wendell Phillips Thanks God for Defeat..."N. Y. Tribune" Defies the National Government—Hen. Wade on Dissolution...The Seceding States follow Ben.'s Advice...C. M. Clay "Spots the Union as It Was"...Beecher Ridicules the "Sheepskin Parchment"...Daniel Webster on the "Grasp of Executive Power"..."Democrats Must Not Clamor for the Union as It Was"...Moulding Public Opinion...Mr. Lincoln in 1854...Mr. Seward and Violence...Mr. Seward on the "Last Stage of Conflict" ...Mr. Seward's Justification for Disunion...The Prefix "National" Stricken from the Republican Cognomen... Banks Predicts a Military Government...Carl Schurz on Revolution...J. P. Hale on Dissolution...Gen. Butler on Reconstruction...Object and Consequences of Slavery Agitation...Prophesies of Eli Thayer...General Conclusions, &c.

A THREAT TO DISPLACE THE PRESIDENT.

In the New York *Independent* of August 9, 1862, under the head of "A Leader for the People," we find the following, with much more of the same import, too lengthy for insertion here. The paragraphs here quoted, indicate as strong as language can, the purpose of the Radicals to depose Mr. LINCOLN by force, unless he yielded to their demands, and issued the Proclamation, and it is but charity to suppose that these and kindred threats, from kindred sources, forced him to reconsider his firm resolve on that subject:

"Let any one compare the State papers, messages, proclamations and orders that have issued from this Administration during the past year and a half, with the documents which preceded and accompanied our own war of Independence. The Bills of Rights of the colonies sparkle with sentiments of humanity, of right, of liberty, The resolves of the old colonial legislatures had in them that which fed the deep love of liberty in the human soul. The remonstrances addressed to the throne— the letters of eminent men—the declarations of Congress—were all aglow with a divine enthusiasm.

"Compare with these the papers that have issued from our Government, during this infernal revolt of slave bred men against free institutions—*they are cold, heartless, dead.* * * * There has not been a line in any government paper *that might not have been issued by the Czar, by Louis Napoleon, or by Jeff Davis.*

"Our State papers *during this eventful period are void of genuine enthusiasm,* for the great doctrines on which this government was founded. *Faith in human rights is dead in Washington.* The Administration have faith in America, in the United States, in a united North, in a *Republican party,* but no faith in that invisible principle which underlies and nourishes them. The people are never called to maintain their historic ideas. The nation is never reminded of its political truths. The people not marched where their enthusiasm, like the sleeping music of the harp strings, lies waiting some touch to bring it forth, to roll over this continent such an anthem as the world never heard, and only a free people can chant. Let one of those grand old documents be brought forth which our fathers issued before this infernal slavery had made man timid of their best faith, and tolerant only of the doctrine of devils. Behold its lofty spirit. See how divine in its inclusion of the whole human family in the right claimed by its authors for themselves. How bold, wise, fearless and consistent!

"Now lay down by its side the pale, cold, lifeless documents that have come forth from the Government of the great people striving for their liberties, and for the very land bequeathed them by their fathers. Why, their State papers of our time are the winding sheets of the old ones—the very shrouds in which to bury the noble lines and sentences of the fathers out of sight of generations whom slavery has misled, or whom a false prudence has intimidated. * * *But we must cease looking*

any more to Government, we must turn to OURSELVES. A time may be near when the people will be called to act with prudence [how cautious the sentence] and courage beyond all precedent. After strength has been frittered away in wooing the manhood of Border State eunuchs, and reverses have come, and our rulers are *fugitives* from the proud capital.— Should they deem the task of maintaining the sanctity and integrity of the national soil hopeless, *then this great people, running through all their States, may yet be called to take up the dispairing work, and carry it to victory!*
"The people must have *leaders*. As yet they have not found them."

"THE UNION AS IT OUGHT TO BE."

The Chicago *Tribune* thus scorns the idea of the Union as it was:
"In his letter to Horace Greeley the President says:
" 'The sooner the national authority is restored, the sooner will be the Union *as it was.*'
"There is much ambiguity in this expression. The 'Union as it was,' is a cant phrase, invented by the famous Vallandigham, and fathered by his dirty tool, Dick Richardson. The meaning they attach to these words is well understood. *But such a Union loyal men do not want to see restored. They prefer a Union as it ought to be.*"

BAYONETS TO DEFY THE PEOPLE.

In the Chicago *Tribune* of Sept. 17, 1862, we find the following:
"Let it be understood that the people have become lukewarm in the cause [abolition of slavery] in which they are contending, and we shall straightway behold them [the soldiers] asserting *their* principles *in defiance of the people.* The bayonets *think.* The bayonets in the American army bristle with ideas."

THE RADICAL CONSPIRACY OF 1862.

It is well known, that following in the lead of the Hartford Conventionists of 1814, several of the New England Governors, in defiance of the spirit of the Constitution, which forbids the states to enter into any alliance, and what states cannot do the Governors of the states cannot rightfully undertake, met at Providence, R. I., in *secret*, and finally adjourned to another secret meeting at Altoona, Pa. All this was done in the summer of 1862, while the radicals were attempting to browbeat Mr. LINCOLN into issuing the proclamation—when he complained of the "terrible pressure" upon him. And it will go down among the legends of history, if even it does not yet appear in bold relief, that those most "Loyal Governors" conspired together with a view to pledge themselves to furnish no more troops for the war unless the President yielded to their demands. Whatever the object of their meetings, true loyalty did not require *secrecy.* The old Hartford Convention sat with closed doors, and intended to keep their aims and purposes secret, but they were at last subjected to the fiery crucible of history, and exhibited in all the infamy of a treasonable attempt to dissolve the Union.

Let us trace the conspiracy of 1862 to its logical conclusions, and make up our verdict from the budget of facts before us.

The following telegraphic dispatch, issued from the very headquarters of the Government just about the time the President was compelled to yield to the radical policy, and who knows that it was not furnished to the press by his order, as a justification of the course he did pursue? At all events, take the whole affair, link by link, and does it not show we had the Hartford Convention revised?

"*The Roundhead Conspiracy—Startling Developments—Conspiracy of the Radicals to Depose the President.*

"WASHINGTON, Sept. 16, 1862.

"Most astounding disclosures have been made here to day, by letters and verbal communications, from prominent politicians, showing that a vast conspiracy has been set on foot by the radicals of the Fremont faction to depose the present administration, and place Fremont at the head of a provisional government; in other words, to make him military dictator. One of these letters asserts that one feature of this conspiracy is the proposed meeting of the governors of the northern states to request President Lincoln to resign, to enable them to carry out their scheme. The writer, in conclusion, says Governor ANDREW and Senator WILSON are at work, and they are probably at the bottom of the movement.— From other well informed sources it is learned that the fifty thousand independent volunteers proposed to be raised under the auspices of the New York National Union Defence Committee were intended to be a nucleus for the organization of the Fremont conspiracy. It was the purpose of those engaged in this movement to have this force armed and organized by the government, and placed under the independent command of their chosen leader, and then to call upon all sympathizers to unite with them in arms to overthrow the present administration, and establish in its stead a military dictatorship, to carry on the peculiar policy they desire the government should execute. Failing in this, it is stated that a secret organization had been inaugurated, the members of which are known by the name of Roundheads.

It is intended that this organization shal number two hundred thousand men in arms, who shall raise the standard of the conspirators, and call General Fremont to the command. They expect to be joined by two-thirds of the army of the Union now in the field, and that eventually one million of armed men will be gathered around their standard. This startling disclosure is vouched for by men of high repute in New York and other northern states. It is the last card of those who have been vainly attempting to drive the President into the adoption of their own peculiar policy."

The following, from the Boston *Courier*, also sheds some light, and offers some valuable suggestions on the subject:

"*The F. emont Conspiracy—Scheme of the New York Jacobins to Depose President Lincoln.*

"If we published our paper in the city of New York, we should be disposed to press the affair of the war committee to all its legitimate results. The ill-tempered letter of Mayor Opdyke, the chairman, to Messrs. Belmont, shows the spirit of the committee, but ought they not to be specifically inquired of, as to certain points demanding explanation? For example, might it not well be asked of this committee:

"1. In what manner did you intend to employ the 50,000 men which you proposed to raise by the authority of the state government, in case the general government refused to allow of such a formidable military organization under command of Gen. Fremont?

"2. For what purpose did a deputation of your committee attend a conference of New England Governors at Providence?

"3. What was the report which they brought back and made to you, after that conference?

"4. Was it not proposed that the army of 50,000 men, which you designed to raise in New York should be reinforced by such recruits as you might be able to obtain in New England? And was not this proposition considered and discussed at the conference in question?

"5. If your object was solely and legitimately to aid the government in the suppression of the rebellion, why did you seek to raise a separate military force without its authority, and if such authority were refused, so to raise it necessarily against its authority?

"6. Do you think that this proceeding could be regarded as encouraging enlistments—or, was it not rather the most direct possible discouragement, by attempting to raise a large force, not for the service of the government, but aside from it?

"7. What was the specific object of raising that military force? Explain, if you please, how it could be employed in any legitimate way?

"8. Why have the sessions of your committee been secret? We do not ask why you may have excluded reporters for the press, or the public generally, while you were engaged in the transaction of committee business—but why is the business of a National War Committee so conducted, that absolute exclusion of the public from all knowledge of the character of its doings is deemed necessary?

"9. Has it occurred to you that the suspicions of the public might justly be roused, lest transactions of which so much has been revealed, combined with the fact of this extraordinary privacy, might be inconsistent with the public peace and safety?

"10. Has any suggestion been made in your committee, as to a government at the north, separate from that of the United States? We do not ask you whether you have formally resolved to secede, in a certain contingency, but wheter that subject has been discussed in your committee—whether it was not discussed at the Providence meeting before referred to—whether your sub-committee did not make a report on this particular subject—and if not, what object it actually was which you wished to raise an army for?

"11. When you proposed to place the army you thought of raising under the command of Fremont, did you have in mind the following lauguage attributed to him, as was used by him while in the service of the United States in Missouri?

"That the people were in the field, and he was at their head, and would have done everything according to their expectations from him; that now we have only extra constitutional government—no civil rights, so to speak—all ordinary peaceful rules were to be set aside, and this thing of red tape must give way very shortly to what the people require of him; that he meant to carry out such measures as they, the people, expected him to carry out, without regard to the red tape of the Washington people."

"12. Are you not aware that large numbers of persons, disaffected as to the policy of the national government, and with whom you have been in political association, are providing themselves with arms in the state of New York and in the New England states?"—*Boston Courier.*

"*The New York 'National War Committee.'*

"The Jacobin club is not, however, idle, although exposed and denounced. Its agents are busily engaged in gathering up secretly the names of all who are willing to enrol themselves in the army of 50,000 men, to be placed under the command of Fremont. It is a repetition of the Wide Awake clubs of 1860, with this difference, that the Jacobin force will be supplied with arms, which they would not probably have the courage to use.

"There is every reason to fear that this bold usurpation is of wider extent than has been supposed. In every city or county of this state there is good reason to believe, similar secret bodies are in existence, with the object of systematically organizing a force that may be used, if the necessity should arise to usurp the power of the government."—*Albany paper.*

The following from the Saint Louis *Anzieger* (Rep.) gives us still further evidence of the means to be employed:

"PROGRAMME OF THE REVOLUTION.— We directed attention, yesterday to the approaching convention of the Western Governors, who, as we learn, in conjunction with some Eastern governors intend to put an *ultimatum* to President Lincoln, and in case of a refusal, withdraw their quota of the troops.

"According to the report communicated to us, this programme will contain the following points:

"1. Immediate and general emancipation of the slaves. [Which was acceded to.]

"2. Dismissal of the Cabinet and formation of a new one from the ranks of the radicals.

"3. Discharge of McClellan and all Democratic Generals [This was acceded to.]

"4. Transfer of the chief command of the entire army to Gen. Fremont. Besides, some other demands of a like character.

"Governors Curtin, Tod, of Ohio, Pierpont, of Virginia, and Morton, of Indiana, have declared themselves against this revolutionary proceeding, and invited the Western Governors to a conference on the 24th, in Pennsylvania. For the present, preliminary consultations are held at Springfield, Illinois, and the project of a revolution, with the removal of Lincoln from the Presidency and the dismissal of his Cabinet, is openly discussed. Unless further decisive victories of General McClellan stifle the project in its birth, we shall soon see the doors open to anarchy, and then woe to the Germans! They will be made the scapegoat, who will have to suffer for every thing."

More of the Conspirators in New York.

The New York *Observer*, a religious sectarian organ, says:

"We speak what we know when we say that a calm, scholarly minister of Christ in this city declared in the house of God, four days ago, that we shall have no success in this war until the President is driven out of Washington, and three of his Cabinet are executed.— This is the revolutionary spirit that is abroad, and the foundations of government and law and society are trembling at its breath.

Here, then, are numerous links, well put together, and forming a chain of almost irresistable evidence. But they are not all. Just leave New England abolitionism for a moment alone in its glory, and turn our attention to evidences of the guilt in the West. The Executive convention at Cleveland worked in harmony with the New York and New England move. Simultaneously all the Western Legislatures were called together, with no visible necessity for the trouble and expense. They all urged substantially the same measures, which were, that the soldiers should be priviledged to vote, and that the States should arm and equip themselves, like independent war powers. Gov. Ramsey, of Minnesota, thus alluded to the voting question:

"It may happen, that unless proper legislative action is taken to prevent it, a day will come when our vast force of volunteers in the field will represent *one set* of principles, while our *government, state and national*. will be controlled by an entirely different set; in other words, the labors and sufferings of a patriotic army may be frustrated, embarrassed and brought to nought by the *machinations of home governments*, wielded by *timid or disloyal spirits*. No mind can estimate the horrors to which such a state of things would lead. It would be armed right contending against *legalized treason*, and its fruit would be a condition of fearful anarchy."

The Chicago *Tribune* of the 17th, said upon the same topic:

"Let it be understood that the people have become lukewarm in the cause for which they are contending, and we shall straightway behold them (the soldiers) asserting *their* principles *in defiance of the people!*"

Here, then, it was directly announced, that any opposition to the wishes of the people (and the radicals claimed to be the people) on the part of the Washington Government would be "legalized treason," and the leading organ of that faction declared the soldiers may find it necessary to assert their principles (here used in the sense of the principles of the radicals) "*in defiance of the people.*"

THE ALTOONA MEETING

[From the Boston Courier, Sept. 27.]

"The further report of the *Herald's* Altoona correspondent is entirely confirmatory of the first one, and there is every reason to believe it is substantially correct. The attempt to cover up the proceedings, or to conceal the designs of the active conspirators, must inevitably fail. The article of the Louisville *Journal* on the subject is impressive, and will command attention and respect. The country has great cause to be thankful that Governor Bradford, of Maryland, set down in some accounts as a "war democrat," but who has always been a Whig, and acted with the Bell and Everett party at the last election, was present. His true loyalty and spirit were of main service at the meeting; and the action of Gov. Tod, of Ohio, and Gov. Curtin, of Pennsylvania, in concert with him, turned the tide of faction and conspiracy.

"Undoubtedly we shall have further developments forthwith, especially as to the persistent malice of Governor Andrew and those who concurred with him in the silly and malignant attempt to press for the removal of McClellan. But he is now out of their reach, and they will suffer the usual consequence of biting files. Under the recent supplementary proclamation of the President, these men could be handily arrested at Washington, whither they are said to have repaired; for their conduct in hostility to the commanding general is, of all things, directly to discourage enlistments and to be guilty of disloyal practices, affording aid and comfort to the rebels, who would like nothing better than to have McClellan removed. Our own Governor, indeed, can be proved to have declared in New York a few days ago that the government should not have a man from Massachusetts until the change in the command of the army was effected.

The *Herald's* correspondent, who was on the spot, informs us that these "Loyal Governors" were in session till *half past one o'clock at night*, and that after the telegraph had informed them the President had yielded, they opened their batteries on Gen. McCLELLAN—made it a part of their programme that he should be removed, and adjourned for Washington in a body, where, no doubt, they received the assurance from headquarters, that as soon as it would *look well* their wishes should be gratified.

This meeting of twelve Governors of twelve states, at such a time, and such an hour, for such purposes, is without a parallel in the annals of traitorous conspiracies. Even the traitorous Federal Governors of 1814, dared not undertake so bold a job in their executive capacities and the Hartford Convention was composed of a set of lay delegates. We relinquish this subject with the melancholy regret that we have men high in office that would combine in a move to coerce the executive of the nation into any measure, and that we have a National Executive that would yield to such a pressure. The precedent is one pregnant with unalloyed danger to our Government, and all true patriots will regret that we had not one in the Presidential chair who would meet all such forestalling efforts with the reply:

"By the Eternal, I run this machine—disperse to your homes, or I will hang you on the first tree as plotters of treason!"

REVOLUTIONARY SPIRIT TAUGHT BY CHARLES SUMNER.

On the 7th of September, 1854, at Worcester, Mass., CHARLES SUMNER made a speech on the birthday of the Republican party in that state. Then and there the party was christened, and Mr. SUMNER in leading it to its baptismal fount, portrayed the objects of its birth, and prophesied of its future career, as the MOSES in the Abolition bull rushes:

"The whole dogma of *passive obedience must be rejected*. In whatever guise it may assume, and under whatever *alias* it may skulk—whether in the tyrannical usurpations of king, parliament, or *judicial tribunal*—whether in the exploded theories of Sir Robert Filmer, or the rampant assumptions of the partizans of the Fugitive Slave bill. The rights of the *civil power* are limited. There are things beyond its province. There are matters out of its control. There are cases in which the *faithful citizen* may say—aye, *must* say, *I will not obey*."

And again:

"I desire to say that no party which calls itself *National*, according to the common acceptance of the word, which leans upon a slave holding wing (cheers), or is in combination with slave holders (cheers) can at this time, be true to *Massachusetts* (Great applause), and the reason is obvious. It can be presented so as to cleave the most common understanding. The essential element of such a party, whether declared or concealed, is *compromise*, but our duties require all constitutional opposition to slavery, and the slave power without *compromise.* * * * As Republicans, we go forth to encounter the oligarchy of slavery! (Great applause.)

MR. SEWARD'S DESPOTISM.

To show that Mr. SEWARD considers himself a Duke of no ordinary pretensions in a great Republican Despotism, we quote from his remarks to the British Lord:

"My Lord, I can touch a bell on my right hand, and order the arrest of a citizen of Ohio! I can touch the bell again, and order the imprisonment of a citizen in New York, and *no power on earth, but that of the President*, can release them! Can the Queen of England, in her dominions, do as much?"

No, Mr. SEWARD, the Queen of England cannot. If she attempted it her head would roll from the block. None but the Czar of Russia, the Sultan of Turkey, the Kahn of Tartary, the Emperor of Austria, the President of the United States, and such autocrats, could accomplish such feats of absolute despotism.

THE CONSTITUTION PRONOUNCED AN "ABSURDITY."

When the bill for dismembering Virginia was up for consideration, in the House of Representatives, THAD. STEVENS thus gave vent to his abhorence of the constitution:

"I will not stultify myself by supposing that we have any warrant in the constitution for this proceeding.

"This talk of restoring the Union as it was, and under the constitution as it is, is one of the absurdities which I have heard repeated until I have become sick of it. There are many things which make such an event impossible. *This Union never shall, with my consent, be restored under the constitution as it is!*"

REPUBLICANS CHEERING FOR DISSOLUTION.

In the Wisconsin *State Journal*, (Rep.) of September 13, 1854, we find the following:

"*Second Edition of Little Giantism in Chicago.*

"Last Saturday, Lieutenant Governor Willard, of Indiana, attempted to convert the political heathens of Chicago to the sublime doctrine of Squatter Sovereignty, and force them into allegiance to the Prophet of the New Dispensation.

"The people listened to his remarks half an hour in silence, when thinking he had made a decided impression, he ventured to stigmatize Horace Greeley as "the first man who attempted opposition to the Nebraska Bill, *and recommended a dissolution of the Union. This brought out the crowd* with *three cheers for Greeley*, and three groans for Douglas! Again, he turns and attacks Benton, and the crowd answered with six cheers for Benton, and three groans for Douglas! Then he attacked the *Know Nothings*, and this brought out *three cheers for that party*, and as usual three groans for Douglas!"

This was not the first or last time the Republicans cheered for those in favor of a dissolution of the Union, and for that pestiferous Know Nothing party.

HAILING EXTERMINATION AND DAMNATION.

The Republicans of Cadiz, Green county, Wisconsin, held a meeting on the 26th of March, 1863, and from their resolutions we select the following:

"*Resolved*, That we will hail any policy of our Government, be it the Proclamation, Annihilation, Extermination, Starvation, and even *Damnation*, could that form a part of its policy," &c.

This is "loyalty" and piety combined.

NULLIFICATION IN OHIO.

When the Oberlin rescuers' case was before the Supreme Court of Ohio, Mr. WOLCOTT, the Republican Attorney General of that State, in arguing for the nullification of law, and trampling the Constitution under foot, used the following language:

"I hesitate to refer to a single point. Yes, I bear it—you hear it—everybody hears it said upon the streets, if this Court shall exercise its unquestionable prerogative in the enlargement of these prisoners, there will be a conflict—a conflict between State and Federal authority. What then? Are we children—are we old women, to be frightened from our propriety by a menace like this? I mean *law*, but not the law of King BOMBA, of Naples. Order—I stand by order, but not the order which reigned in Warsaw, after the massacre. Peace is most desirable, but not the peace which survives liberty, and subsists under a despotism. If there is to be a conflict, let it come now, when I can meet it. I would leave no such conflict as a legacy to my children."

This false appeal to patriotism, to destroy our Government, and override its laws, was heartily endorsed by all the Republican press. The Milwaukee *Sentinel* said of WOLCOTT's appeal, "it is well expressed."

NO RESTORATION—'TIS A "CRIME."

The President issued a proclamation appointing a day of fasting and prayer, in which occurred this sentence:

"Let us then, rest humbly in the hope, authorized by the Divine teachings, that the united cry of the nation will be heard on high, and answered with blessings no less than the pardon of our national sins, and the restoration of our now divided and suffering country, *to its former condition of unity and peace*"

Upon this, the Boston *Commonwealth*, the home organ of CHARLES SUMNER, commented as follows:

"It is *cool assumption* of the President that the pardon of our national sins has any kind of connection with the restoration of our country to '*its former happy condition of unity and peace!* " Our own opinion is, that if God had resolved not to pardon us at all, he would *prove it by allowing the restoration of that old* 'unity of peace.' *That unity was crime;* that *peace worse than war!* "

And the aforesaid sheet proceeds to invoke a curse on the President, and all who shall join in praying for the aforesaid "restoration," as follows:

"*May the tongue be withered, ere it is answered*, that prays for a restoration of that old state of things, from which God in His mercy seems willing to rescue us—than which His fiercest wrath could find no more *terrible doom*, for a blind nation, led by blind rulers!"

The above is but an echo of that resolution passed by the Massachusetts Senate forty-nine years before, that it was

"unbecoming in a moral and religious people to rejoice over the victories obtained by our arms."

One would think that forty-nine years was a period long enough to bleach out the treasonable impiety, so ingrained in Puritanical blood, but it is a trite old saying that

"What is born in the bones, rarely leaves the flesh."

THE SOUTH NOT WORTH A COPPER.

In 1859, the Milwaukee *Free Democrat*, in a long article, endeavoring to educate the public mind to the idea that it was for the *interest* of the North to dissolve the Union, favored us with the following Republican conclusion:

"We repeat the assertion, *that the Union is not worth a copper to the North in any point of view*, but is a perpetual sacrifice of both money and morals, [?] an assertion which we can make good."

"NO WISH FOR RECONSTRUCTION."

The New York *Tribune*, in February, 1863, in a long leader, had the following:

"Speaking for ourselves, we can honestly say for the old Union, which was kept in existence by Southern menaces and Northern concessions, we have no regrets, and no wish for its reconstruction.

"Who wants a Union which is nothing but a *sentiment to lacquer Fourth of July orations*, withal!

"If by change, in ancient times the criminal felt the loathsome corpse, which justice had tied upon his shoulders, slipping off, he did not, we fancy, cry out: 'O, wretched man that I am! who will fasten me again *to the body of this death?*' If we are, in the Providence of God, to be delivered from unnatural alliances —if the January of slavery is no longer to chill by natural embraces the May of human hope, who is there wicked and weak enough to forbid *the righteous divorce!*"

The Boston *Commonwealth*, SUMNER's organ, says:

"How dare any man pray for the return of that festering wrong—that sin and shame—the Union as it was? It is like breaking the tables of the Eternal Law, and dashing them in the face of Jehovah!"

Mr. BINGHAM, an abolition orator, while stumping Connecticut for the Republicans, in 1863, said:

"Who in the name of God wants the cotton States, or any other State this side of perdition, to remain in the Union, if slavery is to continue?"

THE CONSTITUTION COMMITTED TO THE FLAMES

The Boston *Liberator* of April 24, 1863 thus gloried in its treason, and hatred of our Constitution:

"No act of ours do we regard with more conscientious approval, *or higher satisfaction* —none do we submit more confidently to the tribunal of Heaven and the verdict of mankind, than when several years ago, on the Fourth of July, in the presence of a great assembly, *we committed to the flames the Constitution of the United States*, because (in the language of John Quincy Adams)—

"'The bargain between freedom and slavery was morally and politically vicious, inconsistent with the principles on which alone our revolution can be justified, and cruel and oppressive, by riveting the chains of the oppressed, and pledging the faith and freedom to maintain and perpetuate the tyranny of the master.'

"And should the present bloody struggle end in any compromise with the South, or in recognizing any constitutional obligations to slaveholders or slave hunters, in the *border states, we shall again give that instrument to the consuming fire*, and renew our protest against it, as '*a covenant with death, an agreement with hell!*' * * * * * * * * * * *

"In the court of *conscience*, and before God, it matters not what slaveholding agreements or compromises may be found in the Constitution or out of it, they are inhuman, unjust and immoral, and *therefore null and void*, and if a man can retain office or be a voter under the Government only on condition of sustaining compromises, then it is certain, that if he would not not do evil, that good may come, he must relinquish office holding, and refuse to cast a vote stained with human blood. His motto is, and must be, as one loyal to right and duty, *no Union with slaveholders.*"

"'Man is more than constitutions—
Better rot beneath the sod
Than be true to church and state,
While we are doubly false to God.'"

Thus, we have a clue to what the opponents of the Democracy mean by "loyalty." It is the touch stone of opposition to the Constitution. Nor need any one tell us this is but the ravings of an ultra Abolitionist. It is the cry of all who claim to be *par excellence* Administration men, not one of whom will consent to retain the Constitution as it is.

Senator HENKLE, of Springfield, Ohio, in a speech at Columbus, in 1863, said in speaking of the Constitution:

"*I would blow it away as a child blows a feather into the air.*"

Per contra, Mr. VALLANDIGHAM, in a speech in the same State, said:

"I am a Democrat—*for the Constitution— for law—for the Union—for liberty.*"

Mr. HENKLE gets a fat office under the conscription law since he uttered his Phillipic against the Constitution, while Mr. VALLANDIGHAM was banished. So that it will be seen, it *pays* better under this Administration to denounce the Constitution than it does to stand by it as "the sheet anchor of our hope," as JEFFERSON termed it.

GOD AND THE NEGRO.

After having spit upon the Constitution— derided its founders—mocked the wisdom of its purposes—trampled it under foot, and committed it to the flames, these impious forerunners of the "New Dispensation" that "is to be" set up the negro, as MOSES did the serpent in the wilderness, and expect the people are to "look and live." A specimen of this impious negro worship we find in the New York *Independent* of January, 1863:

"Congress is in dispute over a bill to arm and equip 150,000 negroes to serve in the war. Let it [Congress] stop the debate. The *case is settled;* the problem is *solved;* the *argument is done.* Let the recruiting sergeants beat their drums! The next levy of troops must not be made in the North, but on the plantations! Marshal them into line by regiments and brigades! The men that have picked cotton, must now pick flints! Gather the great third army. For two years the government has been searching in an enemy's country for a path to victory—*only the negro can find it.* Give him gun and bayonet, and let *him* point the way. The future is fair—*God and the negro are to save the Republic!* [The army is nowhere in this programme.]

"The interval between the destruction and salvation of the Republic is measured by two steps—one is emancipation—the other military success. The first is taken—the other delays. How is it to be achieved? There is but one answer—*by the negro.*

"*The negroes are the final reliance of the Government. They are the forlorn hope of the Republic! They are the last safe keepers of the good cause. We must make alliance with them, or our final success is imperiled!*"

Thus does this *religio-political* apostle hold up the *negro* as our only Savior. Look to him and live, all ye "loyal" sons of freedom! Great God, what mockery! In the light of the civilized world, for twenty millions of white men, with abundance of wealth, power, intelligence, and prestige of the old government to back them, cowardly acknowledging their impotence before eight millions of "paupers," and calling on the semi-savage, down-trodden sons of Ham to come to their relief, lest they perish.

But, the *Independent* has an object—and that object is to invest the negro with undue importance, to the end that he may have his full *political* weight in the political part of this conflict. This is the drama we are now playing to "crowded houses." It is for the benefit of political tricksters.

BLOODTHIRSTY VENOM OF THE "LOYALISTS."

During the summer of 1863, according to the Washington *Chronicle*, JIM LANE, a Republican United States Senator from Kansas, made a speech in Washington, in which he gave utterance to the following bloodthirsty sentiments:

"I would like to live long enough to see every *white man* in South Carolina, *in hell*, and the negroes inheriting their territory. [Loud applause.]

"It would not wound my feelings any day to find the dead bodies of rebel sympathizers [this is the term applied by the radicals to all democrats] pierced with bullet holes in every street and alley of Washington. [Applause.] Yes, I *would* regret this, for I would not like to witness all this waste of powder and lead. I would rather have them hung, and the ropes saved! Let them dangle until their stinking bodies rot and fall to the ground piece by piece. [Laughter and applause.]

THE UNION "HATED BY EVERY PATRIOT."

The Chicago *Tribune* thus puts on record its detestation of the Constitution and Union:

"The Union as it was will never bless the vision of any pro-slavery fanatic or secession sympathizer, and it *never ought to!* It is a thing of the past, *HATED BY EVERY PATRIOT*, and destined never to *CURSE an honest people,* or *BLOT THE PAGE OF HISTORY AGAIN!*"

"Better recognize the Southern Confederacy at once, and stop this effusion of blood, than continue this ruinous policy, or have even a restoration of the Union as it was."—*Cassius M. Clay.*

"Conway of the Boston *Commonwealth* writes home [from England] to say that he 'had rather have heard of a defeat at Vicksburg than the declaration of Gerrit Smith, that the Union must be saved, even though slavery be saved with it.'"—*Albany Journal*, (*Rep.*)

AMALGAMATION AND NEGRO EQUALITY.

This is what is now aimed at by the radicals. Many conservative Republicans still revolt at the idea, but time, and the "policy" of the "powers" and coming events will cure them of that, as it has of former repugnance to many other radical "ideas" they now swear by. In a speech by WENDELL PHILLIPS, in 1863, that "leader of this progressive age," came out flat-footed for amalgamation.

FRED DOUGLAS, whom the Tiltonians prefer to MCCLELLAN, for President, addressed a Republican meeting at Brooklyn, in 1863, on the subject of amalgamation, in which he said:

"There is not much prejudice against color now, because, in coming down Broadway, the other day, I saw a white lady riding beside a colored man. It is true the colored man had a bit of tinsel around his hat, but nobody seemed to notice it, and the lady did not show any signs of disgust. A few days since a white lady asked me to walk down Broadway with her, and insisted on taking my arm. On walking along, every one we met stared at us as if we were some curious animals. What was the reason the people did not stare at the coachman in the same manner. Simply because he was a servant, and I was walking with a friend. By and by you will get over *all this nonsense.* (Cheers.) You ought to see me in London, walking down Broadway with a white *lady* on each arm, and nobody stared at us, as if they thought it strange. And *it will soon be so here,* and then we will be all the nobler and better. (Cheers.)"

WENDELL PHILLIPS, at the Tremont Temple, Boston, said:

"Thank God, for McClellan, for Cameron—thank God for *defeat*. With a *man* for President, we should have put down the Rebellion in ninety days, and left slavery *where it was!*"

SALMON P. CHASE, the present Secretary of the Treasury, made a speech in Ohio, August 19, 1854, in which he said:

"We have rights which the Federal Government *must not invade*—rights *superior to its power*, on which our sovereignty depends, and we do mean to assert these rights against all tyrannical assumptions of authority."

In 1854, in speaking of the delivering up of BURNS, the fugitive, the New York *Tribune* said:

"There is power enough in the anti-fugitive law masses of Massachusetts, when properly directed, to *defy the whole force of the national government*, if that force were exerted for the enforcement of the statute."

DEN. WADE WILLING TO LET THE SOUTH GO.

The Hon. BENJ. WADE, Republican U. S. Senator from Ohio, made a speech in the Senate, December 4, 1856, in which he coined the following:—[*Cong. Globe*, 3d Sess. 34th Cong. p. 25.

"But Southern gentleman stand here and in almost all their speeches, speak of the dissolution of the Union, as an element of every argument, as though it were a peculiar condescension on their part that they permitted the Union to stand at all. If they do not feel interested in upholding the Union—if it really trenches on their rights—if it endangers their institutions to such an extent that they cannot feel secure under it—if their interests are violently assailed by means of this Union, I am not one of those who expect that they will long continue under it. I am not one of those who would ask them to continue in such a Union. It would be doing violence to the *platform of the party to which I belong*. We have adopted the old Declaration of Independence as the basis of our political movements, which declares that any people when their Government ceases to protect their rights—when it is so subverted from the true purposes of Government as to oppose them, have the right to recur to fundamental principles, and if need be, to *destroy the Government under which they live*, and to erect on its *ruins* another more condusive to their welfare. I hold that they have *this right. I will not blame any people for exercising it*, whenever they think the contingency has come. * * * You cannot forcibly hold men in this Union, for the attempt to do so, it seems to me would subvert the first principles of the Government under which we live."

If this be the correct doctrine, we cannot see what objection Mr. Senator WADE can have to the following response to his own doctrine:

"We, the people of South Carolina, in Convention assembled, do declare and ordain, and it is hereby declared and ordained, that the ordinance adopted by us in convention, on the 23d day of May, A. D. 1788, whereby the Constitution of the United States of America, was ratified, and also all acts and parts of acts of the General Assembly of this State ratifying amendments of the said Constitution, are hereby repealed, and the Union now existing between South Carolina and other States, under the name of the United States of America, is hereby dissolved"—ayes 169, noes 0.

And if this does not satisfy the Honorable Senator, let us copy the Preamble to the Alabama Act of Secession, which is a perfect transcript of the substance of the Senator's remarks:

"*Whereas*, The election of Abraham Lincoln and Hannibal Hamlin to the offices of President and Vice President of the United States of America by a sectional party, avowedly hostile to the domestic institutions, and to the peace and security of the people of the State of Alabama, following upon the heels of many and dangerous infractions of the Constitution of the United States [This is the language of the ordinance of secession of Wisconsin—resolutions of 1859] by many of the states and people of the Northern section, is a political wrong of so insulting and menacing a character, as to justify the people of the State of Alabama in the adoption of prompt and decided measures for their future peace and security, "*Therefore*, be it ordained," &c.

Now, had not South Carolina, Alabama, and others, a right to infer from the speech of Senator WADE, that they would not be molested in their withdrawal from the Union? WADE certainly announced the doctrine before they acted on it. He gave the license, based on his party's "platform"—a license which they also found in Mr. LINCOLN's speech in 1848—a ilcense in the secession speeches, editorials, memorials sermons, resolves, &c., of Massachusetts forty-nine years ago—and of Wisconsin five years ago. Still, all of these should not have induced the secession of the Southern states. They ought to have been more politic than to have followed the example of the Northern secessionists.

"SPOT THE UNION AS IT WAS."

CASSIUS M. CLAY, a pet of the Administration, made a speech at Brooklyn, New York, during the canvass in 1862, and this is the way he manifested his revolutionary spirit:

"So far from finding fault with Abraham Lincoln, he rather found fault with him that he had not suspended the *habeas corpus*—not by a dash of the pen, but *by ropes round the necks of the traitors.*

"A voice—We'll hang them yet.

"Mr. Clay—Yes, sir, *the hanging of such men as Seymour and Wood would have saved thousands of honest lives.*

"A voice—That is so.

"Mr. Clay—That is true philosophy. (Applause and laughter.)"

Quite in keeping with this Robesperrean spirit from this Republican expounder, in the same speech:

"It was a delusion to suppose that liberty could be established on this continent, when the President of the United States and the people of the United States had not the courage to do what was right. Therefore, spot not Gen. Boyle; spot the President of the United States; spot the heads of the Departments; spot your military chieftains; *spot those who would have the Union as it was!*"

IS THE PRESIDENT THE GOVERNMENT?

This question is thus settled by that pious thunderer, in Plymouth Church, the Rev. Political HENRY WARD BEECHER:

"I know it is said that the President is not the government; that the Constitution is the government. What! a sheepskin parchment a government? I should think it was a very fit one for some men that I hear and see sometimes. What is a government in our country? It is a body of living men ordained by the people to administer public affairs according to laws that are written in a constitution and in the statute books, and the government is the living men that are administering in a certain method the affairs of the nation. [The elementary writers say a government is the system of laws by which a nation is governed—but then the elementary writers don't know much!] It is not a dry writing or a book. President Lincoln, his Cabinet, the heads of the executive departments, are the government, and men have got to take their choice whether they will go against their government or go with them."

The first object of tyrants who seize power, is to show that they do it *legitimately.* No despotism was ever erected over any people, except through a slow yet sure process of false reasoning and plausible pretexts. ROBESPERRIE, DANTON, ST. JUST, and other despots, who figured in the French Revolution, and were the authors of that Reign of Terror that caused the soil of France to drink up the blood of five millions of innocent victims, pleaded their justification in public—in "Military Necessity"—all to preserve the "liberties of France." "*Necessity*" has been the tyrant's plea the world over, to build despotisms on the ruins of constitutional government.

We cannot do better, in this connection, than to quote the following just sentiments from DANIEL WEBSTER, the "Great Expounder," who in speaking of the value and sacredness of our constitution said:

"The contest for ages has been to rescue liberty from the *grasp of executive power.* On the long list of champions of human freedom, there is not one name dimmed by the reproach of advocating the extension of Executive authority. [Mr. W. had evidently not studied Beecher.] On the contrary, the uniform and steady purpose of all such champions has been to limit and restrain it. Through all the history of the contest for liberty, executive power has been regarded as a lion that must be caged. So far as being the object of enlightened, popular trust; so far as being considered the natural protection of popular right, it has been dreaded as the great object of danger.

"Our security is our watchfulness of Executive power. It was the construction of this department which was infinitely the most difficult in the great work of erecting our government. To give to the Executive such power as should make it useful, and yet not dangerous; efficient, independent, strong, and yet prevent it from sweeping away everything by its military and civil power, by the influence of patronage and favor; this, indeed, was difficult. They who had the work to do saw this difficulty, and we see it If we would maintain our system, we should act wisely, by using every restraint, every guard the Constitution has provided—when we and those who come after us, have done all we can do, and all they can do, it will be well for us and them, if the Executive, by the power of patronage and party, shall not prove an overmatch for all other branches of Government. I will not acquiesce in the reversal of the principles of all just ideas of Government. I will not degrade the character of popular representation. I will not blindly confide, when all my experience admonishes to be jealous. I will not trust Executive power, vested in a single magistrate, to keep the virgils of liberty. Encroachment must be resisted at every step, whether the consequence be prejudicial or not, if there be an illegal exercise of power, it must be resisted in the proper manner We are not to wait till great mischief comes; till the Government is overthrown, or liberty itself put in extreme jeopardy. We would be unworthy sons of our fathers were we so to regard questions affecting freedom."

In 1862 the Racine (Wis.) *Journal*, in an article looking to the "new order of things," said:

"Let the main disposition be to aid the army, the Congress, the Cabinet and the President, in every bold and proper method to put down the rebellion. *The Democrats must not clamor for the Union as it was. The thing is absurd and never will be seen again."*

MOULDING PUBLIC OPINION.

Says the Boston *Liberator:*

"The Republican party is moulding public sentiment in the right direction for the specific work the Abolitionists are striving to accomplish, viz: *the dissolution of the Union, and the abolition of slavery throughout the land.*"

MR. LINCOLN IN 1854.

Mr. LINCOLN made a speech at Peoria, Illinois, on the 16th of October, 1854, in which he said:

"What I do say is this: that no man is good enough to govern another man without the other's consent.—*Howell's Life of Lincoln, p.* 279.

MR. SEWARD AND VIOLENCE.

Mr. SEWARD, in the Senate, March, 1858, one year before the John Brown raid, said:

"The interests of the white race demand the ultimate emancipation of all men. Whether that consummation shall be allowed to take effect with needful and wise precautions against sudden change and disaster, or ☞ *be hurried on by violence,* is all that remains for you to decide."

MR. SEWARD ON THE "LAST STAGE OF CONFLICT."

Mr. SEWARD made speech at Boston, 1860, in which he thus foreshadowed the purpose of the Abolition party :

"What a commentary upon the history of man is the fact that eighteen years after the death of John Quincy Adams, the people have for their standard bearer, Abraham Lincoln, *conferring the obligations of the Higher Law,* which the Sage of Quincy proclaimed, and contending for weal or for woe, for life or death, in the impressible conflict between freedom and slavery, I desire only to *say that we are in the last stage of the conflict,* before the great triumphant inauguration of this policy into the government of the United State."

MR. SEWARD'S JUSTIFICATION FOR DISUNION.

Mr. SEWARD, in the Senate, threw this firebrand at the South:

"Then the Free States and Slave States of the Atlantic, divided and warring with each other, would disgust the Free States of the Pacific, and they would have *abundant cause and justification for withdrawing* from the Union, productive no longer of peace, safety, and liberty to themselves," &c.

"NATIONAL" STRICKEN OUT.

In the Republican Convention of Chicago, 1860, at which Mr. LINCOLN was nominated, we find the following among the proceedings, as published in the New York *Tribune* of May 18, 1860:

"Judge Jessup said that he desired to amend a verbal mistake in the name of the party. It was printed in the resolutions '*National* Republican party.' He wished to strike out the word '*National,*' as that *was not* the name by which the party was properly known."

The correction was made. And does not this, of itself, show the sectional, disunion aims of the leaders? They could not bear to be called National, because that implied fealty to the Union.

BANKS PREDICTS A MILITARY GOVERNMENT.

N. P. BANKS, in a speech in Massachusetts, in 1856, thus predicts a "Military Dictatorial Government":

"I can conceive of a time when this Constitution shall not be in existence—*when we shall have an absolute military dictatorial Government,* transmitted from age to age, with men at its head who are made rulers by military commission, or who claim an hereditary right to govern those over whom they are placed."

CARL SCHURZ ON REVOLUTION.

Mr. SCHURZ, in 1860, said:

"May the God in human nature be aroused and pierce the very soul of our nation with an energy that shall sweep, as with the besom of destruction, this abomination (slavery) from the land. You call this revolution. *It is.* In this we *need revolution;* we *must,* we *will have it.* Let it come!"

JOHN P. HALE ON DISSOLUTION.

On the 12th of July, 1848, JOHN P. HALE said:

"All the terrors of *dissolution* I can look steadfastly in the face, before I could look to that moral Union which must fall upon us when we can so far prostitute ourselves as to become the pioneers of slavery in the territories."

In the Senate, February 26, 1856, Mr. HALE in speaking of the conflict said:

"Good! good! Sir, I hope it will come, and if it comes to blood, let it come. No, sir, if that issue must come, let it come, and it cannot come too soon."

GENERAL BEN. BUTLER FOR "MODERN IMPROVEMENTS."

An "ovation" was given to General BUTLER, on his return from New Orleans, by the Republicans, in New York. The General of course made a speech, and of course took ground which pleased his admirers. He said:

"And now my friends, I do not know but that I shall commit some heresy; but as a Democrat, and as an Andrew Jackson Democrat, [God save the mark.] I say, *I am not for the Union as it was*, I have the honor to say, as a Democrat, that I am not for the Union to be again as it was. * * I am not for the reconstouction of the Union as it was. I have spent tears and blood enough on it, in conjunction with my fellow citizens, *to make it a little better*. * * The old house was good enough for me, but as they have pulled down the early part, I propose that we *rebuild* it, with *all the modern improvements!*" [That is the "Strong Government" Abolition "improvements."]

THE OBJECTS AND CONSEQUENCES OF ABOLITION AGITATION.

The Hon. ELI THAYER, an "old line Whig" and a conservative Republican, addressed a Union meeting in New York, in 1859, in which he set forth the objects and consequences of the slavery agitation in its true light. We make room here for a valuable extract, as showing the well grounded fears of the conservative Union men of that day, in reference to this "wolf," which JEFFERSON said we had "by the ears, and can neither hold him nor safely let him go," and also to show that the agitators of that day had their eyes open—that knowing the consequences, they persisted in the course of dissolution—as we believe using the slavery imbroglio as a *means* to effect their *ends*—the dissolution of the Union. Mr. THAYER said:

"To come, then, squarely up to the issue, to grapple with it fiercely and without parley— what is the present aspect and position of the slavery question between the South and the North? I think that it is comprehended in this—that wherever the anti-slavery sentiment is introduced into politics and made the *sole base* of party organization and action, it becomes *abolitionism*. (prolonged applause.) It may not be altogether such in the outset, but that is its tendency, and must of necessity be its result."

At this period, be it remembered, the Republicans indignantly spurned the idea that they had any sympathy with abolitionism; but let us see how very like its father Mr. THAYER perceived their likeness.

"The anti-slavery sentiment as a *moral conviction and opinion* in the *minds and consciences* of men, no matter how strong is a passive sentiment, and remains such, until introduced into politics. It then becomes an active agency, and if it *alone* constitutes a *party*—if there is nothing of the party but what is based on this, then we must see what is its antagonism—what it is directed against—for every party is an active, opposing force, formed for positive and *aggressive action*. Now, will you tell me what there is for a party, based solely on anti-slavery to oppose, to fight against? Not certainly the extension of slavery in the territories—that contest is ended. (Applause.) Not the revival of the slave trade—for this finds too few advocates to make an issue. (Applause.) Then certainly it *must oppose slavery, as it exists*, or its office is at an end—"Othello's occupation is gone." (Applause.) [How strictly this has been verified.] There will of course be many classes under this general head—as many different shades of Abolitionists as there are colors in the African race—varying from real jet of Mrs. Stowe's ·Uncle Tom' to the *Octoroon* of Bourcicault. (Applause.) Some, only a few, I hope, if they would not engage in it, would countenance an insurrection, [see John Brown raid at a sample] would *furnish* arms, if they did not *use* them. [Just what they did do.] Many will intensify and inflame the bitter hatred to slavery and slave holders, [this they did do] till the very weight of animosity and aversion engendered *will make the Union unbearable!*"

No prophecy in the Book of Jeremiah ever proved more true than this. Indeed, all penetrative minds could not have failed at that time, to have seen the *result* from *causes* then maturing. The radicals knew that envy would be the parent of hate—that hate would beget crimination,—that crimination would propogate its own species, and that the progeny of all these would be dissolution. They *knew* this fact. They could not have been ignorant of it. It was the main count in the indictment, and the Supreme Court of History will render its verdict of "guilty"—guilty in the first degree, of attempting to compass the life of their country.

CHAPTER XXI.

ABOLITIONISTS SHOW THEIR PURPOSE TO DESTROY THE UNION.

The Various Efforts at Compromise...Compromise the Basis of all Governments...General Principles of, Applied... The Compromises of the Constitution : What were They ?...Messrs. Yates and Lansing Retire from the Convention of 1787...Compromise between Delaware, Maryland and Other States...The First Draft...Luther Martin on Compromise...The Large and Small Small States at War on Suffrage...Compromise on Slave Trade and Navigation Acts...An Original Plan of Constitution...The Great Suffrage Question...Mr. Martin's Explanations... Compromise between Slavery and Navigation,..The New England States Favor the Slave Trade...Official Proof... Hypocrisy of Abolition States...Massachusetts Stealing Negroes...The Virginia and New Jersey Plan of Government...Predictions of Geo. Mason...The Missouri Compromise...General Propositions...Jackson and Clay on Compromise...Compromise of 1832-3...Compromise of 1850...Why the Radicals would not Compromise in 1861.

In this connection we will introduce to the reader sundry facts concerning

THE VARIOUS EFFORTS AT COMPROMISE.

Compromise is a talismanic word. It presupposes a controversy, and then it assures us of a settlement.

"COMPROMISE:—To adjust and settle a difference by mutual agreement, with concessions of claims by both parties, &c."

This is WEBSTER's definition.

Compromise is, indeed, the *basis* of all governments. No government could exist an hour without compromise. Its "usual signification," says WEBSTER, is, "mutual agreement—adjustment." Now, let us place all men back to first principles—on their *natural* rights. No one man has any control over another, of right. The aggregate of all is society, and the aggregate of societies or communities form states—states make up nations. But by what process is it all accomplished? A nation must have a system of laws—a governing principle. How is this to be accomplished? If all thought exactly alike, there would be no need of laws or rulers. But all do not—cannot think alike. The good and bad—the wise and the foolish—promiscuously mix. Who shall make laws, and set the machinery of government in motion? Why, the people, of course (in a Democratic Republican Government). But how can the people act? Why, by choosing Representatives to make laws, and somebody to adjudicate and administer them. Perhaps all may agree to the necessity of this, but the *manner*—the mode—the *how* to do it—will be a question of conflicting views. One says by ballot—another by *viva voce*. One has objections to an aggregate poll—another will not consent to a multitude of polls. One has his mode of making returns—another his, and so on, until a thousand and one objections arise, and plans are projected, forming a Baabel of ideas, making confusion worse confounded.

What is to be done? A *Government* is absolutely necessary. All concur in that, but the mode and manner of getting at it—the system and details to be adopted are the points on which minds do and will differ. A *knows* he is right and will not yield to B. B swears he is right, and scorns to yield to A, while C believes both A and B to be wrong, and sets up a theory of his own, warranted to be perfect. Here, we have a trio of ideas, each in conflict with the other. The strong bent of *human nature*, and the pride of opinion, breed a struggle and a contest, for each considers his opinions and wishes as of much consequence, and nearer right than his neighbors, therefore, a complete yielding cannot be expected by either party. What then? Why, the very law of our existence will suggest—*a compromise*, whereupon—

A says to B, Now this obstinacy is wrong. We all agree that we need a government, and yet our differences about the *mode* of securing that government, are likely to finally deprive us of its blessings. As we cannot all agree as to the exact *mode*, let us compromise the matter. I will agree to a portion of *your* plan, *you* to a portion of mine, while we will both agree to a portion of C's. Now, A has touched the subsoil of conciliation, for while he invites a little yielding from others, he himself yields. And this is the basis of amity. It is compromise. Mutual concessions take away the sting of the shout of victory—neither party feels vanquished or humiliated—*compromise* has accomplished its work, and the organization of government begins.

All this is in strict accordance with the theory of the Declaration that Governments ought to be founded on the "consent of the governed." No such Government can be formed, except by compromise.

A Government of *force*—established by the sword, neither seeks or yields to compromise. A tyrant usurps power by restraining the people of the liberty to compromise. The sword is his means—usurpation his purpose—a servile obedience his object.

We have thus been led to advance these

views, because many seem to argue that any compromise in reference to the affairs of Government is the highest of crimes, but it will be our purpose to show that these very men enjoy their liberty to denounce compromises from the very fact that our fathers did compromise—yea, and compromised, too, the slavery question.

As illustrating something of the nature of controversies arising in forming and operating a Government, and the necessities of compromise, we feel justified in presenting copious extracts from early publications, which will shed sufficient light, we trust, on the difficulties and dangers attending the formation of our present Union, to enable those anti-compromisers of the present day to appreciate the *value* and *necessity* of conceding something to obtain much. WASHINGTON's advice to frequently have recourse to "fundamental principles," is as good to follow now as ever, and while the world is convulsed because our people have ceased to study the fraternal precepts of WASHINGTON, let us consider

THE COMPROMISES OF THE CONSTITUTION.

The struggle in the National Convention of 1787 for a supremacy of "ideas" and principles, good and bad, was as vigorous as any contest that has transpired since that epoch. Men of that day were governed by all the ambition and qualities of mind that distinguish men of the present era. All parties of all sections endeavored to secure the most for *self and location.* The larger States strove to overreach the smaller ones, while the smaller ones were jealous of their more powerful neighbors.

As already stated, in another portion of this work, the National Convention was divided in sentiment as to the nature of the Government to be adopted. There was the extreme Democratic element, in favor of shearing the power of the General Government to the lowest dimensions; the Democratic Republican party, in favor of uniting a Democratic and a Republican form of Government as near as might be. so as to give sufficient strength to the Union to make it serviceable for the purposes intended; a Federal party, in favor of confederating power in a General Government, under the Republican form, and a party of Monarchists, in favor of a monarchical government, having unlimited sway over the States and the people. As might be expected, these clashing elements were hard to harmonize, and nothing but a spirit of compromise could do it.

For weeks, said FRANKLIN, the contest hung in doubt, as to whether any government would be formed, and at one time dissolution and eternal separation seemed inevitable.

Two members from New York, Mr. YATES and Mr. LANSING, left the convention, to return no more, because they failed to carry certain points, and in a joint letter to Governor CLINTON, they say:

"Thus circumstanced, under these impressions, to have hesitated would have been to be culpable. We therefore gave the principles of the Constitution, which has received the sanction of the majority of the convention, our decided and unreserved dissent. We were not present at the completion of the new constitution; but, before we left the convention, its principles were so well established as to convince us that no alteration was to be expected to conform it to our ideas of expediency and safety. A persuasion that our further attendance would be fruitless and unavailing, rendered us less solicitous to return."

Now, supposing that all the members of that convention, who were displeased with some portion of its results (and we believe there was not one but that objected to some part of the instrument adopted) had left the convention because their views were not accepted by the majority, we should have had no Constitution, and of course no Union, but compromise brought the Convention together—compromise kept it together—compromise preserved it from wild disorder and dissolution—compromise saved its labors to bless posterity.

Many of the delegates were trameled by instructions. Those from Delaware were instructed to "yield no point that did not secure equal suffrage, as by the original articles of confederation"—which was an *equal* vote in Congress, under the new government, with any other state. This, of course, was preposterous, for a state hardly the size of some of the counties in others, to demand equal power and voice in the new government. But Delaware was *sovereign* then, and had a sovereign right to demand conditions. But other states would not grant these conditions. Here was a dead lock, to begin with. Supposing that all the other states should have said we will yield nothing of the kind—would not that have been an end of the matter, unless one or the other party receded, which was not to be expected. The matter was of course *compromised*, by giving Delaware an equal voice in the Senate, and her relative power in the popular branch.

This claim set up by Delaware then, was the cause of that particular feature of representation in our Constitution.

Maryland contended that Virginia had claimed more than her share of the power of suffrage [see *Luther Martin's Letter in Elliott's Debates*, v. 1, p. 346] and that her representation was too large, while Virginia contended that such was not the case. This matter was *compromised* in the system of suffrage agreed upon—Virginia yielding a little, and her sister states receding a little—neither victorious—neither vanquished.

The Convention agreed by resolution to consider propositions as well as a schedule for the whole Constitution in the committee of the whole House, and that after the committee had agreed upon any plan or system, any member might offer amendments or new propositions in open convention.

To show the compromising spirit that followed, we present here a plan for a constitution which passed the committee of the whole, and which the spirit of opposition on one side and compromise on the other materially modified, as the reader will see by comparing this with the constitution as adopted.

"1st. *Resolved*, That it is the opinion of this committee that a National Government ought to be established, consisting of a Supreme, Legislative, Judiciary and Executive.

"2d. That the Legislature ought to consist of two branches.

"3d. That the members of the first branch of the National Legislature ought to be elected by the people of the several States, for the term of three years, to receive fixed stipends, by which they may be compensated for the devotion of their time to public service, to be paid out of the National Treasury; to be ineligible to any office established by a particular State, or under authority of the United States, except those particularly belonging to the functions of the first branch, during the term of service and under the National Government, for the space of one year after its expiration.

"4th. That the members of the Second Branch of the Legislature ought to be chosen by the individual Legislatures, to be of the age of 30 years, at least, to hold their offices for a term sufficient to insure their independency, viz.: seven years, one third to go out biennially, to receive fixed stipends, by which they may be compensated for the devotion of their time to public service, to be paid out of the National Treasury; to be ineligible to any office by a particular state, or under the authority of the United States, except those peculiarly belonging to functions of the Second Branch, during the term of service, and under the National Government, for the space of one year after its expiration.

"5th. That each branch ought to possess the right of originating acts.

"6th. That the National Legislature ought to be empowered to enjoy the Legislative rights vested in Congress by the Confederation, and moreover to legislate in all cases, to which the seperate states are incompetent, or in which the harmony of the United States, may be interrupted by the exercise of individual legislation, to negative all laws passed by the several states [this was the extreme Federal scheme] contravening in the opinion of the Legislature of the United States, the articles of Union, or any treaties subsisting under the authority of the Union.

"7th. That the right of suffrage in the first branch of the National Legislature ought not to be according to the rule established in the Articles of Confederation, but according to some equitable rate of representation, viz.: in proportion to the whole number of white and other free citizens and inhabitants of every age, sex and condition, including those bound to servitude for a term of years, and three fifths of all other persons, not comprehended in the foregoing description, except Indians, not paying taxes in each state.

"8th. That the right of suffrage in the second branch of the National Legislature ought to be according to the rule established in the first.

"9th. That a national Executive be instituted, to consist of a single person, to be chosen by the National Legislature for the term of seven years, with power to carry into execution the national laws—to appoint to offices, in cases not otherwise provided for—to be ineligible a second time, and to be removable on impeachment, and conviction of malpractice, or neglect of duty—to receive a fixed stipend, by which he may be compensated for the devotion of his time to public service—to be paid out of the National Treasury.

"10th. That the National Executive shall have a right to negative any legislative act which shall not afterwards be passed, unless by two-thirds of each branch of the national legislature.

"11th. That a national judiciary be established, to consist of one supreme tribunal, the judges of which to be appointed by the second branch of the national legislature, to hold their offices during good behavior, and to receive punctually, at stated times, a fixed compensation for their services, in which no increase or diminution shall be made, so as to affect the persons actually in office at the time of such increase or diminution.

"12th. That the national legislature be empowered to appoint inferior tribunals.

"13th. That the jurisdiction of the National Judiciary shall extend to cases which respect the collection of the National revenue—cases arising under the laws of the United States—impeachments of any National officer, and questions which involve the National peace and harmony.

"14th. *Resolved*, That provision ought to be made for the admission of states lawfully arising within the limits of the United States, whether from a voluntary jurisdiction of Government terrritory or otherwise, with the consent of a number of voices in the National Legislature less than the whole.

"15th. *Resolved*, That provisions ought to be made for the continuance of Congress, and their authority and privileges, until a given day after the *reform* of the articles of Union shall be adopted, and for the completion of all other engagements.

"16th. That a Republican Constitution and its existing laws ought to be guaranteed to each state of the United States.

"17th. That provision ought to be made for the amendment of the articles of Union whenever it shall seem necessary.

"18th, That the Legislative, Executive and Judiciary powers within the several states ought to be bound by oath to support the articles of the Union.

"19th, That the amendments which shall be offered to the Confederation by this Convention ought at a proper time, or times, after the approbation of Congress, to be submitted to an assembly or assemblies, recommended by the Legislatures, to be expressly chosen by the people, to consider and decide thereon."—*pp.* 356-7-8 *1st v. Elliott's Debates.*

In commenting on this framework for a Constitution, before the Legislature of Maryland, Mr. Luther Martin, a National Delegate, thus exposed the jealousies that existed on the subject of usurping power by the large states:

"Hence, these three states (Virginia, Pennsylvania, and Massachusetts) would, in reality, have the appointment of the President, Judges, and all other officers. This President and these Judges, so appointed, we may be morally certain, would be citizens of one of those three states, and the President, as appointed by them, and a citizen of one of them, would espouse their interests and their views when they came in competition with the views and interests of the other states."

Under the old Confederation, the States exercised suffrage in the National Congress as *individual* States, and not on the basis of popular suffrage among the *people*—that is, each State had just one vote on all matters, and if the representation of delegates happened to be even in number and equally divided (as was often the case), the State had no vote and its power was wholly neutralized. This subject was one of the bones of contention in the National convention. On the vote being taken, it was found that Connecticut, New York,* New Jersey, Delaware and Maryland,† (the smaller states) were for equal *State* suffrage, as under the Confederation, while the larger States, of Massachusetts, Pennsylvania, Virginia, North Carolina and South Carolina, were for popular suffrage. Here was a dead lock.— The States were equally divided, and what was to be done? If neither party had yielded "an inch," of course it would have been an end to the whole matter, for it was a vital point. But *compromise* saved the nation from anarchy and dissolution. Be it remembered, the States had the same votes in the convention they did in Congress, under the Confederation—each one vote. As we have seen, the difficulty, which at one time seemed insurmountable, was compromised by the larger States yielding to the smaller equal *State* representation in the Senate, and the smaller States yielding to the larger equal representation in the popular branch. Who will say this was not a just course.

The way and manner this compromise was affected is so appropos to the *application* we are making that we feel justified in letting Mr. MARTIN, a delegate from Maryland, tell the story in his own way:

"Thus, sir, on this great and important part of the system—the Convention being equally divided—five states for the measure, five against and one divided—there was a total stand; and we did not seem very likely to proceed any farther. At length it was proposed that a select committee should be balloted for, composed of a member from each state, which committee should endeavor to devise some mode of reconciliation, or compromise. I had the honor to be on that committee. We met and discussed the subject of difference. The one side insisted on the inequality of suffrage in *both* branches; the *other side equality* in both. Each party was tenacious of their sentiments [as is alwas the case in controversies.] When it was found that *nothing* could induce *us* to yield the inequality in *both* branches, *they* at length proposed, by way of comprise, if *we* would accede to *their* wishes as to the *first* branch, *they* would agree to an equal representation in the *second.* To this it was answered that there was no merit in the proposal; in was only consenting,'after they had struggled to put both their feet on our necks, to take one of them off, provided we would consent to let them keep the other on; when they knew, at the same time, that they could not put one foot on our necks, unless we would consent to it, and that by being permitted to keep on that

---

*New York in population was then below many of the other States.

†Mr. MARTIN was the only delegate present from Maryland, which carried the vote for *State* suffrage. Had the delegation been full it would have been divided.

one foot, they should afterwards be able to place the other foot on whenever they pleased.

"They were also called upon to inform us what security they could give us, should we agree to this compromise, that they would abide by the plan of government formed upon it, any longer than suited their interests, or they found it expedient. The *States* have a *right* to an equality of representation. This is *secured* to us by our present articles of confederation. We are in possession of this right. It is now to be torn from us. What security can you give us, that, when you get the power the proposed system will give you—when you have men and money—you will not force from the States that equality of suffrage in the second branch, which you now deny to be their right, and only give up from actual necessity? Will you tell us we ought to trust you because you now enter into a solemn compact with us? This you have done before, and *now* treat with the utmost contempt. Will you now make an appeal to the Supreme Being, and call on Him to guarantee your observance of the Articles of Confederation, which you are now violating in the most wanton manner? [This argument might well be addressed to the radicals to-day.]

"The same reason which you *now* urge for destroying our *present* Federal Government, may be urged for abolishing the system you propose to adopt: and as the *method* prescribed by the Articles of Confederation is now totally disregarded by you, as little regard may be shown by you to the rules prescribed for the amendments of the *new system!* [This was prophetic.] Whenever, having obtained power by the Government, you shall hereafter be pleased to discard it entirely, or so to alter it as to give yourselves all that superiority which you have *now* contended for, and to obtain which you have shown yourselves disposed to hazard the Union!

"Such, sir, was the language used on that occasion; and they were told that, as we could not possibly have a stronger tie on them for the observance of the new system than we had for their observance of the Articles of Confederation, (which had proved totally insufficient,) it would be very imprudent to confide in them. It was further observed, that the inequality of the representation would be daily increasing—that many of the states, whose territory was confined, and whose population was at this time large in proportion to their territory, would probably, twenty, thirty or forty years hence, have no more representatives than at the introduction of the Government; whereas, the states having extensive territory, whose lands are to be procured cheap, would be daily increasing in the number of inhabitants, not only from propogation, but from the emigration of the inhabitants of the other states, and would soon have double, or perhaps treble the number of Representatives that they are to have at first, and thereby enormously increase their influence in the National councils.

"However, the majority of the select committee at length agreed to a series of propositions by way of *compromise*—part of which related to the representation in the First Branch—nearly as the system is now published (in the adopted Constitution) and part of them to the second branch, securing in that equal representation; and reported them as a *compromise*, upon the express terms that they were to be wholly adopted or wholly rejected. Upon this *compromise* a great number of the members so far engaged themselves, that if the system was proceeded upon agreeably to the terms of compromise, they would lend their names by signing it, and would not actively oppose it, if their states should be inclined to accept it. Some, however, in which number was myself, who joined in that report, and agreed to proceed upon these principles, and see what kind of a system would ultimately be formed upon it, yet reserved to themselves in the most explicit manner, a right of finally giving a solemn dissent to the system, if it was thought by them inconsistent with the freedom and happiness of their country. This, sir, will account why the gentlemen of the Convention so generally signed their names to the system—not because they thought it a proper one—not because they thoroughly approved, or were unanimous for it—but because they thought it better than the system attempted to be forced upon them. This report of the select committee was, after long discussion, adopted by a majority of the Convention, and the system was proceeded in accordingly. I believe near a fortnight—perhaps more—was spent in the discussion of this business, during which *we were on the verge of dissolution, scarce held together by the strength of a hair*, though the public papers were announcing our extreme unanimity."

Such were some of the difficulties encountered by our fathers in reference to only one point of issue then pending. The same species of opposing views and clashing interests arose on almost every section of the Constitution—all of these discordant elements had to be met by the spirit of compromise.

COMPROMISE BETWEEN SLAVERY AND NAVIGATION.

We have not room in this connection to notice, even by reference, any other point of difference and the compromises thereon, save that pertaining to the slave trade and the navigation laws.

Some portions of the South were very anxious to be protected in the slave trade for a considerable period, in order, as they said, to compensate them for the losses of slave property during the Revolution. On the other hand, New England was very jealous lest the non commercial states should place some obstacles on commerce and navigation, and when the slave trade clause came up for consideration, and was referred to a committee, New England delegates were not slow in using their influence to send the clause pertaining to navigation to the same committee. The blending of these two dissimilar subjects shows the real object to make the one act as a weight to compromise in favor of the other. We will let a member of the Convention and the Committee (Mr. MARTIN) explain the mode of doing this:

"By the 9th section of this article, the importation of such persons as any of the states now existing shall think proper to admit, shall not be prohibited prior to the year 1808, &c.

"The design of this clause is to prevent the General Government from prohibiting the importation of *slaves*, but the same reason which caused them to strike out the word "National," and not admit the word "stamps," [because at that time these words were odious.] influenced them here to guard against the word "slaves." They anxiously sought to avoid the admission of expressions which might be odious in the ears of Americans, although they were willing to admit into their system those things which the expression signified; and hence it is, that the clause is so worded, as really to authorize the General Government to impose a duty of ten dollars on every foreigner who comes into a state to be a citizen, whether he comes absolutely free, or qualifiedly as a servant; although this is contrary to the design of the framers, and the duty was only meant to extend to the importation of slaves.

"This clause was the subject of a great diversity of sentiment in the Convention. As the system was reported by the Committee of Detail, the provision was general, that such importation should not be prohibited, without confining it to any particular period. This was rejected by eight states, Georgia, South Carolina, and, *I think*, North Carolina voted for it.

"We were then told by the delegates of the two first of these States, that their States would never agree to a system which put it in the power of the General Government to prevent the importation of slaves, and that they, as delegates from those States, must withhold their votes from such a system.

"A committee of one member from each State was chosen by ballot, to take this part of the system under their consideration, and to endeavor to agree upon some report, which *would reconcile these States.* To this committee also was referred the following proposition:

"No navigation act shall be passed without the assent of two-thirds of the members present in each House."

A proposition which the staple and commercial States were solicitous to retain, lest their commerce should be placed too much under the power of the *Eastern* States, but which these last States were anxious to reject. This committee, of which I have had the honor

to be a member—met—and took under consideration the subjects committed to them. I found the *Eastern States, notwithstanding their aversion to slavery were very willing to indulge the Southern States,* at least with a temporary liberty to prosecute the slave trade, *Provided,* the Southern States would, in their turn, gratify *them, by laying no restriction cn navigation acts,* and after a very little time the committee, by a great majority, agreed on a report, by which the General Government was to be prohibited from preventing the importation of slaves for a limited time, (1800), and the restriction relative to navigation acts, was to be omitted."—*Elliott's Debates, Vol.* 1, *p.* 373.

MASSACHUSETTS FAVORS THE SLAVE TRADE.

Thus have we a clue to the compromise of the Constitution on the slavery question. Recollect that the original committee of thirteen had recommended that the constitutional license to the slave trade should cease at the period of 1800. But this did not suit the avarice of some of the New England states, and we copy from the secret record of the debates, kept by Mr. Yates, a member from New York. [*See Elliott's Debates, v.* 1, *p.* 264-5.

"It was moved and seconded to amend the report of the committee of eleven, entered on the Sournal of the 24th [August 1787] inst., as follows:

"To strike out the words 'the year eighteen hundred,' and insert 'the year eighteen hundred and *eight.*'

"Which passed in the affirmative,

"YEAS.—*New Hampshire, Massachusetts, Connecticut,* Maryland, North Carolina, South Carolina and Georgia.—7. "NAYS.—New Jersey, Pennsylvania, Delaware and Virginia—4."

To show that what Mr. MARTIN said above was true, that many states did not wish to incur the "odium" of inserting the word "slave" in the Constitution, yet were willing to reap the pecuniary benefit from the *thing itself,* we copy further, continuously from this official report:

"It was moved and seconded to amend the first clause of the report to read—

"The importation of *slaves* into such of the states as shall permit the same shall not be prohibited by the Legislature of the United States prior to the year 1808.

"Which was passed in the negative,

"YEAS.—*Connecticut,* Virginia and Georgia.—3. "NAYS.—New Hampshire, Massachusetts, Pennsylvania, Delaware, North Carolina and South Carolina.—6. "DIVIDED—Maryland—1.

This was the same proposition as that which followed, except it contained the word "*slave.*" It seems that even *Connecticut* had then no scruples about that word being in the Constitution, while all but two of the slave states had.

Now, mark the hypocrisy of the three New England Abolition states that voted to continue the inhuman slave trade for *eight years* longer than some of the slave states desired. We continue our quotation:

"On the question to agree to the first part of the report, as amended, viz:

"'The migration or importation of *such persons* as the several states now existing shall think proper to admit, shall not be prohibited by the Legislature [Congress] prior to the year 1808'—

"It passed in the affirmative:

"YEAS—*New Hampshire, Massachusetts, Connecticut,* Maryland, North Carolina, South Carolina and Georgia—7.
"NAYS—New Jersey, Pennsylvania, *Delaware* and *Virginia*—4."

Thus, it will be seen that if the three states which have all along been willing to break up the Union, on account of slavery, had went with their Northern sisters, and with the *slave states* of *Delaware* and *Virginia*, the vote would have stood right the reverse—4 for and 7 against the eight *additional* years of the trade which has been declared *piracy* by the laws of civilized nations.

If there be efficacy in prayer, we trust that all good people will pray that Massachusetts, Connecticut and New Hampshire may cast the black beam out of their own eyes before they declare they see "*disloyalty*" in every *mote* in their neighbor's eyes. A little going back to "first principles" might teach them to be humble, even as a peacock doth drop his plumes when he beholds his own dirty feet!

We raise no complaint, even at this mode of compromising. It cannot be objected to even on such a subject, for without a compromise, no Union could have been effected. We only object to the subterfuge and subsequent display of hypocrisy.

The question may be raised as to the *motive* that then induced the three principal New England States to engage in the slave trade at all, or to desire its continuance. The answer is summed up in one compound word—*self-interest*, which is the mainspring of all commercial transactions. For more than a century the ships of Massachusetts, Connecticut, and others, had been profitably engaged in the slave trade, which it was hard to relinquish, and twenty years promised more profits than twelve years. The very fact that they agreed to suppress it at all, shows that they *then* knew it to be as wrong as it is to-day.

MASSACHUSETTS STEALING NIGGERS.

Thus, for twenty years after the Constitution was formed, did Massachusetts, and the other New England states, prosecute the slave trade. Their slave merchantmen piratically tore from the coast of Guinea thousands of the unoffending natives, transported them through the horrors and suffocation of the "Middle Passage," and sold them for gold to the planters of South Carolina, Georgia, &c., and ever since the constitutional prohibition began to run they have been endeavoring to break up the Union, because the Southern states owned and worked the very slaves these abolition humanitarians stole from Africa and sold to them. Enough! We have no heart to further pursue so dark a subject.

There were dozens of plans submitted to the original National Convention, embracing almost every conceivable variety and form of Government. We have not space to notice them all in detail, but will note the difference between two plans submitted by Virginia and New Jersey, respectively, as a sample of the whole, that the reader may see something of the difficulties in the way of compromise.

The Virginia plan proposed two branches of Congress ;

New Jersey a single branch.

Virginia—Legislative powers derived from the people ;

New Jersey—same from the States.

Virginia—a single Executive ;

New Jersey—more than one.

Virginia—that a majority of Congress could act ;

New Jersey—a small majority could control.

Virginia—Congress to legislate on all National concerns ;

New Jersey—only on limited objects.

Virginia—Congress to negative all State laws ;

New Jersey—Giving power to Executive to compel obedience by force.

Virginia—To remove Executive by impeachment ;

New Jersey—On application of majority of States.

Virginia—For establishment of inferior judicial tribunals ;

New Jersey—No provision.

PREDICTION OF GEO. MASON.

" This Government will commence in a moderate aristocracy : It is at present impossible to foresee whether it will, in its operations produce a monarchy or a corrupt, oppressive aristocracy—it will most probably vibrate some years between the two, and then terminate in one or the other.

"GEO. MASON."
[See Elliott's Debates, 1, p. 406.

Our Government was not only created on the basis of compromise, but it has only been kept together up to the election of ABRAHAM LINCOLN by that spirit of compromise which brought its form and substance from the chaos of the Confederation.

THE MISSOURI COMPROMISE.

In 1819 the cloud of dissolution arose from behind the Missouri question. Missouri asking and demanding to be admitted with her slavery constitution on the one hand, while the Abolitionists of the North declared she should never be admitted as a slave state. Here was two extreme propositions. Neither party would yield wholly to the other, for that cannot be expected in any controversy. At least, few instances of the kind have been recorded by history. Both parties must yield something, or war and dissolution followed.

MR. CLAY'S COMPROMISE.

Thus matters stood when Mr. CLAY, the great American champion of compromises, brought forth his celebrated Missouri compromise, which was finally incorporated into the Missouri Act of Admission, as the 8th section, and which consisted in drawing an imaginary line of 36 deg. 30 min. north latitude, to the western boundary of Missouri, and providing that slavery should never exist north of that line. This is what the Southern party yielded to the Northern party, in consideration of the Admission of Missouri as a slave state, with another condition that the article in the constitution prohibiting free blacks from settling in that State, should be stricken out. Under these provisions, Missouri was admitted as a State, by proclamation of President MONROE, in the summer of 1821—the people of Missouri, in the mean time having voted to accept the conditions of the compromise.

Thus, the Missouri imbroglio blew over, while parties busied themselves in getting up a new cause of irritation. They were not long in maturing their mischievous plans.

The tariff of 1828, passed while the "Federal Republicans" were in power, was excessively offensive to the South, and especially to South Carolina. And in 1832 that state positively bid defiance to the General Government, and resolved to resist its revenue law of 1828. At one time civil war seemed inevitable, but the firm, yet compromising spirit of General JACKSON, aided by the accommodating spirit of HENRY CLAY, soon allayed discontent and restored the relations of peace and obedience to law. South Carolina was opposed to all tariffs. The manufacturing states were for a high "protective" (prohibitory) tariff. Here was the two extremes. If neither had yielded, war was inevitable. One could not in "honor" yield *wholly* to the other. Hence, the "protectionists" yielded so as to bring the tariff to the supposed standard of revenue, while the nullifiers yielded their opposition to *all* tariffs, so as to consent to the revenue standard—and here was the common mean between the two extremes. Compromise accomplished in this what perhaps half a million of lives and five thousand millions of property could not accomplish, while subsequent history demonstrated the fact that that the basis of actual settlement was really more beneficial to both parties than either extreme would have been to either party.

GEN. JACKSON ON COMPROMISE.

As the *spirit* in which Gen. JACKSON treated this embroglio may be of some service to those who are not too mad to reason, we introduce it here, in the language of Col. BENTON:

"Such was the message which President Jackson sent to the two Houses in relation to the South Carolina proceedings, and his own to counteract them, and it was worthy to follow the proclamation, and commenced in the same spirit of justice and patriotism, and therefore wise and moderate. * * * His proclamation, his message, and all his proceedings, therefore, bore a two-fold aspect—one of relief and justice, in reducing the measure to the wants of the Government, in the economical administration of its affairs—the other of firm and mild authority, in enforcing the laws against offenders. * * * Bills for the reduction of the tariff—one commenced in the Finance Committee of the Senate, and one reported from the Committee of Ways and Means of the House of Representatives, and both moved in the first days of the session, and by committees politically and personally favorable to the President, *went hand in hand with the exhortations in the proclamation*, and *the steady preparations for enforcing the laws. if the extension of justice and the appeals to reason and patriotism should prove insufficient* Many thought that he ought to relax in his civil measures, for allaying discontent, while South Carolina held the military attitude of armed hostility to the United States, and among them Mr. Quincy Adams. But *he adhered steadily to his purpose of going on with what justice required for the relief of the South, and promoted by all the means in his power the success of the bills to reduce the measure*, especially the bill in the House, and which being framed upon that of 1816, (which had the support of Mr. Calhoun,) and which was (now that the public debt was paid,) sufficient both for revenue and the incidental protection which manufacturers required, and for the *relief of the South*, must have had the effect of satisfying every honest discontent, and of exposing and estopping that which would not."—*Thirty Years, p.* 308.

This was the noble, yet firm and patriotic stand taken by Gen. JACKSON to cast water instead of pitch on the flames of civil discontent.

HENRY CLAY ON THE SAME SUBJECT.

The manly and patriotic sentiments uttered by Mr. CLAY when he introduced his compromise tariff bill, is a noble model of enlightened statesmanship, which is worthy of being framed in gilt to garnish the best statesman's library on the globe. He said:

"Sir. I repeat, that I think South Carolina has been rash, intemperate, and greatly in the wrong, but I do not want to disgrace her, nor any other member of this Union. No, I do not desire to see the lustre of one single star dimmed of that glorious confederacy which constitutes our political system. Still less do I wish to see it blotted out and its light obliterated forever. Has not the state of South Carolina been one of the members of this Union in days that 'tried men's souls?' Have not her ancestors fought alongside our ancestors. Have we not conjointly won many a glorious battle. If we had to go into a civil war with such a state how would it terminate? Whenever it should have terminated, what would be her condition? If she should ever return to the Union what would be the condition of her feelings and affections? What the state of the heart of her people? She has been with us before, when her ancestors mingled in the throng of battle, as I hope our posterity will mingle with hers for ages and centuries to come, in the united defense of liberty, and for the honor and glory of the Union. I do not wish to see her degraded or defaced as a member of this Confederacy."

Mr. CLAY's second speech in defense of his compromise bill was equally honorable and patriotic. Such a speech, made by the same man, now-a-days, would be pronounced, in "loyal" nomenclature, as "copperhead treason." Mr. CLAY said:

"This, or some other measure of *conciliation*, is now more than ever necessary since the passage through the Senate of the Enforcing Bill. * * * It appears to me, then, Mr. President, that we ought not to content ourselves with passing the Enforcing Bill only.— Both that and the Bill of Peace seem to me to be required for the good of our country. * * The difference between the friends and the foes of the compromise under consideration, is, that *they would*, in *the enforcing act send forth ALONE a flaming sword—we would send out that, but along with it the Olive Branch, as a messenger of peace*. They cry out, "The law! The law!! The law!!! Power! Power!! Power!!!" We, too, revere the *laws*, and bow to the supremacy of its obligation, but we are in favor of the law *executed in mildness*, and *power tempered with mercy*. * * * We want no war—above all, no *civil war*—no family strifes. We want to see no sacked cities— no desolated fields—no smoking ruins—no streams of American blood shed by American arms.

Pass this bill—tranquolize the country, restore confidence and affection in the Union, and I am willing to go home to Ashland, and *renounce public service forever.* * * * Yes. I *have* ambition! but it is the ambition of being the humble instrument in the hands of Providence, to reconcile a divided people—once more to revive concord and harmony, in a distracted land. The pleasing ambition of contemplating the glorious spectacle of a free, united, prosperous and practical people!"

The settlement of the South Carolina controversy left peace and all its fraternal blessings to flow uninterruptedly for eighteen years, till 1850—but the spirit of discord and the demon of dissolution were at work; and scarcely a month passed of this eighteen years that did not witness the utterance of some treasonable sentiment in favor of dissolution.

In the progress of events, and the fullness of our history, a war with Mexico, not only settled a long pending controversy, over repeated insults, injuries and wrongs, but gave us New Mexico and California. The immediate and almost providential discovery of rich fields of gold in our newly acquired Pacific possessions, stimulated emigration to such extent that California put in motion the whole machinery of a State Government, and asked admission into the sisterhood of states, as a free state.

The claims of that State were resisted by the slavery "balance-of-power" men of the South, because there happened to be no slave State ready for admission as an offset, to keep up the political equilibrium between the two sections of our common country, so basely divided by political agitators on both sides of the line between slave and free states. In this the South had no constitutional cause of complaint, because she had no constitutional right to demand that this "equilibrium" should be kept up. But the "occasion" gave to her politicians a pretext for complaint, which they lost no time in entangling with the slavery agitation generally. The bad faith of the North in reference to the rendition of fugitive slaves—the personal liberty bills that virtually rendered nugatory the fugitive law of 1793—were made to play their part in the budget of complaints, claims and counter claims, until the controversy became mixed with merit and demerit on both sides. The crisis at one time became alarming, when again shone forth, in all their brilliancy, and not in the least dimmed by age, the compromising qualities of CLAY, who with WEBSTER, CRITTENDEN, DOUGLAS, and such old Nestors of patriotic fame, became active to still once more the noises of faction, and who endeavored to dry up the fountains of discord by the system of compromise adopted in 1850. The measures known as the "compromise measures" (or omnibus) of 1850, were as follows:

1st, The admission of California, with her free Constitution. [In this the South yielded.]

2d, The erection of the territory of Utah, leaving the people to regulate their own affairs [No particular yielding on either side.]

3d, The creation of New Mexico into a territorial government, with like provisions, [No particular yielding on either side.]

4th. The adjustment of the Texas boundary question. [Claimed by abolitionists to have been a concession to the South.]

5th. Abolition of the slave trade in the District of Columbia. [Concessions by the South to the North.]

6th. The amendments to the Fugitive Slave Law. [A concession in mode of operating, to the South, but no concession as to principle.]

These measures received the concurrence of such men as CLAY, WEBSTER, CASS, DOUGLAS, BENTON, DICKINSON, &c., and were considered as settling the whole controversy. Both the Democratic and Whig National Conventions of 1852, agreed most solemnly to stand by these compromises. But the radical element in the Whig party was turbulent, and refused to acquiesce, and immediately the agitation began. The radicals took the field with BINNEY at their head, in 1852, when the Whigs found themselves severely beaten. The party vainly struggled on, with little vitality, for two years, when it disbanded, and the "Free Soil" or abolition party drank in most of its members, and from that day to this the agitation has continued, wholly on a *sectional* basis. The result need not be portrayed by us. But it remains for us, in this chapter, to perform the unpleasant duty of considering

THE FRUITLESS EFFORTS TO COMPROMISE IN 1861.

Alas, CLAY, WEBSTER and BENTON—the heroes of the compromise of 1850—were gone to their final account. DOUGLAS was prostrate, and soon followed his old compeers—CASS, at a ripe old age, had been retired from the National counsels. Political agitators and cheap politicians occupied their once honored places.

The hour of trial came—the crisis, long accumulating its virus, had broken forth—the shock of dissolution was terribly felt. The *causes* that produced or hastened the black evils of the hour, belong not for us to canvass here. Go to the first fifty pages of this work and read for yourself. There you will find the cause. There, every line is a sermon—every sentence an oration—almost every extract an obituary. Could the authors of "all this riot" be induced to filter and settle the waters they had riled—could prattling youth, stern manhood, ripe old age, or pleading wives, or agonized daughters and sisters, by the loud tones of discontent, or the mute expostulations of fear, move the guilty authors of the impending calamities to make an *effort* to retrace their steps—to desist from acts of effrontery that stimulated exasperation, and heated to a boiling temper the mad spirit of faction—could these agitators be induced to pour oil on the troubled waters—in short, to *compromise* the jarring claims of faction, so as to bless the world with peace? No, they could not, and we are left the mournful task of recording the reasons

WHY THE RADICALS WOULD NOT COMPROMISE IN 1861.

When the cloud of war broke forth in all its fury, as JEFFERSON predicted in 1821, all patriotic lovers of the Union strove to avert the evils, and to turn the tide of fratricidal war. Various were the efforts, and numerous the propositions to compromise our national differences, and to go on once more in the brotherly path of peace, possessing the manifold objects which invited us to untold blessings and happiness. But the tide of the destoyers of the Union was at its flow—the crisis they had long sought to create, had arrived, with the additional advantage of having the reigns of Government in their power, so that while they might not be able to control the storm, they could direct the course of the ship of state, with a view to cause sufficient damage to justify in their belief a *general overhauling and repairs*, with "all the modern improvements," as expressed by Gen. BUTLER in New York.

The following full history of the CRITTENDEN compromise, and the action of the Republican party thereon was compiled by a distinguished patriot, and we here present it in detail. We can well afford the space it occupies, as it covers the most *important* history of our country.

CHAPTER XXII.

THE RADICALS DETERMINED TO PREVENT A SETTLEMENT.

Could the Present War have been Avoided...Complete History of the Crittenden Compromise...Votes, Resolves, Propositions, &c.

COULD THE PRESENT WAR HAVE BEEN AVOIDED—HISTORY OF THE CRITTENDEN COMPROMISE.

"We know of no great revolution which might not have been prevented by compromise early and graciously made. Firmness is a great virtue in public affairs, but it has its sphere. Conspiracies and insurrections, in which small minorities are engaged, the outbreakings of popular violence unconnected with any extensive project or any durable principle, are best repressed by vigor and decision. To shrink from them is to make them formidable. But no wise ruler will confound the pervading taint with the slight local irritation. No wise ruler will treat the deeply-seated discontents of any party as he treats the conduct of a mob which destroys mills and power-looms. The neglect of this distinction has been fatal even to governments strong in the power of the sword. * * * In all movements of the human mind which tend to great revolutions, there is a crisis at which moderate concessions may amend, conciliate and preserve."—*Macaulay*.

No truer words were ever uttered by any historian; and had we had a wise ruler instead of the present weak-minded Chief Magistrate, we should not now have to lament the deplorable condition to which the country is reduced by the want of those timely concessions, which would have conciliated and preserved. To show to a people how they have been made the dupes of a class of men "whose hostility," in the language of the lamented Douglas, "to slavery is stronger than their fidelity to the Constitution, and who believed that the disruption would draw after it, as an inevitable consequence, civil war, servile insurrections, and, finally, the utter extinction of slavery in all the Southern States," we have made up from the record a history of the "Crittenden Compromise." It will develop the great crime that has been committed against liberty, civilization and humanity, by men, who, unfortunately for the American people, had, for over two years past, the direction of our national affairs.

On the 18th day of December, 1860, Senator Crittenden, of Kentucky, introduced into the Senate of the United States a series of resolutions as a basis of settlement of the difficulties between the North and the South—difficulties, which at that time, threatened the peace of the country and the integrity of the Union. [*Congessional Globe*, Part 1, session of 1860-61, page 114]

Senator Hale (Abolition) led off in a speech in opposition to the resolutions, declaring it to be his opinion that the remedies of our troubles were not in Congressional action. He said:

"I do not know that this Congress can do anything; but this controversy will not be settled here."

He was right. The controversy was not settled there. Would to God it had been! But we all know that the reason why it was not settled there was, the Republicans would not permit it. Douglas told them, on the floor of the Senate, that the responsibility of the failure was with them. The Republican Senators and Representatives acted on the idea of Senator Chandler, of Michigan, who declared that without a little blood-letting the Union would not be worth a rush.

No further action was had on these resolutions, except ordering them to be printed, until January 2d, 1861, (South Carolina having seceded Dec. 20, and her delegation withdrawn from Congress Dec. 24, 1860) when Mr. Crittenden introduced them anew with a different preamble, in which shape they read as follows: (Page 237,)

"WHEREAS, The Union is in danger, and owing to the unhappy divisions existing in Congress, it would be difficult, if not impossible, for that body to concur in both its branches by the requisite majority, so as to enable it either to adopt such measures of legislation or to recommend to the States such amendments to the Constitution as are deemed necessary and proper to avert that danger; and whereas in so great an emergency the opinion and judgment of the people ought to be heard, and would be the best and surest guide to their representatives; therefore

"*Resolved*, That provisions ought to be made by law, without delay, for taking the sense of the people, and submitting to their vote the following resolutions, as the basis for the final and permanent settlement of those disputes that now disturb the peace of the country, and threaten the existence of the Union.

"*Resolved by the Senate and House of Representatives of the United States of America, in Congress assembled, two-thirds of both Houses concurring*, That the following articles be and are hereby proposed and submitted as amendments to the Constitution of the United States, which shall be valid to all intents and purposes as part of said Constitution, when ratified by Conventions of three-fourths of the several States:

"Article 1. In all the territory of the United States now held, or hereafter acquired, situated north of latitude thirty-six degrees and thirty minutes, slavery or involuntary servitude, except as a punishment of crime, is prohibited while such territory shall remain under territorial government. In all the territory now held, or hereafter acquired, south of said line of latitude, slavery of the African race is hereby recognized as existing, and shall not be interfered with by Congress; but shall be protected as property by all the departments of the Territorial government during its continuance: and when any territory north or south of said line, within such boundaries as Con-

SCRAPS FROM MY SCRAP-BOOK.   185

gress may prescribe, shall contain the population requisite for a member of Congress according to the then Federal ratio of representation of the people of the United States it shall if its form of government be republican, be admitted into the Union on an equal footing with the original States, with or without slavery, as the Constitution of such new State may provide.

"Art. 2. Congress shall have no power to abolish slavery in places under its exclusive jurisdiction, or within the limits of States that permit the holding of slaves.

"Art. 3. Congress shall have no power to abolish slavery within the District of Columbia, so long as it exists in the adjoining States of Virginia and Maryland, or either, nor without the consent of the inhabitants, nor without just compensation first made to said owners of slaves as do not consent to such abolishment. Nor shall Congress at any time prohibit officers of the Federal Government or members of Congress, whose duties require them to be in said District, from bringing with them their slaves, and holding them as such during the time their duties may require them to remain there, and afterward taking them from the District.

"Art. 4. Congress shall have no power to prohibit or hinder the transportation of slaves, from one State to another, or to a Territory in which slaves are by law permitted to be held, whether that transportation be by land, navigable rivers, or by sea.

"Art. 5. That in addition to the provisions of the third paragraph of the second section of the fourth article of the Constitution of the United States, Congress shall have power to provide by law, and it shall be, its duty so to provide, that the United States shall pay to the owner who shall apply, for it the full value of his fugitive slave, in all cases when the Marshal, or other officers whose duty it was to arrest said fugitive, was prevented from so doing by violence or intimidation, or when, after arrest, said fugitive was rescued by force, and the owner thereby prevented and obstructed in the pursuit of his remedy for the recovery of of his fugitive slave, under the said clause of the Constitution and the laws made in pursuance thereof. And in such cases when the United States shall pay for such fugitive, they shall have the right in their own name to sue the county in which said violence, intimidation, or rescue, was committed, and to recover from it, with interest and damages the amount paid by them for said fugitive slave. And the said county after it has paid said amount to the United States, may, for its indemnity, sue and recover from the wrong-doers or rescuers, by whom the owner was prevented from the recovery of his fugitive slave, in like manner as the owner himself might have sued and recovered.

"Art. 6. No future amendment of the Constitution shall effect the five preceding articles, nor the third paragraph of the second section of the first article of the Constitution, nor the third paragraph of the second section of the fourth article of said Constitution, and no amendment shall be made to the Constitution which will authorize or give to Congress any power to abolish or interfere with slavery in any of the States by whose laws it is or may be allowed or permitted.

"AND, WHEREAS, also, besides those causes of dissension embraced in the foregoing amendments proposed to the Constitution of the United States, there are others which come within the jurisdiction of Congress, and may be remedied by its legislative power; and, whereas, it is the desire of Congress, as far as its power will extend, to remove all just cause for the popular discontent and agitation which now disturb the peace of the country, and threaten the stability of its institutions; therefore,

"*Resolved, by the Senate and House of Representatives of the United States of America, in Congress assembled,* That the laws now in force for the recovery of fugitive slaves are in strict pursuance of the Constitution, and have been sanctioned as valid and constitutional by the Supreme Court of the United States; that the slaveholding states are entitled to the faithful observance and execution of those laws, and that they ought not to be repealed or so modified or changed as to impair their efficiency; and that laws ought to be made for the punishment of those who attempt, by the rescue of the slaves, or other illegal means, to hinder or defeat the due execution of said laws.

"2. That all State laws which conflict with the Fugitive Slave Acts, or any other constitutional act of Congress, or which, in their opinion impede, hinder or delay the free course and due execution of any of said acts, are null and void by the plain provisions of the Constitution of the United States. Yet those State laws, void as they are, have given color to practices and lead to consequences which have obstructed the due administration and execution of acts of Congress, and especially the acts for the delivery of fugitive slaves, and have thereby contributed much to the discord and commotion now prevailing. Congress, therefore, in the present perilous juncture does not deem it improper, respectfully and earnestly to recommend the repeal of those laws to the several States which have enacted them, or such legislative corrections or explanations of them as may prevent their being used or perverted to such mischievous purposes,

"3. That the act of the 18th of September, 1850, commonly called the Fugitive Slave Law, ought to be so amended as to make the fee of the Commissioner, mentioned in the eighth section of this act, equal in amount, in the case decided by him, whether his decision be in favor or against the claimant. And, to avoid misconstruction, the last clause of the fifth section of said act, which authorizes the person holding a warrant for the arrest or detection of a fugitive slave to summon to his aid a posse comitatus and which declared it to be the duty of all good citizens to assist him in its execution, ought to be so amended as to expressly limit the authority and duty in cases in which there shall he resistance, or danger of rescue.

"4. That the laws for the suppression of the African slave trade, and especially those prohibiting the importation of slaves into the United States, ought to be made effectual, and ought to be thoroughly executed, and all other enactments necessary to those ends ought to be promptly made."

On the 15th of January, 1861, Senator Clark (Abolitionist) moved to strike out all of Mr. Crittenden's proposition, after the preamble and the word *Resolved*, and insert in lieu thereof the following:

"That the provisions of the Constitution are ample for the preservation of the Union, and the protection of all the material interests of the country; that it needs to be obeyed rather than amended; and that an extrication from the present dangers is to be looked for in strenuous efforts to preserve the peace, protect the public property, and enforce the laws, rather than in guarantees for particular difficulties, or concessions to unreasonable demands.

"*Resolved,* That all attempts to dissolve the present Union, or overthrow or abandon the present Constitution, with the hope or expectation of constructing a new one, are dangerous, illusory, and destructive; that in the opinion of the Senate of the United States, no such reconstruction is practicable; and therefore, to the maintenance of the existing Union and Constitution, should be directed all the energies of all the departments of the Government, and the efforts of all good citizens."

The object of the introduction of that resolution was very plain: it was to kill Mr. Crittenden's plan without taking a direct vote on it. Mr. Clark's motion prevailed by the following vote:

AYES.

Anthony,	Durkee,	Seward,
Baker,	Fessenden,	Simmons,
Bingham,	Foote,	Sumner,
Chandler,	Foster,	Ten Eyck,
Clark,	Grimes,	Trumbull,
Collamer,	Hale,	Wade,
Dixon,	Harlan,	Wilkinson,
Doolittle,	King,	Wilson,

25.—All Republicans.

NAYS.

Bayard,	Green,	Powell,
Bigler,	Lane,	Pugh,
Bragg,	Latham,	Rice,
Bright,	Mason,	Saulsbury,
Clingman,	Nicholson,	Sebastian,
Crittenden,	Pearce,	
Fitch,	Polk,	

23.—All Democrats and Americans.

Mr. Crittenden's proposition was thus defeated for the present. At a subsequent hour of the same day, Senator Cameron. who had voted for the Clark amendment, moved a reconsideration of the vote by which the Crittenden proposition was killed. The vote on this motion was not taken until the 18th of January, 1861. The following was the result: (Page 443.)

"YEAS.

Bayard, Gwin, Pearce,
Bigler, Hunter, Polk,
Bragg, Johnson of Ark., Powell,
Bright, Johnson of Tenn., Pugh,
Clingman, Kennedy, Rice,
Crittenden, Lane, Saulsbury,
Douglas, Latham, Sebastian,
Fitch, Mason, Slidell.—27.
Green, Nicholson,

NAYS.

Anthony, Doolittle, Seward,
Baker, Fessenden, Simmons,
Bingham, Foote, Sumner,
Cameron, Foster, Ten Eyck,
Chandler, Grimes, Wade,
Clark, Hale, Wigfall,
Collamer, Harlan, Wilkinson
Dixon, King, Wilson.—24.

It will be seen that Mr. Cameron voted against his own proposition. The motion to reconsider having prevailed, the question then was on agreeing to Mr. Clark's substitute for the Crittenden plan. The final vote was not taken, on agreeing directly to the Crittenden proposition, until the 3d of March, the day preceding the close of the Congress and the inauguration of Mr. Lincoln. The Clark amendment was first disposed of; the debate preceding the vote on which, we give:

Mr. Clark—"It might be expected, as I offered that substitute, that I would say something in its support; but, as the session is drawing so near a close, though I am prepared, I shall waive the opportunity, and let the vote be taken.

Mr. Wilson—"We have voted on that several times, and I suggest that it be withdrawn, and let us vote directly on the resolutions.

The Presiding Officer—"It cannot be withdrawn, the yeas and nays having been ordered.

"The Secretary proceeded to call the roll.

Mr. Anthony (when his name was called)—"Without any reference to the merits of this amendment, I shall vote against it for the purpose of allowing the Senator from Kentucky to obtain a vote on his resolutions. I vote nay.

Mr. Baker (when his name was called)—"Without reference to the merits of this amendment, I shall vote against it in order to get an opportunity to vote against the resolution of the Senator from Kentucky.

"The result was announced—yeas 14, nays 22, as follows:

"YEAS.

Bingham, Fessenden, Sumner,
Chandler, Foote, Trumbull,
Clark, Harlan, Wade,
Doolittle, King, Wilkinson.—14.
Durkee, Morrill,

NAYS.

Anthony, Foster, Mason,
Baker, Gwin, Nicholson,
Bayard, Hunter, Polk,
Bigler, Johnson, of Tenn. Pugh,
Bright, Kennedy, Rice,
Crittenden, Lane, Sebastian,
Dixon, Latham, Ten Eyck—22.
Douglas,

So Mr. Clark's amendment was rejected. (Page 1404.)

The question then recurred on adopting the Crittenden plan of compromise. It was defeated by the following vote: (Page 1405.)

YEAS.

Bayard, Johnson, of Tenn. Polk,
Bigler, Kennedy, Pugh,

Bright, Lane, Rice,
Crittenden, Latham, Sebastian,
Douglas, Mason, Thomson,
Gwin, Nicholson, Wigfall.—19.
Hunter,

NAYS.

Anthony, Fessenden, Sumner,
Bingham, Foote, Ten Eyck,
Chandler, Foster, Trumbull,
Clark, Grimes, Wade,
Dixon, Harlan, Wilkinson.
Doolittle, King, Wilson—20.
Durkee, Morrill,

Of the nineteen who voted yea, seventeen were Democrats and two Americans. The latter were Senators Crittenden, of Kentucky, and Kennedy, of Maryland. The twenty who voted in the negative were all Republicans.

In the House of Representatives.

On the 27th of February, 1861, [*see page 1261*,] Mr. Clemens, of Virginia, proposed to the House of Congress that the Crittenden compromise should be submitted to a vote of the people for adoption or rejection. He proposed the following joint resolution:

"WHEREAS, The Union is in danger; and owing to the unhappy division existing in Congress, it would be difficult, if not impossible, for that body to concur, in both its branches, by the requisite majority, so as to enable it either to adopt such measures of legislation, or to recommend to the States such amendments to the Constitution as are deemed necessary and proper to avert that danger; and

"WHEREAS, In so great an emergency, the opinion and judgment of the people ought to be heard, and would be the best and surest guide to their representatives; therefore

"*Resolved by the Senate and House of Representatives of the United States of America in Congress assembled,* That provisions ought to be made by law, without delay, for taking the sense of the people, and submitting to the vote the following resolutions (Crittenden's) as the basis for the final and permanent settlement of those disputes that now disturb the peace of the country and threaten the existence of the Union."

[Here followed Mr. Crittenden's resolutions.

The proposition of Mr. Clemens was rejected by the following vote: yeas 80, nays 113.

YEAS.

Adrian, D, Florence, D, Moore, T. Am.
Anderson, W.C. Am Fourke, D, Morris, I, N, D.
Avery, D. Garnette, D. Nelson, Am.
Barr, D. Gilmer, Am. Niblack, D.
Barrett, D. Hamilton, D. Noell, D.
Babcock, D. Harris, J, M, Am. Peyton, D.
Boteler, Am. Harris, T, J, D. Phelps, D.
Bouliguey, Am. Hatton, Am. Pryor, D.
Brabson, Am. Holman, D. Quarles, Am.
Branch, D. Howard, William, D Riggs, D.
Briggs, Am. Hughes, D. Robinson, J. C, D.
Bristow, Am. Jenkins, D. Rust, D.
Brown, D. Kunkel, D. Sickles, D.
Burch, D. Larnbee, D. Simms. D.
Burnett, D. Leach, J, M, Am. Smith, William, D
Clark, H. F. D. Leake, D. Smith, W, H.N, Am
Clark, J. B. D. Logan, D. Stevenson, D.
Cochrane, John, D Maclay, D. Stewart, J, A, D,
Cox, D. Mallorry, Am. Stokes, Am.
Craig, James, D. Martin, C, D, D. Stout, D.
Burton, D. Martin, E, S. D. Thomas, D.
Craig, D. Maynard, Am. Vallandigham, D.
Davis, J, G, D, McClernand, D. Vance, Am.
Dejarnette, D. McKentey, D. Webster, Am.
Dimmick, D. Millson, D. Whitney, D.
Edmundson, D. Montgomery, D. Winslow, D.
English, D. Laban, Am. Woodson, D.
80—Democrats, 61; Americans, 19. Wright, D

SCRAPS FROM MY SCRAP-BOOK. 137

"NAYS.

C. F. Adams, R.   Foster, R.   Pettit, R.
Aldrich, R.   Frank, R.   Porter, R.
Alley, R.   French, R.   Potter, R.
Ashley, R.   Gooch, R.   Pottle, R.
Babbitt, R.   Graham, R.   E. R. Reynolds, R.
Beale, R.   Grow, R.   Rice, R.
Bingham, R.   Hale, R.   C. Robinson, R.
Blair, R.   Hall, R.   Royce, R.
Blake, R.   Helmick, R.   Scranton, R.
Braytou, R.   Hickman, R.   Sedgwick, R.
Buffington, R.   Hindman, D.   Sherman, R.
Burlingame, R.   Hoard, R.   Somes, R.
Burnham, R.   W. A. Howard, R. Spaulding, R.
Butterfield, R.   Humphrey, R.   Spinner, R.
Campbell, R.   Hutchins, R.   Stanton, R.
Carey, R.   Irvine, R.   Stevens, R.
Carter, R.   Junkin, R.   W. Stewart, R.
Case, R.   F. W. Kellog, R. Scratton, R.
Coburn, R.   W. Kellog, R.   Tappan, R.
C. B. Cochrane, R. Kenyon, R.   Thayer, R.
Colfax, R.   Kilgore, R.   Theaker, R.
Conkling, R.   Killinger, R.   Tompkius, R.
Conway, R.   DeWitt C. Leach, R. Train, R.
Corwin, R.   Leo, R.   Trimble, R.
Covode, R.   Longnecker, R.   Vandever, R.
W. H. Davis, A'n. Loomis, R.   Van Wyck, R.
Dawes, R.   Lovejoy, R.   Terree, R.
Delano, R.   Marston, R.   Wade, R.
Duell, R.   McKean, R.   Waldron, R.
Dana, R.   McKnight, R.   Walton, R.
Edgerton, R.   McPherson, R.   C. C. Washburne, R.
Edwards, R.   Morehead, R.   R. B. Washburne, R.
Elliot. R.   Morrill, R.   Wells, R.
Ely, R.   Morse, R.   Wilson, R.
Etheridge, A'n.   Nixon, R.   Windham, R.
Farnsworth, R.   Olin, R.   Wood, R.
Fenton, R.   Palmer, R.   Woodruff. R.
Ferry, R.   Perry, R.

113. Republicans, 110; Americans, 2; Democrats, 1.

Such was the recorded action of the two houses of Congress, at the most critical and momentous period of our history, on a measure that would have saved us from civil war had the representatives of the party that had just been elected to power adopted it in season.

It is denied by some of the leaders and presses of the Republican party, that such would have been the result of the adoption by Congress of the Crittenden Compromise; but they produce no proof to sustain their assertion. On the other hand, we have as high testimony as could be desired or needed, to show that had the Crittenden Compromise been adopted in season, it would have saved the country from civil war.

Senator Douglas, on the 3d of January, 1861 speaking of his own plan of adjustment, which he had introduced into the Senate, said: (See Appendix Con. Globe, 1860, 1861, page 41.)

"I believe this (his own plan) to be a fair basis of amicable adjustment. If you of the Republican side are not willing to accept this, nor the proposition of the Senator from Kentucky, Mr. Crittenden, pray, tell us what you are willing to do. I address the inquiry to the Republican alone, for the reason that in the Committee of Thirteen, a few days ago, every member from the South, including those from the cotton States, (Messrs. Toombs and Davis,) expressed their readiness to accept the proposition of my venerable friend from Kentucky, Mr. Crittenden, as a FINAL SETTLEMENT of the controversy, *if tendered and sustained by the Republican members*. Hence, THE SOLE RESPONSIBILITY *of our disagreement* and the ONLY DIFFICULTY *in the way of an* AMICABLE ADJUSTMENT *is with the* REPUBLICAN PARTY."

When Mr. Douglas made that speech, he made it in presence and in the hearing of Jeff. Davis and Toombs, and other Southern Senators, except those from South Carolina, who had retired from Congress; and no one denied the truth of his statement. Nor did any of the Republican members of the Committee of Thirteen deny its truthfulness. They must, therefore, all be taken as having concurred in its correctness, viz: that the Southern Senators would have received the Crittenden plan, if tendered and sustained by the Republican members, as a final settlement of the slavery controversy; and, that therefore, the only difficulty in the way of an amicable adjustment was with the Republican party, and on it would rest the sole responsibility of the disagreement and its consequent horrors of civil war.

But there is other proof. On the 7th of January, 1861, Mr. Toombs made a speech (see p. 270) in which he corroborated the statement of Mr. Douglas, so far as he was concerned. He said:

"But, although I insist upon this perfect equality in the territories, yet when it was proposed, as I understand the Senator from Kentucky now proposes, that the line of 36 deg. 30 min. shall be extended acknowledging and protecting our property on the south side of that line, for the sake of peace—permanent peace—I said to the Committee of Thirteen, and I say here, that, with other satisfactory provisions, I would accept it. * * I am willing, however, to take the proposition of the Senator, as it was understood in committee, putting the North and the South on the same ground, prohibiting slavery on one side, acknowledging slavery and protecting it on the other, and applying that to all future acquisitions, so that the whole continent to the North Pole shall be settled upon the one rule, and to the South Pole under the other."

But that is not all. By reference to the same *Congressional Globe*, part 2, page 1300. will be found a speech made by Mr. Pugh, on the 3d of March, 1861. In the course of that speech, Mr. Pugh said:

"The Crittenden proposition has been indorsed by the almost unanimous vote of the Legislature of Kentucky. It has been indorsed by the Legislature of the noble old Commonwealth of Virginia. It has been petitioned for by a larger number of electors of the United States than any proposition that was ever before Congress. I believe in my heart to-day that it would carry an overwhelming majority of the people of my State—ay, sir, and of nearly every other State in the Union. *Before the Senators from the State of Mississippi left this Chamber, I heard one of them, who now assumes, at least, to be President of the Southern Confederacy, propose to accept it and to maintain the Union if that proposition could receive the vote it ought to receive from the other side of the Chamber.* Therefore, of all your propositions, of all your amendments, knowing as I do, and knowing that the historian will write it down, at any time before the 1st of January, a two-thirds vote for the Crittenden Resolutions in this Chamber would have saved every State in the Union but South Carolina."

Mr. Pugh said that in the presence and in the hearing of Republican Senators, and no one denied the truth of his assertion. Mr. Douglas was present and followed Mr. Pugh in a speech, remarking: (Page 1391.)

"The Senator has said that if the Crittenden Proposition could have passed early in the session, it would have saved all the States except South Carolina. I firmly believe it would. While the Crittenden Proposition was not in accordance with my cherished views, I avowed my readiness and eagerness to accept it, in order to save the Union, if we could unite upon it. No man has labored harder than I to get it passed. I can confirm the Senator's declaration, that Senator Davis himself, when on the Committee of Thirteen, was ready, at all times, to compromise on the Crittenden Proposition, I will go further, and say that Mr. Toombs was also."

10

We think nothing could be more conclusive than that testimony, unless the actual experiment itself, by the adoption of the plan itself and a trial under it, which the Republican members would not permit Senator Crittenden's opinion as to the effect the adoption of his plan would have had, was expressed by him, in a letter to Larz Anderson, Esq., of Cincinnati, dated Frankfort, March 27, 1861, in which he said:

"Those resolutions were proposed in the true spirit of compromise, and with the hope of preserving or restoring to the country peace and union. They were the result of the joint labors of, and consultation with friends, having the same object in view; and I believe if those measures thus offered had been, at a suitable time, promptly adopted by the Congress of the United States, *it would have checked the progress of the rebellion and revolution and SAVED THE UNION.*"

Some of the leaders finding the proof against their party to be so conclusive and overwhelming, endeavor to avoid its force by stating that, had the Southern Senators remained in their seats and voted, the Crittenden plan of Compromise would have passed Congress. That is not true. Under no circumstances could it have passed the House, which was Republican. With a full Senate, and every Senator present and voting, it would have required forty-four votes to pass the Crittenden Compromise, being a two-thirds vote, which is required on amendments to the Constitution. Had the thirty Senators from the Slave States been present and voted, they, with the ten Democrats from the Free States, would have made but forty, which would not have been enough by four votes. It is not true, therefore, that had the Southern Senators remained in their seats and voted, the Crittenden Compromise would have passed the Senate even. As we have already remarked, the House being Republican, it could not have received a majority vote in that body, let alone a two thirds vote.

But unanimity of opinion was necessary to have secured the success of the Crittenden plan with the states, had it even passed Congress. The Southern Senators, in the Committee of Thirteen, felt the necessity of that unanimity, and therefore it was that Mr. Douglas said, that "every member from the South, including those from the Cotton States, (Messrs. Toombs and Davis,) expressed their readiness to accept the Crittenden Compromise as a *final settlement* of the controversy, IF TENDERED AND SUSTAINED BY THE REPUBLICANS." If not tendered and sustained by the Republicans, the Southern Senators, as did everybody else, knew that the adoption, by Congress, of the Crittenden Compromise, would, in the end, be perfectly nugatory, as it would be defeated in the State Legislatures by the Republicans. Had it been tendered and sustained by the Republican members of Congress, the Southern people would have had a strong assurance, amounting almost to certainty, of its success in the State Legislatures; for the two great parties would then have been for it. But the managing, leading Republicans wanted no compromise at all, and least of all did they desire any that would be acceptable to the South.— They wanted a disruption of the Union, and civil war, in order to overthrow slavery. The testimony of Mr. Douglas on that point is overwhelming. In a letter to S. S. Hayes, Esq., of Illinois, he said:

"WASHINGTON, December 20, 1860.

"MY DEAR SIR: *   *   *   You will have received my proposed amendments to the Constitution before you receive this. *The South would take my proposition if the Republicans would agree to it.* But the extreme North and South hold off, and are precipitating the country into revolution and civil war.

"While I can do no act which recognizes or countenances the doctrine of secession, my policy is peace, and I will not consider the question of war until every effort has been made for peace, and all hope shall have vanished. When that time comes, if unfortunately it shall come, I will then do what it becomes an American Senator to do on the then state of facts. *Many of the Republican leaders desire a dissolution of the Union*, and URGE WAR AS A MEANS OF ACCOMPLISHING DISUNION; while others are Union men in good faith. We have now reached a point where a COMPROMISE on the basis of MUTUAL CONCESSION, or DISUNION and WAR, are INEVITABLE. I prefer a fair and just compromise. I shall make a speech in a few days.   S. A. DOUGLAS.
"S. S. HAYES, ESQ."

On the same day Mr. Douglas addressed a letter of like import to the Hon. John Taylor, of New York. To that gentleman, Mr. Douglas wrote:

"WASHINGTON, Dec. 20, 1860.

"MY DEAR SIR:—Pressure of business has prevented an earlier acknowledgment of your kind letter. The prospects of our country are gloomy indeed, but I do not despair of the Republic. We are now drifting rapidly into civil war, which must end in disunion. *This can only be prevented by amendments to the Constitution*, which will take the slavery question *out of Congress, and put an end to the strife*. Whether this can be done DEPENDS UPON THE REPUBLICANS. Many of their leaders *desire disunion on party grounds, and here is the difficulty.* God grant us a safe deliverance is my prayer.

"Very truly your friend,
"S. A. DOUGLAS.
"Hon. JOHN TAYLOR."

Mr. Douglas made his speech four or five days after the date of that letter, in which he avowed his readiness and eagerness to accept the Crittenden Compromise in order to save the Union; thereby endorsing it as "a fair and just compromise." But there were too many Republican leaders, who desired a dissolution of the Union, and urged war as a means of accomplishing disunion, to permit either Mr. Douglas' plan or Mr. Crittenden's plan, or the Peace Conference plan to pass; and so the country was precipitated into civil war.

Early in February, 1861, Mr. Douglas, in a letter to the editors of the Memphis *Appeal*, drew more fully the portrait of the managing Republicans. He said:

"WASHINGTON, February 2, 1861.

"MESSRS. EDITORS: *   *   *   You must remember that there are disunionists among the party leaders at the North as well as at the South, men, whose hostility to slavery is stronger than their fidelity to the Constitution, and who believe that the disruption of the Union would draw after it, as an inevitable consequence, civil war, servile insurrection, and, finally, the utter extermination of slavery in all the Southern States. They are bold, daring, determined men; and believing, as they do, that the Constitution of the United States is the great bulwark of slavery on this continent, and that the disruption of the American Union involves the inevitable destruction of slavery, and is an inseparable necessity to the attainment of that end, they are determined to accomplish their paramount object by any means within their power.

"For these reasons the Northern Disunionists, like the Disunionists of the South, are violently opposed to all compromises or constitutional amendments, or efforts at conciliation, whereby peace should be restored and the Union preserved. They are striving to break up the Union under the pretence of unbounded devotion to it.— They are struggling to overthrow the Constitution, while professing undying attachment to it, and a willingness to make any sacrifice to maintain it. They are trying to plunge the country into civil war as the surest means of destroying the Union, upon the plea of enforcing the laws and protecting the public property. If they can defeat every kind of adjustment or compromise, by which the points at issue may be satisfactorily settled, and keep up the irritation, so as to induce the Border States to follow the Cotton States, they will feel certain of the accomplishment of their ultimate designs.

"Nothing will gratify them so much, or contribute so effectually to their success, as the Secession of Tennessee and the Border States. Every State that withdraws from the Union increases the relative power of Northern Abolitionists to defeat a satisfactory adjustment, and bring on a war which, sooner or later, must end in final separation and recognition of the independence of the two contending sections."

That Mr. Douglas drew a correct portrait of the managers of the Republican party is proved by the letter written by Senator Chandler, of Michigan, to Austin Blair, then Governor of that State. This letter was written a few days after the date of Senator Douglas's letter to the editor of the Memphis *Appeal*. Here it is:

"WASHINGTON, Feb. 11, 1861.

"MY DEAR GOVERNOR:—Governor Bingham and myself telegraphed to you on Saturday, at the request of Massachusetts and New York, to send delegates to the Peace or Compromise Congress. They admit that we were right and they were wrong; that no Republican State should have sent delegates; but they are here and now it is for us. Ohio, Indiana and Rhode Island are caving in, and there is some danger of Illinois, and now they beg us, for God's sake, to come to their rescue and save the Republican party from rupture. I hope you will send stiff-backed men or none. The whole thing was gotten up against my judgment and advice, and will end in thin smoke. Still, I hope, as a matter of courtesy to some of our erring brethren, that you will send the delegates.

"Truly your friend, Z. CHANDLER.
"His Excellency AUSTIN BLAIR.

"P. S.—Some of the Manufacturing States think that a fight would be awful. Without a little blood-letting this Union will not, in my estimation, be worth a curse."

That letter is full of point. It opens to the public gaze the motives upon which the Republican managers acted. Virginia had solicited a conference of the states to see if some plan could not be devised and agreed upon, to save the Union and prevent civil war. Sincere patriots were anxious to save the Border States— Delaware, Maryland, Virginia, Kentucky and Missouri, together with North Carolina and Tennessee—and therefore favored the assembly of this Peace Conference. The Republican managers were opposed to it Massachusetts and New York sent delegates, but when the plan of the Republican managers was explained to them, they repented of their haste, acknowledged their error, admitted that the managers were right and they wrong, and that no Republican state should have sent delegates. They, therefore begged for God's sake, for the Governor of Michigan to come to the rescue, and save the Republican party—not the Union—from rupture. The Governor was requested to send stiff backed men or none—none who were likely to favor any plan of conciliation. In the opinion of Chandler, the Union would not be worth a curse, without a little blood letting.

As far back as December 23, 1860, Mr. Toombs issued an address to his constituents, of Georgia, in which he says, speaking of the Crittenden Compromise:

"A vote was taken in the Committee of Thirteen on amendments to the Constitution, proposed by the Hon. John J. Crittenden, and each and all of them were voted against harmoniously by the Black Republican members of the Committee. In addition to these facts, a majority of the Black Republican members of the Committee *declared distinctly that they had no guarantees to offer,* which was silently acquiesced in by the other members."

Mr. Toombs afterward, January 7, 1861, made his speech in the Senate, in which he said he would accept the Crittenden Compromise as a final settlement of the slavery question. But, as Senator Hale, a leading Republican, said, on the floor of the Senate, when Mr. Crittenden presented his plan to the Senate, the controversy was not to be settled by Congress. The Republican managers did not mean to permit it to be settled there. They wanted, in the language of Senator Douglas, a disruption of the Union, believing a disruption "would draw after it, as an inevitable consequence, civil war, servile insurrections, and, finally, the utter extermination of slavery in all the Southern states." They are the great criminals upon whose backs the scorpion whips of a duped and outraged people should be applied.

But for these men, we might have continued a united and prosperous people. Their devilish spirit demanded war, blood-letting, and the land has been gorged with the blood of brethren, shed by the hands of brothers Desolation and death, humiliation and tears and sorrow, have been our portion since these Republican managers have had the direction of public affairs at Washington. They are the cabal that have controlled the President from the start.— To what condition the country will be reduced by the time their power shall cease, on the retirement of Mr. Lincoln, can be imagined from its present deplorable state, under their manipulation. All our troubles might have been avoided but for their determination that there should be NO COMPROMISE. What a price the country is paying for the Abolition whistle!

CHAPTER XXIII.

REPUBLICANS OBSTINATE AND REFUSE TO COMPROMISE.

The Conduct of the Abolitionists in the Wisconsin Legislature...Radical Reasons for not Compromising...The Chicago' Platform Good Enough for the Radicals... Tenacity of the Wouldn't-Yield-An-Inchers...Effort of Democrats to send Commissioners to the Compromise Congress...Republicans Claim to have "Struggled Manfully against the United Democracy"...Carl Schurz and "Our Side"...Republicans of Sauk City opposed to Compromise...A Candid Admission...Edward Everett on Compromise...Lord Brougham on Coercion...Plan of Adjustment by the Peace Congress...Franklin's Substitute..."New York Post" on Effect...Greeley against Compromise...General Conclusions, &c.

WISCONSIN LEGISLATURE ON COMPROMISE.

In addition to the foregoing, we have sorted out the following from the proceedings of the Wisconsin Legislature, as samples of the *general* course of the Republicans, and as showing their *general* purposes and designs. With this we consider the "record complete."

In the Senate of Wisconsin, Jan. 25th, 1861, the following resolution was passed:

"*Resolved*, (*if the Assembly concur*,) That the following resolution, reported by a minority of the select committee of 33 in the Congress of the United States, and signed by Messrs. Tappan of New Hampshire, and Washburn of Wisconsin, reflects the judgment and sentiments of the Legislature of Wisconsin, and that its views and patriotic conclusions should be adequate to restore permanent peace and prosperity to our glorious Republic.

"*Resolved*, That the provisions of the Constitution are ample for the preservation of the Union; and the protection of all the material interests of the country; that it needs to be obeyed rather than amended; and that extrication from present difficulties should be looked for in efforts to protect and preserve the public property, and the enforcement of the laws, rather than in new guaranties for particular interests or compromises and concessions of unreasonable demands."

Mr. BRADFORD, (Rep.) introduced the following in the Assembly:

"*Resolved*, That we, as the representatives of the people of Wisconsin, are opposed to each and all the schemes of compromise which have been proposed or may hereafter be devised recognizing slavery as in accordance with the Constitution, or, in any way tending to extend, diffuse or perpetuate so peculiar and odious an institution, and which has been well said to be "the sum of all villainies."

Mr. KEOGH (Dem.) offered the following, [which was intended to be a gentle reminder to the Chairman of the Committee on Federal Relations, (Mr. SPOONER, now Lieutenant Governor,) who managed to have all peace resolutions referred to his Committee, where they were kept, as was believed, to prevent action:]

"*Resolved*, That the Committee on Federal Relations be instructed to report within one week on the preamble and resolutions No. 8, A., referred to them on yesterday, as to the policy or impolicy of the action therein proposed, and also whether the state of Wisconsin ought or ought not, in the opinion of said Committee, take any action in reference to the dangers that now threaten our Union, and whether, if any action is deemed necessary, it should be pacificatory *first*, before warlike, or whether it is our policy as a state to declare against all concessions, and for blood and strife.

"*Resolved*, That the 'poet,' in giving the history of our early strife with the mother country, and the object of our forefathers in reference to the white and black man's rights, &c., expresses just and wise sentiments, as follows:

"'The Tableaux change, and Brother J. proposes
To 'boot' the King, and ring his soldiers' noses!
Now, George this 'insult' with gallant scorn resented,
(Though 'tis due to state he afterwards repented;)
And, of course, a long and sanguinary war ensued,
And brother's hands with brother's blood imbued!
Those were the times, as their history now unfolds,
That friccasied men's bodies—and tried their souls!
Then, we had 'Tragedians,' all first class 'Stars,'
Who, true to heroic life, delineated Mars;
No phosphorous lightning—no sheet iron thunder!
Then shook the Thespian Temple with false wonder!
No incandescent flash—no pyrotecnic blaze!
Such as school boys muster in nocturnal plays;
No 'fancy fencing, with stub-shod iron swords—
No ratan muskets flourished on THOSE 'Boards:'
But the real 'Old Flint Lock' and Damascus Steel,
Made the 'claret' flow, and flesh and muscle *feel*
And on every bloody field the patriots' bayonets
Pierc'd the tinseled helmets of Gen'ral and Brevets!
Nor were our fathers fighting, like hypocrites and knaves,
Under *pretense* of giving 'freedom' to their slaves!
Nor were they guilty, in their 'Bill of vested rights,'
Of classing Ethiopians with their brother whites!
They left to God the gen'ral purpose of his plan,
To apportion as He will'd the proper 'Rights of Man!'
Of which self-gov'ment—more potent than the rest—
Each prevailing Race make laws that suit *them* best.
Since God himself wisely hath partition'd races—
Assigned to each their *superior* and *inferior* places—
What right hath mortals to change His holy plan,
And *legislate* the *inferior* to the *superior* man?'"

On the 26th of January, the propositions of Virginia for a Peace Congress, were transmitted to the Legislature by Governor RANDALL. These propositions were conceived in a worthy spirit, and evidently showed an earnestness to compromise and save blood shed. They were imploring but not dictatorial. They were treated with general respect, by some Republicans, but evidently detested and scorned by the mass of the party. The Democracy to a man were in favor of immediate action, and a favorable response. For days the question was argued, in various forms, in both Houses, and finally, by the schemes of Republican party leaders, the proposition to send Commissioners was defeated. Below we present some of the opinions expressed in the course of debate by leading Republicans, though it is due to state that some Republicans *appeared* to honestly favor action:

"Senator Hutchison, (Rep.) believed that we should meet with the representatives of Virginia around the family altar. There is never danger to him whose cause is just, meeting with his adversary. It was at first thought that the delegation in Congress should act as commissioners, but upon further reflection, and as it was for a specific purpose, it was thought better to send special commissioners. He inserted Mr. Washburne's name, as he had been on the committee of 33, and it might be gratifying to have his action endorsed.

"Senator Bartlett, (Rep.,) thought that slavery was sufficiently guarantied by the Constitution in the State of Virginia. If we appoint a committee in accordance with the Virginia resolutions we meet with her commissioners on the basis that they present. *As a Republican party we debauch* ourselves if we place ourselves on the record, as these resolutions require. It's worse than folly to make a mere show of amity by sending commissioners to Washington, bound by instructions not to grant the demands of the South, and nothing but an insult to those with whom we treat. If we were prepared to admit that south of 36 deg. 30 min. should be given up to slavery and that it should be perpetual, then indeed might we consistently treat. The Senator from the 30th, Hutchinson, thinks it an alarming thing that we cannot meet the Southern States round the family altar, but it is true that at this time they are engaged in acts of treason and he thought the resolutions showed a lack of moral courage, and he as a Republican, did not wish to be put in such an anamolous position as they would place him in. Moral courage, sir, is that kind of courage which enables a man to *take his stand on principle and do right.* This is what alone can save the country in the present crisis. We cannot look to the shattered columns of the Democracy of the North for salvation. Nothing but firmness and integrity on the part of the *Republicans* will carry the country safely through the present crisis. No good can arise from such a conference as is proposed.

"There can be no moral influence in the course advocated by Senator Hutchinson as it bears a lie on its face. We should also look to the *expense* of this commission, and believing that no good can result from the expense, I cannot go in for it. He that is wasteful of the people's money is also wasteful of principle."

February 1, '61, the following action was had in the Senate, on the Commissioner proposition:

"Senator Gill then spoke against the adoption of Senator Hutchinson's amendment: He was tired of hearing of Union savers. Too many eulogies had already been pronounced on such men as Alexander H. Stevens, of Georgia. He reiterated at length that the Virginia resolutions called for Commissioners from this state, with the words explicitly stating that they were required to deliberate on amendments to the Constitution, and if they went they would find themselves deluded and in a snare.

"Senator Worthington followed in a pointed and deliberate argument against the appointment of commissioners. He said that the position of Senator Gill was invulnerable, and that he very much doubted, from what he knew of the sentiments of some of the intended Commissioners of their accepting the commission. He agreed with the remarks made by his colleague on the committee, Senator Bartlett.

"Senator Cole, as one of the committee on Federal relations, was impelled by a full consideration of the Virginia resolutions, to vote for the amendment as amended.

"Senator Joiner, in some brief and sensible remarks, stated his intention, notwithstanding the grand flourishes of some gentlemen to the contrary that he had heard during the argument, of voting for the amendment.

"The resolutions introduced by Senator Hutchinson, and as amended by Senator Virgin, were then adopted by

AYES.

A. I. Bennett,	Ferguson,	Quentin,
Cole,	*Hutchinson,*	Sweat,
Cunning,	Joiner,	Sweet,
Decker,	Kingston,	*Virgin—*14.
Egan,	Maxon,	

NAYS.

Bartlett,	Crane,	*Montgomery,*
Bean,	Foot,	*Stewart,*
Geo. Bennett,	Gill,	Utley,
Carey,	Hazelton,	*Worthington—*14.
Cox,	Kelsey,	

Republicans in italic.

"The Lieutenant Governor giving his vote in the affirmative, which occasioned much applause.

The Lieut. Governor (Rep.) was denounced by his party press for giving this casting vote.

On the same day the following debate was had in the Assembly:

"Mr. Rugee (Rep.) spoke in favor of his amendment, and was in favor of acting up to the requirements of the 21,000 majority in this state. He was satisfied that the Democratic party would not swallow the Republican platform, and he could see no propriety in sending a Democrat among the Commissioners, unless he is willing to conform to the Republican platform.

"Mr. C R. Johnson (Rep.) said the question used to be, 'Have we a Bourbon amongst us?' It might now be rendered, 'Have we a Republican party?' He believed the Republican party was a Union party. He was a Union man. He could not appreciate the expression, that 'in these revolutionary times it is ridiculous to talk of the Chicago platform' was not an emanation from a Republican breast. He was in favor of instruction if we must send commissioners. Mr. J. proceeded for some time to enforce his views, taking strong ground against this action. He went in for the Chicago platform.

"Mr. D. H. Johnson, (Rep.,) thought it important that we should have a free interchange of sentiment, with a view to a better understanding. He was sorry to see a spirit of disappointment and opposition here. He alluded to the gentleman from Rock, [Mr. Graham, which brought that gentleman to his feet in explanation.] Mr. J. proceeded to discuss at considerable length the propriety of not including the Chicago platform in his action.

"Mr. Rugee, (Rep.,) said if any Republican would show anything bad in the Chicago platform he would withdraw it.

"Mr. D. H. Johnson rejoined.

"Mr. Bradford, (Rep.,) said that he discovered that his Democratic friends were as calm as turtle doves, while many of the Republicans seemed to be trembling in their boots. [Laughter.] He predicted that to send commissioners would end in a conventional bubble, and would explode, amounting to nothing. He knew when Virginia asked anything she meant to have it or nothing. He was decidedly opposed to the proposition of sending commissioners. He cautioned the *Republicans against leaving out the Republican platform* if they did they would leave out many of the party.

"Mr. Atwood, (Rep.) said that several gentlemen had endeavored to impress upon this House that they were Republicans. He believed that where he lived no one questioned his Republicanism. This question was not one of party; it was not to advance Republicanism as such—it was to save our country, and party had nothing to do with it. He could meet the Democrats and act with them on this matter, and never stop to enquire whether they ever had a platform or not. In giving the "21,000 majority," so much referred to here, we did not expect these dreadful realities which now surround us. We must now act upon the facts and circumstances as they surround us. These commissioners could go to Washington and act independent of any other state. They would no doubt act with reference to the sentiment of the people of the state as much as possible. He was opposed to any positive instructions, though he should have no objection to have the commissioners required to communicate with the legislature.

"Mr. Rugee again rejoined, taking strong ground in favor of sending the Chicago platform to Washington.

"Mr. Graham, (Rep.) said he had intended to be content with a silent vote against this measure, but he could hardly sit still since so much had been said, and his proposition had been voted down. He believed the northern Democrats were as loyal to the constitution and government as the Republicans, and he should not object to see a Democrat appointed, if the commissioners should be raised. He should vote for Mr. Rugee's proposition to instruct, *for the purpose of killing the motion.*—

He spoke against the idea that slaves are property. [Why not have raised this question on the Ripon speech before electing Judge Howe? —REPORTER.]

"Mr. Atwood said he respected the frankness of the gentleman from Rock in declaring he would go for the amendment *to kill the proposition.* He thanked him for that. He liked the Chicago platform as much as any one, but he could not consent to tack that and state constitutions on propositions of this kind.— He believed this move would do good. He believed it would do good for a parley to be held. It could do no harm—it might do good."

From the Assembly Debates on the 4th we take the following:

"Mr. Dwight (Rep.) was at first in favor of sending commissioners, but the arguments he had heard had convinced him of his error, and he was not ashamed to own it. He did not propose to get down on his knees when the South had a club over his head, and eat a 'large piece of pumpkin pie.' His children were all girls, and therefore he could stand the war very well. He wished he was in the Chair, he would show the South a little of Old Jackson. In short, he was opposed to all concessions and all compromise.

"Mr. Lindsley (Rep.) was opposed to this commission. He believed we had already given the South an intimation of what we would do, and he was opposed to going any further. He would favor the submission of our personal liberty bill to a judicious committee, and if found to be unconstitutional, to repeal it, but he was opposed to meeting the South for any such purpose as this. Much as he loved peace and quiet he would willingly sacrifice his life *to abolish slavery.* He loved the Union, and he would be willing to make any reasonable sacrifices to save it, but he would not vote for this resolution.

"Mr. Spooner, (Rep.) was opposed to the amendment. He saw where the opposite side met the difficulty. They find it necessary to ignore the expressed will of the people. His constituents had instructed him not to back down in the least, and to yield nothing. So far as he was concerned, he should stand by his instructions. He could vote for no such propositions and go back to his constituents."

A correspondent of the *Milwaukee Sentinel* (rep.) of February, said:

"My sympathies on this occasion were all with the Republicans, who struggled manfully against the *united Democracy*, aided by members from their own ranks, to defeat this proposition; and who were finally overcome only by the casting vote of the Lieutenant Governor, who, representing the *whole* state, nevertheless preferred to vote with the *six* Republicans who favored the proposition, rather than the *fourteen* who opposed it. Vengeance is not mine."

CARL SCHURZ was at Norwalk, Ohio, during this controversy. He, with CHANDLER, of

SCRAPS FROM MY SCRAP-BOOK. 143

Michigan, was opposed to compromise, and believed that to send "stiff-backed Republicans," who were opposed to it, as commissioners, was the only way to prevent compromise, and *save the Republican party* The following dispatch explains itself:

"To Gov. Randall:
"By Telegraph from NORWALK, OHIO, Feb. 1, 1861.
"Appoint Commissioners to Washington conference—myself one, to strengthen our side.
"CARL SCHURZ."

The Republicans in various portions of the State soon began to act, and wire pullers pulled the strings to prevent compromise. A "Union" meeting was held by the Republicans of Sauk City, Sauk county, Wisconsin, in February, and from among their resolutions we select the following:

"*Resolved*, That we, as Republicans, will not submit to compromises at the sacrifice of principle."

"There was a Brutus once, that would have brook'd
The eternal devil, to keep his State in Rome,
As easily as a King."—*Julius Cæsar.*

No one doubts that BRUTUS had the courage to do much that he lacked the power. We find many here that would "brook the eternal devil" to carry their points, but they would no doubt end where BRUTUS did, with the loss of liberty and power. With the following, from King Henry IVth, we will leave our readers to "heed or bleed."

"A Peace is of the nature of a Conquest!
For then *both* parties nobly are subdued,
And neither party loser."

A CANDID ADMISSION.

The Milwaukee *Sentinel*, in February, 1861, made the following admission:

"Had the election of last November resulted in favor of that party, [the Democracy,] we should have heard nothing of 'Secession;' no complaints about 'Personal Liberty Laws;' no denunciation of Northern fanaticism; no talk of a 'Southern Confederacy.' South Carolina indeed, might have made more or less fuss, as usual; but she would have stood alone, and her fit would have soon passed over."

This was very true, but the Democracy did not succeed; hence the necessity for compromise.

EDWARD EVERETT ON COMPROMISE.

A large and enthusiastic Union meeting was held in Faneuil Hall, Boston, February, 1861, at which the CRITTENDEN proposition was endorsed *unanimously*. The following letter was read to the meeting from the Hon EDWARD EVERETT:

"WASHINGTON, Feb. 2, 1861.
"MY DEAR SIR—I much regret that it is not in my power to be present at the meeting to be held in Faneuil Hall next Tuesday. I have yielded, at the sacrifice of personal convenience, to the advice and request that I would prolong my stay at Washington, with a view to conference with members of Congress and other persons from various parts of the Union, who are uniting their couns-ls and efforts for its preservation.

"The crisis is one of greater danger and importance than has ever before existed. Six states have declared their separation from the Union; and the withdrawal of the seventh is a probable event. The course of the remaining Southern States will be decided in a few days. They are under opposing influences. A strong conservative sentiment binds them to the Union; a natural sympathy with the seceding states draws them in an opposite direction.

"If they adhere to the Union there will be no insuperable difficulty in winning back the sister States, which have temporarily withdrawn from us, but if the border states are drawn into the Southern Confederacy the fate of the country is sealed. Instead of that palmy prosperity which has made us for two generations the envy of the civilized world, we shall plunge into the road to ruin. We must look forward to collision at home—fierce, bloody, deadly collision—not alone between the two great sections of the country, but between neighboring States—town and country, and embittered parties in the same city—and abroad we must submit to the loss of the rank we have hitherto sustained among the family of nations. Human nature is the same in all ages, and the future, now impending over our once happy country, may be read in the mournful history of the Grecian and Italian republics, and in the terrific annals of the French revolution. To expect to hold fifteen States in the Union by force is preposterous. The idea of a civil war, accompanied, as it would be, by a servile insurrection, is too monstrous to be entertained for a moment. If our sister states must leave us, in the name of heaven let them go in peace. I agree in the sentiment that the people alone can avert these dire calamities. Political leaders, however well disposed, are hampered by previous committals and controlled by their associates. The action of Congress, unless accelerated by an urgent impulse from the ultimate source of power, is too much impeded by the forms of legislation and tediousness of debate. There is no hope from the political parties of the country—agencies unhappily too potent for mischief, but, in the present extremity, powerless for good. except by a generous sacrifice of all party views, interest and ambition to the public weal.

"No; it is only by the loud, emphatic, unanimous utterance of the voice of the people, that the danger can be averted. Let the cry go forth from Faneuil Hall, and ring through the land, that the Union must and shall be preserved! (Great cheering.) "Your friend and fellow citizen, "EDWARD EVERETT."

LORD BROUGHAM ON COERCION.

The venerable Lord BROUGHAM, one of the wisest and most conservative men of England, thus wrote on the 19th of March, '61—a just rebuke to those who would sustain something they have dubbed a Platform, and make shipwreck of the Constitution and Union:

"The alarm felt by all the friends of human improvement at the risk of disunion in America, are naturally uppermost in one's mind at the present time. How much it is to be wished that the contending parties in both Italy and America would take a leaf out of our books, and *learn the wisdom as well as virtue of compromise and mutual concession*."

PLAN OF ADJUSTMENT ADOPTED BY THE PEACE CONGRESS.

"Sec. 1. In all the present territory of the United States, north of the parallel of thirty-six degrees thirty minutes of north latitude, involuntary servitude, except in punishment of crime, is prohibited. In all the present territory south of that line the status of persons held to service or labor, as it now exists, shall not be changed. Nor shall any law be passed by Congress or the territorial legislature to hinder or prevent the taking of such persons from any of the States of this Union to said territory, nor to impair the rights arising from said relation. But the same shall be subject to judicial cognizance in the Federal courts according to the common law. When any territory north or south of said line, with such boundary line as Congress may prescribe shall contain a population equal to that required for a member of Congress, it shall, if its form of government be republican, be admitted into the Union on an equal footing with the original States, with or without involuntary servitude, as the constitution of such State may provide.

"Sec. 2. No territory shall be aquired by the United States except by discovery and for naval and commercial stations, depots, and transit routes, without the concurrence of a majority of all the Senators from the States which allow involuntary servitude, and a majority of all the Senators from States which prohibit that relation; nor shall territory be acquired by treaty, unless the votes of a majority of the Senators from each class of States hereinbefore mentioned be cast as a part of the two-third majority necessary to the ratification of such treaty.

"Sec. 3. Neither the constitution nor any amendment thereto, shall be construed to give Congress power to regulate, abolish or control, within any state or territory of the United States, the relation established or recognized by the laws thereof touching persons bound to labor or involuntary service in the District of Columbia, without the consent of Maryland, and without the consent of the owners, or making the owners who do not consent just compensation; nor the power to interfere with or prohibit representatives and others from bringing with them to the city of Washington, retaining and taking away, persons so bound to labor or service, nor the power to interfere with or abolish involuntary service in places under the exclusive jurisdiction of the United States within these states and territories where the same is established or organized; nor the power to prohibit the removal or transportation of persons held to labor or involuntary service in any state or territory of the United States to any other state or territory thereof, where it is established or recognized by law or usage; and the right, during transportation by sea or river, of touching at ports, shores and landings, but not for sale or traffic, shall exist; nor shall Congress have power to authorize any higher rate of taxation on persons held to labor or service than on land. The bringing into the District of Columbia of persons held to labor or service for sale, or placing them in depots to be afterwards transferred to other places for sale as merchandize, is prohibited, and the right of transit through any state or territory against its dissent, is prohibited.

"Sec. 4. The third paragrah of the second section of the fourth article of the constitution shall not be construed to prevent any of the states, by appropriate legislation, and through the action of their judicial and ministerial officers, from enforcing the delivery of fugitives from labor to the person to whom such service or labor is due.

"Sec. 5. The foreign slave trade is hereby forever prohibited, and it shall be the duty of Congress to pass laws to prevent the importation of slaves, coolies or persons held to service or labor. into the United States, and the Territories from places beyond the limits thereof.

"Sec. 6. The first, third and fifth sections, together with this section six of these amendments, and the third paragraph of the second section of the first article of the constitution, and third paragraph of the second section of the fourth article thereof, shall not be amended or abolished without the consent of all the states.

"Sec. 7. Congress shall provide by law that the United States shall pay to the owner the full value of his fugitives from labor, in all cases where the Marshal or other officer whose duty it was to arrest such fugitive, was prevented from so doing by violence or intimidation from mobs or riotous assemblages, or when, after arrest, such fugitive was rescued by like violence or intimidation, and the owner thereby prevented and obstructed in the pursuit of his remedy for the recovery of such fugitive. Congress shall provide by law for securing to the citizens of each state the privileges and immunities of the several states."

SCRAPS FROM MY SCRAP-BOOK. 145

MR. FRANKLIN'S SUBSTITUTE.

The substitute offered in the Peace Conference by Mr. FRANKLIN, of Pennsylvania, for the first article of the Guthrie Basis, and which was adopted by the vote of all the states represented, except Virginia, North Carolina, Tennessee, Delaware and Missouri, is as follows:

"Art. 1. In all the present territory of the United States, not embraced in the Cherokee Treaty, North of the parallel of thirty-six degrees and thity minutes of North latitude, involuntary servitude, except in punishment of crime, is prohibited. In all the present territory South of that line, the status of persons held to service or labor, as it now exists, shall not be changed by law, nor shall the rights arising from said relation be impaired; but the same shall be subject to judicial cognizance in the Federal Courts, according to the common law. When any territory North or South of said line within such boundary as Congress may prescribe, shall contain a population equal to that required for a member of Congress, it shall, if its form of government be republican, be admitted into the Union on an equal footing with the original states, with or without involuntary servitude, as the Constitution of such state may provide."

THE EFFECT OF IT.

The failure of Wisconsin, says the Milwaukee *Sentinel*, to appoint commissioners is likely to have a decidedly opposite effect from what the opponents of such action have intended. The N. Y. *Post* says:

"In the conference four strongly Republican states remain unrepresented. Michigan, Wisconsin, Minnesota and Kansas have neglected or refused to send commissioners. Of the twenty states represented, three of the free, Rhode Island, New Jersey and Pennsylvania, will join the seven slave states in any propositions which the latter desire. Thus, snould the slave states unite for Guthrie's plan, the vote would probably be a tie, ten to ten. The four free states not represented in the Peace Conference owe it to the country to repair their neglect and authorize the attendance of commissioners."

GREELEY STRIVES TO PREVENT COMPROMISE.

The following appeared in the New York *Tribune* while the peace negociations were pending. It was designed to frighten off the partizans:

"For a man or a party to win a Presidential election under false pretences, is an offense as much more heinous than obtaining money under false pretenses, as the administration of the affairs of a great nation is of more consequence to the world than the question whether John Doe or Richard Roe shall possess a certain ten dollar bill. The Republican party obtained power in the recent Presidential contest by professing certain clearly defined principles upon the subject of slavery in the territories. Being about to assume the seals of office, eminent men, of whom it had a right to expect better things, counsel that it repudiate its platform of principles, confess itself a common cheat, turn its back upon those who elevated it to place, and convict itself of having either been a rank hypocrite before the election, or of being a skulking craven now. Such counselors should know that men and parties which attain power by professing one set of principles, and then, when in office, sacrifice them, and carry out another set, always break down and go to perdition, amid the jeers of the foes whom they beat in the contest, and the execrations of the friends whom they afterwards betrayed. And yet this sort of grand larceny, this stealing into power by false tokens, this playing the 'confidence game' on the broad theatre of a nation, is sometimes called statesmanship! The Republican party can better afford to lose than keep the authors of such statesmanship in its ranks. Let them go!"

The *Tribune* followed this up by declaring the right of secession. On the 2d of March, '61, it said:

"We have repeatedly said, and we once more insist, that the great principle embodied by Jefferson in the Declaration of Independence, that governments derive their just powers from the consent of the governed, is sound and just; and that, if the slave states, the cotton states, or the Gulf states only, choose to form an independent nation, *they have a moral right to do so!*"

We might fill a dozen volumes with corelative testimony, all going to show that the Republicans were determined that no compromise should be affected. Most of their leading presses and orators treated all who favored compromise as little, if any better than traitors.

Little did they think that *compromise* is written on the face of nature itself, and that their very existence is the result of compromise.

The yielding and compensating principles between heat and cold, wet and dry, earth and air, attraction and repulsion, positive and negative, in the mental and physical, good and bad, in the moral and political, wise and unwise principles in the material world, are all the result of *compromise*. Without this accommodating principle, or virtue of yielding partially to opposing forces, to secure results otherwise unattainable, no human government could be formed, no laws could be enacted, no laws executed, no society maintained, and even no family happiness secured.

No compromise, said the Republicans, and as they looked upon their Wide-Awake battalions, "panting for the fray," they bid defiance to conciliation, and looking to the South as Cæsar viewed the Persians across the Hellespont, like Shakespeare's hero they exclaimed:

"Let them come!
They come like sacrifices in their train,
And to the fire-eyed maid of smoky war,
All hot and bleeding, we will offer them!
The mailed Mars shall on his altar sit,
Up to his ears in blood!"

But, happy for them, if in the sequel they do not feel inclined, in the language of Henry VI to exclaim:

"Ah! vain Republicans, these days are dangerous!
Virtue is choked with foul ambition,
And charity chased hence by rancor's hand—
Foul subordination is predominant,
And equity exiled our native land;
The gods of party rule the fatal hour,
And mock all efforts to reprieve the victims!"

CHAPTER XIV.

REPUBLICAN EFFORTS TO STIMULATE DISSOLUTION—THEIR DISLOYALTY AND TREASON.

The Morrill Tariff as a Means to Hasten Dissolution... Opinions of the "Cincinnati Commercial," "New York Times," and "New York World"...From the "London Times"...The Tables Turned on the Charge of "Disloyalty"...Rules of Testimony, and the Proof of Republican Disloyalty...Testimony of Andrew Johnson...Senator Wilson on "Setting up with the Union"...What Constitutes a "Traitor" and a "Copperhead"...Mr. Lincoln on the Stand: His Preaching contrasted with his Practice...Congress on the "Object" of the War... "Indianapolis Sentinel" ditto...Thad. Stevens against the Constitution as it is...Mr. Chase Declares the Union Not Worth Fighting For...Frank Blair on Chase...Thurlow Weed on Mob Theirs...Being for the Union as it was Declared an "Offense"...The Present Programme Blocked Out Just After Lincoln's Nomination...Dawson's Letter to the "Albany Journal"...Giddings in the Chicago Convention; His Radical Doctrine Voted Down There; How Acted On...Lincoln's Letter of Acceptance...Lincoln and the Chicago Platform in Juxtaposition...Sumner Opens the Radical Ball..."New York Post" and Other Papers fear it was Premature...The Other Class of Disunionists...Treason of the "Chicago Tribune"...The Crittenden Resolutions...The Proclamation and Emancipation: Conclusions Thereon..."New York Tribune" and Other Sheets" Predict Good Things ...The "Pope's Bull Against the Comet"...The Object to Divide the North, &c...Gov. Andrew Before and After the Proclamation...Choice Inconsistencies, &c... Money and Not the Proclamation Required to Make the "Roads Swarm'"...Greeley Down on Old Abe... Seward Pronounces the Proclamation Unconstitutional.

THE MORRILL TARIFF AS A MEANS TO HASTEN SECESSION AND DISSOLUTION.

The passage of the MORRILL tariff, with its high pressure demands, just in the nick of time, when the Southern fever was at boiling pitch, was not only calculated to hasten secession and dissolution, but that act was passed under such circumstances, as to leave little doubt of its intent. We submit the following testimony:

REPEAL OF THE TARIFF.

The Cincinnati *Commercial* (Rep.) says:

"Our new and supremely idiotic Tariff is a great lever placed in the hands of the Secessionists, and they are employing it with tremendous effect to pry off the border slave states from the Union. *It is vastly more efficient than the negro question.* The negro cry had lost its effect in the border states, for it was plain that the negro interest was better off within than it would be without the Union. But the cry of oppressive revenue laws in the North, enacted for the benefit of special interests, and that there is more freedom of trade in the South, will convince multitudes that they would improve their condition by going out of the Union. There is no necessity so pressing and exacting as the repeal of the Tariff abomination. It was intended to protect a few interests, and it will be ruinous to all. The system of favoritism in legislation is always pernicious. In these revolutionary times *it is fatal.* There should be an extra session of Congress immediately, and within the first hour after its organization a bill should be introduced repealing the Tariff. The moment an extra session is called, and we think the call inevitable, petitions must be circulated throughout the West, praying and demanding the instant repudiation of the miserably short-sighted and 'puerile' policy of Pennsylvania. Every movement toward perfect freedom of trade with direct taxation for the support of the Government, is in the right direction.

A GLOOMY PICTURE!—EFFECT OF THE MORRILL TARIFF—THE GOVERNMENT UNABLE TO ENFORCE ITS LAWS, &c.

The New York *Times*, (Rep.) draws the following gloomy picture under the caption of 'Breakers Ahead:'"

"The enactment of a highly protective tariff on the heel of the last session of Congress, without the least provison made for its enforcement, and *at the very time when secession was so fully matured* as to indicate its character and purpose, was an act of *reckless folly* unparalleled in our legislative history. The measure is equally bad in every point in which it can be viewed. It is not a revenue tariff.— Its object was to discourage importations. It cannot be enforced on more than three thousand miles of interior line. We treat the seceding States as a portion of our Confederacy. A ship may lawfully enter their ports and put its goods in warehouse. In seizures for condemnation, the case would be tried in the United States Courts, and before a "local" jury. No such jury exist. If they did it would be difficult to tell how the jury would decide. The President has no power whatever in the premises. His guides are well established laws which contemplated nothing like the present state of affairs. The spectacle of a great nation unable to enforce a law enacted with all due solemnity and upon the observance of which the exercise of all its functions depend, is humiliating to the last degree.

"Whatever may be the ultimate aims of the seceding states, a present advantage is of the utmost importance as a lever for future operations. A tariff is highly unpopular in the border states. The one just enacted is the strongest argument yet addressed to them to go to the seceding ones, and is telling with great effect. No matter how absurd may be the statements and arguments used, they none the less effect what we would avoid. We do not at the present moment wish to give an opportunity to draw an ill-natured picture of the Northern capitalist seeking by legislation to add to his gains, by increasing the cost of everything the poor man uses. No step could have been taken, so well calculated to alienate the border states, at the very moment it has been our policy to conciliate them.

"The seceding states have us at equal disadvantage in the foreign Courts. The nations of Europe with whom we have the most intimate commercial relations are earnest advocates of free trade. Yet at the very moment that we most desire their sympathy and co-operation, we insult their conviction and strike the severest blow in our power at their interests. The seceding states will take instant advantage of our blunder, and will make every effort to secure their will, if not an actual recognition, by adopting a commercial policy in harmony with their own. It was for this purpose, undoubtedly, that the enactment of the new tariff was postponed, to await the report of the Commissioners just sent abroad.

"At home and abroad, we are already feeling the effects of our gratuitios folly. Both English and French journals are teeming with ill-natured and unfavorable remarks; with contrasts either openly stated or implied in favor of the seceding states.

"Never was a nation in greater embarrassment. We confess our inability to enforce the most important law we enact, and sit passively down and see them violated, without raising a finger. How can we maintain any national spirit under such humiliation? We take the step of all others most calculated to alienate the border states and foreign nations. We can neither collect our revenue or afford protection. Who, under such circumstances, would dare to embark in any enterprise? How much revenue can be collected in Northern ports? No one can answer these questions. Is not such uncertainty the greatest of all evils? A state of war would be almost preferable. It would be the beginning of an end. Thus far we seem to be without direction or purpose, or the means of enforcing our purpose, if we had any."

THE SHEER TOMFOOLERY OF THE NEW TARIFF.

The New York *World* said:

"To say that this new tariff is simply impotent for good, goes but a small way toward marking its folly. It teems with mischief. It widens the chasm between the revolted states and the Government, by introducing anew a system which has always been obnoxious to them, and which would be sure to repel them now did they have any disposition to return to their old line of duty. It weakens the hands of the Union men of the border states, who already find it hard enough to keep their mortal enemies at bay. It greatly disaffects England and France, alienating the good will which the Federal Government might otherwise surely reckon on, and presents them a direct inducement to recognize, at the earliest day, the independence of the states which reject both it and the policy on which it rests. It imposes new troubles and burdens upon the administrators of the law at a time when it was hard to see how they could efficiently and honorably discharge those which already pressed upon them. It paralyzes the authority of the Government, and puts it in a helpless and ridiculous position, like Œpidus in rags, or Belisarius at the wayside, at a time when, if ever, it needed its whole prestige, its strongest moral force. If Congress was bent on fastening this measure upon the country, it should at least have armed the President with power to enforce it, either by enabling him to abolish contumacious ports of entry, or to collect the revenues outside the harbor To make law, yet withhold the means of its execution, is sheer tomfoolery."

THE MORRILL TARIFF IN ENGLAND.

The London *Times* said:

"We do not say that the tide has turned, but we say that matters are just in that state which imposes a very grave responsibility on friendly nations and especially on Great Britain. It is quite possible to forecast and arm ourselves against the consequences of the revolutionary movement, so far as they affect this island, without treating it as a *fait accompli*. We shall not be deterred, for instance, by the wrath of a New York cotemporary from looking for new sources of cotton supply, and drawing, if necessary upon the resourses of our own colonies, to save our manufacturers from ruin. On the other hand we cannot fail to see, and it is our duty to point out, the tendency of a retrograde commercial policy in the North to divert European trade from Boston and New York to Charleston and New Orleans. These are matters of business, and the warmest friends of the Union cannot expect our merchants to celebrate its obsequies by self-immolation."

This is the way we are "making history." To say that this measure was not *intended* to widen the breach, and *drive* away the South, would be a poor compliment to the intelligence of the leaders who were responsible for the Morrill Tariff. That the rebels in Congress either voted for this Tariff or silently permitted it to pass, shows that they were as anxious to have this "irritating scheme" passed, as its Northern friends were to pass it, and probably for the same purpose—as a common lever to move a common object.

We would have charity, and would not condemn our fellow men of so gross crimes, without sufficient evidence; but we submit it to the scrutinizing ordeal of history, which shall, without bias, apply all the foregoing facts, and what may yet follow in these pages, to determine whether *all* the conspirators against our Government *left* the Union *under* the Southern ordinances of secession.

THE TABLES TURNED ON THE CHARGE OF "DISLOYALTY."

Disloyalty, in its political signification, means unfaithfulness to one's government, or "system of laws," which constitute the Government. This is the only test that can be made in this country. In monarchial governutsme. loyalty to the *person* of the monarch is required, because a monarch or despot assumes to be the government, but in this country, according to the code adopted by our fathers, loyalty to our "system of laws" is all that can be required, and he who is unfaithful to that "system of laws" is disloyal to the government. By that "system of laws" is meant any law that may be passed in "pursuance" of the constitution, which is the fountain license of power.

Here, then, is the correct definition of "loyalty" used in a political sense (though in fact no such word belongs to the nomenclature of a Republican Government) and as we have already shown from innumerable speeches, resolves, addresses and editorials, by the radical leaders of the party in power, to be not only denunciatory of the constitution and such laws passed under it, as they do not relish, but that they have raised the standard of "positive defiance" and hence have shown *their disloyalty* to their government.

Not only this, but we believe, and will endeavor to prove, by a chain of circumstantial and and positive evidence, as strong as would be required in a court of justice to convict one charged with murder in the first degree, that the political leaders of the party in power desire, and will accomplish, if they can, a dissolution of the Union. This is a serious charge, we know. If true, the guilty should be placed in a higher grade of crime, if that be possible, than the Southern rebels, because to the same crime they (the radicals) add deception and hypocrisy.

If we were Prosecuting Attorney in court, and it was our official duty to prosecute a man for wilful murder, on circumstantial evidence, and if we should succeed in proving—

1st. A *motive* for the *crime*.
2d, *Opportunity* to commit it.
3d, *Threats* to accomplish it.
4th, That the weapon of death had been found in the prisoner's possession.
5th, That blood had been found upon his person.
6th. That it was for his interest, either pecuniarily or otherwise to have the deceased out of the way.
7th. Frequent admissions by the prisoner that he had attempted to take the life of the deceased.

If we had proved all these facts, we should have a clear conscience to ask the jury for a verdict of "guilty"—we should cite the court to innumerable cases, where conviction was had on weaker testimony than this—we should ask the court for instructions on this point—the court would give them—the jury would render a verdict of guilty, if unbiased, without leaving their seats.

Now, what is the evidence before us?

The leaders of the party in power are prisoners before the bar of public opinion, charged with the crime of not only disloyalty, but treason to the Government. What is the evidence?

1st. We have shown their *motive for dissolution*, as exhibited through a long series of years—to divide the Union, and multiply the officers, so as to give a fewer number a greater opportunity at the spoils—to build up an aristocracy; wherein the poor shall pay constant tribute to the rich, by way of enormous taxes for interest on a monstrous public debt, which they have claimed to be a "public blessing."

2d. Is not the present the fairest *opportunity*, to destroy the Union and civil liberty, on the pretext of military necessity?

3d. *Threats*—Search the preceding pages, and you will find *threats* without number to dissolve the Union.

4th. Have these marplots not been found with the *weapons* of dissolution in their hands, —to-wit: the slavery agitation, to say nothing of other weapons? Read the *testimony* given by themselves.

5th. Has not *blood* been found upon their persons? Were not their garments stained with the blood of poor BACHELDER in Boston, in 1854, in the discharge of his duty? Wore not their whole garments dripping with human gore, when they deified JOHN BROWN, and indorsed his insurrection and murders?

6th. Have they not often declared it was for their *interest*, pecuniary and otherwise, to have the old Union out of the way?

7th. Have they not time and again *admitted* that they have attempted to take the life of the Union? Do they not even now tell us, with lips steeped in clammy treason, that *the* Union shall live no more?

We might stop here and "rest" our case as having been made out by the admissions of the implicated ones themselves, but we will present accumulative circumstantial and positive evidence.

It will be recollected that when Sumter had been fired on, and the shock of battle reverberated through the land, the whole North, as one man (that is, without distinction of party) rose in its might to shake off the incubus of disunion. Democrats forgot the animosities engendered by the political contest but six months before, and did not stop to enquire whether they were to be commanded by political friend or foe. Men of all parties rushed to the standard of their country, asking no conditions but the privilege of fighting to preserve the Union as it was. Now for the testimony.

WHAT ANDREW JOHNSON SAYS.

ANDY JOHNSON, the Military Governor appointed by President LINCOLN for Tennessee, bears witness as to the policy of the Administration party, as follows:

"There are two parties in existence who want dissolution. Slavery and a Southern Confederacy is the hobby. Sumner wants to break up the Government, and so do the Abolitionists generally. They hold that if slavery survives the Union cannot endure. Secessionists argue that if the Union continues slavery is lost. Abolitionists want no compromise, but they regard peacable secession as a humbug. The two occupy the same ground. Why, abolition is dissolution; dissolution is secession; one is the other. Both are striving to accomplish the same object. One thinks it will destroy, the other save slavery."

"SITTING UP WITH THE UNION."

Here is what Senator Wilson, one of the big chiefs of the Republican party, said in a recent speech:

"This extra anxiety about the Union is the merest cant. The country is sick of it. The sad fate of the chiefs of this Union cry for the past three years must convince even the member from Windham that *this sitting up with the Union does not pay expenses*."

WHAT CONSTITUTES A TRAITOR OR COPPERHEAD.

A very common practice prevails among the Republicans to call all persons "traitors," "copperheads," who cannot vote for, or continue to support their theories. They disclaim having changed in their principles since the beginning of our national troubles, but such as choose to stand on the principles that we all occupied in 1861, and cannot follow the doctrines of fanaticism, are denounced as disloyal—branded with the epithet of "traitor," "copperhead," &c. Now, let us review the past, and see if these SO CALLED UNION partizans stand by the professions of 1861, as they continuously claim not to have changed; but all who refuse to vote with them, have suddenly become "DISLOYAL," "traitors," and "COPPERHEADS." We will call Mr. LINCOLN on the witness stand first, and see how he stood at the time of his inaugural. There we read thus:

"Apprehensions seem to exist among the people of the Southern states, that by the accession of a republican administration, their property, and their peace and personal security are to be endangered. *There has never been any reasonable cause for such apprehension.* Indeed, the most ample evidence to the contrary has all the while existed and been open to their inspection. It is found in nearly all the written speeches of him who now addresses you. I do but quote from one of those speeches when I declare that *I have no purpose, directly or indirectly, to interfere with slavery in the states where it exists*—I BELIEVE I HAVE NO LAWFUL RIGHT TO DO SO, AND I HAVE NO INCLINATION TO DO SO. Those who nominated me did so with full knowledge that I had made this and many similar declarations and had never recanted them.

"And more than this, they placed in the platform for my acceptance, and *as a law* to themselves and to me, the clear and emphatic resolution, which I now read:

"*Resolved*, That the maintainance inviolate of the rights of the States, *and especially the right of each State to order and control its own domestic institutions, according to its own judgment exclusively*, is essential to the balance of power, on which the perfection and endurance of our political fabric depends; and we denounce the lawless invasion by armed force of the soil of any State or Territory, no matter under what pretext, as AMONG THE GRAVEST CRIMES."

"I NOW REITERATE THESE SENTIMENTS; and, in doing so, I only press upon the public attention the most conclusive evidence of which the case is susceptible, that the *property*, peace and security of no section are to be in any wise endangered by the new incoming Administration. I add, too, that all the protection which, consistently with the Constitution and laws, can be given, will be cheerfully given to all the states when lawfully demanded, for whatever cause—as cheerfully to one section as to another. I take the official oath to-day with *no mental reservations*, and with no purpose to construe the Constitution and laws by any hypocritical rules."

Such was the language of Mr. LINCOLN on the 4th of March, 1861, standing upon the steps of the Capitol, about to take the most solemn oath, calling GOD to witness his sincerity, to faithfully perform the duties of his office, and uphold the constitution and laws of our country. Men who favored Mr. LINCOLN's sentiments in 1861, are called "traitors," and "copperheads," because they firmly believe the same doctrine, and will not change, and cannot vote with the Republicans.

Mr. LINCOLN, in his message to congress (extra session), July 3d, 1861, after the war had begun, said:

"Lest there be some uneasiness in the minds of candid men as to what is to be the course of the Government toward the Southern states, AFTER the rebellion shall have been suppressed, the Executive deems it proper to say, it will be his purpose then, as ever, to be guided by the Constitution and laws, and that he probably will have no *different understanding* of the powers and duties of the Federal Government relative to the rights of the states and the people, under the Constitution, THAN THAT EXPRESSED IN THE INAUGURAL ADDRESS. He desires to preserve the Government, that it may be administered for all, *as it was administered by the men who made it.* Loyal citizens everywhere have a right to claim this of their Government; and the Government has no right to withhold or neglect it. It is not perceived, that in giving it, there is any coercion, any conquest, or any subjugation, in any just sense of these terms."

Now, reader, this same doctrine is TRAITOROUS in 1864, if we do not happen to vote the so-called UNION ticket.

CONGRESS ON THE OBJECT OF THE WAR.

Let us now notice some resolutions passed in the House as recorded in the Congressional Globe, which received the unanimous support of the republicans, on the 11th of Feb., 1861:

"*Resolved*, That neither the Federal Government, nor the people, or Governments of non-slave holding states, have a purpose or a Constitutional right to legislate upon, or interfere with slavery in any of the States of the Union.

"*Resolved*, That those persons in the North who do not subscribe to the foregoing propositions, are too insignificant in numbers and influence to excite the serious attention or alarm of any portion of the people of the Republic; and that the increase of their numbers and influence does not keep pace with the increase of the aggregate population of the Union."

Nothing short of a Copperhead Congress could pass such resolutions in 1864.

Again, see *Congressional Globe*, after Bull Run battle, July 23d, 1861; Congress with the almost unanimous Republican vote passed the following resolution:

Resolved, That the war is waged by the government of the United States, not in the spirit of conquest or subjugation, nor for the purpose of overthrowing or interfering with the rights or institutions of the states, but to defend and maintain the supremacy of the constitution, and to preserve the Union with all the dignity, equality and rights of the several States unimpaired; and that as soon as these objects are accomplished, the war ought to cease.

Now, in 1864, we who claim to cherish the sentiments of this resolution are traitors and copperheads.

Again, the Indianapolis *Sentinel*, a leading Republican state organ, which has not been accused of disloyalty by its party, under date of September 24th, 1861, says:

"The President is right in his treatment of Fremont's Proclamation. Congress, at the recent session, with direct reference to the negro question in the rebellion, having prescribed a precise rule of action for the Government, the Government must necessarily adhere to this rule of action. To disobey it, or to transcend it, ever so little, is to treat the law-making power with contempt, and to make the President liable to impeachment. It is immaterial, in this regard, whether the rule prescribed is right or wrong; it is prescribed by the only power which has authority to prescribe it, and it must stand and command obedience until that power shall abolish or alter it."

Who dare assert, in 1864, that the exercise of power in issuing the proclamation, establishing a limited monarchy, are deemed as traitors and copperheads. We who believed in the above principles in 1861, and were loyal, and still sincerely believe them right in 1864, are denounced as disloyal, traitors—copperheads, because we choose not to change our opinions, and fall in with a fanatical party, under the sanctimonious name of Union, and adopt Greeley's doctrine—that of Negro Emancipation—and Thad. Stevens, the leader of the late Republican Congress, who, in a speech, said:

"The Union as it was, and the Constitution as it is—GOD FORBID IT! We must conquer the Southern States, and hold them as conquered provinces."

And yet there are none but loyalists and patriots in this new party! Well, the world does move.

MR. CHASE PRONOUNCES "THE UNION NOT WORTH FIGHTING FOR."

A Mr. BLOW, in St. Louis, not relishing the manner in which Gen. FRANK P. BLAIR deals with the Jacobins in Missouri and with the restrictions imposed upon trade on the Missisippi, read that gentleman a lecture a few weeks since. The general has replied, and we copy from his rejoinder the following notice of the Secretary of the Treasury. As the General is "loyal," we presume "loyalists" will accept him as authority:

"I know Mr. Chase tolerably well. With very great ability, and all the good looks, polished manners, and gentlemanly bearing that Mr. Blow claims for him, he is as thoroughly selfish and narrow as any public man in the country.

"When the rebellion broke out, Mr Chase held this language: '*The South is not worth fighting for.*' Several gentlemen of high position in the country heard him utter this sentiment, substantially. He was at that time Secretary of the Treasury. Jeff. Davis exclaimed as he left the Senate, 'All the South wants is to be let alone,' and Mr. Secretary Chase was, in effect, declaring 'The South is not worth fighting for.' Jeff. Davis said, 'Let us alone.' Chase said, 'Let them alone.' The difference between them in fact, although their motives are wide apart, was the difference between tweedledum and tweedledee. One wanted a Southern and the other a Northern Confederacy, each believing his own chances best in that sort of a division."

WEED ON THE MOB INCITERS.

Mr. THURLOW WEED wrote a letter expressing his indignation at the cowardly treatment of the unoffending negroes by the New York mob. He inclosed a check of $500 for their relief, and said:

"For the persecution of the negro there is a divided responsibility. The hostility of Irishmen to Africans is unworthy of men who themselves seek and find, in America, an asylum from oppression. Yet this hostility would not culminate in murder and arson, but for the stimulants supplied by fanatics. Journalists who persistently inflame and exasperate the ignorant and lawless against the negro, are morally responsible for these outrages. But what cares Wendell Phillips how many negroes are murdered, if their blood furnished material for agitation? There is abundant occasion for the public abhorence of mob violence. But when all the circumstances have been reviewed, the popular condemnation of those who, while the nation is struggling for existence, thrust the unoffending negro forward as a target for infuriated mobs, will become general and emphatic. Ultra abolitionists were hailed, in South Carolina, as the "best friends" of secession. Practically, they are the worst enemies of the colored man. But for the "malign influence" of these howling abolitionists, in Congress and with the President, rebellion would not, in the beginning, have assumed such formidable proportions; nor, in its progress, would the North have been divided, or the government crippled."

WHY SENATOR LATHAM WAS DEFEATED.

The Chicago *Tribune*, in alluding to the defeat of Senator LATHAM, of California, for the United States Senate, said:

"He was in favor of the Union as it was. No other offense was alleged against him."

Thus, we have the allegation that to be in favor of the "Union as it was" is an "offense."

MR. CHASE AN OLD ABOLITIONIST.

On the 9th of September, 1844, Mr. SALMON P. CHASE issued, through the columns of the Ohio *Columbian*, an Abolition paper, what he termed the "Liberty Man's Creed," from which we select the following:

"I believe that whenever the judiciary of the United States shall cease to be the creature of the slave power, and the judges shall receive their appointment from a Liberty President and Senate, slavery will be declared to be unconstitutional in the District of Columbia, in Florida, and in all states created out of territories.

"*I believe that slavery in the United States will not survive the accession of the Liberty party to power a single year.*"

Can any one doubt his original purposes?

THE PROGRAMME BLOCKED OUT JUST AFTER LINCOLN'S NOMINATION.

Mr. LINCOLN was nominated in May 1860. The friends of Mr. SEWARD declared that the Convention in throwing over SEWARD and taking up LINCOLN, had but followed their instinct of *policy* to obtain votes they could not otherwise receive.

On this subject we quote a letter from Mr. GEO. DAWSON, junior editor of the Albany *Journal* (SEWARD organ) written from the Chicago Convention to that paper:

"CHICAGO, May 19, 1860.

"Misrepresentation has achieved its work. The timid and credulous have succumbed to threats and perversions. To please a few thousand men of equivocal principle and faltering faith, millions of loyal hearts have been saddened. The recognized standard-bearer of the Republican party has been sacrificed upon the altar of availability.

This sacrifice was alike cruel and unnecessary. No man in the Republican party has greater strength than Wm. H. Seward. No man deserves more at the hands of that party, or possesses greater fitness for the high office for which its national tribunal has declared him unworthy. His platform is that of the Republican party and was *before* it. He, more than any other man, initiated the principles which called it into being, and which gave, and which still gives it all its vitality. No other man's history so distinctly embodies the grand idea which brought together those who originally entered into the Republican organization; and the world's verdict was, that good faith, common honesty and the future history and well-being of the Redublican party demanded his nomination as its standard-bearer in the present canvass.

"But this verdict has been reversed. The inflexible virtues, the unwavering integrity, the heroic courage, the profound sagacity, and the exalted statesmanship which endeared him to the people, constituted "the stumbling block and the rock of offence" to the convention. He was deemed too pure, too consistent, too heroic, too wise, and too thoroughly and too conspicuously imbued with the distinctive principles of Republicanism, to succeed.

"Mon, no single proportion of whose heart ever beat responsive to the principles of the Republican party, must be conciliated; and to do so William H. Seward must be sacrificed. Localities where Republicanism never had vitality to breathe were coveted; and to encourage the effort to achieve what is unattainable, William II. Seward was sacrificed. States who have never yet inhaled sufficient of the free spirit of Republicanism to assume its name, demanded the immolation, and they were gratified. Love of consistency, admiration for a long life of devotion to freedom, and a heroic purpose to stand or fall by the noblest embodiment of undiluted and undefiled principle, all had to succumb to fancied expediency and bitter hate.

"The result is less a defeat of William II. Seward than a triumph of his personal enemies. The sentiment which culminated in his rejection was chiefly manufactured by those whose dislike of the man was infinitely in advance of their principles. For years he has been their Mordecai, at the king's gate; and by feeding the doubts of some, by exciting the apprehensions of others, and by the industrious utterance of misrepresentations to all, they have like their ancient prototype, seemingly attained the end they have so ardently coveted, and secured the discomfiture of those who have, for long years, looked and hoped for the coming day when William H. Seward should attain the exalted position for which no man living is so worthy. I know very well that many of those by whose hands his immolation was actually consummated did not share in the spirit of envy and hate, but enough did to turn the scale, and I have no wish to withhold from them this acknowledgement of their right to the commendations which they will covet from those who are in sympathy with them."

JOSHUA R. GIDDINGS was a member in good standing of the Chicago convention. We copy the following from its proceedings to show that they voted down anything like Sewardism, for fear they could not catch the "conservative" vote. LINCOLN, at Freeport, had declared in favor of the Fugitive Slave Law, and his nomination was calculated to cater to the "pro-slavery" sentiment. But read the following by the light of subsequent events, and tell us whether you can escape the conclusion that *policy and deception* was combined in the Chicago convention:

"Mr. Giddings—Mr. President, I propose to offer, after the first resolution as it stands here, as a declaration of principles, the following:

"That we solemnly re-assert the self-evident truths that all men are endowed by their Creator with certain inalienable rights, among which are those of life, liberty, and the pursuit of happiness, (cheers) that governments are instituted among men to secure the enjoyment of these rights."

"Mr. Carter, of Ohio, interrupted—Mr. President, I—

"Mr. Giddings—My colleague will ask no favors of me, I take it. (Applause.) I will detain the convention but a moment. Two hundred years ago the philosophers of Europe declared to the world that human governments were based upon human rights, and all Christain writers have sustained that doctrine until the members of this convention. Our Fathers impressed with this all permeating truth, that right of every human being to live and enjoy that liberty, whichenables him to obtain knowledge and pursue happiness, and no man has the power to withhold it from him. (Prolonged cheers.)

"Our fathers embraced this solemn truth; laid it down as the chief corner stone, the basis upon which this Federal Government was founded. of all parties, the Supreme Court included, these were the primitive, life-giving, vitalizing principles of the Constitution. It is because these principles have been overturned denied and destroyed by our opponents, that we now exist as a party. (Cheers.) At Philadelphia we called on them to meet it. They have not met it. They put forward the Supreme Court to meet it. The Court denied those principles, but the Democratis party to this day dare not deny them; and through the campaign and for four years, no Democrat has stood before the world denying that truth, nor will they. Now, I propose to maintain the doctrines of our fathers. I propose to maintain the fundamental and primeval issues upon which the Government was founded. I will detain this Convention no longer. I offer this because our party was formed upon it. It grew upon it.—It has existed upon it—and when you leave out this truth you leave out the party."

The amendment was rejected by a large majority.

LINCOLN'S LETTER ACCEPTING THE NOMINATION.

Now read Mr. Lincoln's letter of acceptance:

SPRINGFIELD, Ill., May 22.

Hon. GEO. ASHMUN, *Prest. of the Republican National Convention:*

"SIR:—I accept the nomination tendered me by the Convention, over which you presided, and of which I am formally apprised in a letter of yourself and others, acting as a committed of that convention, for that purpose.— The declaration of principles and sentiments which accompanies your letter, *meets my approval*, and it shall be my care *not to violate them*, or disregard *them in any particular.* Imploring the assistance of Divine Power, and with due regard to the views and feelings of all who were represented in the convention, *to the rights of the States*, and Territories and people of the nation *to the in violability of the Constitution,* and the perpetual union, harmony and prosperity of all, I am most happy to co-operate for the practical success of the principles declared by the convention.

"Your obliged friend and fellow citizen,
"ABRAHAM LINCOLN."

Now read the following in juxtaposition, and see if you can arrive at Mr. LINCOLN'S aims:

Extract from Lincoln's speech, June 17, 1858.
"In my opinion it (slavery agitation) will not cease, until a crisis shall have been reached and passed. A house divided against itself cannot stand. I believe this government cannot endure permanently half slave and half free. I do not expect the Union to be dissolved—I do not expect the house to fall—but I do expect it will cease to be divided. It will become all one thing or all the other."

Resolution adopted at the Chicago Convention.
"That to the Union of the states (half slave and half free) this nation owes its unprecedented increase in population—its surprising development of material resources—its rapid augmentation of wealth—its happiness at home and its honor abroad; and we hold in abhorrence all schemes for Disunion, come from whatever source they may. * * And we denounce those threats of disunion, in case of a popular overthrow of their ascendancy, as denying the vital principles of a free government, and as an avowal of contemplated treason, which it is the imperative duty of an indignant people sternly to rebuke and for ever silence."

SUMNER OPENS THE RADICAL BALL.

On the 4th of June following, Mr. SUMNER made a violent speech in the Senate, which gave the key note to the purposes of the party, when successful. In concluding, he said:

Thus, sir, speaking for freedom in Kansas, I have spoken for *freedom everywhere*, and for civilization; and, as the less is contained in the greater, so are all arts, all sciences, all economies, all refinement, all charities, all delights of life, embodied in this cause. You may reject it, but it will be *only for to-day*. The sacred animosity between freedom and slavery can *end only* in the *triumph* of freedom. The same question will soon be carried before that high tribunal, *supreme over Senate and Court*, where the Judges will be *counted by millions*, and where the judgment rendered will be the solemn charge of an *aroused people*, instructing a new President, in the name of Freedom, to see that civilization receives no detriment.

The "judges" here referred to, that could be "counted by millions" and which were to be the "high tribunal" that were to bear down and reign "supreme over Senate and Court," were the great army of Wide Awakes.

This was letting the cat out of the bag. SUMNER was a leader in the Republican counsels, and although that party *has* carried out thus far, the programme here laid down by SUMNER, yet for fear it would "hurt" their cause pending the election, many of the radicals mildly denounced—not the doctrine—but its utterance at that time. The New York *Post* said:

"No one, we presume, can fail to admire the ability and cogency of this address; but whether the peculiar line of argument was called for *at this time*, or whether it will aid in the passage of the Kansas admission bill, may admit of doubt. It seems to us, that its invective can have little other effect than to irritate the objects of it, and to render their prejudices more inveterate and stubborn. Mr. Chestnut, in his ill-natured and ungentlemanly reply, illustrated perhaps the truth of many of Mr. Sumner's remarks upon the manners of slave-masters, but he illustrated also the spirit in which those remarks are likely to be received. Few of the Southerners will give heed to Mr. Sumner's *convincing array of facts*, while all of them will be repulsed and offended by the unsparing tone of his criticism."

Upon which the Wisconsin *State Journal* (which published SUMNER's speech) remarked:

"Mr. Sumner's speech presents a very marked contrast to those of Mr. Seward. The latter is always *scrupulously careful*, while pointing out the wrong and the impolicy of slavery, and assailing the system with the irresistible force of his logic, not to wound and esperate the personal feelings of his opponents. The same may be said of Mr. Lincoln. Both he and Mr. Seward, while their arguments are no less pointed and unanswerable than those of Mr. Sumner, preserve an imperturable good nature and self-possession. In this way, *without kindling the angry feelings* of their opponents to the same extent, their advocacy of the restriction of slavery is more formidable and dreaded than the more impassioned and rhetorical fulminations of the Senator from Massachusetts."

Thus, it will be seen, that neither of these papers speak against Mr. SUMNER's declared policy, but they only regret that he could not have better concealed the purpose of his party. All this is in keeping, as we have charged, with the original design of that party to destroy the Union—to break over the law and "triumph" over the ruins of the Constitution.

THE OTHER CLASS OF DISUNIONISTS.

The following letters from two notable disunionists will show schemes similar in object and management to the disunionists of the North:

"SELMA, NEAR WINCHESTER, (Va.,) Sept. 30, 1856.

"*My dear Sir:*—I have a letter from Wise of the 27th, full of spirit. He says the Governors of North Carolina, South Carolina and Louisiana, have already agreed to the rendezvous at Raleigh, and others will—this in your *most private ear*. He says further, that he had officially requested you to exchange with Virginia, on fair terms of difference, percussion for flint muskets. I don't know the usuage or power of the Department in such cases, but, if it can be done, *even* by liberal construction, I hope you will accede.

"Was there not an appropriation at the last session for converting flint into percussion arms? If so, would it not furnish good reasons for extending such facilities to the States?—Virginia probably has more arms than the Southern States, and would divide in case of need. In a letter, yesterday, to a Committee in South Carolina, I gave it as my judgment, in the event of Freemont's election, that the South should not pause, but proceed at once to "immediate, absolute, and *eternal* separation." So I am a candidate for the first halter. Wise says his accounts from Philadelphia are cheering for Old Buck in Pennsylvania. I hope they may not be delusive. *Vale et salaete.*

Colonel DAVIS.   J. M. MASON.

"MONTGOMERY, June 15, 1858.

"DEAR SIR: Your kind favor of the 15th is received. I hardly agree with you that a general movement can be made that will clear out the Augean stable. If the Democracy were overthrown it would result in giving place to a greater and hungrier swarm of t s.

"The remedy of the south is not 'n such a process. It is a diligent organization of her true men for prompt resistance to the next aggression. It must come in the nature of things. No national party can save us; no sectional party can ever do it. But if we can do s our fathers did—organize 'Committees of Safety' all over the cotton States (and it is only in them that we can hope for any effective move-

ment)—we shall fire the Southern heart, instruct the Southern mind, give courage to each other, and, at the proper moment, *by one organized concerted action, we can precipitate the cotton States into revolution.*

"The idea has been shadowed forth in the South by Mr. Ruffin; has been taken up and recommended in the *Advertiser*, (the Montgomery organ of Mr. Yancey,) under the name of 'League of the Southerners,' *who, keeping up their old party relations on all other questions, will hold the Southern issue paramount, and will influence parties, Legislatures, and Statesmen.* I have no time to enlarge, but to suggest merely.

"In haste- yours, &c.   W. L. YANCEY.
"To JAMES S. SLAUGHTER, Esq."

Now, let the candid reader compare these fulminations with that of CHARLES SUMNER, and tell us, if he can, that one is less guilty than the other.

The following, from the Chicago *Tribune*, is off the same piece of treason with the rebel letters above:

"Give us a rebel victory, let our enemies be destroyed, Maryland conquered, Washington captured, the President exiled, and the Government destroyed; give us these and any other calamities that can result from defeat and ruin, sooner than a victory with McClellan as General."

Can any one doubt, on reading such articles as these, the treasonable purposes of the radical party?

THE CRITTENDEN RESOLUTION—OBJECT OF THE WAR DECLARED.

Early in the war, Congress, the authoritative mouth-piece of the nation, passed, with only two dissenting votes, the Crittenden Resolution, which pledged the country as to the objects and purposes of the war on the part of the North. The resolution reads as follows:

"*Resolved, by the House of Representatives of the Congress of the United States,* That the present deplorable civil war has been forced upon the country by the disunionists of the Southern States, now in arms against the constitutional government, and in arms around the Capitol; that in this National emergency, Congress, banishing all feeling of passion or resentment, will recollect its duty to the whole country; that this war is not waged on their part, in any spirit of oppression, or for any purpose of conquest or subjugation, or purposes of overthrowing or interfering with the rights or established institutions of those states, but to defend and maintain *the supremacy of the constitution, and to preserve the Union* with all the dignity, *equality* and rights of the several States, unimpaired, and that as soon as those objects are accomplished, *the war ought to cease.*"

This was the pledge given by the Republican Congress. It was all the Democrats asked. Under that pledge they did not stop to enquire who elected Mr. LINCOLN, or what were his political views. It was enough for them to know that their country was imperiled, and that they were required to fight in its defence —not merely to shed their blood that the White House might remain unmolested, that a certain man might occupy it for four years— not merely to protect any given measure relative to *land* or territory, but to preserve and defend the *institutions* of our country—the "supremacy of the constitution."

THE PROCLAMATION—EMANCIPATION.

But, no sooner had Congress voluntarily offered this pledge to the country, and the armies of the Union having been voluntarily filled—and to spare—on the strength of that pledge—than the radicals raised a hue and cry for a proclamation abolishing slavery, and thus to violate the congressional pledge not to "interfere with the established institutions" of the South.

The radicals claimed the issuance of this proclamation as a "military necessity." They offered no fact or arguments to show that it would do any good, so far as aiding our armies to quell the rebellion—they only *asserted*, without proof, that such would be its result. But, THE GREAT SECRET OF THE PROCLAMATION was to break down the *unanimity* at the North. So powerful and universal was the sentiment for the war to preserve the Government, that it was likely to soon overthrow the Southern rebels. This would not do. The war *must not end too soon*. Why? Because slavery and the Union might still exist. Hence, the proclamation was wanted—not to crush the South—*but to divide the North—unite the South, and make union impossible!*

"Thank God," says PHILLIPS, "for Bull Run." How often have we heard similar expressions from the leaders of that party of similar import, and does this not all prove the very essance of our charge, that the radicals gloried in reverses to our armies, as the best means to finally accomplish their diabolical purpose of dissolving the Union? Does it not show that DOUGLAS in his last speech in the Senate was correct, when he charged that the Republicans desired dissolution, provided it could be accomplished, and not directly make them chargeable for the result?

The radicals knew the issuing of the proclamation would divide the North and unite the South, and hence they clamored for it as the *means* to accomplish dissolution. They pretended to urge that measure as a "military necessity," and affected to believe that it would soon end the rebellion, yet when read by the light of subsequent events, the reader cannot fail to see the treasonable motive.

THE NEW YORK TRIBUNE ON THE PROCLAMATION.

As a specimen of the great things claimed for the proclamation, we give the following seven reasons:

[From the N. Y. Tribune, Aug. 13, 1862.]

"1st. The hearty good will of three millions of people now doing the necessary work of the rebellion. Ignorant, degraded, imbruited, as many of them are, these three millions of Southerners uniformly, intensely desire to be free. Assure them that they will be free from the moment they escape from their masters to us, and they will begin at once to watch their opportunities for absconding. Even though but few should at first succeed in escaping, many will attempt it, and the rebel masters of all will be rendered suspicious and uneasy.— Thousands will be diverted from shooting Union soldiers, to watching suspected slaves—to the great adveantage of the Union cause.

"2d. Negroes by the thousands can at once be enlisted to scout, spy, cook, dig, chop and team for the Union cause, and to *fight* for it also, if we choose. They will ask no bounty. They will not flee to Canada to escape a draft; they will wait for their pay, so that they be fed and armed and set to work for the liberation of their brethren. One hundred thousand of them can at once be usefully employed in the Union armies, even though they do not fight. And we cannot doubt, that ten black regiments, with arms and equipments for twenty or thirty more would excite more alarm among the rebels of any cotton or sugar growing section than twice as many white ones.

"3d. The liberal sentiment of Christendom would be fixed and intensified on the side of the Union by such a decree. At present, any champion of the rebel cause, who rises to speak in Parliament or elsewhere, begins by solemnly asservating that slavery has nothing to do with the contest—that the North is fighting for slavery as well as the South, and quoting our dispatches, resolves and speeches to sustain that position. A decree of emancipation would effectually squelch that falsehood. And the approbation of the good is a genu'ne power. No foreign country but Dahomey would venture to side with the Davis Confederacy, if it were made clear that it was fighting for slavery, while we were fighting against it. Now, moral, if not physical intervention to our prejudice, is a serious, and by no means a remote, danger.

"4th. Hundreds of thousands of true patriots would sacrifice property, ease, luxury, safety itself, for the Union cause, with a freedom and joy yet unknown, *if* they could realize that in so doing they were certainly aiding to rid their beloved country evermore of the curse and blight of slavery.

"5th. Thousands of dangerous and noble spirits would flock from every christian land to fight for liberty and Union, *who feel but a languid interest in a struggle for the Union alone.*

"6th. Scores of army officers whose hearts are with the rebels, have threatened to resign if (in their phraseology) this "is made an abolition war." Some would do it, and this would be an immense gain to our cause. Had Gen. Patterson done this a week before Bull Run, the rebellion would have been long since extinguished. The disaster at Ball's Bluff would have been averted by the resignation of a few officers of this sort.

"7th. Finally, having identified the Union cause irrevocably with that of humanity, (?) justice and universal freedom, we might reverently look for the blessing of God to crown our efforts with success—and would hardly look in vain."

[From the New York Tribune, Aug. 22, 1862.]

"Let it be proclaimed to-morrow from the White House, and re-echoed from every Union camp, that every slave fleeing to us from the rebels is thenceforth a freeman, and the knell of treason will have been sounded.

"Let every fugitive who comes to us from Jeffdom, be welcomed as a freeman, and *the war cannot last till Christmas.*"

[From the New York Tribune, Sept. 6, 1862.]

"With such a policy the traitors must be called, in good part, from their armies, *to defend and secure their own firesides.* With such a policy [the proclamation] our troops will never lack information, but will be abundantly provided with guides, scouts and spies. With such a policy, in good faith adopted, and thoroughly carried out, *we believe that sixty days would amply suffice to break the back-bone of the slave-holder's rebellion.*"

[From the New York Tribune, Sept. 24, 1862—after the Proclamation.]

"By a single blow he [the President] has palsied the right arm of the rebellion. Slavery is the root of the rebellion: he digs it up by the roots. *The Proclamation of Emancipation will bring out the full strength,* and the Union as it *should* be, will date from the day of its consummation."

[From the Janesville (Wis.) Gazette, summer of 1862.]

"Can he (the President) not see, as we see, that a Proclamation of Emancipation, made last spring, and an invitation to the slaves to come to our armies, would so have unsettled the social fabric of the South, as to have prevented the cultivation of their crops for food, and produced such alarm in the minds of Jeff Davis' soldiers that *they would have fled homeward to save their families,*" &c.

The Waukesha (Wis.) *Freeman*, just previous to the issuing of the Proclamation, said:

"But let the slaves be confiscated or freed, and *the rebellion will be killed stone dead in a fortnight.*"

The Boston *Liberator* thus issued its threatening fiat to force the issuance of the Proclamation:

"The men who are sending out, within a single year, more than a million and a quarter of their fellows to dare the dangers of the battlefield, and who have not winced under the prospective taxation which must follow the expenditure of a thousand millions of money, all for the maintenance of the institutions which our fathers established, though they may not now betray the anger and loathing which the new propositions excite, or the contempt which the *cowardice of the Administration* inspires, will, when the hour of trial comes, show these bad men who, like thieves at a fire," &c.

Now, the facts which subsequent history has developed, do not confirm the good things prophesied of the Proclamation, and it is a wonderful stretch of charity to believe those who uttered them had any confidence in their statements.

THE POPE'S BULL AGAINST THE COMET.

To show that even the President himself had no confidence that any good could come from his proclamation, we quote as follows from his declaration to the Chicago Divines, who called upon him as a religious body, to add the force of *religion* to fanaticism. This was but a few days previous to the issuing of the proclamation. The President said:

"What *good* would a proclamation of emancipation from me do, especially as we are now situated? I do not want to issue a document that the world will see must necessarily be inoperative, like the Pope's bull against the comet. Would *my word* free the slaves, when I cannot even enforce the Constitution in the rebel states? Is there a single court, or magistrate, or individual that would be influenced by it there? And what reason is there to think it would have any greater effect upon the slaves than the late law of Congress, which I approved, and which offers protection and freedom to the slaves of rebel masters who come within our lines. Yet I cannot learn that that law has caused a single slave to come over to us.— And suppose they could be induced, by a proclamation of freedom from me to throw themselves upon us, *what shall we do with them?* How can we feed and care for such a multitude? General Butler wrote me, a few days since, that he was issuing more rations to slaves who have rushed to him than all the white troops under his command. They *eat*, and that is all."

Of course, no sane man could see any good to the Union cause that could possibly result from the emancipation. Our armies had been successful almost everywhere. The Union armies had been successful prior to the 22d of September, the date of the proclamation, in *ninety-four* battles and heavy skirmishes, and had lost but *eight*, with two drawn battles. The rebels had been nearly driven out of Missouri, Arkansas, Kentucky, West Tennessee, a portion of Mississippi, the forts below New Orleans, and that city itself, together with Baton Rouge, had fallen into our hands. The whole North Carolina coast, with Beaufort, S. C.,—sundry places of importance in Georgia—the Florida coast—the Potomac cleared of obstructions—the rebel army driven from the Peninsula, and Washington was not menaced by any adequate force for its reduction. In short, everything was going on smoothly for the Union cause. But this was just what the Radicals did not want. They desired to divide the North, so as to make union more improbable, and they set about every means in their power to accomplish this result. They coaxed, flattered, denounced and prophesied. They were not satisfied to let well enough alone, but the Union must be divided, and they saw that could not be done without *dividing the North.* They knew the proclamation and other revolutionary, to say nothing of unconstitutional measures, would do it.

HORACE GREELEY pledged 900,000 troops to leap forth the moment the proclamation should see the light.

GOV. ANDREW'S CONDITIONS.

Gov. ANDREW was appealed to by the War Department for troops, in great haste. The order is signed by Adjutant General THOMAS, and dated May 19, '62, and directed to Gov. ANDREW:

"The Secretary of War desires to know how soon you can raise and organize three or four infantry regiments, and have them ready to be forwarded here, to be armed and equipped. Please answer *immediately*, &c.

To which the Governor responds under the above date:

"A call sudden and unexpected, finds me without materials for an intelligent reply.— Our young men are all pre-occupied with other views. Still, if a real call for three regiments is made, I believe we can raise them in forty days. The arms and equipments would need to be furnished here. Our people have never marched without them. They go into camp while forming into regiments, and are drilled and practiced with arms and march as soldiers. To attempt the other course would be to dampen enthusiasm and make these men feel that they were not soldiers, but a mob. Again, if our people feel that they are going into the South to help fight rebels who will kill and destroy them by all means known to savages, as well as civilized men, who will deceive them by fradulent flags of truce, and lying pretenses, as they did the Massachusetts boys at Williamsburg, and will use their negro slaves against them, both as laborers and fighting men, while they themselves must never fire at the enemy's magazines, I think they will feel the draft is heavy on their patriotism; but if the President will sustain Gen. Hunter, recognize all men, even black men, as legally capable of that loyalty the blacks are wanting to manifest, and let them fight, God and human nature on their side, the roads will swarm, if need be, with multitudes whom New England would pour out to obey your call. Always ready to do my utmost, I remain, most faithfully,

Your obedient servant
(Signed,) JNO. A. ANDREW."

Well, the Proclamation *was* issued—the thing *was* fixed to the Governor's liking—the roads didn't "swarm" with the "multitudes" promised. But the subsequent chapter in this Abolition drama may be read in the following telegraphic dispatches:

EXTRA SESSION OF THE MASSACHUSETTS LEGISLATURE—GOV. ANDREW'S MESSAGE.

BOSTON, Nov. 11, 1863.

The extra session of the Massachusetts Legislature assembled at noon, to-day.

Governor Andrew, in his message, reviews the legislative acts regarding bounties for recruits, and says:

"It has been represented to me by officers engaged in the recruiting service, as well as by many citizens and magistrates, that these bounties do not offer sufficient pecuniary inducements to enable the required number to be raised within the two months which scarcely remain to us.

"At the request of several municipal governments, and of divers patriotic and public spirited people of the commonwealth, I have, therefore, called together the general court for the simple and special purpose of devising plans to secure the contingent of volunteers assigned to Massachusetts, and to take such action in the premises as in its wisdom may be found expedient."

"In relation to volunteering Governor Andrew says:

"I am prepared, therefore, to assist in committing the commonwealth to a policy for the payment of regular wages to the Massachusetts volunteers in addition to all other pay allowances, bounties, and advantages hitherto enjoyed."

"The employment of colored soldiers is strongly advocated in the address, and the bravery of the Fifty-fourth Massachusett's colored regiment in making the assault upon Fort Wagner is eloquently referred to in proof of their fitness for infantry service.

BOSTON, November 11.

"In the legislature to-day the governor's address was referred to a special legislative committee, which met immediately after the House adjourned.

"A bill was introduced proposing to give all soldiers who hereafter enlist or re-enlist twenty dollars per month from the State Treasury instead of the bounties now offered. Action upon this proposition was deferred until to-morrow."

So, it seems after all, that *money* lies at the bottom of Massachusetts patriotism. What a commentary on the "Bull against the comet."

But, we have another from GREELEY, just previous to the "Bull against the Comet:"

"Leading men from the East and the West alike express grave doubts whether their states will promptly furnish their respective quotas of men under the forthcoming call of the President. There would be no difficulty, they say, if the people were sure that the war was to be conducted with a single eye to the suppression of the rebellion, whether slavery went down with that which it caused or not.

"A war for the maintenance of slavery, as this seems in some quarters to be—a war in which the recruiting officers are instructed to accept no loyal men whose complexions are 'dark—is not one they think likely to make enlistments rapid. Some name sixty or ninety days as the periods within which it will be possible to raise the number required, while others say that their citizens will demand an anti-slavery policy before they will fill up the regiments."

MR. SEWARD PROVES THE PROCLAMATION UNCONSTITUTIONAL.

Mr. SEWARD, in his letter of instructions to Minister ADAMS, in April, 1861, said:

"The condition of slavery in the several states will remain just the same, whether the revolution succeeds or fails. There is not even a pretext for the complaint that the disaffected states are to be conquered by the U. S., if the revolution fail; for the rights of the states, and the condition of every human being in them, will remain subject exactly to the same laws and forms of administration, whether the revolution shall succeed, or whether it shall fail.— In the one case, the states would be federally connected with the new Confederacy; in the other they would, as now, be members of the U. S.; but their constitutions and laws, customs, habits and institutions, in either case, will remain the same.

"It is hardly necessary to add to this incontestible statement the further fact that the new President, as well as the citizens through whose suffrages he came into the administration, has always repudiated all desire whatever, wherever imputed to him of them, of disturbing the system of slavery as it is existing under the Constitution and laws. The case, however, would not be fully presented if I were to omit to say that *any such effort* on his part would be *unconstitutional*, and all his actions in this direction would be prevented by the judicial authority, even though they were assented to by Congress and the people."

Was Mr. SEWARD a traitor—a Copperhead—when he penned these instructions?

CHAPTER XXV.

DISLOYALTY AND "TREASON" OF THE RADICALS.

How the Radicals "Opposed the Government" before the Proclamation...Parker Pillsbury..."New York Times" Before and After the Election..."New York Post"—"Opposes the Government"..."New York Times" Again... "Chicago Tribune" Denounces the President...Wisconsin Home League on "Imbecility and Cowardice"...Predictions of "New York Tribune"...Democratic Predictions...Gov. Stone admits this an "Abolition War"...A Short Tack after the Gale of 1862..."New York Tribune" ...More Prophecies by False Prophets...Wendell Phillips as a Prophet..."New York Post" as a Prophet..."National Intelligencer" a True Prophet...Gov. Andrew's Prophesies..."New York Tribune's" Prophesies...The "900,-000," &c...Remarks of "National Intelligencer" on Same...The Proclamation in a Nut Shell...Belief in the Proclamation a Test of Loyalty...Forney Thereon...Senator Wilson's Address..."Disloyalty" of "Janesville, (Wis.) Gazette"..."Waukesha, (Wis.) Freeman"..."New York Tribune" on "Blunders"...Wendell Phillips on the "Lickspittle Administration"..."Milwaukee Sentinel" Disloyal to the "Government"..."Slate Journal" Ditto ...Phillips Again...Beecher on the "Government"...Testimony of Senator Browning..."Milwaukee Wisconsin" Throws a Javelin at Seward..."Chicago Tribune" Corrects Old Abe..."New York Independent" on the Administration..."New York Times" Scores the "Government"..."Chicago Tribune" Ditto..."Milwaukee Sentinel" Ditto..."Buffalo Express" Ditto..."Pittsburgh Chronicle" Ditto...."Anti-Slavery Standard" Ditto... "New York Post" on "Mistakes," &c...The Loyal Siamose Twins..."New York Tribune" on "Cabbage Head" Halleck.

HOW THE RADICALS OPPOSED THE "GOVERNMENT" BEFORE THE PROCLAMATION.

Since we have heard so much about "disloyalty" and the charge of "copperheadism" against everybody that did not endorse all the measures and policies of the "Government," we will here present some specimens of abuse and opposition to the "Government," so that the style of then radicals may be know when they were displeased with the policy.

PARKER PILLSBURY, whom the Republicans have so tenderly petted, thus vented his spleen and "discouraged enlistments," for which the administration never even talked of having him arrested and sent over the lines:

"Hasten back to a recognition of your own manhood—of your divine origin and destiny.— Believe yourselves too sacred to be shot down like dogs by Jeff. Davis and his myrmidons, and all in the cause of slavery! *Die, rather at home*, in the arms of loving mothers and affectionate sisters. Nay, be shot down, if you must, *at home*, and die like a Christian, and have a decent burial, rather than go and *die in the cause of a Union and a Government based on slavery*, which should never have been formed, and which are blistered all over with the curses of God for wrongs, outrages and cruelties it has inflicted on millions of his poor children. Speak in tones of thunder to the Government, until it hear, and declares a policy and purpose of such a character as that, if you must die in battle, it shall at least be in the cause of justice and liberty."

Did Vallandigham ever utter treason like this? No, never! But, PARKER PILLSBURY don't vote the Democratic ticket, which makes all the difference in the world.

BEFORE AND AFTER THE ELECTION.

Before the election the New York *Times* (Abolition) declared that opposition to the proclamation was infidelity to the Government. After the election it talks in this wise:

"The heaviest loads which the friends of the Government have been compelled to carry through this canvass has been *the inactivity and inefficiency* of the Administration. We speak from a knowledge of public sentiment in every section of the State, when we say that *the failure of the Government* to prosecute the war with the vigor, energy and success which the vast resources at its command warranted the country in expecting at its hands, has weighed like an incubus upon the public heart. With every disposition to sustain the Government—with the most profound conviction that the only hope of the country lies in giving it a cordial and effective support—its friends have been unable to give a satisfactory answer to the questions that have come up from every side: Why has the war made so little progress? Why have our splendid armies achieved such splendid successes? Why have they lain idle so long, and why have the victories they have won been so utterly barren of decisive results? The war has dragged on for a year and a half. The country has given the Government over a million of men, and all the money they could possibly use; yet we have made scarcely any progress toward crushing the rebellion. The rebel armies still menace the capital. The privateers defy our navy, and spread increasing terror among our peaceful traders on the seas. *What is the use of trying to sustain an administration which lags so far behind the country, and seems so indifferent and incompetent to the dreadful tasks committed to its hands?*"

The world does move.

[From the New York Post, Radical Rep.]

"A little more than a year ago, the people of every loyal state rushed together with unparalleled *unanimity* and enthusiasm to devote 'their lives, their fortunes and sacred honors,' to the support of the government and the maintenance of the integrity of the nation. That this was no transient outburst of feeling, but the utterance of a calm and determined purpose, has been proved by their persistent and indefatigable efforts to accomplish even more than they had promised. They have twice given to the authorities an army of over half a million of men; they have opened their purses and allowed those authorities to take money as it was wanted; and they have submitted to derangements of business, to a currency of sticking plasters, to heavy taxation, and to disasters in the field, and not merely with patience and without dismay, but with a cheerfulness and hope for the future that has enlisted the wonder of Europe, and finds no example in the annals of any other nation.

"All this arose from the sincere, earnest and invincible devotion of the people to their institutions and particularly to that Union by which these institutions are guaranteed and vivified. But that devotion is no less strong now than it was a year and a half ago; we are still forwarding troops to the army; we are still contributing money, we are still determined that the rebellion shall be suppressed; and we are still confident that no power on earth, neither our own divisions nor the malignant hatred of the old monarchies, will succeed in separating this once proud and harmonious republic into a multitude of factions and warring states. What, then, means the singular revolution of political sentiment which is testified by the elections in nearly all the middle states? Are Ohio, Indiana, Illinois, Pennsylvania and New York weary of the war? Are they willing to say to the states in rebellion, "Wayward sisters, go in peace!" Are they ready to confess that all their past efforts have been causeless and in vain, and to recall their gallant soldiers from the battle field? Not at all—not at all! But they do say, in emphatic and imperative tones, that they are wholly dissatisfied with the manner in which the war has been conducted."

It is refreshing to get a glimpse of so much truth and candor in a Radical Abolition paper:

A little further on, the same paper in summing up the *causes* that have led to the defeat of the Administration and its policy, remarks:

"Let the authorities at Washington be rebuked significantly, it is said on all sides, and they will do better for the future.

"We trust they will; we trust the incidents of the day have impressed upon their minds two solemn and important lessons: First, that war, when it has been undertaken, is to be fought as war, according to war principles, and not as politics, according to the interests of localities or classes, or the schemes of wily intriguers and managers. The mistake of the administration, from the beginning has been that it has regarded the war not as a deadly and inevitable encounter between two forms of society struggling for the mastery of a continent, but as a neighborhood feud, which must end in a compromise, mutual conciliation, and a final shaking of hands."

SUPPORTING THE "GOVERNMENT."

When any Democrat criticises any act or measure of the Administration, its organs send up one united chorus of "copperhead opposition to the government." The Democracy throw no obstacles in the way of necessary war measures—indeed, they have from the start, aided all such war measures in every possible way. But in the beginning, when the danger of losing our national capital was imminent, the radical press were savage on the "government." The New York *Times* is one of this class. It daily abused and threatened the President until he changed his policy; but now it is foremost in denunciations against all who complain of any act or measure, no matter how despotic and subversive of our liberties, We copy the following as a remonstrance:

[From the New York Times, April 24, 1861.]

It is stated on the authority of Mayor Brown, of Baltimore, that the President has consented that no more troops shall pass through Maryland, and that a regiment from Pennsylvania has been turned back pursuant to this arrangement. Our correspondent gives a very different account of the decision of the President. It is possible the Mayor's account may not be entirely reliable.

"Under this belief we abstain from such comments as such an agreement on the part of the President would naturally provoke. We will simply remark that the President runs no small risk of being *superceded* in his office, if he undertakes to thwart the clear and manifest determination of the people to maintain the authority of the government of the United States, and to protect its honor. We are in the midst of a revolution, and in such emergencies, the people are very apt to find some *representative* leader, if the forms of law do not happen to have given them one. It would be well for Mr. Lincoln to bear in mind the possibility of such an event."

THE PRESIDENT DENOUNCED AS THE AUTHOR OF THE NEGRO RIOTS.

The Chicago *Tribune*, a sheet that has said more unmanly and libelous things against those who felt it their duty to fairly criticise the acts and policy of the Administration, than any other paper in the land, thus inserted its "Copperhead" fangs in Old Abe, because he did not "bow and scrape," and act the excessive genteel to a lot of negroes that called upon him in 1861.

"The interview between the President and the representatives of the colored race, in which they are honestly told that we cannot tolerate them among us, that they must leave our communities and seek a home elsewhere, constitutes a wide and gloomy background of which the foreground is made up of the riots and disturbances which have disgraced within a short time past our northern cities. It is the last struggle of oppression and chattelism. It is the attempt to construct and patch anew the quaking Bastile of the negro drivers by saying to its victims that as freemen they can be received nowhere. That with them it must be slavery or a worse degradation.

The Wisconsin *Home League*, a radical sheet, thus alludes to the President's order revoking the suppression of the Chicago *Times:*

"Compared with the wicked and pestiferous Chicago *Times*, Vallandigham is a pure and spotless Saint ; and for the President to revoke the order suppressing the *Times* and not recall the Ohio traitor, is indicative of imbecility or cowardice, or both. An Administration that succumbs to its powerful enemies, and punishes its weak ones, deserves the contempt and pity of all brave and honorable men.

GREELEY'S PREDICTION OF GOOD THINGS.

The New York *Tribune* of September 27, 1862, five days after the first Proclamation, put on record the following predictions, which need only a comparison with the actual facts, to make them appear ridiculous and absurd:

"1. We predict that the 1st of January, 1863, will prove a most important and auspicious era in the history of the country.

"2. We predict that Jeff Davis will think twice before he gives effect to his well known purpose of denuding the Cotton States of their able bodied whites, up to the age of even fifty years, in order to hurl them on the Union armies along the frontier.

"3. We predict that it will be found much easier to induce the slaves on the great plantations to stop work next Christmas for their annual saturnalia, than to go back to their unpaid tasks on the morning after New Year's.

DEMOCRATIC PREDICTIONS.

The following predictions by the Chicago *Times*, just after the Proclamation, when read by the light of subsequent history, demonstrate the fact that Democrats had a clearer perception of the *effect* of the Proclamation than their opponents. These predictions are a sample of the universal predictions of the Democratic masses, everywhere.

"No President of the United States has ever received a more generous, sincere and earnest popular support than President Lincoln received in the prosecution of the war, from the Democratic party, up to the issuing of the

Emancipation Proclamation. The support was without condition save in *one* respect. The sole condition was, that the war should be conducted to the end, as it had been professedly undertaken, *for the preservation of the constitution and the restoration of the Union,* with all the rights to the *states* unimpaired.

"This generous, earnest and sincere support has not yet been wholly withdrawn, though it must be confessed it has been greatly diminished. It has not yet been wholly withdrawn, because the Proclamation of the 22d of September was only preliminary, and the threatened manifesto on the 1st of January, might be withheld.

"If the threatened manifesto shall be issued, *it will change the whole character of the war.* [A truth that subsequent history has vindicated.] It will make it a war to destroy the constitution and the Union. [True, again.] It will make it a war not only of subversion of the political constitution of the country, but sudden, radical and inevitably ruinous in the industrial and social relations of the people. [This has been proved too true.] It will make it a war to liberate and enfranchise four millions of semi-savage negroes, and to establish them as the people of the sovereign States."

The truth of this has been admitted. Read the remarks of Gov. STONE, of Iowa, in a previous chapter, when he declares:

"I admit this is an abolition war."

A SHORT TACK AFTER THE GALE OF 1862.

The radicals, after the fall elections of 1862, began to fear that the proclamation was working badly for their main purpose—that it was likely to wrench power from their hands, and thus present the consummation of their desires to break up the Union, began to haul in their horns, and to claim that the proclamation would have no effect on the status of Southern institutions, and this is the way the New York *Tribune* states the case:

"Our original conviction, that our Government is to-day at perfect liberty to accept the unconditional return to loyalty of any state or states now in rebellion, and that *those states will thereupon become supreme over their inhabitants not in the service of the United States,* has been nowise shaken, nor do we perceive a necessity for any new arguments to establish it."

About the same date the Albany *Journal* echoed the same note:

"If this position is right, slavery in the states will be in no way affected by the proclamation, but that institution will be as completely re-established, under the reconstructed Union, as if the proclamation had never been issued."

MORE PROPHECIES FROM FALSE PROPHETS.

The great Hebrew law giver, in reply to the question: "*How* shall we know the word which the Lord hath spoken?" replied:

"When a prophet speaketh in the name of the Lord, if the thing follow not nor come to pass, that is the thing which the Lord hath not spoken, but the prophet hath spoken it presumptuously; thou shalt not be afraid of him."

" When wicked men make promises of truth, 'Tis weakness to believe them."
[*Howard's Scanderburg.*

Let us apply the test of the Hebrew lawyer to the speech of WENDELL PHILLIPS, Feb. 17, 1861, wherein he prophecied:

"The South cannot make war on any one.— Suppose the fifteen states hang together a year —which is almost an impossibility:

"1st. They have given bonds in two thousand millions of dollars—the value of their slaves—to keep the peace.

"2d. They will have enough to do to attend to the irrepressible conflict at home. Virginia, Kentucky, Missouri, will be their Massachusetts; Winter Davis, Blair, and Cassius Clay their Seward and Garrison.

"3d. The Gulf States will monopolize all the offices. A man must have Gulf principles to belong to a healthy party. Under *such* a lead, disfranchised Virginia in opposition, will not have much heart to attack Pennsylvania."

If these things prophesied of have come to pass, let us annoint WENDELL as a veritable prophet, if not, is it not "weakness to believe him?"

THE NEW YORK POST AS A PROPHET.

Just *prior* to the issuing of the Proclamation, the New York *Evening Post* set up shop as a wholesale prophet:

"How strange that our great men and rulers should not see that the stomach is the weak point of the enemy! He will have little stomach to fight the bad fight of rebellion on an empty stomach. When the great words of liberty and freedom shall be sounded from the high-places of power like a trumpet through the land, the knell of the rebellion will be tolled. But we are asked how the negroes on the plantations are to be informed of such a decree of the Government. How little do those who ask such questions know of the negro character. The negroes are familiar with every swamp and mountain pass, through glen and forest, and at night, guided by the stars, the gospel of freedom would be circulated from cabin to cabin almost with telegraphic swiftness. *The plow would stand still in the furrow the ripened grain would remain unharvested, the cows would not be milked, the dinners would not be cooked,* but one universal hallelujah of glory to God, echoed from every valley and hill-top of rebeldom, would sound the speedy doom of treason."

Upon which the *National Intelligencer* remarks:

"Have these predictions been fulfilled? And yet it is on the fulfillment of such predictions that the anti-slavery prognosticators have suspended their repute for sagacity.

"Reproducing such representations as these in our columns on the 31st of July, 1862, before any proclamation of freedom had been issued, we wrote as follows:

"There is one aspect of the question which rather inclines us to wish the President might find it compatible with his convictions of public duty to issue some such paper as these complainants ask at his hands. We are well assured that it would prove *brutum fulmen*, but its demonstrated inefficiency might perhaps open the eyes of amiable and sanguine philanthropists, who, until the experiment is tried, will continue to credit such representations."

As we have seen, the prophet, Gov. ANDREW, prophesied that the "roads would swarm" with "Brave Boys."

The people have not yet "seen it."

The New York *Tribune* of July 17, 1862, prophesied that

"Our enemies must henceforth [if the Proclamation be issued] devote half their strength to keeping the rest back."

The people have failed to "see it."

The same sheet of July 19, 1862, prophesied

"A speedy and overwhelming Union triumph."

The people have not yet "seen it."

The same prophetic organ of August 2, 1862, prophesied that the proclamation would stimulate—

"three times three hundred thousand born and naturalized Yankees, who never smelt battle, all join in the grand old chorus of human nature, and its own clear, musical, glorious, burning, self-evident words, the old chorus of liberty forever, all join in and march on, knowing, every blessed mother's son of them, that what is going to be done now is to save the country."

The people have failed to "see" this grand outpouring of 900,000, even with all the natural stimulants of patriotism, individual, county, city, state and national bounties, to say nothing of the thumb screws of conscription —iron hand cuffs and cold lead for deserters.

The same organ, on the 6th of August, 1862, prophesied that the Emancipation Proclamation would

"pierce the very vitals of the revolt."

Does anybody "see it" in that light?

Again, on the 8th of the same month, the same prophet predicted that the proclamation would—

"just lift the nation right off its feet, and surprise it into one unanimous yell of enthusiasm."

We don't "see" anything of the sort yet, but it cannot be doubted that the slaughter house butcheries of Fredericksburg, December 13, following, came very near putting the Union *hors du combat*.

Again says this prophet, on the 11th of the same month, the proclamation:—

"Would give an immediate reinforcement to the Union armies equal to a hundred veteran regiments and fifty well-served batteries?"

If the proclamation can do all this, why did it not, and thus save the people the horrors of conscription, which even with all its force has failed to help the proclamation out?

Again, on the 27th of Sept. 1862, this prophetic seer continued his predictions.

"We predict that the sympathizers in the Free States with the slaveholders' rebellion will have hard work *to keep up the courage of their Southern brethern through the next three months, and that earnest efforts will be made by these compatriots to bring about an accommodation before the day of emancipation*."

Upon which the *National Intelligencer* remarks:

"The time has passed when each of these prophecies enables us to test the inspiration of the seer. The 1st of January, instead of being a "most important and auspicious era in the history of our country," was remarkable only for the utterance of another paper proclamation. Instead of "thinking twice" before denuding the Cotton States of their able-bodied whites," the Confederate authorities propose to make their conscription law still more stringent and comprehensive. The negroes in the Insurgent States, so far as we are informed, went back to "their unpaid tasks on the morning after New Year's" with as much generality and alacrity as ever. And, lastly, the only persons who have done hard work "to keep up the courage of their Southern brethren," and to put forth efforts to bring about an "accommodation," are the authors and abettors of propositions looking to the mediation of Switzerland, and avowing their readiness to "bow to our destiny and *make the best attainable peace*," "if three months more of earnest fighting shall not serve to make a serious impression on the rebels."

"And yet these discredited prophets continue to vex loyal citizens with their croakings, as though any body could stand in awe of their denunciations. They assure the President that he will live to regret the decision he has made in regard to Missouri. Assuming to be guides of mankind when their every pretension to leadership has been exploded by 'the things that have not come to pass,' they should at least learn to speak with some reserve and not provoke any further inquiry into their credentials. We cheerfully concede to them the "liberty of prophesying," but, in view of the long line of their unfulfilled predictions, we hope it is no impiety to disbelieve them."

THE PROCLAMATION IN A NUT-SHELL.

Secretary CHASE, in one of his late speeches, asserts that "the rebellion would have succeeded but for the proclamation of freedom." The *National Intelligencer*, in an elaborate discussion of his position, presents the following theories which show what Mr. Chase will have to do in order to substantiate his assertion:

"Slavery was everywhere destroyed by the hostile presence of our armies *before* the proclamation was issued.

"Slavery was everywhere destroyed by the hostile presence of our armies *since* the proclamation has been issued.

"Required to prove that it is the proclamation which destroys slavery."

And again:

"The hostile presence of a military force where the proclamation *does* not apply, (as in New Orleans, for instance,) produces the destruction of slavery;

"Where the proclamation *does* apply, but where there is no hostile presence of military forces, (as in Alabama) slavery remains undisturbed.

"Required to prove that it is the proclamation which damages slavery."

BELIEF IN THE PROCLAMATION THE TEST OF LOYALTY.

We have already uttered our belief, and sustained that belief with ample proof, that Mr. LINCOLN was badgered into the issuing the Proclamation *for the purpose* of dividing the North, and by such division, to finally overthrow the old Government.

JOHN W. FORNEY, the acknowledged mouthpiece of the powers that be, like the dog Cerberus, that guarded the gates of the Plutonian regions, has, not like that sulphurous watchdog, three heads, but he has two organs—the Philadelphia *Press* and the Washington *Chronicle*. In the latter this watch-dog is pleased to denominate the fight for the Proclamation as—

"The coming struggle for a great principle. * * * This question of enforcing the President's Emancipation Proclamation is rapidly approaching that point at which it will be the *test of popular loyalty!*"

Our fathers taught us that the only "test of loyalty" was a due observance of the constitution, but here we have a new *test*. All who do not subscribe to it, are to be tabooed as disloyal! Disloyal to what? Why, to a measure to break up and destroy the government.

The *Chronicle* also quotes and highly commends the following from the

ADDRESS BY SENATOR WILSON.

"The practical issues before the nation are the suppression of the rebellion by the hand of war, the extinguishment of its cause by the inforcement of the Emancipation Proclamation. These are the vital issues, and they are to meet the sternest resistance—to pass through trials that will test the fidelity and endurance of their supporters, as their fidelity and endurance were never before tested. I tell you, sir, and the men who believe in the Emancipation Proclamation, who mean to make it a practical reality, the irrepealable law of the nation, that they must prepare for a mighty conflict that will stir the country to its profoundest depths. Beside this transcendent question of the inforcement of the proclamation in the rebel states, all other questions, growing out of the existence of slavery, sink into utter insignificance; for its success carries with it everything else—ultimate emancipation in Delaware, and Maryland, Kentucky and Tennessee, fugitive slave law and all. Let then, the anti-slavery men of united America, by thought, word, and deed, support the President in suppressing the rebellion, and in enforcing the proclamation. Let them raise no immaterial issues, no trifling questions to distract or to divide their counsels, or to impede their advance to the achievement of the crowning victory that shall bring along with it unity to a now dismembered country, peace to a wounded and bleeding nation, justice to a wronged race, and a future radiant with the elevating and refining inspirations of equal and impartial freedom."

This shows that these radicals intended to bring on a conflict here at the North "that will stir the country to its profoundest depths," and who can doubt the object?

There was no need of such a conflict. If saving the Union was the real object, these marplots would have striven by all means in their power to have kept the North united, for in unity there is strength, but knowing that in a conflict there would be weakness, they have inaugurated that "conflict" and made it as "irrepressible" as possible, that it might be fulfilled, which was spoken of by DOUGLAS in his last speech in the Senate—that the Republicans desired disunion, whenever they could effect it without making themselves directly responsible.

"DISLOYALTY" OF THE RADICALS.

The standard lately set up by the radicals will do to try them by. They now declare that it is "disloyal" to find any fault with the President or his policy. Let us see what they did prior to the promulgation of the proclamation.

We select the following from the Janesville (Wis.) *Gazette:*

"It may be wisdom in the present administration to keep its own counsel and submit to misrepresentations rather than avow its policy. We know there are good and tried men in the cabinet. Such a representative as Mr. Chase, Ohio, may hold in check the manifestation of a feeling that needs but little incentive to break into an open expression. *But it is useless to attempt to conceal the fact that fear if not distrust is creeping too fast into the minds of too many undoubted Republicans to be pleasant in present contemplation or hopeful in prospect.*"

And again, from the same sheet:

"Gen Halleck is waiting till his officers have hunted out all the contrabands in his army, and delivered them up to their owners, and Gen. Buell, in Kentucky, is waiting for Halleck to move down the Mississippi before he advances into Tennessee. Some are waiting to see if Parson Brownlow will not be rescued for toasting some of 'our friends over there,' &c.

And once more this organ vented its spleen at the administration:

"MODEST.—The Legislature of Kentucky has passed a resolution asking President Lincoln to dispense with Secretary Cameron, on account of his views as to the confiscation of slave property belonging to persons in rebellion to the Government. We should not wonder if the request was complied with, as the Kentucky Unionists seem to have control of the policy of the administration. A pretext for Cameron's removal can be as easily found as for the sacrifice of Fremont on account of his proclamation."

The Waukesha (Wis.) *Freeman* said:

"Just so long as the North (meaning the administration) fights the slaveholders, and holds four millions of human beings in bondage for them to build their fortifications and cultivate their lands, just so long will the South be able to prosecute the rebellion. But let the slaves be confiscated or freed, and *the rebellion would be killed stone dead in a fortnight.*"

THE NEW YORK TRIBUNE ON BLUNDERS.

The pious New York *Tribune* thus pitched into the Administration:

"The history of this war, on the part of both government and people, is little more than a record of the discovery of mistakes and the ratification of blunders. Among the most pernicious blunders which have embarrassed our warlike operations has been the blunder of underrating the strength of the rebels. As a matter of course we have overrated the strength of the loyal States."

And yet GREELEY said this about the same time he was clamoring for the proclamation as a certain means to crush the rebellion "before Christmas."

WENDELL PHILLIPS ON THE "LICK SPITTLE" ADMINISTRATION.

At a Republican meeting in Boston, called to express their disgust at the conduct of the "Government" in modifying CAMERON, Mr. PHILLIPS remarked:

"The President, with senile, lick-spittle haste runs before he is bidden to revoke the Hunter Proclamation. If Hunter had issued a pro-slavery proclamation, be sure the government would have waited for red tape. It showed the old pro-slavery leaning of the Government. Mr. P. believed that President Lincoln's decree in relation to the Hunter Proclamation had lost a quarter of the chances of preserving the Union. (Phillips talk about preserving the Union—*bosh!*) What were the anti-slavery people to do now? They must *educate* public opinion, that was all, and *force the Government* up to the proper anti-slavery point. Emancipation won't save the Union now—confiscation must save it. * * The President and the Cabinet of the United States were *treasonable* in their delay. The people want the Government to take a position. The President and Secretary of War *should be impeached* for allowing Mercier to go down to Richmond, with their consent, to confer with the rebel leaders. That Minister had no right for any such purpose, to hold conference with the rebels in arms, and where is the Government that would have allowed it, but this?"

The Milwaukee *Sentinel*, though at a later date, thus exhibits its faultfinding propensity:

"When an officer like Halbert E Paine, as good as the Government has in its service, and whose men are attached to him, as much as it is possible for men to be attached to an officer, is put under arrest for the cause he was, (for disobedience of orders), *how is it possible to enlist men for service?*"

The Wisconsin *State Journal* said:

"Verily, the policy upon which this war is conducted *must be changed* for a policy more earnest, thorough and effective."

We would say amen to that, if some one would guarantee us immunity from arrest as disloyal to the "Government."

Wendell Phillips made a speech before the Republicans at Abbington, Massachusetts, August 1, 1862, in which occurs this language:

"We shall never have peace until slavery is destroyed. As long as you keep the present *Turtle* at the head of the Government, you make a pit with one hand, and fill it with the other. * * * If any man present believes he has light enough to allow him, let him pray that *Davis may be permitted to make an attack on Washington City, within a week!*"

BEECHER ON THE "GOVERNMENT."

The New York *Independent* of August 9, 1862, contained a most savage diatribe against the "Government." We select the following:

"There has not been a line in any Government paper [under Lincoln] that might not have been issued by the Czar, by Louis Napoleon, or by Jeff Davis.

"Our State papers, during this eventful struggle, are void of genuine enthusiasm for the great doctrines on which this Government was founded. Faith in human rights is dead in Washington!"

TESTIMONY OF SENATOR BROWNING.

Senator Browning, whom Governor Yates, of Illinois, appointed to fill the unexpired term of the lamented Douglas, and who ought to be good Republican authority, made a speech at Quincy, Illinois, soon after his return from Congress, in which he daguerreotyped sundry Republican journals; from which we select the following:

"Among these journals is the Chicago *Tribune* and the Quincy *Whig*. He read an article from the *Tribune*, and denounced it as the most infamous treason that had appeared in any paper in the United States since the war began. Of the editors of the *Tribune* he had the most contemptuous opinion. He did not believe them to be loyal, and if they should take an oath to support the Government, he would not believe their oath."

The Milwaukee *Wisconsin* thus stabbed one branch of the "Government:"

"In the War Department he (Seward) has mixed in on almost every occasion. It is *well known that he favored the inaction of the Grand Army*—when events have proved it would have been comparatively easy to take Richmond. Seward's military policy has been a blotch and a blunder. It has consolidated the rebel Government into its present formidable power."

The Chicago *Tribune* pitched into the President after this style for his expressions to Greeley:

"'*The Union as it Was.*'—In his letter to Horace Greeley, the President says:

'The sooner the national authority is restored, the sooner the Union will be *the Union as it was.*'

"There is much ambiguity in this expression. The 'Union as it was' is a cant phrase, invented by the famous Vallandigham, and fathered by his dirty tool, Dick Richardson. * * * But such a Union loyal men don't want to see restored. They prefer a Union as it *ought to be*. What patriotic citizen desires the 'Union as it was' under Buchanan's administration. [Bosh!] If that is the Union to which Mr. Lincoln refers, he should dismiss his present Cabinet and send for Cobb, Floyd, Thompson, Toucey," &c.

For further information on this head, we refer the reader to a previous chapter on the radical conspiracy against the President:

THE NEW YORK INDEPENDENT ON THE ADMINISTRATION.

We copy as follows from the New York *Independent*:

"There is no need of rousing the patriotism of the people. It is an inexhaustible quality. It underlies their very life. The Government itself is buoyed by it, and rides upon it like a ship upon the fathomless ocean.

"No! It is the *Government* that needs rousing. We do not need meetings on the Hudson, but *motion* on the Potomac. * * There is no use concealing it—the people are beginning to distrust their rulers. * * The President seems to be a man without any sense of the value of time. * * Armies are perishing. Months are wasting. We are in the second year of the rebellion. We have been *just on the eve of doing something for sixteen months.*

"The people cannot but see that the success of our arms has been *in the ratio of their distance from the Seat of Government!* In all the Great West, *where the Government could not meddle*—on the sea board, in North Carolina, at Beaufort, S. C., at New Orleans, we have had success. But in Virginia, *within reach of the influence of Washington* we have had *all our delays and all our misfortunes.*

"We looked from stand to stand in the great meeting on Tuesday, with a sadness we could not disguise. The necessity for such a 'meeting was a mortification. *What President was ever so royally backed;* [stick a pin here.]— What resources, what enthusiasm, what *unity of feeling* ; [just as we mentioned in previous pages.] What eagerness of men to be enrolled, what confidence in the Administration!— And *one* year has so nearly wasted all this that the Government is resorting to *unusual measures* to secure enlistments. Is patriotism dead? Is the love of national unity grounded? Why are such meetings needed to draw up recruits? We are obliged to say, Mr. Lincoln, the fault *is not with the people.*"

Cannot Mr. Beecher see some reason for

this apathy among the people, in the system of arbitrary arrests without accuser, judge or jury—and the negro policy?

"The war line rose up in its majesty to punish rebellion. It put a magnificent army into the President's hands. For one year that army was besieged in the capital! * * and in the second year of the war! And how long will it be before every nation in Europe will have a *right* to say the South has shown itself able to maintain its independence? * * * But one thing is sure, unless there is more purpose and vigor *at Washington*, all the public meetings in the land will not save this country from shame and disaster."

THE HEAVY LOAD OF THE ADMINISTRATION.

The New York *Times*, before the election in 1862, declared that all who did not sustain *every act of the administration*, were traitors. After the election it thus made the administration the scape goat for the sins of its party defeat:

"The heaviest load which the friends of the Government (administration) have been compelled to carry through this canvass, has been *the inactivity and inefficiency of the administration*. We speak from a knowledge of public sentiment in every section of the state, when we say that the failure of the Government to prosecute the war with a vigor, energy and success which the vast resources at its command warranted the country in expecting at its hands, has weighed like an incubus upon the public heart. With every disposition to sustain the Government, with the conviction that the only hope of the country lies in giving it a cordial and effective support, its friends have been unable to give a satisfactory answer to the questions that have come up from every side. Why has the war made so little progress? Why have our splendid armies achieved such slight successes? Why have they lain idle so long? And why have the victories they have won been so wholly barren of decisive results? The war has dragged on for a year and a half. The country has given the Government over a million of men, and all the money they could possibly use, yet *we have made scarcely any progress towards crushing the rebellion*. The rebel armies still menace the capital. The privateers defy our navy and spread increasing terror among our peaceful traders on the seas: What is the use of trying to sustain an administration which lags so far behind the country, and seems so *indifferent and incompetent* to the dreadful task committed to its hands?"

The Chicago *Tribune* threw this fling at the Administration:

"*Influence of Traitors at Washington*.—The recent unrebuked presence in Washington of Mrs. Lay, whose husband was formerly on Gen. Scott's staff, but who is now an Inspector in the rebel army, and Mrs. Campbell, wife of the Assistant Secretary of War of the rebel government, and their unimpeded return to Richmond, have provoked much comment. Many people cannot see why female spies are thus permitted to visit the Capital of the country, and after obtaining whatever information is accessible—usually an ample store—be allowed to return at pleasure through our lines to Richmond, laden with their valuable freightage."

Would the *Tribune* thus cast reproach on the Administration, after the issuing of that wonderful Proclamation? Doubtful.

This same sheet of April 10, '63, takes the New York *Post* to task for its "attacks on the President" for retaining McCLELLAN so long, notwithstanding the *Tribune* admits in the same article to have done the same thing. (Probably before the proclamation.)

The Milwaukee *Sentinel* of April 18, 1863, pitches into the President's "scatteration" policy, in sending BANKS off to the Rio Grande, &c. It says:

"The scattering of large armies at various points along a lengthy line of attack, and too far apart for mutual support, or speedy concentration, seems opposed, not only to the maxims of great military attributes, but to the dictates of common sense. * * * We have more and better men than the rebels. With a military policy *as correct as theirs*, we could not fail to whip them even with our present armies."

But the *Sentinel*, since that time, has obtained a new editor, and probably will "sin no more."

The Buffalo *Express*, a strong Administration paper, in a long doleful article on the failure of the Potomac Army to accomplish anything, says:

"Either we must have generals who can blossom in the shade, for Generals do not thrive under the drip of the Capitol At thirty-six hours distance from Washington, armies and Generals succeed. At twenty-four hours they just held their own; but within six hours they are as dead as a field of wheat under the shadow of a upas tree."

The Pittsburg *Chronicle*, a most radical sheet, in speaking of Rosecrans' movements, says:

"That while the rebels are at their old game of concentration, Halleck is at his of 'scatteration.' Can any sensible man tell why Grant's main army is idle at this moment, or why our best troops are wasted in *idle and Quixotic* expeditions to those distant and God forsaken countries, Texas and Arkansas? Do the vitals of the rebellion live away out among the Camanches or Creek Indians, or in Georgia, Alabama, Mississippi and Virginia? We are again hacking away at the fingers and toes of the rebellion, while Rosecrans' spring at its very heart is turned aside by want of numbers and concentration.''

Perhaps the *Chronicle* is one of those weak minded concerns that believe it is the object of those in power to put down the rebellion, and save the Union. It may be guilty of such weakness.

The anti-slavery *Standard* offers the following mutterings:

"By the time the Government gets ready to do anything, the time for it has passed. This has been the case too often in the past. We need vigor, more vigor, and still more vigor, and Mr. Stanton needs to learn that bullying men as he used to juries, is not vigor.''

The Cincinnati *Gazette*, an extremely loyal paper, as will be seen by a quotation from it in reference to the Mexican war (in a previous chapter) thus utters its complaints:

"The great army of the West lies useless on the Mississippi, while the great shock of armies in the West will soon take place in Tennessee. This is the whole situation, and it would be difficult to describe a more total helplessness of a great power *for want of an intelligent director*. It is hard to account for the apathy of a military Director at Washington, under this state of affairs. * * *

"The rebels have adopted the policy of concentration. Our military Director persists in *scattering*. * * * In its (the war) present arrangement there is nothing to inspire hope, but everything to create disaffection and despondency.''

The New York *Post* says:

"The Government has made mistakes; it has at times pursued an illogical, weak and timid policy; it has done some things calculated to alienate popular sympathy,'' &c.

For saying no more than this, any Democratic paper would have been called "copperhead.''

THE TWO "LOYAL" SIAMESE TWINS.

Booth, the great Wisconsin martyr, and leader of the Wisconsin Republican mobs, takes its yoke fellow, the Milwaukee *Sentinel*, to task as follows. It is like Satan rebuking sin. Says the Milwaukee *Daily Life* (Booth's paper):

"The *Sentinel* man denounces the conciliatory war policy of the Administration for the first twelve months of the war'' as "miserable and disgraceful.'' It says:

"The volunteer soldiers of our army were degraded—their morals and enthusiasm impaired, and their Northern manhood insulted by this miserable half-war and half-peace policy, and it advises any who have forgotten how much violence toward Union men, and how much masterly inactivity were the results of this policy—to take the files of any good newspaper, and wade through the shameful record of subservience, tenderness and patriotism on our side, and of insolence, ingratitude and treachery exhibited by the slave owners of the Border States.''

"The *Sentinel*, during these same 'twelve months,' defended this very 'miserable half-war and half-peace policy,' and denounced those who criticised it, declaring that our paper ought to be suppressed, for finding fault with this policy. But now it turns round, with a facility of sumersaulting, on a brazen faced impudence worthy of the New York *Herald*, and denounces the very policy it then defended, in far stronger language than we used, when it accused us of treason to the Government.''

[From the New York Tribune, of Nov. 22, 1863.]
"Great is Halleck. Yes, great is Halleck! Had he never been called to the post that he fills—that of General-in-Chief—his Order No. Three, and his everlastingly memorable siege of Corinth would have secured for him that mention in history that is not unfrequently denied to daring and worth. In this commonsense world, *and in the country of ours where common-sense is almost sure to win its way*, blank stupidity is always to be mentioned:—Halleck will fill a volume.

"Halleck is General-in-Chief. *To him the planning of campaigns is referred*—to him as a West Pointer, and presumptively a man of science. He, under the President, who does not pretend to know the hidden mysteries that lie within inner and outer circles, is the ultimate authority. *His fiat is conclusive.* "I am the army,'' he may say with just as much truth as Louis XIV. used to say, "I am the State!'' And now behold what he has ordered: An expedition to Brownsville of—we know not of how many men—an expedition that might be in order when all the other enemies of the Republic are put down; but which is now sadly out of keeping with the exigency of the national situation. He is for nipping the rebellion on its edges, while its heart beats loud and strong. He is the champion of exterior lines. Besides this the expedition of Washburn, Texasward, by way of Opelousa—what is that but a stroke of genius of which Order No. 3 was but the premonition—genius that triumphs over swamps, bayous and timber though it may not conquer the enemy? And while these expeditions are floundering, the one in the surf and the other in the mud, we see what we want elsewhere.

"Burnside, beleagured by a superior force, cries for help that cannot reach him, and *Grant shut up at Chattanooga at the head of an army that is battered and bruised by a late encounter, cannot move a peg*. *Meade cannot go forward and cross the Rapidan*, because his force weakened by the sending off detachments to the Cumberland, has not the strength to overcome the obstacles opposed! Defeat stares the armies in the face, because our forces are divided and sent off on Tomfool's errands—to do something that will have no influence on the final and much desired result. Had Grant half of the men that are butting their brains out against cypress trees in that Opelousas country, he could push on; and his first move would call back to his front the columns that now, under Longstreet, threaten Knoxville and the continuity of our line. Hooker and his corps would have been saved to Meade and the fortifications that his army could not have safely assaulted, could not have been turned. Meanwhile a dozen gunboats on the Mississippi could have kept every rebel on the west side of that stream Five hundred men afloat could have done the work of five and thirty thousand in the field. Is not the wisdom, the foresight and necessity of Order No. 8 vindicated in what we relate?

"The country inquires why is it that Halleck *with that cabbage head of his*, retains his place—why is he not permitted to retire to his ancestral krout gardens on the Mohawk, and there, among his kindred, find, in the killing of cut-worms and the care of his cabbage crop, the employment for which his genius is fitted. And if *Burnside is gobbled up, and Grant is forced to retreat, that inquiry will grow into a demand that will be sure to make itself heard.* We, who do not care for all the epauletted dignity that the President can confer on mediocrity, press the demand now. Cabbages for Halleck, and war for those who have genius to comprehend it!"

In a subsequent number of the same paper, we find the following:

"We know no reason, outside of the inefficiency and incompetency of General Halleck, why this array of evils should now confront the country and send a chill down to the soles of every loyal man's boots. And we know of no remedy save that heroic one of sending Halleck, who is responsible for the army's movements, back to the captaincy for which he is best fitted, or to the Mohawk and the cabbages among which he was raised. The disaster now threatening has been foreseen for more than a month, It has been the constant theme of the rebel papers, and their loudest boasts. There is not a man in the land who did not know of the movement intended. There is not, save one at Washington, a General-in-Chief, who would not have made a counter movement to check it. If Knoxville falls, and Burnside is destroyed, let the hero of Corinth —the author of Order No. 3—look out. Not even Presidential favor can save him!

[From the New York World, Nov. 11, 1863.]

"'The greatest folly of my life was the issuing of the Emancipation proclamation.' Such were the words of President Lincoln to Wendell Phillips last January, according to the testimony of the latter in a speech he made last week at the Music Hall in New Haven. Before the issuing of that document, President Lincoln gave it as his opinion that it would be of no more effect than the 'Pope's bull against the comet;' and after he had given it to the world he regards it as 'the greatest folly of his life,' and did not scruple to so inform one of the most influential leaders of the fanatical faction who had forced him into the objectionable measure. President Lincoln has made many notable remarks since he has been in office, but none that is likely to attract so much attention as the above.'"

CHAPTER XXVI.

THE PROCLAMATION...THE RADICAL WAR POLICY.

Mr. Lincoln's Letter to the Utica-Springfield Meetings Editor's Remarks on the Negro Policy..."New York Tribune" Pledges the President, &c ...John P. Hale's Bill to Abolish the Constitution...The Proclamation in England..."New York Tribune" on "Servile Insurrections"...Opinions of English Abolitionists...Mr. Wilberforce on the Folly of the Proclamation...Wendell Phillips on the Rampage...The Proclamation Confessed a Failure...Caleb B. Smith Pledges the Administration against the Proclamation...Mr. Madison on Emancipation...Lord Dunmore's Proclamation...Bancroft, the Historian on the Same...Thurlow Weed's Prediction...Mr. Lincoln on Federal Authority...The Chicago Platform... General Remarks...Post Master General Blair as a Witness...His Rockville Speech.

THE PROCLAMATION AND THE PRESIDENT'S WAR POLICY.

The following is President LINCOLN's letter to the Union Mass Meeting at Springfield, Illinois, and Utica, New York:

"EXECUTIVE MANSION, }
"August 26th, 1862. }

"To Hon. James C. Conklin:

"MY DEAR SIR:—Your letter inviting me to attend a mass meeting of Union men, to be held at the Capitol of Illinois on the third day of September, has been received. It would be very agreeable to me thus to meet my old friends, at my own home, but I cannot just now be absent from this city so long as a visit there would require.

"The meeting is to be of those who maintain unconditional devotion to the Union, and I am sure that my old political friends will thank me for tendering, as I do, the Nation's gratitude to those *other* noble men, whom no partisan hopes make false to the Nation's life.

"There are those who are dissatisfied with me. To such I would say, you desire peace, and you blame me that we do not have it: but how can we attain it? There are but three conceivable ways:

"First—To suppress the rebellion by force of arms. This I am trying to do. Are you for it? If you are, so far we are agreed.

"If you are not for it, a second way is to give up the Union. I am against this. If you are not for force nor yet for dissolution, there remains only some imaginable compromise. I do not believe that any compromise under the maintenance of the Union is now possible. All that I learn, tends directly to the opposite belief—that the strength of the rebellion is in its military—its army; and that the army dominates all the country and all the people within its range. Any offers, if made by any man or men within that range, in opposition to that, ar simply nothing, for the present, because such man or men have no power whatever to enforce their side of a compromise, if one be made with them.

"To illustrate: Suppose refugees from the South and peace men from the North should meet in convention and frame a proclamation or compromise embracing a restoration of the Union, in what way can that compromise be used to keep Gen. Lee's army out of Pennsylvania? Gen. Meade's army can keep Gen. Lee's army out of Pennsylvania, and I think ultimately drive it out of existence. But no paper compromise, to which the controllers of Lee's army are not agreed, can at all effect that army. In an effort at such a compromise we would waste time that the enemy would improve to our disadvantage, and that would be all. A compromise to be effective must be made either with those who control the rebel army, or with the people liberated from the dominion of that army by the success of our army.

"Now, allow me to assure you that no word or intimation from the rebel army, or from any of the men controlling it, in relation to any peace compromise, has ever come to my knowledge or belief. All charges or intimations to the contrary are deceptive and groundless, and I promise you that if any such proposition shall hereafter come, it shall not be rejected and kept secret from you.

[This is certainly apochryphal. See the Wood-Lincoln correspondence]

"I freely acknowledge myself to be the servant of the people according to the bond of the service, the United States Constitution, and as such I am responsible to them. But, to be plain, you are dissatisfied with me about the negro. Quite likely. There is a difference between you and myself upon the subject. I certainly wish all men could be free, while you, I suppose, do not. Yet I have neither adopted or proposed any measure which is not consistent with even your view, provided you are for the Union.

"I suggested a compensated emancipation, to which you replied that you wished not to be taxed to buy negroes, but I had not asked you to be taxed to buy negroes except in such a way as to save you from greater taxation, in order to save the Union exclusively by other means. You dislike the emancipation and perhaps would have it retracted. You say it is unconstitutional. I think differently. I think the Constitution vests its Commander-in-Chief with the law of war in time of war. The most that can be said, if so much, is that slaves are property. Has there ever been any question, that by the laws of war, property, both of enemies and friends, may be taken when needed? and is it not needed whenever the taking of it helps us or hurts the enemy? Armies, the world over, destroy the enemy's property when they cannot use it, end even destroy their own to keep it from the enemy. Civilized belligerants do all in their power to help themselves or hurt the enemy, except in a few things regarded as barbarous and cruel. Among the exceptions are the massacre of vanquished foes and non-combatants, male and female. But the proclamation as a law is valid or not valid. If it is not valid, it wants no retraction. If it is valid it cannot be retracted any more than the dead can be brought to life.

"Some of you profess to think that retraction would operate favorably to the Union. Why better after the retraction than before the issue? There was more than a year and a half of trial to suppress the rebellion before the proclamation was issued, the last one hundred days of which passed under an explicit notice that it was coming unless averted by those in revolt returning to their allegiance.

"The war has certainly progressed as favorably to us since the issue of the proclamation as before. I know, as fully as one can know the opinions of others, that some of the commanders of our armies in the field, who have given us our most important victories, believe the emancipation policy and the aid of colored troops constitute the heaviest blows yet dealt to the rebellion, and that at least one of those successes could not have been achieved where it was, but for the aid of black soldiers.

[We'd like to see the *proof* of this.]

"Among the commanders holding these views are some who have never had any affinity with what is called abolitionism, or the Republican party politics, but who hold them purely as military opinions. I submit their opinions, as being entitled to some weight against the objections often urged that emancipation and arming blacks are unwise as military measures, and were not adopted as such in good faith.

"You say that you will not fight to free negroes; some of them seem willing enough to fight for you, but no matter. Fight you then exclusively to save the Union. I issued the proclamation and propose to aid you in saving the Union. Whenever you have conquered all resistance to the Union, if I shall urge you to continue fighting, it will be an apt time then for you to declare [that you shall not fight to free negroes. I thought that in your struggle for the Union, to whatever extent the negroes should cease helping the enemy in his resistance to you. You think differently.

"I thought that whatever negroes can be got to do as soldiers, leaves so much less for white soldiers to do in saving the Union. Does it appear otherwise to you? But negroes, like other people, act upon motive. Why should they do anything for us if we will do nothing for them? If they stake their lives for us they must be prompted by the strongest motive, even the promise of freedom, *and the promise being made must be kept.*

"The signs look better. The Father of Waters goes unvexed to the sea, thanks to the Great Northwest for it. Nor yet wholly to them. Three hundred miles up they met New England, the Empire and Keystone states and New Jersey, hewing their way right and left. The sunny South too, in more colors than one, lent a hand. On the spot, their part of the history was jotted down in black and white.— The job was a great one, and let none be barred who bore an honorable part in it. And while those who have cleared the great river, may well be proud, yet even that is not all.— It is hard to say that anything has been more bravely and better done than at Antietam, Murfreesboro, Gettysburg and on many fields of less note.

"Nor must Uncle Sam's webbéd feet be forgotten. At all the water's margins they have been present. Not only on the deep sea, the broad bay, and the rapid river, but also up the narrow mud bayou, and wherever the ground was a *little damp* they had been and made their tracks.

"Thanks to all; for the great Republic; for the principles by which it lives and keeps alive; for man's vast fortune—thanks to all! Peace does not appear so distant as it did. I hope it will come soon, and come to stay, *and so come as to be worth the keeping in all future time.* It will then have been proved that among freemen there can be no successful appeal from the ballot to the bullet, and that they who take such appeal are to lose their case and pay the cost. And then there will be some black men who can remember that with silent tongue, and with clenched teeth, and with steady eye, and well-poised bayonet, they have helped mankind to this great consummation; *while I fear that there will be some white men, unable to forget that with malignant heart, and deceitful speech they have striven to hinder it.*

"Still let us not be over-sanguine of a speedy and final triumph. Let us be quite sober, and let us diligently apply our means, never doubting that a just God, in His own good time will give us the rightful result.

Yours very truly,
[Signed.] "A. LINCOLN."

THE NEGRO SOLDIER POLICY.

We have given above the whole of Mr. LINCOLN's epistle to the Utica-Springfield meetings—not that it was necessary for our purpose, but that his friends may not say we have done him injustice by partial extracts. He is here on record as wedded to the policy which the radicals forced him into.

The object of this policy lies deeper than a desire to render aid to white soldiers. This might have been done by employing the negroes as servants and helpers, in camps and ditches. In fact, this is the only way that negroes might be serviceable, to which no one has objected. But Sambo must be used as a *political* machine, and hence he must wear the blue uniform, and become subservient to the military power—not that he has or can do any military service, commensurate with the trouble and expense of his equipment and military training. No, the negro as a soldier has made no record in this war, notwithstanding we are told the nation has expended millions for arming, equipping, feeding and clothing some 200,000 negro troops, be the same more or less, and we do not remember to have heard of Sambo. amid the din of battle, save at Milliken's Bend, where a black regiment was forced to the front by a wall of bayonets, in white hands, behind them. True, we have heard in the radical papers of wonderful prodigies performed by the sable sons of Mars, and some officials have even gone so far as to extol their merits above that of the white soldiers, but in all this, they have failed to furnish us with the *history* of facts and circumstances.

But, do you ask how the negro as a soldier, is to be used to favor political objects? Let us see.

The Proclamation did not assume to liberate slaves everywhere. Certain districts were excluded. Slavery was still unmolested in the loyal Border States. The radicals insisted on some *coup de main* to abolish slavery in the border States. How could this be done? Why by the black soldier system. How by that? Let us see. The moment the black soldier system had been established, thousands of enlisting agents took up their positions in the border States, where they went to enlisting the slaves of loyal masters. They created alarm and brought out protests from the Governors of Maryland and Kentucky, but all to no purpose. The enlistments went on, and the general promise was thrown out, as a tub to the whale, that the slaves thus taken should be paid for. But this did not satisfy the loyal slaveholder. He saw in the movement an undisguised effort and determination to abolish slavery in all the localities excepted by the Proclamation, by *indirection*—a kind of whip-the devil-round-the-stump game.

The radicals saw that if they could, under the protecting ægis of the "military power" seize all the able-bodied slaves in the border States as soldiers, the people from necessity would give up the balance, and thus the negro soldier business would have answered its end. But as for negroes fighting or being of actual use in military operations, the evidence is entirely wanting. If this theory does not solve the negro soldier scheme, then it must remain unsolved till the end of time, for from past history, we have no data to solve it on the *black fighting* hypothesis.

The following from the New York *Tribune,* of December, 1863, is unequivocal, and pledges the President to abolish slavery in all places, without a why or wherefore:

"Slavery, the wicked, wanton fomenter of this horrible strife, must die, or the peace will be but a hollow, delusive truce, to be soon followed by another desolating war. * * * Such is our President's programme, and we indorse every word of it."

A BILL TO ABOLISH THE CONSTITUTION.

As carrying out this view, Senator JOHN P. HALE introduced the following in the Senate, December 14, '63:

"*Be it enacted, &c.,* That hereafter all persons within the United States of America are equal before the law; and all claims to personal service, except those founded on contract and the claim of a parent to the service of a minor child, and service rendered in pursuance of sentence for the punishment of crime, be and the same are hereby forever abolished, anything in the constitution or laws of any State to the contrary notwithstanding."

THE PROCLAMATION IN ENGLAND.

One of the main arguments in favor of the Proclamation, by the radicals, was, that it would bring the English people to our aid; but the following, from the London *Herald,* does not wear so favorable an aspect. That paper says:

"Another symptom of increasing ferocity—a new source of frightful crime, on the one side, and provocation to horrible vengeance on the other, [just what we have seen as the father of all the difficulties in reference to exchange of prisoners, whereby thousands of our brave men have been forced to starve and rot in Southern prisons, all on account of the negro punctilio red-tape-ism of our Government,] is disclosed in the demand made in New York for the Abolitionist Proclamation. So far as its nominal purport goes. this would be as futile as Mr. Lincoln's other edicts. Before he can emancipate the Southern negroes, he must conquer the South [just what he himself said to the Chicago divines]. But the demand is not made with a view to the real liberation of the slaves. It is meant to diminish the rebel army, by calling away many officers and men to the defense of their homes. [This failed entirely.] The object is not negro emancipation, but servile insurrection [this was argued by the New York *T ibune*]—not the manumission of slaves, but the subornation of atrocities, such as those at Cawnpore and Meireut against women and children of Southern families.

"For the negro the Northerners care nothing, except as a possible weapon in their hands, by which the more safely and effectually to wreak a cruel and cowardly vengeance on the South. Inferior in every respect to the Sepoys, the negro race would, if once excited to rebellion, outdue them in acts of carnage, as they would fall below them in military courage. They may be useful as assassins and incendiaries; as soldiers against the dominant race, they would be utterly worthless. Fortunately, there is no probability that the North will be able to kindle any general or extensive negro insurrection. On the lines of the Mississippi there might be occasional outbreaks and numerous desertions; a good many plantations might be fired, and a number of fugitives might be added to the Federal army. But neither the issues of the struggle, nor the fate of the servile race would be thereby altered. The war would only be made more ferocious, and the condition of the slaves more miserable. * * These new Abolitionists do not conceal their motives; they have not the decency to pretend conviction; they seek, avowedly, nothing but an instrument of vengeance on their enemy, and an instrument so dastardly, involving the commission of outrages so horrible. that even a government which employs a Mitchell and a Butler must shrink from such a load of infamy."

OPINIONS OF THE ABOLITIONISTS OF ENGLAND.

The London correspondent of the New York *Times* (Radical) wrote as follows to that paper, in 1862:

"We have still another object of British sympathy—the everlasting negro. We have the most doleful pictures of his unhappy situation, deprived of his Southern home and its comforts. and turned out to freeze and starve. Rejected from some of the Free States, and scorned in all, what is the poor negro to do? *It is a fact that the leading Abolitionists in England are reproaching the National Government for bringing upon the negroes the calamity of sudden and unprovided freedom.* It is costing millions—tasking the resources of a great nation—to feed the idle operatives in Lancashire How then. they say, can you provide for four millions of slaves, who become free by the Proclamation of President Lincoln on the 1st of January? *The great mass of the abolitionists in England would ra her trust the negroes to their masters,* than have them run the chances—or rather, meet, what they consider, *the certain miseries of a forced and immediate emancipation. The abolition policy of the Government has utterly failed,* so far as I have been able to learn, of finding *any sympathy on this side of the Atlantic.*"

MR. WILBERFORCE ON THE PROCLAMATION.

Mr. WILBERFORCE, son of the late and famous Emancipationist, lately wrote a letter to the London *Times*, in which he says:

"Allow me then to say, that if my father's life had been prolonged, I am certain on the one hand that his abhorance of slavery, and zeal for emancipation would not have lessened, and equally certain on the other hand, that he would have considered it a grievous crime to stir up insurrection and civil war; doubly so if it were done, not from mistaken benevolence, but from selfish political purposes. This, as Mr. Bexton truly says, is the only meaning of Mr. Lincoln's proclamation, if it has any meaning at all."

WENDELL PHILLIPS ON THE RAMPAGE.

WENDELL PHILLIPS made a speech at the Cooper Institute, December 22, 1863. We select the *cream* of said speech:

* * * " What Grant has not done he will do. Not now. Every ounce of food his men eat is brought to them fifteen miles over the hills, and that arm of the service needs rest as well as the others. He may not be heard from for sixty or ninety days. But be assured of this—he won't sit down and dig. [Long continued applause.] When he does move, it will be to see the South retreat to the real Gulf States—Georgia, Alabama, Mississippi. They have no means of bringing food to this army, and the army must go to the food. But when they have reached it, when five or six millions of men make up their minds that the forlorn spot is reached, then be sure the war is not yet ended. The South is a brave people. Four years ago I said to you under this roof, "The South is no coward," and you laughed at me. You know now, that however deluded, the South does believe a lie, and is willing to fight for it. The last forlorn refuge for such a people is a bloody fight. The war does not touch its end, and yet its end is certain, and we may now read it in the light of our power and our own perseverance. The Union is to be reconstructed with a cement that laughs all interference to scorn. Daniel Webster said the cement of the Union was the fugitive Slave bill. Sin never cemented anything. The cement of this Union is to be the mutual respect of the sections, bred of that blood which has mingled on bravely contested fields. The South thought of the Yankees as one who knew only how to cheat—she met him at Chattanooga and changed her mind The North thought of the South as only gasconade—she has struggled with her for four years, and learned to respect her sincerity if not her intelligence. Out of that mutual respect is to grow a Union as indestructible and as indivisable as the granite that holds up the continent. The question is here at the North, how far we will go. All civil wars are ended by compromise. There never was a civil war in history in which one party gained a clear victory. The only question is, what shall we compromise on? Once launched on the stormy, turbid waters of politics, you cannot tell.—

To-day the helm is in our hands, and you and I, if faithful, can say this to the nation, and the future: You may compromise when and where you please, with one exception, and that is, that the tap root of slavery shall be cut. [Applause.] Let thirty Senators and Representatives enter Congress under the proclamation, and what will be their first attempt? It will be, gentlemen, fund our debt. Your Representatives will want a tariff to pay Mr. Chase's interest. The reply of the South will be, "Granted, provided that you tack on to it, by way of rider, a tariff that will pay our interest too; only upon that condition shall you have a policy that is not tantamount to repudiation." Do you say that is not possible? Let me see. The builders of private ships in England have some $100,000,000 of this scrip. Suppose they come to the doors of your reconstructed Congress and say, "This paper is not worth five cents on the dollar, but we will give you $20,000,000 of it if you will make the other $80,000,000 worth par." Did you ever know a Congress that could not be bought for $20,000,000? Do you ever hope to see one? The first item of compromise, then, will be three or four thousand million dollars debt. I do not object to that particularly myself. It is the atonement which God demands of this nation for twenty years of sin. No sin is washed out in words. You cannot cheat the devil of his due. Our fathers sinned against that victim race; and God mortgages the hand of every living man, and every child that is to be born for the next half century, to atone for the nation's iniquity. There will be other compromises. One is the first element of Mr. Lincoln's project of reconstruction, which is this: He puts his own act and all the acts of Congress at the feet of the Supreme Court, and says the South is to swear to support the various acts of the government so far as the Supreme Court holds them to be valid. I do not say that he could say anything else. I am only telling you what he does say. What does his proclamation of January 1st, 1863, mean? Some members of the Cabinet say it means that any negro that can get hold of it is free. Mr. Chase says that every negro down to the Gulf that ever sees the flag is free. I asked the shrewdest member of the House of Representatives what he would give for the proclamation before the Supreme Court? "Little or nothing," he said. A prominent New England Senator said to me the greatest danger to the proclamation was from the Supreme Court. Leading Republicans in my State say there is no law in it, that it is not worth the paper on which it is written. Mr. Lincoln says, as he ought to say, nothing. He cannot say anything. The meaning of that proclamation nobody knows until the Supreme Court has decided it. In other words, the proclamation of January 1, 1863, is to be filtered through the secession heart of a man in Baltimore, but his soul, if he has got one, is in Richmond. [Laughter.] It is to pass the ordeal of a Bench of Judges who made the D ed

Scott decision, and announced that a negro has no rights that a white man is bound to respect. It is to pass the ordeal of a set of Judges the majority of whom came out of the wickedness of Polk, Pierce, and Buchanan; and of the only two who refused to sanction the Dred Scott decision, one is in his grave, and the other has resigned. God help the negro if he hangs on Roger B. Taney for his liberty.— [Sensation.] I am not here to speak of the portentous power of the Supreme Court. You know what it is, the Gibraltar of our system, the point where our democratic machine touches nearest to despotism. Taking our system of bowing to precedents, it is a system in which the opinion of the present day is checkmated by the prejudices of men who were appointed fifty years ago, and who are pledged to respect the prejudices of men who have been in their graves a hundred years. That is the meaning of the Supreme Court of the United States. That is the only hope that Mr. Lincoln's project holds out to you of the validity of the act of Congress and of his proclamation of September and January last. As Commander-in-Chief and author of these two instruments. I am not finding fault with Mr. Lincoln. Suppose you are tenant in a house. Your chimney smokes; but your lease is out in thirty days. You throw up the window to make a draft. But the landlord remodels the chimney. Mr. Lincoln is a tenant at will, and goes out shortly. His proclamation is throwing up the window to make a draft. As the landlord, let the nation say we want him to remodel the chimney. We want a platform which the Supreme Court cannot touch. [Applause.] As the *quid pro quo* for this war, I want something of which I know the value to-day without consulting Judge Wayne, Judge Grier, Judge Taney, Judge Clifford, or Judge Catron, secessionists from the top of their heads to the soles of their feet. [Hisses.] If you don't think so, go and examine them; that's all. [Hisses and applause.] If they have reformed and repented, I shall be glad to know it. I judge them by the record—by their decisions. The New York *Times* asks me to-day whether I would not trust the negro where all white men have been trusted for the last seventy years. If I had no protection but the bond of the Supreme Court, I should have been in jail seven years ago; and as for the negro, that court has announced that he has no rights white men are bound to respect. What I ask of Mr. Lincoln in his behalf is, an amendment of the constitution, which his advice to congress would pass in 60 days, that hereafter there shall be neither slavery nor involuntary servitude in any State of this Union. [Prolonged applause.] Mr. Seward wants the Mississippi chairs—the Senate chamber filled. So do I. He is for having them filled as they are. I am for making them so hot that a slaveholder cannot sit in them.''

THE NEW YORK TRIBUNE ON SERVILE INSURRECTION.

In this connection, a word from the New York *Tribune*, may not be out of place, as a foundation for the articles just quoted from the London *Herald*. The *Tribune* says:

"The rebels, not with the phantom, but with the *reality of servile insurrection*, by the sudden appearance in arms, in the region selected, of a body of no less than 5000 negroes, properly led by whites, and supported by regular troops, communication has been opened and kept up for some time by trustworthy contrabands with the bondsman of the *chosen field of operations*, and they know when the liberating hosts will appear, and *are ready to raise in thousands, and swell it to a wave so mighty that it will sweep both rebellion and slavery out of existence*, wherever it may roll.''

THE PROCLAMATION CONFESSED A FAILURE.

The Springgeld (Mass.) *Republican*, a warm administration paper, frees its mind after the following fashion, in reference to the utter failure of the proclamation, March, 1863:

"A great many expectations have been disappointed, and a great many confident predictions have failed of realization in the progress of this war. In nothing has the disappointment been greater than in the results expected from the emancipation war policy, by those most clamorous for it. They were very certain that the proclamation would give the Union cause a quick and sweeping triumph, and the President was fiercely denounced by politicians and persons of his own party, for allowing the 'sacrifice of Northern men' to go on when with a stroke of his pen he could remove the 'cause' of rebellion, and make it impotant for mischief. It was said that as soon as liberty should be proclaimed to the negroes, we should see the Southern soldiers scattering to their homes to look after the chattels and the negroes generally revolting and hastening to enlist under the standard of the Union, and so the necessity for further fighting on our part was to be removed. The predictions were made and repeated with so much confidence, that before the President issued his proclamation, many of his own party had come to consider him guilty, almost to the extent of treason, in delaying to speak the word which was to act like magic in the salvation of the Union. The style of menace in which the President was addressed on the subject is fresh in public recollection, although some who used it would now be glad to have it forgotten.

"Well, it is more than five months since the President announced his intention to proclaim emancipation, and two months since the proclamation was formally made, and the negroes still remain quietly on the Southern plantations. The rebel armies have not dispersed to hunt flying negroes, but are larger and stronger than ever before. The market price of negroes is at its highest—the negroes within our lines show no passionate eagerness to fight, and even Gen. Hunter has been obliged to resort to *forcible conscription* to fill up his negro regiments, and that too, where the expedient of making negro soldiers has been longest in operation. Neither are the promises of the dreadful effect of the proclamation upon the people of the North realized Gov. Andrew's 'swarms' do not throng the roads of Massachusetts, and volunteering has been at a stand still. As to the political effect of the proclamation, at the North, nothing can be said. The enthusiasm it has evoked, *has all been on the wrong side*, and some of the most ardent advocates of emancipation have been so disheartened by this, that they began before the proclamation had been out a month, to talk about letting the South go, if we cannot subdue the rebellion before May. [That was Greeley.] The pretext of our malcontents, that the proclamation is powerless, because it does not declare free the slaves in the loyal states, is not even specious; it is merely absurd."

CALEB B. SMITH PLEDGES THE ADMINISTRATION.

During the time which the Hon. CALEB B. SMITH acted as Mr. LINCOLN's Secretary of the *Interior*, he addressed the Republicans of Providence, R. I., and from that address we make the following selections, to show what the "Government" pledged its good faith to the people on this subject:

"It is the question of domestic servitude that has rent asunder the temple of liberty. What is there in this question of slavery that *should* divide the people? [Sure enough.] * * * The theory of the Government is, that the states are *sovereign* within their proper spheres. The Government of the United States has no more right to interfere with the institution of slavery in South Carolina, than it has to interfere with the peculiar institutions of Rhode Island, whose benefits I have enjoyed to-day. * * * It has been my fortune to be selected as one of his [the President's] constitutional advisers. I have had the honor of being connected with this Administration since its commencement, and I tell you to-night, that you cannot find in South Carolina a man more anxious, religiously and scrupulously, to observe all the features of the Constitution, relating to slavery, than Abraham Lincoln. * * * My friends, we make no war upon Southern institutions. We recognize the right of South Carolina and Georgia to hold slaves, if they desire them. But, my friends, we appeal to you to uphold the great honor of our glorious country, and to leave the people of that country to settle their domestic matters according to their own choice, and the exigencies which the times may present. * * *

"It *is not the province of* the Government of the United States to enter into a crusade against the institution of slavery. I would proclaim to the people of the states of this Union, the right to manage their institutions in their own way. I know that my fellow citizens will recognize that as one fundamental principal on which we commenced this contest.

Let us not give our opponents any reason to complain of in this respect. Let us not bring to bear upon them the *power of despotism*, but the power of a people of a Republican Government, where the people rule."

Mr. SMITH was no doubt honest in the above sentiments, but the utterance of them cost him his seat in the Cabinet, for from that day the radicals gave the President no rest until his exodus was made certain.

We have thus given a pretty full chapter of the rise, progress and decline of the Administration, in its negro policy, and if that policy shall have no worse effect than to demonstrate the inconsistencies and idiosyncrasies of hotbed politicians, then we may thank God for the power of a saving grace, that can check the most sinister machinations of fallen man!

MR. MADISON ON EMANCIPATION.

Mr. MADISON, the "father of the Constitution," in a debate on this subject, in the Constitutional Convention of 1787, used the following language. [*See Elliott's Debates, v.* 3, *p.* 621.

"I was struck with surprise when I heard him (Mr. Wythe) express himself alarmed with respect to the emancipation of slaves. Let me ask, if they (the North) should even attempt it, if it would not be *a usurpation of power. There is no power to warrant it in that paper*, (the Constitution). If there be, I know it not. But, *why* should it be done? Says the honorable gentleman, 'for the general welfare;—it will infuse strength into our system.' Can any member of this committee suppose that it (emancipation) will increase our strength? Can any one believe that the American congress will come into a measure which will strip them of their *property*, and discourage and alienate the affections of five-thirteenths of the Union? Why was nothing of this sort arrived at before? I believe such an idea never entered into an American heart, nor do I believe it ever will enter into the heads of those gentlemen who substitute unsupported suspicions for reasons."

This was the harshest language used by Mr. MADISON in all the debates of the first Constitutional Convention. The idea of emancipation was so absurd to him that he could not conceal his indignation, notwithstanding he was at that time making a Constitution for a state of war, as well as peace, with the experience of a long and bloody struggle before him.

LORD DUNMORE'S PROCLAMATION.

During the Revolution, Lord DUNMORE issued a proclamation to excite the negroes against the Colonists. We refer the reader to

SCRAPS FROM MY SCRAP-BOOK.   175

the Eighth Volume of BANCROFT's History of the United States, where the historian thus sets forth the matter:

"Encouraged by 'this most trifling success,' Dunmore raised the King's flag, and, publishing a proclamation, which he had signed on the 7th, he established martial law, required every person capable of bearing arms, to resort to his standard, under penalty of forfeiture of his life and property, and declared freedom 'to all indentured servants, negroes or others, appertaining to rebels,' if they would 'join for the reducing the colony to a proper sense of its duty.' The effect of this invitation to convicts and slaves to rise against their masters, was not limited to their ability to serve in the army. 'I hope,' said Dunmore, 'it will oblige the rebels to disperse to take care of their families and property.' (But it didn't.) The men to whose passions he appealed were either criminals, bound to labor in expiation of their misdeeds, or *barbarians*, some of them freshly imported from Africa, with tropical passions seething in their veins, and frames rendered strong by abundant food and out-of-door toil; they formed the majority of the population—at tide-water—and were distributed among the plantations, in clusters, around the wives and children of their owners, so that danger lurked in every house. * * * At Dunmore's proclamation, *a thrill of indignation* ran through Virginia, *effacing all differences of party*, and rousing one strong, impassioned purpose to drive away the insolent power by which it had been put forth. * * *

"But, in truth, the cry of Dunmore did not rouse among the Africans a passion for freedom, [nor does it to-day.] To them, bondage in Virginia, was not a lower condition of being than their former. They had no regrets for ancient privileges lost; their memories prompted no demand for political changes; no struggling aspiration of their own had invited Dunmore's interposition; no memorial of their grievances had preceded his offer. [And this was precisely the case with Mr. Lincoln's proclamation.]

"What might have been accomplished had he been master of the country, and had used an undisputed possession to embody and train the negroes, cannot be told; but as it was, though he boasted that they flocked to his standard, [just as the abolitionists do now,] none combined to join him from a longing for an improved condition, or even for ill-will to their masters."

THURLOW WEED'S PREDICTION.

THURLOW WEED, in a letter to the New York *Commercial Advertiser*, thus records his predictions relative to the "Bull against the Comet."

"The solicitude is now intensified by the attitude, arrogance and insolence of abolition journals, representatives and lecturers. In assuming to discover, in the President's proclamation a 'new policy,' and one which converts and perverts the war, waged in defense of the Government and Union into a crusade against slavery, *I see sure and swift destruction!* In Wendell Phillips' avowal, that the abolition motto is '*Death to Slavery or the Union*,' endorsed by the *Tribune* and *Independent*, I see, unless the treasonable sentiment be rebuked, a *divided North*, [The very thing we charged as the object,] with two-thirds of the people against this fanaticism."

MR. LINCOLN ON FEDERAL AUTHORITY.

On the 6th of March, 1862, Mr. LINCOLN transmitted to Congress his message, recommending remuneration for slaves by appropriation from Congress, &c., in which he speaks of initiating an emancipation scheme on the free will basis of state action and national pecuniary aid. He says:

"I say initiatory, because, in my judgment, gradual and not sudden emancipation is better for all. In the mere financial or pecuniary view, any member of Congress, with the census tables and the Treasury reports before him, can readily see for himself how very soon the current of expenditure of the war would purchase, at a fair valuation, all the slaves in any named state. Such a proposition on the part of the General Government sets up *no claim or right by Federal authority to interfere with slavery within state limits*, referring as it does the absolute control of the subject in each case to the state and its people immediately interested."

THE CHICAGO PLATFORM.

The above when read in connection with the following plank in the Chicago Platform, does not well comport with the subsequent action of the President and his friends. This is the 4th plank in said platform:

"4. That the maintenance *inviolate* of the rights of the *States*, and especially the right of each State to order and control its own domestic institutions, according to its own judgment, *exclusively*, is essential to that balance of power, *on which the perfection and endurance of our political fabric depends*."

Here it is laid down as a political axiom that the "maintenance inviolate" of the right of each State to regulate its own domestic concerns in its own way, is *essential*—that is—necessary—to that "balance of power" on which the "*perfection and endurance* of our political fabric depends."

Well, as this right is now disputed by the radicals, and ignored by the Administration, we have a right to infer that it is in contemplation to destroy the "perfection and endurance" of our political fabric. In other words, to dissolve the Union. For, if the Republican *thesis* was right in 1860, their conduct now is not only wrong, but aims at dissolution, for are they not destroying what they declared in 1860 to be "*essential*" to Union? No other corolary can be drawn from the proposition and conduct of the Administration.

POSTMASTER GENERAL BLAIR AS A WITNESS.

Fortunately we were not left to our own opinion or *ipse dixit*, but will refer the reader to the speech of Post Master General BLAIR, at Rockville, Md., October 3, 1863. His speech seems to have been in reply to the Article in the *Atlantic Monthly*, by CHARLES SUMNER, which advocated the "State Suicide" doctrine. We do not endorse *all* that Mr. B. says, but give his reasons in full, that they may be compared with the conduct of the Administration, to which he is officially attached:

SPEECH OF HON. MONTGOMERY BLAIR AT ROCKVILLE, MD., OCT. 3, 1863.

"*Fellow Citizens:*—I congratulate you on the hopes just inspired by the circumstances under which we have met to-day. The progress of our armies gives us good reason for believing that peace will soon be restored to our country, and that when it comes it will be an enduring peace, because obtained by preserving the integrity of the government, and because it will be followed by the early suppression from our system of the institution of domestic slavery, which occasioned most of the difficulty in the founding of the government, and has been the only cause which ever seriously endangered its existence. But even whilst we are indulging in these well founded hopes that our country is saved from destruction by rebellion, we are menaced by the ambition of the ultra abolitionists, which is equally despotic in its tendencies, and which, if successful, could not fail to be alike fatal to republican institutions.

"The slaveocrats of the South would found an oligarchy, a sort of feudal power, imposing its yoke over all who tilled the earth over which they reigned as masters. The abolition party, whilst pronouncing phillippics against slavery, seek to make a caste of another color, by amalgamating the black element with the free white labor of our land, and so to expand far beyond the present confines of slavery the evil which makes it obnoxious to republican statesmen, and now, when the strength of the traitors who attempted to embody a power out of the interest of slavery to overthrow the government is seen to fail, they would make the manumission of the slaves the means of infusing their blood into our whole system by blending with it "amalgamation, equality and fraternity." The cultivators of the soil must then become a hybrid race, and our government a hybrid government, ending, as all such unnatural combinations have ever done, in degraded, if not in abortive generations, and making serfdom for the inferior caste—the unmixed blood of the conqueror race inevitably asserting a despotism over it. To facilitate this purpose a concerted appeal is now made to the people of the free states through the press to open the way to this daring innovation, beginning in the Southern states, unhappily now brought under the ban by the Calhounite conspirators.

"With this view it is proposed to declare the State governments vacated in that section where they are restored to the Union, and all the loyal men of the South whom the treason of Presidents Pierce and Buchanan, in complicity with southern traitors, has subjugated, are to come under absolute submission to the representatives of the Northern States in Congress, without vestige of a State right, a State law, or constitution to protect them—nay, not even the franchise of a vote to send a solitary representative to the Legislative body to which their destiny is to be committed. Simultaneously three leading organs—the *Chronicle*, at Washington, boasting a sort of official sanction; the *Missouri Democrat*, the ultra abolisher of Fremont graft, at St. Louis, and the *Atlantic Monthly*, which lends to the parent stock, at Boston, all it can boast of literary strength and elegance—have struck the key-note of revolution, the sheer abolition of State constitutions in the region suffering under the rod of the rebellion.

"The article in the *Atlantic Monthly* may justly be quoted as the programme of the movement. It presents the issue on which the abolition party has resolved to rest its hope of setting up its domination in this country. The boldness that marks the announcement of its design to assume for Congress absolute power over the states recovered to the Union, without allowing representation for them in the body, argues much for the confidence of those who never attained an ounce of political weight until they threw themselves into the scale of the republican party adjusted at Chicago, wherein state rights, even the most doubtful one asserting exclusive power over the subject of slavery was recognized.

[¶] ["And now in this discussion (says the new ukase) we are brought to the practical question which is destined to occupy so much of public attention. It proposed to bring the action of Congress to bear directly upon the rebel states. This may be by the establishment of provisional governments, under the authority of Congress, or simply by making the admission or recognition of the states depend upon the action of Congress. The essential feature of the proposition is, that Congress shall assume jurisdiction of the rebel states."

"One would suppose that "the action of Congress" had been already brought to bear "directly on the rebel states," by the armies which Congress has raised and sent against the rebel states; or to use exact language, the states in which the rebels enforce a usurpation over the loyal people.

"But it is not over the states in the hands of rebels that the abolition programme proposes to assume jurisdiction; but over the states when wrested from the usurpation of rebels, and in condition to be restored to the control of the loyal people. Against these political military bodies now exerting the force of government in that portion of the United States in which the rebellion reigns for the time triumphant, the Union wages war, but it does not wage war upon the loyal people, upon the constitution they recognize—or the true constitution—upon the pirit and forms of their government, upon its archives or property. On the contrary, the whole system as part of the Union subsists and is respected by the nation, and only remains in abeyance where the rebels hold sway by force of arms. It is against this rebel organization, against the persons and property, the means and instrumentalities of the rebels, that the United States make war, in defence of the loyal men and loyal governments.

"The assumption that certain states of the south are extinct—annihilated by the rebellion—and that a Congress composed of representatives from the states in which the rebellion does not exist has the right to consider the sister Republics where the insurrection for the moment prevails as dead bodies, to be disposed of as they please when they get possession, *is abhorrent to every principle on which the Union was founded*. No member of the Union, nor the government of the whole, can act upon any of the States in the mode prescribed by the constitution. They are all bound to guarantee to each a republican form of government, and that is a government adopted by the people, for it is the essence of republican government that it shall emanate from the people of the State.

"The Federal Government derives its power from the same source, and it is on the people and through the people that it must act as a nationality, and not upon the states, blotting them out of existence by a supposition, while their constitutions, laws, archives, property, all survive, and a loyal people to give them activity the moment that constraint is thrown off. The abolition programme assumes, on the contrary, that because violence has trodden down state governments and state rights, they have ceased to exist; that a loyal people. in whom they still survive and have being, and to whom the United States stands pledged to guarantee them forever, must also have perished, and that a Congress of the other states may step in and take absolute authority over the whole region, as vacated states, territory. and legislate for it:—founding this new assumption upon fictions as absurd as those on which rebellion founds itself.

"The abolition programme ascribes all our calamities to 'the pestilent pretension of State rights.' The discontent with the treaty between the United States and Great Britain, called Jay's treaty, originated in 'pestilent state rights.' The famous resolutions of Virginia and those of Kentucky usually known as the resolutions of '98, sprung from 'pestilent state rights.' The Missouri controversy about the prohibition of slavery, the first South Carolina outbreak, the contest in Congress about abolition petitions, about the recognition of Hayti, about Texas, about the Wilmot proviso, about the admission of California, the discussion of the compromise of 1850, the Kansas question—'all this audacity was in the name of state rights.' If we except from this aggravated list charged to 'pestilent state rights,' the incipient treason of the South Carolina ordinance, there was nothing beyond the wholesome discussions incident to parties in free governments, in which state rights made no resistance to national authority. This denunciation of the party influence derived through appeals to state rights during this eventful and prosperous period of our history, proves that it *proceeds from a party hostile at heart to free debate*, the canvasses, the active employment of the checks and balances of our complicated system of national and state governments which are *essential to the vitality of all its parts*, and enables all to take a just share of the power which moves the whole machinery. In their view our history is a pestilence from Washington's time to this hour, when it is proposed to annihilate state rights as the remedy. We are told that this is effected first by 'state suicide.'

"The states themselves committed suicide, so that as states they cease to exist, leaving their whole jurisdiction open to the occupation of the United States under the Constitution."

"Burke is quoted to make good this position.

"When men," says Burke, "therefore break up the original compact or agreement which gives its corporate form or capacity to a state, they are no longer a people.— They have no longer a corporate form or existence," &c.

"The programme adds:

"If that great master of eloquence could be heard, who can doubt that he would blast our rebel states as senseless communities, who have sacrificed that corporate existence which makes them living corporate members of our union of states."

Burke might blast the "rebel States," but would he blast Missouri, Arkansas, Louisiana, Mississippi, Tennessee, and all the rest of that noble sisterhood of States which, with their loyal people, have in succession been trodden under foot by a military force? Have the people who resisted at the polls, and who still resist in arms, united with their brethren under the flag of the Union wherever it appears, sacrificed that corporate existence which identifies themselves and their States as "living component members of our Union?" Is not the Union and its constitution identified as "that corporate existence" with the States which makes them all—those trodden down and those standing up—component members of our Union States? How can the Union, which is the guarantee of the government of every republic of which it consists, admit while it lives that any part of it is dead? It does not admit it. It is at war in every State of the Union at this moment, co-operating with the loyal in each entitled to its special sovereignty, to crush the traitors who violate it. As members of the Union, the States assailed by treason may be said to be paralyzed; but they live in all their vital powers, ready for resurrection, in the persons of their loyal people, the moment the stone is rolled away. The traitors only will have committed political suicide.

"The man recovered from the bite,
The dog it was that died."

"I allow that "it is a patent and undisputed fact that this gigantic treason was inaugurated with all the forms of law," and that "the states pretended to withdraw bodily in their corporate capacities," which is the ground work of the second proposition of the programme, viz:

"That the states, by their flagrant treason, have forfeited their rights as states, so as to be civilly dead."

"But the Federal Government is very far from admitting that "the forms of law" employed by the rebels, or the fact that "the states pretended to withdraw bodily" *affected in the least the legal status of the states in question.* Treason was committed *not by any State*, but by the individuals who made use of the forms of the state governments and attempted to dismember the National Government.— The suggestion that states, guaranteed by the Constitution as under the shield of the Union, can in no way be held responsible for this treason, and subjected to a forfeiture of their rights as a consequence, shows *affinity of the abolitionists to the nullifiers*. Calhoun's whole scheme was based on the proposition they now adopt, that the states could "withdraw bodily in their corporate capacity."

"The true doctrine, as laid down by the fathers of the constitution, is, that the employment of the forms of the state governments, and the pretense of withdrawing them in their corporate capacity out of the pale of the national authority, does not shift the responsibility from the traitors to the people. Hamilton, in the *Federalist*, marks the change on this point effected by the adoption of the constitution. He says:

"The great and radical vice in the construction of the existing Confederation is the principle of legislation for states or governments in their corporate collective capacities, and as contra distinguished from the individuals of whom they consist."

"He emphasizes this proposition in the strongest manner, by the use of capitals, in order to condemn the policy of acting on states instead of criminal individuals of whom they consist.

"The aim of the abolitionists is now to accomplish this very thing *in defiance of the Constitution*. They demand that Congress shall attach the treason in the south, plotted in secret and sprung upon the nation by a body of oath-bound conspirators, to the people of the whole region, and insist that they have forfeited their rights in their corporate and collective capacities for the treason of these individuals. It asserts the power of legislation over the states or governments, instead of applying the law of treason to the guilty individuals to whom alone in the very nature of things it is applicable. No learning is necessary to enable one to see that a *state cannot be guilty of treason* or *any other crime*. Only common sense is wanted to comprehend that guilt cannot be imputed to any but a sentient being. and only common honesty is required to perceive the injustice of disfranchising loyal citizens on account of the offences committed by the disloyal.

"But the manifesto I am considering comes at last to the conclusion that these modes of retiring the states out of the Union are unsatisfactory.

" 'I discard (says the writer) all theory, whether it be of state suicide or state forfeiture, or state abolition, on the one side, or state rights, immortal and unimpeachable, on the other side. Such discussions are only endless mazes in which a whole Senate may be lost.'

"Verily, such contemptuous flinging away of states and state rights as of no better stuff than may be overlaid with cobwebs and dust—such flimsy arguments as state suicide, state forfeiture, state abdication, might, if indulged in, reduce the Senate to a lost condition. And the process of this scheme shows how readily it might be merged into a consolidated head.— Here is the recipe which disposes of states and senators without resorting to the troublesome fiction of state suicide, state forfeiture or state abdications.

"The ukase continues:

"And, in discarding all theory, I discard also the question of *de jure*—whether for example, the rebel states, while the rebellion is flagrant, are *de jure* states of the Union, with all the rights of states. It is enough that, for the time being, and in the absence of a loyal government, they can take no part and perform no function in the Union; so that they cannot be recognized by the national government. The reason is plain. There are in those states no local functionaries bound by constitutional oaths—so that there are, in fact, no constitutional functionaries—and, since the state government is necessarily composed of such functionaries there can be no state governments."

"This is summary reasoning, but it begins by an assumption that there are no other states but rebel states, cutting out of the question the existence of the states de jure, which have subsisted since the foundation of the government to this hour, and the existence of which the United States are bound to guarantee and maintain, and is at this moment fighting the bloodiest battles known to modern annals to support, against the most excuseless treason and shameless counterfeit authority that ever put on the mask of government. It may be readily conceded that 'rebel states' are not de jure states of the Union, with all the rights of states, and that 'as they can take no part and perform no function in the Union, so they cannot be recognized by the general government.' But does it follow that states are wrenched from the Union because the usurpers hold a disputed tottering power within their territorial limits? States every day recognized as states in the Union, states whose constitutions, laws, archives, loyal citizens, public edifices, lands, and properties of all sorts, are recognized and held sacred, not only in the hearts of loyal patriots of this and every other civilized country, but which the government of the nation recognizes as forming a member of it in every official act, and by every officer at home and abroad, who has occasion to refer to them.

"More than a million of brave men have left their homes, and one hundred thousand of them, at least, have laid down their lives to put down the conspirators and lift up the loyal men in whose sacrifice it was designed to sacrifice the Union. To what purpose have our glorious soldiers devoted themselves? To destroy the rights of the true men they went to save, together with the rights of these states consecrated to the Union by memory of the renown that belongs to our history? And on what pretext is it that states which fought the battles of our independence—states older than the Union, and which labored in its construction, are to be disfranchised of the rights that Union is pledged to guarantee to them under a Republican form of government as equal in the Confederation?

"Congress is to take to itself parliamentary powers—disfranchise certain states, declare others to be mere territories, having no government, and this because 'there are in those states no local functionaries bound by constitutional oaths,' so that in fact there are no constitutional functionaries, and since the state government is necessarily composed of such functionaries, there can be no state government. And what fatal results come upon the states from the want of local functionaries bound by constitutional oaths. Therefore, 'no constitutional functionaries!' Therefore, 'no state governments.' And, finally, the want of 'local functionaries bound by constitutional oaths' extinguishes the states in one-third of the Union, and their destiny is sealed with this *pronunciamento*—'the whole broad rebel region is *tabula rasa*, or a clean slate, where Congress, under the constitution, may write the laws.'

"It is strange that a party bases such immense power on such an immaterial fact that it might be mistaken as to the existence of the fact. The states involved in insurrection have multitudes of magistrates, state and United States Judges, and other sworn functionaries, ready to resume their functions the moment the rebel military duress is removed, and the whole machinery of the state governments will be put in motion by the election of representatives and all civil officers as soon as the military power of the Union has accomplished its duties. In the meantime, are not the state governments in the hands of their appropriate functionaries, bound by constitutional oaths, when the army of the nation is in their midst? Then our army and its officers are at this instant executing in all the states proposed to be disfranchised their most appropriate functions in breaking the rebel power and lifting up and invigorating the state authority everywhere.

"In this way the most potent recognition the Union can afford is given to the Union. Not only army and navy and President give this recognition, but Congress, in voting men and money to erect this grand retinue, pays its homage to the endangered States, of whose maimed condition the ultra abolitionists would take advantage to reduce to territories and strip them of the rights of republican government. In this Congress proves its just appreciation of our Federal system as conceived by its authors. Madison, in the *Federalist* says:

"The State governments may be regarded as constituent and essential parts of the Federal government, whilst the latter is no wise essential to the operation or organization of the former. Without the intervention of the State Legislatures, the President of the United States cannot be elected at all. They must in all cases have a just share in his appointment, and will, perhaps, in most cases of themselves determine it," &c.

"The consequence of this imposed as a duty on the part of the general government to each state a guarantee of a republican form of government, which supposes a pre-existing government of the form which is to be guaranteed, and in effecting this guarantee, both Madison and Hamilton unite in saying the Union may interpose in crushing the dominant majority in a state. Madison thus touches this point:

"At first view it might not seem to square with the Republican theory to suppose either that a majority have not the right, or that a minority will have the force to subvert a government, and consequently that the Federal interposition can never be required but when it would be improper. But theoretic reasoning in this as in most cases must be qualified by the lessons of practice. Why may not illicit combinations for purposes of violence be formed as well by a majority of a state, especially in a small state, as by a majority of a county or district of the same state, and if the authority of the state in the latter case to protect the local magistracy, ought not the Federal authority of the state ought in the latter case to protect the local magistracy, ought not the Federal authority in the former to support the state authority? Besides, there are certain parts of state constitutions interwoven with the Federal Constitution that a violent blow cannot be given to the one without communicating the wound to the other," &c.

"He asks again:

"Is it true that force and right are necessarily on the same side in republican governments? May not a minor party possess such a superiority of pecuniary means, of the military talents and experience, or of secret success from foreign powers, as will render it superior also in an appeal to the sword? May not a more compact and advantageous position turn the scale on the same side against a superior number so situated as to be less capable of a prompt and collected exertion of its strength? Nothing can be more chimerical than to imagine that in a trial of actual force victory may be calculated by the rules which prevail in a census of the inhabitants, or which determine an election."

"Hamilton, in his paper, shows the propriety of the Union interposing by force to protect a state government against internal foes, upon the score that usurpers, clothed with the forms of legal autority, can too often crush the opposition in embryo. Against this anticipated danger he points to our happy federation of state governments for safety. He says:

"'Power being almost always the rival of power, the General Government will at times stand ready to check the usurpation of state governments, and these will have the same disposition towards the General Government.—The people, by throwing themselves into either scale, will infallibly make it preponderate. If their rights are invaded by either, they can invoke the aid of the other as the instrument of redress. How wise will it be in them, by cherishing the Union, to preserve to themselves an advantage which cannot be too highly prized.'

"And yet the abolitionists would begin the work of demolishing this system, by disfranchising one throwing out one-third of the states at the very moment the Union is working out the salvation of the nation in the mode prescribed in its charter

"The abolition manifesto protests against "The instant restoration of the old state governments in all their parts through the agency of loyal citizens, who, meanwhile, must be protected in this work of restoration."

"And why may not the loyal citizens perform this most esential and patriotic duty?

"Because," adds the paper, "it attributes to the loyal citizens of a rebel state, however few in numbers—it may be an insignificant minority—a power clearly inconsistent with the received principle of popular government, that the majority must rule. The seven votes of old Sarum were allowed to return two members to Parliament, because this place, once a Roman fort, and afterwards a sheep walk, many generations before, at the early casting of the House of Commons, had been entitled to this representation; but the argument for state rights assumes that all these rights may be lodged in voters as few as ever controlled a rotten borough in England."

"The argument of Madison, which I have already quoted, indicates the principle of the Constitution which sends the masses of the United States into a state to assert the rights of a loyal minority over an usurping majority there. But the sneer at the loyalty of the South in the suggestion of Old Sarum is unjust. Notwithstanding the conspiracy at work in secret societies and in public bodies throughout the United States to undermine the loyalty of the South for thirty years; notwithstanding two Northern Presidents joined this conspiracy—the one wielding the powers of the Federal Government to add Kansas as a state to reinforce it, and the other sending the navy into distant seas to give it security, and the army into the remote West, to be surrendered, with all the posts, forts, navy-yards, mints, munitions of war, custom-houses, national edifices, and wealth of all sorts—thus, in effect, making the nation itself an ally of treason, notwithstanding the President of the United States thus betrayed the states of the South into the hands of the conspirators with the means of the nation to strengthen them in the possession of the governments they usurped; the President declaring by message to Congress, that they could not be coerced, still the traitors could not bring a majority of the voters to the polls in any of the states but South Carolina to countenance the usurpation.

"In Louisiana, Arkansas, Missouri, Kentucky, Tennessee, Maryland and Virginia, a majority voted against secession, in defiance both of the lurking armed conspirators who pervaded the whole South to control its will, and the insulting taunts of the Abolitionists, who now wish to disfranchise them—to 'let them go.' Does it become any party in this country, pretending fealty to republican government, to sneer at a loyalty which has passed through such an ordeal, and which still bears up under the cruelty of an armed tyranny, which has improved on its experience in the school of slavery—treating the loyal men of the South worse than slaves?

"I turn from the abolition programme to that which is presented by President Lincoln. The issue is made; we must choose one or the other. His plan is simple. He would dishabilitate the rebels and their usurpation called a Confederacy of the States, and rehabilitate the loyal men and their States and republican governments. To do this he must break the power of the conspirators; crush or expel them from the region of the insurrection, restoring in the persons of loyal citizens within the confines of their respective states the republican governments which now have their administration committed to our loyal armies and loyal citizens who have their protection. As soon as this protection is needless, the state governments resume their functions under officers chosen by citizens who have been true to it, and by such others as may be comprehended in an amnesty, and who have given in a sincere adhesion to it and the government of the Union and the measures taken in its maintenance.

"Missouri, whose Governor, Legislature and Judicial officers betrayed her, expelled her faithless representatives with the aid of the Federal government, and filled their places with loyal men, abolishing slavery as an earnest of her abhorrence of the means and the ends for which the conspirators against the Union labored. Kentucky, temporarily paralyzed by the treachery of her Governor, was soon put right by the people when furnished with arms by the government, carried to them by the lamented and gallant Nelson. In Maryland the attempt to turn her over to the rebels was crushed by the arrest of treasonable legislators. Virginia was overwhelmed for a time; but Western Virginia, being delivered from the armed brigands, called a convention, elected a Legislature for the whole state (the greater part of it being still held by the rebels), was recognized as the law making power of the whole state, as such divided the state and set up a new state in the west.

"This exemplifies the President's mode of saving the Union. He saves the States, putting the powers of the government as soon as they are redeemed into the hands of loyal men, and then the State resumes its place in the councils of the nation with all its attributes and rights. He has signified his purpose of inviting Tennessee and Louisiana—now in preparation—to follow these examples, and every other State, as soon as it can be rescued from the rebel armies, will be aided to come in and reintegrate the grand family of republics.

"Now, what is the pretext for abandoning this safe and healing policy of the President? So far it has worked well, and secured the approbation of all well-wishers of the country.— The abolition programme shows somewhat of the motive for converting states into territories, and carrying them back into colonial bondage, to take law from Congress without representation. The reasons assigned:

" 'Slavery,' says the programme, 'is impossible within the exclusive jurisdiction of the national government.'

"For many years I have had this conviction, and have constantly maintained it. I am glad to believe that it is impossible, if not expressed in the Chicago platform. Mr. Chase, among our public men, is known to accept it sincerely. Thus, slavery in the territories is unconstitutional; but if the rebel territory falls under the exclusive jurisdiction of the national government, then slavery is impossible there. In a legal and constitutional sense, it will die at once. The air will be too pure for a slave. I cannot doubt but that this great triumph has been already won. The moment that the states fell, slavery fell also, so that without any proclamation of the President, slavery had ceased to have a legal or constitutional existence in every rebel state.

"In concert with the elaborate article in the *Atlantic Monthly*, a department organ, the *Chronicle*, at Washington, strikes the key note of state annihilation, in a leading editorial:

"There is (says this print) a conflict of authorities—of State and Federal authorities—and it is clear that one or the other must be annihilated. If the State succeeds, the Federal authority is gone forever; nothing can restore it; not even the State itself which destroyed it; for in this case the Federal authority would become subordinate to the State authority, and be no government at all. For the same reason, if the Federal authority prevails, and succeeds in putting down the rebellious states, must the authority be destroyed."

And then the case is put of the present conflict:

"In which several states combine against their common Federal Government.

"Here the power to be overcome is not only greater, but, in a moral point of view, far more dangerous to the Federal government. Hence when such a rebellion is subdued, it is not only necessary to destroy the treasonable element in such rebellious state, but also the power which these states had to combine against the Federal authority," &c.

"In conjunction with these movements at Washington and Boston to annihilate the state governments which preceded and helped to create that of the nation itself, the coadjutors of Presidential schemers in St. Louis and throughout Missouri are endeavoring to throw that state into the cauldron of revolution, that it, too, may be annihilated or declared vacated as one or the other of the counts of "state suicide," "state forfeiture," "state abdication," the *"tabula rasa"* or clean slate on which Congress may write the laws it pleases.

"Does not the extreme anxiety evinced in certain quarters in these forces, efforts to prevent the states dropped out of the Union by conspirators from returning under the auspices of the President, the patriotic army of the Republic, and the loyal citizens who would, through them maintain their own and the rights of the states in question indicate something of a design to command a great event in prospect by revolutionary measures. Is a ban upon one-third of the states, marking them for exclusion from the Union, when treason is defeated and the traitors expelled, as just, as wise, as constitutional, as likely to end the troubles of the country, as that marked out and pursued by the President?

"It is manifest now that the President must steer his course through the strong conflicting tides of two revolutionary movements—that of the nullifiers, to destroy the Union and set up a Southern Confederacy, and that of the ultra abolitionists, which has set in to dischanfrize the South on the pretext of making secure the emancipation of the slaves. The attempt of the nullifiers is rebuked from the cannon's mouth, and the proposal of France to secure their object for her friendly mediation is put aside by the President telling the Emperor that he will confer with the rebels through no indirect medium; that Senators and Representatives in Congress coming from the Southern States, and bringing with them an earnest of returning loyalty, will be met as equals and admitted to the councils that are to dispose of the destiny of the nation.

"Alterations in its laws must be made by Congress; changes in the constitution by delegations in convention from all the states, according to the terms of that instrument. This is the final response of the President to the rebels and to the French Emperor. To the revolutionary demand for the disfranchisement of the southern states, the President's reply from his first message to the last, and all his published letters, has been uniform. It is couched in the words I read you from his proclamation:

"Hereafter, as heretofore, the war will be prosecuted for the object of practically restoring the constitutional relation between the United States and each of the states, and the people thereof, in which states that relation is or may be suspended or disturbed."

"The proclamation answers the demands for the enfranchisement of the slaves. It is conceded from the necessity of growing out of the rebellion, and to quell it. But it closes with this salve for the loyal sufferers under this decisive measure:

"The Executive will in due time recommend that all citizens of the United States who have remained loyal thereto throughout the rebellion shall, upon the restoration of relations between the United States and the people, if that relation shall have been suspended or disturbed, be compensated for all losses by acts of the United States, including the loss of slaves."

"The issues are thus made up between the President and the rebels and their foreign sympathizers, who would revolutionize our government to create a separate government in the South, on the one hand, and on the other hand between the President and the ultra abolitionists, who would disfranchise the southern section of our country. It is not improbable that the latter, though aiming at a different result, will be found co-operating in the end with conspirators of the South and their foreign allies. They may prefer parting with the South to partnership and equality under the constitution."

CHAPTER XXVII.

CONFISCATION—VIOLATION OF THE CONSTITUTION, &c.

The Confiscation Scheme...The Constitution Ignored...Testimony of Senator Cowan...Political Extremes Compared...Postmaster General Blair on Secessionists and Abolitionists...Comments of "National Intelligencer"...Senator Doolittle on Colonization and Emancipation...The Three "Solutions": Of Calhoun, John Brown, (the same as Radicals), and Jefferson...Doolittle on Confiscation...Also, on Same and Abolition Denunciations of the "Government"...A Republican Journal on Senator Doolittle.

THE CONFISCATION SCHEME.

We will not offer opinions of our own on this subject, but will be content to favor the reader with a few gems from Republican sources.

Hon. Mr. COWAN, a Republican Senator from Pennsylvania, made a speech in the Senate on the Confiscation bill, on the 4th of March, 1862. We give his remarks at great length, not fearing to be called "traitor," for we quote from one who votes the Republican ticket:

"This bill proposes to go forward and strip the whole population of the South of their property, and reduce them to poverty—and while yet 400,000 of them have arms in their hands. If there is anything calculated to make that entire people our enemies always, it will be the promulgation of such an act as this.—Will they yield to us any sooner in view of such a destruction? What would we ourselves do under any such circumstances? I need hardly ask that question of men who have descended from sires who refused to pay a paltry tax on tea, and from grandsires who raised a revolution rather than pay twenty shillings ship money—that I think was the amount demanded from Hampden—a revolution which cost King Charles' head. No such sweeping measure as this has ever been enacted, even in the days of William the Conqueror. The proud Norman and his barons were content with the fiefs and castles of the Saxon leaders. They did not dare to strip the people of their property, nor even much increase their burdens. They knew that, victorious as they were, they would have involved themselves in a far more dangerous struggle, in which every peasant would have been a principal combattant — The English in their contest with, and bills of attainder against, the Irish never attempted to touch the possessions of the common people—but only the property of the nobles. This bill goes farther, and attempts to confiscate another species of property which cannot be put into the coffers of the conqueror. I mean the property of slaves. I dont intend to stop to discuss the question of property of this kind. It is enough for me to say that all the South seem to agree as to the kind of property with wonderful unanimity, and to resent any interference with it. This bill proposes to liberate 3,000,000 of slaves—truly the most tremendous strike for universal emancipation ever attempted in the world. Indeed, I think it virtually liberates the whole 4,000,000. What is to be the effect of this upon the war? Shall we be stronger, or shall we find that we have only doubled the number of these men in arms against us? They now have no *cause* for rebellion. Will not this furnish them one? [That was precisely what the Radicals were driving at.] Let the loyal men of that section who know them, answer this question. I will abide the answer.

"I submit again that no deliberative Assembly ever before sat in judgment on so stupendous an issue. Yes, as if to blind us still more, this bill has a proposition of still greater difficulty; that is, to take these millions and transfer them to some tropical clime, and to to protect them there with all the rights and guaranties of freemen. *I find this all provided for in a single section, and a single section of nine lines!* Truly, we must recently have transported ourselves from the domain of practical facts and set down in the romantic regions of Eastern fiction Do the advocates of the measure propose to confer upon the President the gold-making touch of Midas? Nothing short of the ring and lamp of Alladin, with their attendant *genii*, would insure the success of such a scheme, unless it is believed that the Treasury note [greenbacks] possesses this power. And even under that supposition, I think the owners of these Southern climes, and the transportation companies, ought to be consulted in regard to the legal tender clause. * * * * Then, again, there is a fourth consideration in this bill, and one of still greater moment, which is, *that it is in direct conflict with the constitution of the United States*, requiring of us, if we pass it, to set aside and ignore that instrument in its most valuable and fundamental provisions—those which guarantee the life and property of the citizen, and those which define the limits and boundaries of the several Departments of this Government. *Pass this bill, and all that is left of the constitution is not worth much*—certainly not worth this terrible war, which we are now waging for it—for be it remembered that this war is waged solely for the preservation of the constitution. [Mr. Cowan must be a Republican copperhead.] I am aware that some think that the Constitution is a restraint upon the conduct of this war, which they suppose could be carried on a great deal better without it. I have no hesitation in saying that no greater mistake has ever been made anywhere. than is made by such people. I am afraid it will amount to a confession that they have not carefully examined the full scope of its provisions. *The greatest danger* is, that these propositions, at the first glance, seem probable, and even plausible. They are not the rolling breakers which every. one may see, *but the sunken rocks, which are all the more dangerous, because they are hidden.* Therefore I am opposed to this bill, and I will proceed to give my reasons, and show, if I can, why I think that in its main provisions, it is unnecessary, impolitic, inexpedient, and, I may add, utterly and totally useless, and I think I can show that the Government has all the power under the Constitution which is necessary to put down this rebellion, and punish the rebels, and that there is not, in reality, any necessity for straining any of its provisions in any way."

Mr. COWAN then goes into a lengthy disquisition, both able and conclusive, to show that the confiscation bill was a clear violation of the Constitution, and that it would weaken, instead of strengthen our cause. We regret that our space will not admit the whole of this able, conservative speech, but we have given enough to show the drift of the honorable Senator's argument.

We know that with a certain class of radical disunionists it is useless to talk about the Constitution. One might as well attempt to whistle down a whirlwind. The radicals are mad. Flushed with power and gorged with spoils, they are determined to break up the Union. It is, in fact, broken up, and never can be restored, except by and through the conservative element of the country. If they continue in power, all such conservative Republicans as Senator COWAN must be jostled aside, to make room for some "first rate second rate" demagogue. Alas, our Constitution is no more. Its demise has been predicted and pronounced by the ablest men that belong to the reigning traitorous dynasty.

POLITICAL EXTREMES COMPARED.

Metaphors are sometimes very useful in illustrating ideas, causes and effects. The Republican *politician* sometimes feels insulted if you call him an Abolitionist, though that reticence is now wearing off, since leading Republicans (Gov. Stone, of Iowa, for *e. g.*) admit this is "an Abolition war." But, as the Republicans and Abolitionists have *acted together* and voted together since 1854, and all now pursue the policy and dogmas that distinguished the Abolisionists years ago, we feel justified in using the metaphor of Col BENTON, who said that the Abolitionists and Republicans were like a pair of shears, working on a common fulcrum, to cut the Union in twain. Doesticks, or some other humorous writer, says there is no more difference between a Republican and an Abolitionist than there is between two links of sausages, made from the same dog! They may also be likened to two persons placed back-to-back at the North Pole, and walking in apparently opposite directions, yet *both* are going *due South*. But, we will let Post Master General BLAIR give his views, which link these two factions with the Southern secession extreme, forming a most baneful trinity.

In Mr. BLAIR's speech at Concord, New Hampshire, he said:

"There are two knots of conspiring politicians at opposite ends of the Union that make slavery a fulcrum on which they would-play see-saw with the Government, and willingly break it in the middle and demolish it to make experiments with the factions in reconstructions suited to their designs, which are only known as hostile to the well-balanced Constitutions inherited by our fathers. The Calhoun and Wendell Phillips Juntos have both sought the accomplishment of their adverse ends by a common means—the overthrow of the Constitution. Calhoun's school would destroy every free principle, because repugnant to the perpetuity and propagation of slavery universally as the only safe foundation of good government—Phillips's school would subject all our systems of goverment to the guillotine of revolutionary tribunals, because they recognise the existence of different races among us, of white, red, and black; because they repudiate the idea of equality and fraternity in regard to citizenship that tends to produce that amalgamation, personal and political, which would make our Government one of mongrel races; and because they authorize legislation, state and national, which may exclude them from taking root in the soil and government of the country. The white man has excluded the Indian race from dominion on this continent, its native-born original inheritor; the African was introduced on it, not as its owner or to give it law, but to be owned and receive law; and under this aspect the white man, as a conqueror, has accommodated the constitutions of the country to his own condition—that of the ruling race. The ground which Wendell Phillips and his followers take is not merely to alter the law and enfranchise the races held under it as inferior to that holding the dominion by right of conquest, but to abolish the constitutions which recognise that right as established, and admit to equal participation those races hitherto excluded as inferiors."

After remarking, says the National *Intelligencer*, that the Free States of the North exclude the manumitted slaves from their soil, avowing the abhorrent feeling of caste as an insuperable bar to the association on any terms, much less of equality, Mr. Blair asks how it can be expected that the people of the Southern States will acquiesce in arrangements which proceed on the assumption that this excommunicated race, surrendered by them as slaves, should be retained, nevertheless, among them, and admitted as equals and as partners in political power, in defiance of the Constitution of the United States, and the laws even of the Northern States, which brand them with the badge of inferiority and political disability? He adds:

"Would not the inextinguishable memory of wrongs on one side, and of admitted mastery on the other, make patient acquiescence on either side impossible? All the bloodiest revolutions of ancient and modern times have been those broached by slaves against enslavers. Our civil war, closing in the manumission of four million of slaves, to take equal rank with six million of enslavers, would be but the prelude to a servile war of extermination. The advocates of this hybrid policy know this, but they think the negro so essential to the selfish purposes of their political ambition that, like Calhoun, they are willing to make him, as well as those who hold him in durance, the victim of their policy."

We place these sayings on record, for the time is at hand when the Democracy can make good use of them.

SENATOR DOOLITTLE ON COLONIZATION AND EMANCIPATION.

Mr. DOOLITTLE, on the 19th of March, 1862, in the United States Senate, delivered the following remarks. Let everybody read them:

"I know it is sometimes said that the objection which is felt on the part of the white population to living side by side on a footing of social and civil equality with the negro race is more prejudice. Sir, it has its foundation deeper; it is in the very instincts of our nature, which are stronger and oftentimes truer than reason itself. Men of wealth and fortune, men of high wrought education, and men of rank and position, who are removed above the trials and sympathies of the great mass of laboring men, may reason and theorize about social and political equality between the white and the colored race; but I tell you as a practical fact, it is simply an impossibility. Our very instincts are against it. Let us look at the facts, and neither deceive ourselves nor deceive anybody else. How do the people of the free states stand on this question? In my state there are so few colored men that there is now no great feeling on the subject one way or the other; but suppose it should now be proposed to distribute the whole negro population equally among the states, which would bring into the state of Wisconsin about one hundred and twenty thousand, say seven thousand to Milwaukee, and from one to two thousand to each of the towns of Racine, Madison, Janesville, Kenosha, Watertown, Oshkosh, Fond du Lac, and other places, what would be the feelings then? What would our people, native and foreign-born, say to that? Sir, they would probably feel and say just what the people of Pennsylvania, Ohio, Indiana and Illinois feel and say on this subject. Illinois has just held a convention and formed a new constitution, which excludes free colored men, as did the old constitution. Indiana has a similar provision, either by constitutional requirement or by legislative enactment. Ohio had until quite recently, a law by which a free colored man was required to give bail for his good behavior. Nor are the people of New England devoid of this same feeling either. By the laws of Massachusetts intermarriages between those races are forbidden as criminal. Why forbidden? Simply because natural instinct revolts against it as wrong. Come down to the practical question whether, if the whole negro population of the United States should be set free, and be apportioned and distributed among the several states, and you would find just as much repugnance in New England as you now see exhibited in Illinois, Indiana, or Pennsylvania. Their humanity would rejoice at their freedom, but their instincts would shrink back at their apportionment.

"Sir, when we come to the thing itself, and look it squarely in the face, it is a very important question what is to be done in relation to this race of people when they are emancipated. Within this District, and within the territories, we have all power and all responsibility. Within the several states, however, it belongs to them and to their people. They have the undoubted right to regulate, as they have always regulated, their own policy upon this subject for themselves. We know how much that policy varies, in free as well as slave states. In some free states they have civil rights alone; in others, political rights, also. In others still, they are forbidden to come at all. The slave states have peculiar policies of their own. In none are free negroes allowed to come. Some will not allow a negro to be emancipated unless he is taken out of the state; and within the last few years some of them have passed most cruel laws to compel those already free to leave the state or be reenslaved and sold at the auction block.

"All this goes to demonstrate that Jefferson knew as much about the question as the new lights of the present day. He, who was himself the author of the declaration of the equal rights of all the races of mankind, declares to you also as a fact indisputable, that the two races upon the same soil, side by side, in anything like equal numbers, cannot and will not live together upon a footing of equality.

"To illustrate this feeling in the slave states still further, I will state another fact not generally known, and I do so upon the authority of Andrew Johnson, of Tennessee, in 1856, when he was Governor, there were fears of a negro insurrection in that state. Large numbers of the non-slaveholding white population called upon him as Governor for arms. For what purpose? To prevent an insurrection of the slaves? This was the alleged purpose; but he ascertained the fact to be that these men were conspiring to massacre the whole negro population in that section of the state, and he was compelled to call out the militia, not to prevent negroes from raising in insurrection, but to prevent the whites from destroying them altogether.

"I know this bill relates only to slaves in the District Columbia, and my amendment to to colonization from this District only; but it naturally opens the whole field of discussion of the true relations of the two races towards each other. Washington, Jefferson, Madison, Monroe, Clay and Jackson, not only loved liberty as ardently as we do, but they understood this question of race in all its bearings. It is well known they all favored emancipation with colonization. I state a fact not generally known, that General Jackson, when President, in Cabinet council, intending to carry out this policy, proposed the purchase of some territory from Mexico, to become the homes of free colored men, to be occupied as a territory for themselves and all who should become emancipated. But the troubles growing out of the treason of Calhoun postponed any definite action.

"But the day for action is at hand; it cannot be postponed. There must be a solution. It belongs, it is true, mainly to the people of the states. Some responsibility, however, rests upon the Federal Government. It has the undoubted power, by treaties with Hayti, Liberia, and other tropical states, to acquire rights of settlement and of citizenship for all free persons of African descent who may desire to migrate to those countries, and thus, with very little expense gain free homesteads for them and their children forever. This would open the way for the slaveholding states, if any of them desire to avail themselves of the opportunity, to emancipate and colonize their slaves, and thus open their own rich fields to be forever the homes of the pure Anglo-Saxon race.

"There are, and there can be, in my judgment but three solutions to this negro question. One is the solution of John Calhoun, one of John Brown, and a third midway and equally removed from both extremes, the solution of Thomas Jefferson.

CALHOUN'S SOLUTION.

"Calhoun and his followers, Toombs and Davis, say, in substance:

"Slavery is a blessing to mankind, black and white.—Extend it everywhere; reopen the slave trade, bring all Africa into Slavery, to christianize and civilize the negro race; buy if you can, if not, seize Cuba and all central and trophical America; plant slavery all around the Gulf of Mexico and the Carribbean Sea, until the slaveholding aristocracy, proclaiming 'cotton as king,' reaching through the valley of the Orinoco to the valley of the Amazon, shall shake hands with the slaveholding empire of Brazil. Then shall slavery, the great Dagon at whose shrine we worship, hold within its embrace a monopoly of the sugar and the cotton of the world."

"This is the solution of southern fanaticism; this is the dream of southern mad ambition.— It is a gigantic dream. Could they have held the Government for one or two administrations more, they would have struggled to realize it.

But the power was wrested from their hands. Their dream is broken, and for that they make war upon the Government they could not hold.

JOHN BROWN'S SOLUTION.

"The second is John Brown's solution. It is based on this idea—that all the negro population of the United States shall be instantly set free, by act of Congress, or by arms, where they now are, side by side with their masters, throughout all the slave states, and placed on a footing of equality, entitled to all the rights of manhood, civil and political of the citizens of those states; at once trampling down the rights of the states, and producing a system of equality which would bring the laboring white man and the laboring colored man precisely upon the same level, to compete for wages in the same market. This, of necessity, where their numbers bear any proportion to each other, must lead to an ''irrepressible conflict'' of race, and to the expulsion of one or the other, or to amalgamation of races, to produce in the Southern States the same condition that exists in Mexico, making them into mulatto states, and thus solve the negro question.

"This is the John Brown solution. The first, through Davis and Toombs, fourteen months ago, said, 'down with the Constitution; give us a new Constitution, to carry slavery all over Mexico and Central America, as fast as we can acquire it, or we will destroy the Government.' The second cries, 'down with the Constitution. It is a covenant with hell. It gives Congress no power to abolish slavery in the states. Make a new Constitution.' Sir, I will not yield to the demands of either.

JEFFERSON'S SOLUTION.

"I have stood and will continue to stand for that solution of the negro question which Jefferson, the author of the Declaration of Independence, himself, proposes, which, while it will in the end give universal liberty to universal man, will gradually and peacefully separate these two races for the highest good and to the joy of both; giving to each in their own place the enjoyments of their rights, civil, social, political. That solution is in accordance with that law of the Almighty by which the black man dominates the tropics, and always will; by which our race dominates the temperate zone, and will forever. It is easier to work with Him than against Him. When we accept the solution of Jefferson, which falls neither into the fanaticism of the one nor the blindness of the other, we shall see the beginning of the end of that irrepressible conflict, more of race than of condition, which has disturbed us so long. Until it be saved, there can be no permanent peace.

"Mr. President, what idea underlies the war now going on? The leaders of the rebellion were goaded to it by mad ambition. Slavery was their pretext; but the great mass of the non-slaveholding people were deluded into it. They were told, and became maddened at the thought, that the purpose of the Republican party is not merely to prevent slavery going into the territories and abolish it in this District, where we have the power, but that its real purpose is to overturn slavery in the states: to put the black man there upon a footing of social and political equality with themselves and their wives and children. They were made to believe that John Brown was its true representative; that if Mr. Lincoln should be elected, the slaves would be set free and armed against their masters. They believed it. That belief brought before their eyes, to be re-enacted at their own homes, all the horrors of St. Domingo—fire, rape, and slaughter; dwellings burned, children butchered, wives and daughters ravished upon the dead bodies of their husbands and fathers. They were made to belive it all. That belief drove them to frenzy. That alone roused in their breasts a passion too strong for their patriotism. That alone made them desert the flag of the Union and take up arms against this Government.

"What we may constitutionally and justly do to confiscate the property, including slaves, of the leading conspirators upon whom this crime rests, which

"Hell, with all its powers to damn,"

can hardly punish, I will not now consider; I may do so on some proper occasion hereafter. I will only now say, that if we now do just what they charged us with intending to do; if, by one sweeping act of Congress, we declare the immediate and unconstitutional emancipation of all the slaves in all the states, to remain forever within the states against the will of the people in those states, we shall make true every prophecy of our enemies against us, and make false the pledges we made in the canvass of 1860, on which we won the victory, and by which alone we brought this Administration into power. This course would make us appear to be false and hypocritical before God and man. For one, I will not consent to do it. I say to my friends here, there is no Republican on this floor who took part in the canvass of 1860, who did not a hundred times over declare that we had neither the constitutional power nor the purpose to interfere with slavery within the states. How then can we now advocate a doctrine in violation of every pledge we then gave, and on which we came into power? Shall we now make true every charge of our enemies against us, charges which we denounced as false and infamous? Shall we make them true instead of false prophets by our actions now?"

SENATOR DOOLITTLE ON CONFISCATION.

Senator DOOLITTLE of Wisconsin, made a speech on the 2d of May, 1862, on the Confiscation bill:

[In the United States Senate, May 2d, 1862.]

"Mr. Doolittle, (rep.) of Wisconsin, said there were never such grave considerations presented in any bill before Congress. The first section might reach thousands of millions of dollars of property, and the second section would emancipate at least 2,000,000 slaves, and indirectly, perhaps, the whole 4,000,000. He thought, at least, half the slaves belonged to rebel masters.

"Mr. Sherman, (rep.) of Ohio, in his seat — Seven-eighths.

"Mr. Doolittle—My friend says seven-eighths. That makes the case still stronger.

"Mr. Wade, (rep.) of Ohio, in his seat— And still better.

"Mr. Doolittle continued, and said the constitution was just as supreme in withholding as granting powers, and if Congress undertakes to trample on the constitution by usurping powers not granted, *it is just as much rebellion and revolution as the acts of the insurrectionary states. If the Federal government can thus usurp power, then the days of the Republic are past, and the days of Empire begun.* Congress has power to punish treason and suppress insurrection. The bill of the Senator from Illinois is framed under the power to suppress insurrection, and the bill of the Senator from Vermont (Mr. Collamer) framed under both these powers. He contended that the limitation of the constitution in regard to bills of attainder prohibits Congress forfeiting real estate, except during life; but does not apply to personal estate. That was absolutely confiscated on conviction of treason, and even before judgment. He quoted from Blackstone and Chitty, and the opinion of Joel Parker, of Massachusetts, in support of his position. He had studied this question anxiously, and he was convinced that Congress had no power to confiscate the real estate beyond the life of the person. It was perfectly clear that when our fathers put the prohibition to confiscate real estate in the constitution they knew what they were doing, and meant what they said. He had introduced a bill, therefore, to reach the real estate by taxation, in which way he thought it could be done. He held that, under the constitution, Congress had the right to declare what shall be contraband of war, and subject to capture as to our own citizens, not foreigners; but real estate was not subject to capture within the meaning of the constitution—such as can be made a prize of; it must refer to personal property."

MR. DOOLITTLE CHARGES THE UNITED STATES SENATE WITH A WANT OF "SYMPATHY" FOR THE ADMINISTRATION.

On the 11th of July, 1862, the Confiscation bill was still pending in the Senate.

Mr. DOOLITTLE made the following remarks in refererence to the same, and also lashed his "loyal" brethren of the Senate for their want of sympathy with the Administration, &c.

"It has been sometimes objected that some of us on this floor have not gone so far on the subject of confiscation as some other gentlemen, because, in the view we take of the Constitution, that instrument expressly forbids the ferfeiture or confiscation of the real estate of traitors beyond their lives. It is in vain that gentlemen, by calling these traitors public enemies in war, attempt to make them anything else than traitors. Treason consists in levying war against the United States, and those who do so are traitors, and nothing more or less than traitors. The very point decided by Judge Swayne was, that rebels in arms against the United States are not enemies within the meaning of the Constitution, but traitors, and nothing else. Congress is forbidden to forfeit the estate of a traitor, except during his life, by attainder of treason, which at common law reached and forfeited his real estate only. I read the authorities bearing on that question on a former occasion, and no gentleman on this floor has offered a single authority to the contrary. The authorities which I quoted were conclusive. They demonstrated that at the common law the real estate of the traitor, which he held in his own right, or over which he had the power of disposition, was the real estate and the only real estate liable to 'forfeiture, and that it was expressly to limit the forfeiture of that during the lifetime of the traitor that our fathers, in making the Constitution, inserted the words, "no attainder of treason shall work corruption of blood, or forfeiture, except during the life of the person attainted."

"As to personal property, including slaves, they are the subjects of capture in war, and Congress is expressly authorized to make rules concerning captures on land and water.

"But the title passes from the owner, not by the enactment of the law, but by the capture, and that until the President, by his military forces, can put down the armed forces of the rebels, and get possession of their country, and make the captures, *the law of Congress will have no more effect in putting down the rebellion than in putting down the rebellion in China.* If a law of confiscation would have such marvelous results as some suppose, why not by act of Congress confiscate the *powder* and *ball* and *muskets* and *cannon* of the enemy, and that would end it at once. Sir, it needs something more than paper shot, acts of Congress, and impassioned speeches of Congressmen. I will not, however, repeat these views, nor dwell upon these authorities at this time.

"But, sir, I feel called upon to notice a remark made the other day by the Senator from Ohio. [Mr. Wade.] He denominated those of us who hold to these opinions, referring to myself and others, 'weak brethren.' Weak in our disposition to prosecute this war against the rebels? Weak in our sympathies for the loyal cause! As if we had a desire to cover up traitors' property and cover up treason! Let me tell that Senator that the most efficient means to put down the rebellion *is not the enactment of unconstitutional laws by Congress, but by marching our military forces upon the rebel enemy; that nothing will do it but ball and bayonet. Nothing can overcome war but war!* War is an appeal to the god of force, and we must bring force against force. It is not by *speeches* here, nor *resolutions,* nor *acts of Congress* that this rebellion can be crushed. It is to be put down at the point of the bayonet. And if from the beginning of this session the only word of Congress had been 'men and money,' and of the Executive, 'forward march, charge bayonet, a little more grape,' and nothing else, we should be nearer the end of the rebellion than we are at this hour. *We have spent too much time and wasted too much energy in finding fault with each other, in criticising our generals in the field, and criticising and thus weakening the confidence of the country in the Administration.* * * *

"Sir, this is the spirit I would infuse into every American heart. In this day of our trial, in this hour of blood, and agony, and tears, when the hearts of this people, disappointed in their expectations before Richmond are stricken, and the hopes of timid men begin to fail, *it is no time for Senators of the United States to be standing here publicly denouncing the Administration, or denouncing the Generals in command.* Now is the time for men of real courage, men of abiding faith in man and truth, and God, whom temporary reverses do not cast down, and dangers do not appal, to speak to the country, to the President, and to the civilized world words of encouragement and good cheer. Let them know that in the midst of apparent disasters, in spite of threatened intervention from abroad, we, the representatives of American states and of the American people, standing fast by the Constitution and the Union, here and now renew our pledge before high Heaven, and swear by Him who liveth, and reigneth forever, that we will put down this rebellion, we will sustain this Constitution, and preserve this Union forever. [Applause in the galleries.]

"The Presiding Officer—Order!

"Mr. Doolittle—This is the word which I would speak, if I had the power, to the hearts of all American citizens, and speak it now.

"Mr. Wilson, of Massachusetts—Will the Senator allow me to ask a question?

"Mr. Doolittle—Certainly.

"Mr. Wilson, of Massachusetts—I want to ask the Senator from Wisconsin this simple question: What has the Administration asked of the American Senate that has not been given cheerfully and freely by the votes of all of us, to carry on the war?

"Mr. Doolittle—I will answer the honorable Senator. What the Administration has asked of this Senate which it has not had, as it ought to have had, is its sympathy, its words of encouragement and support. Instead of that, it has often received speeches denunciatory in their tone, on this floor, denouncing the policy of this and the policy of that, when the President's hand and heart have been aching and almost crushed under the load of these great responsibilities, which God, in his providence, has thrown upon him. I complain of that.— But what is past is past; let us hear no more of it. I do not say that you have not voted men and money. They have been voted with a lavish hand; but he wants more: he wants the hearts of the Senate to sustain him. Let our hearts go out towards him, to fight with him, and fight for him"

As the foregoing sentiments were uttered by a strong defender of the Administration, it may be safe for Democrats sometimes to quote them. We are aware that Mr. DOOLITTLE does not suit all his "constituents," and as a sample of their displeasure at the utterance of the foregoing sentiments, we introduce the late editor of the Racine (Wis.) *Journal*, who said:

"We can stand a great deal, but we submit that classing Senator Doolittle among the Abolitionists, is altogether too cool for the season. It should be remembered that Mr. Doolittle is a politician, [Few now dispute it since his speeches later than the above, to be seen elsewhere] and is not particularly accountable for anything he says. When it is for his interest to say, as he did in Union Hall (Racine) *that slavery is a divine institution, established and sanctified by the Diety*, and should never be abolished, he says it for some purpose. When he votes against giving freedom to a slave, who did the government great service (as he did in the Senate last summer) he does it for a purpose. When he votes with the friends of the rebels, against confiscating their property, as he did last summer in the Senate, he has an object in view; and, when he gets up in this Senate and endorses every abolition doctrine that we have promulgated for the last twenty years, he has an object in view; when he whines out his pious platitudes, and prates over his 'honest heart,' and his 'plain spoken manner,' then is the time he is seeking afresh some profitable office, at the hands of the people."

Notwithstanding this, the Abolition Legislature of 1863 re-elected him to the Senate.

CHAPTER XXVIII.

INDIRECT MODE TO VIOLATE AND NULLIFY LAWS.

The Personal Liberty Bills of the Various States...Sundry Provisions to Nullify the Fugitive Law...A Radical Organ admits the Purpose...Schemes of the Plotters exposed.

THE PERSONAL LIBERTY BILLS—ANOTHER NORTHERN MEANS TO "PRECIPITATE" REVOLUTION.

We have thought it proper to record for future use the provisions of Northern statutes, passed to virtually abrogate the fugitive act. These we have collated as briefly as possible, that the reader may see that the Southern secessionists had plenty of Northern allies. The provisions of the Northern "personal liberty bills," as these laws were styled, clearly indicate both the cowardice and *animus* of the party that gave them vitality. Let them speak for themselves:

MAINE.—*R. S.*, *Title* 8, *chap.* 80, *page* 491.

§ 53, provides that no Sheriff or other officer of the state shall arrest or detain any person on claim that he is a fugitive slave. The penalty for violating the law, is a fine not exceeding one thousand dollars or imprisonment not less than one year in the County Jail.

NEW HAMPSHIRE.—*Laws of* 1857. *chapter* 1966, *page* 1876.

§ 1. Admits all persons of every color to the rights and privileges of a citizen.

§ 2. Declares slaves, coming or brought into the state, with the consent of the masters, free.

§ 3. Declairs the attempt to hold any person as a slave within the state, a felony with a penalty of imprisonment not less than one nor more than five years. *Provided, that the provisions of the section shall not apply to any act lawfully done by any officer of the United States or other persons in the execution of any legal process.*

VERMONT.—*R. S.*, *Title* 27, *chap* 101, *p.p.* 536.

§ 1. Provides that no Court, Justice of the Peace or Magistrate shall take cognizance of any certificate, warrant or process under the fugitive slave law.

§ 2. Provides that no officer or citizen of the state shall arrest, or aid, or assist in arresting, any person for the reason that he is claimed as a fugitive slave.

§ 3. Provides that no officer or citizen shall aid or assist in the removal from the state of any person claimed as a fugitive slave.

§§ 4 and 5. Provide a penalty of $1,000, or imprisonment five years in the State Prison for violating this act.

§ 6. This act [§§ 1 to 5] shall not be construed to extend to any citizen of this state acting as a *judge of the circuit or district court of the United States, or as marshal or deputy marshal of the district of Vermont, or to any person acting under the command or authority of said courts or marshal.*

§ 7. Requires the state attorney to act as counsel for alleged fugitives.

§§ 9 and 10. Provide for issuing a *habeas corpus* and the trial by jury of all questions of fact in issue between the parties.

SCRAPS FROM MY SCRAP BOOK. 189

CONNECTICUT.—*Revised Statutes*, Title 51, page 798.

§ 1. Every person who shall falsely and maliciously declare, represent or pretend, that any FREE PERSON *entitled to freedom* is a slave or owes service or labor to any person or persons, with intent to procure or to assist in procuring the forcible removal of such free person from this State as a slave, shall pay a fine of $5,000, and be imprisoned five years in the Connecticut State Prison.

§ 2. Require two witnesses to prove that any person is a slave or owes labor.

§ 3. Provides a penalty of $5,000 against any person seizing, or causing to be seized, any free person with intent to reduce him to slavery.

§ 4. Depositions not to be admitted as evidence.

§ 5. Witnesses testifying falsely are liable to $5,000 fine, and five years' imprisonment.

RHODE ISLAND.—*R. S.*, Title 30, chap. 213, page 532.

§ 17. Forbids the carrying away of any person by force out of the State.

§ 18. Forbids any judge, justice, magistrate or court from officially aiding in the arrest of a fugitive slave under the fugitive law of 1793 or 1850.

§ 19. Forbids any sheriff or other officer from arresting or detaining any person claimed as a fugitive slave.

§ 20. Provides a penalty of $500, or imprisonment not less than six months, for violating the act.

MICHIGAN.—Title 37.

§ 1. Requires the State Attorney to act as counsel for fugitives.

§§ 2, 3 and 4. Grant *habeas corpus*, and provide for trial by jury.

§ 5. Forbids the use of jails or other prisons to detain fugitives.

§ 6. Provides a punishment of not less than three nor more than five years for falsely declaring, representing or pretending any person to be a slave.

§ 7. Provides a fine of not less than $500, or more than $1,000, and imprisonment in State Prison for two years, for forcibly seizing or causing to be seized any free person, with intent to have such person held in slavery.

§ 7. Requires two persons to prove any person to be a slave.

WISCONSIN—*R. S.*, chap. 158. sec. 51, &c., page 312, &c.

§§ 1, 52, 53, and 54 provide for the issuing of the *habeas corpus* in favor of persons claimed as fugitive slaves.

§§ 55, and 56, direct how proceedings shall be conducted and grant a trial by jury.

§ 57, provides a penalty of $1,000, and imprisonment not more than five nor less than one year, against any person who shall falsely and maliciously declare, represent or pretend that any free person within the State is a slave or owes service or labor, with the intent forceibly to remove such person from the State.

§ 58, requires two witnesses to prove a person to be a slave.

§ 59, depositions not to be received in evidence.

§ 60, judgment under fugitive slave act not to be liens upon real estate. This however, can only apply to decree of State courts.

THE ANIMUS ADMITTED.

As exhibiting the real *animus* of these laws, and their aim and purpose to nullify the act of Congress and the decision of the Supreme Court thereon, we select the following, among a numerous class of admissions, from the Wisconsin *State Journal*, of Sept. 19, 1854, when such nullification was openly demanded by the radical press of the country. The *Journal* said:

"The modification (of the State law) proposed, will practically prove an abrogation of the law. (The Fugitive Law.) *This must be understood by those who favor it.* (That is, the proposed 'modification.') Few slave owners will desire to incur the cost of reclaiming a fugitive. While the nation bears the expense, and the free men of the North are compelled to pay the larger portion, slave catching may be a pleasant business enough for Southern 'impersonations of the high born aristocrat.' But, compel them to foot the bill, on the old principle that those who dance must pay the fiddler, and the fugitive slave act would become as inoperative, in most portions of the Union, as it *is now in Wisconsin*. The average cost of reclaiming a fugitive, is more than the best proportioned man, or even the most delicate and perfect sample of Creole beauty, will bring in the shambles of Southern aristocracy.

"It is not, then, through any tenderness for the chivalry that this modification is proposed, but *merely to accomplish the same end without openly avowing the purpose.* * * *

"We may discourse, it matters not, how eloquently, of the *sacredness of law*, and of the necessity of respecting *all laws*, but there is not a man among us, *except the most depraved and unprincipled*, who would not rather openly resist its (the fugitive law) *execution*, or avoid complying with its provisions, virtually disobeying it. We ought not then be *particularly delicate* in choosing phrases to express our determination of ridding ourselves of it if possible!"

Thus the Northern plotters had not the courage to advocate laws *directly* annulling the fugitive act, but like cowards, they advocated the "personal liberty acts" to "accomplish the *same end!*"

CHAPTER XXIX.

ARBITRARY POWER—MILITARY ARRESTS, &c.

Introductory Remarks...Loyalty and Patriotism of the North...Arbitrary Power used to Destroy the Northern Unanimity...Senator Fessenden on Stopping Enlistments...Senator Wilson on same...General Conclusions... The Cause and the Effect...Mr. Lincoln's claim to Unlimited Power...Order No. 38...Trial of Vallandigham.... Resolves of the Democratic Meeting at Albany...Their Protest to the President...The President's Reply...The Rejoinder...Protest of the Ohio Committee...President's Reply...Committee's Rejoinder...The Law of the Case, from the "National Intelligencer"...Personal and Legal Rights...Crittenden's Views...Abolitionist Feel Uneasy...Administration Condemned by its own Organs... Views of the N. Y. "Post" and "Tribune"...Judge Duer on Usurpations of the Administration...From the "N. Y. World."

ARBITRARY POWER—MILITARY ARRESTS— THE WAR POWER AND "MILITARY NECESSITY."

[In the great mass of articles, taken promiscuously from a great variety of sources, and at various times, it is quite difficult, in our haste to furnish copy for the printer, as the same shall be needed, to properly arrange and assort the evidences under this head, so as to exactly conform to chronological order. We will, however, endeavor to place the whole easy of access for reference. That is our main object.—ED.]

As a prelude to what follows, it is but due to remark, here, that the Democracy of the country do not, nor have they ever objected to any of those extreme military measures that experience and the laws of war have demonstrated as necessary to good discipline, a well regulated military police, and to prevent and punish crimes and breaches of martial law—*within the lines of army operations*—in short, that the rigor of war may exist *wherever war is.* But the Democracy and all conservative men do protest against visiting peaceful and loyal states and communities, hundreds of miles away from hostile foes and army operations, with all the rigors of arbitrary, martial law, without even a necessity or excuse being shown for it.

This class of wrongs has been interpreted by the people as an effort *solely designed to divide and distract the North, with a view to make peace and Union impossible.* God has given us no prerogative to judge of motives, except by and through the medium of *acts*, and when judged by this standard, we cannot see how it is possible that the unbiased mind can acquit those in power from the design charged herein. Before the system of arbitrary arrests was inaugurated, the whole North was a *unit.*— There was not so much as a ripple on the surface of popular feeling—no popular disturbances manifested themselves, to arouse fear or excite alarm. The people everywhere in the North were not only loyal, but they were more—they formed themselves into one solid wall of military power, to resist and subdue rebellion. In every nook and corner of the great, busy and powerful North—in the agricultural and in the manufacturing districts— from Aroostook to the San Joquin—all was astir in common rivalry to see which state, which county, which town or ward should be the first to answer their country's summons. In short, the whole North was one great military camp.

The whole people, forgetting party—forgetting domestic comfort and happiness—forgetting all save their imperiled country, gathered up their wealth, extended their utmost credit, collected their sons, their fathers and their brothers, and throwing them all at the feet of the President, bad him use them as best he might to save liberty, protect and defend the Union. In a spirit of generous confidence that has no parallel in the world's history, the people at once resigned to the President the entire dominion over the purse and the sword, asking no conditions, save the defense of personal and civil liberty, and protesting the Union of their fathers from wanton destruction. We heard then no criminations about "laggards," "shirks," or "sneaks." The only complaints (and they were many) that afflicted officials in the discharge of their duties, came from the thousands of companies and hundreds of regiments and parts of regiments that were disbanded and turned away, denied the high and noble privilege of offering their sacrifices upon their country's burning altar.

250,000 TROOPS TOO MANY.

Even as late as March 29th, 1862. [*see Globe of that date*] Senators FESSENDEN and WILSON thought it their duty to stop enlistments, because of some 250,000 soldiers under pay more than were needed.

Mr. FESSENDEN said (March 28th):

"There are more men than the Government knows what to do with, here, on the Potomac, to-day. What occasion is there to send for others? * * We have 750,000—if that is the number—250,000 more than we ever intended to have. * * What is the reason why we should go on and appoint Generals to correspond with a number of men that are not needed and are not used? * * I offered a proposition the other day *to stop all enlistments* until we should get *down* to the number we wanted and no more. My friend from Massachusetts (Wilson) said we should have a bill soon where I could put on my amendment, I have not seen his bill yet. As soon as he brings it along, so that I can put on my amendment, I will, and hope it will be forthcoming very soon. I understand, however, that the Department has absolutely stopped enlistments. But whether that be so or not, it is best to reduce it to shape, and have a law on the subject.

SENATOR WILSON ON SAME SUBJECT.

Mr. Wilson (Rep. of Mass.)—"The Senator from Maine (Mr. Fessenden) the other day proposed to reduce the number of men authorized by law down to 500,000. I agree with aim in that. Still, we have not been able to do it. It was suggested also that we ought to stop recruiting. *I agree to that.* I have over and over again been to the war office and urged upon the Department *to stop recruiting in every part of the country*. We have had the promise that it should be done, yet, every day, in different parts of the country, we have accounts of men being raised and brought forth to fill up the ranks of regiments. The papers tell us that in Tennessee and other parts of the country where our armies move, we are filling up the ranks of the army. I believe we have to-day 250,000 more men under the pay of the Government than we need or can well use. I have not a doubt of it, and I think it ought to be checked. I think the War Department ought to issue peremptory orders, *forbidding the enlistment of another soldier* into the voluntary force of the United States, until the time shall come when we need them. We can obtain them at any time when we need them."
—[*See Cong. Globe, March 29, '62.*

Senator WILSON was Chairman of the Committee on Military Affairs, and of course thought he spoke by card. He had no fears that we could not obtain all the men needed, when their services were required. The unanimous action of the people was an earnest of this.

But, what followed? At once, without excuse, cause or palliation, the State and War Departments commenced their system of arbitrary arrests. Victims in large numbers were dragged from their peaceful abodes, at the criminal hour of midnight and without accusation, judge or jury, were bundled off to some loathsome cell or military fort, kept there from one to twelve months, and finally "honorably discharged" without ever being made acquainted with the charge or character of the "suspicion" against them.

These arbitrary, despotic and wholly unnecessary acts, justly aroused, as we believe it was *intended*, the fears and indignation of the people. The North was all ablaze with excitement, and as the arrests were wholly confined to those who professed the Democratic faith, it very naturally aroused a most intense political excitement, and from that hour parties became arrayed against each other.

Not content with letting well enough alone—not content with the patriotic devotion to the country which induced Democrats everywhere to forget party and remember only their country—not content to rely on that mighty avalanche of strength that had in eight months surfeited the Union camps with 250,000 more men than the chairman of the committee on Military Affairs knew what to do with—not content to raise an army of more than twice the size of that which the Great Napoleon led to Moscow, all for the asking—not content to tolerate a united North—this despotic Fire Brand being but the forerunner of its twin measure, the proclamation—was cast into the inflamable materials at the North. It was unnecessary—it was wanton, and hence believed to be the work of design, and that design— *a division of the North*—for *a purpose*, and that purpose has already been divined.

THE CAUSE AND THE EFFECT.

The *cause* is easily traceable to its legitimate *results*. The North has been divided. Voluntary enlistments were entirely suspended, and within a month's time after these firebrands were cast into the great Northern magazine, and for the first time, the cry of a *Draft* was heard! A draft came up from Washington. No one can say that the Democracy were in the least at fault in this, *for the Republicans themselves immediately stopped enlisting.*

When the "powers" at Washington saw this disastrous result, what did they do? Did they stop the *cause* they had set in motion? No, but they gave it new impetus; they aggravated it;

they re-enected the old French code, or "law of suspected persons," and caused wide spread alarm among the people by their new leviesto fill the *LaForce* and the *Conceigeirre* of despotism. If in all this, any necessity had been shown—if the public had been favored with any reasons adequate to the steps taken, the case would have been different. The public in the plentitude of their patriotism, would have overlooked "mistakes," or "errors," or would even have excused hasty acts or false accusations, if there had appeared any desire to calm the popular fears, by assurances that these acts of despotic power had *some* foundation. But, no attempt at explanation has ever been offered. Thousands who were thrown into prison, after months of suffering, in their persons, their property, and their reputations, were turned loose, without remuneration, without redress, and even without ever knowing the charges against them. And not only this, but the Radical Congress, in order to add insult to injury, passed that bold act of despotism, by which all officers, their aiders, abetors, spies and informers, were exonerated from trial and punishment.

And not only this, but Mr. LINCOLN, in his reply to the Albany and Ohio committees, in reference to the despotic arrest and deportation of VALLANDIGHAM, claimed the right to do these things, without being accountable to any power, save his own will and purpose. The doctrine asserted by the President in his reply to these committees is, that there is no limit to arbitrary power, save the *will* of the one who happens to be Commander-in-Chief.

MR. LINCOLN'S CLAIM OF ARBITRARY POWER.

We must be pardoned for the following copious extracts, for as covering the *principle* involved, they are really of more consequence than any given number of special cases.

THE VALLANDIGHAM CASE—IN COURT AND OUT OF COURT.

As the principles involved in this case cover the whole ground, and as the people have been so thoroughly aroused and excited on this subject, we will principally confine our quotations to this particular case.

THE BURNSIDE ORDER No. 38.

This will be our first witness on the stand, because we have good reasons for believing this order was issued expressly, and for no other purpose than to form an excuse to arrest and punish Mr. VALLANDIGHAM, so far as the latter clause is concerned. Certain it is, that we have heard of no other victim being arrested under this order, though hundreds of others said harsher things than Mr. VALLANDIGHAM. This order reads as follows:

"HEADQUARTERS DEPARTMENT OF THE OHIO, CINCINNATI, April 1863.
"*General Order No.* 38.

"The Commanding General publishes, for the information of all concerned—

"That hereafter all persons found within our lines who commit acts for the benefit of the enemies of our country, will be tried as spies or traitors, and, if convicted, will suffer death. This order includes the following classes of persons:

"Carriers of secret mails.
"Writers of letters sent by secret mails.
"Secret recruiting offices within the lines.
"Persons who have entered into an agreement to pass our lines for the purpose of joining the enemy.
"Persons found concealed within our lines belonging to the service of the enemy; and in fact all persons found improperly within our lines who *could* give private information of the enemy.
"All persons within our lines who harbor, protect, conceal, feed, clothe, or in any way aid the enemies of our country.
"The habit of declaring sympathies for the enemy will no longer be tolerated in the department. Persons committing such offences will be at once arrested, with a view to being tried as above stated, or sent beyond our lines into the lines of their friends.

"It must be distinctly understood that treason, expressed *or implied*, will not be tolerated in this department.

"All officers and soldiers are strictly charged with the execution of this order.
By command of Major General A. E. BURNSIDE:
LEWIS RICHMOND,
Assistant Adjutant General.

When it is known that any criticism on the conduct of the Administration, however just and pertinent, was held by the radicals as "declaring sympathies for the enemy," we are enabled to read this order in its true meaning. Take what followed under this order, and compare it with the old, justly odious Sedition law, and the reader will be astonished at the mildness of that law which hurled the Federals from power in 1801. [*See Sedition law on p.* 36.

SPIES SENT OUT.

After issuing this order, General BURNSIDE sent out a couple of spies to track and hunt down Mr. VALLANDIGHAM, who attended the Democratic meeting at Mount Vernon, Ohio, on the 1st of May, 1863, for the purpose of

SCRAPS FROM MY SCRAP-BOOK. 193

evesdropping—catching pa.ts of sentences, distorting others, and garbling the whole, with a view to make out a case. These spies reported at headquarters, and Mr. VALLANDIGHAM was arrested at 2 o'clock at night. His domicil at Dayton, Ohio, was surrounded by 100 soldiers, broken into and himself seized and carried by force to Cincinnati, and to give the full history of this transaction, we present,

THE TRIAL OF C. L. VALLANDIGHAM.

The Charge and Specifications—Testimony for the Prosecution and Defense.—Protest of Mr. Vallandigham, &c.

FIRST DAY.

WEDNESDAY, May 6, 1863.

The commission convened at 10 o'clock a. m.
The Judge Advocate read the General Order from the headquarters of the Department of the Ohio, appointing the following officers a commission to try all parties brought before it, and Mr. Vallandigham was asked whether he had any objections to offer to any member of the court.
The following officers compose the court:
Brig. Gen. R. B. POTTER, President.
Capt. J. M. CUTTS' Judge Advocate.
Col. J. F. DECOURCEY, 16th O. V. I.
Lieut. Col. E. R, GOODRICH, Com. Sub.
Major VAN BUREN, A. D. C.
Major BROWN, 10th Kentucky Cavalry.
Major FITCH, 115th O. V, I.
Capt. LYDIG, A. D. C.
Mr. Vallandigham said he was not acquainted with any of the members of the court, and had no objection to offer to them individually, but he protested that the Commission had no authority to try him, he being neither in the land or naval force of the United States, and was not therefore triable by such a court, but was amenable only to the judicial courts of the land.
The members of his court were then sworn to try his case impartially.
The Judge Advocate then read the following charge and specification:

THE CHARGE.

Charge—Publicly expressing in violation of General Orders No. 38, from Headquarters Department of the Ohio, his sympathies with those in arms against the government of the United States, declaring disloyal sentiments and opinions, with the object and purpose of weakening the power of the government in its efforts to suppress an unlawful rebellion.

THE SPECIFICATION.

Specification—In this, that the said Clement L. Vallandigham, a citizen of the State of Ohio, on or about the 1st day of May, 1863, at Mount Vernon, Knox county, Ohio, did publicly address a meeting of citizens, and did utter sentiments in words, or in effect, as follows: Declaring the present war a "wicked, cruel and unnecessary war," a war "not being waged for the preservation of the Union," "a war for the purpose of crushing out liberty, and erecting a despotism," "a war for the freedom of the blacks and the onslaving of the whites," stating "that if the administration had so wished, the war could have been honorably terminated months ago," that "peace might have been honorbly abtained by listening to the proposed intermediation of France;" [that*"propositions by which the Southern states could be won back, and the south guaranteed their rights under the Constitution, had been rejected the day before the late battle of Fredericksburg, by Lincoln and his minions;"]* meaning thereby the President of the United States and those under him in authority; charging that "the government of the United States was about to appoint military marshals in every district to restrain the people of their liberties,to deprive them of their rights and privileges;" characterizing General Order No. 38, from headquarters department of the Ohio; as "a base usurpation of arbitrary authority," inviting his hearers to resist the same by saying, "The sooner the people inform the

*The portion enclosed in brackets was struck out.

minions of usurped power that they will not submit to such restrictions upon their liberties the better;" declaring that "he was at all times upon all occasions resolved to do what he could do to defeat the attempt now being made to build up a monarchy upon the ruins of our free government;" asserting that "he firmly believed," as he said six months ago, "that the men in power are attempting to establish a despotism in this country more cruel and more oppressive than ever existed before."
All of which opinions and sentiments he well knew did aid, comfort and encourage those in arms against the government, and could but induce in his bearers a distrust of their own government and sympathy for those in arms against it and a disposition to resist the laws of the land.
G. W. CUTTS,
Captain 11th Infantry, Judge Advocate, Department of the Ohio.

Mr. Vallandigham was asked by the Judge Advocate, what his plea was.
Mr. Vallandigham refused to plead, and asked time to consult his counsel, and for process to compel the attendance of Fernando Wood, of New York city, who should be required to bring with him the letter which he received from Richmond in relation to terms offered for the return of southern Senators to their seats in Congress, with the letter of the President declining to entertain the proposition.
Mr. Vallandigham continued to refuse to plead to the charge, the President directed that the plea of "not guilty," be entered on the record.
The court then gave Mr. Vallandigham time to consult his counsel, and for that purpose ordered a recess to half past 1 o'clock.
The court was then cleared for deliberation, as to whether the delay asked for by Mr. Vallandigham should be granted, and remained closed until near noon.
The court again met pursuant to adjournment, and the doors were opened.
The president asked Mr. Vallandigham whether he desired to appear with counsel.
Mr. Vallandigham said he did not. His counsel, Geo. E. Pugh, Geo. Pendleton, and Alexander Ferguson, remained in the adjoining room.

THE TESTIMONY.

The Judge Advocate announced that the case would be proceeded with, and called the first witness for the prosecution.
Capt. H. R. H'll, of the 115th O. V. I., who was sworn.
Question by Judge Advocate—Were you present at a meeting of citizens of Mount Vernon, on May 1st, 1863?
A.—I was.
Q.—Did you hear accused address that meteing?
A.—I did.
Q.—What position did you occupy at the meeting, and were you near enough to hear all he said?
A.—I was leaning against the end of the platform on which he was speaking. Was about six feet from him. I remained in this position during the whole time he was speaking.
By Judge Advocate—State what remarks he made in relation to the war; what he said about the President of the United States and the orders of military commanders.
Witness—In order that I may bring in events as they were referred to by the speaker, I ask permission of the court to refresh my memory from the notes which I took at the time.
President—You can read from your notes.
Witness—The speaker commenced by referring to the canopy under which he was speaking—the stand having been decorated with an American flag—the flag under the Constitution—
Witness—After finishing his exordium, he spoke of the designs of those in power to erect a despotism. That it was not their intention to effect a restoration of the Union That previous to the battle of Fredericksburg an attempt was made to stay this wicked, cruel and unnecessary war. That the war could have been ended in February last. That a day or two before the battle of Fredericksburg a proposition had been made for the re-admission of southern Senators into the United States Congress, and that the refusal was still in existence over the President's own signature, which would be made pulic as soon as the ban of secrecy imposed by the President was removed. That the Union could have been saved if the plan proposed by the speaker had been adopted; that the Union could have been saved upon the basis of reconstruction; but that it

would have ended in the exile or death of those who advocated a continuance of the war. He then referred to Forney, who was a well known correspondent of the Philadelphia *Press*, and said he had no right to speak for those who were not connected with the administration. That some of our public men, rather than bring back some of the seceded states would submit to a permanent separation of the Union. He stated that France, a nation that had always shown herself to be a friend of our government, had proposed to act as intermediator; but that her proposition, which, if accepted, might have brought about an honorable peace, was insolently rejected.

Mr. Vallandigham here corrected the witness. The word he used was "instantly," not "insolently."

Witness...I understood the word he used to have been "insolently." That the people had been deceived—that 20,000 lives had been lost at the battle of Fredericksburg, which might have been saved. In speaking of the objects of the war, he said it was a war for the liberation of the blacks, and the enslavement of the whites. We had been told it would be terminated in three months—then in nine months—and again in a year. That the war was still in progress, and that there was no prospect of its being ended. That Richmond was theirs; that Charleston and Vicksburg were theirs; that the Mississippi was not opened, and would not be so long as there was cotton on its banks to be stolen, or so long as there were any officers to enrich. That a southern paper had denounced him and Cox and the peace Democrats as having done more to prevent the establishing of the Southern Confederacy than 10,000 soldiers could do. That they proposed to operate through the masses of the people in both sections who were in favor of the Union. That it was the purpose or design of the Administration to suppress or prevent such meetings as the one he was addressing. [This very trial proved the truth of this.] That military marshals were about to be appointed in every district, who would act for the purpose of restricting the liberties of the people; [did not this prove true?] but that he was a freeman. That he did not ask David Tod, or Abraham Lincoln, or Ambrose E. Burnside for his right to speak as he had done, and was doing. That his authority for so doing was higher than General Order No. 38—it was General Order No. 1—the Constitution. That General Order No. 38 was a base usurpation of arbitrary power—[a greater truth no man ever uttered]—that he had the most supreme contempt for such power. He despised it and spit upon it. He trampled it under his feet.

That only a few days before a man had been dragged from his home in Butler county by an outrageous usurpation of power and tried for an offence not known to our laws by a self-constituted court martial; tried without a jury, which is guaranteed to every one...that he had been fined and imprisoned. That two men were brought over from Kentucky and tried, contrary to express laws for the trial of treason, and were now under sentence of death. That an order had just been issued in Indiana denying to persons the right to canvass or discuss military policy, and that if it was submitted to would be followed up by a similar order in Ohio. That he was resolved never to submit to an order of a military dictator, prohibiting the free discussion of either civil or military authority. The sooner that the people inform the minions of this usurped power that they would not submit to such restrictions upon their liberties, and that they would not cringe and cower before such authority, the better. Let them not be deluded by the image of liberty when the spirit is gone. He proclaimed the right to criticise the acts of our military servants in power. That there never was a tyrant in any age who oppressed the people further than he thought they would submit to endure. That in the days of Democratic authority Tom Corwin had, in the face of Congress hoped that our brave volunteers in Mexico "might be welcomed with bloody hands to hospitable graves," but that he had not been interfered with. It was never before thought necessary to appoint a Captain of cavalry as Provost Marshal as was now the case in Indianapolis, or military dictators as were now exercising authority in Cincinnati and Columbus....

That a law had recently been enacted in Ohio, as well as in some other states, regulating the manner in which soldiers should vote, that the officers have to be judges of the election.

Judge Advocate objected to this part of the testimony as irrelevant.

Mr. Vallandigham desired the court to permit the witness to go on with this testimony.

Witness...The speaker closed by warning the people not to be deceived. That an attempt would shortly be made to enforce the conscription law, and to remember that the war was not for the preservation of the Union, but that it was a wicked abolition war, and that if those in authority were allowed to accomplish their purposes, the people would be deprived of their liberties and a monarchy established; but, as for him, he was resolved that he would never be a priest, to minister at the altar on which his country was being sacrificed. [Is this implied treason?]

Question by J. A...What other flags or emblems were used in decorating the stage?

A...There were banners made of frame-work, and covered with canvass, which were decorated with butternuts, and bore inscriptions. One banner, which was carried at the head of a delegation which came in from a town in the country, bore the inscription, "The copperheads are coming."

Mr. Vallandigham...The South never carried copper cents.

[What *greatness* for an administration to punish a man for speaking at a meeting where butternuts were worn!]

Judge Advocate...But butternuts are a southern emblem.

Mr. Vallandigham shook his head, and said they were not.

Q. by J. A....Did you see any persons have emblems on their persons?

A...Yes, I saw hundreds of persons wearing butternut and copperhead badges.

Mr. Vallandigham...The copper badges were simply the head cut out of the common cent coins with pins attached.

Mr. Vallandigham...Did you notice what inscription those copperhead badges bore?

A...No, I did not look at them.

Mr. Vallandigham...The inscription on them was "Liberty?"

Q. by J. A...Did you hear any cheers in the crowd for Jeff. Davis?

Mr. Vallandigham...That is not in the specification.

A....I did not hear cheers for Jeff. Davis, but I heard a shout in the crowd that Jeff. Davis was a gentleman, and that was more than the President was. [Did Mr. V. commit treason by proxy?]

CROSS-EXAMINATION BY MR. VALLANDIGHAM.

Q.—Did not I refer in my speech to the Crittenden compromise propositions, and condemn their rejection?

As the witness was about answering the Judge Advocate objected to the question on the ground that it was bringing in a matter foreign to the charge and specification. The court allowed the question to be answered.

A.—When endeavoring to show that the party in power had not the restoration of the Union in view in conducting the war, and that that was not their object, he stated a number of means by which that could have been accomplished, and, from the fact that none had been adopted, he considered it proof that that the restoration of the Union was not the object for which the war was being waged.

Q.—Did I not quote Judge Douglas' declaration that the rejection—

Mr. Vallandigham.—I desire to prove that in my speech I stated that Mr. Douglas had said that the responsibility for the rejection of the Crittenden propositions was with the republican party.

The Judge Advocate stated that his objection was that the question was bringing in political opinions and discussions with which the court had nothing to do.

The room was cleared for deliberation, and the doors closed.

After an interval of fifteen minutes the doors were again opened, and then the Judge Advocate announced, that the question would not be admitted.

Q...When speaking in connection with Forney's *Press*, did I not say that if other democrats in Washington and myself had not refused all idea and suggestions of some prominent men of the party in power, to make peace on terms of disunion, that I believed the war would have been ended in February?

A...When speaking of the propositions before referred to, and that this war was not being carried on for the restoration of the Union, he stated that if the Democrats in Washington had united in influence for the permanent separation of the Union, it would have been accomplished in February.

Q...Did I not refer expressly to myself in that connection, and say that I had refused and always would refuse,

SCRAPS FROM MY SCRAP-BOOK.

to agree to a separation of the states, in other words, to peace on terms of disunion?

A...Well, that idea is not exactly as it was expressed.—*He stated something to that effect.* That he wished to have a voice in the manner in which the Union was to be reconstructed, and that our southern brethren should also have a voice in the matter.

Q...Referring to the Richmond *Enquirer* article, did I not say that it, Jeff. Davis', organ, had called Dictator Lincoln to lock up Mr. Cox, Senator Richardson and myself in one of his military prisons, because of our doing so much against southern recognition and independence?

A...*That is substantially what he said.*

Q...Referring to General Order No. 38, did I not say that in so far as it undertook to subject citizens not in the land or naval forces of the United States, or militia of the United States in actual service, to trial by court martial or military commission, I believed to be unconstitutional and a usurpation of arbitrary power?

A...Yes, except in the words "in so far."

Q...Referring to two citizens of Kentucky tried by military court in Cincinnati, did I not say that if what they were charged with was actual treason, punishable by death, and that if guilty the penalty by state law which was hanging, that they ought to be hung, after being tried by a judicial court and a jury, instead of which they had been tried by a military court, and, as I understood, sentenced to a fine and imprisonment—one of them $300 fine?

A...I don't think he put those "if's" in. I think he said they were improperly tried, and by a usurpation of power.

Mr. Vallandigham...Strike out the "if's" then.

Witness...That was substantially what he said.

Q...Did I not say, in that connection, that the rebel officer who was tried as a spy by the military court at Cincinnati, was legally and properly tried, according to the rules and articles; tried and convicted—that that was a clear case, where the court had jurisdiction?

A...It is my recollection that he denounced the court as an unlawful tribunal, and did not make the distinction.

Q. by Judge Advocate...Did he refer to the case of Campbell, the rebel spy, and make any distinction?

A...No. He denounced the court first, and then gave the instances, which I have already related in my direct testimony.

Q. by Vallandigham...Do you not remember my speaking of the Campbell case, and saying that he was properly tried?

A...He may, but I do not recollect it. He probably did refer to the Campbell case.

Q...May I not have made the distinction and you not have heard it?

The Judge Advocate said he would admit that the accused did draw the distinction between the cases, and that he admitted the right of the court to try the spy. In other words, that he condemned the trial of the Butler county man, and approved the case of the spy who was tried and convicted.

Q...Did I not distinctly, in the conclusion of the speech, enjoin upon the people to stand by the Union at all events and that, if war failed, not to give up the Union, but to try by peacable means, by compromise, to restore it as our fathers made it, and that, though others might consent, or be forced to consent, I would not myself be one of those who would take any part in agreeing to a dissolution of the Union?

A...Yes. He said that he and the peace men were the only ones who wished the restoration of the Union.

Q...Did not one of the banners you refer to as decorated with butternuts bear the inscription, "The Constitution as it is and the Union as it was"?

A...The banners were numerous. One of them, I believe, did bear that inscription.

Q...Do you mean to be understood to say that I heard the reference to Jeff. Davis in the crowd or gave any assent to it whatever?

A...*I cannot say that he did. Did not see or hear him give any assent to it.* There were many other remarks of that character uttered.

Q...What was the size of the crowd assembled there?

A...I did not know the proper estimate but the crowd was very large.

The Court then adjourned to Thursday morning at 10 o'clock.

SECOND DAY.

The court met at 10 o'clock, A. M. Present as before. Yesterday's proceedings and testimony were read and approved, and were signed by the President.

Capt. Hill was again called to the stand, and his cross examination was resumed by Mr. Vallandigham.

Q...In speaking of the character of the war, did I not expressly say as Mr. Lincoln in his proclamation, July 1st, 1862, said, "This unnecessary and injurious civil war?"

Judge Advocate...So, Mr. Vallandigham, was that used in your speech as a quotation from the President's proclamation?

Mr. Vallandigham...Yes, it was.

Witness...I do not recollect that he did. The language he made use of I understood to be his own.

Mr. Vallandigham...Of course I could not put the quotation marks in my speech.

[So that no speaker must repeat Mr. Lincoln's jokes or aphorisms, unless he puts in the quotation marks.]

Q...Again, in speaking of the character of the war, did I not expressly give as proof the President's proclamation of September 22, 1862, and January 1, 1863, declaring the emancipation of the slaves in the southern seceded states, as proof that the war was being waged for that purpose?

The witness was about to answer, when the Judge Advocate checked him. He said it was bringing matters which were foreign to the charge and specification, and that the court was not called upon to pass upon the merits of the President's proclamation. He then desired that the court should be closed for deliberation.

Mr. Vallandigham...I desire to show this fact, in explanation of the purpose and object of my declaration as to the present character of the war, and as my authority for the statement, for I assume that the President is not disloyal.

The Judge Advocate insisted that the question required the cour t to pass judgment upon the merits of the President's proclamation, and not whether he (Mr. V.) was expressing his own sentiments or those of the President.

The Judge Advocate said the question would not be admitted.

Q...Did you continue at the same place during the delivery of the whole speech?

A...I did.

Q...Were your notes taken at the time or reduced to writing afterward?

A...They were taken at the time, and as they fell from the speaker's lips.

Q...Were you not in citizen's clothes; and how came you to be at Mount Vernon that day? Did you go to Mount Vernon for the purpose of taking notes and reporting the speech?

Judge Advocate...I object to this question, on the ground of its immateriality.

Mr. Vallandigham insisted on the question, on the ground that it explained the temper and spirit of the witness, and his prejudices, and as showing that the notes were taken with reference to the arrest and prosecution before this Commission, he being a Captain in the service, and his regiment at Cincinnati.

The question was objected to by the Judge Advocate, and the court was cleared for deliberation.

On opening the doors again, the Judge Advocate announced that the question would be allowed.

A...I was in citizen's clothes, *and I went up for the purpose of listening to any speech that might be delivered by him.* [A self-convicted spy.] I had no order to take notes or report.

Q...Did you go provided with pencil and paper?

The Judge Advocate objected to the question. Of course the witness had pencil and paper.

Q...Did you take notes of any other speech?

A...I commenced taking notes of Mr. Cox's speech, but considered it harmless, and stopped. I took no notes of any other speech.

Q...Were you not sent expressly to listen to my speech?

A...I was not any more than any other speech.

Q...By whom were you sent or requested to go?

A...By Capt. Andrew C. Kemper, Assistant Adjutant General of the military commandant of the city.

Q...From whom did you obtain leave of absence?

Judge Advocate...He did not need any leave of absence; the order was enough.

Mr. Vallandigham...Then strike out the words "or requested" from the answer for it leaves it ambiguous.

Q...Did you make report to Capt. Kemper on your return?

The Judge Advocate objected to the question, but the court allowed it.

A...On my return I did not report to Kemper.

Q...To whom did you report?

A...To Col. Eastman himself, and he sent me to headquarters Department of the Ohio.

This closed the testimony of Capt. Hill on both the direct and cross examination.

The Judge Advocate called Capt. John A. Means, 115th O. V. I., who was sworn. He was asked by the Judge Advocate if he was at the Mount Vernon meeting, and whether he heard Mr. Vallandigham speak, and, if so, what he said of the war, &c.

Witness...I was present at the meeting, and heard Mr. Vallandigham address the people. I was in two or three positions most of the time, and about five or ten feet from the stand. I heard the whole speech.

By the Judge Advocate...State what remarks you heard him make, and give us, as near as you can, his language.

Witness...He stated that the war was not carried on for the restoration of the Union, and that it might have been stopped some time ago, and the Union restored, if the plans which had been submitted had been accepted.

Mr. Vallandigham objected to this testimony, on the ground that he had applied for a subpœna to compel the attendance of Fernando Wood, who would produce the written evidence of what he (Mr. V.) had asserted about the return of Southern Senators to their seats in Congress.

Judge Advocate...I will strike from the specification that part which refers to the propositions by which the Southern States could be won back, &c.

To the Witness...You will omit that part of your testimony.

Witness continued. "If the plans he had proposed himself had been adopted, peace would have been restored, the Union saved by a reconstruction, the North won back, and the South guaranteed her rights. That Richmond, Charleston, and Vicksburg had not been taken, and the Mississippi was not opened, and could not be as long as there was cotton on the banks to be stolen or officers enriched. He said that after the rebuke which the administration received at the last fall election, no more volunteers could be had, and the Administration had to resort to the French conscription law. *But he would not counsel resistance to military or civil law.* That was not needed. The people were not deserving to be free men who would submit to such encroachments on their liberties.

Mr. Vallandigham...What was I referring to, when I made the remarks you say I did?

Witness...He was speaking of the conscription act.... He said he believed that the Administration was attempting to erect a despotism, and in less than one month. Mr. Lincoln had plunged the country in this cruel, bloody, and unnecessary war. He stated that General Order No. 38 was a usurpation of power that he despised...he spit upon it and trampled it under his feet. That he for one would not regard it. He styled the officers of the administration and officers of the army as Lincoln minions.... He said he did not ask Lincoln or Burnside whether he might speak; that he was a free man and spoke as he pleased. He stated the military orders and proclamations were intended to intimidate the people and prevent them from meeting as they had done that day. He claimed the right to discuss and criticise the actions of civil and military authorities.

Q...Did he advise the people to take any steps to obtain their rights?

A...At the close of his speech he advised the people to come up together, and at *the ballot-box* to hurl the tyrant from his throne. In one part of his speech he styled the President as King Lincoln.

CROSS-EXAMINATION BY MR. VALLANDIGHAM.

Q...Did you take any notes at all during delivery of the speech, or are you testifying solely from memory?

A...I took no minutes during the delivery of the speech. After Pendleton commenced speaking, I went and wrote out what I heard. It was perhaps an hour and a half after I heard the speech.

Q...About what was the length of the speech?

A...I think about an hour and a half.

Q...You made no short-hand report of it I suppose. Did you ever report in short hand?

Judge Advocate...The witness has already said he made no report of the speech.

Mr. Vallandigham wanted to know if he was accustomed to reporting speeches.

The Judge Advocate objected to the question.

Q...You speak of my saying the *North* might be won back—was it not the *South* might be won back? Mr. Vallandigham said he noticed that the witness used the word "North" in place of the "South." It was the South he referred to.

—...No. I noticed this particularly. It struck me very forcibly.

Q...You say that I said that I would not counsel resistance to military or civil law. Did not I expressly counsel the people to obey the constitution and the laws and to pay proper respect to men in authority, but to maintain their political rights through the ballot-box, and to redress personal wrongs through the judicial tribunals of the country and in that way to rebuke and put down administrations and all usurpations of power.

A....Not in that connection. He said, at the last of his speech, to come up to the ballot-box and hurl the tyrant from power.

Q...Do you recollect the whole connection in which the sentence was used?

A...I did not understand him to advise submission at all times.

Q...Do you recollect the sum and substance of what I said?

A...I remember part of it, but I cannot remember *the language or substance so as to answer the question.*

Q...Did I not say that my authority to speak to the people in public assemblages on all public questions was not derived from General Order No. 38, but from General Order No. 1—the Constitution of the United States, George Washington commanding?

A...I understood him to say that his authority to speak to the people was higher than General Order No. 38, by that military despot, Burnside. It was Order No. 1, signed Washington. I did not hear him say "Constitution."

Q...Were not the names of Tod, Lincoln and Burnside used in the same connection, and that I did not ask their consent to speak?

A...At another time he did use these words.

Q...Were not the remarks you say I made about despising, spitting and trampling under foot, expressly applied in reference to arbitrary power generally, and did I not in that connection refer to General Order No. 9 of Indiana, signed by General Hascall, denying the right to criticise the war policy of the Administration?

A...The remarks in regard to despising and spitting upon were in direct reference to Order No. 38. Some time afterwards, in speaking of the tyranny of the administration, he did refer to Order No. 9, and of the right to criticise the acts of the Administration, and said that, if submitted to, it would be followed by civil war in Ohio.

Q...Did I approve of condemn the order?

Judge Advocate...The question, I think, has been already answered.

Q...Will you undertake to give any connected or methodical statement of my speech of over one hour and a half long?

A...I simply remember parts of it. I do not pretend to give the speech just as he spoke it.

Q...Were you not present in citizen's clothes, and how came you at Mount Vernon that day, by whose order, and were you sent for the purpose of listening to and reporting the speech?

A...I was there in citizen's clothes by order of Colonel Eastman. *I was sent to listen to the speech* and to give my careful attention and get his language as near as I could.

Q...Did you make such a report?

A...I did; to Col. Eastman.

Q...Did you make report of any other speeches on that occasion?

A...I did. I got the substance of Cox and Ranney's speeches.

Q...Were you directed to go to Mount Vernon and make a report of my speech, with reference to the prosecution under General Order No. 38.

A....I was not.

Q...Were any reasons given you why you should go? The Judge Advocate objected to the question, as the answer had been sufficiently given before.

Q...Was any object stated to you, and if so what, for your going there in citizen's clothes, listening to, and reporting the speech?

A...There was not any.

The cross-examination here closed, and the Judge Advocate stated that he did not propose to introduce any further testimony on the part of the prosecution.

Mr. Vallandigham asked for a few minutes to consult with his counsel, which was granted, and the court took a recess of fifteen minutes.

THE DEFENCE.

On the re-assembling of the court Mr. Vallandigham called Hon. S. S. Cox, who was sworn. He was examined by Mr. Vallandigham.

Q...Were you present at a public political meeting of citizens of Ohio, at Mount Vernon, on Friday, May 1st, 1863, and if so, in what capacity?
A...I was present as one of the speakers.
Q...Did you hear the speech of Mr. Vallandigham on that day made to the assemblage?
A...I did.
Q...State where your position was during its delivery; what your opportunities for hearing were; whether you heard it all; and whether and why your attention was particularly directed to it?
A...Before the speaking began I was on the stand, a few feet from Mr. Vallandigham, and was most of the time standing near him, so that I could not fail to hear all that he said. I do not think my attention was distracted unless for a few minutes during the whole speech. I had not heard Mr. Vallandigham speak since the adjournment of Congress, and as I came in from a different direction from the West, I did not know that he was to be there. I took an especial interest in listening to his speech throughout. Having to follow him, I naturally noted the topics which he discussed. I believe that answers the question.
Q...Did you hear any allusions to Gen. Burnside, by name or description, and if so, what were they?
A...The only allusion that he made to the General was, I think, near the beginning of his speech, in which he said he was not there by the favor of David Tod, or Abraham Lincoln, or Ambrose E. Burnside.
Q...Were any epithets applied to him during the speech?
A...No, sir. If there had been, I should have noticed them, because Gen. Burnside was an old friend of mine. I should have remembered any odious epithets applied to him.
Q...Did you hear the reference to General Order No. 38, and, if so, what was it?
A...The only reference made in that speech to that Order was something to this effect: that he did not recognize (I do not know that I can quote his language) Order No. 38 as superior to General Order No. 1, of the Constitution, from George Washington, commanding. It was something to that effect. I thought at the time that it was a handsome point. I remembered that, because Mr. Vallandigham used the same expression in the debate in Congress on the conscription bill, or in some debate, somewhere else, when I heard him speak.
Q....Were any violent epithets, such as spitting upon, trampling under foot, or the like, used at any time in the speech, in reference to that Order No. 38; and if any criticism was made upon it, what was that criticism?
A...I cannot recall any denunciatory epithets applied to that order, I did not hear them, and if I had I should have remembered them. The criticism upon the order was made as I have stated before.
Q....In what connection did I use the strong language?
A....Mr. Vallandigham discussed the order very briefly, in order to get away on the four o'clock train, and occupied most of his time in discussing other propositions.... It was in connection with remarks about closing the war by separation of the Union. He charged that the men in power had the power to make peace by separation. He exhausted some time in reading proofs of this; one was from Montgomery Blair and another from Forney's *Press*. He also said there were private proofs which time would disclose. He said they pursued this thing until they found that the Democrats were unwilling to make any peace except on the basis of the restoration of the whole Union.
Q...Do you remember to what, if at all, in connection with future usurpations of power he applied his strongest language?
A....I cannot say as to the strongest language, for he always spoke pretty strongly. He denounced in strong language any usurpations of power to stop public discussions and the suffrage. He appealed to the people to protect their rights, as the remedy for every grievance. Twice in his speech he counseled and warned against violence or revolution. By the peaceful means of the ballot-box, all that was wrong of a public nature might be remedied and that the courts would remedy all grievances of a private nature. I cannot quote the language, but that is the substance.
During his speech he referred to those in power having rightful authority, and that they should be obeyed. He counseled no resistance except what could be had at the ballot-box.
Q...Was anything said by me at all looking to forcible resistance of either law or military orders?
A....Not as I understand it.
Q...What was the sole remedy that I urged upon the people?
A....The sole remedy was, as I have stated, in the courts and in the ballot-box. I remember this distinctly, because I had been pursuing the same line of remark at Chicago and Fort Wayne and other places where I had been speaking, and for the purpose of repressing any tendency toward violence among our democratic people.
Q...Was anything said by me on that occasion in denunciation of the conscription bill or looking in any way to resistance to it?
A...My best recollection is that Mr. Vallandigham did not say a word about it.
Mr. Vallandigham....Not one word.
Q...Did I refer to the French conscription law, and if not, by whom was reference made to it?
A...He did not. I did in this connection.
The Judge Advocate objected to what Mr. Cox had said as not being competent evidence.
Mr. Cox desired to say to the Court, in explanation of what he said about the Conscription law, that he had just before the meeting been talking with Judge Bartley about the Conscription law having been copied from the French law, and I merely referred to that in my speech.
Q...Do you remember my quoting from President Lincoln's proclamation of July 1st, 1862, the words "unnecessary and injurious war."
A...I do not. He may have done so, but I did not hear it.
Q...Did you hear similar language used by me?
A...I cannot recollect it.
Q...Do you remember my comments on the change of the policy of the war some year or so after its commencement, and what reference was made by me in that connection?
A...He did refer to the change in the policy of the war, and I think devoted some time to show that it war carried on for the abolition of slavery, and not for the restoration of the Union.
Q...What did he claim to have been its original purpose, and did he refer to any measure or proclamation of the President in that connection?
A...He referred in that defense to the Crittenden proposition, declaring the war was for the restoration of the Union, and not to break up the States.
Q...Did I counsel any other mode in that speech, of resisting usurpations of arbitrary power, except by free discussion and the ballot-box?
A...He did not.
Mr. Vallandigham...As I understand that portion of the specification which relates to the proposition from Richmond has been stricken out, I will ask no questions about it.
Q...Were any denunciations of the officers of the army indulged in by me, or any offensive epithets applied to them?
A...Well, occasionally, Mr. Vallandigham used the word "The President and his minions," but I did not think he used it in any other than the general acceptation of that term. He did not use it in connection with the army.
Mr. Vallandigham...I did not use it in connection with the officers of the army.
Mr. Cox...It was in connection with arbitrary arrests perhaps, that he used it.
Q...Was it not in connection with army contractors and speculators?
The Judge Advocate objected to the question and said the witness had distinctly stated that he did not think Mr V. had applied it to the officers of the army.
Q...Do I understand you to say that the denunciations to which you refer, were chiefly in reference to arbitrary arrests?
A...My recollection is that that was the connection in which it was used. He used strong epithets towards spies and informers, and did not seem to like them very much.
Mr. Vallandigham...As the court has admitted that I did make a distinction between the Butler county case and the Kentucky spy, I will not refer to it now.
Q...Do you remember the connection in which words to this effect were used at the close of the speech: "In regard to the possibility of a dissolution of the Union," and of his own determination in regard to such a contingency, and his "declining to act as a priest?"
A...I cannot give the exact words, but I remember the metaphor, "that he would not be a priest to minister at the

altar of disunion." It was as he wound up his speech. He was speaking about disunion and his attachment to the Union.
Q...What counsel did I give the people on the subject of the Union at the close of my speech?
A...He invoked them under no circumstances to surrender the Union. I think he said something about leaving it to our posterity.
Q...Do you remember my rebuke of arbitrary court martials, and was it in connection with the Butler county case?
A...Yes; I so understood it.
Q...What was the general character of my remarks on that subject?
A...He denounced the applause of Jeff. Davis by that party, and said there was a mode by which this man could be tried.
Mr. Vallandigham asked whether the rebuke had not reference to, and was spoken in connection with the Butler county case. He desired a distinct answer to this.
Mr. Cox...He was speaking of the Butler county case, and he pointed out a mode by which such a man could be tried.
Q...Was anything said in my speech in reference to the war, except in condemnation of what I claimed to be the policy upon which it was now being waged, and as a policy which I insisted could not restore the Union, but must end finally in disunion?
A...I can only give my understanding. I do not know what inference other people might draw from it. I understood his condemnation of the war to be launched at the perversion of its original purpose.
Mr. Vallandigham...I do not remember anything further just now. I have some other witnesses whom I desire to examine on this point, who are not yet here.
Judge Advocate...I have no questions to put to the witness.
To Mr. Vallandigham...Has not this witness sufficiently developed the purpose and spirit of your speech?
Mr. Vallandigham...I have called but one witness, and I understand the court has several more to corroborate what their first witness has testified.
Judge Advocate...The court will not be influenced by the number of witnesses. The number has nothing to do with the case.
Mr. Vallandigham...I did not counsel any resistance in my speech, and there were three witnesses on the stand, one of whom was the presiding officer and one a reporter, who is accustomed to reporting speeches, though he did not report on that occasion, whom I have telegraphed for and expect here at 4 p. m.
The Judge Advocate suggested that Mr. Pendleton, who was now present, was at the meeting at Mount Vernon, and that he might be called to the stand.
Mr. Vallandigham...Mr. Pendleton has been engaged in this case, and I would prefer not to call him, as I have other witnesses. I also desire to show that the witnesses in my speech were not in reference to General Order No. 39.
Judge Advocate...The witness has just said so.
Mr. Vallandigham...If the court will admit that, then I will not call other witnesses.
Judge Advocate...I will admit that the language might not have been used, especially toward General Order No. 38, but it had been proved that such language was used in the Mount Vernon speeches, in reference to military orders.
Mr. Vallandigham...I want to prove that it was not used in relation to General Order No. 38.
Judge Advocate...I will admit that the language was not used in regard to General Order No. 38, but generally to military orders.
Mr. Vallandigham said he desired time to prepare a defence covering this testimony, and would, according to the rules governing court martials, submit it in writing.
The Judge Advocate said he might cover 100 or 200 pages of foolscap in reviewing the case, but this would take time. He (the Judge Advocate) did not propose to say anything on the evidence, but would leave it with the Court. Mr. Vallandigham might say what he desired in defence verbally, and it could be reported in short hand, and thus save time.
Mr. Vallandigham preferred to have the record correct, as it would have to go before another tribunal.
The Court then took a recess to half past four o'clock.
The Court reconvened at five o'clock. P. M.
The Judge Advocate stated that the witnesses for the accused, who were expected, namely, Lickey Harper, J. F. F. Irwin and Frank H. Hurd, had not arrived, and that he had agreed with the accused to admit, as it would avoid a continuance, that if they were present and under oath, they would testify substantially the same as Mr. Cox had done.

Thereupon Mr. Vallandigham said he had no more testimony to offer, and the case closed .

The Judge Advocate now announced that the testimony was all in.

At the request of Mr. Vallandigham, the testimony of Mr. Cox was read over.

Mr. Vallandigham...Gentlemen of the Court, very briefly and respectfully I offer the following protest:

MR. VALLANDIGHAM'S PROTEST.

Arrested without due "process of law," without warrant from any judicial officer, and now, in a military prison, I have been served with a "charge and specifications," as in a court martial or military commission.

I am not in either "the land or naval forces of the United States, nor in the militia in the actual service of the United States," and therefore am not triable for any cause by any such court, but am subject, by the express terms of the Constitution, to arrest only by due process of law, judicial warrant, regularly issued upon affidavit and by some officer or court of competent jurisdiction for the trial of citizens, and am now entitled to be tried on an indictment or presentment of a Grand Jury of such court, to a speedy and public trial by an impartial jury of the state of Ohio, to be confronted with witnesses against me, to have compulsory process for witnesses in my behalf, the assistance of counsel for my defence, and evidence and argument according to the common law and the ways of judicial courts.

And all of these I here demand as my right as a citizen of the United States, and under the Constitution of the United States.

But the alleged "offence" itself is not known to the Constitution of the United States, nor to any law thereof. It is words spoken to the people of Ohio in an open and public political meeting, lawfully and peaceably assembled under the Constitution and upon full notice. It is words of criticism of the public policy of the public servants of the people, by which policy it was allegded that the welfare of the country was not promoted. It was an appeal to the people to change that policy, not by force, but by free elections and the ballot-box. It is not pretended that I counseled disobedience to the Constitution or resistance to laws and lawful authority. I never have. Beyond this protest I have nothing further to submit.

C. L. VALLANDIGHAM.
Cincinnati, Ohio, May 7, 1863.

FINDING AND SENTENCE.

The Commission, after mature deliberation on the evidence adduced and the statement of the accused, find the accused Clement L. Vallandigham, a citizen of the State of Ohio, as follows:

Of the specification except the words: "That propositions by which the northern states could be won back, and the South guaranteed their rights under the constitution had been rejected the day before the last battle of Fredericksburg, by Lincoln and his minions,"—meaning, thereby, the President of the United States, and those under him in authority; and the words, "asserting that he had firmly believed, as he asserted six months ago, that the men in power are attempting to establish a despotism in this country, more cruel and more oppressive than ever existed before" "Guilty."

And as to these words, "Not guilty."

Of the charge "Guilty."

And the commission do therefore sentence him, the said Clement L. Vallandigham, a citizen of the State of Ohio, to be placed in close confinement in some fortress of the United States, to be designated by the commanding officer of this department, there to be kept during the continuance of the war.

II. The proceedings, finding, and sentence in the foregoing case are approved and confirmed, and it is directed that the place of confinement of the prisoner, Clement L. Vallandigham, in accordance with the said sentence, be Fort Warren, Boston Harbor.

By command of Major General BURNSIDE.

LEWIS RICHMOND,
Assistant Adjutant General.

Here is the finding and the sentence. We place them on record, so that all posterity may see *just what* Mr. V. was adjudged guilty of; that is, 1st: for saying that Lincoln and his minions (meaning the president and those acting under him in the character of spies, &c.) had prevented Union by rejecting certain propositions for peace, &c. (This was stricken out, rather than expose WOOD's testimony) 2d, the uttering the *belief* that those in power were attempting to establish a Despotism. (Did not this very trial furnish the *proof* of this?) If this be treason, then traitors may be counted by the millions. The writer hereof, it is but proper to remark, has ever opposed Mr. V's peculiar peace views, as both premature and useless, yet, he believes the means used to put down that gentleman, while CONWAY and hundreds of other republicans, who have directly advocated dissolution, and committed well-defined acts of treason, without so much as a gentle rebuke from official quarters, is not only a gross outrage, but is intensifying the sting of despotism by an unmistakable display of political partiality.

We have not the patience to comment on *such* a trial, and the punishment inflicted on *such* charges, and *such* proofs, to say nothing of the spy system, through the criminal farce as inaugurated.

"Suspect! that's a *Spie's* office!—*Byron*

"Rather confide, and be deceived,
A thousand times, by treacherous foes,
Than once accuse the innocent,
* Or, let suspicion mar repose."—*Mrs. Osgood.*

It would puzzle the most astute and patriotic man that ever lived, to pick out a sentence uttered by Mr. V., on the occasion, and distort it to mean anything like treason against the Government—or anything the half so disloyal as the hundreds of extracts from republican speeches, in the preceding pages of this work. One of the main charges against Mr. V. it seems, was the repetition of a phrase used by Mr. Lincoln in his proclamation of July,'62. To punish citizens for repeating expressions used by him who applies the punishment, in the language of Edward Livingston, in 1798, is "a refinement on despotism."

As we have given our opinion that Order 38 was issued expressly to reach VALLANDIGHAM, so we record our belief that he was virtually sentenced before he was tried. This would not be without a precedent, for the bloody annals of *La Force* and other Bastiles during the Reign of Terror in France, teach us that the following order was often observed:

1st. Suspicion.
2d. Dig the grave.
3d. Procure the coffin.
4th. Arrest of the suspected.
5th. A five minutes trial.
6th. Sentence of death.
7th. Execution.
8th. Use of the coffin and the grave.

The forms of trial, &c, over, the next thing was to sentence and punish Mr. V. BURNSIDE was graciously pleased to sentence the victim to confinement, which the President, in the plenitude and magnanimity of His Majesty's power, commuted, by substituting banishment —a punishment unknown before, on this free continent—a punishment so long the disgrace to British Statutes, but no longer known to the English criminal code.

The arrest and deportation of Mr. V. aroused the most intense excitement throughout the north. The people saw in it a rapidly germinating despotism, and public meetings were held in numerous places—calm, yet firm and decided resolves were adopted, protesting to the President against the usurpation of power, and the striking down at one blow, the last barrier between despotism and civil liberty. The following resolves and "correspondence with the President, are self-explanatory.

THE ALBANY RESOLUTIONS AND THE PRESIDENT'S REPLY.

Letter of the Committee and Resolutions.

ALBANY, May 19, 1863.

To His Excellency the President of the United States:
The undersigned, officers of a public meeting held at the city of Albany on the 16th day of May instant, herewith transmit to your Excellency a copy of the resolutions adopted at the said meeting, and respectfully request your earnest consideration of them. They deem it proper on their personal responsibility to state that the meeting was one of the most respectable as to numbers and character, and one of the most earnest in the support of the Union ever held in the city.

Yours, with great regard,
ERASTUS CORNING, President.
ELI PERRY, Vice President.
PETER GANSEVOORT, Vice President.
PETER MONTEATH, Vice President.
SAMUEL W. GIBBS, Vice President.
JOHN NIBLACK, Vice President.
H. W. McCLELLAN, Vice President.
LEMUEL W. ROGERS, Vice President.
WM. SEYMOUR, Vice President.
JEREMIAH OSBORN, Vice President.
WM. S. PADDOCK, Vice President.
J. B. SANDERS, Vice President.
EDWARD MULCAHY, Vice President.
D. V. N. RADCLIFFE, Vice President.
WM. A. RICE, Secretary.
EDWARD NEWCOMB, Secretary.
R. W. PECKHAM, JR., Secretary.
M. A. NOLAN, Secretary.
JOHN R. NESSEL, Secretary.
C. W. WEEKS, Secretary.

Resolutions Adopted at the Meeting held in Albany, N. Y., on the 16th of May, 1863.

Resolved, That the Democrats of New York point to their uniform course of action during the two years of civil war through which we have passed, to the alacrity which they have evinced in filling the ranks of the army, to their contributions and sacrifices as the evidence of their patriotism and devotion to the cause of our imperiled country. Never in the history of civil wars has a government been sustained with such ample resources of means and men as the people have voluntarily placed in the hands of the administration.

Resolved, That as Democrats we are determined to maintain this patriotic attitude, and, despite of adverse and disheartening circumstances, to devote all our energies to maintain the cause of the Union, to secure peace through victory, and to bring back the restoration of all the states under the safeguard of the Constitution.

Resolved, That while we will not consent to be misapprehended on those points, we are determined not to be misunderstood in regard to others not less essential. We demand that the administration shall be true to the constitution; shall recognize and maintain the rights of the states and the liberties of the citizen; shall everywhere, outside of the lines of necessary military occupation and the scenes of insurrection, exert all its powers to sustain the supremacy of the civil over military law.

Resolved, That in view of these principles we denounce the recent assumption of a military commander to seize and try a citizen of Ohio, Clement L. Vallandigham, for no other reason than words addressed to a public meeting, in criticism of the course of the administration, and in condemnation of the military orders of that General.

Resolved, That this assumption of power by a military tribunal, if successfully asserted, not only abrogates the right of the people to assemble and discuss the affairs of government, the liberty of speech and of the press, the right of trial by jury, the law of evidence, and the privilege of *habeas corpus,* but it strikes a fatal blow at the supremacy of law and the authority of State and Federal constitutions.

Resolved, That the constitution of the United States... the supreme law of the land...has defined the crime of treason against the United States to consist "only in levying war against them, or adhering to their enemies, giving them aid and comfort;" and has provided that "no person shall be convicted of treason, unless on the testimony of two witnesses to the same overt act, or on confession in open court." And it farther provides that "no person shall be held to answer for a capital or otherwise infamous crime, unless on the presentment or an indictment by a grand jury, except in cases arising in the land and naval forces, or in the militia, when in actual service in time of war or public danger;" and farther, that, "in all criminal prosecutions, the accused shall enjoy the right of a speedy and public trial by an impartial jury of the State and district wherein the crime was committed.

Resolved, That these safeguards of the rights of the citizen against the pretensions of arbitrary power were intended more especially for his protection in times of civil commotion. They were secured substantially to the English people after years of protracted civil war, and were adopted into our constitution at the close of the revolution. They have stood the test of seventy-six years of trial, under our republican system, under circumstances which show that while they constitute the foundation of all free government, they are the elements of the enduring stability of the Republic.

Resolved, That, in adopting the language of Daniel Webster, we declare, "It is the ancient and undoubted prerogative of this people to canvass public measures and the merits of public men." It is a "home-bred right," a fire-side privilege. It has been enjoyed in every house, cottage and cabin in the nation. It is as undoubted as the right of breathing the air or walking on the earth. Belonging to private life as a right it belongs to public life as a duty, and is the last duty which those representatives we are shall find us to abandon. Aiming at all times to be courteous and temperate in its use, except when the right itself is questioned, we shall place ourselves on the extreme bounds of our own right and bid defiance to any arm that would move us from our ground. "This high constitutional privilege we shall defend and exercise in all places—in time of peace, in time of war, and at all times. Living, we shall assert it; and should we leave no other inheritance to our children, by the blessing of God we will leave them the inheritance of free principles and the example of a manly, independent and constitutional defence of them."

Resolved, That in the election of Gov. Seymour, the people of this State, by an emphatic majority, declared their condemnation of the system of arbitrary arrests, and their determination to stand by the constitution. That the revival of this lawless system can have but one result: to divide and distract the North, and to destroy its confidence in the purposes of the administration. That we deprecate it as an element of confusion at home, of weakness to our armies in the field, and as calculated to lower the estimate of American character and magnify the apparent peril of our cause abroad. And that, regarding the blow struck at a citizen of Ohio as aimed at the rights of every citizen of the North, we denounce it as against the spirit of our laws and constitution, and most earnestly call upon the President of the United States to reverse the action of the military tribunal which has passed a "cruel and unusual punishment" upon the party arrested, prohibited in terms by the constitution, and to restore him to the liberty of which he has been deprived.

Resolved, That the President, Vice-Presidents, and Secretary of this meeting be requested to transmit a copy of these resolutions to his Excellency the President of the United States, with the assurance of this meeting of their hearty and earnest desire to support the government in every constitutional and lawful measure to suppress the existing rebellion.

Mr. Lincoln's Reply.

EXECUTIVE MANSION,
WASHINGTON, June 12, 1863.

Hon. Erastus Corning and others:

GENTLEMEN—Your letter of may 19, inclosing the resolutions of a public meeting held at Albany, New York, on the 16th of the same month, was received several days ago.

The resolutions, as I understand them, are resolved into two propositions—first, the expression of a purpose to sustain the cause of the Union, to secure peace through victory, and to support the administration in every constitutional and lawful measure to suppress the rebellion; and, secondly, a declaration of censure upon the administration for supposed unconstitutional action, such as the making of military arrests. And from the two propositions a third is deduced, which is, that the gentlemen composing the meeting are resolved on doing their part to maintain our common government and country, despite the folly or wickedness, as they may conceive, of any administration. This position is eminently patriotic, and, as such, I thank the meeting and congratulate the nation for it. My own purpose is the same; so that the meeting and myself have a common object and can have no difference, except in the choice of means or measures for effecting that object.

And here I ought to close this paper, and would close it, if there were no apprehensions that more injurious consequences than any merely personal to myself might follow the censures systematically cast upon me for doing what, in my view of duty, I could not forbear. The resolutions promise to support me in every constitutional and lawful measure to suppress the rebellion, and I have not knowingly employed, nor shall knowingly employ, any other. But the meeting, by their resolutions, assert that certain military arrests, and proceedings following them, for which I am ultimately responsible, are unconstitutional. I think they are not.

The resolutions quote from the constitution the definition of treason, and also the limiting safeguards and guarantees therein provided for the citizen on trials for treason, and on his being held to answer for capital or other infamous crimes, and, in criminal prosecutions, his right to a speedy and public trial by an impartial jury. The proceed to resolve

"That these safeguards of the rights of the citizen against the pretensions of arbitrary power were intended more *especially* for his protection in times of civil commotion."

And, apparently to demonstrate the proposition, the resolutions proceed:

"They were secured substantially to the English people *after* years of protracted civil war, and were adopted into our constitution at the close of the revolution."

Would not the demonstration have been better if it could have been truly said that these safeguards had been adopted and announced during the civil wars and during our revolution, instead of after the one and at the close of the other? I, too, am devotedly for them after civil war, and before civil war, and at all times, "except when, in cases of rebellion or invasion, the public safety may require" their suspension. The resolutions proceed to tell us that these safeguards

"Have stood the test of seventy-seven years of trial, under our republican system, under circumstances which show that while they constitute the foundation of all free governments they are the elements of the enduring stability of the Republic."

No one denies that they have so stood the test up to the beginning of the present rebellion if we accept a certain occurrence at New Orleans; nor does any one question that they will stand the same test much longer after the rebellion closes. But these provisions of the constitution have no application to the present case we have in hand, because the arrests complained of *were not made for treason*—that is, not for the treason defined in the constitution, and upon the conviction of which the punishment is death—*nor yet were they made to hold persons to answer for any capital or otherwise infamous crimes*; nor were the proceedings following, in any constitutional or legal sense, *"criminae Prosecutions."* [In this connection we call the readers attention to the speech of Edward Livingston, on a subsequent page.] The arrests were made on totally different grounds, and the proceeding following accorded with the grounds of the arrest. Let us consider the real case with which we are dealing, and apply to it the parts of the constitution plainly made for such cases.

Prior to my installation here, it had been inculcated that any state had a lawful right to secede from the national Union, and, that it would be expedient to exercise the right whenever the devotees of the doctrine should fail to elect a President to their own liking. I was elected contrary to their liking; and accordingly, so far as it was legally possible, they had taken seven states out of the Union, had seized many of the United States forts, and had fired upon the United States flag, all before I was inaugurated; and, of course, before I had done any official act whatever. The rebellion thus began, soon ran into the present civil war; and, in certain respects, it began on very unequal terms between the parties. The insurgents had been preparing for it more than thirty years, while the government had taken no steps to resist them. The former had carefully considered all the means which could be turned to their account. It undoubtedly was a well-pondered reliance with them that in their unrestricted efforts to destroy Union. constitution and law, all together, the government would, in a great *degree* be restrained by the same constitution and law from arresting their progress. Their sympathizers pervaded all departments of the government and nearly all communities of the people. From this material, under cover of "liberty of speech," "liberty of the press," and *"habeas corpus"* they hoped to keep on foot amongst us a most efficient corps of spies, informers, suppliers, and aiders and abettors of their cause in a thousand ways. They knew that, in times such as they were inaugurating, by the constitution itself, the *"habeas corpus"* might be suspended; but they also knew they had friends who would make a question as to who was to suspend it; meanwhile their spies and others might remain at large to help on their cause. Or if, as has happened, the Executive should suspend the writ, without ruinous waste of time, instances of arresting innocent persons might occur, as are always likely to occur in such cases, and then a clamor could be raised in regard to this which might be at least of some service to the insurgent cause. It needed no very keen perception to discover this part of the enemy's programme so soon as, by open hostilities, their machinery was fairly put in motion. Yet, thoroughly imbued with a reverence for the guaranteed rights of individuals, I was slow to adopt the strong measures which by degrees I have been forced to regard as being within the exceptions of the constitution and as indispensible to the public safety. Nothing is better known to history than that courts of justice are utterly incompetent to such cases. Civil courts are organized chiefly for trials of individuals, or, at most, a few individuals acting in concert; and this in quiet times, and on charges of crimes well defined in the law. Even in times of peace, bands of horse thieves and robbers frequently grow too numerous and powerful for the ordinary courts of justice. But what comparison in numbers have such bands ever borne to the insurgent sympathizers even in many of the loyal States? Again, a jury too frequently has at least one member more ready to hang the panel than to hang the traitor. And yet, again, he who dissuades one man from volunteering, or induces one soldier to desert, weakens the Union cause as much as he who kills a Union soldier in battle. Yet this dissuasion or inducement may be so conducted as to be no defined crime of which any civil court would take cognizance.

Ours is a case of rebellion—so called by the resolutions before me—in fact, a clear, flagrant and gigantic case of rebellion; and the provision of the constitution that "the privilege of the writ of *habeas corpus* shall not be suspended unless when, in case of rebellion or invasion, the public safety may require it," [But the writ had not then been suspended;] is the provision which specially applies to our present case. This provision plainly attests the understanding of those who made the constitution, that ordinary courts of justice are inadequate to "cases of rebellion"—attests their purpose that, in such cases, men may be held in custody whom the courts, acting on ordinary rules, would discharge. *Habeas corpus* does not discharge men who are proved to be guilty of defined crime; and its suspension is allowed by the constitution on purpose that men may be arrested and held *who cannot be proved to be guilty of defined crime,* "When, in case of rebellion or invasion, the public safety may require it." This is precisely our present case—a case of rebellion, wherein the public safety does require the suspension. Indeed, arrests by process of courts, and arrests in cases of rebellion, do not proceed together altogether upon the same basis. The former is directed at the small percentage of ordinary and continuous perpetration of crime, while the latter is directed at sudden and extensive uprisings against the government, which at most will succeed or fail in no great length of time. In the latter case, arrests are made, not so much for what has been done, *as for what probably would be done.* [O. Moses, what a rule.] The latter is more for the preventive and less for the vindictive than the former. In such cases the purposes of men are much more easily understood than in cases of ordinary crime. The man who stands by and *says nothing* when the peril of his government is discussed cannot be misunderstood. If not hindered, he is sure to help the enemy; [so that Vallandigham was arrested for what he *might* do!] much more if he talks ambiguously—talks for his country with "*buts,*" and "*ifs,*" and "*ands.*" Of how little value the constitutional provisions I have quoted will be rendered, if arrests shall never be made until defined crimes shall have been committed, may be illustrated by a few notable examples. General John C. Breckinridge, General Robert E. Lee, General Joseph E. Johnston, General John B. Magruder, General William B. Preston, General Simon B. Buckner and Commodore Franklin Buchanan, now occupying the very highest places in the rebel war service, were all within the power of the government since the rebellion began, and were nearly as well known to be traitors then as now. Unquestionably, if we had seized and held them the insurgent cause would be much weaker. But no one of them had then committed any crime defined in the law. Every one of them, if arrested, would have been discharged on *habeas corpus* were the writ allowed to operate. In view of these and similar cases, I think the time not likely to come when I shall be blamed for having made too few arrests rather than too many.

By the third resolution the meeting indicate their opinion that military arrests may be constitutional in localities where rebellion actually exists, but that such arrests are unconstitutional in localities where rebellion or insurrection does not actually exist. They insist that such arrests shall not be made "outside of the lines of necessary military occupation and the scenes of insurrection." Inasmuch, however, as the constitution itself makes no such distinction, I am unable to believe that there is any such constitutional distinction. I consider that the class of arrests complained of can be constitutional only when, in cases of rebellion or invasion, the public safety may require them; and I insist that in such cases they are constitutional wherever the public safety does require them, as well in places to which they may prevent the rebellion extending as in those places where it may be already prevailing, as well where they may restrain mischievous interference with the raising and supplying armies to suppress the rebellion, as where the rebellion may actually be; as well where they may restrain the enticing men out of the army, as where they could prevent mutiny in the army; equally constitutional at all places where they will conduce to the public safety, as against the danger of rebellion or invasion. Take the particular case mentioned by the meeting. It is asserted, in substance, that Mr. Vallandigham was, by a military commander, seized and tried "for no other reason than words addressed to a public meeting, in criticism of the course of the administration, and in condemnation of the military orders of the General." Now, if there be no mistake about this; if this assertion is the truth and the whole truth; if there was no other reason for the arrest, then I concede that the arrest was wrong. But the arrest, I understand, was made for a very different reason. Mr. Vallandigham avows his hostility to the war on the part of the Union; and his arrest was made because he was laboring, with some effect to prevent the raising of troops, to encourage desertions from the army, and to leave the rebellion without an adequate military force to suppress it. [Nothing of this kind appears in evidence against him.] He was not arrested because he was damaging the political prospects of the Administration or the personal interest of the Commanding General, but because he was damaging the army, upon the existence and vigor of which the life of the nation depends. He was warring upon the military, and this gave the military constitutional jurisdiction to lay hands upon him. If Mr. Vallandigham was not damaging the military power of the country, then his arrest was made on mistake of fact, which I would be glad to correct on reasonably satisfactory evidence. [General BURNSIDE himself furnished the President the best evidence on this point, when he said that the army would "tear to pieces" any man who should talk as Vallandigham did. The fact and corolary do not lay together.—ED.]

I understand the meeting, whose resolutions I am considering, to be in favor of suppressing the rebellion by military force—by armies. Long experience has shown that armies cannot be maintained unless desertion shall be punished by the severe penalty of death. The case requires, and the law and the constitution sanction, this punishment. Must I shoot a simple-minded soldier boy who deserts, while I must not touch a hair of a willy agitator who induces him to desert? This is none the less injurious when effected by getting a father, or brother, or friend into a public meeting, and there work upon his feelings till he is persuaded to write the soldier boy that he is fighting in a bad cause, for a wicked administration of a contemptible government, too weak to arrest and punish him if he shall desert. I think that in such a case to silence the agitator and save the boy is not only constitutional, but withal a great mercy.

If I be wrong on the question of constitutional power, my error lies in believing that certain proceedings are constitutional when, in cases of rebellion or invasion, the public safety requires them, which would not be constitutional when, in the absence of rebellion or invasion, the public safety does not require them. In other words, that the constitution is not in its application in all respects the same in case of rebellion or invasion involving the public safety, as it is in times of profound peace and public security. The constitution itself makes the distinction; and I can no more be persuaded that the government can constitutionally take no strong measures in time of rebellion, because it can be shown that the same could not be lawfully taken in time of peace, than I can be persuaded that a particular drug is not good medicine for a sick man because it can be shown that it is not good for a well man. Nor am I able to appreciate the danger apprehended by the meeting that the American people will, by means of military arrests during the rebellion, lose the right of public discussion, the liberty of speech and the press, law of evidence, trial by jury and *habeas corpus* throughout the indefinite peaceful future which I trust lies before them, any more than I am able to believe that a man could contract so strong an appetite for emetics during temporary illness as to persist in feeding upon them during the remainder of his healthful life.

In giving the resolutions that earnest consideration which you request me, I cannot overlook the fact that the meeting speak as "democrats." Nor can I, with full respect to their known intelligence, and the fairly presumed deliberation with which they prepared their resolutions, be permitted to suppose that this occurred by accident, or in any other way than that they preferred to designate themselves "democrats" rather than "American citizens." In this time of national peril I would have preferred to meet you upon a level one step higher than any party platform, because I am sure that, from such more elevated position, we could do better battle for the country we all love than we possibly can from those lower ones where, from the force of habit, the prejudices of the past and the selfish hopes of the future, we are sure to extend much of our ingenuity and strength in finding fault with and aiming blows at each other. But since you have denied me this, I will yet be thankful, for the country's sake, that not all Democrats have done so. He on whose discretionary judgment Mr. Vallandigham was arrested and tried is a Democrat, having no old party affinity with me; and the Judge who rejected the constitutional view expressed in these resolutions, by refusing to discharge Mr. Vallandigham on *habeas corpus*, is a Democrat of better days than these, having received his judicial mantle at the hands of President Jackson. And still more, of all those Democrats who are nobly exposing their lives and shedding their blood on the battle-field, I have learned that many approve the course taken with Mr. Vallandigham, while I have not heard a single one condemning it. I cannot assert that there are none such. And the name of President Jackson recalls an instance of pertinent history. After the battle of New Orleans, and while the fact that the treaty of peace had been concluded was well known in the city, but before official knowledge of it had arrived, General Jackson still maintained martial or military law. Now, that it could be said that the war was over, the clamor against martial law, which had existed from the first, grew more furious. Among other things a Mr. Louaillier published a denunciatory newspaper article.— General Jackson arrested him. A lawyer by the name of Morel procured the United States Judge Hall to order a writ of *habeas corpus* to relieve Mr. Louaillier. Gen. Jackson arrested both the lawyer and the Judge. A Mr. Hollander ventured to say of some part of the matter that "it was a dirty trick." Gen. Jackson arrested him. When the officer attempted to serve the writ of *habeas corpus*, Gen. Jackson took it from him, and sent him away with a copy. Holding the Judge in custody a few days, the General sent him beyond the limits of his encampment, and set him at liberty, with an order to remain until the ratification of peace should be regularly announced, or until the British should have left the southern coast. A day or two more elapsed, the ratification of the treaty of peace was regularly announced, and the Judge and others were fully liberated. A few days more, and the Judge called Gen. Jackson into court and fined him a thousand dollars for having arrested him and the others named. The General paid the fine, and there the matter rested for nearly thirty years, when Congress refunded principal and interest. The late Senator Douglas, then in the House of Representatives, took a leading part in the debates, in which the constitutional question was much discussed. I am not prepared to say whom the journals would show to have voted for the measure.

It may be remarked, first, that we had the same constitution then as now; secondly, that we then had a case of invasion, that the permanent right of the people to public discussion, the liberty of speech and of the press, the trial by jury, the law of evidence, and the *habeas corpus* suffered no detriment whatever by the conduct of General Jackson, or its subsequent approval by the American Congress.

And yet, let me say that in my own discretion I do not know whether I would have ordered the arrest of Mr. Vallandigham. While I cannot shift the responsibility from myself, I hold that, as a general rule, the commander in the field is the better judge of the necessity in any particular case. Of course, I must practice a general directory and revisory power in the matter.

One of the resolutions expresses the opinion of the meeting that arbitrary arrests will have the effect to divide and distract those who should be united in suppressing the rebellion, and I am specifically called on to discharge Mr. Vallandigham. I regard this as, at least, a fair appeal to me on the expediency of exercising a constitutional power which I think exists. In response to such appeal I have to say it gave me pain when I learned that Mr. Vallandigham had been arrested—that is, I was pained that there should have seemed to be a necessity for arresting him and that it will afford me great pleasure to discharge him as soon as I can by any means, believe the public safety will not suffer by it. I farther say that, as the war progresses, it appears to me, opinion and action, which were in great confusion at first, take shape and fall into more regular channels, so that the necessity for strong dealing with them gradually decreases. I have every reason to desire that it should cease altogether, and far from the least is my regard for the opinions and wishes of those who, like the meeting at Albany, declare their purpose to sustain the government in every constitutional and lawful measure to suppress the rebellion. Still I must continue to do so much as may seem to be required by the public safety.

A. LINCOLN.

To which the committee replied in the following

Scathing and Conclusive Rejoinder.

STATEMENT.

At a public meeting held at the Capitol, in the city of Albany, on the 16th of May, 1863, to consider the arbitrary arrest of Mr. Vallandigham, certain resolutions were adopted, copies of which were by the direction of the meeting, transmitted by its officers to President Lincoln, who, in a communication dated the 12th of June, 1863, addressed to the gentlemen referred to, which has appeared very generally in the public prints, discussed the resolutions and controverted certain positions which they maintained in regard to personal rights and constitutional obligations.

On the receipt of this communication, the Hon. Erastus Corning, chairman of the meeting referred to, addressed the President, informing him, in substance, that the special duty assigned to the officers of the meeting had been fulfilled by sending the resolutions to his Excellency; but adding that, in view of the importance of the principles involved, and the public interest which the matter had assumed, he had deemed it proper to submit the President's letter to the committee who reported the resolutions, for such action as in their judgment it might demand.

The committee, having considered the subject, and the questions at issue as of the gravest importance, replied to the President's communication, which reply is now laid before the public. At the request of the committee, it was sent to the President by the officers of the meeting, in a letter under their signatures, of which the following is a copy:

"To His Excellency the President of the United States:

"SIR:—The undersigned, officers of the public meeting held in this city on the 16th day of May last, to whom your communication of the 12th of this month, commenting on the resolutions adopted at that meeting, was addressed, have the honor to send to your Excellency, a reply to that communication by the committee who reported the resolutions. The great importance to the people of this country of the questions discussed must be our apology, if any be needed, for saying that we fully concur in this reply, and believe it to be in entire harmony with the views and sentiments of the meeting referred to.

"We are, with great respect, truly yours.

"ERASTUS CORNING, President.

[This was also signed by the entire Committee.]

"ALBANY, June 30, 1863."

To His Excellency ABRAHAM LINCOLN, President of the United States:

SIR—Your answer, which has appeared in the public prints, to the resolutions adopted at a recent meeting in the city of Albany, affirming the personal rights and liberties of the citizens of this country, has been referred to the undersigned—the committee who prepared and reported those resolutions. The subject will now receive from us further attention, which your answer seems to justify, if not to invite. We hope not to appear wanting in the respect due to your high position; if we reply with a freedom and earnestness suggested by the infinite gravity and importance of the question upon which you have thought proper to take issue at the bar of public opinion.

You seem to be aware that the constitution of the United States, which you have sworn to protect and defend, contains the following guarantees, to which we again ask your attention. (1.) Congress shall make no law abridging the freedom of speech or of the press.— (2.) The right of the people to be secure in their persons against unreasonable seizures shall not be violated, and no warrant shall issue but upon probable cause, supported by oath. (3.) No persons except soldiers and marines in the service of the government shall be held to answer for a capital or infamous crime, unless on presentment or indictment of a grand jury, nor shall any person be deprived of life, liberty or property, without due process of law. (4.) In all criminal prosecutions, the accused shall enjoy the right of a speedy and public trial by an impartial jury of the State or district in which the crime shall have been committed, and to be confronted with the witnesses against him.

You are also, no doubt, aware that, on the adoption of the constitution, these invaluable provisions were proposed by the jealous caution of the states, and were inserted as amendments for a perpetual assurance of liberty against the encroachments of power. From your earliest reading of history, you also know that the great principles of liberty and law which underlie these provisions were derived to us from the British constitution. In that country they were secured by *Magna Charta*, more than six hundred years ago, and they have been confirmed by many and repeated statutes of the realm. A single palpable violation of them in England would not only arouse the public indignation, but would endanger the throne itself. For a persistent disregard of them Charles the First was dethroned and beheaded by his rebellious subjects.

The fact has already passed into history that the sacred rights and immunities which were designed to be protected by these constitutional guarantees have not been preserved to the people during your administration. In violation of the first of them, the freedom of the press has been denied. In repeated instances newspapers have been suppressed [in the loyal states, because they criticised, as constitutionally they might, those fatal errors of policy which have characterized the conduct of public affairs since your advent to power. In violation of the second of them, hundreds, and we believe thousands, of men have been seized and immured in prisons and bastiles, not only without warrant upon probable cause, but without any warrant, and for no other cause than a constitutional exercise of freedom of speech In violation of all these guarantees, a distinguished citizen of a peaceful and loyal state has been torn from his home at midnight by a band of soldiers, acting under the order of one of your Generals, tried before a military commission, without judge or jury, convicted, and sentenced without the suggestion of any offence known to the constitution or laws of this country. For all these acts you avow yourself ultimately responsible. In the special case of Mr. Vallandigham, the injustice commenced by your subordinate was consummated by a sentence of exile from home pronounced by you. That great wrong more than any other which preceded it, asserts the principles of a supreme despotism.

These repeated and continued invasions of constitutional liberty and private right have occasioned profound anxiety in the public mind The apprehension and alarm which they are calculated to produce have been greatly enhanced by your attempt to justify them, because in that attempt you assume to yourself a rightful authority possessed by no constitutional monarch on earth. We accept the declaration that you prefer to exercise this authority with a moderation not hitherto exhibited. But, believing as we do, that your forbearance is not the tenure by which liberty is enjoyed in this country, we propose to challenge the grounds on which your claim of supreme power is based. While yielding to you as a constitutional magistrate the deference to which you are entitled, we cannot accord to you the despotic power you claim, however indulgent and gracious you may promise to be in wielding it.

We have carefully considered the grounds on which your pretensions to more than legal authority are claimed to rest; and, if we do not misinterpret the misty and clouded forms of expression in which those pretensions are set forth, your meaning is, that, while the rights of the citizens are protected by the constitution in time of peace, they are suspended or lost in time of war, when invasion or rebellion exists. You do not, like many others in whose minds reason and the love of regulated liberty seem to be overthrown by the excitements of the hour, attempt to base this conclusion upon a supposed military necessity existing outside of and transcending the constitution,—a military necessity behind which the constitution itself disappears in a total eclipse. We do not find this gigantic and monstrous heresy put forth in your plea for absolute power, but we do find another equally subversive of liberty and law, and quite as certainly tending to the establishment of despotism.— You claim to have found, not outside, but within the constitution, a principle or germ of arbitrary power, which, in time of war, expands at once into an absolute sovereignty, wielded by one man; so that liberty perishes, or is dependent on his will, his discretion, or his caprice. This extraordinary doctrine you claim to derive wholly from the clause of the constitution which, in case of invasion or rebellion, permits the writ of *habeas corpus* to be suspended. Upon this ground your whole argument is based.

You must permit us to say to you, with all due respect, but with the earnestness demanded by the occasion, that the American people will never acquiesce in this doctrine. In their opinion, the guarantees of the Constitution, which secure to them freedom of speech and of the press, immunities from arrest for offences unknown to the laws of the land; and the right of trial by jury before the tribunals provided by those laws, instead of military commissions and drum-head courts martial, are living and vital principles IN PEACE AND IN WAR, at all times and under all circumstances. No sophistry or argument can shake this conviction, nor will the people require its confirmation by logical sequences and deductions. It is a conviction deeply interwoven with the instincts, the habits, and the education of our countrymen. The right to form opinions upon public measures and men, and to declare those opinions by speech or writing, with the utmost latitude of expression: the right of personal liberty unless forfeited according to established laws, and for offences previously defined by law, the right, when accused of crime, to be tried where law is administered and punishment is pronounced only when the crime is legally ascertained; all these are rights instantly perceived, without argument or proof. No refinement of logic can unsettle them in the minds of freemen; no power can annihilate them, and no force at the command of any Chief Magistrate can compel their surrender. So far as it is possible for us to understand from your language the mental process which has led you to the alarming conclusions indicated by your communication, it is this: The *habeas corpus* is a remedial writ, issued by courts and magistrates to inquire into the cause of any imprisonment or restraint of liberty; on the return of which and upon due examination the person imprisoned is discharged if the restraint is unlawful, or admitted to bail if he appears to have been lawfully arrested and held to answer a criminal accusation. Inasmuch as this process may be suspended in time of war, you seem to think that every remedy for a false and unlawful imprisonment is abrogated; and from this postulate you reach at a single bound the conclusion that there is no liberty under the constitution which does not depend on the gracious indulgence of the Executive only. This great heresy once established, and by this mode of induction, there springs at once into existence a brood of crimes or offences undefined by any rule, and hitherto unknown to the laws of this country; and this is followed by indiscriminate arrests, midnight seizures, military commissions, unheard of modes of trial, and punishment; and all the machinery of terror and despotism. Your language does not permit us to doubt as to your essential meaning, for you tell us that

"arrests are not made so much for what has been done, as for what probably would be done."

And again:

"The man who stands by and says nothing when the peril of his, government is discussed cannot be misunderstood. If not hindered [of course by arrest,] he is sure to help the enemy, and much more if he talks ambiguously —talks for his country with 'buts,' and 'ifs,' and ands.'"

You also tell us that the arrests complained of have not been made "for the treason defined in the constitution," nor "for any capital or otherwise infamous crimes, nor were the proceedings following in any constitution or legal sense criminal prosecutions." The very ground, then, of your justification is, that the victims of arbitrary arrest were obedient to every law, were guiltless of any known and defined offense, and therefore were without the protection of the constitution. The suspension of the writ of *habeas corpus*, instead of being intended to prevent the enlargement of arrested criminals until a legal trial and conviction can be had, is designed, according to your doctrine, to subject innocent men to your supreme will and pleasure. Silence itself is punishable according to this extraordinary theory, and still more so the expression of opinions, however loyal, if attended with criticisms upon the policy of the government. We must respectfully refuse our assent to this theory of constitutional law. We think that men may be rightfully silent if they so choose, while clamorous and needy patriots proclaim the praises of those who wield power; and as to the "buts," the "ifs," and the "ands," these are Saxon words and belong to the vocabulary of freemen.

We have already said that the intuition of a free people instantly rejects these dangerous and unheard of doctrines. It is not our purpose to enter upon an elaborate and extended refutation of them. We submit to you, however, one or two considerations, in the hope that you will review the subject with the earnest attention which its supreme importance demands. We say, then, are you not aware that the writ of *habeas corpus* is now suspended in any of the peaceful and loyal states of the Union. An act of Congress approved by you on the 3d of March, 1863, authorized the President to suspend it during the present rebellion. That the suspension is a legislative, and not an executive act, has been held in every judicial decision ever made in this country, and we think it cannot be delegated to any other branch of the government. But, passing over that consideration, you have not exercised the power which Congress attempted to confer upon you, and the writ is not suspended in any part of the country where the civil laws are in force. Now, inasmuch as your doctrine of the arbitrary arrests and imprisonment of innocent men, in admitted violation of express constitutional guarantees. is wholly derived from a suspension of the *habeas corpus*, the first step to be taken in the ascent to absolute power ought to be to make it known to the people that the writ is in fact suspended, to the end that they may know what is their condition. You have not yet exercised this power, and, therefore, according to your own constitutional thesis, your conclusion falls to the ground.

It is one of the provisions of the constitution and of the very highest value, that no *ex post facto* law shall be passed, the meaning of which is, that no act which is not against the law when committed can be criminal by subsequent legislation. But your claim is, that when the writ of *habeas corpus* is suspended, you may lawfully imprison and punish for the crime of silence, of speech and opinion. But, as these are not offences against the known and established law of the land, the constitutional principal to which we now refer plainly requires that you should, before taking cognisance of such offences, make known the rule of action, in order that the people may be advised in season, so as not to become liable to its penalties. Let us turn your attention to the most glaring and indefensible of all the assaults upon constitutional liberty, which have marked the history of your administration. No one has ever pretended that the writ of *habeas corpus* was suspended in the state of Ohio, where the arrest of a citizen at midnight, already referred to, was made, and he placed before a court martial for trial and sentence, upon charges and specifications which admitted his innocence according to the existing laws of this country. Upon your own doctrine, then, can you hesitate to redress that monstrous wrong?

But, sir, we cannot acquiesce in your dogmas that arrests and imprisonment, without warrant or criminal accusation, in their nature lawless and arbitrary, opposed to the very letter of constitutional guarrantees, can become in any sense rightful by reason of a suspension of the writ of *habeas corpus*. We deny that the suspension of a single and peculiar remedy for such wrongs brings into existence new and unknown classes of offences, or new causes for depriving men of their liberty. It is one of the most material purposes of that writ to enlarge upon bail persons who, upon probable cause, are duly and legally charged with some known crime. and a suspension of the writ was never asked for in England nor in this country except to prevent such enlargement when the supposed offence was against the safety of the government. In the year 1807, at the time of Burr's alleged conspiracy, a bill was passed in the Senate of the United States, suspending the writ of *habeas corpus* for a limited time, *in all cases where persons were charged on oath with treason or other high crime or misdemeanor* endangering the peace or safety of the government. But your doctrine undisguisedly is, that a suspension of this writ justifies arrests without warrant, without oath, and even without suspicion of treason or other crime. Your doctrine denies the freedom of speech and of the press. It invades the sacred domain of opinion and discussion. It denounces the "ifs" and "buts" of the English language, and even the refuge of silence is insecure.

We repeat, a suspension of the writ of *habeas corpus* merely dispenses with a single and peculiar remedy against an unlawful imprisonment; but, if that remedy had never existed, the right to liberty would be the same, and every invasion of that right would be condemned not only by the constitution, but by principles of far greater antiquity than the writ itself. Our common law is not at all indebted to this writ for its action of false imprisonment, and the action would remain to the citizens if the writ were abolished forever. Again: every man, when his life or liberty is threatened without the warrant of law, may lawfully resist, and, if necessary in self-defence, may take the life of the aggressor. Moreover, the people of this country may demand the impeachment of the President himself for the exercise of arbitrary power. And, when all these remedies shall prove inadequate for the protection of free institutions, there remains, in the last resort, the supreme right of revolution. You once announced this right with a latitude of expression which may well be considered dangerous in the present crisis of our national history. You said:

"Any people, anywhere, being inclined and having the power, have the right to raise up and shake off the existing government and form a new one that suits them better. Nor is this right confined to cases where the people of an existing government may choose to exercise it.... Any portion of such people that can may revolutionize and make their own of so much of the territory as they inhabit. More than this, a majority of any portion of such people may revolutionize, putting down a minority intermingled with or near about them, who may oppose their movements."...(*Volume 19, Congressional Globe,* p. 94.)

Such were your opinions, and you had a constitutional right to declare them. If a citizen now should utter sentiments far less dangerous in their tendency, your nearest military commander would consign him to a dungeon, or to the tender mercies of a court martial, and you would approve the proceeding.

In our deliberate judgment, the constitution is not open to the new interpretation suggested by your communication before us. We think every part of that instrument is harmonious and consistent. The possible suspension of the writ of *habeas corpus* is consistent with freedom of speech and of the press. The suspension of the remedial process may prevent the enlargement of the accused traitor or conspirator, until he shall be legally tried and convicted or acquitted; but in this we find no justification for arrest and imprisonment without warrant, without cause, without the accusation or suspicion of crime. It seems to us, that the sacred right of trial by jury, and in courts where the law of the land is the rule of decision, is a right which is never dormant, never suspended, in peaceful and loyal communities and states. Will you, Mr. President, maintain that, because the writ of *habeas corpus* may be in suspense, you can substitute soldiers and bayonets for the peaceful operation of the laws, military commissions and inquisitorial modes of trial, for the courts and juries prescribed by the constitution itself? And, if you cannot maintain this, then let us ask where the justification is for the monstrous proceeding in the case of a citizen of Ohio, to which we have called your attention? We know that a recrant Judge, whose name has descended to merited contempt, found the apology on the *outside* of the supreme and fundamental law of the constitution. But this is not the foundation on which your superstructure of power is built.

We have mentioned the act of the last Congress professing to authorize a suspension of the writ of *habeas corpus*. This act now demands your especial attention, because, if we are not greatly in error, its terms and plain intention are directly opposed to all the arguments and conclusions of your communication. That act, besides providing that the *habeas corpus* may be suspended, expressly commands that the names of all persons theretofore or thereafter arrested by authority of the President, or his cabinet ministers, *being citizens of states in which the administration of the laws has continued unimpaired*, shall be turned over to the courts of the United States for the district in which such persons reside, or in which their supposed offenses were committed; and such return being made, if the next grand jury attending the court does not indict the alleged offenders, then the Judges are commanded to issue an order for their immediate discharge from imprisonment. Now, we cannot help asking wheather you have overlooked this law, which most assuredly you are bound to observe, or whether it be your intention to disregard it? Its meaning certainly cannot be mistaken. By it the national legislature has said that the President may suspend the accustomed writ of *habeas corpus*, but at the same time it has commanded that all arrests under his authority shall be promptly made known to the courts of justice, and that the accused parties shall be liberated, unless presented by a grand jury according to the constitution, and tried by a jury in the ancient and accustomed mode. The President may, possibly, so far as Congress can give the right, arrest without legal cause or warrant. We certainly deny that Congress can confer this right, because it is forbidden by the higher law of the constitution. But, waiving that consideration, this statute, by its very terms, promptly removes the proceedings in every case into the courts where the safeguards of liberty are observed. and where the persons detained are to be discharged, unless indicted for *criminal offences* against the established and ascertained laws of the country.

Upon what foundation, then, permit us to ask, do you rest the pretension that men who are not accused of crime may be seized and imprisoned or banished at the will and pleasure of the President or any of his subordinates in civil and military positions? Where is the warrant for invading the freedom of speech and of the press? Where the justification for placing the citizen on trial without the presentment of a grand jury and before military commissions? THERE IS NO POWER IN THIS COUNTRY WHICH CAN DISPENSE WITH ITS LAWS The President is as much bound by them as the humblest individual. We pray you to bear in mind, in order that you may duly estimate the feeling of the people on this subject, that, for the crime of dispensing with the laws and statutes of Great Britain, our ancestors brought one monarch to the scaffold and expelled another from his throne.

This power which you have erected in theory is of vast and limitable proportions. If we may trust you to exercise it mercifully and leniently, your successor, whether immediate or more remote, may wield it with the energy of a Cæsar or Napoleon, and with the will of a despot and a tyrant. It is a power without boundary or limit, because it precedes upon a total suspension of all the constitutional and legal safeguards which protect the rights of the citizen. It is a power not inaptly described in the language of one of your Secretaries. Said Mr. Seward to the British Minister in Washington:

"I can touch a bell on my right hand and order the arrest of a citizen of Ohio. I can touch the bell again, and order the imprisonment of a citizen of New York, and no power on earth but that of the President can release them. Can the Queen of England, in her dominions, do as much?"

This is the very language of a perfect despotism, and we learn from you, with profound emotion, that this is no idle boast It is a despotism unlimited in principle, because the same arbitrary and unrestrained will or discretion which can place men under illegal restraint or banish them can apply the rack or the thumbscrew, can put to torture or .o death. Not thus have the people of this country hitherto understood their constitution. No argument can commend to their judgment such interpretations of the great charter of their liberties. Quick as the lightning's flash, the intuitive sense of freemen perceives the sophistry and rejects the conclusion.

Some other matters which your Excellency has presented demand our notice.

In justification of your course as to Mr. Vallandigham, you have referred to the arrest of Judge Hall at New Orleans by order of Gen. Jackson: but that case differs widely from the case of Mr. Vallandigham. New Orleans was then, as you truly state, under "martial or military law." This was not so in Ohio, where Mr. Vallandigham was arrested. The administration of the civil law had not been disturbed in that commonwealth. The courts were open, and justice was dispensed with its accustomed promptitude. In the case of Judge Hall, Gen. Jackson in a few days sent him outside of the line of his encampments and set him at liberty; but you have undertaken to banish Mr. Vallandigham from his home. You seem also to have forgotten that Gen. Jackson submitted implicitly to the judgment of the court which imposed the fine upon him; that he enjoined his friends to assent,

"as he most freely did, to the decision which had just been pronounced against him."

More than this, you overlook the fact that the then administration (in the language of a well-known author) "mildly but decidedly rebuked the proceedings of Gen. Jackson," and that the President viewed the subject with "surprise and solicitude." Unlike President Madison, you, in a case much more unwarranted, approve the proceedings of your subordinate officer, and, in addition, justify your course by a carefully considered argument for its support.

It is true that, after some thirty years, Congress, in consideration of the devoted and patriotic services of Gen Jackson, refunded the amount of the fine he had paid. But the long delay in doing this proved how reluctant the American people were to do anything which could be considered as in any way approving the disregard shown to the majesty of the law, even by one who so eminently enjoyed their confidence and regard.

One object more, and we shall conclude.— You expressed your regret that our meeting spoke "as Democrats;" and you say that,

"In this time of national peril, you would have preferred to meet us upon a level, one step higher than any party platform."

You thus compel us to allude to matters which we should have preferred to pass by. But we cannot omit to notice your criticism, as it casts, at least an implied reproach upon our motives and our proceedings. We beg to remind you that when the hour of our country's peril had come, when it was evident that a most gigantic effort was to be made to subvert our institutions and to overthrow the government, when it was vitally important that party feelings should be laid aside, and that all should be called upon to unite most cordially and vigorously to maintain the Union; at the time when you were sworn into office as President of the United States, when you should have urged your fellow citizens in the most emphatic manner to overlook all past differences and to rally in defence of their country and its institutions, when you should have enjoined respect for the laws and the constitution, so clearly disregarded by the South; you chose for the first time, under like circumstances, in the history of our country, to set up a party platform, called "the Chicago platform" as your creed, to advance

it beyond the constitution, and to speak disparagingly of the great conservative tribunal of our country, so highly respected by all thinking men who have inquired into our institutions—THE SUPREME COURT OF THE UNITED STATES.
Your administration has been true to the principles you then laid down. Notwithstanding the fact that several hundred thousand democrats in the loyal states cheerfully responded to the call of their country, filled the ranks of its armies, and by "their strong hands and willing arms," aided to maintain your Excellency and the officers of government in the possession of our national capital; notwithstanding the fact that the great body of the democrats of the country have, in the most patriotic spirit, given their best efforts, their treasure, their brothers and their sons to sustain the government and to put down the rebellion; you, choosing to overlook all this, have made your appointments to civil office, from your Cabinet officers and foreign Ministers down to the persons of lowest official grade among the tens of thousands engaged in collecting the revenues of the country, exclusively from your political associates.
Under such circumstances, virtually proscribed by your administration, and while most of the leading journals which supported it approved the sentence pronounced against Mr. Vallandigham, was our true course, our honest course, to meet as "Democrats" that neither your Excellency or the country might mistake our antecedents or our position.
In closing this communication, we desire to reaffirm our determination and we doubt not that of every one who attended the meeting which adopted the resolutions we have discussed, expressed in one of those resolutions, to devote "all our energies to sustain the cause of the Union."
Permit us, then, in this spirit, to ask your Excellency to re-examine the grave subjects we have considered, to the end that, on your retirement from the position you now occupy, you may leave behind you no doctrines and no farther precedents of despotic power to prevent you and your posterity from enjoying that constitutional liberty, which is the inheritance of us all, and to the end, also, that history may speak of your administration with indulgence, if it cannot with approval.

We are, &c. with great respect, yours truly,
JOHN V. L. PRUYN,
Chairman of Committee.
[Signed also by the entire Committee.]
ALBANY, June 30, 1863.

CORRESPONDENCE WITH THE OHIO COMMITTEE.

The following is a correct copy of the correspondence between President Lincoln and the committee appointed by the Ohio Democratic State Convention to ask for permission for Hon. C. L. Vallandigham to return to Ohio:

The Letter to the President.

WASHINGTON CITY, June 26, 1863.
To His Excellency the President of the United States:

The undersigned, having been appointed a committee, under the authority of the resolutions of the state convention, held at the city of Columbus, Ohio, on the 11th instant, to communicate with you on the subject of the arrest and banishment of Clement L. Vallandigham, most respectfully submit the following as the resolutions of that convention, bearing upon the subject of this communication, and ask of your excellency their earnest consideration. And they deem it proper to state that the convention was one in which all parts of the state were represented, and one of the most respectable as to character and numbers, and one of the most earnest and sincere in support of the Constitution and Union ever held in that state.

Resolved, 1. That the will of the people is the foundation of all free government; that to give effect to this will, free thought, free speech and a free press are absolutely indispensable. Without free discussion there is no certainty of sound judgment; without sound judgment there can be no wise government.

2. That it is an inherent and constitutional right of the people to discuss all measures of their government, and to approve or disapprove, as to their best judgment seems right. That they have a like right to propose and advocate that policy which in their judgment is best, and to argue and vote against whatever policy seems to them to violate the Constitution, to impair their liberties, or to be detrimental to their welfare.

3. That these and all other rights guaranteed to them by their constitutions are their rights in time of war as well as in time of peace, and of far more value and necessity in war than in peace, for in peace liberty, security and property are seldom endangered; in war they are ever in peril.

4. That we now say to all whom it may concern, not by way of threat, but calmly and firmly, that we will not surrender these rights nor submit to their forcible violation. We will obey the laws ourselves, and all others must obey them.

11. That Ohio will adhere to the Constitution and the Union as the last, it may be the last, hope of popular freedom, and for all wrongs which may have been committed or evils which may exist will seek redress, under the Constitution and within the Union, by the peaceful but powerful agency of the suffrages of a free people.

14. That we will earnestly support every constitutional measure tending to preserve the Union of the states. No men have a greater interest in its preservation than we have—none desire it more; there are none who will make greater sacrifices or endure more than we will to accomplish that end. We are, as we ever have been, the devoted friends of the Constitution and the Union, and we have no sympathies with the enemies of either.

15. That the arrest, imprisonment, pretended trial, and actual banishment of Clement L. Vallandigham, a citizen of the State of Ohio, not belonging to the land or naval forces of the United States, nor to the militia in actual service, by alleged military authority, for no other pretended crime than that of uttering words of legitimate criticism upon the conduct of the administration in power, and of appealing to the ballot-box for a change of policy —said arrest and military trial taking place where the courts of law are open and unobstructed, and for no act done within the sphere of active military operations in carrying on the war—we regard as a palpable violation of the following provision of the Constitution of the United States:

1. "Congress shall make no law * * * * abridging the freedom of speech or of the press, or the right of the people peaceably to assemble, and to petition the government for a redress of grievances."

2. "The right of the people to be secure in their persons, houses, papers, and effects, against unreasonable searches and seizures, shall not be violated; and no warrants shall issue, but upon probable cause, supported by oath or affir-

mation, and particularly describing the place to be searched and the persons or things to be seized."

3. "No person shall be held to answer for a capital or otherwise infamous crime unless on a presentment or indictment of a grand jury, except in cases arising in the land or naval forces, or in the militia, when in actual service in time of war or public danger."

4. "In all criminal prosecutions, the accused shall enjoy the right to a speedy and public trial, by an impartial jury of the state and district wherein the crime shall have been committed, which district shall have been previously ascertained by law."

And we furthermore denounce said arrest, trial and banishment, as a direct insult offered to the sovereignty of the people of Ohio, by whose organic law it is declared that no person shall be transported out of the state for any offence committed within the same.

16. That Clement L. Vallandigham was, at the time of his arrest, a prominent candidate for nomination by the Democratic party of Ohio, for the office of governor of the state: that the Democratic party was fully competent to decide whether he is a fit man for that nomination, and that the attempt to deprive them of that right, by his arrest and banishment, was an unmerited imputation upon their intelligence and loyalty, as well as a violation of the Constitution.

17. That we respectfully, but most earnestly, call upon the President of the United States to restore Clement L. Vallandigham to his home in Ohio, and that a committee of one from each congressional district of the state, to be selected by the presiding officer of this convention, is hereby appointed to present this application to the President.

The undersigned, in the discharge of the duty assigned them, do not think it necessary to reiterate the facts connected with the arrest, trial, and banishment of Mr. Vallandigham—they are well known to the President, and are of public history—nor to enlarge upon the positions taken by the convention, nor to recapitulate the constitutional provisions which it is believed have been contravened; they have been stated at length, and with clearness in the resolutions which have been recited. The undersigned content themselves with brief reference to other suggestions pertinent to the subject.

They do not call upon your excellency as suppliants, praying the revocation of the order banishing Mr. Vallandigham, as *a favor;* but, but by the authority of a convention representing a majority of the citizens of the State of Ohio, they respectfully ask it as a *right* due to an American citizen, in whose personal injury the sovereignty and dignity of the people of Ohio, as a free state, have been offended.— And this duty they perform the more cordially from the consideration, that, at a time of great national emergency, pregnant with danger to our Federal Union, it is all important that the true friends of the Constitution and the Union, however they may differ as to *the mode* of administering the government, and *the measures* most likely to be successful in the maintenance of the Constitution and the restoration of the Union, should not be thrown into hostile conflict with each other.

The arrest, unusual trial and banishment of Mr. Vallandigham, have created wide-spread and alarming disaffection among the people of the state, not only endangering the harmony of the friends of the Constitution and the Union, and tending to disturb the peace and tranquility of the state, but also impairing that confidence in the fidelity of your administration to the great landmarks of free government, essential to a peaceful and successful enforcement of the laws in Ohio.

You are reported to have used, in a public communication on this subject, the following language:

"It gave me pain when I learned that Mr. Vallandigham had been arrested—that is, I was pained that there should have seemed to be a necessity for arresting him; and that it will afford me great pleasure to discharge him, so soon as I can by any means believe the public safety will not suffer by it."

The undersigned assure your excellency, from our personal knowledge of the feelings of the people of Ohio, that the public safety will be far more endangered by continuing Mr. Vallandigham in exile than by releasing him. It may be true, that persons differing from him in political views may be found in Ohio, and elsewhere, who will express a different opinion. But they are certainly mistaken. Mr. Vallandigham may differ with the President, and even with some of his own political party, as to the true and most effectual means of maintaining the Constitution and restoring the Union; but this difference of opinion does not prove him to be unfaithful to his duties as an American citizen. If a man devotedly attached to the Constitution and the Union conscientiously believes that from the inherent nature of the federal compact the war, in the present condition of things in this country, cannot be used as a means of restoring the Union; or that a war to subjugate a part of the states, or a war to revolutionize the social system in a part of the states, could not restore, but would inevitably result in the final destruction of both the Constitution and the Union, is he not to be allowed the right of an American citizen to appeal to the judgment of the people for a change of policy by the constitutional remedy of the ballot-box?

During the war with Mexico many of the political opponents of the administration then in power thought it their duty to oppose and denounce the war, and to urge before the people of the country that it was unjust, and prosecuted for unholy purposes. With equal reason it might have been said of them that their discussions before the people were calculated to discourage enlistments, "to prevent the raising of troops," and to induce desertions from the army and leave the government without an adequate military force to carry on the war. If the freedom of speech and of the press are to be suspended in time of war, then the essential element of popular government to effect a change of policy in the constitutional mode is at an end. The freedom of speech and of the press is indispensable, and necessarily incident to the nature of popular government itself. If any inconvenience or evils arise from its exercise they are unavoidable. On this subject you are reported to have said further:

"It is asserted, in substance, that Mr. Vallandigham was, by a military commander, seized and tried 'for no other reason than words addressed to a public meeting in criticism of the course of the administration, and in condemnation of the military order of the general.' Now, if there be no mistake about this, if there was no other reason for the arrest, then I concede that the arrest was wrong. But the arrest, I understand, was made for a very different reason. Mr. Vallandigham avows his hostility to the war on the part of the Union; and his arrest was made because he was laboring, with some effect, to prevent the raising of troops, to encourage desertions from the army, and to leave the rebellion without an adequate military force to suppress it. He was not arrested because he was damaging the political prospects of the administration, or the personal interest of the commanding general, but because he was damaging the army, upon the existence and vigor of which the life of the nation depends. He was warring upon the military, and this gave the military constitutional jurisdiction to lay hands upon him. If Mr. Vallandigham was not damaging the military power of the country, then his arrest was made on mistake of facts, which I would be glad to correct on reasonable satisfactory evidence."

In answer to this, permit the undersigned to say, first, that neither the charge, nor the specifications in support of the charge, on which Mr. Vallandigham was tried, impute to him the act of laboring either to prevent the raising of troops, or to encourage desertion from the army; secondly, that no evidence on the trial was offered with a view to support, or even tended to support, any such charge. In what instance, and by what act, did he either discourage enlistments or encourage desertions from the army? Who is the man who was discouraged from enlisting, and who encouraged to desert by any act of Mr. Vallandigham? If it be assumed that perchance some person might have been discouraged from enlisting, or that some person might have been encouraged to desert, on account of hearing Mr. Vallandigham's views as to the policy of the war as a means of restoring the Union, would that have laid the foundation for his conviction and banishment?

If so, upon the same grounds, every political opponent of the Mexican war might have been convicted and banished from the country. When gentlemen of high standing and extensive influence, including your excellency, opposed, in the discussions before the people, the policy of the Mexican war, were they "warring upon the military," and did this "give the military constitutional jurisdiction to lay hands upon" them? And, finally, the charge, in the specifications upon which Mr. Vallandigham was tried, entitled him to a trial before the civil tribunals, according to the express provisions of the late acts of Congress, approved by yourself, July 17, 1862, and March 3, 1863, which were manifestly designed to supercede all necessity or pretext for arbitrary military arrests.

The undersigned are unable to agree with you in the opinion you have expressed, that the Constitution is different in time of insurrection or invasion from what it is in time of peace and public security. The Constitution provides for no limitation upon, or exceptions to, the guarantees of personal liberty; except as to the writ of *habeas corpus*. Has the President, at the time of invasion or insurrection, the right to engraft limitations or exceptions upon these constitutional guarantees, whenever, in his judgment, the public safety requires it?

True it is, the article of the constitution which defines the various powers delegated to Congress, declares that "the privilege of the writ of *habeas corpus* shall not be suspended unless where, in cases of rebellion or invasion the public safety may require it." But this qualification or limitation upon this restriction upon the powers of Congress has no reference to, or connection with, the other constitutional guarantees of public liberty. Expunge from the Constitution this limitation upon the power of Congress to suspend the writ of *habeas corpus*, and yet the the other guarantees of personal liberty would remain unchanged.

Although a man might not have a constitutional right to have an immediate investigation made as to the legality of his arrest upon *habeas corpus*, yet his "right to a speedy and public trial by an impartial jury of the state and district wherein the crime shall have been committed," will not be altered; neither will his right to the exemption from "cruel and unusual punishments;" nor his right to be secure in his person, houses, papers, and effects, against unreasonable seizures and searches; nor his right not to be deprived of life, liberty, or property, without due process of law; nor his right not to be held to answer for a capital or otherwise infamous offense, unless on presentment or indictment of a grand jury, be in any wise changed. And certainly the restriction upon the power of Congress to suspend the writ of *habeas corpus*, in time of insurrection or invasion, could not affect the guarantee that the freedom of speech and of the press shall not be abridged.

It is sometimes urged that the proceedings in the civil tribunals are too tardy and ineffective for cases arising in times of insurrection or invasion. It is a full reply to this to say, that arrests by civil process may be equally as expeditious and effective as arrests by military orders. True, a summary trial and punishment are not allowed in the civil courts. But if the offender be under arrest and imprisoned, and not entitled to discharge on writ of *habeas corpus*, before trial, what more can be required for the purposes of the government? The idea that all the constitutional guarantees of personal liberty are suspended throughout the country at a time of insurrection or invasion in any part of it, places us upon a sea of uncertainty, and subjects the life, liberty and property of every citizen to the mere will of a military commander, or what he *may say* that he *considers* the public safety requires. Does your Excellency wish to have it understood that you hold that the rights of every man throughout this vast country, in time of invasion or insurrection, *are subject to be annulled whenever you may say that you consider the public safety requires it?*

You are further reported as having said, that the constitutional guarantees of personal liberty have

"No application to the present case we have in hand,

because the arrests complained of were not made for treason—that is, not for the treason defined in the Constitution, and upon the conviction of which the punishment is death—nor yet were they made to hold persons to answer for capital or otherwise infamous crime; nor were the proceedings following in any constitutional or legal sense 'criminal prosecutions.' The arrests were made on totally different grounds, and the proceedings following accorded with the grounds of the arrests," &c.

The conclusion to be drawn from this position of your Excellency is, that where a man is liable to "a criminal prosecution," or is charged with a crime known to the laws of the land, he is clothed with all the constitutional guarantees for his safety and security from wrong and injustice; but that, where he is not liable to a "criminal prosecution," or charged with any crime known to the laws, if the President or any military commander shall say that he considers that the public safety requires it, this man may be put outside of the pale of the constitutional guarantees, and arrested without charge of crime, imprisoned without knowing what for, and any length of time, or be tried before a court-martial and sentenced to any kind of punishment, unknown to the land, which the President or the military commander may see proper to impose.

Did the Constitution intend to throw the shield of its securities around the man liable to be charged with treason as defined by it, and yet leave the man, not liable to any such charge, unprotected by the safeguards of personal liberty and personal security? Can a man not in the military or naval service, nor within the field of the operations of the army, be arrested and imprisoned without any law of the land to authorize it? Can a man thus, in civil life, be punished without any law defining the offense and prescribing the punishment? If the President or a court martial may prescribe one kind of punishment unauthorized by law, why not any other kind? Banishment is an unusual punishment, and unknown to our laws. If the President has the right to prescribe the punishment of banishment, why not that of death and confiscation of property? If the President has the right to change the punishment prescribed by the court-martial, from imprisonment to banishment, why not from imprisonment to torture upon the rack, or execution upon the gibbet?

If an indefinable kind of constructive treason is to be introduced and engrafted upon the constitution, unknown to the laws of the land, and subject to the will of the President whenever an insurrection or invasion shall occur in any part of this vast country, what safety or security will be left for the liberties of the people? The constructive treasons that gave the friends of freedom so many years of toil and trouble in England, were inconsiderable compared to this. The precedents which you make will become a part of the Constitution for your successors, if sanctioned and acquiesced in by the people now.

The people of Ohio are willing to co-operate zealously with you in every effort, warranted by the Constitution, to restore the Union of the states; but they cannot consent to abandon those fundamental principles of civil liberty which are essential to their existence as a free people.

In their name, we ask that, by a revocation of the order of his banishment, Mr. Vallandigham may be restored to the enjoyment of those rights of which they believe he has been unconstitutionally deprived.

We have the honor to be, respectfully, yours, &c.,

M. BIRCHARD, Chairman, 19th Dist.
DAVID A. HOUK, Sec'y 3d Dist.
GEO. BLISS, 14th Dist.
T. W. BARTLEY, 8th Dist.
W. J. GORDON, 18th Dist.
JOHN O'NEILL, 13th Dist.
C. A. WHITE, 6th Dist.
W. E. FINCK, 12th Dist.
ALEXANDER LONG, 2d Dist.
J. W. WHITE, 16th Dist.
JAS. R. MORRIS, 15th Dist.
GEO. S. CONVERSE, 7th Dist.
WARREN P. NOBLE, 9th Dist.
GEO. H. PENDLETON, 1st Dist.
W. A. HUTCHINS, 11th Dist.
ABNER L. BACKUS, 10th Dist.
J. F. MCKINNEY, 4th Dist.
F. C. LE BLOND, 5th Dist.
LOUIS SCHAFFER, 17th Dist.

The Reply.

WASHINGTON, D. C., June 29, 1863.

Messrs. M. Burchard, David A. Houck, George Bliss, T. W. Bartley, W. J. Gordon, John O'Neill, C. A. White, W. E. Fink, Alexander Long, J. W. White, George H. Pendleton, George L. Converse, Hanza P. Noble, James R. Morris, W. A. Hutchins, Abner L. Backus, J, F. McKinney, P. C. LeBlond, Louis Schafer.

GENTLEMEN: The resolutions of the Ohio Democratic State Convention, which you present me, together with your introductory and closing remarks, being in position and argument mainly the same as the resolutions of the Democratic meeting at Albany, New York, I refer you to my response to the latter as meeting most of the points in the former. This response you evidently used in preparing your remarks, and I desire no more than that it be used with accuracy. In a single reading of your remarks, I only discovered one inaccuracy in matter which I suppose you took from that paper. It is where you say:

"The undersigned are unable to agree with you in the opinion you have expressed that the Constitution is different in time of insurrection or invasion from what it is in time of peace and public security."

A recurrence to the paper will show you that I have not expressed the opinion you suppose. I expressed the opinion that the Constitution is different *in its application* in cases of rebellion or invasion, involving the public safety, from what it is in times of profound peace and public security; and this opinion I adhere to, simply because by the Constitution itself things may be done in the one case which may not be done in the other.

I dislike to waste a word on a merely personal point, but I must respectfully assure you that you will find yourselves at fault should you ever seek for evidence to prove your assumption that I "opposed in discussion before the people the policy of the Mexican war."

You say,

"Expunge from the Constitution this limitation upon the power of Congress to suspend the writ of *habeas corpus*, and yet the other guarantees of personal liberty would remain unchanged."

Doubtless if this clause of the Constitution, improperly called as I think a limitation upon the power of Congress, were expunged the other guarantees would remain the same; but the question is, not how those guarantees would stand, with that clause *out* of the Constitution, but how they stand with that clause remaining in it, in cases of rebellion or invasion, involving the public safety. If the liberty could be indulged of expunging that clause, letter and spirit, I really think the constitutional argument would be with you. My general view on this question was stated in the Albany response, and hence I do not state it now. I only add that, as seems to me, the benefit of the writ of *habeas corpus* is the great means through which the guarantees of personal liberty are conserved and made available in the last resort; and corroborative of this view, is the fact, that Mr. Vallandigham in the very case in question, under the advice of able lawyers, saw not where else to go but to the *habeas corpus*. But by the Constitution the benefit of the writ of *habeas corpus* itself may be suspended when in cases of rebellion or invasion the public safety may require it.

You ask in substance, whether I really claim that I may override all the guaranteed rights of individuals, on the plea of conserving the public safety—when I may choose to say the public safety requires it. This question, divested of the phraseology calculated to represent me as struggling for arbitrary personal prerogative, is either simply a question *who* shall decide, or an affirmation that *nobody* shall decid, what the public safety does require in cases of rebellion or invasion. The Constitution contemplates the question as likely to occur for decision, but it does not expressly declare who is to decide it. By necessary implication, when rebellion or invasion comes, the decision is to be made, from time to time; and I think the man whom, for the time, the people have, under the Constitution, made the commander-in-chief of their army and navy, is the man who holds the power and bears the responsibility of making it. If he uses the power justly, the same people will probably justify him; if he abuses it, he is in their hands to be dealt with by all the modes they have reserved to themselves in the Constitution· [But how can this be done when free discussion is arbitrarily forbidden?]

The earnestness with which you insist that persons can only in times of rebellion be lawfully dealt with, in accordance with the rules for criminal trials and punishments in times of peace, induces me to add a word to what I said on that point in the Albany response. You claim that men may, if they choose, embarrass those whose duty it is to combat a giant rebellion, and then be dealt with only in turn as if there were no rebellion. The Constitution itself rejects this view. The military arrests and detentions which have been made, including those of Mr. Vallandigham, which are not different in principle from the other, have been for *prevention*, and not for *punishment*—as injunctions to stay injury—as proceedings to keep the peace—and hence, like proceedings in such cases, and for like reasons, they have not been accompanied with indictments, or trials by juries, nor, in a single case, by any punishment whatever beyond what is purely incidental to the prevention. The original sentence of imprisonment in Mr. Vallandigham's case was to prevent injury to the military service only, and the modification of it was made as a less disagreeable mode to him of securing the same prevention.

I am unable to perceive an insult to Ohio in the case of Mr. Vallandigham. Quite surely, nothing of the sort was or is intended. I was wholly unaware that Mr. Vallandigham was, at the time of his arrest, a candidate for the Democratic nomination for governor, until so informed by your reading to me resolutions of the convention. I am grateful to the State of Ohio for many things, especially for the brave soldiers and officers she has given in the present national trial to the armies of the Union.

You claim, as I understand, that, according to my own position in the Albany response, Mr. Vallandigham should be released; and this because, as you claim, he has not damaged the military service by discouraging enlistments, encouraging desertions, or otherwise; and that if he had, he should have been turned over to the civil authorities under recent acts of Congress. I certainly do not *know* that Mr. Vallandigham has specifically, and by direct language, advised against enlistments, and in favor of desertion and resistance to drafting.

We all know that combinations, armed in some instances, to resist the arrest of deserters, began several months ago ; that more recently the like has appeared in resistance to the enrollment preparatory to a draft ; and that quite a number of assassinations have occurred from the same animus. These had to be met by military force, and this again has led to bloodshed and death. And now, under a sense of responsibility more weighty and enduring than any which is merely official, I solemnly declare my belief that this hindrance of the military, including maiming and murder, is due to the course in which Mr. Vallandigham has been engaged, in a greater degree than to any other cause ; and is due to him personally in a greater degree than to any other one man.

These things have been notorious, known to all, and, of course, known to Mr. Vallandigham. Perhaps I would not be wrong to say they originated with his especial friends and adherents. With perfect knowledge of them, he has frequently, if not constantly, made speeches in Congress and before public assemblies; and if it can be shown that with these things staring him in the face he has ever uttered a word of rebuke or counsel against them, it will be a fact greatly in his favor with me, and one of which, as yet, I am totally ignorant. When it is known that the whole burden of his speeches has been to stir up men against the prosecution of the war, and that in the midst of resistance to it he has not been known in any instance to counsel against such resistance, it is next to impossible to repel the inference, that he has counseled directly in favor of it.

With all this before their eyes, the convention you represent have nominated Mr. Vallandigham for governor of Ohio; and both they and you have declared the purpose to sustain the national Union by all constitutional means. But of course they and you, in common, reserve to yourselves to decide what are constitutional means, and, unlike the Albany meeting, you omit to state or intimate that in your opinion an army is a constitutional means of saving the Union against a rebellion, or even to intimate that you are conscious of an existing rebellion being in progress with the avowed object of destroying that very Union. At the same time your nominee for governor, in whose behalf you appeal, is known to you and to the world to declare against the use of an army to suppress the rebellion. Your own attitude, therefore, encourages desertion, resistance to the draft and like, because it teaches those who incline to desert and to escape the draft to believe it is your purpose to protect them, and to hope that you will become strong enough to do so.

After a short personal intercourse with you, gentlemen of the committee, I cannot say I think you desire this effect to follow your attitude, but I assure you that both friends and enemies of the Union look upon it in this light. It is a substantial hope, and by consequence a real strength to the enemy. It is a false hope and one which you would willingly dispel. I will make the way exceedingly easy. I send you duplicates of this letter, in order that you or a majority of you may, if you choose, indorse your names upon one of them, and return it thus endorsed to me, with the understanding that those signing are thereby committed to the following propositions, and to nothing else:

1. That there is a rebellion now in the United States, the object and tendency of which is to destroy the national Union, and that, in your opinion an army and navy are constitutional means for suppressing that rebellion.
2. That no one of you will do anything which, in his own judgment, will tend to hinder the increase or favor the decrease, or lessen the efficiency of the army or navy while engaged in the effort to suppress that rebellion, and
3. That each of you will, in his sphere, do all he can to have the officers, soldiers and seamen of the army and navy, while engaged in the effort to suppress the rebellion, paid, fed, clad, and otherwise well-provided and supported.

And with the further understanding that, upon receiving the letter and names thus indorsed, I will cause them to be published, which publication shall be, within itself, a revocation of the order in relation to Mr. Vallandigham.

It will not escape observation that I consent to the release of Mr. Vallandigham upon terms not embracing any pledge from him or from others, as to what he will or will not do. I do this because he is not present to speak for himself, or to authorize others to speak for him,

and hence, I shall expect, that on returning, he would not put himself practically in antagonism with the position of his friends. But I do it chiefly because I thereby prevail on every influential gentleman of Ohio to so define their position as to be of immense value to the army —thus more than compensating for the consequences of any mistake in allowing Mr. Vallandigham to return, so that on the whole the public safety will not have suffered by it. Still in regard to Mr Vallandigham and all others, I must hereafter, as heretofore, do so much as the public safety may seem to require. I have the honor to be respectfully yours, etc.,

A. LINCOLN.

The Rejoinder.

NEW YORK CITY, July 1, 1863.

To His Excellency the President of the United States:

SIR:—Your answer to the application of the undersigned for a revocation of the order of banishment of Clement L. Vallandigham, requires a rerly, which they proceed, with as little delay as practicable, to make.

They are not able to appreciate the force of the distinction you make between the *Constitution* and *the application* of the Constitution. whereby you assume that powers are delegated to the President at the time of invasion or insurrection in derogation of the plain language of the Constitution. The inherent provisions of the Constitution remaining the same in time of insurrection or invasion as in time of peace, the President can have no more right to disregard their positive and imperative requirements at the former time than at the latter.— Because some things may be done by the terms of the Constitution at the time of invasion or insurrection which would not be required by the occasion in time of peace, you assume that *anything whatever*, even though not expressed by the Constitution, may be done on the occasion of insurrection or invasion which the President may choose to say is required by the public safety. In plainer terms, because the writ of *habeas corpus* may be suspended at the time of invasion or insurrection, you infer that all other provisions of the Constitution having in view the protection of the life, liberty and property of the citizen may be in like manner suspended.

The provision relating to the writ of *habeas corpus*, being contained in the first article of the Constitution, the purpose of which is to define the powers delegated to Congress, has no connection in language with the declaration of rights, as guarantees of personal liberty, contained in the additional and amendatory articles. And inasmuch as the provision relating to *habeas corpus* expressly provides for its suspension, and the other provisions alluded to do not provide for any such thing, the legal conclusion is, that the suspension of the latter is unauthorized. The provision for the writ of *habeas corpus* is merely intended to furnish *a summary* remedy, and not the means whereby personal security is conserved, in the final resort; while the other provisions are guarantees of personal rights, the suspension of which puts an end to all pretense of free government. It is true Mr. Vallandigham applied for a writ of *habeas corpus* as a summary remedy against oppression. But the denial of this did not take away his right to a speedy public trial by an impartial jury, or deprive him of his other rights as an American citizen. Your assumption of the right to suspend all the constitutional guarantees of personal liberty, and even of the freedom of speech and of the press, because the summary remedy of *habeas corpus* may be suspended, is at once startling and alarming to all persons desirous of preserving free government in this country.

The inquiry of the undersigned; whether

"you hold that the rights of every man throughout this vast country, in time of invasion or insurrection, are subject to be annulled, whenever you may say that the public safety requires it,"

was a plain question, undisguised by circumlocution, and intended simply to elicit information. Your affirmative answer to this question throws a shade upon the fondest anticipations of the framers of the Constitution, who flattered themselves that they had provided safeguards against the dangers which have ever beset and overthrown free governments in other ages and countries. Your answer is not to be disguised by the phraseology that the question

"is simply a question *who* shall decide, or an affirmation that *nobody* shall decide what the public safety does require in cases of rebellion or invasion."

Our government was designed to be a government of *law*, *settled* and *defined*, and not of the arbitrary will of a single man. As a safeguard, the powers granted were divided, and delegated to the legislative, executive, and judicial branches of the government, and each made co-ordinate with the others, and supreme within its sphere, and thus a mutual check upon each other, in case of abuse of power. It has been the boast of the American people that they had a *written Constitution*, not only expressly *defining*, but also *limiting* the powers of the government, any providing effectual safeguards for personal liberty, security, and property. And to make the matter more positive and explicit, it was provided by the amendatory articles, nine and ten, that "the *enumeration* in the Constitution of *certain rights* shall not be construed to *deny* or *disparage* others retained by the people," and that "the powers not delegated to the United States by the Constitution, nor prohibited by it to the states, or reserved to the states respectively or to the people." With this care and precaution on the part of our forefathers who framed our institutions, it was not to be expected that, so early a day as this, a claim of the President to arbitrary power, limited only by his conception of the requirements of the public safety, would have been asserted.

In derogation of the constitutional provisions making the President strictly an executive officer, and vesting all the delegated legislative power in Congress, your position, as we understand it, would make *your will the rule of act-ion*, and your declarations of the requirements of the public safety the law of the land. Our inquiry was not, therefore,

"simply a question *who* shall decide, or the affirmation that *nobody* shall decide what the public safety requires."

Our government is a government of *law*, and it is the *law-making* power which ascertains what the public safety requires, and prescribes the rule of action; and the duty of the President is simply to execute the laws thus enacted and not *to make or annul laws*. If any exigency shall arise, the President has the power to convene Congress at any time, to provide for it; so that the plea of necessity furnishes no reasonable pretext for any assumption of legislative power.

For a moment contemplate the consequences of such a claim to power. Not only would the dominion of the President be absolute over the rights of individuals, but equally so over the other departments of the government. If he should claim that the public safety required it, he could arrest and imprison a judge for the conscientious discharge of his duties, paralyze the judicial power, or supercede it, by the substitution of courts-martial, subject to *his own will*, throughout the whole country. If any one of the states, even far removed from the rebellion, should not sustain his plan for prosecuting the war, he could, on this plea of the public safety, annul and set at defiance the state laws and authorities, arrest and imprison the governor of the state, or the members of the Legislature, while in the faithful discharge of their duties, or he could absolutely control the action, either of Congress or of the Supreme Court, by arresting and imprisoning its members; and, upon the same ground, he could suspend the elective franchise, postpone the elections, and declare the perpetuity of his high prerogative. And neither the power of impeachment, nor the elections of the people, could be made available against such concentration of power.

Surely it is not necessary to subvert free government in this country in order to put down the rebellion; and it *cannot be done* under *the pretense* of putting down the rebellion. Indeed, it is plain that your administration has been weakened, greatly weakened, by the assumption of power not delegated in the Constitution.

In your answer you say to us:

"You claim that men may, if they choose, embarras those whose duty it is to combat a giant rebellion, and then be dealt with in turn only as if there were no rebellion."

You will find yourself at fault if you will search our communication to you, for any such idea. The undersigned believe that the Constitution and Laws of the land, properly administered, furnish ample power to put down an insurrection, without the assumption of powers not granted. And if existing legislation be inadequate, it is the duty of Congress to consider what futher legislation is necessary, and to make suitable provision by law.

You claim that the military arrests made by

your administration are merely *preventive remedies* "as injunctions to stay injury, or proceedings to keep the peace, and *not for punishment.*" The *ordinary* preventive remedies alluded to are authorized by established law, but the preventive proceedings you institute have their authority merely in the will of the executive or that of officers subordinate to his authority. And in this proceeding a discretion seems to be exercised as to whether the prisoner shall be allowed a trial; or even be permitted to know the nature of the complaint alleged against him, or the name of his accuser. If the proceeding be merely preventive, why not allow the prisoner the benefit of a bond to keep the peace? But if no offense has been committed, why was Mr. Vallandigham tried, convicted and sentenced by a court-martial? And why the actual punishment, by imprisonment or banishment, without the opportunity of obtaining his liberty in the mode usual in preventive remedies, and yet say, it is not for punishment?

You still place Mr. Vallandigham's conviction and banishment upon the ground that he had damaged the military service by discouraging enlistments and encouraging desertions, &c.; and yet you have not even pretended to controvert our position, that he was not charged with, tried or convicted for *any such offense* before the court-martial.

In answer to our position that Mr. Vallandigham was entitled to a trial in the civil tribunals, by virtue of the late acts of Congress, you say:

"I certainly do not know that Mr. Vallandigham has specifically and by direct language advised against enlistments and in favor of desertions and resistance to drafting," &c.

And yet, in a subsequent part of your answer, after speaking of certain disturbances which are alleged to have occurred in resistance of the arrest of deserters, and of the enrollment preparatory to the draft, and which you attribute mainly to the course Mr. Vallandigham has pursued, you say, that he has made speeches against the war in the midst of resistance to it, that "he has never been known, in any instance, to counsel against such resistance," and that "it is next to impossible to repel the inference that he has counseled directly in favor of it." Permit the undersigned to say, that your information is most grievously at fault. The undersigned have been in the habit of hearing Mr. Vallandigham speak before popular assemblages, and they appeal with confidence to every truthful person who has ever heard him, for the accuracy of the declaration that he has never made a speech before the people of Ohio in which he has not counseled submission and obedience to the laws and the Constitution, and advised the peaceful remedies of the judicial tribunals and of the ballot-box for the redress of grievances, and for the evils which afflict our bleeding and suffering country. And, were it not foreign to the purposes of this communication, we would undertake to establish, to the satisfaction of any candid person, that the disturbances among the people to which you allude, in opposition to the arrest of deserters and the draft, have been occasioned mainly by the measures, policy and conduct of your administration, and the course of its political friends. But if the circumstantial evidence exists, to which you allude, which makes,

"It is next to impossible to repel the inference that Mr. Vallandigham has counseled directly in favor"

of this resistance, and that the same has been mainly attributable to his conduct, why was he not turned over to the civil authorities to be tried under the late acts of Congress? If there be any foundation in fact for your statements implicating him in resistance to the constituted authorities, he is liable to such prosecution. And we now demand, as a mere act of justice to him, an investigation of this matter before a jury of his country; and respectfully insist that fairness requires, ether that you retract these charges which you make against him, or that you revoke your order of banishment and allow him the opportunity of an investigation before an impartial jury.

The committee do not deem it necessary to repel at length the imputation that the attitude of themselves or of the Democratic party in Ohio "encourages desertions, resistance to the draft and the like," or tends to the breach of any law of the land. Suggestions of that kind are not unusual weapons in our ordinary political contests. They rise readily in the minds of politicians heated with the excitement of partisan strife. During the two years in which the Democratic party of Ohio has been constrained to oppose the policy of the administration and to stand up in defense of the Constitution and of personal rights this charge has been repeatedly made. It has fallen harmless, however, at the feet of those whom it was intended to injure. The committee believe it will do so again. If it were proper to do so in this paper, they might suggest that the measures of the administration and its changes of policy in the prosecution of the war have been the fruitful sources of discouraging enlistments and inducing desertions, and furnish a reason for the undeniable fact, that the first call for volunteers was answered by very many more than were demanded, and that the next call for soldiers will probably be responded to by drafted men alone. The observation of the President in this connection, that neither the convention in its resolutions, nor the committee in its communication, intimate that they "are conscious of an existing rebellion being in progress with the avowed object of destroying the Union," needs, perhaps, no reply. The Democratic party of Ohio has felt so keenly the condition of the country, and been so stricken to the heart by the misfortunes and sorrows which have befallen it, that they hardly deemed it necessary by solemn resolution, when their very state exhibited everywhere the sad evidences of war, to remind the President that they were aware of its existence.

In the conclusion of your communication, you propose that, if a majority of our committee shall affix their signatures to a duplicate copy of it, which you have furnished, they shall stand committed to three propositions therein at length set forth; that you will publish the names thus signed, and that this publication shall operate as a revocation of the order of banishment. The committee cannot refrain from the expression of their surprise, that the President should make the fate of Mr. Vallandigham depend upon the opinion of this committee upon these propositions. If the arrest and banishment were legal, and were deserved; if the President exercised a power clearly delegated, under circumstances which warranted its exercise, the order ought not to be revoked, merely because the committee hold, or express, opinions accordant with those of the President. If the arrest and banishment were not legal, or were not deserved by Mr. Vallandigham, then surely he is entitled to an immediate and unconditional discharge.

The people of Ohio were not so deeply moved by the action of the President, merely because they were concerned for the personal safety or convenience of Mr. Vallandigham, but because they saw in his arrest and banishment an attack upon their own personal rights ; and they attach value to his discharge chiefly, as it will indicate an abandonment of the claim to the power of such arrest and banishment. However just the undersigned might regard the principles contained in the several propositions submitted by the President, or how-much-soever they might, under other circumstances, feel inclined to endorse the sentiments contained therein, yet they assure him that they have not been authorized to enter into any bargains, terms, contracts, or conditions with the President of the United States to procure the release of Mr. Vallandigham.

The opinions of the undersigned, touching the questions involved in these propositions, are well known, have been many times publicly expressed, are sufficiently manifested in the resolutions of the convention which they represent, and they cannot suppose that the President expects that they will seek the discharge of Mr. Vallandigham by a pledge, implying not only an imputation upon their own *sincerity* and *fidelity* as citizens of the United States, but also carrying with it by implication a concession of *the legality* of his arrest, trial, and banishment, against which they, and the convention they represent, have solemnly protested. And while they have asked the revocation of the order of banishment not as *a favor*, but as *a right*, due to the people of Ohio, and with a view to avoid the possibility of conflict or disturbance of the public tranquility, they do not do this, nor does Mr. Vallandigham desire it, at any sacrifice of their dignity or self-respect.

The idea that such a pledge as that asked from the undersigned would secure the public safety sufficiently to compensate for any mistake of the President in discharging Mr. Vallandigham is, in their opinion, a mere evasion of the grave questions involved in this discussion, and of a direct answer to their demand.— And this is made especially apparent by the fact that this pledge is asked in a communication which concludes with an intimation of a disposition on the part of the President to repeat the acts complained of.

The undersigned, therefore, having fully discharged the duty enjoined upon them, leave the responsibility with the President.

M. BIRCHARD, 19th district, Chairman.
DAVID HOUK, Secretary, 3d district,
GEO. BLISS, 14th district,
T. W. BARTLEY, 8th district,
W. J. GORDON, 18th district,
JNO. O'NEILL, 13th district,
C. A. WHITE, 6th district,
W. E. FINCK, 12th district,
ALEXANDER LONG, 2d district,
JAS. R. MORRIS, 15th district,
GEO. S. CONVERSE, 7th district,
GEO. H. PENDLETON, 1st district,
W. A. HUTCHINS, 11th district,
A. L. BACKUS, 10th district,
J. F. McKINNEY, 4th district,
J. W. WHITE, 16th district,
F. C. LeBLOND, 5th district,
LOUIS SCHEFFER, 17th district,
WARREN P. NOBLE, 9th district.

As showing how reckless the party in power were, and how little regard they paid to the law of their own making, we copy the following article from that old, substantial and candid journal, the *National Intelligencer:*

"THE LAW OF THE CASE.

"As much confusion seems to prevail with regard to the legal aspects of the arrest, trial, and conviction of Mr Vallandigham, on the charge of giving aid and comfort to the enemy, we think it proper, in view of the interest attaching to this question, considered as one of law rather than of military caprice, to place distinctly before our readers the points on which it turns. [Here follows the charge and specification, see page 193.]

"It will thus be seen that the charge and the specification, even if entirely sustained by the evidence, (as to which, in this inquiry, we raise no question,) seek to convict Mr. Vallandigham, a citizen of Ohio, of 'giving aid and comfort to the enemy.'

"Now, this offence has, by the recent legislation of Congress, been made expressly cognizable by the Courts of the United States. This will appear from the following statute, being

"An Act to suppress insurrection, to punish treason and rebellion, and confiscate the property of rebels, and for other purposes,"

approved July 17, 1862, and found in vol. 12th, chapter 195, page 589, of the Statutes at Large, as printed by order of Congress. We cite the the sections relative to this topic, as follows :

"Sec. 2. *And be it further enacted,* That if any person shall hereafter incite, set on foot, assist, or engage in any rebellion or insurrection against the authority of the United States, or the laws thereof, or shall give *aid or comfort thereto,* or shall engage in or give *aid or comfort to any such existing rebellion or insurrection,* and be convicted thereof, such person shall be punished by imprisonment for

15

a period not exceeding ten years, or by a fine not exceeding ten thousand dollars, and by the liberation of all his slaves, if any he have; or by b..th of said punishments, at the discretion of the court.

"Sec. 3. *And be it further enacted,* That every person guilty of either of the offences described in this act shall be forever incapable and disqualified to hold any office under the United States."

"The tribunal to take cognizance of such cases and questions distinctly appears from the concluding section of this statute, as follows:

"Sec. 14. *And be it further enacted,* That the courts of the United States shall have full power to institute proceedings, make orders and decrees, issue process, and do all other things necessary to carry this act into effect."

"This is conclusive as to the jurisdiction of the courts of the United States, and of them alone, over the offence alleged to have been committed by Mr. Vallandigham.

"But the last Congress did not stop here. As if to shut the door against any such proceedings as those instituted by Gen. Burnside, it passed an act, approved March 3d, 1863, expressly

"relating to habeas corpus and regulating judicial proceedings in certain cases."

"The sections of this act relevant to the case of Mr. Vallandigham may be found on page 755 of the volume of the Statutes at Large as just printed by order of Congress, and are as follows. [See this law on p 109.

"The reader can easily educe from these provisions the law of the question raised by the arrest of Gen. Burnside. They will perceive that proceedings under the writ of *habeas corpus* are to be suspended by the courts whenever and wherever the privilege of this writ has been suspended by the President, which is not the case in the State of Ohio. Judge Leavitt, in refusing to grant the writ sued out in behalf of Mr. Vallandigham, stated that he had not seen this law, which was cited in court by Mr Pugh, the attorney of Mr. Vallandigham We infer from this fact that Judge Leavitt does not deem it necessary to have a knowledge of the laws which it is his sworn duty to administer, or that his means of procuring information under this head are more limited than those possessed by layman who read journals which are authorized to publish the laws of the United States officially, or who possess a sufficient interest in such matters to purchase the volume printed by the eminent publishers, Messrs. Little & Brown, of Boston, under the authority of Congress. His ignorance of the laws may be his best excuse for not doing his duty under them.

"And when a judge of the United States is found ignorant of the legislation of Congress on this head, surely Gen. Burnside may be excused for not knowing that Congress, by the act of July 17th, 1862, had expressly provided for the trial by the courts of the offence he alleges against Mr Vallandigham. Nor is it any answer to say, as Gen. B. urges in his statement made to the Judge, that

" we are in a state of civil war, and an emergency is upon us which requires the operations of some power that moves more quickly than the civil,"

for it was precisely in view of such an "emergency" that Congress passed the act of last July 17th, already cited, and it was to exclude the possibility of the arbitrary detention of persons held

"as prisoners of the United States by order or authority of the President of the United States, as state or political prisoners, or otherwise than as prisoners of war,"

that Congress passed the act approved on the 3d of March last, and the sections of which, so far as they relate to this case, we have cited above. The intervention of a court-martial, illegally charged with the trial of a citizen, does not alter the nature of the imprisonment of Mr. Vallandigham, who, while deprived of his liberty, must be regarded *in law* as one

"imprisoned by the order or authority of the President, acting through the Department of War."

"If it be true, as is said, that Mr. Vallandigham has been imprisoned in Fort Warren by order of Gen. Burnside, confirming the sentence of the court martial illegally charged with the trial of a citizen for an offence made cognizable by the courts, it follows that Mr. Vallandigham is now held as a "state or political prisoner," within the terms of the act of March 3d, 1863, and it will therefore be the duty, as we doubt not it will be the pleasure, of Mr. Secretary Stanton to report the name of Mr. Vallandigham to the Judge of the United States Circuit or District Court which has local and legal jurisdiction of the place for which Mr. Vallandigham is now irregularly detained, that he may be put on trial according to the statutes made and provided for precisely such offences as he is alleged to have committed. His conviction, under such circumstances, would carry with it the sanction of *law*, and as such would receive the assent of law abiding citizens, and be a terror to evil doers."

PERSONAL AND LEGAL RIGHTS.

DANIEL WEBSTER thus defines the prerogatives of the people, in times of peace, and in times of war:

"It is the ancient and undoubted prerogative of this people to canvass public measures and the merits of public men. It is a 'home-bred right'—a fireside privilege. It hath been enjoyed in every house, cottage, and cabin in the nation. It is not drawn into controversy. It is as undoubted as the right of breathing the air, or walking on the earth. Belonging to the private life as a right, it belongs to public life as a duty, and it is the last duty which those whose representatives I am shall find me to abandon. Aiming at all times to be courteous and temperate in its use, except when the right itself is questioned, I shall place myself on *the extreme boundary of my right, and bid defiance to any arm that would move me from my ground.* This high constitutional privilege I shall defend and exercise within this house and in all places; *in time of peace, in time of war, and at all times.* Living I shall assert it, and should I leave no other inheritance to my children, by the blessing of God, I will leave them the inheritance of free principles and the example of a manly, independent, and constitutional defence of them."

MR. CRITTENDEN ON THIS CASE.

Mr. CRITTENDEN thus spoke in reference to this case:

"Neither on this nor any other occasion has it been my habit to make an outcry and clamor; but when usurpations of power are made dangerous, and when encroachments upon my liberty and the liberty of my constituents, and upon the Constitution intended to guard the liberties of us all are made, I would have every man have spirit enough to declare his opinions and offer his protests. Without this freedom of speech there can be no lasting liberty—the republic cannot exist. If every man should close his lips. and not venture even a word against violated rights, who could maintain a free Goverument? Nobody. A people who cannot discuss the public measures of the nation, and apply the necessary rebuke to secure correction of wrongs, cannot be a free people, and do not deserve to be. But it is not necessary that it be done with passion. You are a portion of the people of the United States; act in a manner becoming your high character. Sedition does not become it; clamor does not become it. Action, at the proper time and in the proper manner, according to legal and constitutional provision, is what we want, and what the world has a right to expect."

THE ABOLITIONISTS FELT UNEASY.

The following was from the *Anti-Slavery Standard:*

"I think there can be doubt that Gen. Burnside committed a blunder in paying any attention to his (Vallandigham's) stump speeches. He should have been indicted and tried in the courts. That is the better way in a free State. For one, I am not going to desert the cause of free speech and good government. Let men like Vallandigham be punished in and by the courts. If any body gets down where there are no courts on the border. where the war rages, let the military power govern him. but it is not quite time yet to let Gen. Burnside direct the newspapers and the politicians of Ohio. If he may do so, the next step will be for Gen. Wool to suppress the newspapers of New York. Those who justify the military arrest of Vallandigham for making excited stump speeches could not deny to Gen. Halleck the right to suppress every newspaper in the country through his subordinates. Gen. Burnside is the sole judge according to this military theory, and of course Gen. Wool would be the only judge in New York. *Let us not admit too much against our own liberties in this terrible attempt to suppress the pro-slavery revolution.*"

To like purport, the Washington correspondent of the New York *Independent* writes as follows:

"It is yet doubtful what will be done with Mr. Vallandigham. It is reported here that Mr. Seward says it was a great mistake for Gen. Burnside to arrest him—that he should have been brought before the courts and tried for treason. If this is Mr. Seward's position, he exhibits his unusual sagacity. The time has not yet arrived when there is a necessity for arresting citizens and trying them by court-martial in the states where the conflict of arms does not rage. If Gen. Burnside may with propriety ignore the civil courts in Ohio, so may Gen. Dix in New York, and the next step will be, perhaps, the arrest of every editor in New York who offends Gen. Halleck by criticisms upon his course. For it must be remembened shat it is the General who arrests, who is sole judge of the necessity, and if a half dozen officers can be found who believe that criticisms upon the General-in-chief tend to evil in the army, then your Washington correspondent and the editors of the *Independent* may soon be sentenced to the Dry Tortugas! There are no liberties for the citizen if the new military doctrine prevails. The better course is to stick to law and order, and in the peaceful states to prosecute men in the civil courts for treasonable acts. The experience of 1862 certainly shows this. The President hesitates, and wisely. He doubtless dislikes to seem to shrink from a collision with the copperheads. If Vallandigham goes free again, all will agree that it was a blunder that the arrest was made; but the President cannot evade the blunder, and he is forced to decide upon its merits."

The Administration Condemned by its own Organs.

[From the Evening Post, May 14.]

BURNSIDE AND VALLANDIGHAM.

"General Burnside's response to the Circuit Court, from which a writ of *habeas corpus* was asked in the case of C. L. Vallandigham, arrested for treasonable words spoken, and tried by a military commission, is published on another page. It is so patriotic in spirit, so decided in its expressions of loyalty, and so nobly bold in taking the responsibility, that we almost dislike to question its propriety.— Yet. we think dangerous fallacies run through it. which ought to be exposed. General Burnside will himself be among the first to rectify his positions as soon as it is made manifest to him that they are wrong.

"He assumes that because he and his soldiers may not indulge in 'wholesale criticisms of the policy of the government,' because it would be an offence in him and his officers to undermine the confidence of the men in the perfect. wisdom and integrity of the administration. therefore no citizen has a right to utter such criticisms. But he forgets that persons 'in the military and naval service of the United States' are subject to military law, while the ordinary citizen is subject exclusively to civil law. Military law is a part of the law of the land as much as the civil law; but it is applicable only to a particular class, and administered only by special tribunals. Soldiers in service, cadets at West Point, servants of officers and citizens within the actual lines of the army may be guilty of offences created by their law and tried by its courts; but we doubt whether it can be extended to others in any case. Mr. Vallandigham does not belong to either of these categories.

"Neither does it seem to us that martial law as it is called by the English and French writers, and the "state of seige" by the French—a different thing from military law—has been proclaimed to exist in the department of the Ohio. Or, even if it has been proclaimed, we doubt whether any authority under it can be exercised against persons who are not immediately within the scope of active military operations. It is at least an arbitrary application of military government—the government of mere force—which substitutes the will of the commanding general for the common or municipal law, and which ought not to be resorted to except in cases of absolute necessity. When domestic turbulence and riot prevent the exercise of the ordinary jurisdictions, when the presence of contending armies drives out the inhabitants, when the behests of law are set at naught by an entire district, there is occasion for the strong hand of military power. But in other social conditions the appeal to it is unnecessary and in all probability hurtful.

"Vallandigham's offences, moreover, have been as yet confined to the use of foolish words. He calls Mr. Lincoln bad names; he denounces the Republican party; he abuses Burnside's new military orders, and his example and his instructions are exceedingly pernicious. But, alas, we cannot, in the spirit of Anacharsis Kloot's demand, hang all the dastards and scoundrels at discretion. Vallandigham has not, that we hear, committed any overt act of treason; he has not resisted the laws, though he has perhaps counselled resistance; and until he does, his silly babbling, like Brooks' and Wood's, must be allowed to pass for what it is worth. It is not likely to persuade more than a few ignorant or malignant men to do wrong. *Besides, no governments and no authorities are to be held as above criticism or even denunciation.* We know of no other way of correcting their faults—spurring on their sluggishness, or restraining their tyrannies—than by open and bold discussion. How can a popular government, most of all, know the popular will, and guide its course in the interests of the community, unless it be told from time to time what the popular convictions and wishes are? Despotisms, like that of Louis Napoleon or the Czar of Russia, have no need of this inspiration and control from the people, because they are not administered in the interests of the people, and look to those of a single man or a family, which can very well manage its own affairs. But a republic lives alone in its fidelity to the sentiments of the whole nation.

"Abuses and licenses of course adhere to this unlimited freedom of public criticism; but these are apparently inseparable from the use, and without the abuse we should scarcely have the use. It is a question, too, who is to draw the line between the use and the abuse outside of the courts established for the election and punishment of all offences. If Vallandigham's peace nonsense is treasonable, may not Greeley's be equally so? If he cannot arraign the conduct of the war, can Mr. Schalk, who has written a book on strategy which is the severest arraignment of it yet printed? If he may not question the justice or the propriety of Burnside's orders, may the *Evening Post* or a thousand other journals venture to hint a doubt of the superhuman military abilities of General Halleck? We know it may be said that his motives are bad and treasonable, while those of the others are loyal; but tribunals and commissions cannot inquire into motives. Deeds are tangible, but not thoughts.

"Our article is already too long, or we should like to add a line of the punishment meted out to this Western demagogue. He has been sentenced, it is said, to two years' confinement to the Tortugas Islands. It is a penalty which will make him a martyr, and rouse his old friends and others to earnest expressions of sympathy. He ought merely, at most, to have been sent beyond our lines, to the rebel friends whom he so much admires and serves, and the change would have been a gain to us, if no great gain to them. Nor, supposing the rightfulness of the jurisdiction, could any one have complained of a sentence which mercifully confines the culprit to the agreeable society of this kind."

[From the New York Tribune, May 15.]

"VALLANDIGHAM.

"General Jackson was doubtless a man of more than average sagacity, yet we do not think he showed it in writing, after taking ample time for cool reflection, that, had he been military commandant in Connecticut in December, 1814, he would have hung the leading members of the Hartford Convention under the second section of the Article of War. We will not here discuss the legality of such execution; but we insist that it would have been most impolitic and unwise. The Hartford Convention did very much to save a timid and feeble administration from falling into general contempt and odium. It gave the country its first look over the precipice of disunion, and impelled it to shrink back shuddering, resolved to bear any temporary ills rather than plunge into the yawning vortex beneath. For a supporter of Madison and the war, to have shot or hung the leading Hartford Conventionists, would have been not merely harsh but ungrateful.

"The copperhead spirit never had a freer development than in the recent Connecticut election, where it harmed none but those it sought to serve. Had the democrats of that State simply renominated their former candidates and held their tongues they must have triumphed. But they placed a prominent copperhead in the front, and had such men as Toucey, Mayor Wood, Brooks, Richardson, Schnabel and Perrin to aid him in the canvass and that settled their coffee. Their adversaries had no power to beat thrm, but they were perfectly able to beat themselves, if the government would only let them. And they did.

"Mr. Clement L. Vallandigham is a pro-slavery Democrat of an exceedingly coppery hue. His politics are as bad as can be. If there were penalties for holding irrational, unpatriotic and inhuman views with regard to political questions, he would be one of the most flagrant offenders. But our federal and state constitutions do not recognize perverse opinions nor unpatriotic speeches, as grounds of infliction of the speeches themselves, and then the hearer suffers the penalty, not the speaker. So we don't exactly see how Mr. V. is to be lawfully punished for making a bad speech, unless by compelling him to make it to empty seats.

"We fully agree with General Burnside that Vallandigham ought not to make such speeches—that he ought to be ashamed of himself—but then he will make them and won't be ashamed —so what will you do about it? "Send him to the Dry Tortugas," says the General--probably as a hint to him to "dry up." "Send him over into Dixie," the President is said to suggest as an alternative. But this is the worst joke Mr. Lincoln has yet made. They don't trouble themselves to try and sentence opposition orators down that way—they kill them on sight, and save a world of trouble. Mr. Vallandigham must be aware that any person making just such speeches in Dixie against the war for secession, as he makes or our side against the war for the Union, could not live out the first day's experiment. He would be shot by the first rebel that could obtain a loaded musket, and that would be the end of him. Sending copperheads down to Jeffdom, where they have speeches only on the side the "powers that be," would set a dozen such tongues wagging for every one so silenced. Beside, "carrying coals to Newcastle" has never been considered politic nor statesmanlike.

VIEWS OF JUDGE DUER ON THE USURPATIONS OF THE ADMINISTRATION.

Martial Law Cannot be Established in the Loyal States—The Courts to be Upheld by Force if Necessary.

"OSWEGO, May 29.

"GENTLEMEN: I received some time ago your letter inviting me to attend the public meeting called to vindicate the right of the people to express their sentiments upon political questions. It was not in my power to be present at the meeting, and illness has prevented me until the present moment from answering your letter. I answer it now, though late, both to explain my apparent incivility, and also because I think that in the present crisis no loyal citizen ought to shrink from the expression of his opinion.

"The action that has taken place since your meeting was held convinces me that it is the intention of the President to crush opposition to their acts by means of force and terror. For this purpose they have established and do now actually enforce martial law in several loyal states, and they will doubtless do the same in New York and everywhere else unless they are made to know that the people will not submit to it.

"To many persons the words "martial law" do not convey any very definite idea. They know that it is something very harsh and rigorous, and summary, but they suppose that it bears some resemblance to all other laws of which they have ever heard or read, in this respect at least; that it defines offenses and fixes their punishment. And I cannot but suppose that many of those who clamor for its establishment are ignorant that it is nothing in the world but the absolute and unrestrained will of a military chieftain. Permit me, then, to give a description of martial law upon the authority of the highest judicial tribunal of our country. The language is that of Judge Woodbury in delivering the opinion of the court in a case determined by the Supreme Court of the United States:

"By it," says the court, "every citizen, instead of reposing under the shield of known and fixed laws as to his liberty, property, and life, exists with a rope round his neck, subject to be hung up by a military despot at the next lamp-post under the sentence of some drum-head court-martial."

"It is true that the Republicans have reason to believe that *they* will be safe from the horrors of this law under a Republican administration. No Republican or Abolitionist has yet been arrested, imprisoned, or banished, and they may reasonably calculate that none ever will be. Such persons are permitted to stigmatise the Constitution as a league with hell, and insist that the war shall be prosecuted, not to restore the Union, but to destroy it, without being regarded as guilty of any "disloyal practice." The only sufferers, so far, have been Democrats. Indeed, the very purpose for which the establishment of martial law is sought by the managers of the clubs and leagues is to destroy the Democratic party.— And we find it declared in an official document emanating from the War Department, that to support the Democratic party is to support the cause of the rebels.

"This terrible engine, then, is to be set in motion by one political party for the persecution of another, arming neighbor against neigbor, and setting issues in every household. The machinery is prepared. Already the secret societies are in motion, bound by what oaths, I know not. That they who design these things design all their dreadful consequences, I dot believe; but they know little of human nature and little of history who cannot discern them. Under a single despot there is equality; from a single despot there may be hope of escape. But the worst form that despotism can assume is that of the tyranny of party over party; and if anything can add to its horrors it is when the dominant faction is inflamed by fanaticism and led by priests.

"What matters it that these men are conscientious, that they act under a sense of duty, of religious duty? I do not impeach their motives. The more conscientious they are, the worse. All factions are conscientious, and it is this that makes their tyranny, of all tyrannies, the most insufferable.

"What we can and ought to do, beyond the mere expression of our sympathy, in aid of our oppressed countrymen in Ohio, Kentucky, and Indiana, is a subject upon which it may be as well at present to say nothing. Let us wait the course of events. We have an immediate question to determine for ourselves, and that is whether we will permit the establishment of the same species of government in our own state; a government which not only no Englishman and no Frenchman would endure, but against which the very lazzaroni of Naples would revolt. I do not speak of exceptional cases of an extreme public necessity, such as we may imagine, though their occurrence is not at all probable; but I speak of systematic acts, done under claim of right, without necessity, upon false pretences—acts which are not only flagrantly unconstitutional, but utterly subversive of liberty and of law, and of which the manifest tendency, if not the purpose, is not to maintain the Union but to destroy it. I am sure that we will not submit to this, and we ought to say so plainly. I have no faith in any petitions, protests, or remonstrances that fall short of this. There is danger in leaving the President ignorant of our purpose. I am not sanguine enough to hope for anything from his sense of justice or respect for the law. The powers that control him, whether spiritual or terrestrial, will do to us whatever we will suffer, but are not likely to attempt that which they know we will not suffer.

"At the same time I deprecate all resistance that is not strictly constitutional. Let us not only submit to but support all proper authority. The President claims the constitutional power to establish martial law over the body of the people in the loyal states. We deny it. Let the courts determine the question. The judicial authority is vested in the courts, and not in the President, the Congress, or the Army. It is as much the duty of the President as of any private citizen to submit to that authority. If he resists it he becomes an usurper, and may himself be lawfully resisted. And on the other hand, if any court or judge, acting under the forms of law, shall sanction his monstrous assumptions, let us in turn submit; not because there may not be judicial as well as executive usurpation, and the same right in extreme cases to resist the one as the other, but on account of the condition of the country, and the double dangers that assail us. In this way there may be occasional acts of tyranny, as has been already, but upon the whole the restraint of the judiciary will be found adequate to our protection, if the President himself will respect it.

"But if any citizen of this state shall be arrested or imprisoned by military men, or by provost marshals or other officers, acting under the authority of the President, and the court before whom the question shall be brought shall determine that he is entitled to his liberty, then, *if in spite of this decision, force shall be used to detain him, there ought to be no hesitation to support the judiciary in opposition to military usurpation and I should regard it as a base and cowardly not to do so unless in the face of such a force as should make resistance quite hopeless.* If it be said that such action would impede the successful prosecution of the war, I answer that it is better that a nation should lose a portion of its territory than its liberty. And if for this cause the rebellious states shall succeed in establishing their independence the fault will be that of the administration; and the people, driven to choose between two evils, will have wisely chosen that which beyond all comparison is the least.

"The times require, in a very high degree, the exercise of the virtues of courage and of prudence. Moderation in our counsels will give us strength and unity in action. Let us accept as our leader him whom not less merit than position designates (the chief magistrate of our state), and follow him and support that moderate and patriotic, but not feeble or unmanly policy which he has recommended and enforced with so much dignity and success, and I shall yet hope that the Union may triumph over both classes of its enemies—the southern secessionist and the northern abolitionist. I remain, gentlemen, very respectfully your servant, WILLIAM DUER.

"To Gideon J. Tucker, John Hardy, and Andrew Mathewson, Esqs."

[From the New York World.]

PRESIDENT LINCOLN'S DEFENSE.

"The President not only admits that citizens have been deprived of their liberty on mere partisan conjectures of their possible intentions, but he confesses that these conjectures have had nothing to rest upon.

"The man who stands by and says nothing when the peril of his government is discussed, cannot be misunderstood."

"Was anything so extraordinary ever before uttered by the chief magistrate of a free country? Men are torn from their homes and immured in bastiles for the shocking crime of—*silence!* Citizens of the model republic of the world are not only punished for speaking their opinions, but are plunged into dungeons for holding their tongues! When before, in the annals of tyranny, was silence ever punished as a crime?

"Citizens who disapprove of the acts of the administration are denied even the refuge of a dignified silence, and, on malicious and partisan conjectures of the motives of such silence, they are deprived of their liberty. Few among us ever expected to live to see such things done; and nobody, we are sure, to see them so unblushingly *confessed.* What must be Mr. Lincoln's appreciation of the public sentiment of the world, when he thus comes before the country with a paper containing statements which sound more like the last dying speech and conversation of a tyrant than like the *justification* of the elected ruler of a free people? "The courts, of course, cannot punish this dreadful crime of 'standing by and saying nothing.' Mr. Lincoln admits this, and assigns a very good reason :

"Because," says he, "the arrests complained of were not made for treason—that is, not for *the* treason defined in the Constitution."

"It is a tolerably safe position, that silence, ' to stand by and say nothing,' is not *'the* treason defined in the Constitution' ; it is a treason which our fathers never thought of providing against; they guaranteed free speech, but they never imagined that free silence could ever stand in need of protection. So far from silence being *'the* treason defined in the Constitution,' it is *'a* treason' invented by Abraham Lincoln. It was reserved for him, in the last half of the enlightened nineteenth century, to hit upon this refinement, which had escaped the acuteness of all preceding tyrants.

"The man who stands by and says nothing,' the president tells us,

"*if not hindered,* is sure to help the enemy; much more if he talks for his country with ·buts' and 'ifs' and 'ands.'"

"While silence is a 'sure' presumptive proof of treason, any exceptions to any of the acts of the administration (for what else does Mr. Lincoln mean by 'buts,' 'ifs,' etc?) is proof conclusive. This is the most amazing statement ever made by a public man."

CHAPTER XXX.
ARBITRARY POWER—MILITARY ARRESTS, &c., (CONTINUED.)

John Adams a Monarchist...What the Early Fathers thought of the Vallandigham Case...Great Speech of Edward Livingston on the Alien Bill, 1798...Terrible Scathing of Assumptions of Arbitrary Power...Who was Edward Livingston ?...Republican Confessions of Gross Abuses of Arbitrary Power...Case of Messrs. Brinsmade and Mahoney...Damaging Admissions by "Milwaukee Sentinel"...General Remarks thereon.

WHAT THE EARLY FATHERS THOUGHT OF THE VALLANDIGHAM CASE.

The world is not ignorant of the fact that the elder ADAMS was a Limited Monarchist. In our early history he published three volumes devoted to this subject. In Vol. 1, p 209, we find this declaration, in reply to the principles of a Republic, as laid down by Plato:

"The aristocracy, or ambitious Republic, becomes immediately an Oligarchy. What shall be done to prevent it? Place two guardians of the law to watch the aristocracy; *one in the shape of a KING*, on one side of it; another in the shape of Democratical Assembly on the other side."

We might quote many pages all to the same purport; this, however, will suffice. In 1797 he became President of the United States, and attempted to enforce his views of a mixed Monarchy, by means of the Alien and Sedition Laws, and concentrating power in the hands of the President, never contemplated by the Constitution or the people who adopted it. For this an dignant people hurled him from power, by the election of 1800. The celebrated Alien bill was before the House of Representatives for discussion on the 21st of June, 1798, when the Hon. EDWARD LIVINGSTON, famous in the early history of our Government, made a speech against it, which for logical reasoning, power and eloquence, has seldom ever been equaled, even in the palmiest days of CLAY and WEBSTER.

This speech so exactly hits every stage and degree of the VALLANDIGHAM and other similar cases, and prophecies these latter day usurpations and acts of despotism, with such minute exactness, that we feel justified in transferring it entire to these pages.

SPEECH OF THE HON. EDWARD LIVINGSTON

On the Third Reading of the Alien Bill, June 21, 1798.

[See American Museum and Annual Register, Pub. 1799, p. 196-7, &c.]

Mr. LIVINGSTON said:—"He esteemed it one of the most fortunate occurrences of his life, that after an inevitable absence from his seat in that House, he had arrived in ·time to express his dissent to the passage of the bill. It would have been a source of eternal regret, and the keenest remorse, if any private affairs, however urgent—any domestic concerns, however interesting—had deprived him of the opportunity he was then about to use, of stating his objections, and recording his vote against an act which he believed was in direct violation of the constitution, and marked with every characteristic of the most odious despotism.

"On my arrival, sir," said Mr. Livingston, "I enquired what subject occupied the attention of the House, and being told it was the alien bill, I directed the printed copy to be brought to me; but to my great surprise, seven or eight copies of different acts on the same subject, were put into my hands, among them it was difficult (so strongly were they marked by the same family features,) to discover the individual bill, then under discussion. This circumstance gave me a suspicion that the principles of the measures were erroneous. Truth marches directly to its end, by a single, undeviating path—error is either undetermined on its object or pursues it through a thousand winding ways. The multiplicity of propositions, therefore, to attain the same general but doubtful end, led me to suspect that neither the object nor the means proposed to attain it, were proper or necessary. These surmises were confirmed by a more minute examination of the act. In the construction of statutes, it was a received rule to examine what was the state of things when it was passed, and what were the evils it was intended to remedy. As these circumstances would be applied in the construction of the law, it might be well to examine them minutely in framing it. The state of things, if we are to judge from the complexion of the bill, must be that a number of aliens enjoying the protection of our government, are plotting its destruction. That they are engaged in treasonable machinations against a people who have given them an asylum and support, and that no provision is found to provide for their expulsion and punishment. If these things be so, and no remedy exists for the evil, one ought speedily to be provided. But even then, it must be a *remedy consistent with the Constitution* under which we act; for as by that instrument it powers not expressly given by it to the Union are reserved by the states, it follows that unless an express authority can be found, vesting us with the power, be the evil never so great, it can only be remedied by the several states who have never delegated the authority to Congress; but this point will be presently examined, and it will not be a difficult task to show that the provisions of this bill are not only unauthorized by the Constitution, but are indirect violation of its fundamental principles, and contradictory to some of its most express prohibitions. At present it is only necessary to ask whether the state of things contemplated by the bill have any existence. We must legislate upon facts, not on surmises; we must have *evidence— not vague suspicions*, if we mean to legislate with prudence. What facts have been produced—what evidence has been submitted to the House? I have heard, sir, of none. But if evidence of facts could not be produced, at least it might have been expected that *reasonable cause of suspicion should be shown*. Here, again, gentlemen were at fault. They could not show even a *suspicion* why these aliens ought to be suspected. We have indeed been told that the fate of Venice, Switzerland and Batavia was produced by the interference of foreigners. But the instances were unfortunate, because all those powers had been overcome by foreign force, or divided by domestic faction; not by aliens who resided among them, and if any instruction was to be gained from those Republics, it would be that we ought to banish, not the aliens, but all those citizens who *did not approve of the Executive acts*. This, I believe, gentlemen are not ready to own, but if this measure prevails, *I shall not think the other remote*. But, if it had been proved that these governments were destroyed by the conspiracies of aliens, it yet remains to show that we are in the same situation, or that any such plots have been detected, or are even reasonably suspected here. Nothing of this kind has been yet done. A modern theseus, indeed, has told us, he has procured a clue that will enable him to penetrate the labyrinth, and destroy this monster of sedition. Who the fair Ariadne is that kindly gave him the ball, he has not revealed—nor, though several days have elapsed since he undertook the adventure, has he yet told where the monster lurks. No evidence, then, being produced, we have a right to say that none exists, and yet, we are about to sanction a most important act, and on what grounds? Our individual *suspicions*— our private fears, and our overheated imaginations. Seeing nothing to excite these suspicions and not feeling these fears, I could not give my assent to the bill, even if I did not feel a superior obligation to reject it on other grounds. As far as my own observation goes, I have seen nothing like the state of things contemplated by the bill. Most of the aliens I have seen, were either traduced Englishmen or Frenchmen, with dejection in their countenances and grief at their hearts, preparing to quit the country and seek another asylum. But, if these plots exist—if this treason be apparent —if these be aliens be guilty of the crimes ascribed to them—an effectual remedy presents itself for the evil. We have already wise laws —we have upright judges, [upright judges are just what Federals and Republicans ever feared] and vigilant magistrates, and there is *no necessity* of arming the Executive with the destructive power proposed by the bill on your table. The laws now in force are competent to punish every treasonable or seditious attempt.

"But, grant, sir, what has not been at all supported by facts,—grant that these fears are not visionary—that the dangers are imminent, and that no existing laws are sufficient to avert them; let us examine whether the provisions of the bill are conformable to the principles of the constitution. If it should be found to contravene them, I trust it will lose many of its present supporters; but, if not only contrary to the general spirit and principles of the constitution, it should also be found diametrically opposite to its most express prohibitions —I cannot doubt that it will be rejected with that indignant decision, which our duty to our county and our sacred oathes demands.

THE ALIEN ACT AND ORDER 3S.

"The first section provides that it shall be lawful for the president

"to order all such aliens as he shall judge dangerous to the peace and safety of the United States, or shall have reasonable grounds to *suspect* are concerned in any treasonable or secret machinations against the Government thereof, to depart out of the United States, in such time as shall be expressed in such order."

"Our Government, sir, is founded on the establishment of those principles which constitute the difference between a free constitution and a despotic power. A distribution of the Legislative, Executive and Judiciary powers, into special hands—a distribution strongly marked in three first and great divisions of the Constitution. By the first, all Legislative power is given to Congress; the second, vests all Executive functions in the President, and the third declares that the Judiciary power shall be exercised by the Supreme and inferior courts. Here, then, is a division of Governmental powers, strongly marked—decisively pronounced, and every act of one or all of the branches that tends to confound these powers, or alter this arrangement, *must be destructive of the Constitution.* Examine then, sir, the bill on your table, and declare whether the few lines I have repeated from the first section. do not confound these fundamental powers of the Government—vest them all in the most unqualified terms in one hand, *and thus subvert the basis on which our liberties rest.* Legislative power prescribes the rule of action; the Judiciary applies that general rule to particular cases, and it is the province of the Executive to see that the laws are carried into full effect.

"In all free governments, these powers are exercised by different men, and their Union in the same hand is the peculiar *characteristic of despotism.* If the same power that makes the law can construe it to suit his interest, and apply it to gratify his vengeance—if he can go further, and *execute* according to his own passions [as Mr. Lincoln did in the case of Vallandigham and others] the judgment which he himself has pronounced upon his own construction of laws which he alone has made, [see "Order No. 38," e. g.] what other features are wanted *to complete the picture of tyranny?* Yet, all this, and more is proposed to be done by this act. [and was done under "Order No. 38."] By it the President alone is empowered to make the law [Precisely the case as under the aforesaid Order]—to fix in his own mind what acts, what words, what thoughts or looks [e. g. the "ifs," the "buts," the "ands" or the "saying nothing," claimed by Mr. Lincoln in his reply to the Albany committeee. as grounds for not only suspicion, but punishment] shall constitute the crime contemplated by the bill, that is, the crime of being "suspected to be dangerous to the peace and safety of the United States. He is not only authorized to make this law [the law of "Order No. 38,"] for his own conduct, [or the conduct of his Generals,] but to vary it at pleasure, [exactly the case of said order,] as every gust of passion—every cloud of suspicion shall agitate or darken his mind. The same power that formed the law then applies it to the guilty or innocent victim, whom his *own suspicions*, or the secret whisper of a *spy.* [e. g the two spies sent out to watch Vallandigham, and take notes of his speech, &c.,] have designated as its object. The President, then. having made the law—the President having considered and applied it—the same President is by the bill [Order 38] authorized to execute his sentence, [see sentence of Vallandigham,] in case of disobedience, by imprisonment during his pleasure. *This, then, comes completely within the definition of* DESPOTISM—a union of Legislative, Executive and Judicial powers.

"But, this bill, sir, does not stop here. Its provisions are a *refinement upon despotism*, and present an image of the most fearful tyranny. Even in despotisms, though the monarch legislates, judges and executes, yet he legislates openly; his laws, though offensive, are known—they precede the offence, and every man who choses may avoid the penalties of disobedience. Yet he judges and executes by proxy, and his present interest or passions do not inflame the mind of his deputy.

"But here the law is closely concealed in the same mind that gives it birth—the crime is *exciting the suspicions of the President;* [That was Vallandigham's *only* crime, as admitted by Mr. Lincoln in his reply to the Albany committee] but no man can tell what conduct will avoid that suspicion! A careless word [such as quoting the language used by the President in his message] perhaps misrepresented or never spoken, may be sufficient evidence. A look may destroy! An idle gesture may insure punishment! [Or the wearing of breast pins by the victim's friends.] No innocence can protect. No circumspection can avoid the jealousy of suspicion. Surrounded by *spies, informers, and all that infamous herd which fatten under laws like this,* [and under Order No. 38] the unfortunate stranger will never know either of the law, the accusation or the judgment until the moment it is put in execution! [Let the thousands of victims of the Bastiles answer for the fulfillment of this prophecy.] He will detest your tyranny, and fly from a land of *delators. inquisitors and spies.*

"This, sir, *is a refinement* on the detestable contrivance of the Decemvirs! They hung the table of their laws so high that few could read them. A tall man. [like the maker in our age] however, might reach—a short one might climb and learn their contents. But here, the law is equally inaccessible to high and low, safely concealed in the breast of its author. No industry or caution can penetrate this recess, or obtain a knowledge of its provisions; nor even if they could, as the rule is not permanent, would it at all avail?

"Having shown that this act is at war with the fundamental principles of our government, I might stop here, in the certain hope of its rejection. but, I can do more. Unless we are resolved to pervert the meaning of terms, I can show that the constitution has endeavored to 'make its surety doubly sure and take a bond of fate,' by several express prohibitions of measures like that you now contemplate. One of these is contained in the 9th section of the first Article—it is at the *head of the Arti*cles which restrict the powers of Congress, and declares:

"That the migration or importation of such persons as any of the States shall think proper to admit, shall not be prohibited prior to the year 1808."

"Now, sir, where is the difference between a power to prevent the arrival of aliens, and the power to send them away as soon as they shall arrive. To me they appear precisely the same. The Constitution expressly says that Congress shall not do this, and yet Congress are about to delegate this prohibited power, and say that the President may exercise it as often as his pleasure may direct. I am informed that an answer has been attempted to this argument, by saying that the article, though it speaks of 'persons' only relates to slaves, but a conclusive reply to this answer may be drawn from the words of the section. It speaks of migration and importation. If it related only to slaves, 'importation,' would have been sufficient; but how can the other word apply to slaves? Migration is a voluntary change of country, but who ever heard of a migration of slaves? The truth is, both words have their appropriate meanings, and were intended to secure the interests of different quarters of the Union. The Middle States wished to secure themselves against any laws that might impede the migration of settlers. The Southern states [as well as Massachusetts, New Hampshire and Connecticut,] in the importation of slaves, and so jealous were they of this provision, that the 5th article was introduced to declare that the constitution shall not be amended so as to do it away.

"But even admit the absurdity that the word 'migration' has no meaning, or one foreign to its usual acceptation, and that the article relates only to slaves—even this sacrifice of common sense will not help gentlemen out of their dilemma. Slaves, probably always, but certainly, on their first importation are aliens. Many people think they are always 'dangerous to the peace and safety of the United States.' If the President should be of this opinion, he not only can, but by the terms of this law, is obliged to order them off, for the act creates an obligation on him to send away all such aliens as he shall judge dangerous to the peace or safety of the United States. Thus according to the most favorable construction, every proprietor of this species of property holds it at the will and pleasure of the President, and this, too in defiance of the only article of the Constitution that is declared to be unalterable.

"But, sir, for a moment, if it be possible, let us imagine that a constitution founded on a division of powers into three hands, may be preserved, although all these powers should be surrendered into one. Let us imagine, if we can, that the States intended to restrict the general government from preventing the arrival of persons whom they were yet willing to suffer that same general government to ship off, as soon as they should arrive. Grant all this, and they will be as far from establishing the constitutionality of the bill as they were at the first moment it was proposed; for, in the 3d Article it is provided

"That all judicial power shall be vested in the Supreme and inferior courts;—that the trial of all crimes shall be by jury."

"Except in case of impeachment, and in the 7th and 8th amendments provision is repeated and enforced by others, which declare that

"'No man shall be held to answer for a capital or otherwise infamous crime, unless on a presentment of a grand jury' and that 'in all criminal prosecutions the accused shall enjoy the right to a speedy and public trial by an impartial jury of the state and district where the crime shall have been committed, which district shall have been previously ascertained by law, and to be informed of the nature and cause of the accusation—to be confronted with the witnesses against him—to have compulsory process for obtaining witnesses in his favor, and to have the assistance of counsel for his defense.'"

"Now, sir, what minute article in these several provisions of the constitution is there that is not violated by this bill? All the bulwarks which it opposed to encroachments on personal liberty fall before this engine of oppression. "Judiciary power is taken from Courts [as in Vallandigham's case,] and given to the Executive. The previous safeguard of a presentment by a grand inquest is removed. [Hits the Vallandigham and other cases exactly.]— The trial by jury is abolished. The 'public trial' required by the Constitution is changed into a secret and worse than inquisitorial tribunal. Instead of giving 'information of the nature and cause of the accusation,' the criminal, alike ignorant of his offense and the danger to which he is exposed, never hears of either, until the judgment is passed, and the sentence is executed. Instead of being 'confronted with his accusers,' he is kept alike ignorant of their names and their existence, and even the forms of a trial being dispensed with, it would be a mockery to talk of 'process for witnesses,' [as it was when Vallandigham was denied the privilege to send for Fernando Wood,] or the 'assistance of counsel for defence.'

"Thus, are all the barriers which the wisdom and humanity of our country had placed between accused innocence and oppressive power, at once forced and broken down. Not a vestige, even, of their form remains. No indictment, [as in the case of Vallandigham,] no jury, [as in the case of Vallandigham and others,] no trial, [as in the case of Vallandigham, unless it be said the solemn mockery of a picked commission was a trial,] no public procedure, [ditto,] no statement of the accusation, [as in hundreds of cases where the victims lay in the Government bastiles,] no examination of witnesses in its support, [ditto,] no counsel for defense, [ditto.] All is darkness, silence, mystery and suspicion. But, as if this were not enough, the unfortunate victims of this law are told in the next section that if they can convince the President that his suspicions are unfounded, [Mr. Lincoln said to the committee that if they could convince him that his suspicions were unfounded, &c.] he may—if he pleases, give them a license to stay! But how remove his suspicions, when they know not on what account they were founded? [but how remove Mr. Lincoln's suspicions, when he has suspended the habeas corpus, and forbids his victims to go before the court—their only resort for legal evidence?] How take proof to convince him, when he is not bound to furnish that on which he proceeds? Miserable mockery of justice!

"Appoint an arbitrary judge, armed with legislative and executive powers, added to his own! Let him condemn the unheard—the unaccused object of his suspicion, and then, to cover the injustice of the scene, gravely tell him—

"'You ought not to complain—you need only disprove facts you never heard—remove suspicions that have never been communicated to you—it will be easy to convince your judge—whom you shall not approach—that he is tyrannical and unjust, and when you have done this, we give him the power he had before, to pardon you—*if he pleases.*'

[A perfect, and by no means overdrawn picture of the case presented by the victims of Forts Henry, Warren, La Fayette, &c.]

"So obviously do the constitutional objections present themselves, that their existence cannot be denied, and two wretched subterfuges are resorted to, to remove them out of sight:—First, it is said the bill does not contemplate *the punishment* of any *crime* [the identical logic given by Mr. Lincoln to the Albany committee] and therefore, the provisions in the constitution relative to criminal proceedings, and judiciary powers, do not apply! But have the gentlemen who reason thus, read the bill, or is everything forgotten in our zealous hurry to pass it? What are the offenses upon which it is to operate? Not only the offence of being

"'Suspected to be dangerous to the peace and safety of the United States, but also that of being concerned in any *treasonable* or secret machinations against the government thereof.'

[Precisely the law of Order 38.] "And this we are told is no *crime!* [Abraham Lincoln agrees with the advocates of the alien law in this respect.] A *treasonable machination* against the Government is not the subject of criminal jurisprudence! [Mr. Lincoln says so.] Good heaven! to what absurdities does an over zealous attachment to particular measures lead us! In order to punish a particular act, we are forced to say that *treason is no crime!* and plotting against our Government [discouraging enlistments] is no offense. And, to support this hypothesis, we are obliged to plunge deeper in absurdity and say, that as the acts spoken of in the bill are no crimes, so the penalty contained in it, is no *punishment!* [precisely Mr. Lincoln's argument] it is only a prevention. That is to say, we invite strangers to come among us—we declare solemnly, that Government shall not have the power to prevent them—we entice them over by delusive prospects and advantages. In many parts of the Union we permit them to hold lands, and give them other advantages, while they are waiting for the period at which we have promised a full participation in all our rights. An unfortunate stranger, disgusted with tyranny at home, thinks he shall find freedom here—he accepts your conditions—he puts faith in your promises—he vests his whole property in your hands—he has dissolved his former connections, and made your country his own. But while he is patiently waiting the expiration of the period that is to crown the work, and entitle him to all the rights of a citizen, the tale of a domestic spy, or the calumny of a secret enemy draws on him the suspicions of the President, and, unheard, he is ordered to quit the spot which he selected for his retreat—the country he had chosen for his own—perhaps the family which was his only consolation in life, he is ordered to retire to a country [now to Dixie] whose Government, irritated by his renunciation of its authority, will receive only to punish him, and all this we are seriously told, is no *punishment!*

"Again: We are told that the constitutional compact was made between citizens only, and that, therefore, its provisions were not intended to extend to aliens; and that this act, operating only on them, is therefore not forbidden by the Constitution. But unfortunately, neither common law, common justice, nor the practice of any civilized nation will permit this distinction. It is an acknowledged principle of the common law, the authority of which is established here, that alien friends (and permit me to observe that they are such only whom we contemplate by this bill, for we have another before us to send off alien enemies) residing among us, are entitled to the protection of our laws, and that during their residence, they owe a temporary allegiance to our Government. If they are accused of violating this allegiance, the same laws that interpose in the case of a citizen must determine the truth of the accusation, and if found guilty, they are liable to the same punishment. This rule is consonant to the principles of common justice, for who would ever resort to another country, if he alone was marked out as the object of arbitrary power? It is equally unfortunate too, for this argument, that the Constitution expressly excludes any idea of this distinction:—it speaks of '*all* judicial power'—'*all* trials for crimes'—'*all* criminal prosecutions'—'*all* persons accused.' No distinction between citizen and alien—between high or low—friends or opposers of the Executive power—republican and royalist. All—all are entitled to the same equal distribution of justice—to the same humane provisions to protect their innocence—all are liable to the same punishment that awaits their guilt. How comes it, too, if the constitutional provisions were intended for the safety of the citizen only, that our courts uniformly extend them to all, and that we never hear it enquired, Whether the accused is a citizen, before we give him a public trial by jury?

"So manifest do these violations of the constitution appear to me—so futile the arguments in their defence—that they press seriously upon my mind, and sink it even to despondency. They have been so glaring to my understanding that I felt it my duty to speak of them in a manner that may perhaps give offence to men whom I esteem, and who seem to think differently on that subject—none however, I can assure them, is intended.

"I have seen measures carried in this House which I thought militated against the spirit of the constitution, but never before have I been a witness to so open, so wanton and undisguised an attack.

"I have now done, sir, with the act, and come to consider the consequences of its operation. One of the most serious has been anticipated when I described the blow it would give to the constitution of our country. We should cautiously beware the first act of violation. Habituated to overleap its bounds, we become familiarized to the guilt, and disregard the danger of a second offence, until proceeding from one unauthorized act to another, we at length throw off all restraints which our constitution has imposed, and very soon not even the semblance of its forms will remain.

"But, if, regardless of our duty as citizens, and our solemn obligations as representatives —regardless of the rights of our constituents, of their opinions and that of posterity—regardless of every sanction, human and divine—if *we* are ready to violate the Constitution we have sworn to defend—will the people submit to our unauthorized acts? Will the states sanction our usurped power? Sir, they ought not to submit—they would deserve the chains which these measures are forging for them, if they did not resist—for, let no man vainly imagine that the evil is to stop here [we have seen the fulfilment of this prophecy]—that a few unprotected aliens only are to be affected by this inquisitorial power. The same arguments which enforce these provisions against *aliens, apply with equal strength to enacting them in the case of citizens*. [Have we not seen this?] The citizen has no other protection for his personal security, that I know, against laws like this, than the humane provisions I have cited from the Constitution. But all these apply in common *to the citizen and the stranger*. '*All crimes*' are to be tried by jury. '*No person*' shall be held to answer, unless on presentment. In all *criminal prosecutions*, the 'accused' is to have a public trial; the 'accused' is to be informed of the nature of the charge—to be confronted with the witnesses against him —may have process to enforce the appearance of those in his favor, and is to be allowed counsel for his defence. Unless, therefore, we can believe that *treasonable machinations*, and the other offences described in the bill, are not *crimes*—that an alien is not a *person*, and that one charged with treasonable practices is not *accused*—unless we can believe all this, in contradiction to our own understandings—to received opinions and the uniform practice of our courts, we must allow that all these provisions extend equally to *aliens* and *natives*, and that the citizen has no other security for his personal safety than is extended to the stranger who is within his gates.

"If therefore, this security is violated in one instance, what pledge have we that it will not in the other? The same plea of necessity [Mr. Lincoln's plea] will justify both. Either the offences described in the act are crimes, or they are not. If they are, then all the humane provisions of the constitution forbid the mode of punishing or preventing them; equally as relates to aliens and citizens. If they are not crimes, then the citizen has no more safety by the constitution than the alien has, for all those provisions apply only to *crimes*. So that in either event, the citizen has the same reason to expect a similar law [and it was given in Order 38] to the one now before you, which subjects his person to the *uncontrolled despotism of a single man*.

"You have already been told of plots, of conspiracies, and all the frightful images that were necessary to keep up the present system of terror and alarm, were presented to you. But who were implicated by these dark hints, these mysterious allusions? They were our own citizens, sir,—not aliens. If there is, then, any necessity for the system now proposed, it is more necessary to be enforced against our own citizens than against strangers, and I have no doubt that either in this or some other shape they will be attempted. [This was a correct prophecy of Order 38.]

"I now ask, sir, whether the people of America are prepared for this?—whether they are willing to part with all the means which the wisdom of their ancestors discovered and their own caution so lately adopted, to secure the liberty of their persons—whether they are ready to submit to imprisonment or exile [like the exile of Vallandigham, for instance,] whenever suspicion, calumny or vengeance shall mark them for ruin? Are they base enough to be prepared for this? No, sir, they will—I repeat it, they will resist this tyrannic system. The people will oppose—the states will not submit to its operation. They ought not to acquiesce, and I pray to God they never may. My opinions, sir, on this subject, are explicit, and I wish they may be known. They are, that whenever our laws *manifestly infringe the Constitution*, under which they were made, the people ought not to hesitate which they should obey. If we exceed our powers we become *tyrants*, and our acts have no effect. Thus, sir, one of the first effects of measures, such as this, if they should not be acquiesced in, will be disaffection among the states, and opposition among the people, to your government. Tumults, violence, and a recurrence to first revolutionary principles [which Mr. Lincoln has argued was right and proper.] If they are submitted to, the consequences will be worse. After such manifest violation of the principles of our constitution the form will not long be sacred. Presently, every vestige of it will be lost, and *swallowed up in the Gulf of Despotism!* But, should the evil proceed no further than the execution of the present law, what a fearful picture will our country present! The system of espionage thus established, the country will swarm with informers, [as we have seen in our day] spies, delators, and all that odious reptile tribe that breed in the sunshine of despotic power—that suck the blood of the unfortunate—that creep into the bosom of sleeping innocence only to wake it with a burning wound. [What a graphic, life-like picture of what we have seen for the two years last past!] The hours of the most unsuspecting confidence—the intamacies of friendship, or the recesses of domestic retirement, afford no security [especially, as we have seen, when a hundred armed men surround the domicile of a man and seize and carry him off at the dead hour of night]—the companion whom you most trust—the friend in whom you confide—the domestic who waits in your chamber, are all tempted to betray your imprudence, or guardless follies—to misrepresent your words; [as the spies and delators did those of Vallandigham] to convey them, distorted by calumny, to the secret tribunal, where jealousy presides—where fear officiates as accuser, and *suspicion* is the only evidence that is heard.

"These, bad as they are, are not the only ill consequences of these measures; among them we may reckon on the loss of wealth, of population, and of commerce. Gentlemen who support the bill, seemed to be aware of this, when yesterday they introduced a clause to secure the property of those who might be ordered to go off; they should have foreseen the consequences of the steps they have been taking; it is now too late to discover, that large sums are drawing from the banks, that a great capital is taken from commerce. It is ridiculous even to observe the solicitude they show to retain the wealth of these dangerous men, whose persons they are so eager to get rid of; if they wish to retain it, it must be by giving them security to their persons, and assuring them that while they respect the laws, the laws will protect them from arbitrary power; it must be, in short by rejecting the bill on your table. I might mention many other inferior considerations; but I ought, sir, rather to entreat the pardon of the house, for having touched on this: compared to the breach of our constitution, and the establishment of arbitrary power, every other topic is trifling; arguments of convenience sink into nothing; the preservation of wealth, the interests of commerce, however, weighty on other occasions, here lose their importance. When the fundamental principles of freedom are in danger, we are tempted to borrow the impressive language of a foreign speaker, and exclaim—"Perish our commerce; let our constitution live:"—Perish our riches; let our freedom live. This, sir, would be the sentiment of every American, were the alternative between submission and wealth; but here, sir, it is proposed to destroy our wealth, in order to ruin our commerce. Not in order to preserve our constitution, but to break it—not to secure our freedom, but to abandon it.

"I have now done, sir; but, before I sit down let me intreat gentlemen seriously to reflect before they pronounce the decisive vote, that gives the first open stab to the principles of our government. Our mistaken zeal, like that of the patriarch of old, has bound the victim; it lies at the foot of the altar; a sacrifice of the first-born offspring of freedom is proposed by those who gave it birth. The hand is already raised to strike, and nothing I fear but the voice of heaven can arrest the impious blow.

"Let not gentlemen flatter themselves, that the fervour of the moment can make the people insensible to these agressions. It is an honest noble warmth, produced by an indignant sense of injury. It will never, I trust, be extinct, while there is a proper cause to excite it; but the people of America, sir, though watchful against foreign agression, are not careless of domestic encroachment; they are as jealous, sir, of their liberties at home, as of the power and prosperity of their country abroad; they will awake to a sense of their danger; do not let us flatter ourselves then, that these measures will be unobserved or disregarded. Do not let us be told, sir, that we excite a fervour against foreign agression, only to establish tyranny at home, that, like the arch traitor, we cry, "*Hail, Columbia,*" at the moment we are betraying her to destruction; that we sing out "*happy land,*" when we are plunging it in ruin or disgrace; and that we are absurd enough to call ourselves "*free and enlightened,*" while we advocate principles that would have disgraced the age of Gothic barbarity, and establish a code, compared with which the ordeal is wise, and the trial by battle is merciful and just"

WHO WAS EDWARD LIVINGSTON?

The author of the foregoing speech was the son of an eminent patriot of the Revolution—was elected twice to Congress from New York city—was appointed by Mr. Jefferson as the United States District Attorney for New York—was elected Mayor of New York in 1801, and Judge of a very important municipal court He was Aid-de-camp to General JACKSON at New Orleans—was the author of the Louisiana code—author of a famous criminal code, which fixed his reputation among the foremost jurists in the land. In 1823 Mr. LIVINGSTON was elected to Congress from Louisiana, which place he held till 1829, when he was elected to the Senate from that state. In 1831 General JACKSON appointed him his Prime Minister, in which capacity he wrote the celebrated anti-nullification message. In 1833, Gen. JACKSON appointed him Minister to France, where he acquitted himself with great credit, and to the entire satisfaction of the hero of New Orleans.

This was the man who in 1798 so eloquently denounced that bold attempt to turn this Government into a despotism, and which has been so faithfully imitated by the present Administration.

REPUBLICAN CONFESSIONS.

The following article was prepared by us, and published in the Wisconsin *Patriot*, Nov. 29, 1862. As it shows both sides, and we might not be able to improve on the arguments presented, we transfer it to these pages:

That the abolitionists deeply feel the effect of the popular verdict against the unblushing tyranny, and usurpation, by which the Administration has filled its bastiles with innocent victims of party hate, is too plain for dispute. When Mrs. BRINSMADE, an artless, beautiful and giddy wife of 22 years, was chased about from city to city and finally arrested without a shadow of suspicion against her and caged with common criminals and burglars in a common police station, in New York, the abolition press heralded her arrest as an evidence that the Administration was sharp after traitors and traitoresses, and much fiendish satisfaction was indulged in by the abolition press at the incarceration of this defenseless female. She was locked up as aforesaid for near fifty days, and closely watched, and all entreaties by respectable ladies of New York and Brooklyn to see her and give her such necessaries as she might be suffering for, were peremptorily refused by the black hearted jacobin who held her a prisoner. She had many respectable and loyal friends, who sought to procure for her a speedy trial, and if she could not be found guilty, to relieve her from her loathsome prison, and thus save reproach on the American character, but all to no purpose. She was held in durance vile until the elections thundered at the gates of criminal power, and then, and not until the thunder of the ballot had been heard all over the land, and the Belshazzars of power began to tremble with very fear, was this lady, guilty of no crime, permitted to "go in peace" with no charges against her. Then the Administration organs began to plead the "Baby Act." They declared the Administration knew nothing of her arrest. But this had better be told to the marines, for the fact of the arrest of this female was heralded through the public press all over the North, and the Administration knew perfectly well that she was a prisoner, and they knew also that no charges had been filed against her, for so the pettifogging journals assert.

Never, since our forefathers baptized the tea in Boston harbor, has our country been so disgraced, as by these arbitrary, *unnecessary*, despotic and unconstitutional arrests. It is too late in the day for the Administration to plead ignorance of specific arrests. It will avail them nothing in that awful blistering history which time is writing out. Queen ELIZABETH often pled ignorance of certain enormities committed by her perjured minions, but history holds her guilty of all, for having planned the general crusade against the personal rights of her subjects.

King RICHARD, the hunchback, pled ignorance of the murder of the Heir-Apparent, in the Tower, and wondered who could have done so foul a deed—after he himself had bribed his ready-made tool, BUCKINGHAM, to the awful regicide. We repeat, it is too late in the day for the pensioned organs of the Administration to plead ignorance on its part, of the infamous enormities committed by a generally unprincipled set of Provost Marshals, appointed without the least public necessity, so far as the loyal North is concerned.

By the plainest principles of the common law, handed down as judicial heir looms, by JUSTINIAN and other law givers, if a man turns loose a vicious animal, he is responsible to his neighbor for any damage that may be committed, though he might have known nothing of the depredations! So with the President of the United States. Without the authority of law—without warrant of any kind—without the poor plea of "military necessity" he has let loose upon our loyal society a set of vagabonds, who have committed the grossest outrages on decency and personal rights, and he must be responsible to an outraged people for the wrongs committed. He has sent the arrow quivering from the bow, and though its poisoned blade hits an object he did not aim at, he must bear the guilt of its ravages.

We have another strong case in point, of Mahoney, editor of the Dubuque *Herald*, who was arrested at two o'clock at night, and hurried off to the Old Capitol building, as a political prisoner, right under the very eye of the president. The Milwaukee *Sentinel*, whose editor is an appointee of the president, and of course pocket-bound to do his bidding, undertakes to put in another Baby-Act plea for the president. In speaking of Mahoney, who was liberated only by the thunder of the ballot box, as mysteriously as Paul and Silas were from the Jewish prison, the stipendiary editor says :

"He has been incarcerated but a short time, and with others, has been set free without question. Were there a disposition to tyrannize on the part of the government, and had Mahoney been arrested under the dictate or impulse of that spirit, it is altogether probable that he would have been detained, and not liberated as he was. The president, nor none of his subordinates, he says, was willing to take the responsibility of his arrest. It is not likely they would have shrunk from any such responsibility, if any disposition to oppress him had caused the arrest.

"The Government is *obliged in existing emergencies* to trust a vast deal of discretion to subordinates—which subordinates have generally from the necessities of the case, been very *hastily appointed*, and in many cases lack the discretion required in the position. They do very foolish things, the arrest of Mahoney and others of the same stamp being among *those foolish things*. But the Government neither endorses or sanctions it. The moment Mahoney's case was reached, and the *groundlessness and foolishness* of the complaints against him *were discovered, he was liberated*. He complains that he does not yet know for what crime he was arrested. By acquitting him without question —the Government *confesses substantially he was guilty of no crime.* The moment the fact is ascertained he is liberated."

This whole plea is as weak as it is babyish. It exhibits an evident consciousness of guilt, and overzealousness to avoid its natural consequences. This paid organ says that MAHONEY "was incarcerated only a short time." If the editor of that sheet was incarcerated, in a loathsome cell, on prison diet for *over three months*, we hardly think he would call it a "short time." But short or long, the principle is the same. And now says this organ: "he, with others, has been set free *without question!*" Exactly! They did not even ask him whether he was guilty or innocent After begging the Administration for over two months to give him a trial, or at least let him know the *pretence* of his arrest or incarceration, and all the while they refusing to do either, they turn him loose, "without question." Did mortal man ever hear of greater mocking of justice and decency? The man who could deliberately pen an excuse for such 'diabolical conduct, would be the last to yield in a quarrel over the vesture of his Savior.

The *Sentinel* attempts to weave the web of probability that the Administration is innocent, by raising the question that if the Administration had really intended oppression, it would not have released Mahoney. What do you call a two months incarceration *without charges of wrong*, but oppression? But the "delivery" has no real merit. It was wrung from the Administration by the ballot-box thunder, as the *Magna Charta* was wrung from King John by his oppressed and determined subjects. If Mahoney had been liberated *before* the election, it would have put a different phaze on the motive of the Administration, but to wait till the great states of the North had demanded by the potent ballot—"formidable to tyrants only"—that the oppressed innocent should go free—the act of liberation was no virtue, but a cowardly necessity.

But, says this Custom House organ:

"The Government is obliged, in *existing emergencies*, to entrust a vast deal of discretion to subordinates; and those subordinates, *hastily* appointed, often lack discretion, and do very foolish things; the arrest of Mahoney being among these *foolish* things," &c.

Now, we deny that the Government is obliged in the existing emergencies, in any state north of the Ohio and Potomac, to appoint—"hastily" or otherwise—any officers to arrest people at their will. The necessity does not, and never has existed. It is not within the power of any organ of the Administration to show that in any single instance, here in the North, the duties of a Provost Marshal are *necessary*. Among all the thousands of victims they have arrested, we have heard of *not one* that has been proven guilty, and we take it no man— even under the pressure of the highest salary —will plead for the necessity of arresting innocent men and women. But the plea of "hasty appointment" is the baby act over. It is worse than a baby's plea, for the appointments have been made with no more *haste* than thousands of other appointments. No, the people will not —cannot—except that plea. But the offer of it shows the crying guilt of the party in power. Men always give their *best* reasons first for evil consequences, and if the Administration has no better reason than its organ tests to the waiting multitude, it might as well own up, first as last, that this Provost Marshal business was organized—not to serve the nation— but to serve the Abolition party as a threatening engine of oppression, to force the weak and timid to support the Abolition party; but, thank God, they have failed. Provost Marshals are no longer wanted. They have done many "foolish things." Let the Administration discharge them, and thus save its credit while it is possible.

"The moment Mahony's case was reached," says the *Sentinel,* "the *groundlessness and foolishness* of the complaints against him *were discovered*, and he was liberated!"

What do you mean by "reaching" the case? That would indicate a kind of *hearing*, but nothing of the kind occurred, and as for the "*groundless and foolishness* of the complaint," that is all moonshine, for no complaint was ever lodged against him, and this the *Sentinel* admits. From the start there was nothing charged against him, and this the Administration knew, for MAHONY was almost daily asking the Administration what he was arrested for. We never knew a weaker argument and a more atrocious case than is here presented. The organ says that "By acquitting without question the government confesses substantially he was *guilty of no crime!*" And the government knew this the moment he was incarcerated, as well as the moment when they gave the order for his release. We hardly think the *Sentinel* will claim that the government arrests its victims in hopes to *hunt up afterwards* charges against them. This would be re-enacting the bloody and damnable deeds of the old *Conceigierre*, in France, where they dug the graves, made the coffins, then sent out their provost marshals to hunt up the victims to fill them. "The moment he is found to be guilty of no crime," says this organ, "he is liberated." Now, how did the government arrive at the conclusion that he was innocent just at that particular time? No court or tribunal had been organized to determine the fact. No witnesses had been sworn—no charges preferred, and yet all at once—just after the election—the Administration found out that MAHONY was guilty of no crime, and he was set at liberty! What a mockery of common sense and justice!

From MAHONY's case, the *Sentinel* offers the Baby Act plea in reference to Mrs. BRINSMADE's case, as follows:

"The case of Mrs. Brinsmade, in New York, is one in point. Some official, (it is not yet certain who, but supposed to be Marshal Kennedy,) took the responsibility of arresting Mrs. Brinsmade and locked her up. The *case was finally* brought to the attention of the authorities, and she was promptly released. None denounce the arrest more heartily and pointedly than the immediate friends of the Administration."

Yes, yes, "some official" did take the responsibility—but he took it from the President's order commanding the arrest of all persons for "disloyal practices"—his appointees to be the sole judges. There is where the responsibility came from. Mrs. B's case "was *finally* brought to the attention of the authorities," eh? Yes, as soon as the elections, had opened their eyes and their ears, and set their hearts to palpitating, then they listened to the appeals of the poor, weak woman, and not before. If so flagitious and iniquitous an arrest had been made, and a young and beautiful female so long imprisoned in a common ward station house, without authority from headquarters, think you the scoundrel who did it would wear the star of office another hour? No, he would be instantly dismissed, and a decent man put in his place, but he is still kept in office, a sufficient fact to our mind to warrant the belief that he is wanted for other nasty jobs But, says the organ, "the immediate friends of the Administration denounce" these outrages, and therefore we must draw the inference that it is guileless. Some of them have denounced them *since* the election, but not before. We challenge a single case to prove they denounced them before election, but many Democrats did, and for doing so were called "traitors" and "tories" by these same organs. Theirs is a death-bed repentance.— The Ryan Address and Gov. SEYMOUR's speech denounced these arbitrary and illegal arrests, and for doing so the *Sentinel* and other abolition sheets—before election—denounced RYAN and Gov. SEYMOUR.

Again, says the Custom-House organ :

"We have felt that a great many foolish, and even oppressive things were being done by these government agents. But the emergency of the government required the creation of agents of the character, and the evils complained of are almost inevitable and inseparable from their appointment. The government, itself, however, has shown no disposition to tyrannize. These agents will learn their duties and learn not to overstep the bounds of a sensible discretion ; or, failing in that, will be speedily displaced, and their places filled with better men."

We have seen no displacement of these bad men as yet. The first part of the above paragraph any man of sense and self-respect will say amen to. But it will be hard to convince any man of ordinary intelligence that any possible "emergency" has arisen, or is likely to arise, in the Northern States, whereby this new batch of officers are, or may be necessary. What act have they done, or can they do, (save to violate law and outrage personal rights,) that may not be done by U. S. Marshals, their deputies, or any other civil, executive officer ?— What possible necessity has arisen, or can arise, in all human probability, in the loyal states, making it necessary, or even excusable, to arrest any man without "due process of law?"— And, what necessity for arresting men without warrant, and suspending the privilege of *habeas corpus*, except it be the intention to "tyrannize" over men for their political opinion's sake? What possble harm *could* come to the government, to *permit* men to be arrested, when charged with some crime, and taken before some competent, civil tribunal, to be tried?— Does any one believe, a man thus arrested, in any loyal state, and proven guilty, would escape punishment? A bare suspicion of such a thing would be an imputation on the loyalty of citizen jurors, and the fidelity of our judiciary.

We therefore insist, that, no matter what the original intentions, this Provost Marshal business is a gross imposition on, the people—an imputation on their loyalty—a political engine, to force political action in violation of political opinions—and until we can be shown some *necessity* for it—the accomplishment of legitimate Government purposes, that cannot be accomplished by other means, we will denounce it in all its phases as not only "foolish" and "oppressive," but a disgrace to the nineteenth century.

In view of the verdict of the people in the overwhelming political revolution, of '62, the *Sentinel* had gravely come to the following quite sensible conclusion:

"The nature of our government, as well as the *temper of the people*, clearly reveal the folly of any attempt at tyranny or abuse of power on the part of those entrusted with the administration."

All of which we endorse without a *but* or an *if*.

In conclusion, let us suggest, that if the Administration believes that Provost Marshals are necessary, and that it does not intend them to overawe the people in the exercise of their civil and political rights, would not the said Administration *remove* all incompetents as soon as their "foolish" incompetency was discovered? Few if any greater crimes can be committed against individual rights than to deprive a man of his liberty without cause. And yet, the President don't remove that miserable tyrant, Kennedy, who arrested Mrs. Brinsmade, nor the contemptible wretch that arrested Mahoney who, the *Sentinel* admits were arrested without cause. Now, if our peacable and law-abiding citizens are to be arrested and plunged into the filth and debris of a military prison, with not even a charge against them, and the President

after *knowing all the facts*, as he does *now* know them, at least, will not remove his appointees who are guilty of such gross outrages, then *he* becomes personally the guilty party, and is inaugurating a system of despotism that may yet cost the loyal North seas of blood to crush out, after it has fairly got a foothold.

One word as to what the *Sentinel* says about the friends of the Administration condemning these "oppressive" outrages. Did the *Sentinel* denounce the arrest of Mrs. BRINSMADE before the election? Not a bit of it. On the other hand, if our memory is not at fault, it glorified in the arrest of a "she secessionist." Did the *Sentinel* or *State Journal* denounce the arrest of MAHONEY *before* the election?— By no means; on the contrary, the latter did, even if the former did not, glory in the arrest of the "traitor MAHONEY." Now, that he is *acknowledged* to have been innocent, that Jacobin organ is *mum*. Not a note has it to sound against the outrage—but O, how the Abolition press howled when BOOTH and DANIELS, of Wisconsin, were arrested for crimes they gloried in—crimes of "*positive defiance*" to law, which are to-day the corner stone of the Republican platform of Wisconsin.

Great God! is this that "liberty" we have heard preached so often from Republican pulpits? Is it that "freedom" so often harrangued from Republican rostrums? Is it that "free speech" so often sung in the Republican cloister and peddled through the columns of the Republican press? Is this party of boasted "freedom" about to turn the oppressors and enslavers of the white race, and impose upon it the necessities of becoming "hewers of wood and drawers of water" for Congo masters? Strange that a great party that no longer ago than 1860 had emblazoned on its victorious banners "Liberty and Freedom," should, at the first moment of its drunken success, raise the standard of worse than Roman slavery. Reader, beware, for we have the lesson of the Quakers to guide us, who for centuries preached religious "freedom" and "toleration," and the moment they got the power, they went to hanging and persecuting all who did not believe in their dogmas. The case of Roger Williams is not forgotten—nor will the political debaucheries and vile salvonic persecutions of Abolitionism be forgotten, so long as debased humanity may steal that oft abused word

16

"Liberty," as a cloak for slavery and oppression.

This chapter has been extended much beyond our original design, but the principles involved are of such vast importance, that we feel justified in going beyond that design, though the largest 12 mo. volume would not contain the half we had selected under this head.

CHAPTER XXXI.

DESPOTISM, USURPATIONS, INALIENABLE RIGHTS TRAMPLED UPON, Etc.

Despotism Seeks the Semblance of Loyalty...Solicitor Whiting perverts Judge Taney's Decision...Provost Marshal Fry Acts Thereon...Star Chamber...Laws by Proclamation in England...Kidnapping in New York... Gov. Hunt on Arbitrary Arrests...The Case of Gen. Stone ...Beecher on Arbitrary Arrests...A Nice Point to Silence a Press...Geo. W. Jones vs. Wm. H. Seward...Judge Clarke's Decision...A Young Lady Fined $15 for Playing the "Bonnie Blue Flag"...Burnside Favors the Arrest of Males and Females that wear Butternut Badges... Opening the Prison Doors...Case of Gov. Tod and Others ...Opinion of Judge Van Trump..."New York Journal of Commerce" on the Powers of the Provost Marshal... Case of Judge Constable...Liberated from the Bastile... Atrocious Sentiments by Senator Wilson...Cincinnati Prison Full...Other Acts of Despotism...General Conclusions...Vallandigham's Acts compared with Leading Republicans...Loyalty of Democrats...Disloyalty of Republicans...$500 Reward for a Disloyal Democrat Not Taken...The Writ of Habeas Corpus the Palladium of Our Liberties...Extracts of the Magna Charta—Wrung from King John...Lord Campbell's Boast...English Bill of Rights..."Body of Liberties" Brought by the Mayflower...The Bill in the Declaration...Virginia Bill of Rights...Massachusetts' "Declaration of Rights" in 1780...From Bill of Rights in Our Constitution...General Remarks on Suspension of the Writ of Habeas Corpus... Law of Suspected Persons...A Leaf from French History, by Allison...Our Parallels...Thiers on French Confiscation...Danton's Prediction...General Remarks...Blackstone on the English Habeas Corpus...Our Constitution Applied...The Ordinance of 1787 Applicable...What Our Fathers Thought of it...Pinckney, Rutledge, Morris and Mlllson on the Habeas Corpus...Judge Curtis on "Loyalty" and Habeas Corpus...A Scathing Speech...Mr. Chase's Opinion of Loyalty...The Roman Law and Personal Liberty...St. Paul on Arbitrary Violations of Law ...Judge Festus and King Agrippa Respected the Roman Law..." New York Independent" on Arbitrary Arrests ...What a Conservative Republican Thinks of it...President's Suspension of the Writ of Habeas Corpus : His Proclamation...Congress on Arbitrary Arrests...Official Vote...Supreme Court of Wisconsin on Suspending the Writ.

DESPOTISM SEEKS THE SEMBLANCE OF LEGALITY.

It is very natural, and has been, in all ages of the world, for Despots to claim they were acting under legal authority. The following "opinion" by Solicitor WHITING is quite in point:

"WAR DEPARTMENT,
"PROVOST MARSHAL GENERAL'S OFFICE,
"Washington, D. C., July 1, 1863.
"Circular, No. 36.

"The following opinion of Hon. William Whiting, Solicitor of the War Department, is published for the information and guidance of all officers of this Bureau:

"*Arrest of Deserters—Habeas Corpus.—Opinion.*

"It is enacted in the 7th section of the act approved March 3, 1863, entitled "An act for enrolling and calling out the national forces, and for other purposes," that it shall be the duty of the Provost Marshals appointed under this act, 'to arrest *all deserters, whether regulars, volunteers, militia men, or persons called into the service under this or any other act of Congress,* wherever they may be found, and to send them to the nearest military commander, or military post.'

"If a writ of *habeas corpus* shall be issued by a State court, and served upon the Provost Marshal while he holds under arrest a deserter, before he has had opportunity 'to send him to the nearest military commander, or military post,' the Provost Marshal is not at liberty to disregard that process. 'It is the duty of the Marshal, or other person having custody of the prisoner, to make known to the Judge, or Court, by a proper return, the authority by which he holds him in custody. But after this return is made, and the State Judge or Court judicially apprised that the party is in custody under the authority of the United States, they can proceed no farther.'

"They then know that the prisoner is within the dominion and jurisdiction of another government, and that neither the writ of *habeas corpus*, nor any other process issued under state authority, can pass over the line of division between the two sovereignties. He is then within the dominion and exclusive jurisdiction of the United States. If he has committed an offence against their laws, their tribunals alone can punish him. If he is wrongfully imprisoned, their judicial tribunals can release him and afford him redress. And, although as we have said, it is the duty of the marshal, or other person holding him, to make known, by a proper return, the authority under which he retains him, it is, at the same time, imperatively his duty to obey the *process* of the United States, to hold the prisoner in custody under it, and to refuse obedience to the mandate or process of any other government. And consequently, it is his duty not to take the prisoner, nor suffer him to be taken before a state judge or court upon a *habeas corpus* issued under state authority. No state judge or court, after they are judicially informed that the party is *imprisoned* under the authority of the United States, has any right to interfere with him, or require him to be brought before them. And if the authority of a state, in the form of judicial process or otherwise, should attempt to control the marshal, or other authorized officer or agent of the United States, in any respect, in the custody of his prisoner, it would be his duty to resist it, and to call to his aid any force that might be necessary to maintain the authority of law against illegal interference. No judicial process, whatever form it may assume, can have any lawful thority outside of the limits of the jurisdiction of the court or judge by whom it is issued, and an attempt to enforce it beyond these boundaries is nothing less than lawless violence.

"The language above cited is that of Chief Justice Taney in the decision of the Supreme Court of the United States, in the case of Ableman vs. Booth. (21 *Howard's Reports*.)

If a writ of *habeas corpus* shall have been sued out from a State Court, and served upon the Provost Marshal while he holds the deserter under arrest, and before he has had time or opportunity

"To send him to the nearest military commander, or military post,"

It is the duty of the Marshal to make to the Court a respectful statement, in writing, as a return upon the writ, setting forth,

"1st. That the respondent is Provost Marshal, duly appointed by the President of the United States, in accordance with the provisions of the act aforesaid.

"2d. That the person held was arrested by said Marshal as a deserter, in accordance with the provision of the 7th section of the act aforesaid. That it is the legal duty of the respondent to deliver over said deserter "to the nearest military commander, or military post," and that the respondent intends to perform such duty as soon as possible.

"3d. "That the production of said deserter in court would be inconsistent with, and in violation of the duty of the respondent as provost marshal, and that the said deserter is now held under authority of the United States.— For these reasons, and without intending any disrespect to the honorable Judge who issued process, he declines to produce said deserter, or to subject him to the process of the court."

"To the foregoing, all other material facts may be added.

"Such return having been made, the jurisdiction of the state court over that case ceases. If the state court shall proceed with the case and make any formal judgment in it, except that of dismissal, one of two courses may be taken. (1) The case may be carried up, by appeal or otherwise, to the highest court of the state, and removed therefrom by writ of error to the Supreme Court; or, (2) the judge may be personally dealt with in accordance with law, and with such instructions as may hereafter be issued in each case.
"JAMES B. FRY,
"Provost Marshal General."

Now, to claim that Chief Justice TANEY, in the Booth-Ableman case, endorsed the arbitrary power claimed in the foregoing is one of the most abomniable stretches of Judicial license we have met with. Judge TANEY simply says that when a state court is made acquainted with the fact that a man is "*imprisoned*" under a "*process* of the United States," such state court can proceed no further. This is good law, and no sound lawyer will dispute it, but when the pettifoggers of the Administration ask us to assume that a military order is a judicial "process," such as Chief Justice TANEY alluded to, it is asking more than can be granted

This shows to what desperation the authors) f despotic power are reduced.

LAWS BY PROCLAMATION IN ENGLAND—OUR STAR CHAMBER.

Lord SOMERS, in denouncing the despotism of the STUARTS, said:

"We had a privy council in England, with great and mixed powers; *we suffered under it long and much:* All the rolls of Parliament are full of complaints and remedies; but none of them effectual till Charles the First's time. *The Star Chamber was but a spawn of our council,* and was called so only because it sat in the usual council chamber. It was set up as a formal court in the third year of Henry the Eighth, *in very soft* words,

"To punish great riots, to restrain offenders too big for ordinary justice."

* * * * *

"*But in a little time it made the nation tremble.* The Privy Council came at last *to make laws by proclamation, and the Star Chamber ruined those that would not obey.*"

The arrest of actual deserters is well enough, and all courts should and would remand them whenever it appeared that they *were deserters*. But the great benefit of the writ is to ascertain the fact whether the accused were in truth deserters, or, whether in fact innocent men had not been arrested through mistake, or through the avaricious desire to get the bounty. The writ is not to encourage guilt, but to protect innocence. The following will illustrate the case in point:

[From the New York World, Nov. 3, 1863.]

"KIDNAPPING IN NEW YORK.

"An instance of the gross injustice which seems inseparable from the arbitrary military system inaugurated by Secretary Stanton has recently come to light. In October, 1861, sixty-two young men were induced to enlist in what they were told was 'Company L, Colonel Serrell's Regiment of Volunteer Engineers,' the pay being for privates seventeen dollars per month. The company, when organized, was, without authority of Governor Morgan, taken to Washington, where for several days neither the War Department nor the General-in-Chief would recognize them. Subsequently, and without any new muster, they were designated as Fourth New York Independent Battery. The men protested in writing, but in vain—the pay is thirteen dollars per month. They have been in eleven actions, and have distinguished themselves. They applied through counsel to the adjutant-general to be attached to Colonel Serrell's regiment, in pursuance of their enlistment, or to be discharged. This was refused; yet neither by statute nor army regulations have the government the power to transfer men from one arm of service to another in the volunteer service.

"Several of the men, feeling that they had been grossly wronged, after the battle of Gettysburg deserted and reached New York. A *habeas corpus* was taken out before Mr. Justice Clerke, they having been arrested as deserters by a sergeant of artillery. Justice Clerke discharged them from the Fourth Independent Battery, for the reason that they never enlisted therein, and also *from the service of* the United States, for the reason that they were enlisted under false pretenses. A copy of this order, certified and under seal, was given to the men. Last week a government detective arrested one of these men, read the order, and sent the man to Governor's Island, from whence, it is said, he has been sent South.

It is very clear that this is a flagrant instance of downright kidnapping, and that by no rule of equity can it be justified. It is monstrous that under our system of laws, in which there are so many provisions for guarding the rights of the citizen and insuring the faith of contracts, men can be compelled to do military service without the slightest regard to law, justice, or their personal rights. Congress ought to investigate this matter.

WASHINGTON HUNT ON ARBITRARY ARRESTS.

The people of New York, without distinction of party, met in Union Square, New York, in May, 1863, twenty-five thousand strong, to take into consideration the subject of personal liberty. There was speaking at four stands.— The following letter was read, from Washington Hunt, whom our opponents have so often supported for high offices in the Empire State:

LOCKPORT, May 16, 1863.

"GENTLEMEN:—I have received your letter inviting me to attend the proposed meeting at Union Square. It is out of my power to come, but I wish to avail myself of the occasion to declare my emphatic condemnation of the recent attempts to subject the people of the loyal states to an irresponsible and arbitrary system of military domination.

"While we are willing to submit to the greatest sacrifices, in a patriotic spirit, for the preservation of the Union, it may as well be understood that we will not consent to be bereft of any of our constitutional rights. We have lost none of these rights in consequence of the southern rebellion.

"The Administration ought to comprehend that it is amenable to public opinion, and that its conduct and policy are a legitimate subject of popular discussion and criticism. It is for the perpetuation of a free constitutional government, and for this only, that the country has been so willing to exhaust its best blood and place its vast resources at the disposal of the national authority. God forbid that the American people should allow the strength thus imparted to be turned against tnemselves, and a military despotism erected on the ruins of public liberty! So far as New York is concerned, let it be proclaimed from the house tops that no man within her borders

"Shall be deprived of life, liberty, or property, without due process of law."

"With great regard, yours truly,
"WASHINGTON HUNT.
"Messrs. Gideon J. Tucker, John Hardy, A. Mathewson, and others."

THE CASE OF GEN. STONE.

"We have a case in point, in that of Gen. Stone, of the great wrong and injustice liable to be done by arbitrary proceedings against individuals. Gen. Stone it is remembered, was arrested while in the exercise of a command, sent to one of the military prisons, denied information as to the cause of his arrest, and refused any opportunity to explain any proceedings of his own which might have seemed unusual. After several months of confinement, he was released without trial, and it is now announced that he was assigned to duty in the Department of the Gulf,—the President being satisfied, of course, that he was wrongfully arrested and imprisoned. How easily could this wrongful arrest and imprisonment have been avoided."

BEECHER ON ARBITRARY ARRESTS.

Even the most radical of all radicals; HENRY WARD BEECHER, sees danger ahead, in the way of arbitrary arrests. In speaking of VALLANDIGHAM's case he said:

"It would be better for the country that ten thousand brave men were slain on the battle field, than that one should be deprived of even the least of his guarranteed rights at this time. The heart of the nation is in no mood to be thus despotically tampered with."

GETTING DOWN TO A NICE POINT.

[From the New York World.]

"We ask all candid liberty-loving American citizens of both parties if the following does not smack rather too much of Venice or Poland for this free country:

"HEADQUARTERS MILITARY GOVERNOR,
"Alexandria, Va., Sept. 16, '63.
"*Proprietor Alexandria Gazette:*

"SIR:—Observing in your issue of this evening an article boldly headed 'Virginia Legislature,' which article contains the proceedings of the Confederate Legislature of Virginia, and hence, is a public recognition upon your part of a state government in Virginia opposed to the federal government, the general commanding directs me to inform you that the repetition of this act will be visited with a suspension of your paper.

"The existence of a paper in Alexandria known to be hostile to the government he represents, will be tolerated so long only as there appears nothing in it offensive to loyal people. Respectfully,
"ROLLIN C. GALE, A. A. G."

Have not things come to a pretty pass when an American newspaper published within a few miles of the capital of the country is threatened with suppression, because the heading to some of the news displeases an ignorant military officer? The phrase "Virginia Legislature" is literally correct, no matter what the political crimes of that body may have been. A gun is a gun, whether in the hands of a federal or a confederate soldier, and an organized state legislature, in or out of the Union, is very properly distinguished by the name of the state it legislates for. The "general commanding" who inspired the above order may have a "bold" head of his own, but it certainly has very little brains or discretion inside of it.

GEO. W. JONES VS. WM. H. SEWARD.

Judge CLERKE, of the Superior Court of the city of New York, in which the case of GEORGE W. JONES *vs.* WILLIAM H. SEWARD, an action for alleged false imprisonment, is pending, has rendered an important decision. The question before the court arose upon a motion to remove the case from the state court to the United States Court for the northern district of New York.

Judge CLERKE, in giving the decision of the court, said:

"The defendant stated in his petition for this order that the action was brought for acts alleged to have been done by him as Secretary of State for the United States of America, under authority derived by him from the President of the United States, in causing the plaintiff to be arrested and imprisoned, or for some other wrong alleged to have been done to the plaintiff under such authority during the present rebellion, and that it therefore comes within the act of Congress of March 3d, 1863, relating to the writ of *habeas corpus*, by which a case may be removed to another court.

"The question to be determined being whether the President of the United States, during a rebellion, can arrest any person not subject to military law, without the process of some court, this was a question that would arise under the constitution of the United States. * * * * * *

"It cannot of course be pretended by the most ardent advocate of this high Presidential prerogative that the constitution confers it in set terms There is nothing in that instrument that can be tortured into the conferring of such power upon the President in his civil capacity, and this, it appears to me, plainly disposes of the question; for it would be asserting the greatest contradiction and strangest anomaly to say that absolute and unlimited power, equal to any exercised by Czar or Sultan, can be implied by a constitution which gives no power to any department that is not specially set forth, except simply the consequent right to employ all legal means necessary to the execution of the power.

"If there is anything beyond all controversy in the constitutional history of the nation it is that the purpose of the constitution and the provisions which it contains were for a considerable time before its adoption thoroughly discussed by their people and their delegates in convention, and any man professing to confer unlimited power on any department of the government, on any pretext, would not have been deemed sane."

After referring to the constitutional history of the United States and England, the learned judge remarks:

"Could it be supposed that the framers of the constitution intended any such power as that claimed in the present case, either express or implied? If they intended a dictatorship to exist *under any emergency*, they would not leave it to the chief-executive to assume it when he may in his discretion declare necessity required it, but would have provided that this necessity should be declared by congress, and that the legislature alone should select the person who should exercise it. That the President can assume such a power is an extravagant assumption which cannot be entertained by any court. No such inquiry can arise under the constitution of the United States. *It does not reach the proportions* or stature of a question.

"Mr. Lincoln as a military commander can possess no greater power than if he were not President. Suppose the constitution vested the commander-in-chief of the army and navy in some person other than the President—could this functionary subvert the constitution and laws under the plea of military necessity? Certainly not."

The learned judge thus concludes:

"The power for which the defendant contends is plainly not necessary for the safety of the nation, and is not conferred by the Constitution. When that safety shall be endangered within the immediate theatre of insurrection or war, the commander-in-chief and his subordinates are judges of the occasion, but beyond that the ordinary course of proceedings in the courts of justice will be sufficient to punish any persons who furnish information, afford aid to an enemy or betray their country. In cases of emergency, caused by invasion or insurrection, the powers expressly given by the constitution, and the acts of Congress to repel the one and suppress the other are ample and effective.— It requires no exercise of an extraordinary power over the sacred rights of personal liberty to accomplish all this. It is manifest that it is beyond all controversy, that those rights in war or in peace, during invasion or domestic violence, even during the hideous rebellion which now confronts us, exist in cases which I have stated and are inviolable.

"The President, therefore, whether in his civil or military capacity as commander-in chief, has no such power as that claimed for him.

"The ground upon which the application is made has no foundation in right. It cannot be entertained as a question in any state, or in the United States court. The only question in this motion worthy of consideration, and which can be entertained, does not arise under the constitution of the United States, but is clearly within the jurisdiction of this court."

A YOUNG LADY FINED FIFTEEN DOLLARS FOR PLAYING A SECESH TUNE ON THE PIANO.

No one act of NAPOLEON III has been more virtuously denounced than the suppression of the Marseilles Hymn, and the punishment of those who sang or played that air. As a part of the correlative history of the times, we give the following from the New Orleans police reports, as it appeared in the New Orleans *Era* of April 29th, 1863:

"*Provost Court*—Judge A. De B. Hughes, presiding.

"Miss Claiborne Massey, arrested for playing the air of the Bonnie Blue Flag at the residence of her parents, was before the Court. The Hon. Michael Hahn appeared to defend her, and remarked that he did not think the playing of the air without the words constituted much of an offense. He said that the watchman had heard the air played, but at the time did not think it necessary to make the arrest. He afterwards consulted the Sergeant, who also thought it was not necessary to make the arrest; but he afterwards went back and made the arrest. Judge Hughes said that in consideration of the high character of the able gentleman who defended the lady, he would be as lenient as the strict requirements of his duties would permit, and therefore fined her only $15.

In the local column we find this notice of the affair:

"A young lady, named Miss Claiborne Massey, of the highest respectability, was arrested last night and locked up for playing the Bonnie Blue Flag. She was released to appear before the Provost Court. This morning she was fined $15."

Is it in the power of the human imagination to conceive of any possible harm for a young lady, accomplished, and of the "highest respectability," playing any tune on a piano? Did Napoleon III. ever exceed this Police demonstration? Young ladies must be careful how they play "Dixie." The substitution of "John Brown's Soul is Marching On," will save their $15.

MORE DISLOYAL PRACTICES.

By the following telegram it appears that all who wear butternut emblems—male or female —are to be arrested:

"Cincinnati, April 20, '63.—Gen. Burnside approves the order issued by Gen. Carrington for the arrest of members of the K. G. C., on the ground that they are enemies to the Government. He also favors the arrest of persons, male or female, wearing butternut emblems.— Arrests are now being made, and examples will be made."

Madness rules the hour. How long will it be before Democrats will be compelled to cut down and burn up any butternut shade trees they may have set out, on pain of being arrested and "made examples of?" It cannot be possible the American people sanction these things.

OPENING THE PRISON DOORS.

The Washington correspondent of the Chicago *Times* says:

"This morning it is announced that the prison doors are open, and that the victims of private malice and official spite are free to depart. Are we to bow down in the dust and thank the man whose name is signed to the order of release? Rather let him tremble; and not him alone. The administration cannot, by this tardy act, atone for the misery they have inflicted, nor can they bring back the happiness they have ruthlessly destroyed. The punishment of tyrants is sure to come, and they cannot escape theirs.

"This act of releasing prisoners of state is a mere caprice. There is no more reason for doing it now than there was three or six months ago. There was no cause for the arrests at first, and there is no cause for the termination of the confinements now that did not exist then."

BELSHAZZAR never trembled till he saw the handwriting on the wall, and *then* he was afraid. Wonder if the Administration did not read on the walls of the old bastile, the dreadful words, "*Mene tekel upharsin?*"

THE CASE OF GOV. TOD AND OTHERS.

It will be remembered that Gov. TOD, of Ohio, was recently arrested upon a charge of kidnapping Doctor OLDS. In the Court of Common Pleas of Fairfield county, in that State, a motion was made by STOUGHTON BLISS, one of the parties arrested in the same case, for a transfer of the cause to the Circuit Court of the United States for the Southern District of Ohio. The motion was based upon the act of Congress of March 3d, 1863, which provided for such transfer, and also provided that the defendants in such cases, by proving that they were "acting under color of authority" from the President, or of officers deriving their authority from him, should be entitled to discharge. Judge VAN TRUMP, before whom the motion was made, in a brief but singularly clear and logical review, showed the unconstitutionality of the law, and overruled the motion. We append an extract of one point made by him, which, to our mind, was alone ample justification for his decision:

"What is the legal *status* of the claim made by the petitioner to remove his case into the Circuit Court of the United States? It is, in my opinion, nothing more or less than an attempt to transfer the criminal jurisdiction of the State Court into that of the Federal tribunals. If such is the scope and effect of this act of March 3d, 1863, then I have no hesitation in pronouncing it unconstitutional. If the Congress of the United States have no constitutional power to modify, abolish or repeal the law of a state crime, it is a logical deduction, in my opinion, from which there is no escape, that they are powerless in changing the forum of trial of such crime. Has not Congress the same power to measure and fix the punishment of crime under a state law, or to enact a code of evidence, or practice, for its prosecution, as to erect the forum of trial?"

POWERS OF THE PROVOST MARSHAL.

The New York *Journal of Commerce* thus sets forth the cunning devices of the conscription act, by means of the created Provost Marshals, to act as spies, detectives, &c.:

"This Provost Marshal General will be one of the most tremendous officials in the country. The bill allows him and the Secretary of War to do pretty much as they please with the rights and liberties of the citizen. There are three things which these Provost Marshals are specially required to do:

"One is, to arrest deserters, and send them to the nearest commander, which is necessary and proper.

"The second is, to enquire into and report all treasonable practices. If this means anything, it means that the Provost Marshal may employ any number of spies, like a veritable little tyrant, to pry into the private affairs of any person whom, in his high mightiness, he choses to suspect of 'treasonable practices.' If he happens to be a fierce radical, he may take the liberty of regarding every conservative as essentially a traitor—this being the prevalent view of the radical organs on that subject. The bill says nothing about the forcible entry of houses; but that will undoubtedly be authorized in the 'rules and regulations' of the great functionary, the Provost Marshal General.

"The third duty of the Provost Marshal is, to 'detect, seize and confine spies.' This is a puzzler, and comes very queerly, after the paragraph authorizing the Provost Marshals to employ spies of their own to any extent. Interpreted literally, and meaning real spies, who come over from the enemy to inspect the strength of our forces, and the armament of our fortifications, it is a just and necessary regulation. The objection to it lies in this fact—that the Provost Marshal, or his superior is made the sole judge of what, and who, is a spy, and can arrest and confine him without judge or jury.

"A Provost Marshal who holds that every conservative is a traitor, may also hold that some conservatives are constructively 'spies.'"

If a Provost Marshal wanted to arrest a conservative and put him in a fort, where he could stay out the balance of the war, nothing would be easier than to make a vague accusation that, at some time or other, he had communicated with some individual who is regarded as being traitorous in his proclivities. This would make the poor man constructively a spy. But the Provost marshal, and those above him, need not give explanations, unless they please. They may presume any man a spy—in the employment and confidence of the enemy, and arrest and imprison him.

"All this is the most odious kind of martial law. It is wrong to impose it on this quiet and peaceful North."

THE CASE OF JUDGE CONSTABLE.

The papers and facts in this case are too voluminous to record in this work. We shall have to content ourself with a brief statement of the facts.

The laws of Illinois declare it kidnapping to arrest a person without authority of law. In March, 1863, two persons were brought before Judge CONSTABLE, of the 4th Judicial Circuit of Illinois, charged with having violated the statutes against kidnapping. The proof against them was conclusive. They had arrested certain persons, without showing any authority therefor. The Judge, as it was his sworn duty, held them for trial. For thus exercising his duty, Judge C. was seized, and forcibly carried away from the duties of his office, and after having been kept in durance a long while, was finally liberated—no proof, or even charge of wrong appearing against him.

LIBERATED FROM THE BASTILE.

The following, from the Pittsburgh *Post* covers a great variety of cases, and we copy it as a sample:

"A number of gentlemen who were incarcerated (Mahony and others) in a loathsome prison in Washington, upon imaginary charges and released the other day, without explanation, passed through our city last evening on their way to their respective homes. These enlarged captives paid us a a visit yesterday, and we refer the reader to our local column for an account of their incarceration, mal-treatment and release. Let the reader peruse this statement, and then reflect that it is not an extract from the history of England during the 'War of Roses,' nor a chapter depicting the horrors of the Bastile of the French Revolution, but a single recital of personal suffering, inflicted by our boasted Government upon *its own citizens*. Let the reader ponder upon this brief narrative, if he has patience, and see how it contrasts with similar persecutions of what we glibely term the 'Dark Ages.' The tales of the Spanish Inquisitions, the English Star Chamber proceedings, have been held up as the scandal of those who sustained them, but we will venture to say that the Spanish Inquisition which was principally used to punish the Moorish enemies of Spain, not her own people, was little worse than the system of persecution invented by our War Department. There was, in fact, some excuse for Spain punishing the Moorish Mahomedans, as she did. Those fierce and fanatical soldiers, had overrun nearly one half of Asia and Africa, when they invaded Spain. For seven centuries they struggled for the mastery of permanently inhabiting portions of the Spanish soil. A different race, wild with the furious belief of the Mousselman, which inflicted unheard-of torments upon the proud Castilians, could expect nothing but the severest retaliation. Whether justified in their proceedings against the Moores or not, the reader will judge for himself. One thing we know, that her inquisition has been held up as among the cruelest of tortures, of even the remote era in which it was established; but, when we reflect on that era and our own, and that country now—on that nation's institutions then, and ours, until a few months ago, we are forced to believe that the proceedings of the Inquisition were excusable, compared to the outrages that have been inflicted by the orders of our War Department upon innocent and loyal people—arrested without a charge, when courts are open, incarcerated without a word of explanation, and dismissed after months of imprisonment, without a hearing, were not bad enough, but the ingenuity of the fanatic invented an oath, which each of his victims is compelled to take, to the effect that *he will not institute, or cause to be instituted any suit against any authority of the United States, for his imprisonment!*

"It would appear, indeed, that human nature is the same always, and that the tortures inflicted by a Robespierre are to be equalled in a more civilized country than that of Paris in his day, but the occasion which produces such monsters always creates an avenger of the people's injuries, and sooner or later vengeance overtakes their oppressors. Heaven grant that there may be no such trial in store for our groaning country, and that no dramatist may hereafter find in the present troubles of our nation incidents upon which to build more bloody dramas than have been written upon the horrid proceedings of the French Revolution, and the atrocious secrets of her Bastile."

ATROCIOUS SENTIMENTS.

During the canvass of 1863, Senator WILSON, of Massachusetts, spoke at Brunswick, Me., on the 27th of August, in the course of which he said:

"The draft in New York is going on. There are forty-four noble and loyal regiments there to help the Government enforce the draft, and there is not a soldier among them who would not *rather shoot a copperhead* [a term applied to the Democrats generally]—*put a bullet through his brains—than a rebel soldier.*"

Such atrocious sentiments might have garnished the bloody nomenclature of a DANTON, a ROBESPIERRE, or a MARAT, but in our free America, they sound like the Indian war whoop that precedes the barbarous carnival of torture. WILSON has no doubt been reading and feeding his blood-thirsty spirit on DANA's Bucchaneers.

THE PRISONS FULL.

The following appeared among the telegraphic items of the date indicated:

"CINCINNATI, June 2d, 1863.
"All the Dayton prisoners, including W. T. Logan, editor of the Dayton *Empire*, have been released from prison. *Two hundred and fifty prisoners are still in confinement.*"

OTHER ACTS OF DESPOTISM.

On the 18th of February, 1863, a political State Convention met at Frankfort, Ky., to nominate state officers. No one ever did or ever could bring a charge, substantiated, against one of the delegates to that Convention, that he or they were disloyal to the Government of the Union. They met as loyal citizens had a right to "peaceably assemble" under the First Article of the Amendments of the Constitution of their country. But one Col. GILBERT, no doubt actuated "By Authority" issued "General Order No. 31" commanding them to Disperse, and forbidding them to make nominations, under penalty of military vengeance. We have the authority of the Chicago *Journal* (Rep.) of February 19, 1863, that this Colonel made a speech, in which he told them it would be useless to nominate, for their nominees should not be permitted to run, or to hold office if elected. We have other evidences of the intention of those in power to plunge us into a Military Despotism, some of which we shall present under another head.

All these acts of despotism were endorsed by the radical press. We have before us, numerous articles in proof, but for want of room we present the following as a sample, from the Janesville (Wis.) *Gazette*, of June 9, 1863.

"Our doctrine is that in war the laws of war

are supreme. Our belief is that we are now at war, *the whole entire country*, and that there is no place within the boundaries of the republic where the court martial may not take the place of civil courts and thrust aside the laws of congress, in all things pertaining to the war.

Our belief further is that the generals in command, subject to the President, are the only judges of the necessity of the time and occasion when such court martial or order may be properly issued, and no civil court can interfere."

This covers the whole ground of despotism, and demands the last sacrifice, and from these extraordinary demands and equally extraordinary exercise of power, we have the "range" of those who are seeking to tyranize over the American people.

GENERAL CONCLUSIONS.

From the foregoing evidences, and fifty times more, which we have in our possession, but are compelled to omit, we cannot escape the general conclusion that it is the purpose of those in power and those who control the Administration, to plunge us into despotism—to finally destroy this old Union, and to build up a government on its ruins, in accordance with the early motives of a privileged aristocracy, or limited monarchy. The Union as it was, we need never look for again. So the despots in power tell us, and if they can prevent it, that fabric of free government reared by the combined wisdom and through the mutual sacrifices of a race of heroes and statesmen, will never be permitted again to shed the luster of its glory on a people that will soon lament the entire loss of civil liberty.

Look at the evidence. Read it by the light of calm reflection, banishing all partizan prejudices, burying all resentment, and tell us, who can, that our liberties are not in danger. Read the evidence that thousands of innocent men and women have been immured in prisons, without charges, without a knowledge of their accusers, without witnesses, judges, jury or trial—kept in durance vile for long months, and then "honorably discharged" and forced, under military duress, to take an oath not to prosecute their persecutors. Can anything be found in the Spanish Inquisition, in the French Reign of Terror, or the Cromwellian "War of Roses," that exceeds this, in the degree of injustice?

Read and ponder the VALLANDIGHAM case step by step. The "law of suspected persons" enacted in Order 38, on purpose to create a crime, that even the last Congress dare not invent (this is saying much)—the system of spies and delators established to carry "law" into effect—the midnight arrest by armed soldiers—the mock trial, by a picked inquisition —the sentence, without a particle of proof to sustain a charge of crime—and the deportation of the victim. Can any man, in his senses, believe that this picked commission had not actually determined on their verdict before a witness was sworn? No trial, even in the Force or old *Conceigerrie*, was ever more predetermined, and *who* was the prosecuting attorney or Judge Advocate? The same who a short time subsequent, was found guilty of secretly watching a lady make her toilet, and was dismissed in disgrace from the office, but was reinstated by the President, probably for his services as prosecutor in the VALLANDIGHAM trial:

But why this outrage on the person of Mr. V.? The President was forced to admit he had committed no offense against the law, and the most that could be said was, that he had *prematurely* advocated peace. Few of his own party endorsed his views, though all would welcome the ends, as soon as honor and a united country would accomplish the purpose.— Mr. VALLANDIGHAM never advocated a dissolution of the Union, but Congressman F. A. CONWAY did, yet the latter was unmolested; while the former was exiled. Mr. V. never denounced the Union as a "lie," nor as a "covenant with death—an agreement with hell." But WENDELL PHILLIPS and LLOYD GARRISON did. Mr. V. never said the Union was "not worth fighting for," but Secretary CHASE did. Mr. V. never said, "the Union as it was, God forbid," but THAD STEVENS did. Mr. V. never advised a person not to enlist, but the Boston *Commonwealth*, the organ of CHARLES SUMNER, did, and so did STEPHEN FOSTER. Mr. V. never said that under any circumstances "dissolution would be no misfortune." The Wisconsin *State Journal* did. Mr. V. never advised resistance to law. Charles Sumner and a great many others did. Mr. V. never said the "Constitution is the cause of all our troubles." HENRY WARD BEECHER did. Mr. VALLANDIGHAM never uttered a sentiment against the Union and the Constitution. Thousands of leading Republicans have done so. Then, why is Mr. VALLANDIGHAM selected as the object of Administration vengeance, and those other men left unmolested. Echo answers, because Mr. V. votes the Democratic ticket, and the others never refused to sustain the Republican organization.

In all the oppressive acts and arbitrary arrests, we do not know of one Republican arrested, nor do we know of one Democrat convicted of a crime against his country.

The tone of the Democracy, through their presses, and their leading speakers, even under all the gross provocations calculated to sting men to madness, has been loyal to their government. We know of not one that has uttered a disloyal sentiment, or a desire to see the Union dissolved. How different their mode of expression from the great array of speeches, resolves, editorials and sermons we have copied from their opponents, ranging through a long series of years, and yet those who oppose the Democracy have the brazen impudence to claim all the loyalty, while they invest the Democracy with every species of disloyalty. But the people have long since learned to judge of things and principles by what they *are* and not what they may *seem* to be.

"The man who dares to dress misdeeds
And color them with virtue's name, deserves
A double punishment from gods and men."
[*Ch. Johnson's Medea.*

A CHALLENGE FOR "LOYALTY."

The following appeared in the Wisconsin *Patriot* of September 15, 1863, and from that day to this no one has claimed the

"FIVE HUNDRED DOLLARS REWARD.

"The above reward will be given to any man who will show that any Democrat, north of Mason's and Dixon's line, by word or deed ever advocated a dissolution of the Union, or who ever expressed a desire, wish or thought, favorable to a dissolution under any circumstances ever likely to take place. Now, if the Democratic party is disloyal, they are disloyal to the government of the Union, for disloyalty can exist in nothing else, and here is a first rate chance to get paid for the trouble of proving the Democracy or any member of the party disloyal, if it can be done. Now, if this cannot be done, and no one claims the reward for the discovery, then the cry of disloyalty against the Democratic party, must be voted a senseless and vile partizan scheme unworthy of honorable men.

"On the contrary, we affirm, and no one dare dispute it, that the following named Republicans and Republican papers, &c., have, in various ways expressed, either directly, or under certain contingencies, a desire for the dissolution of the Union, viz:

M. D. Conway, Mass.,
F. A. Conway, Kan.,
Horace Greeley, N. Y.,
E. O. Ingersoll, Ill.,
Owen Lovejoy, Ill.,
Wendell Phillips, Mass.,
Republican State Convention, Mass.,
Wm. Davis, Pa.,
F. A. Pike, Me.,
W. P. Cutler, Ohio,
J. M. Ashley, Ohio,
J. P. C. Shanks, Ind.,
John Hutchings, Ohio,
Republicans of Green Co., Wis.,
C. M. Clay, Ky.,
C. F. Sedgwick, N. Y.,
J. H. Rice, Mich.,
Geo. W. Julian, Ind.,
David Wilmot, Pa.,
Horace Mann, Mass.,
State Journal, Wis.,
C. L. Sholes, Wis.,
S. M. Booth, Wis.,
Lebanon (O.) Star,
Warren (O.) Chronicle,
Xenia (O.) Torch Light,
Senator Chase, Ohio,
R. P. Spaulding, Ohio,
Erastus Hopkins,
H. M. Addison,
R. W. Emerson,
Boston Chronotype,
New York Tribune,
Anson Burlingame, Mass.,
Z. Chandler, Mich.,
Thad. Stevens, Pa.,
Rev. Dr. Bellows, N. Y.,
Chicago Tribune,
J. A. Bingham, Ohio,
A. G. Riddle, Ohio,
Lloyd Garrison, Mass.,
Sen. Wade, Ohio.
J. P. Hale, N. H.,
Ch. E. Hodges, N. Y.,
78 Republicans, endorsers of the Helper Book,
Milwaukee Free Democrat,
Gov. Andrews, Mass.,
Gerrit Smith, N. Y.,
Gov. Reader, Pa.,
H. W. Beecher, N. Y.,
J. R. Giddings, Ohio,
Wm. O. Duvall, N. Y.,
J. Watson Webb, N. Y.,
Boston Republican, 1859,
Chas. Sumner, Mass.,
Free American, Pa.,
Mass. Gazette,
Boston Liberator,
Senator Wilson, Mass.,
Cincinnati Gazette,
Kennebec (Me.,) Journal,
N. H. Statesman,
Haverhill (Mass.) Gazette,
Boston Sentinel.
Fred Douglas,
Kansas Redpath.

"Now, all the foregoing are leading Republicans, and the list might be almost indefinitely extended. We will not dodge behind a mere empty charge, without proof that these men and presses are disloyal to the Government of this Union. We have their blistering record, as written by themselves before us. We have given that record to the public, and our Republican cotemporaries know we can do it again. Hence, they will not call on us for the proof, but being the guilty ones—being disloyal themselves—they seek to escape the indignation of the people by crying 'Copperhead,' and 'disloyalty' against the Democracy, just as the thief attempts to escape detection by crying 'stop thief.'

"Now, then, if it be true, and we dare any man to the test, that no man in the Democratic party can be found, who has ever expressed a desire, in any form, for a dissolution of this Union, and all the above named Republicans have expressed disloyal sentiments, is it not true that the Democratic party is the loyal and the Abolition the disloyal party? We challenge any man to a full scrutiny of these facts."

THE WRIT OF HABEAS CORPUS—THE PALLADIUM OF OUR LIBERTIES.

The privilege of the writ of *habeas corpus* is the most sacred that pertains to human liberties. Sir WILLIAM BLACKSTONE hails it as "the glory of the British Constitution." The right existed in some form all through the primeval and mature existence of civilized Greece and Rome, and the right to be heard in self defense was the corner stone of the Pandects. When tyrants and oppressors abridged, and annually banished this inestimable right from the Peninsular, the Roman Empire faded into obscurity. When the Saracens were driven out of Gaul, the *habeas corpus* was snuffed out and the sun of liberty sat to rise no more for long years. The Normands under the Feudal Dynasty refused to recognise this sacred right, and its denial cost more than one tyrant his head, and convulsed Europe for ages, until the Anglo Saxon spirit rose in the majesty of its strength, and wrung from King JOHN over six hundred years ago, the *Magna Charta* o' British liberty. The people had] been seized and imprisoned without accusation or trial, and rising as one man, demanded a constitutional pledge that their personal liberties] should be secured from such outrages. That trembling monarch at first refused and scorned the public clamor and complaints, but when he saw the block from which his guilty and tyranical head was soon to roll, he yielded, and thus was wrung from him the following pledge, which has ever been the pride, the boast and the "key stone" of English liberty:

"No freeman shall be arrested or imprisoned, or dissiezed (of property), or outlawed, or banished, *or any ways injured*, nor will we pass sentence upon him, nor send trial upon him, *unless by the legal judgment of his peers, or by the law of the land.*"

"The denial of this right," says a distinguished statesman, "cost one English Monarch his head, another his crown, and a third his most valuable colonies, and to-day if Queen Victoria should attempt to suspend it by telegraph, or by Executive order, of privy council, in any way, she would be a refugee in a foreign land in less than a fortnight." Nearly half a century later this inestimable right was confirmed, and the people were protected by their sovereign immunity from arrests without trial. In 1626, the great law giver, Lord Coke, drew up the celebrated "Petition of Rights," which again confirmed and extended this inestimable right, as follows:

"No man, *of what estate or condition that he be*, shall be put out of his land or tenements, nor *arrested nor imprisoned*, nor disinherited, nor put to death, without being brought to answer BY DUE PROCESS OF LAW."

And it was further provided that no "commissioners" should be appointed to try any one "not in the army" by martial law,

—"lest by color of them, any of his Majesty's subjects be destroyed or put to death, contrary to the laws and franchises of the land."

Then, in 1679 came the *habeas corpus*, &c., upon which Lord CAMPBELL remarked, and we fear Americans must blush to own the truth of that proud boast, that

—"personal liberty has been more effectually guarded in England than it has in any other country in the world."

In 1689 came the English "Bill of Rights," matured and enacted by the most profound statesmen and pure patriots that ever breathed in England. These great and exalted men, after they had driven the tyranical James II. from the throne for his repeated violations of the rights of Englishmen, declared him guilty of subverting the laws of the Kingdom, and attempting to destroy the liberties of the people, and in their "true. bill" of indictment they thus arraign the would-be tyrant before the British people and the world:

"1. By assuming and exercising a power of dispensing with and *suspending of laws* and the execution of laws *without consent of a Parliament.*

"2. By committing and prosecuting divers worthy prelates, for humbly petitioning to be excused from concurring to the said assumed power.

"By violating the freedom of election of members to serve in Parliament.

"All of which," say they, "are utterly and directly contrary to the known laws and statutes and freedom of this realm."

These, fellow readers, are the sacred liberties of Englishmen. Their violation has proven fatal to more than one head, garnised by the diadems of power, and yet from time to time these rights in England have been partially secured. The great Charter of English freemen was outraged in various ways by the succeeding reigning monarchs, who sought to control the lives and property of persons as well as the government, nor was this great right completely sacred until the beginning of the present century. It was the partial refusal of this right, and sundry and divers enormities committed in violation of the "Great Charter" that sent the Mayflower and its refugee pilgrims to Plymouth Rock who brought over with them, sealed in their liberty-loving hearts, the *Magna Charta* of English liberty, the key stone of which was the *habeas corpus* and a proper trial for all alleged offence. Twenty years after their landing, in 1641, the infant colony enacted in their "Body of Liberties," that

"No man's life shall be taken away, no man's honor or good name shall be stained, *no man's person shall be arrested*, restrained, banished dismembered nor any ways punished, no man shall be deprived of his wife and children, no man's goods or estate shall be taken away from him, nor any way endangered under color of law or countenance of authority, unless it by virtue or equity of some express law of the country warranting the same, &c.

"No man's person shall be restrained or imprisoned *by any authority whatsoever*, before the law hath sentenced him thereto, if he can put in sufficient security, bail or mainprise," &c.

Thus was sown the seeds of English liberty on American soil. But for a long series of years prior to the declarations of Independence King George had been riveting the chains of servitude on the American colonies, who had borne it until forbearance ceased to be a virtue, when on the 4th of July, 1776—135 years after the first declaration of American liberties —the American colonies by their Deputies, put forth the immortal Declaration, drawn by the inspired pen of Thos. Jefferson. It will be seen that among the many complaints, on which should stand or fall our claim to separation and freedom, the rendering the military independent of, and superior to the civil power, the denial of the right of trial by jury, and transporting us to foreign lands to be tried for pretended offences were not among the least.

"He has affected to render the military independent of, and superior to the civil power.
"For depriving us, in many cases, of the benefits of trial by jury.
"For transporting us beyond the seas to be tried for pretended offenses."

Reader, have you seen nothing of late that Savors of outrages thus complained of in *our Magna Charter* of freedom?

And again: in the Virginia "Bill of Rights" of 1776, written also by JEFFERSON, it is declared that—

"All power is invested in, and consequently derived from the people, that magistrates are their trustees and servants, and at all times amendable to them.

"All power of suspending laws, or the execution of laws, by any authority, *without consent of the representatives of the people*, is injurious to their rights, and ought not to be exercised.

"*In all cases* the military should be under strict subordination to, and governed by, the civil power.

"Freedom of the press is one of the great bulwarks of liberty, and can never be restrained, but by the despotic governments."

And yet again: in the "Declaration of Rights" in Massachusetts, in 1780, it is laid down that—

"No person shall be held to answer for any crime or offense, until the same is fully and plainly, substantially and formally described to him. And *no person shall be arrested or imprisoned*, or despoiled or deprived of his property, immunities or privileges, put out of the protection of the law, or deprived of life, liberty or estate, *but by the judgment of his peers or the law of the land.*

"Every person has a right to be secure from all unreasonable searches and seizures of his person, his house, his papers and all his possessions.

"The liberty of the press is essential to the security of freedom in a state.

"The people have a right to keep and bear arms for the common defense. The military shall *always* be held in *exact subordination* to the civil authority and be governed by it.

"The people have a right in an orderly and peaceable manner to assemble to consult upon the common good.

"The power of suspending the laws ought never to be exercised *but by the Legislature*, or by authority derived from it, to be exercised in *such particular cases only* as the Legislature shall expressly provide for.

"No person can, *in any case*, be subjected to *law martial*, or to any penalties or pains by virtue of that law except those employed in the army or navy, and except the militia in actual service, *but by authority of the Legislature.*"

Such, reader, were understood to be American rights, in our Revolutionary period, the men loved their country for the sake of the common blessings to flow from its just and wise laws, honestly administered. Such the liberty of the inaugurating that good system of fundamental law that pervades the Constitution of the United States and every State in the Union. Let us look at the "Great Charter" of the Union. Here is enough to *settle* the point without bloodshed.

"The judicial power shall extend to *all cases* in law and equity arising under this Constitution, the laws of the United States, and treaties made, or which shall be made, under their authority.

"The trial of all crimes, except in cases of impeachment, shall be by jury, and such trial shall be held in the State where the said crimes shall have been committed.

"Treason against the United States shall consist ONLY in levying war against them, or in adhering to their enemies, giving them aid and comfort. No person shall be convicted of treason unless on the testimony of two witnesses to the same *overt act*, or on confession in open court.

"Congress shall make no law respecting an establishment of religion, or prohibiting the free exercise thereof; or abridging the freedom of speech, or of the press; or the right of the people peacably to assemble, and to petition the Government for a redress of grievances.

"The right of the people to keep and bear arms, shall not be infringed.

"The right of the people to be secure in their persons, houses, papers and effects against unreasonable searches and seizures, shall not be violated, and no warrant shall issue but upon probable cause, supported by oath or affirmation, and particularly describing the place to be searched and the persons and things to be seized.

"No person shall be held to answer for a capital or otherwise infamous crime, unless on a presentment or indictment of a grand jury, except in cases arising in the land and naval forces, or in the militia, when in actual service, in time of war and public danger; *nor shall be deprived of life, liberty or property, without due process of law;* nor shall private property be taken for public use without just compensation.

"In all criminal prosecutions the accused shall enjoy the right to a speedy and public trial by an impartial jury of the State and District wherein the crime shall have been committed, which District shall have been previously ascertained by law; and to be informed of the nature and cause of the accusation; to be confronted with the witnesses against him; to have compulsory process for obtaining witnesses in his favor, and to have the assistance of counsel for his defense

"The powers not delegated to the United States by the Constitution, nor prohibited by it to the States, are reserved to the States respectively, or to the people.

"All Legislative powers herein granted, shall be vested in a Congress of the United States.

"The privilege of the writ of *habeas corpus* shall not be suspended, unless when in case of rebellion or invasion the public safety requires it."

To the last paragraph we would devote a word or two. So great has been the desire to see the rebellion crushed, and no impediment put in the way of those who would honestly do it, that many Democrats justified the act of the President in suspending the writ in Maryland, before that state was brought under the full control of the U. S. power. It was then an open question, whether the President or Congress had the full or concurrent power to suspend this writ. Republican great men and Democratic statesmen differed on the subject. But that matters not for our present purpose. All agree that our fathers, in framing the Constitution, did conceive of a possible necessity that might require the suspension of this inestimable right, and they provided that somebody might use it when necessary. But the reasonable construction is, that no man has a right to suspend that writ in districts where the civil power is loyal, and is not impeded or menaced by hostile forces. All know that in a state of actual conflict, within hostile lines, the civil power however loyal may be its agents, is not safe to trust with the trial and punishment of traitors, who may be leagued in such vast numbers as to defy all civil process. Especially where the judicial agencies are justly suspected of disloyalty, it is proper to suspend this writ but *never* —NEVER—NEVER in a district where the civil power is omnipotent. Nor is it a safe doctrine to hold that if Congress has the power to suspend the writ (and that is now the conceded fact), that power can be delegated to the President, or to any other branch of government agencies. For if Congress can delegate power in this instance, it may in all, and it may invest the President with every other power it pleases—the making of laws, treaties, trial of impeachments, &c. In fact, Congress may declare the President supreme law giver and dictator. This proposition is too absurd to require argument to enforce it, and yet, it is precisely what Congress has attempted, in delegating a portion of its power to the President. Suppose that any man in either of the loyal states should be arrested on suspicion of being disloyal to the Government. Does any one believe it would be unsafe to trust any judge in his county, or his state, even, to hear and determine the charges, and that if he was really proven guilty, does any man believe any judge in his state would connive at his release? Such an idea would be monstrous to entertain. There is no excuse then, in the loyal states for suspending this writ. Not a man in the loyal North, (save a host of leading Republicans) has raised his voice against the Government, and all, save those disunionists, would fight, if necessary, to defend it.

All, then, have one common interest in seeing the laws and all legal orders obeyed. But under the late order, the best man, the purest patriot we have in any state may be "suspected" by some personal enemy, and by false accusations arrested for "disloyal practices," and bundled off to a foreign bastile, without ever being informed what he was arrested for. We have hundreds of such cases to fill up the black list of tyranny and personal revenge.— 'Tis but a few days since we heard of General

Prince, of the army, who was liberated from Fort Lafayette, and for the first time acquainted with the charge against him, which was for stealing horses he was taking over the line, when he pulled out a "pass" for the identical horses, which he had in his pocket at the time, and which he could have shown at the time, if permitted to know the charges against him, showing that the horses *were his own*. Thus, with the evidence of his innocence in his pocket from a high commanding officer, he was arrested without charges, and locked in loathsome dungeons for months, as a test of the tyrant's power. Reader, your turn may come next. As you sit reading this, some secret personal enemy may be plotting your arrest, and you may be sent to some foreign Bastile, and there waste away in duress, without ever knowing the charges against you.

Is this the "freedom" our early fathers proclaimed, in 1641, on the historical Rock of Plymouth, and for which they risked their lives, their fortunes, and their most sacred honors, during the fearful period that ushered in the freest of the free among the families of nations? Is this the kind of "freedom" we have heard so much about for the last twenty-five years, sung in the school room, chanted in the cloister, doled from the press, preached from the pulpit, and thundered from the Abolition Vaticans? Is this the "freedom" we are now fighting for? Let us see if we find any warrant for such belief in our own *Magna Churta*, the Constitution, which is but a reflex of all preceding state constitutions on this "free" continent, whose tap root reaches down through a long line of freedom's consanguinity, o the Great Charter wrung from King John, by a crude, though outraged people. Here are a few gems from our Bill of Rights—from Article I:

"All persons are born equally free and independent, and have certain inalienable rights; among these are life, liberty and the pursuit of happiness."

"Every person may freely speak, write and publish his sentiments on *all* subjects, being responsible for the abuse of that right, and no laws shall be passed to restrain or abridge the liberty of speech or the press."

"The right of the people to assemble to consult for the common good, and to petition the Government or any Department thereof, *shall never be abridged*."

"The right of trial by jury *shall remain inviolate*."

"No person shall be held to answer for a criminal offense unless upon the presentment or indictment of a Grand Jury, except in cases of impeachment, or in cases cognizable by Justices of the Peace, or arisinging *in* the Army or Navy or in the Militia, *when in actual service* in time of war or public danger."

"The privilege of the writ of *habeas corpus* shall not be suspended, unless when in cases of rebellion or invasion the public safety may require it."

Now, no one will pretend the loyal North is "invaded," or that we have a "rebellion" within our borders and yet the writ of *habeas corpus* is suspended.

"Treason against the state shall consist *only* in levying war against the same, or in adhering to its enemies, giving them aid and comfort."

We deny that there is a man in the loyal states, known to any person, who comes under this definition of treason.

"The military shall be in strict subordination to the civil power."

Now, who has a right to disobey these fundamental commands? Are our liberties safe when our inalienable rights are set aside? Who can contemplate the parallel history of Jacobinism and red Republicanism in France, without a shudder. The Peninsular wars and the French Revolution all furnish us material for the most serious alarm. Read the 10th and 14th chapter of Allison's History of Europe, and read the "Law of Suspected persons." Here is an extract that now suits our "commissioner" trial system to a T. [*See Allison's History of Europe, vol.* 1, *p.* 219.

"Thenceforward, the committee of public safety at Paris exercised, without opposition, all the powers of government; it named and dismissed the Generals, the judges and the juries; appointed the intendants of the provinces; brought forward all public measures in the convention [like our abolitionists] and launched its thunder against every opposite faction. By means of its *commissioners* [like our commissioners to try for alleged offences] it ruled the Provinces Generals and armies [see our own condition] with absolute sway; and soon after, the *Law of Suspected Persons* [the same as here] placed the personal freedom of every subject at its disposal [the same here.] The revolutionary tribunal rendered it the master of every life, the requisition and the maximum of every fortune; the accusations in the conventions of every member of the Legislature.

"The Law of Suspected Persons [see Fort Lafayette, &c.] which gave this tremendous power to the Decemvirs, passed on the 17th of Sept. [the anniversary of which the Republicans of the Wisconsin Legislature celebrated by their action on the infamous army voting scheme.] It declared all persons liable to arrest who, either by their conduct, their relations, their conversations, or their writings [or 'any disloyal practices,' eh?] have shown themselves partizans of tyranny, [yes, even French Red Republicans denounced tyranny while they waded knee deep in human gore!] or of federation, with the enemies of freedom [the same kind of 'freedom' we are threatened with, perhaps,] all persons who have not discharged their debts to the country, all nobles, the husbands, wives, parents, children mothers, sisters or agents of emigrants, [those who fled from the reign of terror] who have not incessantly manifested their devotion to the Revolution. Under this law no person had any chance of safety but in going the utmost length of Revolutionary fury."

We learn from this history that all France was divided into 12 classes, as follows:

1. "All those who in the assemblies of the people discouraged their enthusiasm by cries, menaces or *crafty discourses*. 2. All those who most prudently speak only of the misfortunes of the Republic, and are always ready to spread bad news with an affected air of sorrow 3. All those who have changed their conduct and language according to the course of events, who were mute on the crimes of the Royalists, [This is equivalent to Mr. Lincoln's crime of "saying nothing,] and loudly exclaim against the slight faults of the Republicans. 10. Those who speak with contempt of the constituted authorities the ensigns of law, the popular societies, or the defenders of liberty, &c., &c."

Are we to be cursed by such a reign of terror that swept away five millions of the French people, and by such brutal contentions as run riot between the bloodthirsty Jacobins and the agrarian Girondists? Are our tribunals to relapse into French Decemvirates, as described by Thiers, the French historian, who says:

"The Tribunal, once the protectors of life and property, have become the organs of butchery, where robbery and murder have *usurped the names of confiscation and punishment!*"

And during all this bloody period, both the Jacobins and Girondins claimed to be acting in behalf of "Freedom" and "Liberty!" Reader, see you not a parallel in the looming shadow before you? GOD forbid that truth, in this land, should compel us to exclaim with the heroic DANTON, when thrown into a French bastile, for predicting the ruin and desolation that speedily followed:

"At last," said he "I perceive, that in Revolutions, the supreme power finally rests with the most abandoned!"

Who that reads the gorey pages of French history, during the reign of terror, that swept away the last vestige of Gaullic liberty, can repress a shudder, lest in the mazes of our Revolution, we may drift into the abyss of contending factions, and be overtaken by the cruelty of a St. Just, the fanaticism of a Couthon, or the crafty tyranny of a Robespierre. History is our monitor. The tortuous pathway of nations is strewn with the bleaching bones of ambitious pretenders, and national epitaphs are graven on every mile stone:—"Enslaved in the name of Liberty!—slain in the name of humanity!"

The people of France yielded inch by inch and suffered their liberties to be invaded, and their rights, one by one, to be swallowed up, in the din of the demagogue's cry of "Liberty," until the Jacobin and Girondin Clubs, the Committee of Public Safety, rioting under the "Law of Suspected Persons," destroyed every vestige of their power, and they were forced to bear the expense of their own execution! May our Nation's Capitol never become a Conciegerrie.

We are for suppressing this rebellion the "shortest way under the constitution." We desire to see the strong arm of power outstretched to crush out treason wherever it exists, but we do not want to see the charter of our liberties destroyed. Violence should not be used except where violence is arrayed against the Government. If our citizens may under any pretext, except in actual rebellion here at home, be arrested, on the *ipse dixit* of any political pretender, and transported to other states, without knowing what charges have been preferred against them, we have no security. Even the Jacobins who persecuted the Girondins may in turn become the persecuted, and thus the *lex talionis* become the watchword for a new French reign of terror. We should profit by the warnings of history. The fate of nations that live only in bloody history, should teach us that human rights cannot long be trampled on with impunity. Cato demanded of his son the suicide's weapon rather than live under the tyranny of the invading Cæsar. May we pray that no necessity shall ever arise where the suicide Cato shall become the homicide Brutus. God protect the right and save the liberties of the people from anarchy and despotism.

BLACKSTONE ON ENGLISH HABEAS CORPUS

A certain lawyer once quoted Blackstone to

a Justice, who had decided a point against him, not, as he said, to change the mind of the Justice, but to show the Court what an old fool Sir WM. BLACKSTONE was. According to our state Constitutions, in order to the preservation of our liberties, frequent recourse must be had to fundamental principles, and as Sir WILLIAM BLACKSTONE is considered pretty good authority, we wish to quote from him, 1, 135:

"By 16 Car. I, c. 10, if any person be restrained of his liberty by order or decree of any illegal court, *or by command of the King's Majesty in person*, or by warrant of the Council Board, *or of any of the Privy Council*, he shall, etc., have a writ of *habeas corpus* to bring his body before the Court of King's bench, or Common pleas, who shall determine whether the cause of his commitment be just," &c.

"Of great importance to the public is the preservation of this personal liberty; for if once it were left *in the power of any*, THE HIGHEST MAGISTRATE, *to imprison arbitrarily whomever he or his officers* thought proper, THERE WOULD SOON BE AN END OF ALL OTHER RIGHTS AND IMMUNITIES. Some have thought that unjust attacks even upon life or property at the arbitrary will of the magistrates are less dangerous to the Commonwealth than such as are made upon the personal liberty of the subject. To bereave a man of life, or by violence to confiscate his estate, without accusation or trial, would be so gross and notorious an act of despotism as must at once convey the alarm of tyranny throughout the whole kingdom. And yet sometimes when the state is in real danger even this may be a necessary measure. But the happiness of our Constitution is that *it is not left to the Executive power* to determine when the danger of the state is so great as to render this measure expedient; for it is the *Parliament or Legislative power*, that, whenever it sees proper, can authorize the crown, by suspending the *habeas corpus* act for a short and limited time, to imprison suspected persons, without giving any reason for so doing."

And, further to enlighten the Court upon the subject of sending men from Iowa to Fort La Fayette or any other Bastile, 1200 miles from their residence, we quote from the same author, same vol. p. 137:

"And by the *habeas corpus* act, (the second *Magna Charta* and stable bulwarks of our liberties,) it is enacted that no subject of this realm who is an inhabitant of England, Wales, or Berwick, shall be sent prisoner into Scotland, Ireland, Jersey, Guernsey, or other places beyond the seas; but that all such imprisonments shall be illegal, that the person who shall dare to commit another, contrary to this law, *shall be disabled from bearing any office*, shall incur the penalty of *praemunire* and be *incapable of receiving the King's pardon*, and the party suffering shall also have his private action against the person committing, and all his aiders, advisers, and abettors; and shall recover treble costs; besides his damages which *no jury shall assess at less than £500.*"

These rights were declared in 1688 to be "the birth right of every Englishman;" and are they not ours by inheritance?

Now look at the Constitution of the United States. Sec. 8 of Art. 1, declares affirmatively the powers of Congress; Sec. 9 defines their powers negatively. If the President can arbitrarily suspend the writ of *habeas corpus* upon the authrity of section 9, equally can he exercise any other of the powers of Congress. Section 10 negatively defines the powers of states. Notice here the connection: 1st What Congress shall have power to do; 2d What Congress shall not have authority to do; and 3d What the States shall not have the right to do, under the Constitution. No other interpretation is plausible.

The Ordinance of 1787 expressly guarantees certain privileges to the inhabitants of the territory embraced, being expressly stated to be

"Articles of compact between the original states in the said territory, and shall *forever remain unalterable*, unless by common consent," to-wit:—"The inhabitants of the said territory shall *always* be entitled to the benefits of the writ of *habeas corpus*, and of the *trial by jury.*"

WHAT OUR FATHERS THOUGHT OF IT.

In the Constitutional Convention of 1787, [Elliott's Debates, vol. 5, p. 484,] we find the following sentiments advanced in reference to the sacredness of the writ of *habeas corpus:*

"Mr. Pinckney, urging the propriety of securing the writ of *habeas corpus* in the most ample manner, moved that it should not be suspended but on the most urgent occasions, and then only for a limited time, not exceeding twelve months.

"Mr. Rutledge was for declaring the *habeas corpus* inviolate. He did not conceive that a suspension *could ever be necessary* at the *same time* THROUGH ALL THE STATES.

"Mr. Gouveneur Morris moved that "the privilege of the writ of *habeas corpus* shall not be suspended, unless when, in case of rebellion or invasion, the public safety may require it."

"[This was the clause finally adopted.]

"Mr. Millson doubted, whether in *any case* a suspension could be necessary, as the discretion now exists with judges, in most important cases, to keep in goal or admit to bail."

The above shows how jealous our fathers were of their rights, and how they feared to risk the suspension of the sacred writ of *habeas corpus* under any circumstances. The record shows that even seven states, New Hampshire, Massachusetts, Connecticut, Pennsylvania, Delaware, Maryland and Virginia, voted for the clause as adopted, while three states, North Carolina, South Carolina and Georgia, voted against the last clause—they being opposed to any suspension of the writ, under any circumstances. Three states were absent.

JUDGE CURTIS ON LOYALTY AND HABEAS CORPUS.

The Hon. GEORGE TICKNER CURTIS, formerly of Boston, now of New York, and one of the soundest jurists in the land, addressed the Democratic Union Association of New York city on the 28th of March, 1863. We are almost tempted to give his remarks entire, lengthy as they were, but our space allotted will not permit us. The following *should be read by everybody*:

"No man, who does not join in a wild, undiscriminating support of the measures and dogmas of a dominant party, can hope to escape detraction and obloquy. The utmost exertions are made to suppress ordinary freedom of speech; every device is employed to misrepresent, and every effort is made to misunderstand the purposes of those who are not in political power. The vocabulary of political slang is exhausted to find terms of reproach and infamy with which to stigmatize men whose motives have in their favor all the ordinary presumptions of purity, and whose arguments and opinions are at least entitled to a respectful hearing. This process, which has been going on for many months with violence unexampled, even among a people whose political discourses are never marked by too much temperance, has culminated from time to time in outrages upon the rights of persons and property, and may do so again. It is no time when one would choose to utter opinions without being impelled by a strong sense of duty.

"But, if we are not prepared to suffer for our convictions, they must be very humble convictions. If we do not love our country and its institutions well enough to encounter all the hazards that may attend an honest effort to save them, our love must be cold, indeed. Such I am sure is not your case or mine. (Applause.) Meaning to utter here nothing but words of truth and soberness—the truth as I hold it, in the soberness that becomes me to accept all the responsibility to public opinion which may justly fall thereon.

"I propose to speak to you to-night upon a subject which seems to me to be strangely misapprehend by many good men, and strangely perverted by many who are not good. I mean the subject of 'loyalty.' The word itself, at least in the sense in which it is used in those countries from which we have borrowed it, can scarcely be said to have an appropriate political and social system. But it is a word at present in great use among us; and we must take it as we find it, and are bound to enquire what are the moral duties which its just and true signification embraces. The injury and the certain consequences of accepting and following out the doctrines which are now forced upon us will form the topics of my discourse to-night.

"The true conditions of American loyalty are not to be found in the passionate exactions of partizan leaders, or in the frantic declamations of the pulpit, the rostrum or the press. (Cheers.) People who do not like my political opinions may howl at me the epithet disloyal, but when they have thrown this missile they have not taken a step towards defining to me and to others, what the true conditions of loyalty are. It is important that this step should be taken; for, whether we are to go on or to cease, in this course of idle and unmeaning abuse, it concerns us all to know what measure of public duty may rightfully be exacted of us. To know the length and depth of of those great virtues which are comprehended in the term 'patriotism'—to feel at once that they are seated in our affections, and enthroned in our reason—is, to 'get wisdom and understanding,' in the largest of earthly possessions. (Great applause.) The true conditions of American loyalty are to be found in the institutions under which we live; in the duties flowing from the Constitution of our country; (applause) in the political system which we have inherited from our fathers, with all its manifold relations, through which we may trace the clear dividing line that separates perfect from imperfect obligations. (Cheers.)

"The text of our fundamental law is the guide, and the sole guide, in all ethical inquiries into the duties of the citizen. To that source all must come, rulers and people alike; to that fountain all must resort. The vague and shifting standards that are drawn from supposed dangers to what is called the 'national life,' or which spring from the conflicting judgments of man respecting public necessities, can determine nothing. Those things can furnish no *rule*. We must have a *rule*, for loyalty is a moral duty; and it must, therefore, be capable of definition. A people whose 'national life' exists only by virtue of a written necessity, can find no rule of loyalty in any of the necessities that lie out of, or beyond the written necessity, can find no rule of loyalty in any of the necessities which their constitution of Government does not cover. They may find grounds of expediency in one or other supposed necessity for destroying their constitution; but, it would be extremely absurd to say that this expediency could be made the object of their 'loyalty.' Let us go, then, to the fountain head—the source of all national obligations.

"The Constitution of the United States itself

prescribes the full measure of our loyalty, in these words:

"*This Constitution, and the laws of the United States which shall be made in pursuance thereof, and all treaties made, or which shall be made, under the authority of the United States, shall be the supreme law of the land.*"

"Observe how precise as well as comprehensive this great rule of our duty is. It expresses without ambiguity the whole of our obligation toward the Federal Government. It makes a *supreme law*—a law paramount to all other human laws—an obligation paramount to all other human obligations. It leaves no room whatever for the intrusion of another, or a rival claimant to our civil obedience. That claimant can neither be a person invested, or uninvested with office, nor an idea of, public necessity, nor an imaginary 'national life' beyond, or apart from the life created under the constitution. The only possible claimant of our obedience is *the law;* for, as that law is made supreme, all other demands or demandants upon our submission are of necessity excluded. (Loud cheers.)

"What, then, does this supreme law embrace? The text on which I am commenting itself furnishes the answer, 'This Constitution,' it says—what *this constitution contains, and the laws that shall be made in conformity with it—these* shall be the supreme law, rising in authority above all other laws. No public necessities, save as they are embodied in the Constitution—no 'national life,' save as it exists under the Constitution—no legislation that is not in accordance with the Constitution—is the supreme law; but what the Constitution ordains or authorizes, *that* is the public necessity—*that* is the national life, because it is the supreme civil obligation. (Applause.)

"Such is the fundamental character of our political system, and so perfect is it in its consistency with itself, and with the rights of all who are subject to it, that it contains a machinery by which the conformity of all acts of the Government with the principles of the Constitution may be peacefully tested, without forcible resistance. If the acts of the Government are complained of as unconstitutional, they may be brought to a judicial test, or the people may themselves pass upon them at the ballot box through the instrumentality of frequent elections. (Applause.)

"Now, when we look into the Constitution of our country, to discover the full scope of the obligations which are embraced in the supreme law of the land, we find that it grants certain political powers and rights to the central or national government, and reserves all other political powers and rights to the states or the people. Hence, it is plain that the reserved rights of the people are just as much comprehended within the duty of our allegiance—just as much for the rightful objects of our 'loyalty' as the powers and rights presented in the national government. If the political existence created by the Constitution is the 'national life,' called into being by the supreme law of the land—and he would be a bold and reckless sophist who should undertake to find that national life anywhere else—then, the rights which the Constitution reserves to the states or the people are equally comprehended it that life, for they are equally declared to be parts of the supreme law of the land. For this reason, all idea of a supremacy of the national rights, or powers or interests, when founded on something not embraced in the Constitution, is purely visionary. No duty of 'loyalty' can possibly be predicated on any claim that is not founded in the supreme law, and our 'loyalty' is not due to them. When we know what are the rights and powers reserved to the states or the people—and we know they are the whole residue of all possible political rights and powers—they are equally the objects of our 'loyalty' for the self same reason, namely—they are parts of the supreme law of the land. (Loud applause.)

"Again, the Constitution not only contains some political powers and rights granted to the Federal Government, and a reservation of all other political powers and rights to the states or the people, but it also embraces rights of person and property, guaranteed to every citizen in his individual capacity; and these are equally made, not by implication, but expressly, parts of the same law of the land, and are therefore equally the objects of our 'loyalty.' All pretense, therefore, of any paramount authority in the Central Government to override these personal rights of the citizen, or to claim our 'loyalty' in disregard of these co-ordinate parts of the supreme law, is a perversion of the very idea of American loyalty. (Cheers.) As well might the citizen claim, because the Constitution has made his personal rights part of the supreme law, that therefore, the loyalty of his neighbor is due to him alone, as the Government can claim that loyalty, is due solely, or chiefly, or principally, or ultimately, to the functions *it* is appointed to perform.— The rights of the Government, the rights of the states, and the rights of individuals, all and equally, are comprehended in the supreme law of the land, and our loyalty is due to that law—to the *whole and to every part of it*—and public officers are in the same sense, and for the same reason, bound to obey every 'jot and tittle of it.' (Great applause.)

"These provisions are very plain and familiar; too familiar, perhaps you will say, to require to be stated. The extravagant language and ideas that are current in the mouths of even sensible people, on this subject of loyalty, would have exceeded all capacity of belief, in any other period than this. If one were to undertake to reduce their language and their ideas to something like a definite, moral proposition, it would be found that the doctrine is something like this:—In a time of war, when there are great public dangers, the rights of States and of individuals, must give way, and if those who administer the government are satisfied that the public necessity requires them to use powers that transcend the limits of the constitution, he who does not acquiesce in their judgment, or who questions their authority, to do particular acts, is a "disloyal" citizen. (Laughter.) This statement of the doctrine is the best I know how to make, for I know not how else to interpret or to apply the denunciations which we find in the proceedings of public meetings, in the columns of party newspapers, and in the common speech and action of very many persons. I need only point to the utter prohibition that is attempted to be placed on all discussion of any plan for bringing this dreadful war to a close, except by the particular method of fighting; or to the manner in which the terms 'traitor' and 'secessionist' are hurled at all who question the authority and lawfulness of the methods pursued by the government in the prosecution of the war. For myself, I do not profess to have, as yet a definite idea concerning several of the modes in which a peace might be sought. But I know not what right I have, legally, or morally, to say that my neighbor shall not discuss such a question, or shall not act upon it at the polls, or shall be denounced as 'disloyal' because his opinions on the subject differ from mine. It is to me very plain that this whole effort of a dominant party to control opinion by such means, can, under such institutions as ours, lead to but one of two results—the establishment of a despotism of a very bad kind, or the overthrow of the power of those who resort to such methods. Either the institutions of the country will perish, or the party which undertakes to repress all freedom of discussion will perish. (Cheers.) I hope we shall make up our minds to destroy the party and save the institutions. (Great applause. 'We will do it.') But of this hereafter.

"Let me return to this new doctrine of 'loyalty,' which requires us to acquiesce in silence in the judgment of public servants, as to what the public necessities require, even to the extent of overlooking great infractions of the Constitution. This doctrine entirely ignores the purpose for which the Constitution imposed certain stringent limitations on the powers of the National Government. In order to explain this, it will be necessary to descend from general reasoning to particular illustrations.

"The Constitution, after enforcing certain defined political powers upon the Federal Government, declares that all other political powers are reserved to the States or the people.— And it further secures to every citizen inalienable rights of person, forever, beyond all possible control of the Government. Now, does any one suppose that this was done without a purpose? Does any one believe that it was done for what is vulgarly called *buncombe*? Do you believe that it was done with mental reservation of the doctrine of 'public necessity' standing behind the Constitution, and ready to strike it down from its supreme control over us and our affairs? Let me suggest to you, my fellow citizens, that you cannot study the Constitution, and the purposes of the great generation who made it, without seeing that the very object of all this careful provision for rights that were placed beyond the reach of the Central Government, was to exclude forever this doctrine of 'public necessity' as a measure of the powers that were conferred upon that Government. (Cheers.) I use this language deliberately. I affirm that when the Constitution repeated the words of *Magna Charta*, not as a statute, but as a fixed provision of the fundamental law, and declared that 'no person shall be deprived of life, liberty, or property, without due process of law,' it meant to make a rule for all times and all circumstances—shutting the door forever against any supposed 'public necessity,' for violating the citizen's rights.* In like manner, I affirm that the Constitution reserved to the states or the people all political power not granted to the Federal Government, it meant to preclude every ground of 'necessity' for the assumption by that Government of the powers thus withheld. (Applause.)

"In fact, the idea of a written constitution— a fixed and supreme law—is utterly irreconcilable with the theory that the administrators of such a government can resort to *their own judgment* of 'public necessity,' and *act contrary to that supreme law*, and that good citizenship requires the people to acquiesce in that judgment. They who set up such a claim for our rulers, claim for them an entirely irresponsible power. We are required, for example, to believe that what are called 'arbitrary arrests,' are 'necessary,' but no one explains to us the grounds of that 'necessity.' No account is rendered. We are to *assume* the existence of causes of justification, but no one tells us *what* these causes are. They may remain forever locked in the bosoms of those who do the acts of which we complain. Why should American citizens, filling high places of public trust, act upon such a principle as this? Can anything be more degrading—more injurious to the public conscience of a people than to form a habit of implicit belief in the existence of necessities which nobody explains, and of which nobody is required to give an account? You may hear a hundred men in a day, speaking of some particular case of this kind, profess its *necessity*, and not one man in the whole hund-

---

* It is in my opinion a monstrous fallacy to suppose that the implied authority for suspending the writ of *habeas corpus* warrants indefinitely the arrest and detention of citizens, without judicial process. This implied authority was given in the original constitution, but after the adoption of that instrument, the people came forward and annexed to it the prohibition of *Magna Charta*, making that provision a part of the supreme law. The two clauses of the constitution must therefore be so construed and applied as not to render nugatory the one last adopted, and so as to give effect to its strongest declarations. These clauses can be reconciled only by such a course of legislation and executive action as will preserve the operation of both. If, under peculiar circumstances of imminent danger, the actual seizures made without judicial process, the prisoner should be immediately charged with an offense by warrant, and then a suspension of the writ of *habeas corpus* may intervene to prevent his discharge from the imprisonment, for causes which would operate to discharge him, if the writ was not suspended. This is the only course of legislation, in my opinion, that can be consistent with all the provisions of the constitution. I do not see how it is possible to contend that a continual imprisonment, founded on mere executive seizure can be authorized by taking away the writ of *habeas corpus*. If *Magna Charta* had not been interposed, there might have been some ground for this pretension, for then there would have been no necessity for process at any time.

red can tell you *what* the necessity was! (Laughter and applause.)

"My friends, these false theories of 'loyalty'—for false I must deem them—are infusing into our national character *a fatal poison*. They are leading those who cherish them to impute factious and interested motives to all pure and manly efforts in defense of the principles of civil liberty. They who indulge in this dangerous work—of deriding the defenders of constitutional rights, can have but a very inadequate conception of the convulsions that must precede the final loss of these rights. They take but a very superficial view of the depth of those feelings which lead men in all free countries to resist every form of mere arbitrary power. They make no account of the principles implanted in our breasts, and cherished into dictates of nature by generations of training in the practice of liberty. These principles on which depend the primary office of an opposition in a free government, and by means of which all constitutional rulers are restrained from abuses of power. Impatient of those restraints, such persons rush to methods which cannot be employed without undermining the foundations of liberty. And, for a supposed temporary advantage, barter away the strength and the supports that sustain the vigor of the body politic. This has been in all ages the downward course of nations, who have substituted for free institutions and systems of fundamental law, a blind and unquestioning faith in 'public necessities,' and have then welcomed some despotic power. Thus did the Roman Empire succeed the Republic, and thus we may be preparing ourselves for a like destiny. Let us be warned in time.

"I have endeavored to state with due precision and fairness one very important part of the conditions of a true loyalty, but I should leave this subject in an imperfect state, if I omitted, on the other hand, to give equal prominence to certain principles of our political system which limit the mode in which states and individuals are to exercise their constitutional rights of opposition to the measures of the Federal government. I have briefly adverted to this already, but a more extended statement of the principle is necessary.

"I will assume then, that a measure, having all the forms of law, is believed upon good grounds, to be a violation of the constitutional rights of States and individuals. What is the rule of action under such circumstances? There is no difficulty whatever, in finding the answer. [The Republican leaders would say 'revolutionize the government.'] By the establishment of a judicial system within the Federal constitution, having ultimate cognizance of all cases arising under that constitution, one mode is provided by which both states and individuals can ascertain whether their reserved rights are invaded by the Federal authorities. [Now, mark the difference between Democrats and Republicans as to the 'mode and measure of redress.'] This remedy is at all times open, and there is no valid reason why a state should forcibly assert its constitutional rights any more than that an individual should do the same thing. While a state remains a member of the Union, it is bound to vindicate its constitutional rights and powers in that mode which is consistent with the preservation of that Union, and it can at any time under any supposed violation of its rights, or the rights of its people, make a case for judicial determination. Forcible resistance [such as Wisconsin and Massachusetts were guilty of] is open revolution, and nothing but an intolerable oppression, cutting off all judicial remedy, can make a revolution a necessity and a duty. (Applause.)

"Again, there is another equally good reason which shows that no popular tumults, and no forcible resistance are either legally or morally justifiable while the ballot box remains untouched. If the people of all the states had reason to believe that measures of the Federal Government are subversive of the Constitution, it is their right to correct the evil by change of their rulers. (Cheers.) In cases of supposed extensive violation of the Constitution, to which the attention of the whole country is called, the remedy of elections is ordinarily to reverse, and is in our system held to reverse erroneous constructions of that instrument, as well as errors of policy. The popular tribunal may not be quite so precise in its action as the judicial, but there can be no mistaking the judgment of the people when it is pronounced upon an issue clearly made, with an Administration which is charged with infringing the Constitution. (Great applause.)

"These principles, no one I presume, will be inclined to dispute, but there is thrust in to intercept their application to the present crisis in our affairs, a doctrine which I for one, distinctly repudiate. That doctrine is in substance, that all questioning of the measures of the Administration should be postponed while we are in a civil war—that there should be but one party, and that all should rally, to an 'unconditional support' of the constitutional authorities. This dogma needs examination. If by an 'unconditional support' of the constituted authorities it is intended to claim that we must all recognize the fact that we are engaged in a civil war, and that we must conduct it while it lasts *through* those authorities, and must hold no irregular intercourse with the public enemy, I readily accede to the proposition; but, if it is meant that we are not to question the *methods* which the Administration pursues in the prosecution of the war—that we have no rightful control over their *measures*—or that we are to refrain from demanding a change in their policy, I reject the doctrine without the slightest hesitation."

S. P. CHASE'S OPINION OF "LOYALTY."

Mr. CHASE, the present Secretary of the Treasury, on the 26th of August, 1857, in a speech in Ohio thus gave his idea of rights which the Government could not invade:

"We have the right to have our state laws

obeyed. We don't mean to resist Federal authority. Just or unjust laws, properly administered, will be respected. If dissatisfied, we will go to the ballot box and redress our wrongs. But we have rights which the Federal Government *must not invade*—right, superior to its power, on which our sovereignty depends, and we do mean to assert these rights against all tyranical assumptions of authority."

THE ROMAN LAW AND PERSONAL LIBERTY.

The Romans had a keen and just appreciation of the liberty of their citizens—in war and in peace, the liberty of the Roman citizen was held sacred, and it would seem that our "rulers" in the latter part of the 19th century have gone back of the age of Roman liberality. By the Roman law no man could be condemned unheard, or thrust into prison without a trial, and an opportunity to meet his accusers "face to face." There were cases when the bigoted Romans, in persecuting the Christians, violated their laws in reference to this subject. The Christians of that day, like the Democrats of this era, were persecuted for opinion's sake. They took PAUL and SILAS, on one occasion, without process of law, and arbitrarily thrust them into prison. But God's power came to the aid of the Roman law—the jail trembled and was fearfully shaken—the doors were opened, and the terrified jailor was thunderstruck to find that his victims had not departed, and the guilty persecutors, fearing a further demonstration of God's wrath, bad the prisoners go, but PAUL being a good lawyer, and knowing he and his compatriot had been illegally dealt by,

"Said unto them, they [the persecutors] have beaten us openly, *uncondemned*, being Romans, and have cast us into prison, and now do they thrust us out privily? Nay, verily; but let them come themselves, and fetch us out."

Our laws were borrowed from the Roman Pandects, which declared that no man should be 'scourged" (punished) uncondemned; and why should not our citizens be treated as fairly as PAUL insisted on being treated by his Jewish, Republican persecutors, who sought to punish him "uncondemned," as Mr. LINCOLN punishes Democrats?

Again, when PAUL was at Ephesus, a Roman silversmith, (no doubt a contractor,) by the name of DEMETRIUS, attempted to stir up sedition against him, because PAUL did not belong to his "party." He attempted to make the people believe that PAUL was in some way "opposing the Government," and the "multi-

tude" (of Union Leaguers, no doubt,) raised a hue and cry against PAUL. But the "Town Clerk" (no doubt a Democrat,) quieted the rabble by telling them if PAUL and his followers had committed anything against the law, the *law* should punish them. He said:

"Wherefore, if Demetrius and the craftsmen [contractors, in the original, no doubt,] which are with him, have a matter against any man, *the law is open*, and there are deputies [law officers]; let them implead one another.

"But if ye imagine anything concerning other matters, it shall be determined in a *lawful* assembly."—Acts XIX—38, 39.

Again, when the clamoring Romans demanded Paul's life before Festus, one of the Supreme Judges, who, in relating the case to King Agrippa, said:

"It is not the manner [law] of the Romans to deliver any man to die before that he which is accused, *have the accusers face to face* and have license to answer *for himself* concerning the crime laid against him."

After His Honor, Judge Festus had laid the case before King Agrippa, the King desired to see this strange man, Paul, and Festus sent for him, and when Paul came into Agrippa's august presence, Judge Festus said:

"King Agrippa, and all men which are here present with us, ye see this man about whom all the multitude of the Jews have dealt with me [they had probably called Paul a 'copperhead'] both at Jerusalem, and also here, crying that 'he ought not to live any longer.'" [Equivalent to the bloodthirsty declarations of Senators Wilson and Jim Lane against the Democrats.]

The last verse, Acts XXVI, reads:

"For it seemeth to me *unreasonable* to send a person, and not without to *signify the crimes laid against him*."

Here was a Roman Judge, near 2,000 years ago, addressing his King, and declaring it not only unlawful, but *unreasonable* to arrest a man charged with no crime, and without giving him a fair trial, and the privilege of confronting his accusers face to face, and this, too, when the Romans were engaged in war.

Would to God that our President and his party would read the New Testament, from which they could drink in the inspiration of reason, honor and law. Even the Jews had more respect for law, with all their religious fanaticism, than do our present rulers.

THE N. YORK INDEPENDENT RIGHT FOR ONCE.

In speaking of the arbitrary arrests of the

Administration, the New York *Independent* remarked:

"These blundering, silly arbitrary arrests have rendered the Administration unpopular in many sections of the country. The people are jealous of their liberties, *and they should be so*. No loyal man objects to the arrest of a traitor, or of a man fairly open to suspicion, but arbitrary arrests of citizens to-day, who are released within a week, without charge, or an investigation, are as wicked and unjustifiable acts as they are foolish and impolitic. Mr. STANTON has been guilty of too many of these acts, for the welfare of the *Administration* and the *Republican party*."

Much of the virtue of the foregoing is dissipated in the over-anxiety for the fate of the "Administration" and the "Republican party!" The cause of Civil Liberty is of little moment, to the Rev. Divine editor, as against the fate of the *Republican party!* Like the penitent thief in the stocks, who did not regret the larceny, but manifested great contrition at having been caught!

WHAT A CONSERVATIVE REPUBLICAN THINKS OF IT.

The Boston *Advertiser*, soon after the election in 1862, said:

"We say, then, that the decision of the people, at the late elections, was a verdict against the course pursued by the radical managers, and a direct avowal of distrust of their policy and guidance. It was a popular condemnation of the confusion which they have caused in military affairs, of the little foresight and wisdom shown by them in legislation; of the indecent haste and declamatory violence with which they have disposed of great public questions; of their factious course as regards the Executive, and their dangerous recklessness as to ordinary *constitutional safeguards*. Against their rule the people had resolved to register a verdict."

PRESIDENT'S SUSPENSION OF THE WRIT OF HABEAS CORPUS.

The following is the Proclamation suspending the writ of *habeas corpus* throughout the United States. We give it entire, as it may be convenient for reference:

"WASHINGTON, September 15, 1863.

"By the President of the United States.

"A PROCLAMATION.

"*Whereas*, The Constitution of the United States has ordained that the privilege of the writ of *habeas corpus* shall not be suspended unless in case of rebellion or invasion, the public safety may require it, and

"*Whereas*, A rebellion was existing on the 3d day of March, 1863, which rebellion is still existing, and

"*Whereas*, By a statute which was approved on that day, it was enacted by the Senate and House of Representatives of the United States in Congress assembled, that during the present insurrection, the President of the United States, whenever, in his judgment the public safety may require, is authorized to suspend the privilege of the writ of *habeas corpus* in any State throughout the United States, or any part thereof, and

"*Whereas*, In the judgment of the President, the public safety does require that the privilege of the said writ shall now be suspended throughout the United States, in cases where, by the authority of the President of the United States, military, naval and civil officers of the United States, or any of the leading persons under their command, or in their custody, as prisoners of war, spies, or aiders and abettors of the enemy, or officers, soldiers or seamen, enrolled, drafted, or mustered, or enlisted in, or belonging to the land or naval forces of the United States, or as deserters therefrom, or *otherwise* amenable to military law, [under Order 38 or 90 this would include everybody and every case] or to the rules and articles of war, or to the rules and regulations prescribed for the military or naval services, by the authority of the President of the United States, or for resisting a draft, *or for any other offences* against the military or naval services [is not this broad enough to cover everything and everybody?]

"*Now, therefore*, I, Abraham Lincoln, President of the United States, do hereby proclaim and make known to all whom it may concern, that the privilege of the writ of *habeas corpus* is suspended throughout the United States, in the several cases before mentioned, and that this suspension shall continue throughout the duration of such rebellion, or until this proclamation shall, by a subsequent one, to be issued by the President of the United States, be modified or revoked

"I do hereby require all magistrates, attorneys and other civil officers, within the United States, and all officers and others in the military or naval services of the United States, to take distinct notice of this suspension, and to give it full effect ; all other citizens of the United States to conduct themselves accordingly, and in conformity to the constitution of the U. States, and the laws of Congress, in such case made and provided. In Testimony, &c.

BY THE PRESIDENT: ABRAHAM LINCOLN.
WM. H. SEWARD.

This proclamation, be it remembered, was issued shortly after the fall of Vicksburg, when our arms were victorious in all the South West —When not a threatening ripple disturbed the placid North—no disturbance—no factious threatenings—no murmurings that boded illicit opposition—no organized menacing of the constituted authorities—no cause of fear—while the brightest rays of victory had penetrated the black and rapidly separating clouds of war

—just when hope began to light up the gloomy horizon—came this proclamation, like a thunderbolt from a clear sky! No explanations are given. No reasons set forth—no "necessity" exhibited. The President takes this delegated power second hand from Congress, with the power to make and adjudicate all laws, added to his own power as Executive.

Is not this, in the language of EDWARD LIVINGSTON, "a refinement on Despotism?"

THE WAY THE MAGNA CHARTA WAS TREATED IN CONGRESS.

We close this chapter with the following, taken from the proceedings of the House of Representatives, Dec. 17, 1863. It will bear preserving for the future:

ARBITRARY ARRESTS.

"Mr. Harrington, (Dem.) offered the following resolutions, and demanded the previous question on their adoption:

Whereas the Constitution of the United States (article one, section nine,) provides: "The priviledge of the writ of *habeas corpus* shall not be suspended, unless when in cases of rebellion or invasion the public safety may require it;" and whereas such provision is contained in the portion of the Constitution defining legislative powers; and not in the provisions defining executive powers, and whereas the Constitution (article four of amendments) further provides: "The right of the people to be secure in their persons, houses, papers, and effects, against unreasonable searches and seizures, shall not be violated," &c.; and whereas the Thirty-Seventh Congress did by act claim to confer upon the President of the United States the power at his will and pleasure to suspend the priviledge of the writ of *habeas corpus* throughout the United States without limitation or conditions; and whereas the President of the United States, by proclamation, has assumed to suspend such privileges of the citizen in the loyal States; and whereas the people of such States have been subjected to arbitrary arrests without process of law, and to unreasonable searches and seizures, and have been denied the right to a speedy trial and investigation, and have languished in prisons at the arbitrary pleasure of the Chief Executive and his military subordinates; Now, therefore

Resolved, by the House of Representatives of the United States, That no power is delegated by the Constitution of the United States, either to the legislative or executive branch, to suspend the privilege of the writ of *habeas corpus* in any State loyal to the Constitution and Government not invaded, and in which the civil and judicial power are in full operation.

2. *Resolved,* That Congress has no power under the Constitution to delegate to the President of the United States the authority to suspend the privilege of the writ of *habeas corpus,* and imprison at his pleasure, without process of law or trial, the citizens of the loyal States.

3. *Resolved,* That the assumption of the right by the executive of the United States to deprive the citizens of such loyal States of the benefits of the writ of *habeas corpus,* and to imprison them at his pleasure, without process of law, is unworthy the progress of the age, is consistent only with a despotic power unlimited by constitutional obligations, and is wholly subversive of the elementary principles of freedom upon which the Government of the United States and of the several States, is based.

4. *Resolved,* That the Judiciary Committee be instructed to prepare and report a bill to this House protecting the rights of the citizens in the loyal States, in strict accordance with the foregoing provisions of the Constitution of the United States.

Mr. Lovejoy, (Rep.)—Mr. Speaker—
The Speaker—Debate is not in order.
Mr. Lovejoy—I want to state a fact—.
The Speaker—Debate is not in order.
Mr. Lovejoy—Would it not be in order to move to refer these resolutions to a committee on Buncombe when it shall be appointed?—[Laughter.]
The Speaker—It would not.
Mr. Fenton, (Rep.)—I move to lay the resolutions on the table.
Mr. Davis, of Maryland, (Rep.)—I beg that gentleman will allow us to have a direct vote on the resolutions and reject them, so as to get done with this work of laying resolutions on the table.
Mr. Fenton—I withdraw the motion to lay on the table.

The previous question was seconded, and the main question ordered.

Mr. Holman called for the yeas and nays on the resolutions.

The yeas and nays were ordered.

The question was taken, and it was decided in the negative—yeas 67, nays 90; as follows:

YEAS.

Allen, James C.
Allen, William J.
Ancona,
Baldwin, A. C.
Bliss,
Brooks,
Brown, James S.
Chandler,
Coffroth,
Cox,
Cravens,
Dawson,
Dennison,
Eden,
Edgerton,
Eldridge,
English,
Finck,
Ganson,
Grider,
Hall,
Harding,
Harrington,
Harris, Benj. G.
Herrick,
Holman,
Johnson, William
Kernan,
King,
Knapp,
Law,
Le Blond,
Long,
Mallory,
Marcy,
McAllister,
McDowell,
McKinney,
Middleton,
Miller, William H.
Morris, James R.
Morrison,
Nelson,
Noble,
Odell,
O'Neill, John.
Pendleton,
Perry,
Radford,
Randall, Samuel J.
Robinson,
Rogers,
Ross,
Scott,
Steele, John B.
Steele, William G.
Stiles,
Strouse,
Sweat,
Voorhees,
Wadsworth,
Ward,
Wheeler,
White, Chilton A.
White, Joseph W.
Winfield,
Wood Fernando
—67

NAYS.

Alley,
Allison,
Ames,
Arnold,
Ashley,
Baldwin, John D.
Boutman,
Blaine,
Blow,
Boutwell,
Brandegee,
Broomall,
Brown, Wm. G.
Clark, Ambrose W.
Clarke, Freeman
Clay,
Cobb,
Cole,
Creswell,
Davis, Henry W.
Davis, Thomas T.
Dawes,
Dixon,
Donnelly,
Driggs,
Dumont,
Eckley,
Eliot,
Farnsworth,
Fenton,
Frank,
Garfield,
Gooch,
Grinnell,
Hale,
Higby,
Hooper,
Hotchkiss,
Hubbard, A. W.
Hubbard, John H.
Hulburd,
Jencks,
Julian,
Kasson,
Kelley,
Kellogg, F. A.
Kellogg, Orlando
Loan,
Longyear,
Lovejoy,
Marvin,
McBride,
McClurg,
McIndoe,
Miller, Sam'l. F.
Moorhead,
Morrill,
Morris, Daniel
Myers, Amos
Myers, Leonard
Norton,
O'Neill, Charles
Orth,
Perham,
Pike,
Pomeroy,
Price,
Randall, Wm. H.
Rice, Alex. H.
Rice, John H.
Rollins, E. H.
Schenck,
Scofield,
Shannon,
Sloan,
Smith,
Smithers,
Spaulding,
Stevens,
Thayer,
Tracey,
Van Valkenburgh,
Washburne, E. B.
Washburne, W. B.
Whaley,
Williams,
Wilder,
Wilson,
Windom,
Woodbridge,—90.

So the resolutions were rejected by a strict party vote

SUPREME COURT OF WISCONSIN ON SUSPENDING THE WRIT.

No one will doubt the extreme "loyalty" of the members of the Wisconsin Supreme Court. That Court, in the celebrated Kemp case, decided that the President of the United States could not suspend the writ. Judges DIXON and PAINE wrote out lengthy decisions. We only have room to quote from Judge P.'s decision, as follows:

"Whether the writ of *habeas corpus* is legally suspended or not, depends entirely upon the question whether it requires an act of Congress to suspend it, or whether it may be done by the President alone; and this has been so fully and ably discussed, that whoever is now called on to decide it, can do little more than to indicate which side of the argument he adopts.—For myself, I entertain no doubt *that it requires an act of Congress.* The power to issue the writ is given by law, and *the President cannot make a law.*"

And Judge PAINE might have added, as he does, virtually, that Congress cannot delegate to the President the law making power.

CHAPTER XXXII.

MORE REVOLUTIONARY SYMPTOMS.

Mobbing of Democrats and Democratic Presses... Schenck's Order Suppressing Newspapers... Hascall's Despotic Note to the "New York Express"... How the Republicans Love Free Speech... Mobbing of Douglas in Chicago... Republican Mob in Green County, Wis.... Federals, Whigs and Republicans in Juxtaposition... Their Line of Consanguinity... Senator Doolittle vs. Political Doolittle... President Lincoln vs. Political Lincoln... Republicans in Congress Suppress Inquiry into Illegal Acts... Their Preaching vs. Practice... The Negro Voted Out of Illinois and Wisconsin... Abolitionists Selling Negroes for Cotton.

MOBBING OF DEMOCRATS AND DEMOCRATIC PRESSES.

Never was the spirit of bigotry, arrogance and intolerance more glaringly developed than in the party opposed to the Democracy. No matter by what name they may hail—not matter whether in or out of power—they have ever been disposed to carry their points and enforce their dogmas by low, vulgar epithets, gross denunciations, or if need be, by mobs and violence. For years they have preached "free soil, free press and freedom," but the moment they came into power, they set about the most proscriptive intolerance, and sought to reduce all who did not endorse their every ism, to abject slavery. They have mobbed Democratic presses in innumerable instances, and sought by military power to suppress the publication of any newspaper that exposed their manifest delinquencies, wrongs and wholesale plunder-ing of the public exchequer.

They sought to silence the Ohio *Crisis* by a military mob—the editors of the Harrisburg *Patriot & Union* were arrested on the most frivolous pretext, and after being kept in durance vile for four weeks, without accusation or proof of wrong, were "honorably discharged" without indemnity. BURNSIDE undertook to place the New York *World* and the Chicago *Times* beneath the iron heel of despotism, but the uprising of an outraged people forced the mad despots to relinquish for the time their insane purposes.

We have not the room to give the details of all the cases under this head, but there is scarcely a moderately sized division of the country that has not been disgraced by outrages upon the liberty of the press. If the official authorities could find nothing in a newspaper, which did not reflect their views, sufficient to build up an excuse for its suppression, by military "order," they managed to set in motion a mob to destroy it, as they did in scores of cases in Iowa, Missouri, Illinois, Indiana, Ohio, &c.

In all these cases, the Republican presses have joined in the cry, and endorsed the outrage. A few of the Abolition presses, of the old stock, to their credit, have not hesitated to denounce this blow at civil liberty.

SCHENCK'S ORDER SUPPRESSING NEWSPAPERS.

As a *sample* of a large class, we place on record the following "Order" by the notorious SCHENCK:

"HEADQUARTERS 5TH ARMY CORPS, }
"Baltimore, June 29, 1863.   }

"The following newspapers have been suppressed within the limits of this Department; and the local press will not hereafter be allowed to publish extracts from their columns.

"By order of the General Commanding

"The New York *World*.
"The New York *Express*.
"The Cincinnati *Enquirer*.
"The Chicago *Times*.
"The New York *Caucasian*.

"[Signed,] W. S. FISH,
"Lieut. Col. and Provost Marshal."

No reason is here given, for the best reason in the world—SCHENCK had no reason to give save his own malignity. We will here drop the curtain on this branch of *free* despotism.

Our "library would not be complete" without the following gem, which bears its own comments:

SCRAPS FROM MY SCRAP-BOOK.

HEADQUARTERS DISTRICT OF INDIANA,
Department of the Ohio,
Indianapolis, May 5th, 1863.

"To the Editors of the New York Express;

"GENTS:—Some one has been kind enough to enclose me a slip from your paper containing a copy of my Order No. 9, and your remarks thereon. They are exceedingly witty and smart, and in your judgment, probably, dispose of the whole case. It may surprise you some to know that the order was issued after mature deliberation and consultation, and is being, and will be, carried out to the letter. *It is fortunate for you that your paper is not published in my District.*

"Very truly yours, MILO S. HASCALL,
"Brig-Gen. Vols., Commanding District."

This demonstrates that kind of cheap despotism which had its orign at Head Quarters, and which has disgraced the age in which we live.

HOW THE REPUBLICANS LOVE FREE SPEECH.

On the 1st of September, 1854, Senator DOUGLAS attempted to speak in Chicago, and to explain the principles of the Kansas-Nebraska bill. The Republicans, in utter ignorance of those principles, refused to listen, and the following, which we copy from the Wisconsin *State Journal*, (Rep.) of Sept. 7, 1854, shows how they managed to prevent Mr. DOUGLAS from discussing the measures which they had so ignorantly denounced.

"Gentlemen, by the Nebraska Bill, the people are allowed the right of self government. (A voice. "who appoints the Governor and Judges?") The President of the United States. (Three groans for Pierce.) He appoints Judges in every State in the Union, why should he not in Nebraska and Kansas? ("Read the section of the bill." "Read the bill.") The bill was published in one of your city papers to-day, and you can read at your leisure.— (Don't take that paper.) (A voice; "what a head.") The best interests of the United States required that my bill should become a law, and that the right of the people to self-regulation should be recognized. (A voice, "let the niggers govern themselves."

"Gentlemen, we are not talking about niggers, we are talking about the Nebraska-Kansas-bill. Gentlemen you have had a Convention lately, in the First Congressional District. (Three cheers for Washburne! Cries for the Harbor bill.) You can't hear anything about the harbor bill to-night, I am talking about the Nebraska bill, and I intend to talk about it. If you think to put a stop to the free discussion of this measure, you are dealing with the wrong person. I shall stay here and talk as long as it suits my convenience. (Chorus: 'We won't go home till morning, till morning, till morning. We won't go home till morning, till daylight doth appear.'")

"The speaker then defied the crowd to put him down, and said that he should speak again and again if necessary. ('Good! good!' 'Do it more!' 'Try it again!') Another attempt to speak on the Nebraska question was succeeded by a perfect typhoon of discordant voices, and cries of 'Small Giant!' 'Little Dug!' 'Millikon!' 'Dr. McVicker!' 'Cook, carry him home!' 'Young America!' &c."

This, be it remembered, was the Republican account. It does not come up to the reality.

THE GREEN CO., (WIS.) MOD.

About the 1st of August, 1862, the Republicans of Green county, Wis., organized themselves into what they termed a Vigilance Committee. They took all matters into their hands, such as defining and punishing treason, &c. They adopted POPE's "Army Oath," and required all to subscribe to it, or be roughly handled. They caught one old, respectable man, loyal and true to his country, and rode him on a rail for refusing to sign the following oath:

"I, ———, of the town of———, in the county of Green, and State of Wisconsin, do solemnly swear that I am a loyal citizen of the United States of America, that I will bear true allegiance to the same, that I will to the utmost of my ability support the government in its efforts to suppress the rebellion; that in rendering such support I will discountenance in every possible manner by word or action every sentiment or expression the tendency of which may be to encourage disloyalty to the government, and that I will not by word or deed, countenance any disloyal, secret organization; and for the violation of this oath may I suffer the just penalty of the crime."

Another by the name of STEVES was roughly handled for the same set, and we let the Rockford (Ill.) *Democrat*, (Rep) tell the story:

"Mr. John Steves, a well known citizen of Durand, and a very radical Republican in politics, [the mob did not know his politics] we understand, had occasion to visit Monroe, Wisconsin, last week, and while there a vigilance committee of which that vicinity boasts had taken into their hands a supposed secessionist of the place to administer to him the oath of allegiance, and if he refused to do so to inflict upon him a proper punishment. The operations of the committee had drawn together a large and excited crowd. Mr. Steves looked on and saw that their victim was an old man, perhaps seventy years old, whom they were handling, as Mr. Steves thought, with a degree of violence which was hardly removed from brutality. To see an old man thus treated aroused his sympathy, and without stopping to consider the merits of the case as charged against the old man, in the name of common humanity remonstrated with the crowd, telling them that they ought to treat him more civilly, and consider upon his case more dispassionately;—that the worst criminal who was to be hanged within the next half hour was entitled to a decent respect and inviolability of his person in the mean time.

"The excited crowd instantly turned upon Mr. Steves, and he found himself in their hands and at the mercy of their excitement. The vigilance committee took his case in hand, as he learned upon being informed that they were then considering as to what should be done with him. In a few moments one of the committee told him that he had one minute left to take the oath of allegiance or leave the town. Mr. Steves told them that he had not one word of objection to the sentiments of the oath and its purport, and as a voluntary transaction would take it a thousand times; but that he had not said a word or done a thing which gave them any reason to suspect his loyalty, and he should decline to take the oath upon compulsion. All that he had said was a plea for commonly civil, personal treatment towards an old gray haired man whom they had taken into their hands, and whom in the excitement of their anger he thought they were treating inhumanly. He asked to see the committee as a body and make a statement to them, believing when they had heard all, they would see his case in the right light, and leave him to himself. The committee refused to see him, and at the expiration of the minute, the crowd took him, placed him upon a rail, and carried him on it to his wagon, and ordered him to leave town immediately. This accomplished, Mr. Steves, at the earnest solicitation of a friend whose goods he had been moving to Monroe, and whom as he was just starting in business there, he (Mr. Steves) did not wish to compromise, volunteered to take the oath of allegiance, and it was accordingly administered to him. Thus relieving himself from the penalty of his refusal, he was allowed to remain in town until next day, and then took his departure for home, satisfied with his visit to Monroe."

FEDERALS, WHIGS AND REPUBLICANS IN JUXTRAPOSITION.

FEDERAL.
1796 to 1814.
DISSOLUTION.

"The Northern States can subsist as a nation—a Republic—without any connection with the Southern. It cannot be contested that if the Southern States were possessed of the same *political ideas*, our Union would be more close than separation, but when it becomes a serious question whether we shall give up our government or part with the States south of the Potomac, no man *North* of that river, whose heart is not *thoroughly Democratic*, can hesitate what decision to make.

"I shall, in the future papers, consider some of the great events, which will *lead to a separation of the United States*—show the importance of retaining their present Constitution, even at the expense of a separation—endeavor to prove the impossibility of a Union for any long period in future, both from the *moral* and *political* habits of the citizens of the Southern States, and finally examine carefully to see whether we have not already approached to the era when they must be divided."
—*From Pelham's Pamphlet*, 1796.

"*The Union has long since been virtually dissolved, and it is full time that this part of the United States should take care of itself.*—p. 19.

WHIG.
1844 to 1848.
DISSOLUTION.

"*Resolved*, Rather than see slavery established on Mexican territory as the result of this accursed war, it were better this Union should be at once dissolved.—*Whig Resolution in Worcester, Mass.*, 1847.

"On the 24th of February, 1842, John Quincy Adams presented a petition in the House of Representatives, signed by a large number of citizens of Haverhill, Mass., for a peaceable dissolution of the Union, 'assigning as one of the reasons, the inequality of benefits conferred upon the different sections.' "—*Blake's History of Slavery*, p. 524.

"We cannot possibly look favorably upon this war. Its first act was a gross outrage upon Mexico. and can it be supposed by Mr. Polk and his advisers, that an error so glaring—a crime so unpardonable, as this Mexican war, can be whitewashed?"—*Mt. Carmel Register*, 1847.

"Were I a Mexican, I would welcome these invaders with bloody hands to hospitable graves." — *Thomas Corwin*, 1847.

REPUBLICAN.
1854 to 1863.
DISSOLUTION.

[Resolution adopted by the American Anti-Slavery Society, New York, December, 1855.]

"*Whereas*, The dissolution of the present imperfect and inglorious Union between the free and slave states would result in the overthrow of slavery and the consequent foundation of a more perfect and glorious Union, without the incubus of slavery, therefore

"*Resolved*, That we invite a free correspondence with the disunionists of the South, in order to devise the most suitable way and means to secure the consummation so devoutedly to be wished."

"*Resolved*, That it is the duty of the North in case they fail in electing a President and Congress that will restore freedom to Kansas, to revolutionize the government!"—*Republicans of Green Co., Wis.* 1856.

Mr. Garrison made a speech in 1856, in which he declared:

"I have said, and I say again, that in proportion to the growth of disunionism, will be the growth of Republicanism. * * The Union is a lie. The American Union is an imposture, and a covenant with death, and an agreement with hell. * * I am for its overthrow. * * Up with the flag of disunion, that

"The once venerable Constitution HAS EXPIRED BY DISSOLUTION in the hands of those wicked men who were sworn to protect it. Its spirit, with the precious souls of its first founders, has fled forever. Its remains, with theirs, *rest in the silent tomb!* At your hands, therefore, we demand deliverance. *New England is unanimous*, and we announce our irrevocable decree, that the tyrannical oppression of those who at present usurp the powers of the Constitution is beyond endurance!—*Address to Hartford Convention*, 1815.

"My plan is to withhold our money and make a separate peace with England."—*Boston Daily Advertiser*, 1814.

OPPOSING THE "GOVERNMENT," ETC.

"On or before the 4th of July, if James Madison is not out of office, *a new form of government will be in operation in the Eastern section of the Union, instantly after, the contest in many of the states will be, whether to adhere to the old, or join the new government!* Like everything else, which was foretold years ago, and which is verified every day, this will also be vilified as visionary. Be it so. But, Mr. Madison cannot complete his term of service if the war continues! It is not possible! and if he knew human nature, he would see it."— *Federal Republican, Nov.* 7, 1814.

"It is a time of day that requires cautious jealousy; not jealousy of your magistrates, for you have given them your confidence. * * Cursed be he that keepth back his sword from blood. Let him that hath none, sell his coat and buy one."—*Sermon of Rev. Dr. Parish, of Boston, July* 4, 1799.

"The full vials of despotism are poured out on your heads, and yet you may challenge the plodding Israelite, the stupid African, the feeble Chinese, the drowsy Turk, or the frozen exile of Siberia, to equal you in tame submission to the powers that be· * *

"Here we must trample on

OPPOSING THE "GOVERNMENT," ETC.

"The voice of lamentation and war, heard all over the country, from homes and firesides made desolate by the slaughter of fathers, and husbands, and brothers, is sweet music to the ears of the President and his friends, and they seem ambitious to swell the chorus by increasing the victims. * * * We rejoice to see a large and respectable number of Whig papers in this and other states taking ground against further appropriations by Congress of men and money for the Mexican cut throating business. This is as it should be."—*Warren (O.) Chronicle*, 1847.

"If there is is in the United States a breast worthy of American liberty, its impulses to join the Mexicans, and hurl down upon the base, slavish, mercenary invaders, who, born in a Republic, go to play over the accursed game of the Hessians on the tops of those Mexican volcanoes, it would be a sad and woful *joy*, nevertheless to hear that the hordes under Scott and Taylor were every man of them swept into the next world! What business has an invading army in this ?"— *Boston Daily Chronotype*, 1847.

we may have a free and glorious Union of our own."

"Tear down the flaunting lie;
Half-mast the starry flag;
Insult no sunny sky
With hate's polluted rag!"
—*New York Tribune*, 1854.

OPPOSING THE "GOVERNMENT," ETC.

Resolution adopted by the Essex County (Mass.) Anti Slavery Society May 10, 1862.

"*Resolved*, That the war as hitherto, prosecuted, is but a wanton waste of property, a dreadful sacrifice of life, and worse than all, of conscience and of character, to preserve and perpetuate a Union and Constitution which should never have existed, and which, by all the laws of justice and humanity, should in their present form, be at once and forever overthrown."

From Parker Pillsbury's Speech, April, 1862.

"I do not wish to see this government prolonged another day in the present form. I have been for twenty years attempting to overthrow the present dynasty. The constitution never was so much an engine of cruelty and crime as at the present hour. I am not rejoiced at the tidings of victory to the northern arms; I would far rather see defeat, etc."

From Stephen F. Forters' Speech, Boston, 1862.

"I have endeavored to dissuade every young man I could from enlisting, telling them that they were going to fight for slavery."

"On account of the repeat-the mandates of despotism, or here we must remain slaves forever."—*p.* 13. *April* 7, 1814.

"Sec. 2. *And be it further enacted,* That if any person shall write, print, utter, or publish, or shall cause or procure to be written, printed, uttered or published, or shall knowingly or willingly aid in writing, printing, uttering or publishing any false, scandalous and malicious writing or writings against the Government (the party in power) of the United States, or either House of the Congress of the United States, or the President of the United States, with intent to defame the said Government, or either House of the Congress, or the said President, &c."— *Sedition Law, July* 17, 1798.

ed expressions of disloyal and incendiary sentiments, the publishing of the newspaper known as the Chicago *Times* is hereby suppressed. — *Burnside's Order No.* 84, *June* 1, 1862.

"That *any order* of the President, or under his authority, made at any time during the existence of the present rebellion, shall be a defense in all courts to any action or prosecution, civil or criminal," &c.—*Extract from act suspending Habeas Corpus, March,* 1863.

KNOW NOTHINGISM.

"The real cause of the war must be traced to the influence of *worthless foreigners* over the press and the deliberations of the Government in all its branches.—*Response to the Message of Gov. Strong, of Mass., by the Assembly, June,* 1814.

KNOW NOTHINGISM.

"If I had the power, I would erect a gallows at every landing place in the city of New York, and suspend every cursed Irishman as soon as he steps upon our shore."—*Remarks of Mathew L. Davis on receiving the news of the Democratic triumph in New York, in* 1852.

"It is our opinion, as our readers well know, that no man of foreign birth should be admitted to the exercise of the political rights of an American citizen."—*Albany Daily Advertiser.*

"We could not find any other remedy against the threatening danger, than a repeal of *all naturalization laws."—Col. Webb, of New York.*

"*All* naturalization laws should be instantly repealed, and the term preceding the enjoyment of civil rights extended twenty-five years."— *Mr. Clark, Whig Mayor of New York.*

KNOW NOTHINGISM.

"Taken altogether, the squatter reception, last evening, fell below what had been promised, but furnished an instance of what a few determined wire pullers can do with a few hundred *voting cattle.*"— (alluding to the Irish and Germans.)—*Chicago Tribune. Oct.* 15, 1860.

"*We unhesitatingly aver that seven-tenths of the foreigners in our land, who bow in obedience to the Pope of Rome, are not as intelligent as the full blooded Africans of our state —we will not include the part bloods."—Cleveland Herald.*

We might proceed almost *ad infinitum,* but the above must suffice. Our only object is to link together the principles of fraternism in a single group, between the old Federals and their progeny, so that the reader might see at a glance how well the three great parties, or rather the one party, with three great names, have agreed, voted, acted and thought alike. The above does not exhibit the *strongest* family resemblance—that feature, in all its various tints and hues, will be found scattered throughout this entire work. Let no Republican say he was not sired by a Federal. We have traced his geneology too clearly to admit of doubt.

SCRAPS FROM MY SCRAP-BOOK.

REPUBLICAN PREACHING VS. PRACTICE.
Senator Doolittle vs. Political Doolittle.

On the 2d day of May, 1862, Senator DOOLITTLE made a speech in the Senate of the United States, in which he maintained that there was ample power under the Constitution for every emergency in war:

LOOK ON THIS PICTURE.

"Sir, I repeat, that never before, in this body, nor in any legislative body the sun ever shone upon, were there graver questions raised than these. And yet, under all this responsibility, there are gentlemen who, in their eagerness to press this measure to a vote, smile at constitutional scruples and responsibilities. Sir, I am not one of those; I confess that I can concur fully in the language of my colleague, and say when I am pressed to act upon questions involving these great responsibilities, that I do so with a fear and apprehension—not the fear of any man here or elsewhere—for I know no man master on earth, but the fear that in the presence of that God, before whom I have taken an oath to support the Constitution, I may be pressed, under the excitement of the moment, when passion rules the hour, to trample it under my feet.

"Mr. President, we are in arms to-day. We are at war. For what!? It is for this very Constitution—to maintain, protect and defend its supremacy in every state, everywhere, from Maine to Texas. To maintain that supremacy we send our sons to the battle field—we stake all we have and all we are, and I should regard myself wanting in manhood, as cowardly, shrinking from the performance of my duty, if, while my sons and my countrymen are in the field, fighting the enemy, meeting danger and death in every form, I should not stand here in the defense of the Constitution, by every power God has given me—let it be assailed from what quarter it may. The only fear I have is, that I may not defend it as I should.

"Mr. president, that constitution, let me say, is just as supreme in reserving powers from this government, as it is in granting powers to it. Just as supreme in withholding as in conferring power. If this government, or any branch of it—if Congress or the Executive, or the Supreme Court shall undertake to overturn its provisions, and to trample under their feet the rights reserved to the States and the people by it, *it is just as much an attempt at revolution and rebellion as when the men in the insurrectionary states undertake to trample under their feet the powers which by it are given to this government. Either is REVOLUTION!* And if either succeeds, it is an end to our whole system of republican government!! If the doctrine shall once prevail, and be acquiesced in by the government, and the people of the United States, that the constitution can be overborne; that this Federal Government can usurp powers which are not delegated, but are expressly reserved to the States—the days of this Republic are already passed—the days of the Empire have begun, and we are preparing to re-enact, on perhaps a grander scale, the history of the decline and fall of the Empire of Rome. [You were right, Mr. D.]

"The maintenance inviolate of the rights of the states and especially the rights of each state, to order and control its own domestic institutions, according to its own judgment exclusively, is essential to that balance of power on which the perfection and endurance of our political fabric depends."—[*From the Chicago Platform.*]

"Without that they cease to be states at all, [Mr. D. did not think then, perhaps, how soon he would be forced into the "state suicide" doctrine] and the Federal Government becomes one vast, consolidated empire. This was as true in the beginning as it was in 1860, when we made it the pledge upon which we came into power, and it will be true, forever, whether men in the heat and passion of this hour shall heed it, or trample it under their feet.

"This Constitution of ours gives to us all the powers which are necessary to meet *even the exigencies of civil war. It is just as perfect in this as in any other respect.* [For claiming this, Democrats have been called "Copperheads."] It meets *all* the necessities of our situation, whether of *war, insurrection* or *peace.* The idea that at any time—for one single hour—this Constitution, because civil war exists, is dissolved, or gives way to martial law, as to something higher, and above itself, at the discretion or caprice of the President or Congress, or both together, is a heresy as fatal to free Government, and as full of evil as the whisperings of Satan to Eve in the Garden of Eden. No, sir, no! The Constitution is just as much above mortal law as it is above civil law. From it alone are derived all the powers of the Government, and under it alone can they be exercised."

NOW LOOK ON THIS.

On the 4th of June, 1863, Mr. political DOOLITTLE made a speech before a meeting in Chicago, called to denounce the President for countermanding BURNSIDE's Order, suppressing the Chicago *Times,* which speech demonstrates the facility with which "first rate *fourth* rate" statesmen can descend from the sublime to the ridiculous; and, here is the manner Mr. political DOOLITTLE proposed to *practice* on the preaching of Mr. senator DOOLITTLE. We quote from the Chicago *Tribune,* of above date:

"He (DOOLITTLE) believed the exercise of the power in any part of the United States, to suppress newspapers, is simply a question of time and necessity. In New Orleans Gen. BUTLER suppressed newspapers, and even executed a traitor. Has anybody found fault with that? In many parts of the North papers have been suppressed, and *justly so.* In my opinion *the Executive is clothed with discretion* in the time of war to do *WHAT HE DEEMS FIT AND PROPER.* He alluded to the revoking order. Probably the President thinks the time has not yet come when Chicago shall be put under martial law. But if any newspaper opposes the enforcing of the conscription law, or *any other order* the President thinks proper to give, that paper will be suppressed, and if need be, martial law proclaimed. We desire, if possible, to have the loyal people of the North united as one man, and we must have it practically so, or it is of no avail. He regretted that there were still two political parties [suppression is a good way to get rid of one]—there should be but one, and that one united with a determination to put down the rebellion, but as it is, the President must control *all men of all parties*, and those that oppose the administration must suffer the consequences. If the time comes, and it becomes necessary, Mr. LINCOLN will declare martial law, even in Chicago."

Now, let the reader judge of Political DOOLITTLE's "heresy," by Senator DOOLITTLE's declaration, above, as to martial law being "fatal to free government." We confess we are naturally too nervous to comment further upon such whiffling inconsistencies. They are degrading to the high character of an American Senator.

PRESIDENT LINCOLN VS. POLITICIAN LINCOLN.

Look on this Picture.

"I have no purpose, directly or indirectly, to interfere with the institution of slavery in the States where it exists. I believe I have *no lawful right to do so*, and I have no inclination to do so.—*President Lincoln in his Inaugural.*

Then on This.

"I order and declare that all persons held as slaves in the said designated states and parts of states, are, and hereafter shall be free.—*Politician Lincoln in the Emancipation Proclamation.*

The Republicans have always professed to be for law and order, and Mr. LINCOLN in his VALLANDIGHAM and Springfield correspondence, scouted the idea that he intended to violate law and the Constitution. This was the *profession.* What of the *practice.*

In defiance of law a military Governor was appointed for the District of Columbia, which by the very terms of the Constitution, was to be forever under the *exclusive* control of Congress.

Mr. WICKLIFFE (Dem.) introduced a resolution in Congress to enquire under what law said Governor was appointed.

Mr. OTIS (Rep.) moved to table the resolution, and thus prevent all enquiry. This was carried by a strict party vote, 85 to 46.

PROFESSIONS OF EQUAL RIGHTS TO THE NEGRO IGNORED IN PRACTICE.

Several years ago the Republicans of Wisconsin passed a law, in pursuance to the Constitution, submitting the question to the people whether the negroes should vote, and notwithstanding the professions of that party to be in favor of the move, and their having 12,000 majority, the negro was voted down by 27,000 majority.

In Illinois the disparity between profession and practice is vastly greater. In 1862 that State voted on a new constitution, two clauses of which related to the negro—one to exclude him from all privileges in the State, to prohibit him from being on Illinois soil. Below is the vote in several intensely negroized counties:

Counties.	Maj. for Negro.	Maj. ag'st Negro.	Rep. Maj.
McHenry		1,507	2,040
Boone	350		1,356
Carroll		1,462	1,222
Cook		10,000	4,000
Henderson		1,443	261
LaSalle		3,151	1,260
Coles		2,530	35

While the Republicans had the vote to defeat the constitution, they voted down the negro, by adopting all the articles against him, some of which by over 100,000 majority.

PRACTICE VS. PREACHING.

Just before the election in Wisconsin, November, 1863, the *Sentinel*, a Jacobin journal printed in Milwaukee, declared that "*he who votes must fight.*"

Fortunately an opportunity occurred to test the sincerity of this vociferously patriotic organ. One of its editors was drafted, and in the next issue of the paper appeared the following:

"While Mr. L., (the editor) would make a tip-top soldier, he is too valuable to be spared for that occupation just now."

This is a specimen of a large class. Mr. TILDEN, of the N. Y. *Independent*, who had been vociferously abusing the "Copperheads" for not going to the war, was among those who drew a "prize" from the wheel of fortune, but instead of following his own precepts, he proved the value of his patriotism to be just $300, under the pressure of a dire "necessity."

REVELATIONS OF COTTON SPECULATION—TRADING NEGROES FOR COTTON.

For years the Abolition politicians have been rocking the cradle of liberty, and singing the lullaby of freedom, and the idea of buying and selling "human flesh" as "chattels" was most terribly shocking to them. The following, from a publication during the summer of 1863, will speak for itself. The matter was hushed up, because Gen. CURTIS was a political General, but "when this cruel war is over" many facts blacker than the following will appear in the great record book of recorded facts:

"A commission is now in session at the west with Maj. Gen. McDowell at its head, investigating the conduct of Maj. Gen. Curtis and other Republican officials, in conducting their military operations so as to secure the largest amount of cotton possible for their own private benefit. One of the richest revelations made is in reference to the trading off of negroes for cotton! The specification alleges that negro slaves had been taken from the plantations *upon the pretense of giving them freedom under the President's "emancipation edict,"* and thus used as a substitute for coin. It has been fully proven before the investigating court. The officer charged with this lucrative speculation was Col. Hovey of Illinois, *formerly the principal of the State Normal School at Bloomington.* The following is the testimony upon the subject.

"Brice Suffield being called and sworn, testified as follows:

"Q. State whether you ever made an expedition for cotton on the steamer *Iatan*, in September, 1862, and if so, state what occurred at that time?

"A. I did. Our company, commanded by Capt. Twining, was ordered out from a camp near Helena, to go down on the steamer *Iatan*. The captain of the boat told us the intention was to take us down to get some wood for fuel. We landed on the Mississippi side of the river, opposite the cut-off—White river. There was aboard the boat one Brown, an overseer of Col. McGee's plantation; he was on the boat when we went aboard. After the boat was tied up, Brown went ashore; this was after dark. Some of our company, supposing him to be a rebel soldier, asked him where he got his clothes. He told them he got them in the Mexican war. He went to the captain of the Loat and told him it was all right—that the cotton would be in, in the course of a few hours. In due time Crown returned, bringing with him twenty-six bales of cotton. After the cotton was delivered, *the boatmen, by order of the captain, put on shore fifteen negroes that had been used as boat hands.*

"After getting them on shore, they *tied them,* after considerable struggling on the part of the negroes. In the tying operation one of the negroes escaped. After they were tied, Brown took them away. I was on picket post, and Brown, with the negroes, stopped at the post and bid me good evening, and then went on. Some time after taking the negroes away, Brown came back and went aboard the boat and stayed till daylight. A member of my company (don't recollect his name) told me he saw Capt. Weaver pay Brown some money—we supposed for the cotton.

"Q. What part did Capt. Twining or soldiers present take in the transaction of putting off the negroes?

"A. Merely acting under orders. They put us out on shore to guard against surprise. We guarded the boat. That was our duty. We had nothing to do with the negroes at all.

"Q. On what date was this?

"A. It was about the 24th of September.

"Q. Was any military officer on board the boat besides the officers of your company?

"A. I think not. There was a man on board, but I don't think he was a commissioned officer. He was acting as aid to Col. Hovey. His name is Washburne.

"Q. How many negroes acting as deck hands were there on board the boat when you went aboard with your company?

"A. Fifteen.

"Q. After these fifteen negroes were put ashore, did any other negroes come back with you as deck hands in the service of the boat?

"A. No sir. *These negroes were taken on an expedition to the same place some weeks before from the same plantation.*

"Q. Under whose charge was that expedition?

"A. Col. Hovey."

It would crowd the dimensions of our volume to unreasonable proportions to continue this chapter to the full; we must therefore close it, to make room for more important matter.

CHAPTER XXXIII.
HAVE WE A MILITARY DESPOTISM?

General Remarks...Educating the Army to the New Role...Adjutant General Thomas Preaching Politics to the Soldiers...Punishes Soldiers for Political Opinions...How the Soldiers View it...Anti-Copperhead Letters and Resolves from the Army...How Manufactured...General Remarks...General Halleck on "Crushing the Sneaking Traitors of the North"...Seward, Chase, Blair, &c., at the Cooper Institute Meeting...Case of Lieut. Edgerly...Abolitionism a Test of a Soldier's Duty...The Conscription Act intended to Ignore the Constitution..."Boston Commonwealth" Admits that the Administration Employed Bayonets to Carry Elections...Difference between Orthodoxy and Heterodoxy...Atrocious Sentiments of Senator Wilson...A Leaf from French History...A Fact by Sallust...Gov. Seymour on the Rotten-Borough System. His Message of Jan. 5, 1864...A Flexible Platform...Henry Clay's Opinion...Free Speech Abolished...Senator Howe on...Petty Despotism...Arrests for Wearing Badges...Several Instances in Point...The Evidences of Approaching Despotism...A Link from "New York Tribune"...To Doubt the Infallibility of the President is "Treason"...Declaration of Independence Revised, &c.

HAVE WE NOT A MILITARY DESPOTISM?

That we have not only a military despotism, but the worst species known to civilized nations, is a fact that will not only soon be generally known, but universally *felt*, unless a swift and radical change takes place in the aims and policy of the Administration. We say this in no spirit of controversy, nor do we utter it with factious feelings or ulterior purposes; but, we declare it in unutterable grief founded on the "logic of events."

We see in the modes and measures of the Administration that silent, yet sure, tiger-like tread in the path so often pursued by the tyrants and despots of the Old World, that we cannot mistake their purpose. The ingenuity of sophistry cannot make white appear black, nor transform a substantive, ponderable reality into a chimera or imponderable phantom. Those that have eyes, not totally blinded by passion, by prejudice, or by self-interest can see; those that have ears may hear—and hearing and seeing give evidence against a world of scepticism.

We complain not of those measures of force necessary to meet and subdue force, when and where it shall be criminally exerted against the government. We grant that the laws of war should govern *where* war exists. We would withhold no necessary power to arrest and punish treason wherever it raised its guilty head. We have heard, in fact, no one complain of the existence of martial law whenever and wherever a hostile force is too powerful for the civil law.

But we do complain, with fear that amounts almost to despair, of the striking down the great "writ of innocence" in states that are loyal, and where no hostile force menaces the courts, or interferes with their peaceful functions. We *know* there is no "necessity" for this.

We do complain at the exercise of that power which seizes any citizen without process or legal charges, and immures him in some bastile, or deports him beyond the reach of our laws, while our courts are free to try all crimes and have power to punish all offences. We complain of this because we *know* there is no "necessity" for it. We do most seriously complain of military interference in elections, because there is not only no "necessity" for it, but such interference is despotism. It is using the terror of the bayonet to prevent the people from choosing representatives opposed to the policy of those in power—a feat that the Emperor Napoleon III has not dared to perform, for it was but a few weeks since the people of Paris—right at the very throne of power—elected representatives opposed to the Emperor, by over six thousand majority. If absolute monarchs suffer a people to poll a free ballot, it seems that it might be tolerated in this land, under the *forms* of Republicanism.

The Indemnity Act which we publish in another portion of this work, is the cap shief of despotism. Under that act the President has unlimited, absolute power over the life and liberty of his "subjects." He may order one of his appointees to seize any man and put him in prison, and keep him there so long as it shall suit his pleasure; or he may order the seizure of his property and the scattering it to the four winds. He may order any man or any number of men, though as innocent as the unborn infant, to be shot and quartered, and there is no power to punish him or to call him to account. If he or the officers under him are prosecuted for malicious arrest, and imprisonment, all that is necessary is, to plead that 'the act was done by order of the President or by one acting under his order. That ends the case.

But says one, that law is unconstitutional, and can never stand the test of judicial scrutiny. We grant it. Any Constitution that could tolerate the exercise of such power in peaceful communities, would be nothing but a charter of despotism. But how are you to get before the proper tribunal to determine the unconstitutionality of that act? You cannot do it; for the same act authorizes the President to suspend the writ of *habeas corpus*, a license he has exercised to the fullest extent; so that no civil powers can have effect.

And this was the very object of that law. No human being can see any necessity for suspending the privilege of the writ of *habeas corpus*, where the courts are free to act—no reason has been given, and none can be given, except the one reason that despotism always finds a means to accomplish its ends.

Our government is undergoing a revolution at the North as well as at the South. The party in power, as we have fully shown in the foregoing pages, have put themselves on record in favor of a different government from that of our fathers. They spit upon and deride the Constitution. But they knew they could not change this government to that of a military despotism, except by and through the means of military power. Hence, they have stricken down the civil and erected the military standard. We are now virtually under martial law. We can exercise no civil functions that do not suit the pleasure of the Military Dictator. This is the land-mark we have reached to-day. No man can deny this fact, and if this power is not exercised in *every* particular, it only shows that the historian was correct when he asserted as a general maxim that

"New born despotism is both timid and cautious, and seldom reaches its altitude at one bound, but chooses rather to approach it by slow but sure degrees."

It is a shrewd *policy* to allow the people for a while some of their rights, lest a counter revolution might be inconvenient and troublesome.

EDUCATING THE ARMY TO THE NEW ROLE.

Look to our army. Has it been only the object of the "powers," to educate that army in the arts and sciences of war, and to make it efficient as against the foe? By no means. That from the first, that army has been tampered with, and more pains has been taken in certain quarters to bring it up to the required standard of political discipline, than to make it efficient in military acquirements cannot be doubted. Let us cite a few facts from the scores we have in store.

ADJUTANT GENERAL THOMAS PREACHING POLITICS TO THE SOLDIERS.

In 1862, Adjutant General Thomas was sent out to the West, ostensibly to look after contrabands, and organize negro regiments; but his real object seems to have been to make political speeches to the soldiers, and to require of them unequivocal recognition of the political policy of the Administration.

About the time when he first made his appearance in the army of the West, the celebrated "anti-copperhead resolutions" began to pour forth from the army, deluging the whole North, with the most blood-thirsty denunciations and threats against a majority of the people at home, threatening that as soon as the army should return they would exterminate the "copperheads" (meaning Democrats,) with fire and sword. These epistles and *resolves*, it is believed were instigated by this Adjutant General THOMAS, who set that ball in motion to effect the Northern elections. But, although many of those bloodthirsty resolves were represented to have been passed by a unanimous vote in most instances, yet it is in proof, and as soon as we dare publish a long array of private correspondence, and not subject good brave soldiers to the severe punishments that would follow their exposure, we shall give to the world evidence that in most cases the soldiers either silently permitted those diabolical resolutions to pass, without protest (for fear of the consequences) or by their silence were claimed as having assented.

HOW THE SOLDIERS VIEW IT.

Below we give an extract from a letter written by a member of the 12th Wisconsin Infantry to his brother in the Legislature of 1863, which was published in the Wisconsin *Patriot*.

"Some of our officers got together last Sunday and passed a number of resolutions, which I presume you have seen before this, for they were sent to the *State Journal** to be published. * * * Some of the resolutions were voted on by some of the soldiers, and some were strongly opposed to them, but they have since come to consider on the political object of the resolutions, and that the real purpose is to keep them longer a fighting for the negro, without one ray of hope for the Union, and all to give certain officers a certain share of the spoils of cotton and other trophies, and from a pretty general conversation with the boys of the regiment, I believed that if called upon to-day to vote on those resolutions, that not five of the rank and file in the whole regiment would vote for them, though from the reign of terror which prevails over the soldier who is not much better in the eyes of the officers than a nigger, they would remain passive, as many of them do, when called upon by shoulder straps to aid political schemes or cotton forays.

"We are all under ban here, but if the soldiers—the 'boys,' I mean, dared to speak their honest sentiments, there would be a hot row in camp. * * I would not dare to speak my sentiments here, as I now write them to you, for if I were not immediately locked up and punished by some picked guard, I should be subject to extra-hazardous services, and in one way or another be made to pay dearly for writing what I *know* to be true," &c.

We have hundreds of such articles before us, but this must suffice as a sample, which demonstrates the fact that the army is being used to propogate political ideas and dogmas.

After Adjutant General THOMAS had succeeded in getting a series of threatening resolutions issued from each camp, he took to harranguing the soldiers, to get expressions from them direct in favor of the political policy of the Administration, punishing such as refused to hurra for such measures. Startle not, reader, for we shall let

GEN. THOMAS SPEAK FOR HIMSELF.

After Adjutant General THOMAS returned to Washington, he rendered his own account in his own way, of his acts in the West:

"I was compelled to speak to the troops, [who "compelled" him, except it was the President, his superior?] along the route—speaking in one day some seven or eight times. During my tour I met an Irish Regiment, the 90th Illinois, from Chicago—men who read the Chicago *Times*. After talking to them awhile,

---

*This paper had published the resolutions as having been unanimously passed.

18

I proposed three cheers for the President of the United States. *These were given heartily.* Three cheers were then proposed *for the settled policy of the United States,* [the Administration] *in regard to negroes.* This was met by cries of 'No!' 'No!'

"The Colonel was absent, and the Lieut. Colonel was in command. I enquired what such conduct meant? The Lieut. Colonel endeavored to excuse the men by saying that they had no opportunity to look over the matter. I replied 'you are not telling the truth, sir! I know that they have been discussing this question for a week past. I know the fact if you do not.' The officer was coniderably mortified. [It is well for Adjutant Gen. Thomas that he did not provoke that kind of "mortification" which an Old Hickory would have manifested.]

"I ordered those who were opposed to this policy of the government, to step forward, and said *I knew the regiment had seen considerble service and fought well!* but I also knew there was but little discipline observed among them —*that I wanted a distinct recognition of this doctrine—that was the first with me. Several stepped forward. They were instantly seized and sent to the guard-house.*

"I then left the regiment, telling them I would give them a week to consider what they would do. At the next Station I met the Col. of the regiment, who begged that I would leave the matter in his hands, and he would see that the men were taught the duty of soldiers. I complied with the request."

Such is the confession (we use the term in its legitimate sense) of this political avant courier—this man, who supported the traitor BRECKINRIDGE on the platform that the constitution carried slavery everywhere, and protected it. This is the man who attempted to abolitionize the army, and what he lacked in offers of promotion he made up in "military discipline," threats and punishment.

Now, let us enquire what right has the Administration to own and control the private opinions of those who fight the battles of the country? This political Ajax admits they fought well—no complaint ever rested against them for any dereliction of military duty—but they were "instantly seized and placed in the guard house," and for what? Because they could not forswear their manhood—deny their political principles—as sacred to them as their religion, and acknowledge what they believed to be a lie.

Who will have the courage to face posterity in the mirror of history, and say this was right? If soldiers "fight well" and obey all the lawful military commands of their superiors, in the name of God and their country, what more ought to be required of them? But no, this will not do. The Administration has a purpose in view. No one can be so foolish and illogical as to believe the "powers" care a fig for the private opinions of soldiers so long as they do not come in contact with the purpose of said "powers." But, suppose we are correct in awarding motives of despotic dominion in the radical leaders, whould we not look for just such measures? A despotism could not be consummated without the aid of the army. That army must be moulded to the very purpose in view. All conservatism must be forced out of the army by the pressure of *discipline,* so that when the time for action shall come, that army can be relied on, in every emergency. If it should become necessary to march into the North and murder the "copperheads" (the Democrats) the soldiers must be first prepared for it. Hence the "anti-copperhead resolutions," committing the army by threats to this very thing. Hence, the bloodthirsty epistles of Secretary STANTON to the Cooper Institute meeting, and the bloodthirsty speeches of Senators WILSON, LANE, and others—hence, the bloodthirsty and inflammatory articles in the radical press.

GEN. HALLECK AS A TUTOR.

The Republicans had a meeting in Union Square, in April, 1863. A great number of Abolition celebrities were there, who threw out bloody threats and hints. Gen. HALLECK was not present, but he wrote a letter from which we seclect the following Robesperrian threat:

"We have already made immense progress in this war—a greater progress than was ever before made under similar circumstances. Our armies are still advancing, and if sustained by the voice of the patriotic millions at home, they will ere long crush the rebellion in the south, *and then place their heels upon the heads of sneeking traitors in the North.*

"Very respectfully, your ob't serv't
"W. H. HALLECK, General-in-Chief."

Not content with uttering this bloodthirsty threat against two millions of voters in the north, as Mr HALLECK, but he adds the weight of his high office, as "General-in-Chief."

OTHER SENTIMENTS AND THREATS.

Mr. SEWARD also wrote a letter in which he remarked, in his most grandiloquent eloquence:

"Let us ask each other no questions about how the nation shall govern itself," or "who shall preside in its councils in the great future," &c.

This is the same syren song, under the narcotic and "*\piatic*" influence of which Greece, Rome and Athens went to sleep, to wake no more.

Mr. CHASE in speaking of slavery to the same meeting said:

"What matter now how it dies? Whether as a consequnce or as an *object* of the war—what matter."

Mr. Post Master General BLAIR also spoke at that meeting, and illustrated the Administration's new definition of "treason;" spoke of the

"Creatures in the Free States * * spared by the clemency of the Administration, that call themselves Democrats. *But these men in the North are only so many men on gibbets.*"

THE CASE OF LIEUT. EDGERLEY.

As exhibiting further the object of the Administration to compel the army through fear of punishment to succumb to the political schemes and purposes of the Administration, we place before the reader the following extract from

"SPECIAL ORDER NO. 119.

"WAR DEPARTMENT, ADJUTANT GENERAL'S OFFICE,
WASHINGTON, March 13, 1863.

"33. By direction of the President, the following officers are hereby dismissed the service of the United States. * * Lieut. A. G. Edgerly, 4th New Hampshire Volunteers, *for circula'ing Copperhead tickets*, and doing all in his power to promote the rebel cause [meaning the Democratic ticket] in his state.

"By order of the Secretary of War.
"L. THOMAS, Adjutant General.
"To the Governor of New Hampshire."

We hardly know how to command language adequate to express the official turpitude of this transaction. Here, the only charge that was brought again t the Lieutenant, was voting the Democratic ticket. For that is just what it amounts to. It is the first time in the history of this or any other government, that the vile nicknames of party have been used in official orders emanating from the high officers of Government. It shows the revolutionary spirit of those in power, and the act itself, demonstrates beyond a cavail, that it is the intention of the "powers that be" to use what power they have to compel the army to become the agent, when the decisive hour shall arrive, to crush out the last remnant of liberty, and to throw a wall of bayonets around the throne of despotism. If this is not the legitimate meaning, aim and purpose of such acts as we have here recorded, then we confess to a lamentable incapacity to read men's intentions by the light of their conduct.

THE CONSCRIPTION BILL.

This act by the last Congress was an unnecessary violation of the Constitution, for the same objects could have been obtained strictly in occordance with the Constitution. But that would not suit the purposes of despotism. The Constitution of the United States clearly places the militia under the control of the states, until called into actual service by the United States.

Section 2, of Art. II., of the Constitution of the United States, declares that the President shall be

"Commander-in-Chief of the army and navy of the United States, and of the militia of the several *States, when called into the actual service* of the United States."

By this it would seem that the militia belongs to the States, and is exclusively under State control, until actually called into the service of the United States.

Subdivisions 14 and 15 of Sec. 8, Art. I., also make similar provisions.

But, the Conscription Act ignores the constitution entirely, (so decided by the Supreme Court of Pennsylvania) because it calls upon the people, and enrols them as the *United States* militia, without reference to the States. This is just what one would expect from those who intended to establish a despotism, for if the soldiers were called for by the mode prescribed in the fundamental law, and it turned out that they were actually being used for despotic purposes, the States might refuse to grant them, and thus the purposes of despotism might be thwarted. But as it is—if the conscription act can be fully carried out, troops may be obtained to any number without asking their consent of the States.

When the conscription bill was on its passage in the House of Representatives—

"Mr. Wickliffe offered an amendment that the men thus called into service shall be by the Governors of the States organized into companies and regiments, with officers to command them, appointed by the authority of each State, according to the provisions of the constitution of the United States Rejected, ayes 55, noes 103."

This clearly demonstrates the real purpose of the radicals—to place the militia of the States at the unlimited command of the President, for any and whatever purposes he chooses to employ them.

We have already alluded to the despotic power by which a Democratic convention was broken up in Kentucky—how the Kentucky election was controlled under martial law—how the sword controlled the elections in Maryland, Delaware, Missouri, &c. These outrages were thus avowed and excused by the organ of Gov. ANDREW and CHAS, SUMNER:

"The Thirty-eighth Congress is about to assemble. The Senate will have a large administration majority, and the House one sufficiently large to elect the caucus nomination for Speaker, Clerk, and other officers. We say this without having carefully examined the tables, for we assume that the administration would not have resorted to its somewhat *extraordinary means* of carrying elections in the Border States, unless it had been sure that these means, successfully used, would give it a working majority. We do not find fault with the machinery used to carry Maryland and Delaware. Having nearly lost the control of the House by its blunders in the conduct of the war from March, 1861, to the fall of 1862, the administration owed it to the country to recover that control *somehow*. To recover it *regularly* was impossible; so irregularity had to be resorted to. Popular institutions will not suffer, for the copperhead element will have a much larger number of members in both branches than it is entitled to by its popular vote. Ohio, with its ninety thousand Republican majority, will be represented by five Republicans and a dozen or more copperheads.— It is fitting that this misrepresentation of popular sentiment in the great state of the West should be offset, if necessary, by a loyal delegation from Maryland and Delaware, *won even at the expense of military interference*. If laws are silent amid the clank of arms, we must take care that the aggregate public opinion of the country obtains recognition, *somehow or other*." —*Boston Commonwealth*.

That is a pretty *bold* defense of villainy.— The *Commonwealth* is an organ of the Gov. ANDREW negro school of politics, and he openly advocates the use of the *bayonet* against the *ballot*. We suppose those who advocate giving Mr. LINCOLN "all the men and all the money he wants," will be highly delighted with this use made of them!

Such despotic acts committed by any other party would be denounced with the most vehement howlings, but being committed by the "loyal" party, they are considered all right, and this reminds us of the answer of the English Bishop to the question:

"Pray, my lord, is it not difficult to trace the exact line between orthodoxy and heterodoxy?"

To which the more honest than discreet divine replied:

"Not at all, nothing can be more simple. Orthodoxy is my doxy, and heterodoxy is any other man's doxy'."

This illustrates the intolerant arrogance of Abolitionism:

WHAT SENATOR WILSON SAID.

In a speech he made during the Maine canvass at Brunswick in that state, just preceding the election, he declared:

"We shall subjugate the rebel states; that's the word—subjugation! And *we will conquer the rebellion in New York. Forty-five regiments are there to do it*, every soldier of which, as I told you before, would sooner shoot a copperhead than a rebel soldier."

A LEAF FROM HISTORY.

The following extracts are from Allison's History of Europe, vol. 1, chap. 14, should be read to be appreciated, by the light of the VALLANDIGHAM trial, and such diatribes as we have quoted from Senators WILSON, LANE, HALLECK, &c.:

"In pursuance of these views, St. Just made a labored report to the general police of the commonwealth, in which 'recapitulated all the stories of conspiracies against the Republic, explaining them as efforts of every species of vice against the austere rule of the people, and concluding with holding out the the necessity *of the government striking without intermission till it had cut off all those whose corruption opposed itself to the establishment of virtue*. "The foundation of all great institutions," said he, "is terror. Where would now have been an indulgent Republic? We have opposed the sword to the sword, and its power is in consequence established. It has emerged from the storm, and its origin is like that of the earth out of the confusion of chaos, and of man who weeps in the hour of nativity." As a consequence of these principles, he proposed a general measure of proscription against all the nobles, as the irreconcilable opponents of the Revolution: "You will never," said he, "satisfy the enemies of the people till you have re-established tyranny in all its horrors. They can never be at peace with you; you do not speak the same language; you will never understand each other. *Banish them* by an inexorable law; the universe may receive them, *and the public safety is our justification*." He then proposed a decree which banished all the ex-nobles, all *strangers* from

Paris, the fortified towns, and seaports of France; and declared *hors la loi* whoever did not yield obedience in ten hours to the order. It was received with applause by the convention, and passed, as all the decrees of government at that time, by acclamation. * * *

"The trial of these unhappy captives was as brief as during the massacres in the prisons "Did you know of the conspiracy of the prisons Dorival?" "No." "I expected no other answer, "Are you not an ex-noble?" "Yes," To a third: "Are you not a priest?" "Yes, but I have taken the oath." "You have no right to speak; be silent." "Were you not architect to Madame?" "Yes, but I was disgraced in 1788." "Had you not a father-in-law in the Luxembourg?" "Yes." Such were the questions which constituted the sole trial of numerous accused; no witnesses were called; their condemnations were pronounced almost as rapidly as their names were called; the law of the 22d Prairial had dispensed with the necessity of taking any evidence, when the court were convinced by moral presumptions. The endictments were thrown off by hundreds at once, and the name of the individual merely filled in; the judgments were printed with equal rapidity, in a room adjoining the court, and several thousand copies circulated through Paris by little urchins, exclaiming, amid weeping and distracted crowds, "Here are the names of those who have gained prizes in the lottery of the holy guillotine."— The accused were executed at leaving the court, or, at least, on the following morning.

"Since the law of the 22d Prairal had been passed, the heads fell at the rate of fifty or sixty a day. "This is well," said Fouquier Tinville; "but we must get on more rapidly in the next decade; four hundred and fifty is the very least that must then be served up." To facilitate this immense increase, spies were sent into the prisons in order to extract from the unhappy wretches their secrets, and designate to the public accuser those who might first be selected. These infamous wretches soon became the terror of the captives. They were enclosed as suspected persons, but their real mission was soon apparent from their insolence their consequential airs, the preference shown them by the jailers, their orgies at the doors of the cells with the agents of the police. They were caressed, implored by the trembling prisoners, and received whatever little sums they had been able to secrete about their persons, to keep their names out of the black list; but in vain. The names of such as they chose to denounce were made up in a list called, in the prisons, "The Evening Journal," and the public chariots sent at nightfall to convey them to the Conciergerrie preparatory to their trial on the following morning.

Says SALLUST,

"All bad actions spring from good beginnings,"

and while the objects as originally declared by Congress, for the prosecution of this war, challenged the respect of every patriot in the land, the "bad actions" that have sprung from the "good beginning" may well turn our attention to the bloody 14th chapter in Allison's History.

GOV. SEYMOUR ON THE ROTTEN BOROUGH SYSTEM.

We had intended to offer some suggestions on the President's last message and proclamation, but Gov. SEYMOUR has said all that is necessary much better than we could say it. We therefore copy that portion of his message devoted to national affairs:

VIEWS OF GOV. HORATIO SEYMOUR.

Expressed in his Annual Message to the Legislature of New York, delivered January 5th, 1864.

The past year has been crowded with events, both civil and military, of the greatest interest. The establishment of a national bank system; the issue of the enormous amounts of paper money, which is made a legal tender; the adoption of a law for coerced military service; the act indemnifying and shielding officials charged with offences against the persons and property of citizens; the suspension of the writ of *habeas corpus* in peaceful and loyal communities, are measures which go far towards destroying the rights of States and centralizing all power at the national capital.

The executive and military officials assume to declare martial law and to arrest citizens where the courts are in undisturbed operation, to try them by military tribunals, and to impose punishments unknown to the customs of our country; to administer arbitrary test oaths; to interfere with the freedom of the press and with State and local elections by military decrees and the display of armed power.

The President claims the right to do acts beyond the civil jurisdiction, and beyond the legislative power of Congress, by virtue of his position as Commander-in-Chief. In this assumption he is sustained by both branches of Congress, and by a large share of the people of the country. The proceedings of Congress and the action of the Executive and military officials have wrought a revolution. The civil power, the laws of States and the decisions of the Judiciary have been made subordinate to military authority. At this time, then, we are living under a military government, which claims that its highest prerogatives spring from martial law and military necessities. These acts have been sustained by the army and acquiesced in by the people. This revolution, if permanently accepted, must be recognized as an overthrow of established and cherished principles of government. Hereafter it will force itself upon the attention of the American people, who will then see and feel its nature and results. To their decision in calmer hours this subject must be referred.

If these measures of military, political and financial consolidation break down, their failure will show the wisdom of the constitution in withholding from the general government powers it cannot exercise wisely and well; and it will establish the rights of States upon a basis firm and undisputed, and will make the general government strong by confining it to one jurisdiction. In the end we shall return to principles from which we have been drifting.

"In the meanwhile, we are threatened with other calamities which demand our immediate attention. The rights of the people and the restraints of the constitution can be reasserted whenever the public shall demand their restoration, but it is believed the power of the popular voice will rescue us from the calamities of national bankruptcy or national ruin, when these have befallen us. The progress of events has brought us to a point where we are compelled to contemplate these calamities and to consider how they may be averted.

"While it is a duty to state plainly my views about public affairs, I shall do so in no spirit of controversy or of disrespect for the opinions of those who differ from me. The questions of of the day are beyond the grasp of any mind to comprehend in their influence or results. We see them from different stand-points, and we reach conflicting conclusions. None but the ignorant, the bigoted, or the designing will make these differences of views occasions for reproach or contumely. The times demand outspoken discussions. When we see good and earnest men, under the influence of some absorbing sentiment, overlooking the great principles of good government, trampling upon usages and procedures which have grown up with the history of liberty in the civilized world, we are warned that none of us can claim to be above the influence of passions or of prejudices. While I do not agree with those upon the one hand who insist upon an unconditional peace, or with those, upon the other extreme, who would use only unqualified force in putting down this rebellion, I demand for them, what I ask for those who concur in the views which I present, a fair, dispassionate, and respectful hearing. Let not the perils of our country be increased by bigotry, by partizan passions, or by an unwillingness to allow opinions to be uttered in forms and modes in accordance with the usages of our people and the spirit of our laws.

Since the outset of the war the national administration has asked for nearly two millions of men. To keep up our armies, the average annual calls have been more than 400,000 men.

In addition to the loss of life, there has been a diversion of labor from peaceful productive occupations to war, which destroys the accumulated wealth of the country.

The Secretary of the Treasury states the national debt will be sixteen hundred millions in July next. This does not include unascertained demands. In our former wars these latent claims have nearly doubled the liabilities supposed to exist during their progress. If the war should cease to-day, the national indebtedness could not fall short of two thousand millions of dollars. To this must be added the aggregate of State, county and town obligations. The cost of carrying on the war hereafter will be increased by larger pay to our soldiers, by interest accounts, by enhanced prices of provisions, transportation and material, growing out of a depreciated currency. The proposed issue of three hundred millions of paper money under the national banking scheme, in addition to the vast sum now put out by government, will add to the inflation of prices.

Conflicting views are held as to the amount of indebtedness which would cause national bankruptcy, and with regard to the length of time the war can go on without causing national ruin. All agree in this: that there is an amount of indebtedness which would overwhelm us with bankruptcy; that there is a duration of war which would bring upon us national ruin. The problem with which we have to grapple is: How can we bring this to a conclusion before such disasters overwhelm us? Those perils must be confronted

Two antagonistic theories are now before the American people for bringing to an end the destructive contest in which we are engaged. The first is that contained in the resolution adopted by Congress and approved by the President at an early day, and upon the faith of which the people of this country, without distinction of party, have furnished more than one million of men to our armies, and vast contributions to the treasure of our country.

This resolution consecrated the energies of war and the policy of the government to the restoration of the Union, the support of our constitution. It was a solemn appeal to the civilized world that the objects thus clearly set forth justify a war which not only concerned the American people, but which also disturbed the commerce and industry of all nations.

The opposite theory prevents the return of the revolted States upon the condition of laying down their arms; it denies them a political existence which enables them to come back upon any terms; it holds that States in the revolted section of the country must be "re-established;" that the States hereafter made may or may not hold the names or boundaries of the States thus destroyed, although "it is suggested as not improper" that these names and boundaries, &c., shall be maintained.

The war, therefore, is not to be brought to an end by the submission of these States to the constitution and their return to the Union, but it must be prolonged until the South is subjugated to the acceptance, not of its duties under the constitution, but of such terms as may be dictated. Until States are thus "re-established" it is held that there are no political organizations which can bring back the people to their allegiance; that if the nine States spoken of lay down their arms, and should return to the performance of their duties, they would not be recognized nor received. This theory designs a sweeping revolution in the section of our country now in rebellion, and the creation of a new political system by virtue of executive decrees.

Is this calculated to stop the waste of blood

and treasure? If the South is revolutionized, its property devastated, its industry broken up and destroyed, will this benefit the North?

Those who urge the restoration of the Union and the preservation of our constitution contend that, in addition to upholding our armies and our navies, every measure of wise statesmanship and conciliatory policy shall be adopted to bring this war to a successful close.

Only the ends for which this war was begun should be sought; because they are the most easily attained, most beneficial when gained, and in their support the most varied, the most enlarged, and the most patriotic influences can be exerted.

On the other hand, it is insisted that the war shall be prolonged by waging it for purposes beyond those avowed at the outset, and by making demands which will excite a desperate resistance. A demand is made that the people of the South shall swear to abide by a proclamation put forth with reluctance, and which is objected to by a large share of northern people as unwise and unjust, as it makes no distinction between the guilty and the innocent.— They are to take an oath to which no reputable citizen of the North of any party will subscribe; that they will uphold any future proclamations relating to slavery. They are to submit themselves to uttered and unuttered opinions and decrees. No longer regarding the war as directed against armed rebellion, it is to be waged against people, property and local institutions! It is held that the whole population within the limits of certain States are stripped of all political rights until they are purged by Presidential clemency.

The disorganization and destruction of the South are not to save us from the cost of war. The plan for the future government of the seceded States demands the maintenance of armies and a continued drain upon the persons and property of our people. Whenever one-tenth of the voters of either of these States shall submit themselves to the conditions imposed, they may form new governments with new or old names and boundaries. This inconsiderable minority is to be supported in the exercise of power by the arms and treasure of the North. There will be no motives on their part to draw the remaining population into the support of the governments thus created.— There will be every inducement of power, of gain, and of ambition, to perpetuate the condition of affairs so favorable to individual purposes. It will also be for the interest of the national administration to continue this system of government, so utterly at variance with a representative policy. Is not this the same mistaken theory upon which other nations have tried to govern their dependencies? Has complete subjugation for centuries produced by the quiet, the obedience to law, the order, the security to life and property, the kindly feelings or the mutual contributions to prosperity which belong to real peace?

Governments thus formed would represent not the interest of their citizens but the wills and interests of the power that creates and sustains them. The nine States thus controlled would balance in the House of Representatives in the choice of President, and at all times in the Senate. New York, Pennsylvania, Ohio, Illinois, Indiana, Massachusetts, Missouri, Kentucky, and Wisconsin, with a united population of 16,533,383, which is more than one-half of that of our whole country. The one-tenth who would accept the proclamation for the price of power would not only govern the States made by Executive decrees, but they would also govern the North. While the plan is harsh to the body of the Southern people, it is still more unjust towards the North. Fourteen hundred men in Florida would balance in the Senate of the United States the power of New York. Less than 70,000 voters in the nine States named in the President's proclamation would wield a power sufficient to weigh down that of the nine most populous States in the Union.

We would thus have, with the nominal States of Eastern and Western Virginia, a system of rotten boroughs which would govern the Union and destroy the representative nature of our government. This, in connection with existing inequalities in State Representation, would be a dangerous invasion of the rights of a majority of the American people. It would enable an administration to perpetuate its power.

It it a fact full of significance that every measure to convert the war against armed rebellion into one against private property and personal rights at the South, has been accompanied by claims to exercise military power in the loyal States of the North.

The proclamation of emancipation at the South, and the suspension of the writ of *habeas corpus* at the North; the confiscation of private property in the seceding States, and the arbitrary arrests, imprisonments, and banishment of the citizens of loyal States; the claim to destroy political organizations at the South, and the armed interference by government in local elections have been cotemporaneous events.

These acts at first were justified upon the ground that they were necessary to save the national existence. We now find that new and more extreme claims to arbitrary power are put forth when it is declared that the strength of the rebellion is broken, and that our armies are about to trample out every vestige of its incendiary fires. More prerogatives are asserted in the hour of triumph than were claimed as a necessity in days of disaster and of danger.

The doctrine of southern disorganization and revolution is a doctrine of national bankruptcy and of national ruin; it is a measure for lasting military despotism over one third of our country, which will be the basis for military despotism over the whole land. It does not contemplate the return of our soldiers to their families, or relief from the cost and sacrifices of war. It will make an enduring drain upon our homes, and impose crushing burthens upon our labor and industry. It will open a wide and lasting field for speculation and fraud. It tends to perpetuate power by making and unmaking States, as the interests of factions may dictate. It will be a source of internal disorder and disquietude, and national weakness in our external relations. It will give dangerous allies to invaders of our soil.

If this war is to make a social revolution and structural changes in great states, we have seen only its beginning. Such changes are the work of time. If they are to be made by military power, it must be exerted through long periods. Whether white or black troops are used, the diversion from labor and the cost of war will be equally prolonged, and we have just entered upon a course of certain cost and uncertain results. No such changes as are now urged have ever, in the world's history, been without struggles lasting through more than one generation of men.

What has government accomplished in the territories wrested from rebellion by the valor of our armies? Has it pacified them? Has it revived the arts of peace? Has quiet and confidence been restored? Is commerce renewed? Are they not held as they were conquered, at the expense of northern blood and treasure? Are not our armies wasted by holding under armed control those who, under a wise and generous spirit, would have been friends? The spirit which prompts the harsh measure of subjugation has driven off many in the border states, who, at the crisis of our country's fate, broke away from their ancient sympathies with the seceding states and clung to the Union. States which, by the elections of the people, ranged themselves upon the side of the constitution, are not allowed the free exercise of the elective franchise. In some quarters discontent has been increased; in no place has the wisdom of government gained us allies.

There is but one course which will save us from national ruin. We must adhere to the solemn pledges made by our government at the outset of the war.

We must seek to restore the Union and to uphold the Constitution. To this end, while we beat down armed rebellion, we must use every influence of wise statesmanship to bring back the states which now reject their constitutional obligations. We must hold forth every honorable inducement to the people of the South to assume again the rights and duties of American citizenship.

We have reached that point in the progress of the war, for which we all have struggled and all have put forth united exertions. Our armies and navies have won signal victories; they have done their part with courage, skill and success. By the usage of the civilized world, statesmanship must now exert its influence. If our cause fails, in the judgment of the world, it will be charged to the lack of wisdom in the Cabinet, and not to the want of bravery or patriotism in the army. The great object of victories is to bring back peace; we can now with dignity and magnanimity proclaim to the world our wish that states, which have long been identified with our history, should resume their positions in the Union. We now stand before the world a great and successful military power. No one can foresee the latent victories or defeats which lie in our course if force and force alone is to be exerted. The past has taught us the certain cost of war and the uncertainties of its results.

In this contest belligerent rights are necessarily conceded to the South. The usages of international warfare are practiced in the recognition of flags and the exchanges of prisoners. Is it wise to put off the end of the war and thereby continue a recognition which tends to familiarize the public mind in our own country, and in the world at large with the idea that we are disunited into two distinct nationalities? A needlessly protracted war becomes disunion.

Wise statesmanship can now bring this war to a close, upon the terms solemnly avowed at the outset of the contest. Good faith to the public creditors; to all classes of citizens of our country; to the world, demands that this be done.

The triumph won by the soldiers in the field should be followed up and secured by the peace-making policy of the statesmen of the Cabinet. In no other way can we save our Union.

The fearful struggle which has taught the North and the South the courage, the endurance and the resources of our people, have made a basis of mutual respect upon which a generous and magnanimous policy can build lasting relationships of union, intercourse and fraternal regard. If our course is to be shaped by narrow and vindictive passions, by venal purposes, or by partisan objects, then a patriotic people have poured out their blood and treasure in vain and the future is full of disaster and ruin.

We should seek not the disorganization, but the pacification of that section of our country devastated by civil war.

In this hour of triumph appeals should be made to States, which are identified with the growth and greatness of our country, and with some of which are associated the patriotic memories of our revolutionary struggle. Every generous mind revolts at the thought of destroying all those memories that cling about the better days of the Republic, that are connected with the sacrifices of the men who have made our history glorious by their services in the Cabinet, in the forum, and in the field.

The victories which have given our government its present commanding position were won by men who rallied around and fought beneath the folds of a flag whose stars represent each State in our Union. If we strike out of existence a single State, we make that flag a falsehood. When we extinguish the name of any one of the original thirteen States, we dishonor the historic stripes of our national banner. Let the treasonable task of defacing our flag be left to those who war upon our government, and who would destroy the unity of our country.

Faith in our armies and to our citizens demands that we keep sacred the solemn pledge made to our people and to the civilized world when we engaged in this bloody war, "that it was not waged in any spirit of oppression, or for any purpose of conquest or subjugation, or purpose of overthrowing or interfering with the rights of established institutions in those states, but to defend and maintain the supremacy of the Constitution, and to preserve the Union with all the dignity, equality, and rights of the several states unimpaired; and that as soon as these objects are accomplished the war ought to cease." HORATIO SEYMOUR.

A FLEXIBLE PLATFORM.

The following platform (says the *Corydon Democrat*) we have arranged to suit all parties. The first column is the Secession platform; the second is the Abolition platform; and the whole read together is the Democratic platform. The platform is like the Union—as a whole, it is Democratic; but divided, one-half is Secession and the other Abolition:

Hurrah for	The Old Union
Secession	Is a curse
We fight for	The Constitution
The Confederacy	Is a league with hell
We love	Free Speech
The rebellion	Is treason
We glory in	A free press
Separation	Will not be tolerated
We fight not for	The negro's freedom
Reconstruction	Must be obtained
We must succeed	At every hazard
The Union	We love
We love not	The negro
We never said	Let the Union slide
We want	The Union as it was
Foreign invention	Is played out
We cherish	The old flag
The stars and bars	Is a flaunting lie
We venerate	The *habeas corpus*
Southern Chivalry	Is hateful
Death to	Jeff. Davis
Abe Lincoln	Isn't the government
Down with	Mob law
Law and order	Shall triumph

THE PURSE AND THE SWORD.

The chief objection of PATRICK HENRY to the ratification of the Constitution, was what he feared would be the yielding of the purse and sword to the President. In a speech in the Virginia Convention he thus replied to a member who attempted to show that the President could never obtain control of the purse and sword under our constitution:

"Let him tell me candidly, where and when did freemen exist when the purse and the sword were given up from the people? Unless a miracle in human affairs interposed, no nation ever retained its liberty after the loss of the purse and the sword. Can you prove by any argumentative deduction that it is possible to be safe without one of them? If you give them up, you are gone."—[*See Elliott's Debates*.

Mr. CLAY, in a debate in the Senate, said:

"The two most important powers of civil government are those of the purse and the sword. If they are seperate, and exercised by different responsibe Departments, civil liberty is safe, but if they are united in the hands of one individual, they are gone."

FREE SPEECH ABOLISHED.

We have seen, as another link in the chain of despotism now forcing for the people, that free speech is no longer tolerated, except as it may suit the pleasure or whim of the President or some of his appointees.

Senator T. O. HOWE in his celebrated Ripon (Wis.) speech said:

"I reply that if free speech be stifled upon any one subject the *Union is already absolutely and inevitably lost!*"

This is none the less true because Senator HOWE now upholds a dynasty that has stricken down free speech—mobbed and destroyed a free press, and claims the right to annihilate both at pleasure.

PETTY DESPOTISM.

The Abolitionists gave to the Democrats the vile nickname of "Copperheads." Finding that such nickname might be typical of "Liberty," they began to wear badges made of the old copper cent, with the profile of WASHINGTON on one side and the word "Liberty" on the other. This badge had nothing to do with the Southern cause—it represented no idea in connection with it, nor did it manifest the least sympathy for that cause, but the radicals, ever ready to summon an *excuse* for their despotic conduct, chose to *say* that the Copperhead badge was an emblem of "disloyalty." The "Government," as in other small matters, joined in with the low grade of cheap politicians and gave orders to arrest all who should be found wearing one of the liberty heads. The following, as a sample, we clip from the Chicago *Tribune* of April, 1863:

"At Cairo, several wearers of Copperhead badges have been arrested, to be dealt with. It has passed beyond a pleasantry, and those who so mark themselves, *will find that they are marked for examination!*"

The following was telegraphed to the Associated Press:

"CAIRO, April 16, 1863.

"Nine persons were arrested here this evening for wearing the Copperhead badge."

Thus did the head officers of a great and magnanimous nation, professing the Christian faith, and boasting of intelligence, league with the miniature politicians to hunt down all who should wear any device to distinguish them from their vile persecutors.

We may search every lane and alley of history for a parallel of this *small* greatness.

THE EVIDENCES OF APPROACHING DESPOTISM.

When COLUMBUS was on his first voyage to America, his faith in the existence of land to the west of him was confirmed by various floating weeds, logs, &c., and the appearance of birds, for he knew those things could not exclusively exist without land. So, in our voyage towards the unknown coast of the future, we know that despotism of some kind lies in our way, for we have seen so many floating evidences of it. As one of those evidences, we cite the following from the New York *Tribune:*

"In times of war every blow struck at the measures of the Government [the Administration] though designed only to affect a change of Administration, really affords aid and comfort to the enemy."

These extravagant claims of unlimited acquiescence in everything the Administration may do or propose, are sure and certain evidences of approaching despotism, for the claim would not be set up, unless it was thought proper to enforce it. If it be true that any opposition to the measures of the Administration is "aid and comfort to the enemy," then it is treason as defined by the Constitution, and no matter what the President may do or propose, the least opposition is treason. Such a doctrine would land us in the lowest depths of despotism.

Again says the *Tribune:*

"To doubt the infallibilty of the royal or ministerial good judgment [of the President] is to doubt the greatness and glory of the country, and the *smallest dissatisfaction becomes a kind of petty treason.*"

We must be near the rocks and breakers of despotism, when we meet such arguments, floating on the tide of popular madness.

DECLARATION OF INDEPENDENCE REVISED.

The following was prepared by the author for a 4th of July occasion, and is here inserted as the most proper way to present the indictment against the radical policy:

When, in the course of political events, it becomes necessary for the people to dissolve the official bands that have bound them to an unjust, unwise and tyranical Administration, and to assume to change that Administration, a decent respect for the opinions of mankind requires that they should declare the causes which impel them to the separation.

We hold these truths to be self-evident, that all citizens of the loyal states, are, by the fundamental law, free and equal, and endowed by their Creator and the *Magna Charta* with certain inalienable rights, that among these are the liberty of speech, liberty of the press, and the liberty to properly criticise the acts of all public officers. *That to secure these rights,* our Government was instituted, deriving its just powers from the *consent of the governed,* and whenever the administration of this government becomes destructive of these ends, it is the right and the duty of the people to change such Administration, basing their policy on such principles and organizing power in such form, under the fundamental law, as to them shall seem most likely to affect their safety and happiness. Prudence, indeed, will dictate that an honorable Administration in times of great public danger, should not be changed for slight and transient causes, and accordingly our experience hath shown that our people are more disposed to suffer while evils are sufferable than to right themselves by any other than constitutional means. But, when a long train of abuses and usurpations, pursuing invariably the same objects, evince the design to reduce the people under absolute despotism, it is their right—it is their duty—to throw off such Administration, and to provide new guards for their future security. Such has been the patient suffering of this people, and such is now the necessity which constrains them to change the administration.

The history of the present Executive is a history of repeated wrongs, injuries and usurpations, all having a direct tendency to the establishment of an absolute tyranny and despotism over these states; to prove which, let facts be submitted to a candid world.

He has obstructed the administration of justice, by requiring his subordinates—creatures of his own will—to resist, *vi et armis*, the legal mandates of the loyal judiciary.

He has arbitrarily usurped power to subject the liberties of our citizens, who acknowledge full allegiance to our laws, to the whim or ca-

SCRAPS FROM MY SCRAP-BOOK.

price of military tribunals, wholly the offspring of his own choice.

He has forcibly arrested and held in durance vile, judges on the bench, while in the exercise of their loyal and legal functions. [See the case of Judge CONSTABLE.]

He has combined with others to subject us to a jurisdiction foreign to our Constitution, and unknown to our laws, by instructing subalterns, subject to his own pleasure, to create by proclamation a criminal code, in direct antagonism to our laws.

He has created a multitude of new offices, and sent hither swarms of officers, to harrass our people, and eat out their substance.

He has affected to render the military independent of, and superior to, the civil power, in direct violation of the fundamental law.

He has, in innumerable instances, deprived our citizens of the benefit of trial by jury.

He has, arbitrarily, and without excuse suspended that great charter of civil liberty, the Writ of Habeas Corpus, in violation of the Constitution, as solemnly declared by the Supreme Court.

He has endeavored to extinguish state sovereignty, by giving his assent to law obliterating state lines, without the assent of the people, thus striking down the last constitutional safeguard of a free people.

He has practically annulled laws enacted over his own signature, providing against arbitrary arrests and illegal seizures.

He has, for many months, pursued a line of policy which, if not arrested, will alter, fundamentally our form of Government.

He has appointed men to fill the highest offices of trust, responsibility and honor, notoriously incompetent and corrupt, as a remuneration for political services.

He has been, and now is, quartering among the loyal people of the North, large bodies of armed soldiery, without apparent necessity, but as it is believed, to sow the seeds of alarm among the people, to inaugurate a conflict, and to create a pretended necessity for a declaration of martil law, for purposes more safely imagined than described.

He has encouraged unprovoked assaults on defenceless citizens by soldiers, incited by officers amenable alone to his power, by neglecting or refusing to issue his proclamation against such abuses, and failing to bring the offenders to justice.

He has invaded the sanctity of private domicils at the dead and criminal hour of night—dragged forth their occupants, guilty of no crime, as he himself publicly affirms—and then after a mock trial, before a picked military commission, that dare not offend their superiors, transported the victim beyond his civil jurisdiction.

He has endeavored to suppress the liberty of speech, and only failed to suppress the liberty of the press through fear of the dreadful consequences.

He has forced citizens into extradition beyond the limits of their own states, and without the pale of laws to which they owed fealty, without charges or legal trial, to be imprisoned in loathsome dungeons, for pretended offences.

He and his radical advisers have endeavored to mould the popular branch of Congress to their own partizan purposes by a no less dishonorable scheme than a "rotten borough" system, so long the standing reproach to the British crown. This has been done by admitting members chosen by small fractions of the people in the seceded states, under military coercion, after first extorting pledges to give their votes for measures the most radical and destructive.

He and his political confrers have rendered the elective franchise a mockery and the ballot-box a fraud, by counting a pretended army vote, given hundreds of miles beyond their state jurisdictions, managed, controlled and returned by partizan zealots, without legal restraint and beyond the reach of sanitary laws—to set aside the known will of the people.

He has sought to render the military—the joint sacrifice and pride of all parties—a political engine, by discharging from the service of their country, and affecting to dishonor and disgrace good and valiant officers, for no other offense than exercising the elective franchise as they deemed proper for the public weal.

He has subjected loyal citizens to harsh and unusual punishment for no other offense than opinion's sake.

He boldly claims the right to exercise summary authority over the personal liberty of every citizen, in defiance of courts and law; thus assuming an autocratic power that no prince or potentate on any other continent, would dare exercise, to render the tenure of personal freedom alone dependant on his will.

He has also, through a subordinate officer, declared martial law on the eve of an important State election, with no other ostensible object than to control the will of the people by the force of bayonets.

He has sought to intimidate the people in the lawful exercise of their political rights, and to prevent their counselling together, by masssing large bodies of armed troops in line of battle, to overawe a peaceful convention of loyal citizens, convened under the broad ægis of the constitution, to deliberate on matters of great public concern, and to petition for redress of grievances.

He has, in one of these loyal states, dispersed by armed force, a political convention called in the usual and time-honored way, to nominate officers of state, thus wickedly and unlawfully employing the military for partizan purposes.

He has also, by orders and edicts of his subordinates, annulled State laws, and prescribed new and unusual tests for exercising the elective franchise, thus rendering the tenure of office dependent on his pleasure.

He has, by proclamation, established a rotten Borough system by which less than 70,000 persons in nine of the rebel states—and for aught that is known, a large portion of these may be enfranchised negroes,—may control over one-half the entire population of all the states, and that 1,400 persons in Florida may have as much power in one branch of our government as the great state of New York, with three millions of people.

He has done numerous and sundry other unlawful and despotic things, against the peace, the dignity, and the quietude of this sorely oppressed people.

In every stage of these oppressions and usurpations, the people have remonstrated in the most humble terms. Their remonstrances have been answered only by repeated wrongs and injuries.

An administration that is thus marked by every act that may define tyrants, is unfit to manage the affairs of a free people, and should be changed, in a peaceful and lawful manner, as soon as our charter will permit.

Nor have the people—the whole people—been wanting in duty to the Administration and the country. During every stage of oppression and insult, they have poured out their blood and their substance, free as the air of heaven; and notwithstanding nearly three years of war's fiery ordeal, that our adversary hovers as near our hearth-stones as ever before, the people are yet willing to bleed and be taxed, in the hope that the God of Battles will, ere it be too late, ordain a change of rulers, when a more enlightened policy shall infuse confidence and vigor into the war for the maintenance of the most liberal system of government on this planet.

And for this purpose, and to break up the most wicked rebellion that ever reared its hydra head against a parent government, we pledge each to the other, our lives, our fortunes, and our most sacred honor.

CHAPTER XXXIV.

MORE OF THE RULE OF DESPOTISM.

Abolition Schemes to Control Elections...Army Voting... Julius Cæsar the Originator of...Dr. Lieber on...Louis Napoleon and Army Voting...Army Vote for...General Tuttle and Vallandigham...Mr. V. Ahead...N. Y. World thereon...Tricks of the Administration to Saddle their Electioneering Expenses on the People...Governor Salomon of Wisconsin in the role...The Army Weakened ...Soldiers sent home to Vote...Proofs in Connecticut... Proofs in New York, &c...Stanton Boasts of sending more Soldiers than Curtin's majority...The Contractors perform their part...Martial Law in Kentucky to force the Election...How a "loyal" Paper Views it...From Louisville Journal...Statements of Clerk of the Election... How a Congressman was elected by an "overwhelming majority"...Further evidences...The Administration carries Maryland by the Bayonet...Gov. Bradford's Proclamation on the Subject...The Great Frauds Practiced on New York by the Enrollment and Quota process... New York Overdrawn as compared with other States... Frauds in the Pennsylvania and Ohio Elections... Punishing officers for Voting the Democratic Ticket... Cass of Capt. Sells...Officers' Threats to control Elections ...Bribery at Elections...War on the "Copperheads "... Republican Organ Justifies Military Interference in Elections...The Politics of this War...Discharging disabled and dying Soldiers from Office of Sutler for Voting the Democratic Ticket...Abolition claim of "Those who Vote must Fight"...Abolition Roorbacks to Effect Elections...The Union League Machinery...Forney on Their Purposes...Dr. Lieber on Soldiers Voting...Gen. Milroy on "Home Traitors"...John Brough's Appeal from the Ballot to the Bullet...More Threats...New York Independent Boasts of the Infamy, &c.

ABOLITION DESPOTISM AND SCHEMES TO CONTROL ELECTIONS.

The facts and documents now before us bearing on this point, would surfeit the largest folio volume. Our already over-crowded space admonishes us to shear down this matter to its lowest dimensions—barely giving here and there samples of the general whole, without particular reference to chronological dates.

That the Administration while crying "no party," has constantly sought to use the Army and every available means—legitimate and illegitimate—within its power, to perpetuate its reign, no man, not absolutely blinded by partizan zeal, can deny.

ARMY VOTING.

Army voting is not a recent invention. Our New York *World* cotemporary gives LOUIS NAPOLEON BONAPARTE the credit of having discovered the art of Army voting, but we trace the discovery to a more remote date. PLUTARCH, in his life of MARCUS CRASSUS, gives a striking illustration of the truth that history repeats itself in all ages, and in no times more fully than in civil wars. The Administration, in its recent interference in the elections, has but followed, not only LOUIS NAPOLEON, but the tricks and intrigues of JULIUS CÆSAR. In speaking of the intrigues and dissensions that marked the Republic of Rome at the time of the Triumvirate of POMPEY, CÆSAR and CRASSUS, PLUTARCH says:

"On Cæsar's coming from Gaul to the city of Lucca, numbers went to wait upon him, and among the rest Crassus and Pompey. These, in their private conferences, agreed with him *to carry matters with a higher hand and to make themselves absolute in Rome.* For this purpose Cæsar was to remain at the head of his army, and the other two chiefs to divide the rest of the army between them. There was no way, however, to carry their scheme into execution, without suing for another consulship, in which Cæsar was to assist by writing to his friends, *and by sending a number of his soldiers to vote in the election.*"

LOUIS NAPOLEON, following in the lead of CÆSAR, set up what he called "universal suffrage," but which Mr. KINGLAKE called a "snare" to "strangle a nation in a night time with a *plebiscite.*" Dr. LIEBER, (whom Mr. LINCOLN has chosen as the author of his army code) commenting on the fraud of which LOUIS NAPOLEON "strangled a nation in a night time," submits the following forcible conclusions:

"Votes without liberty of the press have no meaning; votes without liberty of press and with a vast standing army itself possessing the right to vote, and considering itself above all law, have a sinister meaning; votes without an unshackled press, with such an army, and with a compact body of officials, whose number with those directly depending upon them or upon Government contracts, amounts to nearly a million, have no meaning whether he who appeals to the people says that he leaves 'the fate of France in the hands of the people' or not."

Substitute the fate of America for the words "the fate of France," and the picture suits our mould to a T.

When LOUIS NAPOLEON had got his "snare to strangle a nation in a night time" fairly set, and had got his army well distributed throughout France, at every poll, it was an easy matter to accomplish the balance of the programme. He then submitted the question to the people—soldiers and all—whether they approved of his breaking his oath, and of the despotism which he proffered in exchange for their Republican Constitution. The vote stood as follows:

The number voting Yes.................................. 7,438,216
The number voting No.................................. 639,737
Annulled votes... 36,820
The number not voting................................. 393,590

No doubt these returns were manipulated by faithful officials, but it was an *object* to show a few votes in the negative, so as to make it *appear* as though the people had voted "freely." And when, soon thereafter NAPOLEON again set the snare which he called "universal suffrage," in submitting the question whether he should assume the royal purple, the *published* returns stood as follows:

Voting Yes... 7,824,189
Voting No... 258,115
Votes declared void.................................... 63,326

Dr. LIEBER, Mr. LINCOLN's martial law giver, from whom the above figures are taken, remarks with commendable sarcasm:

"This is a state of harmony to which people of the Arylican tribe, with all their calmer temper, we venture to say, have never yet attained,"

and yet we have cases of still greater "harmony" in our army voting.

GEN. TUTTLE AND VALLANDIGHAM IN THE ARMY.

We select these two persons as the *extremes,* and give sufficient of the army vote for each to indicate the fact, that no matter how "loyal" and patriotic a candidate might be, if he did not *vote* with the Administration partizans, he stood no more chance than the worst "copperhead." Gen. TUTTLE, the Democratic candidate for Governor of Iowa, stood upon a platform that was the *ne plus ultra* of war and loyalty. It was as strong "war to the knife," and support of the Administration in the conduct of the war, as any Republican ever could ask. No one doubted Gen. T.'s patriotism, for he had "won his spurs" in the field, at the head of the brave Iowa boys, with whom the General was a popular favorite, while Col. STONE, his opponent, was under a cloud, and was neither popular at home or in the army. Such was the standing and character of Gen. TUTTLE. Now, let us take a view of Mr. VALLANDIGHAM's position, as candidate for Governor of Ohio. He was denounced as the "prince of copperheads"—had been seized and banished by the Administration, as one too disloyal to be among loyal people, and every epithet that hate or ingenuity could invent, was heaped upon him. Officers were dismissed the service for speaking in his favor—soldiers were punished in the guard house for voting for him—and yet, after all these disparaging circumstances, he polled more votes, as will be seen below, in proportion to the number cast, than did Gen. TUTTLE, not only in the army, but also on the home vote:

OHIO AND IOWA VOTE.

The following are specimens of each:

OHIO.

Brough, Abolition.		Vallandigham, Dem.
115th (Regiment)	371	25
100th	475	18
114th	460	4
118th	480	180
25th	169	7
62d	272	41
67th	233	29
107th	25	none.
Hospital, Cairo	66	4
Soldiers in Martinsburg	650	70
	3231	387

IOWA.

Stone, Abolition.		Gen. Tuttle, Dem.
37th	520	30
18th	297	6
20th	93	13
4th	294	13
5th	302	12
6th	176	9
7th	559	10
9th	327	5
10th	280	37
14th	238	88
17th	177	49
25th	207	10
21st	84	2
Hospital, Cairo	38	2
Soldiers in St. Louis	482	42
Second Cavalry	571	107
First Battery	54	
	4693	434

Thus, it will be seen, that Mr. V. has 88 more votes than his *proportion*, on the number above given.

The New York *World* thus pertinently refers to this subject.

"That the present administration would not scruple to interfere with the suffrage of the soldiers and use it as an instrument for perpetuating its power, is proved by its unwarrantable interference with the right of suffrage in the states. An administration that cashiered Lieutenant Edgerly, of New Hampshire, for distributing Democratic ballots at his own home, will tolerate no free suffrage in the army much less the free discussion and untrammeled political action without which voting is a fraudulent mockery. An administration that commissions major-generals, and then, instead of assigning them commands, uses them to carry elections in states of which they are not residents, will have no scruples in using the officers and sutlers of the army for similar purposes. Within the lines of the army, where no intelligence circulates but by its permission, where speaking disrespectfully of Government officials is a penal offense, where its control over the pay and comfort of the soldier is complete, and its power of life and death over them is nearly absolute, voting ought, under no circumstances to be allowed, unless accompanied by safeguards against its abuse.

"How easy it is for the administration to control votes in the army without exercising much seeming constraint is proved by the voting of Wisconsin soldiers, when the administration had no strong motive to exert its infuence.

THE TRICKS AND FRAUDS OF THE ADMINISTRATION TO SADDLE THEIR ELECTIONEERING EXPENSES ON THE PEOPLE.

The following appeared under the telegraphic head of

"CAIRO, ILL, Oct. 27, '63.

"A short time before the recent elections a superannuated individual made his appearance at headquarters with a letter from Gov. Saloman, of Wisconsin, saying that he was traveling on the business of the Sanitary Commission, and asking for such assistance as the military could afford him in the prosecution of his philanthropic purposes. While the officers were debating among themselves, the propriety of giving him transportation *at the expense of the government*. they asked him some questions whereupon he acknowledged that he was provided with election tickets for the soldiers of the different states, and on his way to distribute them, as had been arranged previously by parties at home. No doubt other agents of the republican party, traveling und r the guise of Sanitary Commission agents and in other ways have been sent, at the people's expense, among the soldiers to distribute black republican ,ickets and documents."

This speaks for itself, and needs no comment. It is but a *sample*.

THE ARMY WEAKENED—SOLDIERS SENT HOME TO VOTE.

We present below a few specimens of that political game which has cost the nation much of its best blood, and vast treasures, by weakening our armies at a most critical juncture and sending them home to vote the Republican ticket.

The following appeared among the news items of New York, of October 26, 1863:

SCRAPS FROM MY SCRAP-BOOK. 279

"In a period of less than forty-eight hours, more than *five thousand soldiers* have arrived in this city on their way from the Army of the Potomac. Not all these, nor a majority of them are invalids or furloughed on account of disability, but sound, able-bodied men sent home to vote the Republican ticket.

"One party of seventy-five, from different companies, were all Republicans but two, and these two were obliged, before getting leave to come home, to pledge themselves to vote the Republican or so-called Union ticket. Most of these were sound men, and made no secret of the fact that they were sent home to vote. Men not willing to pledge themselves thus could not obtain a furlough."

[From the Hartford Times.]

"The following letter is from a soldier, who when in Hartford, always voted the Republican ticket:

"ARLINGTON HEIGHTS, April 3, 1863.

"DEAR WIFE:—I did not go home with those who went home to vote. I expected to go, but the furloughs were given to a picked crowd, that would pledge themselves to vote for Buckingham. I never want to take any such oath as this, although I think I should vote for Buckingham myself if I had been there; but I could not now at any rate, for I call this a damnably mean game. If I had come, I did'nt mean to let you know of it until I came in and took you by surprise; but this game has turned me, and all the rest of the regiment, too. I think half of the regiment would have come out again if this had not occurred; now, they won't come at any rate; and I don't blame them. You can tell all my Republican friends that I am no more a Republican if they carry on elections in such away as this.

Here is another which appeared in the Hartford *Times:*

BUCKINGHAM LEGION, 20TH REGIMENT C. V.
Camp near Stafford Court House,
April 3, 1863.

Editors Times:—Col. Ross is acting Brigadier General, Col. Wooster is in command of the regiment. To-morrow morning about twenty-five men leave here for Connecticut. All that go are pledged to *vote the Republican ticket.* There are men in the regiment who have done no duty during the last three months. The doctors say they ought to be discharged. These cannot go, and the reason is they will not pledge themselves to vote for Buckingham.

The following is from the Cincinnati *Commerical* (Rep.):

"COLUMBUS, O., Oct. 9, 1863.

"Nearly two thousand soldiers are in the city to-night, from Camp Chase, receiving transportation to their different counties, to enable them to vote on Tuesday next. They are given ten days furlough, and are jubilant over their visit home, shouting lustily for Brough and the Union. They are now besieging Quartermasters Burn's office, determined not to allow the employees to leave until each and all have their tickets."

[From the Troy Press.]

THE PROSCRIPTION OF DEMOCRATS.

"We have in our possession a letter from a friend, a non-commissioned officer in the army of the Potomac, whose word was never questioned in the neighborhood where he lived, stating that he applied for a furlough at the time when so many were being allowed to go home and visit their friends, and the reply was that he could have a furlough *on condition that he would vote the so-called Union ticket,* but as he had always been a Democrat, and was so still, he could not agree to such terms, and therefore *was compelled to remain on duty* while many of his companions had gone home.

"We have also another letter from the army of the Potomac, dated October 8th, which is as follows:

"DEAR PARENT:—It would give me the greatest pleasure to visit you, as some of our boys are taking furloughs for twenty days, which is to give them a chance to vote at the election. But there is a condition upon which these furloughs are given with which I cannot comply. Any one of us that will pledge our vote for Gov. Curtin can have twenty days to visit friends. Father, this I cannot do.— The boys call us, who refuse, foolish, but we think otherwise. They promise to deliver our letters to our friends while they visit theirs."

The shameful act of using one part of the army to vote, and the other—not of the administration school of politics—to fight, is again and again being presented. The New York *Journal of Commerce* says:

"Several thousand more soldiers arrived from Washington Friday. They were pouring through some of the streets from morning to night, making their way to the railroad depots and steamboat landings, where they could take passage home to vote. When asked how many are on the route, they laugh, and say that,

"It's only begun to sprinkle yet, but a smart shower may be looked for on Saturday, Sunday, and Monday."

"Within the last two days from 6,000 to 8,000 reached this city, and it may be inferred from the size of the advance guard, how large an army will be distributed throughout the state by Monday next?"

A Sergeant in BATES' Battery, on his way through Albany boasted he

"Had brought on sixty-nine soldiers—all Republicans—on their way to Utica to vote, and had left every d—d Democrat behind to take charge of the battery and horses."

Mr. STANTON boasted that he had elected Gov. CURTIN, for said he:

"I sent him 15,000 votes more than his majority."

Says the *World:*

"It is pretended that no soldiers are 'brought from the front.' The battle of Chickamauga was lost in order to carry the Ohio election. General Meade was left to be driven into retreat by General Lee in order that the administration might carry the Pennsylvania election. In the face of these glaring facts, it is no wonder that the Abolition journals try to make it appear that nothing is lost to our effective strength in the field by this fresh depletion of the Army of the Potomac to carry the New York election."

THE CONTRACTORS PERFORM THEIR PART.

The following cases in Connecticut, bear their own comments, and are but samples of a large class:

"In Williamantic, some 65 voters having dependent families, were forced to vote the Republican ticket against their will. Yellow ballots were used, and employers stood by the ballot box, watching to see if any 'freemen' dared to disobey their openly proclaimed orders! From 60 to 70 workmen, thus watched, in that place alone voted abolition against their own wishes! One poor old man, not employed in any of the mills, and too infirm for work, voted a white ticket, for the party with whom he had acted for half a century. The malignant abolition wretches could not discharge him because they had not employed him, but the old man had a daughter in one of the mills, whose daily labor was the support of the family. *Her they wreaked their vengeance upon, and discharged her at once!*—and not satisfied with this, they ordered the old man and his family out of the tenement in which they lived! A subscription was set on foot by the democrats to save them from suffering. The names of the free speech men who discharged this inoffensive girl, are Hayden—managers of the 'Smithville Co. Mill.'

"The same infamous proceedings changed some 600 votes in other towns in Windham county, and nearly as many each in New London and Tolland counties. Colored ballots to 'spot' workmen—open proclamation of proscription as the consequence if they dared to vote as their conscience dictated—this, with wholesale bribery and the votes of 3,000 picked and selected soldiers, sent home on a promise to vote abolition, was the way in which the disunion party worked in every county in the State.

"In Colt's Pistol Factory this same tyranny made at least 100 of the democratic workmen vote the abolition ticket.

"In Plymouth, a man having refused the abolition command to vote that ticket, his family in his absence, were turned out of the house, the furniture and bedding thrown out, and a family of negroes put in the house! Legal action will be taken in this case.

"In many towns the abolitionists, aided and encouraged by the 'Loyal Women's League,' have stopped all dealings with Democrats, and pass their former friends and neighbors without recognizing them in the street. Such are the legitimate results of fanaticism.

"A day is coming when these persons will regret this shameful conduct."

MARTIAL LAW IN KENTUCKY—ORDER "NO. 120."

The following is BURNSIDE's order suspending civil law in reference to elections,

just four days prior to the election in that State:

HEADQUARTERS DEPARTMENT OF THE OHIO, }
CINCINNATI, Ohio, July 31, 1863. }
Order No. 120.

Whereas, The state of Kentucky is invaded by a rebel force, with the avowed intention of overawing the judges of elections, of intimidating the loyal voters, keeping them from the polls, and forcing the election of disloyal candidates at the election on the 3d of August; and

Whereas, The military power of the government is the only force that can defeat this attempt, the state of Kentucky is hereby declared under martial law, and all military officers are commanded to aid the constituted authorities of the state in support of the laws and of the purity of suffrage, as defined in the late proclamation of his Excellency, Governor Robinson.

As it is not the intention of the Commanding General to interfere with the proper expression of public opinion, all discretion in the conduct of the election will be as usual in the hands of legally appointed judges at the polls, who will be held strictly responsible *that no disloyal person be allowed to vote,* and to this end the military power is ordered to give them its utmost support.

The civil authority, civil courts, and business will not be suspended by this order. It is for the purpose only of protecting, if necessary, the rights of loyal citizens, and the freedom of election.

By command of Major Gen. Burnside.

LEWIS RICHMOND, A. A. G.

No subsequent fact demonstrated that any such combination as is here referred to existed in the state, or that there was any cause to suppose that such was the case. Of course, an election under such an "edict" was a farce, which the voluminous documents before us amply prove. We have only room for the following.

The following appeared in the *War Eagle* at Columbus, Kentucky, three days before the election. This sheet was published under military control.

"We now warn the people to beware of these traitors, for if they, in defiance to the will of Government, go to the polls and vote for Trimble, or any other man who has not publicly avowed himself as an unconditional Union man, they will hereafter be treated as enemies, and as men deserving on their guilty heads all the punishment which the Government has in reserve for traitors.

"Other persons of lesser magnitude have announced themselves as candidates for the State Senate, and for Representatives in the State Legislature, who are occupying the same position that Wickliffe and Trimble occupy. The people are warned not to vote for such men, as they are enemies, and are running in direct violation of Special Order No. 159, issued from Headquarters, 16th Army Corps, and General Order No. 47, issued by Gen. Asboth, commanding the District of Columbus. We tell the people of the District that their only *safety and protection depends on voting the straight-out Union ticket*. The issue is in your hands, and on your conduct next Monday depends your future peace and protection. When you vote for traitors, you can of course expect no protection from the Federal Government."

[From the Louisville Journal.]

"He who would make use of force to prevent freedom of election is a traitor to all the principles of civil liberty. To accomplish a temporary object, he would invoke a power which will destroy not only the liberties of his fellow-citizens, but eventually his own. The horse in the fable, to wreak his vengeance on the stag, permitted the man to saddle him, and was ridden ever after, till the day of his death. We consider ourselves superior to our English ancestors six hundred years ago; but many men in this age may learn a lesson from the times of Edward the First. "And because elections ought to be free," says a statute of that time, "the king commandeth, upon great forfeiture, that no man, by force of army, nor by malice, or menacing, shall disturb any to make free elections."

A FEW ACTUAL SPECIMENS.

The following is a statement of the polls in Mount Washington, at 9 o'clok a. m.:

"Wickliffe 21, Bramlette 3, Green 21, Samuels 3, Frazier 21, Dawson 3.

"Voting on the Wickliffe ticket was stopped *by military order* at 9 o'clock in the morning. The polls opened at about 8 o'clock in the morning.   ROB'T. HALL, Clerk,"

The following is a true statement of the polls in Mount Washington at the close for dinner, at 11½ o'clock:

"Bramlette, 15; Jacobs, 17; Harlan, 15; Garrard, 16; Samuels, 15; Stephens, 15; Harding, 17; Thompson, 24; Hogland 12.

"P. S.—There were four or five of the above votes cast before the interference of military authority.   R. HALL, Clerk."

The New Albany (Ind.) *Ledger* in its report printed on the afternoon of election day, said:

"Numerous arrests of persons pointed out by the "spotters" at the polls as rebels have been made, the parties arrested being placed in the military prison. Files of soldiers are stationed at all the polls, and we saw several pieces of artillery, with horses hitched and the men at the guns, ready for action at a moments notice.

"In Portland, at 12 o'clock, the vote stood: Bramlette, 30; Wickliffe, 2. The two votes for Wickliffe at this poll were cast before the soldiers arrived.

"The Wickliffe men are overawed, and it is probable but few of them will attempt to vote this afternoon."

19

HOW A CONGRESSMAN WAS "ELECTED BY AN OVERWHELMING MAJORITY."

"PADUCAH, Ky., Aug. 16, 1863.
"To the Editor of the Chicago Times:

"In your paper of the 13th inst. you gave to your readers the oath which the detestable tools of the administration at Washington were wont to cram down the throats of the democrats of Kentucky. Herewith I give you another item that will be of interest to the mighty army of democrats in the free States who read your excellent paper.

"It is now announced, with all Puritan innocence and godlike simplicity, that L. Anderson, Esq., of the 1st Congressional district, is 'elected by an overwhelming majority.' Now, let me show you how this 'overwhelming majority' was attained. At our Precinct, No. 3, we did *not vote at all*. Why? Let the following answer:

"PRECINCT, No. 3, Aug. 3, 1863.
"Be it known that we, the undersigned voters of McCracken county, Ky., did, on this day, appear at our Precinct No. 3 to vote, in accordance with the laws of the Commonwealth, and the proclamation of the Governor thereof, dated July 20, 1863, but that we have been prevented from so voting by reason of the fact that the Judges could not execute the duties of their office in accordance with the laws of the State, and at the same time obey the military orders respecting the manner in which our elections shall be conducted; and, to said military orders, a squad of armed soldiers are here present, to deter the Judges from doing their duty. Therefore, we, the undersigned, voters of McCracken county, declare it to have been our purpose and intention to vote at this time and place the *democratic ticket* headed by Wickliffe for Governor, &c., and that we have been prevented from so doing for the reasons hereinbefore stated.

"(Signed by 35 voters)."

Extract from a letter dated:

BLOOMFIELD, Ky., Aug. 4, 1863.
"Bloomfield is a small town, twelve miles from Bardstown, in the midst of a fine country, where Democrats abound. On Monday morning (election day), Capt. Sea, formerly of Chicago, but now an Indiana Captain of cavalry—an Abolitionist who voted for Lincoln, avowed himself in favor of the emancipation and negro-arming policy of the President, and defines 'loyalty' to be a support of all the President's measures—with a squad of twenty-five soldiers, armed with carbines, sabres, and revolvers, took possession of the polls. He informed the judges that they were under martial law, and would have to conduct the election according to his directions, which he had received from his superiors. He then declared Hon. C. A. Wickliffe a disloyal man, and that no vote should be cast for him. He furnished State, Congressional, and county tickets, which he declared to be 'loyal,' and said that 'loyal men' might vote for them. At a later period he stated that votes of 'loyal men' might be cast for other candidates, provided the judges would *indorse the loyalty of the candidates*, admonishing them, at the same time, that they *would be held responsible for all men voted for;* and that if any of them should hereafter be declared 'disloyal' by the military authorities, *the judges would be punished;* but what the punishment might be he was not authorized to say. The judges, overawed by the military,

being acquainted with only a few of the long list of candidates, and warned of exposure to an undefined military punishment if by chance a disloyal man should be voted for, concluded to receive votes only for the *military ticket*, of which Bramlette, for Governor, was the head. A few Democrats offered to vote for Mr. Wickliffe, but were met with the assurance of the Indiana, Abolition, negro-arming Captain, with his revolver conspicuously displayed, that

"Mr. Wickliffe is a disloyal man, and that in no case shall a vote be cast for him."

"The Democrats then gave up the contest and resigned the polls to the military and the "loyalty." About nine-tenths of this precinct is democratic, and would have so appeared on the poll-books, if we had been allowed to vote; but the military decreed otherwise, and like our beloved brethern, the northern democrats, when they get in a tight place, "we are a law and order people." "But for our forbearance, blood would have been shed," as our northern brethern say when they allow the adolitionists to "spit upon them and rub it in." That is to say, we quietly submitted to have our rights wrested from us, and the soldiers had no occasion to "shed the blood" of so docile a people.

"The whole number of votes cast was *nineteen*—all for the Bramlette ticket. If the democrats had been allowed to vote Mr. Wickliffe's majority would perhaps have been 120 or more The entire "bogus Union" strength was polled, except, perhaps two votes.

"Old men who have been voting for forty and fifty years were yesterday refused the privilege of voting, while mere youths, just out of their minority, freely voted. An aged minister of the Gospel, who has been a legal voter, but not a politician, *for fifty-seven years*, was denied a vote; while a young man, without sufficient intelligence to read his ticket, and *known to be a thief*, voted Bramlette & Co. Men of large wealth and high character, who pay heavy taxes to State and national governments, could not vote, while "squatters" and "sponges" freely voted, who will probably never pay a dime to support the national government, and nothing more than head tax to the state government.

"Thus did the military officer aid the constituted authorities in support of the laws and of the purity of suffrage,' under Gen. Burnside's order proclaiming martial law. Thus did the commander of Indiana troops in Nelson county fulfil his promise, made in flaming capitals, that the people shall 'NOT BE MOLESTED IN ANY WAY,' and shall be protected in their sovereign rights.'

"At Bardstown and other parts of the county the same scene was enacted. The same was done in several other counties heard from. And yet the Louisville *Journal* and *other* abolition papers will claim a brilliant victory achieved.

"At Chaplain, in this county, the judges, supported by a few citizens, 'overawed' a diminutive specimen of a Captain and his squad of men, and voted for Wickliffe, Bramlette securing only 'six' votes, and Wickliffe more than one hundred.   A KENTUCKIAN."

We ask not to be excused for publishing the following entire. It bears its own comment:

GOV. BRADFORD VS. GEN. SCHENCK—THE GUBERNATORIAL PROCLAMATION.

"STATE OF MARYLAND, EXECUTIVE DEPARTMENT, }
"Anapolis, Nov. 2, 1863. }

"*Proclamation by the Governor.*

"To the Citizens of the State, and more especially the Judges of Election:

"A military order issued from the headquarters of the 'Middle Department,' bearing date the 27th ult., printed and circulated, it is said through the State, though never yet published here, and designed to operate on the approaching election, has just been brought to my attention, and is of such a character, and issued under such circumstances, as to demand notice at my hands.

"This order, reciting

"That there are many evil disposed persons now at large in the State of Maryland who have been engaged in rebellion against the lawful government, or have given aid and comfort, or encouragement to others so engaged, or who do not recognize their allegiance to the United States, and who may avail themselves of the indulgence of the authority which tolerates their presence to embarrass the approaching election, or through it to foist enemies of the United States into power,"

proceeds among other things to direct

"all Provost Marshals and other military officers to arrest all such persons found at or hanging about or approaching any poll or place of election, on the 4th of November, 1863, and to report such arrests to headquarters."

"This extraordinary order has not only been issued without any notice to, or consultation with, the constituted authorities of the State, but at a time and under circumstances when the condition of the State and the character of the candidates are such as to preclude the idea that the result of that election can in any way endanger either the safety of the government or the peace of the community.

"It is a well-known fact that, with perhaps one single exception, there is not a Congressional candidate in the state whose loyalty is even of a questionable character, and in not a county of the state outside of the same Congressional district is there, I believe, a candidate for the Legislature or any State office whose loyalty is not equally undoubted. In the face of this well known condition of things, the several classes of persons above enumerated are not only to be arrested *at*, but "*approaching any poll or place of election*." And who is to judge whether voters thus on their way to the place of voting have given "aid, comfort or *encouragement*" to persons engaged in the rebellion, or that they "do not recognize their allegiance to the United States," and may avail themselves of their presence at the polls "to foist enemies of the United States into power?" As I have already said, in a very large majority of the counties of the States there are not to be found among the candidates any such "enemies of the United States," but the Provost Marshals—created for a very different purpose—and the other military officials who are thus ordered to arrest approaching voters, are necessarily made by the order the sole and exclusive judges of who fall within the prescribed category; an extent of arbitrary discretion under any circumstances the most odious, and more especially offensive and dangerous in view of the known fact, that two at least of the five Provost Marshals of the State are themselves candidates for important offices, and sundry of their deputies for others.

"This military order, therefore, is not only without justification when looking to the character of the candidates before the people, and rendered still more obnoxious by the means appointed for its execution, but is equally offensive to the sensibilities of the people themselves and the authorities of the state, looking to the repeated proofs they have furnished of an unalterable devotion to the government. For more than two years past there has never been a time when, if every traitor and every treasonable sympathizer in the state had voted they could not have controlled, whoever might have been their candidates, a single department of the state, or jeopardized the success of the general government. No state in the Union has been or is now actuated by more heartfelt or unwavering loyalty than Maryland—a loyalty identified and purified by the ordeal through which it has passed; and yet looking to what has lately transpired elsewhere, and to the terms and character of this military order, one would think that in Maryland and nowhere else is the government endangered by the 'many evil disposed persons that are now at large.'

"Within less than a month the most important elections have taken place in two of the largest s'ꞌ es of the Union; in each of them candidates were before the people charged by the particular friends of the government with being hostile to its interests, and whose election was deprecated as fraught with the most dangerous consequences to its success. One of the most prominent of these candidates was considered so dangerously inimical to the triumph of the national cause that he has been for months past banished from the country, and yet hundreds of thousands of voters were allowed to approach the polls, and to attempt "to foist" such men into power, and no Provost Marshals or other military officers were ordered to arrest them on the way, or, so far as we have ever heard, even to test their allegiance by any oath.

"With these facts before us, it is difficult to believe that the suggestion that the enemies of the United States may be foisted into power at our coming election was the consideration that prompted this order; but whatever may have been that motive, I feel it to be my duty to solemnly protest against such an intervention with the privileges of the ballot-box, and so offensive a discrimination against the rights of a loyal state.

"I avail myself of the occasion to call to the particular attention of the judges of election the fact that they are on the day of election clothed with all the authority of conservators of the peace, and may summon to their aid any of the executive officers of the county, and the whole power of the county itself, to preserve order at the polls and secure the constitutional rights of the voters.

"It is also made their 'special duty' to give information to the State's Attorney for the county of all infractions of the State laws on the subject of elections, and by these laws it is forbidden to any

"commissioned or non-commissioned officers quartered or posted in any district of any county of the state, to muster or employ any of said troops or march any recruiting party within the view of any place of election during the time of holding said election."

"I need not, I am sure, remind them of the terms of the oath they are required to take before entering upon their duties, and according to which they swear

"to permit all persons to vote who shall offer to poll at the election, etc., who, in their judgment, shall, according to the directions contained in the constitution and laws, be entitled to poll at the same election, and not to permit any person to poll at the same election who is not in (their) judgment qualified to vote as aforesaid."

"It is the judgment of judges of election alone, founded upon the provisions of the constitution and laws of the state, that must determine the right to vote of any person offering himself for that purpose. I trust and believe they will form that judgment, and discharge their duty, as their conscientious convictions of its requirements, under the solemn obligations they assume shall dictate, und.ierred by any order to Provost Marshals to report them to 'headquarters.'

"Whatever power the state possesses shall be exerted to protect them for anything done in the proper execution of its laws.

"Since writing the above I have seen a copy of the President's letter to the chairman of the Union State Central Committee, bearing the same date with the order, and evidently showing that the order was unknown to him, that it would not have been approved by him if he had known it, and that it is therefore all the more reprehensible.

"By the Governor. A. W. BRADFORD.
"WM. B. HILL, Sec'y of State."

"After the above was in print, at 3 o'clock this afternoon, I received from the President the following dispatch:

"I revoke the first of the three propositions in General Schenck's General Order No. 53, not that it is wrong in principle but because the military, being of necessity exclusive judges as to who shall be arrested, the provision is liable to abuse; for the revoked part I shall substitute the following:
'That all Provost Marshals and other military officers do prevent all disturbances and violences at or about the polls, whenever offered by such persons as above described, or by any other person or persons whomsoever; the other two propositions I allow to stand; my letter at length will reach you to-night.

"A. LINCOLN."

"Whilst this modification revokes the authority of the Provost Marshals and military officers to arrest the classes of persons enumerated in the preamble to the order

"Found at or hanging about or approaching any poll or place of election,"

It directs them to prevent all violence or disturbance about the polls, &c.

"To meet such disturbances, the judges of election, as I have already stated, are clothed with ample power, and I had received no previous intimation that there was any reason to apprehend a disturbance of any kind at the polls on the day of election. In the absence of any military display, there would certainly seem to be a little cause for such apprehensions as ever before existed. A preparation by the government, by military means to provide for such a contingency, will be quite as likely to provoke as to subdue such a disposition.— Not only so, but the military thus required to prevent violence or disturbances about the polls must necessarily be empowered to arrest the parties they may charge with such disorder, and they are still left, in effect, "the exclusive judges as to who shall be arrested"—a power they may as readily abuse as any other.

"I regret, therefore, that I can perceive no such change in the general principles of the order as to induce me to change the aforegoing proclamation. A. W. BRADFORD.

"Baltimore, Monday evening, Nov. 2, 1863."

Be it remembered, that the tyrant, SCHENCK forbid the newspapers to publish this proclamation, and Gov. BRADFORD was forced to print it in handbill form, and then the "military authorities" suppressed it. Is not this a "refinement on despotism," when a loyal Governor of a loyal state is denied the privilege of proclaiming to the official agents of his state, their sworn duties under the laws thereof, and those laws are trampled under foot by military candidates for civil offices? And yet, the President had the magnanimity to modify General SCHENCK's order—*not because he thought it wrong*—but to make it just as despotic—and that modification was suppressed, and the officers who did it were not even censured. Under the infliction of such villainous despotism, we confess our faith in *free* government is very much shattered.

In Delaware, the Democrats finding their rights usurped by military authority—the laws under which they lived, trampled under foot, came out in an address, (which we have before us, but must omit) declining to go through with the farce of voting by *bayonet*, and thus their rights went by default.

THE CONSCRIPTION—ITS UNFAIRNESS—IS NOT THIS A POLITICAL WAR?

In New York, and we presume elsewhere, the draft is being used as a political machine —to draft more Democrats than Republicans. This is shown upon the face of things, and when we consider the fact that the names of Democrats have been known to be placed in duplicates, and in some instances in triplicates,

while many leading Republicans are left out altogether—when we consider these facts, it is by no means unfair to suppose that the abolitionists intend to so arrange the draft as to draw at least two Democrats for one Republican. "To prove which, let facts be submitted to a candid world."

The following table exhibits the blistering facts concerning twelve congressional districts of the State of New York—six Democratic and six Republican. The figures are based on the last gubernatorial vote of 1862:

District.	What constitutes district. Counties.	Population.	Total Popul'n of Dists.	Draft.	Canvass 62. Wads	Sey'r	Total Vote.
29	Genessee	32,189					
	Niagara	50,399					
	Wyoming	31,906	114,556	1,707	11,198	8,984	20,182
17	St. Lawrence	83,680					
	Franklin	30,837	114,526	1,838	12,020	5,879	17,902
23	Onandaga	90,686					
	Cortland	26,294	116,980	2,088	12,809	9,645	22,454
28	Monroe	100648					
	Orleans	28,717	129,365	2,013	11,470	9,539	21,009
16	Rensselaer	86,328					
	Washington	45,904	232,331	2,200	11,968	11,148	23,115
27	Chemung	26,917					
	Steuben	66,090					
	Alleghany	41,881	135,488	2,418	15,440	10,447	25,852
30	Erie	141971	141,971	2.538	9,642	11,780	21,423
	Odell's Dist. King's Co. Brooklyn. Wards.						
3	First	6,967					
	Second	9,817					
	Third	10,084					
	Fourth	11,760					
	Fifth	17,400					
	Seventh	12,090					
	Eleventh	28,851					
	Thirteenth	17,958					
	Fifteenth	10,500					
	Nineteenth	9,607	129,217	2,697	7,506	8,915	16,421
	Kallfleische Dis, Kings Co. Wards.						
2	Sixth	27,710					
	Eighth	9,190					
	Ninth	17,343					
	Tenth	25,258					
	Twelfth	11,083					
	Fourteenth	15,475					
	Sixteenth	21,181					
	Seventeenth	7,934					
	Eighteenth	4,316	151,951	4,140	5,381	10,580	15,967
	Towns.						
	Flatbush	3,471					
	Flatlands	1,652					
	Gravesend	1,286					
	New Lotts	3,271					
	New Utrecht	2,781					
	Wards of City of N.Y.						
6	Ninth	44,385					
	Fifteenth	27,587					
	Sixteenth	45,170	117,148	4,531	5,936	6,942	12,877
8	Eighteenth	57,462					
	Twentieth	57,519					
	Twenty-first	40,017	175,988	4,892	5,570	9,625	15,195
4	First	18,148					
	Second	2,500					
	Third	3,757					
	Fourth	21,994					
	Fifth	22,337					
	Sixth	26,006					
	Eighth	39,400	131,854	5,881	4,535	7,826	12,363

It will be seen that in the six Democratic districts, with a total vote of 94,248; and a Democratic aggregate majority of 17,108, the draft calls for **24,688,** while in the six Republican districts the total vote is 130,414—or 36,266 more votes than in the six Democratic districts, and the Republican majority is 19,228, the draft only calls for 12,387—or within a fraction of just one half the number to be drawn from the six Democratic districts, containing nearly 40,000 less voters.

If this is not a clear case of political fraud, then there is no such thing as fraud.

Again, it will be seen that New York, which is "intensely Copperhead," according to the chaste diction of the Abolitionists had furnished an excess *over all* calls of 22,761, exclusive of the militia, which have at different times been furnished for short periods, while many of the intensely Republican districts were short, by large odds. Still, the Administration insisted on drawing from "Copperhead" New York city 12,580 more.

The following table shows what New York had done under the four calls:

Call for	Quota of State.	State Furnished.	Quota of City.	City Furnished.
75,000	13,250	20,000	2,784	14,433
500,000	100,000	89,755	20,966	42,934
300,000	60,000	87,507	12,580	13,468
300,000	60,000	2,734	12,580	830
1,175,000	233,250	210,127	48,910	71,671

And yet the disloyal Abolitionists cry give us more. On this subject the New York *World,* from which we obtained the above figures, remarks:

"The citizens of New York protest against the inequality and injustice of this distribution of a very onerous burden, which must be accompanied by so many cases of individual hardships. They protest against this attempt to use the military power of the government as a party engine to get rid of political opponents who cannot be voted down. We maintain that when the government resorts to a method of raising troops which is, to say the least, of doubtful constitutionality, it ought to give evidence of pure and honest intentions, and an eye single to the public advantage.

The National *Intelligencer,* one of the most candid papers in the Union, and which was never charged with being a Democratic paper, in commenting on these facts, says:

"In order that every reader may see for himself the bases of the calculations from which we educe the conclusion that the quota assigned to New York is excessive, we cite the figures, giving the representative population and the aggregate population of the following states, together with the quota assigned to each. It is needless to say that if the quotas have been correctly distributed among the several states, they ought to bear something like a uniform ratio to the population of the states. Instead of this, we find by the rule of proportion that *the ratio of New York is largely in excess over that of other states.*

States.	Population.	Reps.	Quota.
Massachusetts	1,231,066	10	15,126
Maine	628,270	5	7,581
New Hampshire	326,073	3	3,768
Vermont	315,098	3	3,331
Connecticut	460,147	4	5,432
Rhode Island	174,620	2	2,034
New York	3,880,735	31	60,378
New Jersey	672,035	5	9,441
Delaware	112,216	1	1,156
Pennsylvania	2,906,115	24	38,268
Ohio	2,349,502	19	32,000
Indiana	1,350,428	11	16,000
Iowa	674,948	6	8,910

"The excess required of New York, estimating it upon the representation in Congress, is as follows:

As compared with Massachusetts	13,488
As compared with Maine	15,376
As compared with New Hampshire	21,442
As compared with Vermont	25,958
As compared with Connecticut	18,280
As compared with Rhode Island	28,581
As compared with New Jersey	1,844
As compared with Delaware	26,650
As compared with Pennsylvania	10,948
As compared with Ohio	8,168
As compared with Indiana	15,288
As compared with Iowa	14,343

"The excess required of New York, estimating it upon the population, is about as follows:

As compared with Massachusetts	12,538
As compared with Maine	13,548
As compared with New Hampshire	15,524
As compared with Vermont	19,342
As compared with Connecticut	14,562
As compared with Rhode Island	15,170
As compared with New Jersey	5,858
As compared with Pennsylvania	9,276
As compared with Delaware	20,396
As compared with Ohio	7,298
As compared with Indiana	14,399
As compared with Iowa	9,146

PALPABLE FRAUDS.

Since 1860 Pennsylvania has sent to the war 164,257 men—not less than 135,000 were voters.

The total vote at the election of 1863	523,669
Total vote in 1860	476,446
Excess over 1860, home vote	47,223

Now, as the excitement was intense in 1860, it is presumable that the full vote was out.— Let us compare three Presidential decades in that state.

In 1852 the total vote was	$366,267
In 1856, total vote	461,246
Increase in four years	74,979
Total vote in 1860	476,446
Increase in four years	15,200
Total vote 1863	523,669
Add for voters gone to the army	135,000
	658,669
Increase in *three* years	182,223

Now let us take Ohio for three Presidential decades:

Total vote of 1852,	353,428
Total vote of 1856,	386,497
Increase in four years,	33,069
Total vote in 1860,	442,441
Increase in four years,	56,944

[This was an unprecedented exciting canvass which brought out a *full* vote.]

Total home vote in 1863,	435,786
Add for voters gone to the war,	120,000
	555,786
Increase in three years,	113,339

The same ratio of increase is exhibited in Maine.

Now, it is impossible to reconcile these blistering facts with honesty and fairness.

Does any sane, fair-minded man believe that Pennsylvania has increased her voting population within the three years last past, 182,223? when her increase from 1852 to 1856 was but 71,979, when emigration was going on swimmingly, and from 1856 to 1860 her voting population increased but 15,200, owing to a falling off, in emigration, yet within the last *three* years when emigration had almost entirely ceased, she is represented by the *vote* forced by shoddy and bayonets, to have increased her voting population over 182,000! This is monstrous. The vote in Ohio was equally monstrous. From 1852 to 1856 her voting population increased but 33,069, and from 1856 to 1860, which epoch called out the fullest vote cast in America, the increase was but 56,944, yet for the last *three* years, with no aid from emigration, the vote which she is represented to have cast, shows an increase of 113,339!— The Democratic vote in Pennsylvania at the recent election, was—

Over that of 1852,	56,333
Over that of 1856,	24,117
Over combined vote of 1860,	59,253

The Democratic vote of Ohio at the election in 1863,

Exceeds that of 1852,	19,350
Over that of 1856,	17,096
Over that of 1860,	1,348

While the Republican Abolition vote of 1863, (adding the soldiers they claim in the field,) exceeds that of 1860 by 195,606!

Further comment is unnecessary.

PUNISHING OFFICERS FOR VOTING THE DEMOCRATIIC TICKET.

An article before us states that more than one half the Ohio soldiers refused to vote in October, 1863, and the following may and no doubt does, show a good reason for their reticence.

Capt. BENJ. F. SELLS, of the 122d Ohio V., Company D, was arrested on the 1st of October, on the

"Charge—Conduct prejudicial to good order and military discipline."

And from the specifications we take the following:

"Specification 4th. In this, that he, the said Captain B. F. Sells, 'D' Company, 122d O. V. I., in the service of the U. S.; did utter and use the following language, to-wit: I am going to vote for Vallandigham, and so are all my company, except a few, or words to that effect. This at or near Martinsburg, Va., on or about the 13th day of August, 1863.

"Specification 8th. In this, that he, the said Capt. B. F. Sells, 'D' Company, 122d Regt. G. V. I., in the service of the U. S., did ply officers and men with arguments in favor of voting for Vallandigham, and did use the following language, to-wit: Vallandigham is a loyal man, and I will vote for him, or words to that effect.

"This at or near Martinsburg, Va., on or about the 14th day of August, 1862.
(Signed)   ORLANDO C. FARQUAR,
Capt. Co. G, 122d Regt. O. V. I.

THREATS FROM SHOULDER STRAPS TO CONTROL THE ELECTIONS.

The future historian will be thunderstruck at reading such threatening diatribes of which the following is but a sample of a large class, stimulated as we have remarked elsewhere, no doubt, by the harangues of Adjutant Thomas.

The following, purporting to have been written to R. B. Charles, by one of the Wisconsin soldiers on the Potomac, appeared with grandiloquent headings and preface in the Fond du Lac (Wis.) *Commonwealth*, of April 29, 1863 :

" *   *   We will attend to the rebels, if
" you will take care of the Copperheads at
" home. When we get home, if moral suasion
" has not taught them better manners we will
" treat them to a dish of our own preparing ;
" for we consider them the worst of traitors.
" There are honorable traitors over the river
" (the Rappahannock), but those in the north
" are the most damnable of the devil's imps.
" We are not lying on the ground for nothing,
" *tell them*. Our business is to exterminate
" traitors ; we shall not consider it finished so
" long as there is a copperhead in the north.
" Our epithets may be harsh, but they are just
" such as a damnable set of traitors bring up-
" on themselves, from every honest tongue,
" whether from soldier or citizen. They have
" belied us by stating that the army of the
" Potomac was 'demoralized,' &c., but we will
" not belie them, although truth sounds harsh."

The following is an extract of a letter over the signature of J. W. McKay, of the 25th Wisconsin Infantry, and published in the Republican papers with approving comments, appeared about the same time as the above:

"We warn Northern "Copperheads" to keep hands off; ruin to their friendship is better than ruin to our country, and if they force us to deal with them as enemies, we shall do our work for all coming time."

Enough! The heart sickens at the recital of such bloodthirsty threats with no higher motive than to gain a few votes.

MONEY USED TO CARRY THE ELECTIONS.

Read the following from the Providence (R. I.) *Post:*

"MONEY.—The Republicans admit that they used $40,000 in this city on Wednesday. We guess they used more. They gave as high as $25 for a vote, and there was no competition, either. We are glad that men who are willing to sell out are beginning to ask a high price.

"In East Providence the price ran high, notwithstanding the fact that our friends did not use a dollar.

"In Warwick the Republicans found Colonel Butler a hard man to beat, and offered thirty dollars for a vote all day.

"In North Providence the Republicans spent fifteen to twenty thousand dollars."

Can a party which sanctions such rascality be a friend to Republican institutions?

PHILLIP, of Macedon, used money to destroy the liberties of the Athenians, and ADDISON in speaking of which says:

"A man who is furnished with arguments from the *Mint*, will convince his antagonist much sooner than one who draws them from reason and philosophy. Gold is a wonderful clearer of the understanding; it dissipates every doubt and scruple in an instant; accommodates itself to the meanest capacities; silences the loud and clamorous, and brings over the most obstinate and inflexible. Philip of Macedon refuted by it all the wisdom of the Republic of Athens, confounded their statesmen, struck their orators dumb, *and at length argued them out of their liberties.*"

History seems to be repeating itself very rapidly and unfortunately for our once great country. Our political opponents now in power seem to only have studied the very worst side of it. The saying that "when the wicked rule the people mourn," originated from just such history as our rulers are repeating.

NO POLITICS IN THIS WAR.

One CASPER HAWES, a disabled soldier, obtained the situation as sutler in the Philadelphia Hospital, and was summarily discharged therefrom, for no other reason, says the Philadelphia *Age*, than appears in the following official note, which was proved a lie just after the election:

HAWES had been crippled for life in the defense of his country, and this was the only means he had of getting a living.

MOWER U. S. GEN'L HOSPITAL,
PHILADELPHIA, Oct. 30, 1863.

"SIR:—Having heard from Mr. Sands, of the Chestnut Hill Union Committee, that you voted the Democratic ticket, and expressed yourself inimical to the present Government, you are hereby notified that after November you can no longer be a sutler to this Hospital. By order of the surgeon in charge.

Very respectfully, your obedient servant,
THOMAS C. BRAINARD,
Ass't Surgeon U. S. A., and Executive Officer.

No politics in this war!

Just prior to the election in Wisconsin, in 1863, the Milwaukee *Sentinel*, the leading Abolition paper of the state, kept standing in its columns, in flaming capitals, this line:

"Those who vote must fight."

This was intended as a fraud on those of our foreign born citizens who had not become sufficiently acquainted with the laws, customs and "regulations" to know its falsity. The object was to create an impression among this class of citizens that the act of voting would of itself send them into the army. In this way thousands of Democratic voters were kept away from the polls. It may be a fine thing to laugh over and to impugn their "loyalty," as the organs of that party were wont to do, but the army records show that this class of citizens have been as free to volunteer as those excessive "loyal" Republicans, who always cry "*go*," but never say "*come.*"

ABOLITION ROORBACKS.

The Abolitionists have been in the habit, just before the elections, of starting some wonderful "roorback," detailing some great Union victory over the rebels, with a view to obtain votes, by making the people believe they were really doing something and were entitled to confidence. Just before the Chicago election, in April, 1863, that party caused it to be telegraphed *west* that Charleston was taken, *when they knew it was not* The knowledge of this false news was charged upon the administration and has never been denied. Similar roorbacks, for similar purposes, were started and circulated about the taking of Vicksburg and other places, when the conspirators knew them to be false.

THE UNION LEAGUE MACHINERY.

JOHN W. FORNEY, early in 1863, stated that

"The Union men—in such organizations as Union Leagues, or whatever capacity they please to act, have opened the campaign, and intend to support the President in 1863, and if possible *to control the election of President in 1864.*"

It will be remembered that all along the radicals had denied that the Union Leagues were a political organization. But FORNEY boldly admits what all outsiders know. Now, how do these Union Leaguers propose to carry the elections? Let them speak for themselves. At one of their meetings in Cincinnati March 1863, Judge WOODRUFF, who presided, said:

"The American flag [Greeley's 'flaunting lie'] and the laws [excepting such as they don't like] maintained, and THE ELECTION CARRIED, EVEN AT THE PRICE OF BLOOD, for upon this everything depended."

Mr. HANCOCK, who disgraced the profession of school teacher, spoke at the same meeting, and declared:

"He believed that mob law was wholesome, sometimes!"

A Col. GUTHRIE also spoke:

"He informed those present that the League was military as well as political—that they were drilling nightly, and were prepared for any emergency."

After appointing delegates to attend the Grand Council of the Union Leagues of the United States at Chicago on the 25th of March, Professor ALLYN, of the Weslyan Seminary a teacher of young ladies, said:

"But this time we must make it all right. and *carry the election by any measures necessary to do it*"

We omit much of the filthiness of low profanity that marked much of what was said, and will close with this League by copying the following proposition they had up for discussion :

" For the members of the Association, and all other Union men, to prohibit all the news boys from conveying and selling any opposition paper ; to note every man that takes and reads it, and forbid him entering your company—give him no employment—run him from your midst—turn him out of your church—mark every man and woman at your boarding house that read it—make it too hot for them to stay there—turn them out."

DR. LEIBER ON SOLDIERS VOTING.

Dr. LEIBER, in his work entitled "Civil Liberty and Self-Government," says :

" An election can have no value whatever if the following conditions are not fulfilled : The question must have been fairly before the people for a period sufficiently long to discuss the matter thoroughly, and under circumstances to allow discussion. * * * The liberty of the press, therefore, is a condition *sine qua non*. * * * * It is especially necessary that the army be in abeyance, as it were, with reference to all subjects and movements appertaining to the question at issue. *The English law requires the removal of the garrison* from every place where a common election for parliament is going on. * *

"All elections must be superintended by election judges and officers, *independent of the Executive*, or any other organized or unorganized powers of the government. The indecency as well as the absurdity and immorality of the government recommending what is to be voted, ought never to be permitted. * * If any one of these conditions be omitted, the whole election or voting is vitiated."

And again, says the Doctor in another part of his celebrated work:

"A perfect dependence of the forces, however, not only requires short approbations and limited authority of the Executive over them, but it is further necessary—because they are under strict discipline, and therefore under a strong influence of the Executive—that these forces, and especially the army, be not allowed to become deliberative bodies, and that they be not allowed to vote as military bodies.— WHEREVER THESE GUARANTEES HAVE BEEN DISREGARDED, LIBERTY HAS FALLEN!!!

GEN. MILROY ON "HOME TRAITORS."

In April, 1863, Gen. MILROY, no doubt per order, (he has certainly never been censured for it) published a letter (a poor way for a General to fight) in which he thus sets forth the bloody purposes of himself and partizans:

"I join with my fellow soldiers of the Union everywhere, in warning these traitors at home [all Democrats who do not vote the Abolition ticket are called "traitors!"] that *when we have crushed armed treason at the South*, and restored the sovereignty of our government over these misguided States, (which under God we are sure to do) we will, upon our return, *while our hands are in, also exterminate treason in the North, by arms, if need be,* and seal, by the blood of traitors, wherever found, the permanent peace of our country and the perpetuity of free [negro] government to all future generations. R. H. MILROY."

What a lovely prospect for the people of the North! "*After* this war is over"—"while our hands are in,"—[blood] we, the partizans of the Administration, in the army, will imbue our hands in the blood of our Northern brothers and neighbors, who have not agreed with all the President has done, or may do! This is literally what these bloodthirsty marplots mean. We *are* making history which "we cannot escape."

BROUGH'S APPEAL FROM THE BALLOT TO THE BULLET.

JOHN BROUGH, the candidate for Governor of Ohio, against Mr. VALLANDIGHAM, in one of his campaign speeches in Ohio, in 1863, said:

"What will be the effect of *electing* Mr. Vallandigham Governor of Ohio? I will tell you what will be the effect of it. *It will bring civil war into your State*—civil war into your own homes—upon the soil of your own State—for I tell you there is a mighty mass of men in the State, whose nerves are strung up like steel, *who will never permit* this dishonor to be consummated in their native State."

In plain language then, this meant that if the people should elect Mr. VALLANDIGHAM BROUGH's friends, and the administration would have inaugurated civil war in the State, and put him down by force. What a commentary on free government!

MORE THREATS.

A Washington correspondent of the Wisconsin *State Journal* (supposed to be a United State's Senator) under date of May 6th, 1863, said:

"The morning papers bring the announcement of the arrest of the notorious Vallandigham who for the last eight months has been flooding the country with treasonable speeches, and no doubt some of his disciples and co-laborers in Wisconsin are already writing long editorials against 'arbitrary arrests,' styling him the martyr of a military despotism. *Their time may come next!* A brilliant success of the army *may save them*, but if our armies *should be repulsed*, let them beware!"

That these threats have not been carried into execution, shows no want of disposition, but only the lack of brute courage.

CONWAY vents open threats right in the very portals of the Capitol, and within its halls, of advocating a dissolution of the Government.— VALLANDIGHAM never uttered a sentiment of that kind, and yet these terrible threats and a black cloud of denunciations are hurled at Mr. V. and his friends, while no Abolitionist has ever asked to have CONWAY punished, or in any manner interfered with. The reason and the only reason is as plain as the sun at midday—CONWAY votes the Republican ticket and is in favor of the Radical scheme to break up this Union—VALLANDIGHAM is right the reverse way of thinking, and has exposed their treason.

MORE THREATS FROM ARMY POLITICIANS.

H. BERTRAM, Colonel of the 20th Wis. Vol., published in the *Wisconsin State Journal* of April 18, 1863, a series of resolutions, which he claims were nearly unanimously passed by said regiment [its officers], from which we select the third resolution, as bloody enough for a MARAT:

"*Resolved*, That those who complain so loudly and so lithly about the suspension of the writ of *habeas corpus* and the institution of martial law in time of actual rebellion, ought themselves to be *suspended between heaven and earth by a few yards of hemp well adjusted around their necks.*"

Neither in France or Austria would such demoniac resolutions be tolerated over the signature of military officers. But in this "free and enlightened" country, anything to obtain votes.

THE WHOLE THING JUSTIFIED.

The Boston *Commonwealth*, in admitting the wicked and unlawful means resorted to by the Administration to carry the elections, attempts to justify the monstrous wrongs:

"We do not find fault with the machinery used to carry Maryland and Delaware. Having nearly lost the control of the House by its blunders in the conduct of the war from March, 1861, to the fall of 1862, the Administration owed it to the country to recover that control somehow. To recover it regularly was impossible; so irregularity had to be resorted to. Popular institutions will not suffer, for the copperhead element will have a much larger number of members in both branches than it is entitled to by its popular vote. Ohio, with its ninety thousand Republican majority, will be represented by five Republicans and a dozen or more Copperheads. It is fitting that this misrepresentation of popular sentiment in the great state of the West should be offset, if necessary, by a loyal delegation from Maryland and Delaware, *won even at the expense of military interference*. If laws are silent amid the clank of arms, we must take care that the aggregate public opinion of the country obtains recognition somehow or other."

THE NEW YORK INDEPENDENT BOASTS OF THE INFAMY.

In speaking of the spring elections, the New York *Independent* said:

"The Administration, for the first time since it came into power, *used its legitimate influence on the right side in the New Hampshire election*, and the second occasion was in Connecticut."

This "infinence" consisted in sending such and only such soldiers home as would pledge themselves to vote the Abolition ticket, and refuse to allow any Democrat to go. And this is that Administration that come into power on the promise of *freedom* and *reform*. God save the mark.

CHAPTER XXXV.

SYMPATHY BETWEEN RADICALS AND REBELS—THE DRAFT, &C.

The Rebels Hate the Democracy and Sympathize with the Radicals...General Remarks...Benjamin's Speech in 1860...Breckinridge Secesbers Toasted with Office, &c...Richmond Examiner on Vallandigham, Cox, &c...Mobile Register on Democrats and Abolitionists....The Draft vs. Volunteering....Volunteering a Success...Wilson's and Fessenden's Admissions....Thad Stevens on "Alarming Expenses"....Too many Troops to pay, but none to Spare McClellan...General Remarks, &c....The number of Men called for....Cameron's Eulogy on Volunteering...Cost of Conscription...Opinions of the Republican Press on the Draft....Albany Statesman....The Draft in Rhode Island ....A candid Statement by a Republican paper....The Conscription in Massachusetts....A mysterious Draft in New York....Result of Draft in ninth District of Massachusetts and eighth District of New York...Thurlow Weed on "Sneaks"....Drafting in the time of the Revolution....Remarks Thereon.

HOW THE REBELS HATE THE DEMOCRACY AND SYMPATHIZE WITH THE ABOLITIONISTS.

That the Southern rebels have from the start hated the Northern Democracy and gave preference to the Abolitionists, because they (the abolitionists) hate the old Union, has been known and appreciated ever since the campaign of 1860. During that campaign it is well known that the secessionists and Republicans worked together, cheek-by-jowl, for a common purpose —that common purpose was a division of the Democratic party, that a division of the Union might follow. This is a hard charge, but when read by the light of *confessions*, which abound in this work, no other proof is wanting.

On the 22d of May, 1860, the great rebel leader, J. P. BENJAMIN, a Senator from Louisiana, made a gross and unprovoked attack on STEPHEN A. DOUGLAS, and called it a speech. This was expressly intended as an electioneering document, and was printed by the million, and circulated throughout the North and the South—the expense being equally divided between the secessionists and the Republicans. The portion of these incendiary documents falling to the Republicans, were sent all over the North, as plentiful as autumn leaves, under the franks of Republican members of Congress. We have one before us that came under the frank of "JAS. R. DOOLITTLE, M. C." Yes, this speech, which contained doctrines that slavery must be protected in all the territories, by law, that it was held sacred there by the constitution, and which also contained the most florid puffs on ABRAHAM LINCOLN, was sent broad-cast over the North by Republicans, acting as twin coadjutors with the Southern rebels. In speaking of the *relative* merits of Mr. DOUGLAS and Mr. LINCOLN, this Southern fire-eater said:

"His (DOUGLAS') adversary (Mr. LINCOLN) stood upon principle in the Illinois Senatorial Canvass), and was beaten, and lo! he is the candidate of a mighty party for the Presidency of the United States."

This was said to the praise of LINCOLN, and the disparagement of Mr. DOUGLAS. Throughout the whole speech, not one word is uttered against Mr. LINCOLN, or what the South pretended to believe his heresies, but DOUGLAS was vehemently denounced. And why was this? Because there had no doubt been an agreement—an understanding between the two wings of Disunionists, to help elect LINCOLN, and as soon as he was elected, this same Benjamin and his rebel followers were to claim the election as a *cause* for secession!

One of the main objections to Mr. DOUGLAS was, as seen on page 4 of said speech, that he had acted "consistent" with his former course. Such were the means resorted to by these twin factions to break the last link (the Democratic party) that existed between the North and the South. All other links—the churches and civil relations, had long before been sundered.

Now, take these facts in connection with the treasonable utterances of the leaders of the party in power—their votes—their resolutions —their anathemas against the Union—in short, their former and their present attitude with regard to the "Union as it was, and the Constitution as it is"—and also take what follows in this chapter—and who that has sense and patriotism combined can doubt that the sad events of the past thirty months have not been the result of an "understanding," clear and well defined, to break up the Union? The mad schemes and disunion purposes of the BRECKINRIDGE faction were as well known (we make a few honorable exceptions for those who were really blinded) as they are now.— The fact that they contemplated disunion was patent, for they boasted of it. Neither BRECKINRIDGE nor his friends would answer the queries of Judge DOUGLAS, propounded at Norfolk, as to their designs at revolution. And still, the Republicans took these traitors to their bosoms. They furnished the means to establish and keep alive newspapers at the North, in the interest of that faction, where they were not numerous enough to keep alive a 7x9 half-penny sheet. In all the state of Wisconsin the BRECKINRIDGE ticket only received some 800 out of near 153,000 votes, and yet an expensive newspaper, called the *Argus & Democrat*, was kept up at Madison, in that state, by Republican money, and it is well known that Republicans paid for and distributed a large number of copies among the people, nor was this all. One CALKINS, who was the willing tool to defame DOUGLAS and advocate the secession platform through its columns, was rewarded by a fat office at the hands of the Republicans. N. B. VAN SLYKE, one of the BRECKINRIDGE electors in the same state, was rewarded by a fat and lucrative office, as one of the military blessings that flowed from Republican hands. Another elector on that ticket, in the same state, H. D. BARRON, has been not only appointed by the Republican Governor as Circuit Judge, but has been twice elected by that party as member of the Assembly, and received as high as 46 votes for Lt. Gouernor, in their State Convention of 1863.

These are sample specimens "away out West." In the East the big leaders of the Breckinridge faction were among the first to be invited to the Abolition feast of spoils. Ben. Butler, who boasted of having voted for Jeff. Davis one hundred times, was rewarded with a Major General's commission, which enabled *his brother* to make a "good thing" in the Department of New Orleans, it is said, to the tune of thirteen millions.

EDWIN M. STANTON, another, who rode the Breckinridge hobby, occupies a seat in the synagogue of ABRAHAM the I. DANIEL S. DICKINSON was rewarded by a high place on the Abolition ticket in New York. Hundreds and thousands of others were likewise rewarded by the abolitionists for their subserviency to the destroyers of our Union, all of which show that it *pays* to have been an advocate of secession candidates and the extreme southern doctrine. Let the student of history draw his own conclusions from these facts.

JEFF. DAVIS' OFFICIAL ORGAN ON DEMOCRATS.

The Richmond *Examiner*, the especial organ of JEFF. DAVIS, in speaking of VALLANDIGHAM and COX, of Ohio, used this expressive language, which shows where their rebel sympathies lie, April, 1863:

"We wish from our hearts they were both already safely chained up at the present writing. *They have done us mose harm*—they and their like—than *ten thousand Sewards and Sumners*, We tremble to see their unwholesome advances, and still more to see a morbid craving here *to respond to them*, under the delusive idea of promoting intestine divisions at the North.

"Oh, Dictator Lincoln, lock ye up those two peace Democrats—together with Richardson— in some of your military prisons!"

THE MOBILE REGISTER SAYS "GIVE US SUCH MEN AS SUMNER," ETC.

The Mobile *Register*, shortly after VALLANDIGHAM'S deportation uttered the following remarkable piece of cozening to the Abolitionists. Read:

"We thank God from the depths of our hearts that the authorities at Washington snubbed Vice President Stephens in his late attempt to confer with them on international affairs, without form or ceremony. It has long been known here that this gentleman thought if he could get to whisper into the ears of some men about Washington, the result might be terms of peace on some sort of *Union* or *reconstruction*. He seemed to forget that Douglas, with whom he used to serve, is dead, and notwithstanding his mantle has fallen, by dividing it into four pieces, upon Richardson and Voorhees, Vallandigham and Pugh, still the Democratic party is not in power now, thank God for it.

"The prospect looked gloomy to the Vice President, whose infirmity of body no doubt cast a shadow over his spirits, and he said that one of two things must be done: either some terms must be made, or the whole militia of the Confederacy must be called out, and immediate alliance proposed with foreign powers. President Davis gave him *full powers to treat on honorable terms*, and started him off to the Kingdom of Abraham. But Father Abraham told him there was an impassable gulf between them, and the Vice President had to steam back to Richmond, a little top fallen.

"We hope this will put a *stop forever* to some croakers about here, who intimate that there are people enough f.iendly to the South in the North, to restore the Union as it was. And we also hope that the government at Richmond will not humiliate itself any more, but from this time will look only to the one end *of final and substantial independence. The North is not less set on a final separation than we are.* The Republican party is not fighting to restore this Union, any more than the old Romans fought to establish the independence of the countries they invaded. The Republicans are fighting for *conquest and dominion,* we for liberty and independence.

"There is only one party in the North who want this Union restored, but they have no more power—legislative, executive or judicial —than the paper we write on. It is true, they make a show of union and strength, but they have no voice of authority. We know that the Vallandigham school wants the Union restored, for he told us so, when here in exile, partaking of such hospitality as we extended to a *real enemy* to our struggle for separation, banished to our soil by *another enemy,* who is *pratically more our friends than he.* And if Vallandigham should by accident or other cause, become Governor of Ohio, we hope Lincoln will keep his nerves to the proper tension, and not allow him to enter the confines of the State.— Ilis Administration *would do more to restore heold Union,* than any other power in Ohio ould do, and therefore, we pray he may be defeated.

"Should a strong Union party spring up in Ohio, the third State in the North, in political importance, it might find a faint response in some Southern States, and *give us trouble.—* But as long as the Republicans hold power, they will think on conquest and dominion ovly, and we, on the other hand, will come up in solid column for freedom and independence, which we will be certain to achieve with such assistance as we now (after the refusal of the Washington Cabinet to confer,) confidently expect before the Democrats of the nation get into power again, and come whispering in our ears *Union, Re-construction, Constitution, concessions and guarantees.* Away with all such stuff. We want separation. Give us rather men like *Thaddeus Stevens and Charles Sumner.* THEY CURSE THE OLD UNION, AND DESPISE IT, AND SO DO WE!! And we now advise these gentlemen, that, as they hate the Union and the accursed Constitution, *let them keep down Mr. Vallandigham and his party in the North,* then they shall never be troubled by us with such *whining* about the Constitution and Union, as they are sending up."

This, then, shows that there is both a fellow-feeling and a fellow-purpose between the rebels and the Abolitionists. The rebels know the radicals do not want the Union restored, and in this they both agree, and the reason why the rebels are so prejudiced against the Democrats, is, that they know every Democrat is in favor of restoration. But enough on this subject.

THE DRAFT VS. VOLUNTEERING.

To say nothing of the fact that nine-tenths of the legal mind of the nation believe the mode adopted to procure soldiers by draft, is unconstitutional, by reason of usurping the rights and power of the states over the militia, and that the conscription act has been decided unconstitutional by the Supreme Court of Pennsylvania, on this and other grounds—to say nothing of this, there are features in the operation and ill-success of the draft, that require a moment's attention.

It is far from our purpose to indulge in a fault-finding spirit, merely for the purpose of finding fault. We would by no means throw an obstacle in the way of any just, constitutional and patriotic effort to put out the fires of the rebellion. We would rather assist, all that may be in our power, and the most effective way to assist the Administration is to candidly point out its errors, wrongs and crimes, with a view to correct and improve.

VOLUNTEERING A SUCCESS

The Administration, so long as it adhered to its first declared policy found no difficulty in getting all the soldiers it wanted. Nearly, if not quite a million of men rushed forth, in vast numbers, so rapidly that Senator WILSON, of Mass., chairman of the Military Committee, became alarmed, and said in his place:

"I have over and over again been to the War office, and urged upon the Department to stop recruiting in every part of the country. We have had the promise that it should be done.— I believe we have to-day 250,000 more men under the pay of the government than we need, or can well use. I think the Department ought to issue peremptory orders forbidding the enlistment of another soldier into the volunteer force."

About the same time Mr. FESSENDEN, of Maine, another abolition Senator, said:

"In every state in the Union, there are men who are paid from month to month, not called into the field for the reason that the Government has no occasion to use them; and yet no step is taked to disband these men. Why not disband them if they are not wanted? We have 250,000 more than we ever intended to have.— It is extravagance of the most wanton kind. I offered a proposition to stop all enlistments."

Thus, we have it from the highest abolition

authority, that our armies were too large for the purpose of subduing the rebellion.

About this time THAD. STEVENS, chairman of the committee on ways and means in the House, denounced the extravagance of so large an army, in the following style:

"We shall have to appropriate more than six hundred million dollars without the addition of a single dollar beyond what is estimated for. New, sir, that in itself is alarming. I confess I do not see how, unless the expenses are greatly curtailed, this government can possibly go on six months. If we go on as we have been doing, the finances, not only of the Government, but of the whole country, must give way, and the people will be involved in one general bankruptcy and ruin. We have already in the field an army of six hundred and sixty thousand men, &c."

Not far from the period at which these men gave the above utterances, Gen. MCCLELLAN was on the Chickahominy asking for a reinforcement of 50,000 troops, with which he said he had not the least doubt he could take Richmond in a few days. But the powers at Washingto had *no troops to spare!* and ordered his retreat from the pursuit of the rebel capital. The Administration and the disloyal and traitorous abolitionists that controlled it, saw that if Richmond was taken it would end the war, and the war ended without the accomplishment of their darling object—the abolition of slavery, would not suit their programme, so our brave and ill-treated army was hauled off, and the rebels given time to again recuperate—the mouse was permitted to gain sufficient strength to entertain those who desired to play with it.

From that day to this the Army of the Potomac has been crushed by the foolhardy and criminal policy emanating from the "throne of power." They have been required to march up the hill and then to march down again, and have not been permitted to accomplish anything worthy of their patriotism and courage, except when the old grannies in and around the White House became frightened for their own individual safety.

The people are fast settling down on the conclusion that those who control the Administration do not want to take Richmond—do not want the war to close until they can provoke a state of despotism which may enable them to abolish slavery, or "let the Union slide." This war is being prolonged—the lives and the fortunes of our people are being sacrificed, beyond any necessity of saving the Union, and all to enable the Abolitionists to carry out their primary designs.

It has been a standing remark, for Republican as well as Democratic papers, that the Army of the Potomac was too near Washington to accomplish anything. This is true, and the reason why they have accomplished nothing is because the radicals had resolved they should accomplish nothing, beyond the bare guarding of Washington. We can now see an object in this. It is a link in the same object that brought on a collision by sending an unarmed vessel to banter the rebels at Charleston to a fight.

The rebellion is now reeling at every step. We have more men in the field now than when WILSON and FESSENDEN clamored for a cessation of enlistments, and the rebels are no stronger, and still the Administration is reaching out after conscripts, and by frauds the most damnable, are endeavoring to draft mostly Democrats, in the hope that they may perpetuate their power. They are determined not to allow the rebels to come back and be good citizes, until they can destroy their state rights, and so cripple their power that they cannot *vote against the Abolition party*. That is the secret of their refusal to accept a surrender, as their leading organ, the New York *Times*, declares they will refuse, if a surrender is offered. Does all this look as though the Administration was laboring to save this Union, and for that only? Does it not show that they care more for the future strength of their party than they do for the Union?

It may be uncharitable, but we must confess that we can see it in no other light. We believe as firmly as we believe in the existence of an All-wise God, that the real purpose of insisting on the draft, is to keep the people of the North embittered and divided by a series of gross frauds on the one hand, and lamentable mobs on the other. If the system of provocation and reaction can be kept up, it is no doubt intended to consummate what DOUGLAS predicted, to dissolve the Union and establish a Dictatorship, whenever it can be done with a show of shifting the responsibility on their opponents, or rendering a military excuse.— Hence, we firmly believe, the draft is held constantly over the heads of the people *in terrorem*, to affect the elections, in those various ways so susceptible to Abolition manipulation by the army of Provost Marshals. We have exhibited some of these objects in former chapters of this work.

NUMBER OF MEN CALLED FOR.

In round numbers, the President has thus far called for about 2,100,000 men, and of these about 1,000,000 have been called for by draft. Of the whole number, about 1,200,000 have been secured, and without pretending to be *exact*, (not having the figures before us), we may safely say, that aside from volunteer substitutes, the Administration has not obtained 20,000 men, as living trophies from the " prize wheel." This is an exceedingly small per cent.

MR. CAMERON'S EULOGY ON VOLUNTEERING.

Mr. Secretary CAMERON, in his first report, before the radical measures had been fully developed, said:

"History will record that men who, in ordinary times, were devoted solely to the arts of peace, were yet ready, on the instant, to rush to arms in defense of their rights when assailed. At the present moment, the government presents the striking anomaly of being embarrassed by the generous outpouring of volunteers to sustain its action. Instead of laboring under the difficulty of monarchical governments, the want of men to fill its armies, *which in other countries has compelled a resort to forced conscriptions*, one of its main difficulties is to keep down the proportions of the army."

He says again:

"I cannot forbear to speak favorably of the volunteer system, as a substitute for a cumbrous and dangerous standing army. * * A government whose every citizen stands ready to march to its defense can never be overthrown; for none is so strong as that whose foundations rest immovably in the hearts of the people."

And the second report from the same office glowed with a no less deserved panegyric on this system.

COST OF THE CONSCRIPTION.

We have seen it stated, though with what degree of facts to back it we know not, that each soldier drafted and *mustered* into the United States forces, has cost the people not less than $3000. This is an enormous sum we know, but when we take into account the vast army of officers who are stationed all over the North, hunting down deserting conscripts, at $15 or $30 per head—the trouble, delay, and vast expense attending on making the enrollment—costing nearly as much as the taking of the census—the support of Draft Commissioners—Examining Boards—provost marshals, spies, delators, and the tens of thousands of officers that must be paid and fed from the public crib —all to procure the *poorest* material for war we cannot doubt the statement. We say "poorest" advisedly, for so far as we have read history and studied human nature, a man *forced* into the ranks against his will, is, in nine cases out of ten, inferior to the volunteer, because his heart is against it.

From the observation we have been enabled to make, of all the facts, we are prepared to hazard the opinion that with less than a third of the expense incurred, the Government could have got all the men it wanted. Had it abolished—or rather never organized—its hordes of enrollment and draft officers and hangers-on, and applied the funds they have absorbed, to liberalizing the soldiers' monthly pay, to— say $25 per month, we should have heard nothing of mobs and riots, and no complaints of a lack of men, even under the present pernicious policy. This is the candid opinion of one who has been in favor of a most vigorous prosecution of the war to crush the rebellion, from the start.

REPUBLICAN OPINIONS.

The Albany *Statesman*, a Republican paper, thus warned the Government against continuing longer to insist upon the enforcement of the draft:

"The Government never committed a more fatal mistake than when it abandoned the volunteer and bounty systems—systems which put into the field a million men in eighteen months. The Government, after it puts down the riot in New York, should take a calm view of the dangers which surround us, and if possible return to a system which has never failed us, and which should never have been abandoned. Every person who wishes to see the southern rebellion promptly put down, should use every exertion to prevent a rebellion from breaking out in the loyal states. We are no alarmist, and yet we candidly think that it will take more troops to enforce the draft in this state than is required to capture Richmond.

" The rioters in New York should and must be crushed. We owe this to the supremacy of the laws. Having done this, we do beseech our rulers to so modify the draft that the loyal States may continue to exhibit an unbroken front against the rebellion. Nothing but this unbroken front can prevent the rebellion from becoming a success. We call upon President Lincoln to save the North from anarchy. God grant that he may be equal to the task. At the

SCRAPS FROM MY SCRAP-BOOK. 295

present time the Republic has more to fear from the follies of the war office than from a pair of armies such as Lee now heads in Maryland."

THE DRAFT IN RHODE ISLAND.

We clip the following from a Rhode Island paper:

"In the First District, Wednesday, 78 obtained permission to go, pay, or find a substitute; and 95 were exempted—49 for disability, 10 were elected by their parents, 9 were aliens, 2 were from families having already two in the service, 6 were of unsuitable age, 4 were only sons of widows, 8 were non-residents, 4 are already in the service, and 3 commuted. In the Second District 24 substitutes were accepted, 51 were exempted for physical disability, and 31 for various other causes."

A statement went the rounds of the press, which we have not seen contradicted, that of all the persons conscripted in the state, but *nineteen* actually entered the service, and some of these were negroes.

A CANDID STATEMENT BY A REPUBLICAN PAPER.

The Springfield (Mass.) *Republican*, a strong supporter of Mr. LINCOLN, from first to last, in speaking of the draft in that State, thus testifies to its failure:

"The daily reports of the results of the draft throughout the country, produce the general impression that it is a *failure*—that it will not add materially to the strength of our armies, and that it will *cost more than it is worth*. This is not absolutely true, but it must be confessed it is too close an approximation to the truth to be contemplated with satisfaction. Evidently the Government will not get one-fourth the number drafted, *counting in the substitutes*. Indeed, some consider one-fifth a large estimate.— [And this is a state where the "roads would swarm" with *volunteers*, if the proclamation should be issued!] Making due allowance for the states exempted from the draft, and the whole number actually drawn will not be over 300,000. One-fourth of this number will be 75,000. But many of the conscripts, as well as substitutes, will make their escape, and the War Department would undoubtedly jump at the chance to exchange the whole lot for 50,000, or even 40,000 volunteers. The draft, it must conceded, if not a failure, *is not a very gr ing success*. If the President could have for en how badly the draft would have been mismanaged, we believe he would have decided to rely upon volunteering to fill up the armies, and as things have turned, he could have done so with safety. The money and effort expended on the conscription would have secured fifty thousand volunteers, there is every reason to believe. And it would have been a glorious thing to record on the pages of history, that the great rebellion was put down entirely by the spontaneous and unforced patriotism of the people."

THE CONSCRIPTION IN MASSACHUSETTS.
[From the Boston Herald.]

"The work of examining conscripts in the different districts in this state has progressed quietly and with good order during the past week. All the Boards of Enrollment have been in session to hear claims for exemption, and we regret to find that so many of those whose names were drawn have been compelled to go before the medical officer to claim exemption—it speaks ill of the climate of New England.

"On reviewing the returns of the Boards of Enrolment for the districts of which Boston is a part, we find that during the week the board in district 3 has exempted 259 men, has received satisfactory evidence that 13 have paid the commutation fee, has received and accepted 54 substitutes, and has held one man to serve who reported at once for duty.

"In the Fourth District 1,135 men have been examined, and of these 938 were declared by the Board to be exempt, 70 had paid the commutation fee, 10 were passed as fit for duty, and 108 substitutes were accepted.

"In the first district, up to Friday night, 256 conscripts had been examined by the Board of Enrolment in this city of whom 29 were accepted and furloughed, 12 furnished substitutes, 21 commuted, and 104 were accepted.

"It is stated that Hon. Caleb Cushing has been retained by the Democratic Association of this state, who propose to test the constitutionality of the Conscription Law. H. W. Paine will be associated with him. Hon B. R. Curtis, whose name has been before mentioned in this connection, may give a written opinion in the case."

A MYSTERIOUS DRAFT.
[From the New York World.]

"The draft which commences in this city to-day and which is about to be enforced all over the North, promises to be a very mysterious business. Instead of ordering a general conscription, and publicly apportioning the quotas to the several states, the administration has privately notified the several district provost-marshals, and the drafting has been begun without the knowledge or information of the public. We believe this secret way of doing business is common in Russia or Austria, but it is quite new in this free country.

So far we have no assurance that it is to be an equal conscription. From the number actually drafted in Rhode Island and Massachusetts, it would seem that the call was for 300,000 men; but the number required of the counties of Warren and Essex is on a basis of 400,000. According to the *Tribune*, the number New York city must raise is 26,000, and Brooklyn 10,000, which is conscripting at the rate of 600,000 for the whole North. Can it be that the administration has so much more confidence in New York copperheads than New England Republicans that it calls for more of the former than the latter? This is really a serious matter, and in the absence of any official announcement by the government of the number of men it requires, how do we know but what the secret instructions of the provost marshals are to conscript heavily in the Democratic districts and lightly in the Republican districts?

Of course it is incredible that they should do this injustice; but the secrecy which marks the machinery of the draft naturally excites comment and uneasiness. A Secretary of War who, on an occasion of great national rejoicing for victories won, is small souled enough and prejudiced enough to malign the majority of his fellow-citizens and apply to them an approbrious party epithet, as Mr. Stanton did at the serenade the other evening, is equal to any injustice towards the people he dislikes. President Lincoln has issued a number of unnecessary and mischievous proclamations, but we think one on this subject is very much needed to avoid misapprehensions."

There is no doubt that the iniquities of the draft in New York was the cause of the disgraceful riots in that city.

RESULTS OF THE DRAFT IN MASSACHUSETTS.

The whole number drafted in the 4th District was 4,198. The account of the Examin- Board stood as follows :

Exempt for various causes	2,857
Absentees	22
Dead	4
Paid commutation	134
Furnished substitutes	196
Held and sent to corps	46
Not reported and deemed Deserters	939
	4,198

RESULT IN THE 8th DISTRICT, NEW YORK.

Whole number exempted	2,582
Whole number examined	2,900
Paid commutation	885
Furnished substitutes	67
Conscripts accepted	63

These were no doubt extreme cases, but few districts have done much better, and the whole shows the system of draft to be a farce, and we are led to record our convictions that the draft is only kept up for *political* purposes, and not to obtain soldiers, for in fact, nearly all the soldiers that have been obtained for the past year have been enrolled by voluntary enlistments.

THURLOW WEED ON "SNEAKS."

The following from the pen of that conservative Republican, Thurlow Weed, is as true as it is "rough" :

" It is to be regretted that leading, boisterous abolitionists who were so free of their abuse of all those who differ with them, fail to justify their precepts by their examples. The editor of the *Independent*, whose zeal for the draft led him to rail at all who questioned its wisdom, when drafted himself, ingloriously shrinks from taking his share of duty and danger.— Shame on such a *sneak*. Subject by law to military duty, and constantly pressing others into the field, Mr. Tilton must be craven in spirit, without patriotism, pride or manhood, to skulk a draft himself, while he is merciless in regard to the mechanic and laborer, who is compelled to leave his wife and children.

" Still more mortifying, if possible, is the course of Mayor Opdyke, whose drafted son, instead of gallantly stepping forward, as an example to poor men, *sneaks!* The Mayor is filled with patriotism at conventions—he is gorged with government contracts! He leans heavily upon the government to make good his profits, but his son, when drafted, is not strong enough to be a soldier. He is, however, strong enough to hold offices, but these offices do not expose him to anything but salary and fees.— Being a soldier is quite a different thing. Out upon such false practices—such cheap loyalty —such bogus patriotism."

This just rebuke hits not only Mayor Opdyke and the editor of the N. Y. *Independent*, but it is a just criticism on the sneaking conduct of nineteen-twentieths of those who have so long and loudly abused all Democrats who did not go to the war, and yet they will "sneak" out of all danger—all responsibility—and if they can only get a fat contract or enjoy fat fees, they set themselves up as extra *loyal!*

We have heard of a very loyal member of the Wisconsin Legislature, who gave his age in the Blue Book as considerably below the maximum for the first class, and yet, when drafted, he claims immunity—and gets it—for over age.— These things will happen among the best regulated advocates of loyalty.

DRAFTING IN THE TIME OF THE REVOLUTION,

We recall to the memory of all who have read the history of the revolution, the action of the Congress at that period in relation to the principle of drafting, and to offer for their digestion the following morsel of history:

On the 26th of February, 1778, the following resolutions were unanimously adopted by Congress:

"*Resolved*, That the several States hereafter named be required *forthwith to fill up, by drafts* from their *militia*, or in any other way that shall be effectual, their respective battalions of *Continental* troops.

"*All persons drafted shall serve* in the *Continental* battalions of their respective States, for the space of nine months from the time they shall respectively appear at the several places of rendezvous hereinafter mentioned unless sooner discharged."

"*Resolved*, That all persons, *in whatever way procured*, for supplying the deficiencies in the Continental battalions unless enlisted for three years, or during the war, shall be considered *as drafted*." etc.

On the 9th of March, 1779, it was again—

"*Resolved*, That it be earnestly recommended to the several states to make up and *complete* their respective battalions to their full complement *by draft*, or in any other manner they shall think proper, and that they have their quotas of deficiencies ready to take the field, and to march to such place as the *Commander-in-Chief shall direct*, without delay."

"Thus, it appears, that during the Revolutionary war, men were drafted to fill up the regular regiments of the line, and were immediately subject to the orders of the Commander-in-Chief, without reference to, or control by, the Governors of the states. We have here, therefore, the most undeniable precedent for the action of the last Congress and that of the President, for raising drafted men and placing them in the army. None but Tories and the friends of the enemy opposed the principle then—none but traitors will do it now.—*Rep. Paper*.

Ah, yes, but you forget one thing. You have offered a *precedent*, but that precedent proves just what you didn't want it to. It proves that under the old Continental sway they never thought of allowing Congress to draft, but required the *states* to fill up their quotas by drafts. That's precisely the Democratic way now. That's just the only way the Democrats believe to be constitutional—the only way to preserve state sovereignty, and state identity.

With the following quotation from BURKE, we will close this chapter:

"I can conceive no existence under heaven, that is more truly odious and disgusting than an impotent, helpless creature, without civil wisdom or military skill—without a consciousness of any but his servility to it, bloated with pride and arrogance," and *calling for battles which he is not to fight.*"

CHAPER XXXVI.

LOYALTY AND PATRIOTISM OF DEMOCRATS.

General Remarks and Facts pertaining to...The Democracy of New York...The Iowa Democracy...Doctrine of the Kentucky Democracy...The Ohio Democracy...The Democracy of Wisconsin...The Minnesota Democracy... Democracy of Pennsylvania...Illinois Democracy....Connecticut Democracy...Democracy of Indiana...Of Columbus, Ohio...Of Madison, Wis....The National Democracy ...Sayings and Doings of Leading Democrats...Governor Seymour's Proclamation...Gov. Seymour's Message... Gov. Parker's Proclamation...Remarks of Hon. H. L. Palmer...Et tu Vallandigham...Democrats Rejoice at our Victories...Testimony of our opponents...New York Times...Mr. Seward, Official...Judge Paine, of Wis.... Administration Compliment Gov. Seymour for his Patriotism, &c.

LOYALTY AND PATRIOTISM OF DEMOCRATS.

Having shown, beyond a cavil, in the foregoing pages that the Republican leaders are disloyal to their goverement, we will now show by the best evidence that man can give or receive, that the Democracy of the country are now, as they ever have been, loyal to their government and true to the Union of their fathers. The best criteria of the aims and purposes of a party or individuals, are their recorded avowals—the actual and logical results of their measures. Having judged of their opponents by these criteria, we will now pass in like review the principal leaders and measures of the Democratic party.

From 1801 to 1861 the Democracy of the nation had been constantly in power in one or all of the different branches of Government, and most of this sixty years they had full control of the entire administration of government. That the Democratic party during this long period, embracing the early pupilage of our government, may have committed errors—that individuals of the party may have perpetrated gross wrongs in the name of that party, perhaps it would be uncandid to deny; but, history, the true arbiter, justifies us in the re petition of the oft reiterated, yet never impeached declaration, that during all this period—while the noble—historical Democracy—have been beset by all the ills that party and flesh are heir to, our country has flourished without a parallel in the annals of human governments. On every recurring national holiday, thousands of candidates for oratorical honors have over-taxed the eulogistic muses, and exhausted the most extravagant panegyrics on the fame and progress of our "Glorious Union." All parties, without exception, appealing to facts and drawing lavishly from the store-house of fancy, had held up our country, in marked contrast with all other lands, as the most free, happy, progressive and prosperous—nor was it safe for foreign pretenders to draw in question Brother Johnathan's panegyrics of the glorious past, or his predictions of the glorious future.

This picture is by no means overwrought, and it shows that high grade of opinion in which, we, at least, hold ourselves, and although the leading maratime powers of Europe may not have been willing to acknowledge that Brother Jonathan, yet scarcely out of his teens, had actually outstripped them in wealth and material greatness, they nevertheless acknowledged our vast and rapidly increasing power, and sent hither millions of their own citizens to be partakers with us of those manifold blessings of personal happiness and civil liberty, for so many centuries denied them on their native soil.

We may safely say, without fear of contradiction, that for all these blessings of our government, so justly celebrated for the wisdom and beneficence of its laws, the partakers were indebted to the Democratic party—for we believe no one will question the fact, or attempt to impeach our veracity, when we state that every general law of general public importance, found on the statute book of the nation, up to December, 1860, had its origin in the Democratic party. Perhaps these laws, or many of them might have been bettered, for no man or party has yet reached the degree of Divine perfection—but such as they were—they constituted the basis of all our national prosperity, so often and so long the lyric's song and the statesman's eulogy.

During this sixty years—embracing a long war with the first maratime power on the globe, and sundry harrassing Indian wars, together with a war with the Republic of Mexico, no man was arbitrarily deprived of his liberty without a remedy—no press was destroyed by the direction or connivance of the administrators or executors of the laws—no system of espoinage, spies and delators was established. No citizen was ever exiled or banished—no suspension of the writ of *habeas corpus* occurred outside of military lines. In short, no constitutional right was denied to the people without a remedy. No Democrat was known to curse this Union as a "league with hell," or any equivalent, impious anathema. No clear and unequivocal infractions of the constitution were suffered. In short, the rights of life, liberty and the pursuit of happiness were guaranteed to all, in strict accordance with the constitution.

Such, in brief, was the history and result of Democratic rule, up to the breaking out of our present troubles, and it becomes us now to enquire, what Democrats and the Democratic party (we mean those and only those who fell not into the snares of secession) have done since that time. Our remarks will apply to the two millions of Democrats in the loyal states. Are they disloyal, or are they not?—Let them answer for themselves.

THE NEW YORK DEMOCRACY.

The following is the pertinent plank in the platform of the Democratic Convention that nominated HORATIO SEYMOUR, September, 1862:

"*First*, That they will continue to render the Government their sincere and united support in the use of all legitimate means to suppress the rebellion, and to restore the Union as it was, and maintain the Constitution as it is—believing that that sacred instrument, founded in wisdom by our fathers, clothes the constituted authorities with full power to accomplish such purpose."

NEW YORK DEMOCRACY IN 1863.

The State Convention that met at Albany, September, 1863, passed the following:

"*Resolved*, That we reaffirm the platform adopted by the Democratic Convention of 1862, viz.: *First*, That we will continue to render the Government our sincere and united support in the use of all legitimate means to suppress the rebellion, and to restore 'the Union as it was,' and to maintain 'the Constitution as it is,' believing that sacred instrument, founded in wisdom by our fathers, clothes the constituted authorities with full power to accomplish such purpose."

THE IOWA DEMOCRACY—1863.

Gen. TUTTLE, the Democratic candidate for Gov. in 1863, issued an address to the people, from which we take the following, and on which he was supported by the Democracy:

"I am in favor of a vigorous prosecution of the war to the full extent of our power, until the rebellion is suppressed, and of using all means that may be in our possession, recognized by honorable warfare, for that purpose. I am for the Union without an *if*, and regardless whether slavery stands or falls by its restoration, and in favor of peace on no other terms than the unconditional surrender of the rebels to the constituted authorities of the government of the United States."

DOCTRINE OF THE KENTUCKY DEMOCRACY.

The following from the message of Governor BRAMLETTE, Sept 1, 1863, is the doctrine not only of the Democracy of Kentucky, but everywhere:

"We affiliate with the loyal men north and south, whose object and policy is to preserve the Union and the Constitution unchanged and unbroken, and to restore the people to harmony and peace with the government, as they were before the rebellion.

"It is not a restored Union, not a reconstructed Union, that Kentucky desires ; but a preserved Union, and a restored peace upon a constitutional basis."

THE OHIO DEMOCRACY.

We select the following from among the planks of the Democratic platform adopted by the convention that nominated VALLANDIGHAM, in 1863:

"That we will earnestly support every constitutional measure tending to preserve the Union of the States. No men have a greater interest in its preservation than we have. None desire it more. There are none who will make greater sacrifices or endure more than we will to accomplish that end. We are, as we ever have been, the devoted friends of the Constitution and the Union, and we have no sympathy with the enemies of either."

THE DEMOCRACY OF WISCONSIN.

The following is from the celebrated "RYAN Address," adopted by the Democracy, in Mass Convention at Milwaukee, September, 1862, and reaffirmed in 1863:

"We claim the right on their behalf and our own, to censure the political acts of the Administration, when we think that they deserve it, and to do all lawfully within our power to sustain the supremacy of the Constitution in all places north or south, and over all persons in office and out of it. And to that end we devote our hearts, minds, estates, *to aid the Administration in the most vigorous and speedy prosecution of the war waged against the Union by the revolted states.* We believe that in so doing we fulfil the most sacred duty we owe to the constitution.

"And to this, we solemnly pledge the faith of our party and ourselves, until the war be ended and the constitution restored, as the supreme law of the land, in every state of the Union."

THE SAME PARTY IN 1863.

The following, among others, was adopted at the Democratic nominating State Convention, in 1863:

"11. *Resolved,* That we are proud of the gallantry and devotion of our fellow citizens serving in the land and naval forces of the United States, and sympathize deeply with all their sacrifices of life, health and comfort. End as the war may, their place in history is one of glory—successful whenever beyond the reach of corrupt political influences surrounding the administration, failing from no fault of their own whenever within the reach of those influences, equally brave and patriotic in either fortune, they are the glorious brothers of our blood and will never make good the brutal boast that when they shall have suppressed rebellion in the south, they will turn their arms against their brethren in the north."

THE MINNESOTA DEMOCRACY.

We select the following from the platform adopted by the Democracy in State Convention July 26, 1863:

"6. That it is the duty of every citizen to obey the laws, and that however unconstitutional and oppressive and unjust the same may appear, he must submit thereto, until such laws are repealed, or declared null and void by the proper tribunals.

"7. That we tender our army, and especially the members of our minnesota regiments, our heartfelt thanks for their patriotic devotion to their country, and we also tender our sympathy to the survivors of the gallant dead, who have offered up their lives as a sacrifice for their country and won for themselves the everlasting gratitude of the nation."

THE PENNSYLVANIA DEMOCRACY.

The following was passed by the Democracy of the House of Representatives of Pennsylvania, against the united votes of the opposition, in 1863:

"That Pennsylvania will adhere to the Constitution and the Union as the best, it may be the last hope of popular freedom, and for all wrongs which may have been committed, or evils which may exist, will seek redress under the Constitution and within the Union, by the peaceful but powerful agency of the suffrage of a free people.

"That while the General Assembly condemns and denounces the faults of the Administration, and the encroachments of the Abolitionists, it does also most thoroughly condemn and denounce the heresy of Secession, as unwarranted by the Constitution, and destructive alike of the security and perpetuity of government and of peace and liberty; the people of the State are opposed to any division of this Union; and will persistently exert their whole influence and power under the Constitution to maintain and defend it."

THE ILLINOIS DEMOCRACY.

The Democracy of the Legislature of Illinois, in 1863, among others, adopted the following:

Resolved, That while we condemn and denounce the flagrant and monstrous usurpations by the Administration, and encroachments by Abolitionism, we equally denounce and condemn the ruinous heresy of secession, as unwarranted by the Constitution, and destructive alike of the society and perpetuity of our government, and the peace and liberty of the people."

THE DEMOCRACY OF CONNECTICUT.

The following we take from the Democratic platform of 1863:

"2d. That while as citizens of Connecticut, we assert our devotion to the Constitution and the Union, and will hereafter, as we have heretofore, support with zeal and energy the authorities of the U. S. in the full constitutional exercise of their powers, we deliberately aver that the liberties of the people are menaced by congressional and federal usurpations, and can only be stopped by energetic action of State authority."

THE DEMOCRACY OF INDIANA.

The following is taken from the address of the Democratic members of the Legislature of Indiana, 1863:

"The Democratic party, if in power to-day, *would put down this rebellion*, and restore the Union as it was in six months, and by the honest and lawful method of subduing combatants, and protecting those not in arms against the government. *It would make no war on States*, and populations. *It would overthrow the guilty rebel wherever found in arms.* It would confiscate nothing that did not belong to a fighting traitor to the Union. * * A Democratic Administration would see that our victorious legions marched wherever there was an armed foe to conquer."

DEMOCRACY OF COLUMBUS, OHIO.

The following clearly defines the position of the Democracy everywhere. It is the first of a series of resolutions passed by the Democracy of Columbus, Ohio, in 1863:

"*Resolved*, That the present war should be carried on to maintain the supremacy of the Constitution and the enforcement of all constitutional laws, and that when this is accomplished, the war ought to cease."

DEMOCRACY OF MADISON, WISCONSIN.

The Democracy of Madison, Wisconsin, in July, 1863, met to celebrate the taking of Vicksburg, and adopted the following resolutions:

"*Resolved*, That the Democracy of the city of Madison and Dane county rejoice "with exceeding great joy," at the surrender of Vicksburg, the great Sebastopol of the Mississippi Valley, and that our thanks are due and hereby tendered to Major General Grant and the brave troops under his command for this glorious achievement—that while we tender our sympathies to those who have been wounded in battle, we embrace the mournful privilege of offering our sympathy and condolence to the friends and relatives of those brave men who have fallen while defending the Constitution and Union of our fathers.

"*Resolved*, That we award a like mede of praise and sympathy for sufferers in the Army of the Potomac, who have so bravely and so heroically defended the soil of Pennsylvania from the polution of rebel invasion.

Resolved, In the spirit of the resolution passed by the last Congress, that the war ought to be vigorously prosecuted for the establishment of the National authority, and the supremacy of the constitution and laws over every foot of our territory, and when that object is obtained the war ought to cease."

THE NATIONAL DEMOCRACY.

On the 28th of June, 1863, the Democratic and conservative members of Congress unanimously passed the following, among other resolutions:

"*Resolved*, That the Constitution and the Union and the laws *must* be preserved and maintained in all their proper and rightful supremacy, and that the rebellion now in arms against them *must* be suppressed and put down, and that it is our duty to vote for all measures necessary and proper to that end."

SAYINGS AND DOINGS OF LEADING DEMOCRATS.

Gov. Seymour's Proclamation.

The following we select from Gov. SEYMOUR's proclamation, issued in response to the President's call for troops, October 29, 1863:

"In this emergency it is the duty of all citizens to listen to the appeal put forth by the President, and to give efficient and cheerful aid in filling up the thinned ranks of our armies. It is due to our brethren in the field, who have battled so heroically for the flag of our country, the Union of the states, and to uphold the Constitution, and prompt and voluntary assistance should be sent to them in this moment of their peril. They went forth in the full confidence that they would at all times receive from their fellow citizens at home a generous and efficient support.

"Every motive of pride and patriotism should impel us to give this by voluntary and cheerful contributions of men and money, and not by a forced conscription or coercive action on the part of the government."

Gov. Seymour's Message.

The following paragraph is taken from the message of Gov. SEYMOUR to the New York Legislature, January, 1863:

"We must accept the condition of affairs as they stand. At this moment the fortunes of our country are influenced by the results of battles. *Our armies in the field must be supported.* All constitutional demands of our General Government *must be promptly responded to!* But, *war alone* will not save the Union. The rule of action which is used to put down an ordinary insurrection is not applicable to a widespread armed resistance of great communities. It is wildness and folly to shut our eyes to this truth. *Under no circumstances can the division of the Union be conceded.* We will put forth every exertion of power. We will hold out every inducement to the people of the South to return to their allegiance, consistent with honor.

"We will guarantee them every right, every consideration, demanded by the Constitution, and by that fraternal regard which must prevail in a common country. *But we can never* voluntarily consent to the breaking up of the Union of these states, or the destruction of the Constitution."

Gov. Parker's Proclamation.

On the 22d of October, 1863, Governor PARKER, of New Jersey, issued a proclamation in response to the President's call for troops, in which occurs the following:

"I earnestly call upon every citizen of this state to use every effort to raise these troops. The time for work is short: but, if the people of New Jersey, who have hitherto never faltered in the discharge of duty, will, unitedly and in the proper spirit, at once enter upon it, with a determination not to fail, they will succeed.

"Our armies should be largely reinforced. A crushing blow at the armed power of the rebellion, if followed by wise, just and conciliatory counsels, will open the door to the peace which we so much desire, and which has thus far eluded us."

Hon. H. L. Palmer's Speech.

The Hon. H. L. PALMER, late Democratic candidate for Governor of Wisconsin, presided at a patriotic meeting at Milwaukee. In addressing the vast assemblage he used the following language:

"A most gigantic and stupendously wicked rebellion has arisen to destroy, with bloody and raricidal hands, this fair fabric raised at the cost of our father's blood; and now we are called upon to put it down and save our loved land. I trust we stand here to-day as Americans only, and that we shall not fail in effective measures to answer the call of our country and to send succor to our brothers in arms and peril in the South."

Et tu Vallandigham.

Even VALLANDIGHAM, who has been so unmercifully and fouly villified as a traitor, uttered the following patriotic sentiments in reply to a charge of the New York *Times* that he counselled resistance to law:

"NEW YORK, March 8, 1863.
"To the Editor of the New York Times:

"Allow me to say that the statement of your reporter that I denied that we owed any obedience to the Conscription act, and your own that I counselled resistance to it by the people of the North, are both incorrect. On the contrary, *I expressly counselled the trial of all questions of law before our judicial courts, and all questions of politics before the tribunal of the ballot-box*. I AM FOR OBEDIENCE TO ALL LAWS—obedience by the people and by men in power also. I am for a free discussion of all questions of law before our judicial courts, and all questions of politics before the tribunal of the ballot-box. I am for a free discussion of all measures and laws whatsoever, as in former times, but *for forcible resistance to none*. The ballot-box, and not the cartridge-box, is the instrument for reform and revolution which I would have resorted to. Let this be understood.

"C. L. VALLANDIGHAM."

Mr. Vallandigham in Congress.

The Abolitionists for months paraded through their columns what purported to be an extract from a speech of Mr. V. in Congress, that he would not vote a dollar for the war, &c. Here is what he did say :

"For my own part, sir, while I would not in the beginning have given a dollar or a man to commence this war, I am willing—*now that we are in the midst of it without any act of ours*—TO VOTE JUST AS MANY MEN AND JUST AS MUCH MONEY AS MAY BE NECESSARY TO PROTECT AND DEFEND THE FEDERAL GOVERNMENT. IT WOULD BE BOTH TREASON AND MADNESS NOW TO DISARM THE GOVERNMENT IN THE PRESENCE OF AN ENEMY OF TWO HUNDRED THOUSAND MEN IN THE FIELD AGAINST IT!"

Democrats Rejoice at our Victories.

The following short extract from an editorial in the Chicago *Post* of July 11, 1863, speaks volumes of praise for the Democracy :

"The best answer to Gen. Singleton's unconditional peace speeches is to be found in the *universal rejoicing* by the democratic papers of the country, over the victories of Meade and Grant. In these rejoicings we have an impression of the true democratic sentiment. They are unconditional rejoicings.— They are not qualified by regrets that the war is not a constitutional one, or that it is a barbarous one, or that it is a war to overturn and destroy the liberties of the people ; but the rejoicings are earnest and universal that the armed rebels against the Constitution and the Union have been beaten, defeated and cut to pieces by the troops of the United States. It is claimed that these victories are as honorable and as brilliant as though they were gained over any other enemy seeking to destroy the American Union. In these victories the democratic papers, and the democratic masses everywhere see a hope that the Administration will learn and profit by the lesson that armed rebellion cannot be crushed except by force of arms ; that paper proclamations and cruel laws only serve to exasperate the enemy, who is to be put down by blows and offers of pardon upon proper submission."

TESTIMONY OF OUR OPPONENTS.

The New York *Times*, after months of idle and slanderous denunciations of the Democratic party, was compelled to make the following admission:

"We have never doubted that the great body of the Democratic party are for preserving the Union and crushing the rebellion, which alone threatens its existence. We do not doubt that they look upon a vigorous prosecution of the war as the only means by which that result can be brought about. And, in spite of all the efforts that may be made to drive or seduce the Democratic party from that position, we believe it will hold it with fidelity and firmness, and will insist upon the adoption of that policy by this administration and by any other that may succeed it. We are well aware that the Democratic party does not indorse very many of the acts of the administration. We have no right to ask such an indorsement at its hands. Upon any of the details of administration, upon any of the measures which the President and Congress may see fit to adopt, that party has a perfect right to its own opinions. It may with perfect propriety protest against the proclamation of emancipation, the policy of arbitrary arrests, the enlistment of negro soldiers and any other measure of the administration."

The Philadelphia *Press*, the court organ of the administration, thus slurs at a Democratic resolution:

"The Lancaster county copperheads had a convention, a few days ago, and adopted a number of platitudes, which they called resolutions. The following is one of the most precious of the number:

"*Resolved*, That the soldiers fighting in our armies merit the warmest thanks of the nation. Living, they shall know a nation's gratitude; wounded, a nation's care; and dying, they shall live in our memories, to tench posterity to honor patriotsanl ··· ··· a;ri.iced their lives upon their country's ;\·.

We copy this especially as a compliment.

MR. SEWARD ENDORSES OUR POSITION.

We find in a cotemporary the following resolution, said to have been adopted by a political Convention in the state of Maryland:

"*Resolved*, That there is no such thing in in times of rebellion as supporting the National Government without supporting the Administration of the National Government; that the administration of the National Government is confided by the Constitution to the President, assisted in his several spheres of duty by the administrative departments, and therefore the measures of the President and the general policy of the Administration should, under the present trying circumstances of the country, be sustained by all true patriots in a spirit of generous confidence, and not thwarted by captious criticism or factious opposition."

As a full reply to this we present the following from the official dispatch of Secretary Seward to our Minister at London, of November 10, 1862:

"From whatever cause it has happened, political debates during the present year have resumed, in a considerable degree, the normal character, and while loyal republicans have adhered to the new banner of the Union party, the democratic party has rallied and made a vigorous canvass with a view to the recovery of its former political ascendency. Loyal democrats in considerable numbers, retaining the name of democracy from habit, and not because they oppose the Union, are classified by he other party as 'Opposition.' It is not nece sary for the information of our representatives abroad that I should descend into any examination of the relative principles or policies of the two parties. It will suffice to say that while there may be men of doubtful political wisdom and virtue in each party, and while there may be differences of opinion between the two parties as to the measures best calculated to preserve the Union and restore its authority, yet it is not to be inferred that either party, or any considerable portion of the people of the loyal States, is disposed to accept disunion under any circumstances, or upon any terms. It is rather to be understood that the people have become so confident of the stability of the Union that partizan combinations are resuming their sway here, as they do in such cases in all free countries. In this country, especially, it is a habit not only entirely consistent with the Constitution, *but even essential to its stability, to regard the administration at any time existing as distinct and separable from the government itself, and to canvass the proceedings of the one without the thought of disloyalty to the other.* We might possibly have had quicker success in suppressing the insurrection if this habit could have rested a little longer in abeyance ; but, on the other hand, we are under obligations to save not only the integrity or unity of the country, but also its inestimable and precious Constitution. No one can safely say that the resumption of the previous popular habit does not tend to this last and most important consummation, if, at the same time. as we confidently expect, the Union itself shall be saved."

JUDGE PAINE AGREES WITH THE DEMOCRACY

Judge PAINE, a most intensely radical abolitionist, and one of the judges of the Wisconsin Supreme Court, addressed a "Union" meeting at Madison, Wisconsin, May 14, 1863, and we take the following from his remarks, as reported in the *State Journal* (Radical) of the following day:

"The speaker thought the President possessed all *necessary powers under the constitution, and that he should be governed by that instrument in war as well as in peace. He agreed with the Democrats in this respect.*"

GOVERNOR SEYMOUR COMPLIMENTED.

Gov. SEYMOUR has been the best abused man in all the nation. No term could be heaped upon him too vile for the tastes and appetites of the radical press. But the following will show that he stands in a much more patriotic light before the world for his prompt responses, than does Gov. ANDREW, who hesitated—held back, and was long months in doing what Gov. S. accomplished in a few hours. The following correspondence will explain itself:

On the 15th of June, 1863, Mr. STANTON telegraphed to Gov. S. as follows:

"To his Excellency, Gov. Seymour:

"The movements of the rebel forces in Virginia are now sufficiently developed to show that General Lee, with his whole army, is moving forward to invade the states of Maryland and Pennsylvania, and other states.

"The President, to repel the invasion promptly, has called upon Ohio, Pennsylvania, Maryland, and Western Virginia, for one hundred thousand militia for six months, unless sooner discharged. It is important to have the largest possible force in the least possible time, and if other states would furnish militia for a short time, to be credited in the draft, it would greatly advance the object. Will you please inform me immediately, if, in answer to a special call of the President, you can raise and forward say twenty thousand militia as volunteers, without bounty, to be credited in the draft of your state, or what number you can possibly raise?

E. M. STANTON, Sec'y of War."

Governor S. promptly sent an affirmative answer, and in a few hours several regiments were under marching orders. The "roads" did "swarm." On the same day he received the following "thanks:"

"WASHINGTON, June 15, 1863.
GOVERNOR SEYMOUR:

"The President desires me to return his thanks, with those of the Department, for your prompt response. A strong movement of your city regiments to Philadelphia would be a very encouraging movement, and do great good in giving strength in that state.
"EDWIN M. STANTON,
"Secretary of War."

The following telegrams, sent at different intervals, under all the circumstances of abuse on Governor S., is a better eulogy than our pen could frame:

"WASHINGTON, June 19, 1863.
"To ADJUTANT GENERAL SPRAGUE:

"The President directs me to return his thanks to his Excellency Governor Seymour, and his staff, for their energetic and prompt action. Whether any further force is likely to be required will be communicated to you tomorrow, by which time it is expected the movements of the enemy will be more fully developed.
"EDWIN M. STANTON,
"Secretary of War."
"JOHN T. SPRAGUE, Adjutant General."

"WAR DEPARTMENT, WASHINGTON CITY,
June 27, 1863.

"DEAR SIR:—I cannot forbear expressing to you the deep obligation I feel for the prompt and candid support you have given to the Government in the present emergency. The energy, activity, and patriotism you have exhibited I may be admitted personally and officially to acknowledge, without arrogating any personal claims on my part to such service, or to any service whatever.

"I shall be happy always to be esteemed your friend,
"EDWIN M. STANTON.
"His Excellency, HORATIO SEYMOUR."

What, a *friend* to the "*friend*" of the New York rioters? Incredible!

CHAPTER XXXVII.
MISCELLANEOUS FACTS AND FIGURES.

Political *sine qua non* of Wisconsin Legislature...Still refuse to yield an inch....N. Y. Round Table on Lincoln's Amnesty Proclamation...Two Millions in Men....Three Millions in Money...Is a National Debt a National Blessing...A Negro Nobility...Effects of a High Tariff...Vicksburg Discipline...Will the Rebellion succeed...1,085,000 Democratic Votes in the Loyal States...Gross Outrage by Abolitionists at Boscobel, Wisconsin.

MISCELLANEOUS.

The following not having been convenient for use under their proper heads, we insert them here, without attempting to link them in argumentative form :

WILL LITSEN TO NO PROPOSITION FOR PEACE.

The following remarkable declaration introduced by a Mr. STARKS in the Wisconsin Assembly, Jan. 21, '64, and adopted by all the Republican votes of that body, shows to what extremes we are drifting :

"*Resolved by the Assembly, the Senate concurring*' That as our country, and the very existence of the best Government ever instituted by man, are imperiled by the most causeless and wicked rebellion the world has ever seen believing, as we do, that the only hope of saving the country and preserving the government is in the power of the sword—we are for the most vigorous prosecution of the war, until the constitution and laws shall be enforced and obeyed in all parts of the United States, and to that end we oppose any *armistice, intervention, mediation or proposition* for peace, from any source whatever, so long as the rebels are found in arms against the government, and we ignore all party lines, names and issues, and recognize but two parties, patriots and tritors.

To show *how* they "ignored all *party* lines," we copy the fourth and last of the series:

"*Resolved*, That we recognize in Abraham

Lincoln, President of the United States, a statesman of liberal and enlarged views, great ability, and unswerving integrity and if the wishes of the people of Wisconsin are complied with by the National Union Convention that assembles to nominate candidates for the Presidency Abraham Lincoln will again be nominated."

This is ignoring party with a vengeance. It shows that the supporters of Mr. LINCOLN are pledged against any peace whatever—and of course against any Union. This is the logic of their conduct.

WHAT LINCOLN'S PROCLAMATION WILL DO.

[From the New York Round Table. (Rep.)

"Not only the overthrow of the rebellion as a military power, but the complete subjugation of the Southern people, until they are so utterly crushed and humbled as to be willing to accept life on any terms, is the essential condition of the President's scheme. It may therefore prolong the war; and after the war is substantially ended, it may defer the day of reunion and each. It cannot be doubted that the President contemplates all this, and that in his mind, the removal of slavery being considered the most essential condition of the most desirable and permanent peace, he felt justified in incurring great evils for the sake of a greater ultimate good.

"In plain English, we are informed, that in order to abolish slavery, the war is to be prolonged, and the day of the restoration of the Union deferred."

TWO MILLIONS IN MEN—THREE MILLIONS IN MONEY.

Here are the several calls of the President for forces, not including naval:

April 16, 1861	75,000
May 4, 1861	64,748
From July to December, 1861	500,000
July 1, 1862	300,000
August 4, 1862	300,000
Draft, summer of 1863	300,000
February 1, 1864	500,000
Total	2,039,748

The last call is supposed to include one of the previous calls.

The known cost of all this it is impossible fully to state, but the following figures show the loans and liabilities authorized by various acts of Congress, as given by the New York presses:

Loan of 1842	$242,621
Loan of 1847	9,415,250
Loan of 1848	8,908,341
Texas indemnity loan of 1850	3,461,000
Loan of 1858	20,000,000
Loan of 1860	7,022,000
Loan of 1861	18,415,000
Treasury notes, March, '61	512,900
Oregon war loan, 1861	1,016,000
Another loan of 1861	50,000,000
Three years treasury notes	139,679,000
Loan of August, 1861	320,000
Five-twenty loan	400,000,000
Temporary loan	104,033,103
Certificates of Indebtedness	156,619,437
Unclaimed dividends	114,115
Demand treasury notes	500,000
Legal tenders, 1862	397,767,114
Legal tenders, 1863	104,969,937
Postal and fractional currency	50,000,000
Old treasury notes outstanding	118,000
Ten-forty bonds	900,000,000
Interest-bearing treasury notes	500,000,000
Total	$2,774,912,818

The sums paid by states, cities, towns and individuals are not included in this record, and must reach many hundred millions more.

IS A NATIONAL DEBT A BLESSING.

We have in a former portion of this work, shown that the early Federals, who were for a semi-monarchial government, advocated a national debt, as the foundation of a national privileged aristocracy. A Washington correspondent of the Milwaukee *Sentinel*, January, 1864, thus shadows forth the predilections of the present monarchial party:

"Great wars make nations rich as a people, although the government may be poor and in debt. A large national debt is a bond of strength, especially if the evidences of that debt drawing interest, are held by the masses of the people. Such has been the result with England. From the day that she began to spend hundreds of millions among her people in carrying on her continental wars, did she begin to develope her resources and increase in wealth and power. So it will be with the United States."

And, to carry out the figure to its legitimate proportions, they writer should have added, that with his aristocratical millennium comes also the millions of paupers.

A NEGRO NOBILITY.

(From the Albany (N. Y.) Argus and Atlas.)

"This country will have no *true dignity*," said Fred Douglas in a recent speech to the Abolitionists, "till the negro is entitled to vote and hold office."

The negroes, says Vandal Phillips, are our "nobility," and we must divide the lands of the South among them, as William the Conqueror partitioned England among the Norman Lords.

All that is very fine—"dignity and nobility"—but Sambo wants something practical, and the Administration proposes to give it to him.

We quote an illustrative incident:

"The colored people of Philadelphia are before the War Department for contracts for Quartermaster's supplies. David Browser and Jacob C. White had an interview with Secretary Stanton on Friday, and offered to engage to deliver in thirty, sixty and ninety days shirts, drawers, haversacks and blouses, to the extent of 300,000 of either.

They received assurances that the colored people should be placed hereafter upon the same footing with whites, in the matter of contracts."

"'Contracts' that is the word in which lies the real patent of nobility—then it is 'dignity!' "When the Haytian monarchy was formed, the black chiefs took the titles of Duke of Lemonade, Count Marmalade and the Marquis of Molasses We see looming in the distance our new nobility—Sir Sambo Shoddy, Count Cuffee Codfish and the Marquis of Mulemeat."

EFFECTS OF A HIGH TARIFF.

The New York *News*, in its money article, gives some statistics to show the effect of high prices upon the quantity of certain articles consumed. The following table shows the prices of coffee and the quantity taken for consumption in the last three years:

Price.	Lbs.	Lbs per head
1861..........14c	187,045,786	9 ℔s. 6 oz.
1862..........21c	88,989,911	4 lbs. 7 oz.
1863..........31c	79,719,641	3 lbs. 15 oz.

Thus, the consumption per head, has declined from 9 lbs 6oz. to 3 lb 15 oz. The 9 lbs. 6 oz. cost in 1861, $1 31, and the 3 lbs. 15 oz. in 1863, cost $1 22. Thus the consumer paid nearly as much money, greenbacks and stamps, as in 1861, but got 5 lbs. 7 oz less coffee for it. The same comparison is made as to molasses:

Price.	Gallons.	Per head.
1862..........2? cts	62,668,400	3 gals.,1 pints.
1863..........44 cts	37,569,088	1 gall.,? pints.

The cost of the three gallons and one pint per individual in 1862, was 92, and of the one gallon and seven pints in 1863, 82 cents.

This is not the worst raid of high tariffs.

VICKSBURG DISCIPLINE.

HEADQUARTERS 17th A. C., DEPT. OF THE TENN.,
 Vicksburg, Miss., Dec. 29, 1863.

General Orders No. 51.

The following circular has been issued by the Major General Commanding, and is now published in general orders for the information and guidance of all parties interested, who will make a note of it, and govern themselves accordingly:

Circular.

HEADQUARTERS 17TH ARMY CORPS,
PROVOST MARSHAL'S OFFICE.
Vicksburg, Miss., Dec. 27th, 1863.

The following named persons, Miss Kate Barnett, Miss Ella Barnett, Miss Laura Latham, Miss Ella Martin and Mrs. Moore, having acted disrespectfully toward the President and Government of the United States, and having insulted the officers, soldiers and loyal citizens of the United States who had assembled at the Episcopal Church in Vicksburg, on Christmas day, for Divine service, by *abruptly leaving said church* at that point in the service where the officiating minister prays for the welfare of the President of the United States and all others in authority, are hereby banished, and will leave the Federal lines within forty-eight hou s, under penalty of imp ison e.t.

Hereafter all pe sons, male or female, by word, d ed or implication, do insult or show disrespect to the President,

Government or flag of the United States, or to any officers or soldiers of the United States, upon matters of a national character, shall be fined, banished or imprisoned, according to the grossness of the offense.

By order of Major General McPherson.
 JAMES WILSON,
 Lt. Col. and Pro. Mar, 17th A. C.
W. T. CLARK, A. A. G.

If these female persons did really intend to show disrespect to Mr. LINCOLN, that is one thing, but if it was really a "military necessity" that caused them to leave, why, that is another thing. The question is, how did the gallant Provost Marshal know the true cause of the necessity?

WILL THE REBELLION SUCCEED?

If what the Abolition disunionists say be true, no power on earth can prevent its success, and let us see why.

They declare that all who vote the Democratic ticket are disloyal to our Government—"sympathisers" with the rebellion, &c. If this be true, let us see how strong the rebels are. The vote of 1860 developed about seven inhabitants to every voter in the land.

Now, there are in the loyal states the following numbers that vote the Democratic ticket, which will not probably vary 5,000 either way—near enough quite, to meet the argument:

California	50,000
Connecticut	40,000
Delaware	8,000
Illinois	135,000
Indiana	125,000
Iowa	50,000
Kentucky	88,000
Maine	51,000
Maryland	45,000
Massachusetts	40,000
Michigan	60,000
Minnesota	12,000
Missouri	100,000
New Hampshire	40,000
New Jersey	60,000
New York	285,000
Ohio	187,000
Oregon	8,000
Pennsylvania	254,000
Rhode Island	8,000
Vermont	12,000
Wisconsin	65,000
	$1,685,000

Here, then, right in the loyal states, are one million six hundred and eighty-five thousand votes that "sympathise with the rebellion," according to Abolition say-so. Multiply this by 7, and you have 11,795,000 persons here at the North who are in "open sympathy with the rebels." Add this vast number to the 10,000,000 in the rebel states, and it gives 21,795,000 "traitors," which, subtracted from the 30,000,000 of the entire white population of the whole Union, and it leaves only 8,205,000 "loyal" people to contend against over twenty-one millions of "secesh."

This argument is not ours. It is only the presentation of the Abolition "argument," and the bare statement shows the malicious absurdity of the Abolition asservation.

Let the Administration once throw out the "copperhead" element, and it will find itself in a wofully decimated dilemma.

DISGRACEFUL OUTRAGE.

The following from our correspondent at Boscobel, gives evidence of another of those disgraceful scenes, of which the murder of poor Bellinger last fall was but a prelude. It is the direct fruits of those bloodthirsty sentiments uttered by bloodthirsty Wilson, in Maine—by bloodthirsty Stanton, to the New York meeting—by bloodthirsty Jim Lane, in his bloodthirsty speech in Washington, and of the bloodthirsty letters and resolutions which were manufactured "to order" in the army, and sent North to garnish the bloodthirsty columns of the bloodthirsty radical press. If such teachings, and the inevitable results of such teachings, which have disgraced our land, do not deluge the North in blood, we are mistaken. It is re-enacting the bloody scenes that ushered in the French Reign of Terror.— Those who have set these diabolisms in motion, aid and abet them, need not be surprised to see and feel their counterparts, when forbearance ceases to be a virtue. It is not in human nature for human beings to stand everything. But to the letter :

TOWN OF HICKORY GROVE, Grant Co., Feb. 11, 1864.
Editor of the Patriot, Madison, Wis.

DEAR SIR:—On last Saturday, the 6th of February, one of the most disgraceful things occurred in the village of Boscobel, Grant county, that any civilized community ought to be ashamed of. Some returned soldiers, home on furlough, headed by the citizens, even a Justice of the Peace, went around town and brought up peaceable citizens, made them take the oath of allegiance, and if they would not do it, they got a pounding. For what did they make them take the oath? For voting last fall the Democratic ticket, or having in their house the Chicago *Times*. The night before they broke in windows and doors, pounded men and abused women when they could not find their husbands, and even abused dumb beasts belonging to what they call "Copperheads," by beating them with clubs.

A pretty pass things have come to that a man's life nor his property is safe under the law that rules our land, and a man cannot vote as he chooses under the present Administration. If the Union party (as they call themselves) is the majority or they cant speak, or even read a paper the Administration allows to be printed and circulated, such works being countenanced by the citizens of Boscobel. The loyal men of the town and country around feeling indignant at such works will not hereafter patronize them with their trade no more than they are compelled to by actual necessity.

The writer of this was an eye witness to a good deal of the proceedings, which can be testified to by a good many, if necessary. S. C.

The Grant Co. *Herald*, received last evening, February 10, 1864, actually confirms all our correspondent has said, in nearly two columns of chuckling doggerel. We clip the following from that sheet, which shows that while no pretence is set up that any provocation was given by the Democrats of Boscobel, except their having voted the Democratic ticket, the editor indulges in a "flow of soul," at the "fun for the boys," but death to Democrats:

BOSCOBEL SCENERY—A SPEC OF THE SPECTRE.—The other day certain amusing scenes were acted at Boscobel, scenes that served well for sport, as in the fable of the boys and frogs, but which may be regretted at a sherer moment; for blossoms those are that promise no good fruit. And if fruits spring therefrom which make bitter the future joys of peace, well may we be cheered by the wise few at least for casting a frost that shall chill and hinder another crop.

Boys of the army, the future masters of our country, see to it that in Boscobel all such work as that the other day shall now be held as finished, not to be resumed at any future time.

And, in another column, the editor says :

Hon. J. Allen Barber came home from Madison on furlough the last of the closing week. He thinks the legislature will be a profitable one, and the work excellent, when the committees report. Mr. Barber was very much struck with the manner the laws and *justice* were being administered at Boscobel, while stopping there on Friday and Saturday, an account of which we have written out.

Now, if this does not do great injustice to "Hon. J. Allen Barber," it makes him out as delighted (" *very* much struck") with the "*justice*" administered by the "boys"—that is, Mr. Hon. J. Allen Barber must have been delighted to see Democrats knocked down with clubs, for no crime but having voted the Democratic ticket. And then, suppose them to have committed the greatest of crimes, what right had these soldiers, led on by bloodthirsty Abolitionists, to take matters into their own hands ? Does the "Hon. J. Allen Barber," who is now aspiring to a seat on the Bench, where he may administer the laws, delight in this ? Impossible ! We cannot believe it, but if it be true, with what grace (if he *should* be elected) can he sit on the bench and try the murderous individuals for their crimes?

We hesitate not to utter our belief that unless the President of the United States shall cause stringent orders to be issued against such bloody raids on peaceable citizens, that we shall see bloody times in the North. For it cannot be expected that people will calmly submit to be murdered (as in the case of Bellinger), and knocked down and beaten with clubs (as in Boscobel)—rode on rails (as in Green county, by the mobocrats there), and not rise up in self defense. If it be the purpose of the Powers that be to murder and exterminate Democrats, let them act honorable about it, at least. Let them give fair warning, so that Democrats may prepare to "sell out" as dearly as possible. If the threats that have been uttered by officials, from members of Mr. Lincoln's Cabinet down to the lowest grade of political Roughs, are to be carried out, let the country be prepared for it at once—let the worst come *now*. For us, in the language of the noble Patrick Henry, we say, "give us liberty or give us death." The liberty to think and vote as we please, is as sacred as life itself.

These evidences of an approaching Reign of Terror, furnish the most gloomy aspect of all our troubles—and if the Administration does not desire to force a terrible bloody conflict here at the North, it should take immediate steps to check these certain *causes*. It can do it, and if it will not, then the country may as well make up its mind for the worst, and every Democrat prepare to avail himself of the first law of nature.

We trust that Gov. Lewis will use his power to prevent these certain provocations to disorder and anarchy.

HENRY CLAY'S PROPHECY FULFILLED.

In speaking of the abolitionists, Mr. Clay said in the Senate:

To the agency of their power of persuasion, they now propose to substitute the power of the BALLOT BOX; and he must be blind to what is passing before us, who does not perceive that the *inevitable tendency* of their proceedings is, if these should be found insufficient, to invoke, finally, the more potent powers of the bayonet.

This prophecy has been fulfilled to the letter.

CHAPTER XXXVIII.

FRAUDS, PLUNDERING, SHODDY AND TAXES.

Poetical applications...General Remarks on...Scions of the old Puritanical stock...New York Custom House Frauds ...Testimony and Facts...Conclusions of committee... Van Wyck's speech on the Development of Astounding Frauds...Collector Barney and his subs...John P. Hale on corruptions of the Departments...Cattle contracts... Cummings' Agency...Charter of the Cataline...General Mania for stealing...Horse contracts...Contract Brokerage...Treasury Department Frauds...Fire Arms Frauds ...George D. Morgan's Operations...Army Transportation...Mr. Dawes on Frauds...A Refreshing Expose...A New York Paper on Van Wyck's Report...The "Record of Infamy" by the Ohio State Journal... Members of Congress take a hand in...Simmons, of Rhode Island, takes $50,000...Jack Hale takes a "fee"...The Horse Swindle...Frauds in the Navy Yard...The Book Swindle...The Grimes Committee...Frauds, Rascality, and Perjury...The Vessel Charter Frauds...The Committee's Conclusions...The Mileage Steal...Stupendous Frauds in New York...Swindling at Cairo...A Defaulter Caught...General Wilcox on Contractors...Mr. Dawes on Larcenies...Millions upon Millions Wasted...
Beauties of Republican Retrenchment...Fremont's Frauds ...Marshal Laman Mr. Lincoln's Right Bower...Honest Old Abe and Simon help their Friends...Mrs. Grimsley, the President's sister-in-law, figures in Fraud Investigations ...Letters from Old Abe and Cameron to Major McKinstry ...Congress Censures...that's all...The Holt and Owen Investigation...The Splendor of Fremont's operations... Frauds! Frauds!! Frauds!!! on every hand...General Remarks...Holy Ministers and Stolen Pictures...Swindling the Soldiers...Hundreds of Millions Swindled...We are all Mortgaged...Our National Debt...The Means to pay it... General Remarks...The Currency Question...Stand from Under...General Remarks on Republican Thieves and Plunderers.

FRAUDS—PUBLIC PLUNDERING—STEALINGS, SHODDY AND TAXES.

"Corruption is a tree, whose branches are
Of an immeasurable length—they spread
Ev'ry where; and the dew that drops from Heaven
Hath infected some stools and chairs of State."
[*Beaumont.*

"Hence, wretched nation! all thy woes arise,
Avow'd corruption—licens'd perjuries—
Eternal taxes—treaties for a day—
Despots that rule and people that obey."
[*Lord Lyttleton--Revised.*

"And though bare merit might in *Rome* appear
The strongest plea for merit—not so *here*;
The 'loyal' form their judgments in another way—
And they will best succeed, who best can *pay*;
Those who'd gain a place 'mong 'loyal' tribes,
Must add to their petitions the force of *bribes*."
[*Churchil—Paraphrazed.*

"Our supple tribes repress their patriot throats,
And ask no questions but the *price of votes*."
[*Dr. Johnson.*

"Common thieves must hang, but he that puts
Into his overgorged and bloated purse,
The nation's wealth: wrung by pinching war,
Is a shoddy hero, and escapes."
[*Cowper's Task—Revised.*

"'Tis pleasant, purchasing the 'loyal' creatures,
And all are to be sold, if you consider
Their passions, and are dext'rous—some by features
Are bought up, others by cotton, or rather shoddy—
Some by a place—all both soul and body—
The most by ready cash—each has his price
From kicks to greenbacks, according to his vice."
[*Byron—Improved.*

* * * "Is there not some chosen curse,
Some hidden thunders in the stores of Heaven,
Red with uncommon wrath, to blast the man,
Who owes his greatness to his country's ruin!"

"Honor among thieves," to use a phrase of the prevailing nomenclature, is "played out." It used to be considered dishonorable to commit a robbery at a funeral, but now, while attending the nation's funeral, the pall bearers —chaplains—grave diggers—mourners—all, have plied the art of theft and robbery on their disabled victim. From plebian to patrician, from beggar to nabob—from the non-commissioned civilian to the generals, (to say nothing of other officers,) Representatives, Senators and Cabinet Ministers. Shoddy takes the lead, while contractors' pockets drip with the fat of honest toil. "Loyalty" is cheap, and is guaged by the rise and fall of Greenbacks! Patriotism is founded on contracts, and the devotee of civil liberty chalks his entire creed on the margin of his commission. The confidence man has turned his attention to providing the government with horses, when some accomplice watches the moment they are "condemned," to place them in some neighboring stall to undergo the process of "*doping*," to be again sold for army use, at a round price, and so on to the end of *that* chapter. Officers who have met with the misfortune of not having their merits appreciated, take the stump to win their spurs, and spout radical nonsense as a *quid pro quo* for having their commissions renewed, or write "anti-Copperhead" letters to win promotion. Grave Senators sell their votes, and call it legal fees—Cabinet Ministers heap upon the bending backs of their cousins, nephews, partizans and "friends," the two per cent.'s of contracts by the hundred millions, with the "margin" in the bargain. Even one of the household of His Excellency, the President, holds a letter of credence from that high functionary for traffic with army contractors and agents. Ministers of the holy gospel have replenished their thin libraries from the well stocked repositories of Secessia. Grooms, suttlers and army hangers-on—all, have fattened among the plunder of the general riot. The wardrobes of Yankee land have been replenished from the georgious mansions of Dixie—Northern tables have groaned under the weight of silver plate and expensive wares from Southern cupboards. The shoddy contractor—a mendicant of the past, now riots at the table of luxury, reposes on beds of ease, and rolls on wheels of splendor, while the needle woman, whose spouse is a knapsack carrier, and who is burdened with a large family of little ones—is turned off with eighteen pence a day, *plus* threats and curses at the least complaint—collectors and surveyors receive in fees, fines and perquisites a cool hundred thousand dollars per annum, while those who make the garments they wear are pinched with want, and grim starvation knocks at every door. Civil officers and contractors are rolling in wealth, while the poor soldier receives a pittance too small to divide with the sutler and keep the wolf away from the door of his distant family.

In short, "loyalty" *pays*. Whoever votes the radical ticket and "runs with the Administration machine" is on the high road to fortune. He sees greenbacks in every bush, and "profits" echo from every "loyal" exclamation. All goes on swimmingly. Those who mak their money (?) easy and don't enlist, but insist that everybody is disloyal but themselves, are but scions of that old Puritanical stock who in 1732:

"*Resolved*, That the earth is the Lord's and the fullness thereof.
"*Resolved*, That the Lord hath given the inheritance thereof to the saints.
"*Resolved*, That we are the saints!"

THE MONSTROSITY OF FRAUDS.

The evidences of vast and flagrant frauds that we have been collecting for two years and a half, and that now lie before us, are so voluminous that it is appalling, and we hardly know where to begin, or what selections to make. The difficulty is not what we shall insert, but to determine what to exclude. We confess our inability to do justice to the subject, without extending this chapter beyond the reasonable limits of this work, and we therefore shall content ourself, in many cases, with a citation of the facts, omitting the evidence, which, in most cases, is conclusive and damning.

It would seem that a banditti of robbers, formidable in numbers, and insatiate in greed, had combined to precipitate war, as thieves conspire to fire cities, with especial view to plunder; nor has the system of robbery been confined to the common thieves, and dabblers in petty contracts, but the evil permeates all classes of the *ins*, from Mule Agents, Shoddy Contractors, up to members of Congress, and even Cabinet ministers—each has vied with the other in the race for the spoils, with a zeal and persistency worthy a better cause.

NEW YORK CUSTOM HOUSE FRAUDS.

The Abolition Congress of 1862 appointed a committee to investigate the frauds of the Custom House. The majority of the committee, Messrs. E. B. WASHBURNE, R. E. FENTON, WM. S. HOLMAN, H. L. DAWES, and W. G. STEELE, made a report on the subject, which was so tame, and intended to excuse the guilty in so many ways that Mr. VAN WYCK (Rep.) submitted a minority report, setting forth the facts, which the Republicans endeavored to suppress. We take the following, however, from the *majority* report, which is bad enough in all conscience. Here are the final conclusions of the majority of the committee.

"F!nally, in regard to the general course of

business in these departments of the public service in New York city, into which the committee were directed to make enquiry, they would say in conclusion, that *there are more or less abuses* of the administration of a system so vast and varied as that under consideration. Some of these abuses have probably crept in by a lapse of time, by *cupidity on the part of officials*, and occasional lack of vigilance. But the committee deem it but just to add in this connection that these abuses *were more numerous now* than they have been heretofore.

E. B. WASHBURNE, Chairman.
R. E. FENTON,
WM. S. HOLMAN,
H. L. DAWES,
W. G. STEELE."

TESTIMONY AND FACTS.

The following, though but a small moity of the testimony and facts, will give some clue to the nature of the patriotism of the office-holders

Samuel G. Ogden sworn, says: The compensation received from the government by the three officers the collector, naval officer, and surveyor, is limited by law. The collector, $6,400; naval officer, $5,000; surveyor, $4,900.— These officers also receive each one-third of the half of the net proceeds of all forfeitures, fines, penalties, &c. I have been acting in the capacity of auditor since 1842. In all such cases the money is paid to me, and I distribute it according to law. The collector, naval officer, and surveyor exercise the authority of adjusting the cases of seizures, &c. Question. What is the object of that mode of adjustment?
Answer. To save costs and delay.
Q. Are not these violations of law sometimes adjusted or compromised for the purpose of avoiding the publicity of legal proceedings; and if so, through the intervention of what officer is such compromise effected? What data are furnished to your office in such a case, and by whom is the money paid to you?
A. To avoid publicity may be an inducement to settle in that way. I have no data of such cases, and am not aware of any such compromises being made, *beyond the mere fact of receiving the money*, which is always paid in the same way.
Q. No sum of money, then, is ever paid to your office, except in one of two ways: either the money comes through a regular judgment of forfeiture, or through what would be called a compromise of the transaction, without the publicity of legal proceedings?
A. It comes in one of these two ways.
Q. If property is seized, then, it is either condemned or released, or the value of the property is paid into your office?
A. Yes, sir.
Q. Will you furnish to the committee a statement of the moneys paid into your office, showing the amounts paid to the collector, naval officer and surveyor?
A. I will furnish such a statement.

From the statements subsequently furnished by the auditor, the following is compiled:

From April 1, 1861, to December, 1862—one year and eight months—the collector received for salary..$10,667 00
For distributive share of fines, penalties, and seizures.. 23,514 98
Through the hands of the cashier the collector receives some $300 per month for services rendered by virtue of his office to the state officers, which adds to the above twenty months... 6,000 00

"In reference to which the following testimony was taken:

Wm. D. Robinson sworn, says; I am known as the cashier of the Custom House.
Q. What commission does the collector of this port receive for the collection of those dues for the state officers?
A. Five per cent. from the harbor masters, three per cent. from the health officers, and two and a half ... the Seamen's Hospital.
Q. What would be the average value of these commissions?
A. I should think about $300 a month.
Q. Do you know whether the moneys so received are in any way accounted for by the collector to the government, or are they simply regarded as a compensation from the officers of the State of New York for the services performed?
A. It is simply a compensation from those particular officers, and the general government has no connection with the matter.
Q. And therefore he makes no report of the money so received?
A. None whatever.

It will be seen by the foregoing statements, that the receipts of the collector for the first twenty months of his official career were $45,571.08, to which let there be added the cotton agency commissions for eight months, amounting to $6,762.91, and the alleged profits realized by the "professional" services of one of his law partners, not less than $1,200 per month—although accounts already published place this *profit* as high as $2,500 per month. In addition to these amounts we find in the testimony of Mr Ogden the following :

Q. Is the collector entitled to a share pending in case of seizure, &c., not disposed of at the time of his retiring from office?
A. Yes, sir. If the case of confiscation was commenced by him, and not disposed of before the expiration of his term of office, he receives his share *whenever it is disposed of*; that is to say, the emoluments from confiscations, fines, penalties, &c., go to the collector in whose term of office the prosecutions were commenced.
Q. You have no means of telling what will finally be received by the collector from pending cases?
A. No, sir. Nobody can tell that ; we never can tell what the courts will decree, or our juries will decide.
Q. How does the amount received by the collector, during his term of office, compare with the amount received by his predecessors?
A. It is *considerably larger* than was received by his predecessors generally.

"On the subject of the proceeds from the prosecutions commenced during the term of the collector, it will be necessary to quote from a report of the Secretary of the Treasury. It says:

Statement of suits brought in the Southern District in the State of New York, for the recovery of fines, penalties and for forfeitures for violation of the revenue laws, &c., during the year: 843 suits were brought for the recovery of $1,323,996.93, The total amount reported collected was $832,433.62—leaving still pending and undecided in this district 233 suits. The chief cause of their not having been brought to trial has been the inability of the judges sitting within the district to hear and determine the immense number of cases brought before them.

"The collector's distributive share of these suits then will amount to $55,405 60, or in the same proportion for twenty months it will reach the sum of $92,342 67. This business has unquestionably been much larger during the term of the present collector.

"In addition to this we have other testimony from the auditor, who says that under the act of July 13, 1861, the fees resulting to the collector, naval officer, and surveyor have amounted to about (at the time he testified) $4000 each, and then further payments were discontinued.
Q. Have there been a great number of vessels of that character seized (vessels belonging to disloyal persons.)

A. There have been many seized.
Q. A process of court is pending against them?
A. In many cases.

"It is alleged that over three hundred vessels were seized, worth, at an average valuation, $400,000, one-sixth of which is claimed by the collector, one-sixth by the surveyor, and one-sixth by the naval officer—being to each $66,666 for the operations in this line during the years 1861 and 1862, which will no doubt be received by the revenue officers if Congress does not make an investigation into the subject.

"The office of the collector of the customs is worth in one year, then, on the authority of the foregoing testimony:

SALARIES AND ENORMOUS PERQUISITES.

Salary... $6,500
Commissions from state officers, harbor masters,&c. 3,000
Cash proceeds from siezures, penalties, &c., (one
  year).. 21,000
Proportion to be derived from suits commenced, (one
  year).. 55,400

Total.. $86,030

INCIDENTAL PERQUSITES, OR STEALINGS.

During the first year of office siezures of vessels belonging to disloyal persons, by the act of the 13th of July, 1861... $66,000.00
"Cotton agency" commissions for eight months 6,702.91

Total.. $73,422.47

IRREGULAR STEALINGS.

Paid to law partner for his "professional" advice, &c., concerning the general order stores, $1,200 per month, (one year).. $14,400.00

"The last item is believed to be much below the actual figures. The testimony before the committee, carefully figured out, reveals this important fact: that the actual regular emoluments of the office reached $86,600 per annum, or $7,219 per month.

"The naval officer's emoluments are $81,930 per annum.

"The surveyor's emoluments are $81,430 per annum.

"The two latter expect to have an opportunity of dividing the proceeds of the sales of vessels seized as being the property of disloyal owners.

"The other testimony relates to the manner in which these seizures are made, and exhibits the perfect machinery used by the collector, naval officer and surveyor, to obtain from luckless importers the large sums that go to make up the fines, seizures and penalties." *

MR. VAN WYCK'S SPEECH—ASTOUNDING FRAUDS DEVELOPED.

Mr. Van Wyck, a Republican Member of Congress from New York was a member of one of the Investigating committees. On the 7th of February, 1863, when an attempt had been made to choke him off, and suppress his re-

* Notwithstanding it is here shown that Collector Barney receives nearly $100,000 per annum. The law of Congress requires each person to make return of his, her or their income, that it may be taxed to help pay government expenses, &c. Collector Barney, under this law, returns his income at *fifteen thousand dollars!* Comment is unnecessary.

port, he made a speech, from which we select the following copious extracts:

"Mr. Van Wyck (Rep. N. Y.) commenced by pointing to the parallel between the 19th of April, 1861, and the 17th of April, 1775—the battle of Lexington, and the murderous slaughter of Massachusetts men in the streets of Baltimore. He pointed out the material and other sacrifices the country had made, and then proceeded to analyze the special case which had come before the committee.

Cattle Contract.

"A contract was made in this city by the Department with Dwyer, Laughman, Sibley & Tyler, for cattle, from 2,000 to 10,000, at $8 per hundred, live weight, delivered here, and $5 75 in Pennsylvania. What facilities had Dwyer & Co. for transportation which the government did not possess? Government could lay its strong arms on railroads, and use them; could plant its gathering armies to guard the bridges and track. At that very time an agent was sent by the Department into Maryland, who, without difficulty, purchased cattle, to be delivered in Washington, at $6 50 per hundred, live weight. Besides, direct navigation with New York, was not obstructed by the Potomac. Still more, if the danger of transportation through Maryland was an excuse for this contract, big with profits, why a provision that a portion should be delivered in Pennsylvania if the Department desired, and why were nearly 1,500 received in Harrisburg, while scarce 800 were delivered in Washington? Notwithstanding the lions in the way, Dwyer & Co. immediately sub-let the contract to New York men, so that without any hazard or perils, they realized $32,000, on about 2,000 head of cattle.

Cummings' Agency.

"On the 21st day of April, the Secretary of War, although he well knew the great ability and experience of Colonel Tompkins, Quartermaster, and Major Eaton, Commissary, in New York city, wrote two letters to Alexander Cummings, Esq. In one, he

"wants him to aid the Commissary in purchasing supplies; to assist the Quartermaster in pushing them forward."

"The other letter says that

"The Department needs at this moment an intelligent, experienced and energetic man, in whom it can rely, to assist in pushing forward troops, munitions and supplies."

"No man knew better than the Secretary that these qualifications were already possessed by the army officers in New York, on whom it was safe to rely. Armed with letters of approval from the War Office, he was for the time supreme in the department marked out for him. Instead of rendering aid and assistance, he effectually superceded the army officers. Major Fatou distinctly informed him that his services were not needed in the purchase of supplies. Still, the Doctor commenced buying over $21,000 worth of straw hats and linen pantaloons, which were worthless to the army, and not required by the regulations. He employed a clerk, of whom he knew nothing, and had never seen before. In his evidence, at first, he did not know who recommended him; then he thought he was recommended by Thurlow Weed; and finally said, 'I remember now that Mr. Weed told me that he knew all about him, and upon his recommendation I took him.' This clerk, Mr. Cummings suffered to do all the business, and make all the purchases, except what were made by Geo. D. Morgan.

Charter of the Cataline.

"Mr. Cummings next appoints Capt. Comstock to purchase or charter vessels. The Captain, with a friend, goes to Brooklyn, inspects the Cataline, and learns that her price is from $15,000 to $20,000. Instead of purchasing, or chartering, or recommending Cummings to do so, from the owners, his friend suggests to Mr. Develin that there 'is a nice opportunity to make something by good management.' Capt. Comstock knew that Cummings was agent for the War Department, still he counsels freely with Mr. Develin about the value of the Cataline, and gives an opinion what will be paid for her charter. Had she been cheap at $18,000, his government was entitled to the purchase. After yielding to Mr. Develin all the time required for the negotiation, on the 25th the boat was chartered by Col. Tompkins, he relying upon Captain Comstock, the authorized agent of Cummings, the agent of the War Department, paying for her use $10,000 per month for three months, and if lost by war risks, the Government to pay $50,000. Col. Tompkins would not sign until Capt. Comstock assured him that she was worth $50,000, and that it was all right. The testimony of Capt. Comstock shows the vast number and almost unlimited power of persons at that time assuming to act as agents for the Government. He says:

"I was sent for by Mr. Weed to come to the Astor House about the time of the commencement of these troubles. He stated that he was agent of the Government, and had troops and munitions of war to go to Washington by way of the Chesapeake, and that he wished to charter vessels for that purpose." * * *
"Afterwards Cummings called on me and showed me the same authority that Weed had shown. It had been transferred to him to perform the same service." * * *
"I should think that Weed chartered from six to ten vessels."

"This testimony was given on the 28th day of December, and up to that time the committee had no evidence or intimation that Mr. Weed had been an agent for the government, or acting as such. The committee are not able to show by whom the vessel was loaded. But Collector Barney swears that, on the 27th April, Mr. Stetson, in whose name the tittle had been taken called on him, declaring a clearance to Annapolis. When asked how she was loaded, and to whom the cargo belonged, he replied, she was loaded with provisions, and belonged to several of his friends. Mr. Barney refused to clear her. Stetson then said the provisions were for the army. Mr. Barney replied that, as the property was not government property, but property of individuals, he would not clear her except at the request of some Government officer. It is just to say here, that Mr. Develin was evidently induced to purchase the vessel at the suggestion of those who were acting for the Government, and that Mr. Stetson, in every thing he did, was frank, candid, and made no concealment. When Mr. Stetson again called on the collector "he brought a note from Mr. Weed, stating that the cargo consisted of supplies for troops, and requesting a clearance" Mr. Barney declined, but saw Mr. Weed and explained why a clearance could not be granted. Mr. Weed said "it was all right and would be arranged in some other way."

"A pass was obtained from Gen. Wool, which he regretted, for he sent an order to the Collector revoking it; but the fugitive had escaped. Her voyage was an unfortunate one; after two month's service she was destroyed by fire. The question recurs, who were the friends referred to by Mr. Stetson as the owners of the cargo? Mr. Freeman, who had one-tenth interest in the profits, swears, after declining to do so, that he received as part security for the purchase money of the Cataline, four notes of $4,500 each, as follows: One note by John E. Develin, endorsed G. C. Davidson; one note by Thurlow Weed, endorsed John E. Develin; one note by G. C. Davidson, endorsed O. B. Matteson; one note by O. B. Matteson, endorsed Thurlow Weed. The only other person besides the captain and crew, was James Larkin, who went on the boat, he said, as purser, although he finally concluded his duty was to act as clerk for the captain. This man was appointed by Mr. Develin, upon the recommendation of Mr. Davidson. No one seemed to take any interest in loading the vessel except Mr. Develin. Col. Tompkins knew nothing of her cargo. The Union Defense Committee knew nothing of her cargo; and Dr. Cummings was asked if he knew anything of her cargo. $2,000,000, by the Secretary of the Treasury, were placed in the hands of a committee of high-toned, honorable men, to be paid out on the order or requisition of Mr. Cummings, without his producing to them any vouchers. Strange as it may appear, while this money was there to respond to his requisition, he draws $160,000 and deposits it in his name, with his private account, in one of the city banks. Stranger still, four months after his agency had ceased, he leaves no vouchers with the War Department. The War Department, in its generous confidence, seeks no settlement nor an inspection of vouchers.

General Mania for Stealing.

"The mania for stealing seems to have run through all the relations of government. Even in the matter of the purchase of two sailing vessels, two men of New York, to the crime of larceny, added the sin of perjury, that they might rob from the Treasury $8,000. In the case of the Stars and Stripes, the President of the New Haven Propeller Company, after taking from the Government $19,000 more than she cost, took of that amount nearly $8,000 to line his own pockets, and, in excuse to his company, pretended that he had to bribe an ex-Member of Congress to gain an audience to the head of the Bureau; and from that institution an honorable, high-toned ex-Member of Congress in Connecticut had been subjected to calumny. The President, before the Committee, testified that after taking $19,000 in profits from his country, he was so anxious to serve her in this, the hour of her extremity, that he appropriated nearly $8,000 of his colleagues' money to his private use, so he could devise some machine to take all the Southern cities and no one get hurt. The Department which has allowed conspiracies, after the bidding had been closed to defraud the Government of the lowest bid, and by allowing the guilty to reap the fruits of their crime, has itself been *particeps criminis*. Who pretends any public exigency for giving out by private contract, without bids, over $1,000,000 muskets, at fabulous prices? Who pretends a public exigency to make a private contract for rifling cannon to the amount of $800,000.

Horse Contracts.

"My colleague on the committee (Mr. Dawes) a few days since spoke of the peace-offerings of Pennsylvania politicians, and referred to the horses of Col. Williams' regiment. There is yet another case. A contract not made upon the responsibility of the Bureau, as the late Secretary said, but by his express order, and refused to be made until so ordered. I refer to the contract to purchase 1,000 horses, to be delivered at Huntingdon, Penn. Such a horse market the world never saw. Horses with running sores, which were seen by the Inspector, and branded; and if one outraged common decency he would be rejected, an opportunity sought the same day to pass and brand him. Immediately the horses were subsisted by private contract to favorites, at 39 cents per day, and they sub-let to farmers at 24 to 26 cents. Over 400 of these horses were sent with Col. Wynkoop's regiment, and the papers at Pittsburg report some actually so worthless they were left on the docks. The remaining 500 were left at Huntingdon for the benefit of contractors. In that single transaction over $50,000 were stolen from the government.

Contract Brokerage.

"The testimony of Mr. John Smith, of Kingston, N. Y., powder manufacturer, shows that in the month of May he proposed to give Mr. Weed a per centage for a powder contract; that he went to the Astor House, met Mr. Davidson, whom he had never seen before; inquired of him for Mr. Thurlow Weed. During the conversation he asked what Mr. Smith wanted of Mr. Weed; on being told, he enquired of Mr. Smith what he could afford to pay; he replied, five per cent.. Mr. Smith also says that Mr. Weed asked him what he could afford to pay. That afterwards, at Washington, he handed his propositions for powder to Mr. Weed, who took them to Mr. Cameron. The result was that Mr. Weed was authorized to write a letter to Gen. Ripley, the head of the Ordnance Department, to divide the contracts for powder between the states manufacturing. It is somewhat strange that the Secretary should appoint Mr. Weed as his messenger to carry his wishes to the different bureaus. Mr. Smith understood that he was to pay Mr. Weed five per cent. Mr. Laflin also testified that his powder firm demurred to paying Mr. Weed five per cent.; that Mr. Weed gave them authority to make 1,000 barrels of powder, but they preferred having the authority from the Government. He also testifies that the patriot Dwyer, who figured in the cattle contract, in May or June, at Washington, told him if he would give five per cent. he would sell all the powder he could make; but Laflin declined.

The Treasury Department.

"Even in the Treasury Department—pure and upright as I believe the Secretary to be—what business man could justify, or who, in his own transactions, would allow that a contract of over half a million expenditure should be competed for by only two firms, who could combine and unite? It is no answer to say that the work is done as cheaply as before ; the spirit of the law has been violated, and the millionaire enriched ; besides the products of all departments of labor are cheapened by the stagnation of business. In this matter of the bank note contract, as in some others, underlings control the affairs of the department—they say who shall approach within the charmed circle, they say whose papers shall be put on file, and whose shall be gladdened by the eyes of the Secretary.

The Purchase of Arms.

"Another remarkable transaction was the sale by the Ordnance Bureau to Mr. Eastman, of 5,000 Hall's carbines, as an arm which needed some alteration to be useful, for $3.50 each. This private sale was made at a time when the Department was buying arms which had been condemned, and sent from the arsenals of Europe. After an expenditure of from 75 cents to $1.26, they were sold to Simon Stevens for $12.50; then to Gen. Fremont for $22. No wonder our expenses are $2,000,000 per day—Government sells at $3.50. and in a short time buys back at $22. Dr. Cummings bought 700 of the same carbines for $15. The evidence of Maj. Hagder shows that Mr. Stevens was an agent or aid of Gen. Fremont. This Mr. Stevens denies. However, the relation was one of a warm personal character. He had probably just left him with instruction to purchase. His dispatch to Fremont was just such as an agent would send, or one who had the assurance of the necessities of the West, and that the arms would be taken. At all events, the bargain was an unconscionable one whereby Stevens was to make about $90,000 in one day, without incurring any risk or investing any capital. Mr. Van Wyck next referred to the Department of the West, and charged that Child, Pratt & Co., made from 25 to 50 per cent. on a contract of $1,000,000.

Geo. D. Morgan's Operations.

"Mr. Geo. D. Morgan has prepared an elaborate paper, showing the benefits of his agency, and relies upon the fact that in nearly every instance he paid a less price than the owner asked. We can test the strength of his position by the Stars and Stripes To build her cost $36,000; by her charter the owner realized $15,000 from Government; they then asked $60,000. Mr. Morgan paid $55,000, $5,000 less than they asked, but $19,000 more than the cost. While with the Potomska and Wamsutta the owners realized $53,000, the Government paid $60,000, although Mr. Morgan's papers allege he was asked $80,000. This seems the reverse of the prosition. The Onward was offered to private parties for $26,-000; Mr. Morgan was asked $30,000, and paid $27,000. These are not the only instances, as the committee will show by a further examination, to which they are invited by the Secretary, and directed by a resolution of this House. Mr. Van Wyck proceeded to give many instances of extortion in the purchase of vessels, and then referred to—

Army Transportation.

"Another item of reckless expenditure was the order of the War Department allowing two cents per mile for the transportation of troops, and liberal prices for baggage and horses. So enormous were the profits that railroad companies in the west bid and paid from $1,500 to $2,500 to nearly every regiment for the privilege of transportation. It is remarkable that the late Secretary, who was himself, by long experience and observation, so conversant with the management of railroads, who rejoiced in the confidence of a friend who was intimate with railroad connections, especially in Pennsylvania, should have allowed railroad companies such large amounts that they could lavish thousands for the transportation of a single regiment. Having referred at length to the magnitude of the struggle, Mr. Van Wyck concluded as follows:

"The dead past from out the page of history is looking down upon us; the living present, throbbing with hope, trembling with fear, is looking down upon us. The oncoming future, the echo of whose millions' footfals in the corridors of time we can almost hear, looking upon, beckoning us, and in silent prayer beseeching that we may be true to ourselves, the great legacy our fathers bequeathed, to the trust placed in our hands, to enjoy and transmit, not to tarnish and destroy. By all the memories of the past; by all the prospects of the present; by all the hopes of the future, let us rid ourselves of the sappers and miners at home; conquer this rebellion and subdue the traitors Do you say we may not succeed? Then let us perish in the attempt. We may vainly die for the land we cannot save? Then be it so. Here let hope and liberty's farewell fight be fought. The pale angel of the grave can at last steer our illdestined bark through the "Gate of Tears."

" ' Our cause may be betrayed,
Our dear loved country made
A land of carcasses and slaves,
One dreary waste of chalus and graves.'

"We cannot, we dare not yield, while heaven has light, or earth has graves.

" ' No—rather houseless roam,
Where freedom and our God may lead,
Than be the sleekest slave at home,
That crouches to the conqueror's creed.'

"No such dreadful fate can be ours, if we are only true to humanity and the God who guides the destinies of nations, the movements of arms, as he does the sparrow in its fall.—Here we make our stand; 500,000 men, a wall of human hearts, to guard the land we love, the flag we honor. If driven hence, even to the ocean and the lakes, we there will stand

" ' Until the last red blade be broken,
And the last arrow in the quiver.' "

COL. VAN WYCK'S TESTIMONY.

In the speech of Col. VAN WYCK, on the subject of Custom House and other frauds, he said: We quote from his speech, as published in the N. Y. *Tribune*, of March 7, 1863. In allusion to the selection of Mr. BARNEY to be cotton agent at that port, the speech says:

"When the Secretary of the Treasury appointed Barney government cotton agent, he did that for which unless explained, he deserves the censure of the people. In the name of a divided country and bankrupt treasury, what has Hiram Barney done for this nation that he should have a *carte blanche* to dive into the treasury as far and as often as he desires? Forty thousand dollars per annum! Must I submit to so glaring an outrage, and be told, as I often have, that the revelation will injure my party and political friends? This is not my party, these are not my political friends, who will allow or tolerate such practices. Did not the Secretary know that the arduous duties of the collector had rendered his mind very weak? Why impose the labor of taking nearly $7,000 more from the treasury on a man already overburdened? It was cruel, indeed it was. Mr. Chase must have known that the collector was very obnoxious to most of the merchants of New York, and many believe that he is entirely incompetent for the duties necessary by virtue of his office. Why then superadd these of cotton agent? Sir, there is but very little difference whether rebels destroy us in front, or polished, amiable gentlemen eat out our subsistence in the rear.

Of the general order stores a Republican member of Congress comments in this wise:

"Mr. Barney is wrong when he says *he se-*

lects and has a rule for selecting; while the truth is, he places the privilege in irresponsible hands, and they vend it to those who will submit to the exaction. Such men would probably sell their country in the markets of the world, if they could give a title. This practice never prevailed under any other collector. *Mr. Barney knew of these extortions;* at least he was written to upon the subject, and never checked the abuse; and thirty per cent. was paid by several merchants as a condition of enjoying the business—a sale of offices of the government for which *Mr. Barney long ago should have been driven from his seat in the customs.* He must have known it; it was his duty to know."

The conclusion of VAN WYCK's comment upon these Republican appointees is as follows:

"Yet, as a member of the Republican party, and a friend of the administration, I feel that we have their sins to carry, and I desire here to remonstrate. The neck begins to chafe where the yoke of this heavy burden is borne. The administration has feared to drive such men from its door, lest hostility should be aroused against it. That which they supposed was strength has been the great source of weakness. With a single exception, when has one of these men been court martialed or punished? *To-day they have injured the Republic more than the South in arms.* Had they been arrested and placed under the gallows or in Fort Lafayette, your army would have been stronger, and your people at home more united. No wonder that your soldiery and their friends are dissatisfied. *They cannot appreciate the patriotism of stealing.*

"Your army, for a mere monthly pittance, deprived of all the luxuries and, at times, of the necessaries of life, endure all the privations of camp and the dangers of battle, while they see base men making mockery of the misfortunes of the nation, unchecked and unpunished, coining gold from the tears and sighs of the people. These things produce more distrust than change of commanders or circulation of newspapers. Some professing friendship for the administration, if they cannot have full sway in shaping its policy, directing its appointments, and controlling its plunder, must be allowed, forsooth, to form new party organizations. Still in this time of trial, loyal men can only hope for better times."

JOHN P. HALE ON "CORRUPTIONS."

Senator HALE, in his place in the U. S. Senate, in speaking of the frauds and corruptions of his own party, said:

"I declare upon my responsibility as a Senator, that the liberties of this country are in greater danger to-day from the corruptions and from the profligacy practiced in the various departments of the Governments, than they are from the enemy in the open field."

MR. DAWES ON FRAUDS.

Mr. DAWES, a Republican Representative from Massachusetts, was also a member of the committee to investigate Army Contracts. On the 13th of July, 1862, he made a speech in Congress, in which he exposed the rottenness of this administration. As great portions of his speech refer to the same topics presented by Mr. VAN WYCK, we will omit such portions, and present such other facts as may be interesting.

A REFRESHING EXPOSE.

Mr. DAWES, after exposing the frauds of the cattle contracts, in which the Secretary of War figures in no amiable light, proceeds:

"I ask the House, at this rate, to consider how long the most ample provisions of the Treasury would be able to meet the simple demands for the subsistence of the army. Sir, poorly as the army is shod to-day, a million of shoes have already been worn out, and a million more are being manufactured, and yet upon every one of these shoes there has been a waste of seventy-five cents. Three quarters of a million dollars have already been worn out, and three quarters of a million of dollars upon shoes is now being manufactured. *In that department of the Government contracts have been so plenty that Government officials have gone about the streets with their pockets filled with them, and of which they made presents to the clergymen of their parishes, and with which were healed old political sores and old political feuds.* Even the telegraph announced that *high public functionaries* have graced the *love feasts* which were got up to *celebrate these political reconciliations*, thus brought about while the hatchet of political animosity was buried in the grave of public confidence, and *the national credit crucified* amongst malefactors."

"We have had reported to us the first fruits of one of these contracts. A regiment of cavalry lately reached Louisville, one thousand strong, and a band of army officers there, appointed for the purpose, have condemned four hundred and eighty-five out of the thousand horses, as utterly worthless. The man who examined these horses, declared upon his oath, that there was not one of them that was worth twenty dollars. They were blind, spavined, ringboned, afflicted with the heaves, with the glanders, and with every disease that horseflesh is heir to. These four hundred and eighty-five horses cost the Government, before they were mustered into the service, fifty-eight thousand two hundred dollars, besides more than an additional thousand dollars to transport them from Pennsylvania to Louisville, where they were condemned and cast off

"Mr. Mallory, (Union,) of Ky., asked what regiment these horses belonged to, and who furnished them.

"Mr. Dawes—They belonged to Colonel Williams' regiment of cavalry, and they were purchased in Pennsylvania, from which state they were forwarded to Louisville, where they were condemned. There are eighty-three regiments of cavalry to-day, one thousand strong. It takes two hundred and fifty thousand dollars to put one of these regiments on foot before it moves. Twenty millions of dollars have thus been expended on these cavalry regiments before they left the encampments where they were mustered into service, and hundreds and thousands of these horses have been condemned and sent back to Elmira, and to Annapolis, and to this city, to spend the winter. Any day hundreds of them can be seen round the city, chained to trees, in various places, having thus been left to die and rot till the committee on the District of Columbia have called for a measure of legislation to protect the city from the danger to be apprehended from these horse Golgothas.

"An ex-governor of one State offered to an ex-judge of another State five thousand dollars to get him permission to raise one of these cavalry regiments, and when the ex-judge brought back the commission, the ex-governor takes it to his room at the hotel, while another plunderer sits at the key-hole watching like a mastiff while he inside counts up forty thousand dollars profit on the horses, and calculates twenty thousand dollars more for the accoutrements, and on the other details of furnishing these regiments. In addition to the arms in the hands of the six hundred thousand soldiers in the field, there are numerous outstanding contracts, made with private individuals—not made upon advertisement, nor made with the knowledge of the public, but made by *ex-members of Congress*, who knew no more of the difference between one class of arms and another, than does a Methodist minister. There are outstanding contracts for the manufacture of Springfield muskets, the first one of which cannot be delivered in six months from this day.

"There is a contract for the supply of one million and ninety thousand muskets, at twenty-eight dollars apiece, when the same quality of muskets is manufactured at Springfield for thirteen and a half apiece; and an ex-member of Congress is now in Massachusetts, trying to get machinery made by which he will be able to manufacture in some six months hence, at twenty-one dollars apiece, those rifled muskets manufactured to-day in that armory for thirteen dollars and a half. * * *

"Besides there are seventy-five thousand five hundred and forty-three sets of harness, to be delivered by-and-by, at the cost of one million nine hundred and seventy-eight thousand four hundred and forty-six dollars. I have not time to enumerate all these contracts, when we appropriated at the last session of Congress, for this purpose, twenty millions of dollars, thirty-seven millions and some thousand dollars had been already pledged to contractors—not for the purchase of arms for the men in the field, not to protect them in fighting their country's battles in this emergency and peril, but for some future occasion, or to meet some present need of the contractors, I don't know which at this moment. And not only the appropriation of last session has been exhausted but seventeen millions put upon it.

"The riot of the 19th of April in Baltimore opened this ball, and on the 21st of April, in the city of New York, there was organized a corps of plunderers of the treasury. Two millions of dollars were entrusted to a poor, unfortunate, honest, but entirely incompetent editor of a paper in New York, to dispense it in the best manner he could. Straightway this gentleman began to purchase linen pantaloons, straw hats, London porter, dried herrings, and such like provisions for the army, till he expended in this way three hundred and ninety thousand dollars of the money, and then he got scared and quit, [Laughter.] There is an appropriation, also, for the supply of wood to the army. This contractor is pledged the payment of seven dollars a cord for all the wood delivered to the different commands; wood collected after the labor of the soldiers themselves had cut the trees to clear the ground for their batteries; and then this contractor employs the army wagons to draw it to the several camps, and he has no further trouble than to draw his seven dollars for a cord, leaving the government to draw the wood.—[Laughter.] It costs two millions of dollars every day to support the army in the field. A hundred million of dollars have thus been expended since we met on the 22d day of December, and all that time the army has been in repose. What the expenditure will increase to when that great day shall arrive when our eyes shall be gladdened with a sight of the army in motion, I do not know. Another hundred millions will go with the hundreds more I have enumerated. Another hundred millions may be added to these before the 4th of March.

"What it may cost to put down this rebellion I care but very little, provided, always, that it be put down effectually. But sir, faith without works is dead, and I am free to confess that my faith sometimes fails—I mean my faith in men, not my faith in the cause. When the history of these times shall be written, it will be a question upon whom the guilt will rest most heavily—upon him who has conspired to destroy, or upon him who has proved incompetent to preserve the institutions bequeathed to us by our fathers. It is no wonder that the public treasury trembles and staggers like a strong man with too great a burthen upon him. A strong man in an air-exhausted receiver is not more helpless to-day than is the treasury of this government beneath the exhausting process to which it is subjected. The mighty monarch of the forest himself may hold at bay the fiercest, mightiest of his foes while the vile cur coming up behind him and opening his fangs gives him a fatal wound, and although he may struggle on boldly and valiantly, the life blood is silently trickling from his heart, and he is at last forced to loosen his grasp, and he grows faint, and falters and dies.

"The treasury notes issued in the face of

these immense outlays, without a revenue from custom houses, from land sales, from any source whatever, are beginning to pall in the market. Already have they begun to sell at six per cent. discount at the tables of the money changers; at the very time, too, that we here exhibit the singular spectacle of fraud, and of a struggle with the Committee of Ways and Means itself, in an endeavor to lift up and sustain the Government of the country. Already the sutler—the curse of the camp—is following the paymaster, as the shark follows the ship, buying up for four dollars every five dollars of the wages of the soldiers paid them in treasury notes. I have no desire to hasten the movements of the army, or to criticise the conduct of its leaders, but in view of the stupendous drafts upon the treasury, I must say that I long for the day of striking the blow which will bring this rebellion to an end Sixty days longer of this state of things will bring about a result one way or the other. * *

"Our pressing duty now is to protect and save the treasury from further wholesale or other system of plundering. In conclusion, he argued against paying for printing Treasury notes, on the ground that the contract was improperly obtained."

Notwithstanding these exposes, the frauds and peculations have been on the increase. No stop has been put to them, and with two or three minor exceptions, no one has been punished. And still, the work of plunder goes on.

A New York paper, in commenting on the VAN WYCK report, says:

"But enough! Enough! Column after column is filled with evidence and detail on these points!

"This *expose*, so bold and so fearless, of Van Wyck's committee, we have but to add, does them infinite credit,—and it is to their honor, *that they dare to make it*. They explicitly "mix up" *both the Secretary of War and the Secretary of the Navy, in a knowledge of these transactions—and in the better days of Republic, neither of them could hold office an hour, upon such a charge from a Committee of Congress, with such an exposition.*

"THE RECORD OF INFAMY."

Congress has raised a great number of investigating committees, which have done no good, save to officially expose frauds already known to the whole country. The Washburn committee produced a massive report of 1515 pages, which is now before us. In commenting on this report, the Ohio *State Journal* (Rep.) thus paints its true character:

"By the politeness of a member of Congress we have been favored with the full report of the Washburne committee, for investigating Government contracts. It is a *prodigious* book—*one thousand one hundred and nine pages!*

—it is a *monstrous* book!—a monstrosity in every respect: monstrous in its hugeness, monstrous in the ugliness of its contents, monstrous in the devilishness of its revelations!—The truths therein shown, by sworn and legal testimony, are infinitely stranger than fiction. This huge and monstrous volume will, perhaps, become a reservoir whence some future Dickens will draw material to exemplify the practice of thieves, and for scrutinizing the utter blackness of darkness that can surround a human soul which permits itself to be cursed by the groveling sin of money-lust."

"Of all the devils that ever entered into the human heart, Mammon is immeasurably the meanest! We could tolerate Lucifer where we would abominate Mammon! And yet, this mean, groveling, despicable spirit of Satanic malevolence has possessed itself the hearts of many *after* whose names the world used to write 'honest,' and *before* which themselves still write 'Honorable!'

"This monstrous book is the great Record of Infamy! Its pages are ban and bar forever against those whose names are coupled with the infamy of its revelations. They will stand attesting to the nation and the world the blighting, searing, scathing ignominy which the nation and the world can heap upon those who would lie, cheat and steal from their country in the moment of its struggle for liberty! The common street thief who rushes to the burning mansion only to rob its owner while the fire opened its doors, is a spirit of angelic purity and nobility compared with those moral vampyres who would suck the last drop of vitality from their expiring country."

MEMBERS OF CONGRESS TAKE A HAND IN.

How can it be expected that a smaller grade of thieves will be punished or even choked off, when members of Congress themselves, attack and seize the public exchequer·

SENATOR SIMMONS TAKES $50,000

Senator SIMMONS, of Rhode Island, a very honest hearted Republican, takes a cool fifty-thousand dollars, as the price of his *influence* —not as a citizen, but as a *Senator*—to obtain a contract for a "friend," amounting to $235,000. The question naturally arises, if the contractor could afford to pay poor *honest* SIMMONS $50,000, how much profits did he, the said contractor realize?

HONEST JACK HALE TAKES A RETAINER.

"Honest JACK HALE" had become an axiom in Republican nomenclature, but it seems that some one wanted JACK's vote, or his "influence" as *a Senator*, and he gives him a "retainer" (doucer, in the original) of $2,000, with the promise of a "fee" besides. All who have been in Washington long enough to see how steals are filtered through Congress, can understand this. Of this transaction the New York *Tribune*, though evidently desiring to shield "Honest JOHN," is obliged to thus present the case :

" Why was $2,000 offered to Mr. Hale for his services in this case? Is he in the habit of receiving a retainer of $2,000 when he is retained as a lawyer? It seems not, from his own account. Why was he offered $2,000 in this case ? *Was it not because it was presumed or hoped that his position as a Senator, his political distinction and influence, would enable him to achieve results which an equally good lawyer, lacking these advantages, would vainly attempt?* We do not know that such was the fact, and yet the case looks as though it were. On the whole, while confident that Mr. Hale intended no wrong, and trusting that he has done none, we decidedly incline to the opinion that Senators ought to leave the defense of alleged peculators and public robbers to members of the bar, whose power to aid them is purely professional, and who have no sort of scruple as to undertaking the defense and pocketing all the fees that may be offered.

THE "MIDDLE MEN" IN WASHINGTON.

It is pretty generally understood, though we believe no official report has directly stated it, that there is a horde of outsiders at Washington who act the part of stool pigeons for high officials. These chaps play the part of "confidence men." They stand about the streets, and the purlieus of that rural Sodom, to have the first talk with contractors. If these are willing to draw a "margin," they can have "audience at court," if not, they are fools to approach one of the Departments. But if they will shell out liberally, then they are sure of contracts, and the bonus is no doubt divided between the "middle men" and the head of the Department. Do not the facts presented by VAN WYCK and DAWES, to say nothing of a vast array of other facts, prove this?

THE HORSE SWINDLE.

The following telegram, which was sent over the wires to the Associated Press, January 11, 1864, is but a *sample* of the swindling the Government in almost every locality:

"Out of eight hundred horses bought in New York, and sent to General Butler, seven hundred were condemned. General Butler has obtained permission to go into the open market."

FRAUDS IN THE NAVY YARD.

[From the New York World, Jan. 1864.]

"The frauds which have just been unearthed n the Brooklyn navy-yard are in keeping with the general corruption which seems to pervade all the departments of the government. Day by day the press of the country chronicles the discovery of new swindles upon the public treasury. So common have these disclosures become that they no longer excite comment, much less indignation. They are taken as a matter of course. Yet we cannot but believe that they will materially injure the administration party in the Presidential contest just opening. The Brooklyn navy yard frauds are not exactly committed upon the government, but upon the workmen employed in the navy-yard and the families of the soldiers in the field. When the war opened, with commendable generosity the carpenters and ship-builders agreed to give one day's wages in each month for the benefit of the families of such of their numbers as entered the service, and they have since the commencement of the war continued to pay in their regular monthly assessments.— It is now discovered that the money, which amounts to a very large sum, has not been given to the volunteers' families, but has found its way into the pockets of some of the leading Brooklyn politicians It further appears that the Republican party of Kings county is kept in motion by assessments levied upon the poor workmen in the navy yard. The shoddy patriots who control the action and monopolize the offices and the gift of the Brooklyn politicians, do not pay a cent toward the party expenses, while the poor workmen, in addition to the heavy assessment they are under to the volunteer fund, are also compelled to supply the large sums which are needed for running the Kings county Republican party. Every feature of this navy-yard business is disgraceful to every person and party connected with it."

THE BOOK SWINDLE.

The Great "reform" Congress of 1863, thinking perhaps it would be their last chance, passed a joint resolution to seize all the books not already disposed of to be divided among themselves, as the thieves divided the vesture of the Redeemer. Secretary UPSHER, in his late report, thus refers to this swindle, and tells the country how he managed to evade it, and thus to break up the vandal conspiracy:

"On the 3d of March, 1863, a joint resolution was enacted authorizing and directing the Secretary of the Interior, and all other custodians thereof, to cause equal distribution to be forthwith made among the members of the two Houses of the then expiring Congress, of all books and documents which had been printed or published at the cost of the Government, and not actually belonging to any public library, or the library kept for use in any department of the government, excepting, however, all such books and documents as were embraced in any existing order for the distribution thereof among the members of either House of Congress I found, on examination, that the number of volumes of the documents referred to, their incompleteness as sets or works, and the uncertainty as to their value, aggregately or separately, were such as to render it wholly impracticable to carry the provisions of the joint resolution into effect; and the subject is therefore respectfully submitted for the further consideration and action of Congress."

THE GRIMES (CRIMES?) COMMITTEE.

Government Transport Frauds — Rascality, Duplicity and Perjury.

Of all the chapters of frauds under this fraudulent Administration, none is more conspicuous than that brought to light by the GRIMES Committee, relative to transports, &c. It seems that the War and Navy Departments have been in the habit of appointing obscure and irresponsible agents to do that which should be done directly with officers of the government. They have pursued precisely the course a man would pursue, if he wanted to make a haul from the treasury, and dare not do it without the aid of an accomplice.—High-minded, responsible, honorable men cannot often be found to play agent in such a business, and hence the Departments have been in the habit of securing the services of the other class. Take, for instance, the case of COBLENS, whom the War Department selected as agent to procure transports for the army. The frauds, perjuries and rascalities in the management of this business, were so bold and palpable that Congress appointed a select committee to "investigate" them, with Mr. GRIMES (Rep.,) at the head. The committee express their regret that time was not allowed for a full investigation, but God knows, they exhumed enough corruption to last a life-time, under any *honest* administration.

A Prussian, and an obscure pedler, horse jockey, and by descent an Israelite, by the name of COBLENS, of Baltimore, who was poor before his appointment as agent to secure Government transports for the army, appeared before the committee as a millionaire—the owner of ten steamers, three barges, and eighty acres of valuable land in the vicinity of Baltimore. He was wholly unfamiliar with commercial pursuits, aside from retailing Yankee notions, and jockying in horses. He admits that he refunded $1,500 to Government, which was obtained by bribing the inspector of horses—that he bribed three of the clerks in Col. BELGER's office, and that he was connected with a sale of damaged corn to the Government.

THE VESSEL CHARTER FRAUDS.

The following table, compiled from the testimony of Mr. COBLENS, Mr. A. C. HALL, and Mr. JOHN F. PICKRELL, and the reports of Col. BELGER and Gen. MEIGS, exhibits Mr. COBLENS' transactions with the Government in the chartering of transports for the War Department:

Name of Vessel.	Cost of Vessel.	Rates of Charter.
Steamer Patapsco	$1,200	$85 per day.
Steamer Baltimore	21,500	250 per day.
Steamer Telegraph	7,000	125 per day.
Steamer Jas. Murray	9,333	100 per day.
Steamer Lioness	5,000	45 per day.
Steamer Edwin Forest	4,500	40 per day.
Steamer Fairy Queen	4,000	40 per day.
Steamer Cecil	5,000	80 per day.
Steamer Haswell	3,000	40 per day.
Steamer Lily		35 per day.
Barge Delaware	2,500	70 per day.
Barge Miss Mary	2,250	25 per day.
Barge John Warner		12 per day.
Total	$65,283	$947 per day.

"The rules of arithmetic (say the committee) show that Mr. Coblens was receiving money from the government at the rate of $344,655, on a capital of $65,283, which is equal to 529½ per cent. on his investment."

In addition to this monstrous swindle, the Department allowed Mr. COBLENS 5 per cent. on receipts, and 2½ per cent. on investments. No wonder that the poor horse-jockey became suddenly rich, and is it any wonder, that when these things are allowed to obscure men, in defiance of all honorable transactions, and without law, that one of the heads of the Departments can afford to present his daughter with a $3,000 shawl, a $35,000 residence, and other things to match.

This whole report is rich in exposures of frauds and evidences of perjury, but for want of room, we must confine ourself to the summing up of the committee. In most of these transactions, the name of JOHN TUCKER, Assistant Secretary of War, figures conspicuously, as a rogue of no small dimensions.

THE COMMITTEE'S CONCLUSIONS.

"The ground covered by this report includes only a small portion of the duty assigned to the committee by the resolution of Dec. 22. As previously stated, the time was too short to afford more than a beginning—an outline of the work, which should be undertaken at once by a competent military commission, and prosecuted through all the channels of the transport service, between the 20th of April, 1861, and the present time. The committee are overwhelmed with astonishment and sorrow by the revelations which have been made, but they believe that nothing which so vitally concerns a free people, should be concealed from them, and they hope that this investigation may tend to a more honest and economical administration of the department of the public service to which their attention has been directed.

The conclusions reached by the committee from the whole examination in which they have been engaged, are

"1st. The vessels to be employed by the Government should always be secured through the regular and legitimate channels upon offers to be made by the owners, or agents of such vessels, in answer to public advertisements.

"2d. That the practice of employing an *Agent* to charter vessels, with unlimited power to fix the rate of charter—to determine the character of the vessels to be employed, with the apparent attempt to fasten the responsibility for such transactions upon another party, or upon another department, as in the case of employing John Tucker, with Capt. Hodges, U. S. A., to charter vessels for the McClellan Expedition, the former to inspect and charter, the latter merely to sign the contracts that they might have the official sanction of the Quarter Master's Department, can neither be justified upon principle, nor upon its results.

"3d. All vessels should be thoroughly inspected at the time of purchase or charter by the Government, by competent experts in their profession, who shall be directly responsible to the military branch of the Government. And it is no apology for the want of such examination to say that the vessel had at some time during the preceeding twelve months been inspected by the agents of the Treasury Department.

"4th. That the monopoly of chartering vessels by Hall, Loper and others, even were it known that their transactions were honest, cannot be justified, and the *officers who know* that Hall and others were extorting commissions from the owners and agents of vessels, and *permitted such monopoly to continue*, deserve the severest censure. [This is a rap at Mr. Stauton.]

"5th. The committee are satisfied that the late Assistant Secretary of War, John Tucker, and Col. James Belger, U. S. A., knew of Hall's transactions, and knowing them, permitted his monopoly, and illegal practices to continue.

"6th. That the practice of allowing any person to act at the same time in the double capacity of broker of ship owners and agents of the Government, to select vessels, in both of which characters *Hall did act*, according to the testimony of Col. Belger, is wholly indefensible.

"7th. That the commissions received by Hall, Loper, Danforth and others, which are estimated by the committee to amount in the aggregate to *several hundred thousand dollars*, [probably not less than $5,000,000,] *rightfully belong to the Government*, and immediate steps should be taken by the War Department to ascertain the amount due from each, and to secure the money." [The fact that no move of the kind has been attempted, is pretty conclusive proof that the "War Department" has had a "portion of the hog."]

"8th. That many of the charters affected by, through, or under the agency of Hall, Loper and others, were secured at exorbitant prices, and are otherwise tainted with fraud. All such charters should be at once annulled [but they were not] and steps taken to restore to the Treasury the sums thus extorted, or fraudulently obtained [that's a thing that has never been attempted under this "honest" administration.]

"9th. That all the charters with Charles Coblens were exorbitant in price, and were tainted with fraud—that both Coblens and Pickrell should be made to disgorge [what an Utopian idea] their ill-gotten gains, and the charters should be annulled.

"10th. That no money should be paid upon charters with Coblens, Hall, Loper, &c., upon vessels owned in whole or in part by them, until the amounts honestly and equitably due to the government, growing out of these transactions, shall be ascertained and paid.

"11th. That the facts heretofore recited, concerning Col. James Belger, are sufficiently grave to warrant their being examined by military court.

"12th. That the sums of money obtained by John B. Danforth, of N. Y., from the owners of the steamer Matamora, and from the owners of other vessels, were obtained in violation of law, and against public feeling, and that steps should be taken to cause it to be paid into the treasury. [This is easier said than done. It might implicate others high in office, hence it has not been attempted.]

"13th. The War Department can only restore confidence in its transactions, by inflexibly adhering to the rule that contracts shall only be made with the owners of vessels, or with their immediate, legitimate, established agents, and that every officer who shall be shown to be influenced in the slightest degree, in according a charter, by fear, force, or of faction, or the hope of reward, or who shall ever give reasonable grounds for suspicion of his conduct, shall be summarily punished, if guilty. [Has this been done in a single instance?]

"14th. The cases of perjury shown in the testimony, taken by this committee, shall become subjects of judicial investigation.

This will do to *talk*, but we believe has in no case been acted on.

THE MILEAGE STEAL.

How can the people expect retrenchment, reform, and that "honesty" so much boasted of by the party in power, when members of Congress take all they can get? Not content with attempting to grab all the books, they took from the treasury a constructive mileage for attendance on the extra session, without traveling a rod. The following from the Chicago *Tribune* will answer under this head:

"THE MILEAGE GRAB.—The members of Congress were guilty of a sneaking, dirty grab on the Treasury, just before adjourning, by which they took out $80,000 to which they were not rightfully entitled. The law allows each member of Congress $8,00 a day the year round,—Sundays included—or $8,000 a year, and mileage at the enormous rate of fifty cents a mile each way. The late Congress has held two regular and one extra session. The law allowed no mileage for the extra session, but the honorable gentlemen set it aside and reached their arms into the treasury and took from thence a third mileage—the Western members getting from $800 to $1,500, and those west of the Rocky Mountains from $5,000 to $6000 apiece."

STUPENDOUS FRAUDS IN NEW YORK.

A commission was appointed by Congress to "investigate" the monstrous frauds in the Subsistence Department. An article from the New York *Times* (Radical) of the 27th of December, 1862, is before us, from which we take the following short extract, as a sample of the whole:

"Mr. Olcott entered upon his investigations on the 1st of November last, and has already discovered frauds to the extent of $700,000 perpetrated in this city, and the prospect is, that they will reach double that amount before the investigation is finished."

Thus it goes; frauds by the million are perpetrated—an investigation is had—the guilty *exposed*—but nobody punished; and still the frauds continue. Still the raid upon the Treasury is unchecked—thieves multiply like the locusts of Egypt—now and then we hear of an arrest, but seldom, if ever the infliction of punishment, They are all so linked together—from the highest to the lowest—that there is scarcely an honest man in power left to prosecute. Now and then we see such articles as the following, floating through the columns of the press, as editorials or telegrams, but they are so frequent as to hardly attract attention.

SWINDLING AT CAIRO.

"The postmasters at Cairo are in a bad way. Robert M. Jennings, the assistant, was arraigned before United States Commissioner L. B. Adams, of Springfield, on Tuesday, on a charge of embezzling, secreting and destroying letters, and upon hearing of the case, was held to bail in the sum of $3,000 for his appearance at the next term of the District Court. John Q Harmon and D. J. Baker, Jr., became his sureties. Mr. Linegar, the postmaster, has been removed, and Col. James C. Sloo appointed in his stead Linegar is said to be behind in his accounts with the government at least $3,000, and also behind with his clerks at least $10,000. Linegar is one of the leading abolition politicians of southern Illinois, and, perhaps, one of the least competent men for postmaster to be found in that section."—*Chicago Post.*

A DEFAULTER CAUGHT.

"Howland, the defaulting Quartermaster, who drew $16,500 on a Government check and then fled, was arrested at Hyacinth, Canada."—*Telegram.*

A Government paymaster (COOK) deposited several hundred thousand dollars in a faro bank at Cincinnati—drank, gambled, and was arrested· He felt sorry, and we have heard nothing of it since.

CONTRACTORS ON THE WAR.

From the Speech of Gen. Wilcox.

"Contractors have carried on this war. The blood of our men, the groans of our wounded, the tears of the orphan and the wail of the widow, have been coined into money.

LARCENIES.

From the speech of Dawes, (rep.) from Massachusetts,

"*The larcenies under this administration have exceeded the entire expenditures of James Buchanan's.*"

MILLIONS UPON MILLIONS WASTED.

From the Chairman of the Republican Congressional Committee.

"We have seen a system of commissions to middle men growing up all over the country, stepping in between the producer and furnisher on one side, and the government upon the other, that has cost the government millions of dollars.

BEAUTIES OF REPUBLICAN RETRENCHMENT.

Mr. DAWES, Republican member of Congress from Massachusetts, in a speech on the subject of the extravagance and frauds of the administration, said:

"In the first year of a Republican Administration, which came into power upon professions of Reform and Retrenchment, there is indubitable evidence abroad in the land, that somebody has plundered the public treasury well nigh in that single year, as much as the entire current yearly expenses of the Government during the Administration which the people hurled from power because of its corruption."

FREMONT'S FRAUDS.

The report of the select committee that traveled all over the western country in 1863, taking testimony—traveling over six thousand miles, and examining over 260 witnesses, is another chapter in the history of these frauds and rascalities, that has branded this Administration as a synonim for peculation and plunder.

The committee condemn the purchase by FREMONT of the Austrian muskets, amounting to $166,000—a total loss, as the committee say they were entirely worthless. The Secretary of War and the Secretary of the Treasury are condemned, and placed between two millions of dollars, which went into the hands of a mere pet, with no security and without warrant of law.

FREMONT's expenditures are severely criticised. It is impossible for us to even notice all the flagrant frauds exposed by this committee. The report itself occupies 136 pages, and the evidence makes a monster volume.— Gen. FREMONT is censured for incompetency, and in speaking of the extraordinary expenditures on the "St. Louis fortifications," the committee say :

"The circumstances surrounding this work are of the most extraordinary character, and are marked by extravagance, recklessness, insubordination and fraud."

And, again :

"The dealings of the Quartermaster's Department at St. Louis, while in the charge of Maj. McKinstry, with the firm of Child, Pratt & Fox, were very extensive, amounting to over $800,000 since the present difficulties

SCRAPS FROM MY SCRAP-BOOK. 321

broke out. This business was not confined to the particular kind of business in which the firm were engaged, who were hardware merchants, but extended to every variety of article and thing which the department had occasion to buy. * * To secure to this firm this monopoly, by which immense private fortunes were taken from the treasury, all provisions of law and army regulations, requiring advertisement for proposals, and the contracting with the lowest bidders, to furnish these articles, *were totally disregarded*, and the most unblushing system of favoritism and exclusiveness established that ever disgraced the service. * * * * Every branch of industry whose products were in any way necessary to the department of the west, was made to pay tribute to the firm of Child, Pratt & Fox. The profits made by this firm out of the United States, by enjoying this monopoly, were enormous. Coligan, its bookkeeper, admitted in testimony that it would reach 35 per cent., which upon a trade of $800,000, secures the princely fortune of $280,000—a tax upon the treasury of the United States, which nothing but the most controlling reasons of military necessity would ever justify."

MARSHAL LAMAN MR. LINCOLN'S RIGHT BOWER

This distinguished individual, whom Mr. LINCOLN took on to Washington with him, for the purpose of giving him the Marshalship of the District of Columbia, is most severely handled by this committee, for his extraordinary "cheek" in charging $40,000 for taking the 37th Illinois regiment from Saint Louis to Williamsport.

HONEST OLD ABE AND SIMON—HELPING THEIR FRIENDS—RICH DEVELOPMENTS.

When Major McKINSTRY was on trial for matters related to above, he produced two letters in court—one from Old Honest Abe and one from Honest SIMON CAMERON, which the Major relied upon for his justification in committing such base plunders, without advertising, &c. The gentleman Mr. LINCOLN so patriotically desired to serve, because of "the patriotism of Illinois," was a *partner of Cameron's son*, residing in *Harrisburg*, Pa., and the other individual, Mr. YOUNG, lived in Middleton, the home of Honest SIMON, himself. The Mrs. GRIMSLEY who figures in the record, was not only in the partnership, but is understood to be a sister of Mrs. LINCOLN.

THE TESTIMONY OF MR. FOX.

"Q. Are you personally acquainted with the President of the United States?
"A. I am.
"Q. How long have you been acquainted with him?
"A. For nearly ten years.

"Q. Are you acquainted with his hand writing?
"A. Yes, sir.
"Q. Do you know James L. Lamb, of Springfield, Illinois?
"A. I do, sir.
"Q. Did not James L. Lamb, of Springfield, accompany you at one time to Maj. McKinstry's office?
"A. I met Mr. Lamb at Maj. McKinstry's office. I did not go with him there.
"Q. On that occasion did not one or both of you present to Maj. McKinstry two letters, one from the President of the United States, and one from the secretary of war?
"A. Not on that occasion, sir.
"Q. Did you or Mr. Lamb at any time present such letters?
"A. Mr. Lamb told me he presented such letters.
"Q. Were you not present on the occasion when these letters were presented?
"A. No, sir, I was not. I will state, however, I carried such letters for Mr. Lamb to Maj. McKinstry.
"Q. Are not those two letters now shown to you, and marked 'A' and 'B,' the same presented on the occasion referred to?
"A. They are.
"Maj. McKinstry here asked the Judge Advocate to read the letters referred to.
"The Judge Advocate read as follows:

Letter from Mr. Lincoln to Major McKinstry.

WASHINGTON, Sept. 10, 1861.
J. McKINSTRY, *Brig. Gen'l. and Quartermaster, St. Louis:*
"Permit me to introduce James L. Lamb, Esq. of Springfield, Illinois.
"I have known Mr. Lamb for a great many years. His reputation for integrity and ability to carry out his engagements are both unquestioned, and I shall be pleased, if consistent with the public good, that you will *make purchases of him* of any army supplies needed in your Department. Your ob't servant,
"A. LINCOLN."

What under officer could resist such an appeal from the Commander-in-Chief of the army and navy?

Honest Simon to Major McKinstry.

"WASHINGTON, Sept. 9, 1861.
J. McKINSTRY, *Brigadier General and Quartermaster, St. Louis:*
SIR:—The bearer of this, James L. Lamb, Esq., of Springfield, Ill., is the personal friend of the *President*, as well as *my own*. He is a gentleman of integrity and business capacity, [Simon was posted on "integrity,"] and any engagement entered into will, no doubt, be faithfully carried out. As Illinois is bearing her burden of the war, both in furnishing men and means, it is the desire of the Administration [an irresistible hint] that the citizens of that state should have a fair share of the Government patronage dispensed in your department. If you can do anything for Mr. Lamb, in purchasing supplies, you will oblige, *provided he will make his prices suit you*.
Your ob't servant,
SIMON CAMERON, Sec'y of War."

Thus, for the first time in the history of the Government, did the President of the Nation and his War Minister, combine to urge a pet and a partner of the household on the favor of those who dispensed the patronage of the Government.

"Q. Did you some time in 1861, make an arrangement with Lamb and others to supply the army with goods?
"A. I made arrangements with Mr. Lamb.

The Judge Advocate here objected to the letters becoming a part of the record, on the ground that they had no reference to any party who was connected with any of the transactions covered by the charges and specifications before the court.

"Major McKinstry said he offered these letters to justify the course pursued by the accused in buying horses and other supplies for the army from Illinoisans, without first advertising for proposals, and further to show that the President of the United States and the Secretary of War knew of the course that was adopted by the accused, in making his purchases, and that the Secretary of War left the matter of fixing the price to the accused.

[Court closed—reopened and decided that the letters should become a part of the record.]

"Q. State who the parties were who made such arrangement.
"A. It was between Mr. Lamb and myself.
"Q. Were not other parties associated with Mr. Lamb and yourself in the contemplated arrangement?
"A. Yes, sir, so Mr. Lamb informed me.
"Q. Who were they?
"A. My conversation with Mr. Lamb was of a confidential character, and I do not wish to state it.
"The Judge Advocate objected to witness answering the question, on the ground that it would be hear say evidence.
"Maj. McKinstry said he would withdraw the question.
"The Judge Advocate said he did not object to the question, and wished to have it remain on the record as it stood.
"Maj. McKinstry—The accused submit that the question the witness is asked to state, is not a privileged question, and that it is not for the witness to decide whether or not he will answer it. The evidence sought by the question is to show the position and interest of other witnesses in behalf of the prosecution, who are either named at the foot of the specification or may be called as witnesses for the prosecution.

"[Court cleared—reopened. Objection not sustained.]
"Question repeated.—A. Mr. E. Bly, of Harrisburg, Pa., and Mr. Young, of Middleton, Pa. They were the parties.
"Q. Was it not stated by Mr. Lamb in your presence, that Mrs. Grimsley was one of the parties?
"A. No, sir.
"Q. In the course of the interview you and Mr. Lamb had with Maj. McKinstry, was not Mrs. Grimsley's name introduced to you?
"A. No, sir.
"Q. Did you not state to Maj. McKinstry that Mrs. Grimsley was to share the profits of your contemplated arrangement?
"A. I did not state so in words.
"Q. What did you state?
"A. I did not convey anything to him in *words* on that subject.
"Q. Did you convey any meaning by writing or otherwise?
"A. I did. Now I will explain. Mr. Lamb and myself joined in an application to Maj. McKinstry as Quartermaster, to supply the government with a large amount of goods. After we had perfected our application, we were discussing the probable amount of profit we would make on the contract if we got it from *Major McKinstry*. After that we were talking over the gossip of our town, and this person's name was mentioned by me, and I proposed to Mr. Lamb to join him in presenting this person a sum of money. One day, while I was at Maj. McKinstry's office, trying to get a contract, (Mr. Lamb committed to me the obtaining the contract, (Maj. McKinstry said to me : 'Before I give that order or contract, I want to know who are all the parties interested.' I wrote upon a slip of paper all the parties interested, and handed it to him. I also wrote to Mr. Lamb and told him what Maj. McKinstry had said to me, and I said to him, 'You had better give to me all the letters you have. He did.—I took them and showed them to Maj. McKinstry.
"Q. Was not Mrs. Grimsley's name on the paper?
"A. It was; and I want to say, I take the whole responsibility of her name being on that paper. Mr. Lamb knew nothing of it.
"Q. Who were the writers of those letters?
"A. The President of the United States and the Secretary of War, Mr. Cameron, and Judge David Davis, of Bloomfield, Ill.

"Here the cross examination was concluded, and witness obtained leave to go home, with the understanding that he return on Monday and submit to a renewal of the direct examination.
" Court adjourned."

Thus it will be seen, that the President had in view the helping his sister-in-law to a good profitable contract, while honest SIMMON, had an eye to the partner of his son. Can we wonder at the brazen impudence of shoddy?

CONGRESS CENSURES—THAT'S ALL.

The House of Representatives passed the following resolve, which had no more effect than the baying of dogs at the moon :

"*Resolved*, That the practice of employing irresponsible parties, having no official connection with the Government—the performance of public duties which may be properly performed by regular officers of the Government and of purchasing by private contract, supplies for the different departments, when open and for competition might be properly invited by reasonable advertisements for proper proposals, is injurious to the public service, and meets the manifest disapprobation of this House."

ONE OF THE COOLEST FRAUDS.

The HOLT and OWEN Investigation developed some extraordinary frauds, from which expose a monster quarto volume could be filled. We have only room for the FREMONT carbine fraud, which, for coolness and audacity, is without a parallel in the criminal police courts of any country. FREMONT was cognizant of the fact that the Government had condemned 5,000 carbines, in New York, as worthless, and ordered them to be sold at $3.50 each. He telegraphs from St. Louis to one SIMON STEVENS, in New York, on the 5th of August, 1861, for 5,000 carbines—just the number the Government had condemned. STEVENS was poor and worthless, and telegraphed back that he had 5,000 carbines, but for some excuse, he could not forward them without an advance of some $17,486—just the amount required to purchase them of the Government—that he would sell them and immediately forward them to FREMONT, at St. Louis, if the Government would advance this amount, which was accordingly done, when STEVENS goes to the officer in charge of the carbines, pays for them at $3 50 each, and immediately bills them to the Government, per Gen. J. C. FREMONT, at $22 each. For further particulars, we will let the committee speak of this transaction in their own way.

"Thus, the proposal actually was to sell to the Government, at $22 each, 5,000 of its own arms, the intention being, if the offer was accepted, *to obtain those arms by purchase from the Government at $3 50 each!* That intention was carried out [lacking four carbines only] the day after Gen. Fremont accepted the offer. It is evident, also, that *the very funds with which this purchase was affected were borrowed on the faith of the previous agreement to sell;* so that if the purchase made by Gen. Fremont is to be regarded as a valid purchase by the United States, the Government sold one day for $17,486, arms which it had agreed the day before to repurchase for **$109,912,** making a loss to the United States on the transaction of **$92,426**—*but virtually furnished the money to pay itself the $17,486, which it received!*"

FRAUDS! FRAUDS!! FRAUDS!!!

Go where you will—look which way you may—among the high and low—the learned and the illiterate—from the highest officer of the Government down to the lowest scullion, who cries "Copperhead" for the small pickings that drip from officials kid gloved fingers, and you hear the cry of frauds, peculations and plunderings. Governors of states, state, county, town and ward officials—wherever the army worm goes, there will be fraud. It is but a short time since the Legislature of Kansas, intensely Republican—was forced to impeach their Republican Governor (Robinson) for gross frauds and other offences, together with the Secretary of State (J. W. Robinson) and State Auditor (Geo. S. Hillyer) for like offences.

In the name of an outraged and plundered people, where and when are these things to stop, and if not soon stopped, who can see a *possibility* of saving the Republic? And how can the people expect to see the smaller thieves choked off, when they see so many glaring examples by the highest in office?

The President in answering the Congressional censure of SIMON CAMERON, declared he was responsible for what his subordinates do. It needed not this declaration to show the people this fact, but the question is, how can his party, if they love honesty, as they pretend, favor the re-election of a man who has so much responsibility on his shoulders?

HOLY MINISTERS AND STOLEN LIBRARIES.

If the old, apothegm is as correct as it used to be, making the "partaker as bad as the thief," what must we think of the New England clergymen, who are thus alluded to by the New York *Christian Enquirer:*

"In several libraries of New England clergymen, we have seen choice volumes of great cost, bearing the names of Southern ministers *to whom they still belong,* although they have been sent North as gifts from Yankee soldiers, who had appropriated them!"

It might be "copperhead" impiety to comment on this fact, yet it is by no means an uncommon affair.

SWINDLING SOLDIERS.

The following from the N. Y. *Tribune,* of April 1863, requires no comment :

" A paymaster's clerk recently made this proposition to a capitalist of this city : "Lend me $20,000; I can make 15 per cent. a month on that amount, in this way: In our office we pay $200,000 a month to soldiers. The funds are not always on hand when the pay falls due. When they are not, I can generally purchase the soldiers' claims at 15 per cent. discount. In order to do it, I must resign my clerkship; but I have a brother in the office, and through him I can always learn when and how to invest. There is no risk of capital; the profits are *sure!* and I will share them with you."

" We have this account from the person to whom the offer was made. He indignantly declined it as a swindle of the basest kind—a proposition to cheat the government and defraud the soldiers. Others, however, were less scrupulous, and the clerk speedily affected an arrangement with a firm considered respectable, and their joint operations are probably in full tide of success."

The question naturally arises, why did the *Tribune* suppress the name? Was it for fear it would hurt the *party?*

HUNDREDS OF MILLIONS SWINDLED.

The New Hampshire *Courier,* a reliable " Government" paper, says:

" Contractors have carried on the war. The blood of the men, the groans of our wounded, the tears of the orphan and widow, *have been coined into* MONEY. They have *swindled the government out of hundreds of millions.* They have piled fortune upon fortune. As a distinguished officer at Washington said, ' All the operations of the war are managed by swindlers!' "

Says the N. Y. *Tribune,* in speaking of the war:

" It has saddled us with a debt that will take bread from the mouth of every laboring man's child for generations, and send millions hungry to bed."

WE ARE ALL MORTGAGED.

Mr. SPAULDING, a Republican member of Congress from the Erie, N. Y., district, made a speech in Congress, in which he said:

"Debt and taxation are the inevitable necessities of war. Every day that the war is prolonged the debt is increased. The daily increasing debt of $2,500,000 must all be raised by taxation in some form, or the debt will not be paid. The Government is spending at a fearful rate, the accumulations of former years of prosperity. Every dollar of debt contracted becomes a first mortgage upon the entire productive property of the country. It affects the farmer, laborer, mechanic, manufacturer, merchant, banker, commission merchant, professional man and retired capitalist. Every pound of tea, coffee, and sugar used, is taxed to pay the expenses of the war, and the persons using these articles of daily consumption pay the tax in the increased price. Every person that uses wine, brandy, whisky, beer, cigars, or tobacco, pays a portion of the war tax.

"All necessary articles of dress, such as shoes, boots, hats and wearing apparel, are taxed in like manner, and all superfluous and unnecessary articles, such as silk, lace, diamonds, and jewelry, are heavily taxed, and I would be glad to see the tax still further increased on them, in order to prevent, if possible, their use at this time. Every person that rides upon the rail-roads, reads newspapers, draws a check, or sends a telegraphic message is taxed for war purposes, but I need not further enumerate the different modes in which everybody is taxed every day to pay the expenses of the war.

"This war debt is a mortgage alike on all the productive industry and property of Republicans, Democrats, Old-line Whigs, Conservatives and Abolitionists."

OUR NATIONAL DEBT—THE MEANS TO PAY IT.

No true patriot would think the price too great, if a virtuous and economical use of every dollar in the nation, was required to save the old Union of our fathers, but in view of the foregoing blistering, damning facts of frauds by the hundreds of millions, the following prediction from the New York *Tribune* of January, 1864, is anything but pleasant to contemplate. Some one in Washington had written to that sheet presenting the necessities of increasing the salaries of clerks, whereupon the editor remarks:

"Now look here:

"Our country is involved in a terrible civil war, which has plunged her into debt about fifteen hundred millions of dollars, and is now rolling up at least seven hundred and fifty millions more per annum. We are likely to owe more rather than less than two thousand millions 'when this cruel war is over,' and to be required to pay at least one hundred millions per annum as interest thereon. Add to this the inevitably enhanced military and naval armaments and expenses of our government, caused by this atrocious rebellion, and our current expenditures can hardly be brought below two hundred millions per annum, instead of the fifty to seventy millions that formerly sufficed. This involves high taxes on everything that will bear taxation—on the luxury and income of the rich, and on the cheap and humble enjoyments of the poor. We have hitherto been among the most lightly taxed people on earth; we shall hereafter rank next highest after Great Britain and perhaps France.

"Such is the *permanent* prospect. For the present we are fighting for our nation's life, and the strain upon our resources and credit is fearful. We get on, and that is about all. We hope to get through; but blind confidence will not carry us through; it must be supplemented and justified by the most rigid economy. Yet we see men who should be foremost in thrift and providence contriving to plunge the government into all manner of canal, railroad and other outlays for objects not indispensable to national triumph in our great struggle, precisely as if we were at peace, with a full treasury and no debt! Are they stark mad?

"But to the clerkships:

"The present struggle imposes burdens on and exacts sacrifices from nearly every American. If this war shall cost twenty-five hundred millions, *somebody* has to pay it. Yet almost everybody acts as though *he* ought not to shoulder a portion of the load! Manufacturers say three per cent. on their products, with another dig at their incomes, is too much. Capitalists think it hard that, after paying taxes on all their property and business, they should be called on for three to five per cent. on their incomes in addition. Rum, tobacco and lager beer think the excise too hard on *them*. Business grumbles at stamps, license-fees, and all sorts of bit-by-bit exactions. And labor thinks it should have its wages raised to balance the enhanced prices of nearly every thing that it buys for consumption. In short, everybody thinks the cost of this gigantic war ought to be borne by somebody else."

According to WENDELL PHILLIPS, our public debt must be now quite *three thousand millions*, including amounts ascertained and unascertained. Indeed, we think when all the bills are settled, this amount will be enlarged, immensely.

This is a monstrous sum, almost beyond the power of man to contemplate in detail. It would require one man, if the whole were in silver dollars, counting sixty per minute, and making ten hours per day, Sundays included, about 2,286 years (should he live so long) to count the whole sum. If the Government was required to pay it in monthly installments, it would require $250,000,000 to be paid every thirty days, or $8,333,333,33 each day. If the amount should be divided equally, according to population, among the Northern states, it would be $150 to every man, woman and child, and to ascertain the amount that would, on this hypothesis, be assigned to each state, county, town, &c., let the reader multiply the number of inhabitants in any given district by 150, and he would have the probable sum which that district is mortgaged for—not wholly to sustain and save the Union—but largely to fill the pockets of thieves and public plunderers.

THE NEW CURRENCY—STAND FROM UNDER.

Old salts say that when the gulls flock about and utter plaintive cries, that a storm is brewing. We see evidences of a storm in the monetary affairs of the country in the plaintive cries of the bankers who are petitioning the Legislatures for "relief." When all is going smoothly, the bankers are quiet, but they are the first to snuff danger from afar, and when they invoke Legislative aid, then look out for squalls. We tell our readers to stand from under, for this bank barometer bodes a storm of dreadful fierceness. Already we see that greenbacks are to go *up* to a premium, when all know that it takes just about $1 60 in in greenbacks to buy one in gold. Still greenbacks are to be quoted at a premium, and why? Simply because of the rotten system of Mr. Chase, by which a portion of the greenbacks are to be withdrawn, and the government wild cat banking currency put afloat. This stuff will be so low, that greenbacks in comparison will be at a premium. Call it what you like, and the result is the same, and to be correct, the matter should, and probably soon will be, stated something like this:

Greenbacks below par.................... 60 per cent.
Common bank paper below Greenbacks,...... 10 " "
National Currency below common bank paper 25 " "

Mr. CHASE, in his splendid "system" will soon have the country in a pretty fix, because his "system" is nothing but an air bubble, and a very poor one at that, and it must burst the moment it is fairly blown up—simply because its "representative value" has been so unmercifully *watered*. Gold is but a *representative* of values—government bonds are but a *representative* (and just now a remote one) of gold, The Banking Bonds are but a representative of Greenbacks, while this new United States currency is to be but a *representative* of government bonds. Thus, these new issues are only to be fourth cousins to a representative, which in fact, is just no security at all, for the national debt is so ponderous now, that if the makers of this new currency should fail to redeem (and not one of them can) their notes would be valueless, because it would be out of the power of the government to redeem, by keeping their Bonds at par. Let us see how easy it will be to make a currency no better than unwashed paper rags, because it will stand on no *available* basis.

A desires to start a bank with the prefix "U. S." to it. He has just enough money to pay for the dies and to put up the "margin" [brokers understand this.] He goes to New York and offers the "per cent." to a Wall street broker to loan him greenbacks, with which to purchase $50,000 in 5-20's. This done, he issues the $50,000 minus the "margin," pays the same over to the broker, and is the proprietor of a bank of $50,000, and so he may keep on till he has a bank of a million circulation. But when called on to redeem—what then? Why, he *can't do it*, for his capital is nothing but air bubbles, and the bonds are then upon the market. The first batch will beget the second, and so on, till the whole shall crumble beneath the ruins and the *basis* will become worthless for use, because it will be brokerized at the lowest figure, and the result will be that the people will, in the end, suffer the loss. And all this to make a false popularity for Mr. Chase, who expects to have the credit of keeping up Greenbacks by bankrupting the people on their second-rate representatives. To this are we coming, depend upon it.

A HIGH OFFICIAL'S TESTIMONY.

Mr. McCulloch, the official Comptroler of the currency at Washington, has addressed a circular to the officers of the new national banks, in which he cautions them to beware of the crash, as follows:

"*Bear constantly in mind, although the loyal states appear superficially to be in a prosperous condition, that such is not the fact.* That while the government is engaged in the suppression of a rebellion of unexampled fierceness and magnitude, and is constantly draining the country of its laboring and producing population, and diverting its mechanical industry from works of permanent value to the construction of implements of warfare; while cities are crowded, and the country is to the same extent depleted, and waste and extravagance prevails as they never before prevailed in the United States, the nation, whatever may be the external indication, is not prospering.

"The war in which we are involved is a stern necessity, and must be prosecuted for the preservation of the government, no matter what may be its cost; *but the country will unquestionably be the poorer every day it is continued.* The seeming prosperity of the loyal states is owing mainly to the large expenditures of the government and the redundant currency which these expenditures seem to render necessary.

"Keep these facts constantly in mind, and manage the affairs of your respective banks with a perfect consciousness that *the apparent prosperity of the country will be proved to be unreal when the war is closed, if not before;* and be prepared, by careful management of the trust committed to you, to help to save the nation from *a financial collapse,* instead of lending your influence to make it more certain and more severe."

To a shrewd, practiced banker's eye, the true meaning of these hints is simply this: be careful and save yourselves when the crash comes—for come it will—for the basis of your currency will be of no avail. In what other light can this be read? Let the people be warned in time. The common "pet banks" already see the storm, and are preparing to take in sail. Keep a constant eye to the shore, and let no *ignus fatuus* lead you on to the breakers of destruction. A currency that cannot fall back on a substantial basis is good for nothing. This move of Mr. CHASE is only shifting the onus of the forthcoming crash from his greenback system to a personal, and infinitely worse one—keep an eye on the altitude of gold. The tornado is not far distant.

REPUBLICAN THIEVES AND PLUNDERERS.

Mr. COVODE and his Republican Congressional Investigating Committee uttered a terrible wailing—almost equal to one of the old-time Kansas shrieks—over the lamentable fact, that there were so many of their political brethren fattening by means of steals and dishonest contracts, upon the griefs and miseries of their country. Even the President himself could write to Gen. FREMONT, when in command at St. Louis, begging him to give a Government contract to a hungry and clamorous expectant. CAMERON and STANTON could make supply contracts, and suffer the country to be swindled out of millions of the public treasure; the Secretary of the Navy could allow his brother-in-law a high per centage for the purchase of vessels for the use of the government, and thus enable him to pocket hundreds of thousands of dollars. CHASE had his JAY COOKE and other favorites, who are pocketing their hundreds of thousands, if not millions of dollars a year; and so it goes, throughout all the departments of the public service. Such is the general understanding everywhere, that government contracts are almost universally of the "shoddy" character, that even novels and poems, not to speak of the thousand of newspaper and magazine squibs and protests are devoted to the ridicule of the shoddy contracts and shoddy cheats, so alarmingly prevalent in the country. The big bugs are getting rich, and the smaller fry are fast following suit, in imitation of their heartless and pampered superiors. And the COVODES shed crocodile tears over this stupendous fattening process on the sufferings and miseries of the country.

The New York Custom House, under the sole management of the most rabid sect of modern Republicans, has become so much a stench and by-word of reeking corruption— even to supplying, by connivance, the rebels with much-needed supplies; that even the corrupt Republican congressional leaders have felt constrained to appoint an investigating committee, which has already discovered some 'big leads' of Republican rascality; while another investigating committee, devoted to more general and miscellaneous Republican robberies and rascalities, has also been appointed by Congress.

Two or three years ago, a batch of Republican Congressmen, MATTESON, of New York; among them, who had accepted bribes, and had failed to keep their guilt as well concealed as their fellows, were expelled; and now the hypocritical Senator HALE, of New Hampshire, acknowledges to having received a rich bribe —he softens the thing down to a "*fee*"—and the Senate had his case on the tapis. Restive under their development, and as misery loves company, HALE concludes to pitch into the Secretary of the Navy, and dig out some rich rascalities in that festering Department of corruption, as we learn from the following extract from the New York York *Tribune* of the 26th of January, 1864:

"On motion of Mr. Hale, his resolution, asking for an investigation of the affairs of the Navy Department, was referred to a special committee of three, consisting of Senators Hale, Grimes and Bucklew, with power to send for persons and papers. Mr. Hale gave the statistics of the annual expenditures of the naval powers of Europe, excluding Italy and Denmark. They amounted last year to $139,-000,000; so that we are now called upon to spend this year more than the combined world, with the exception of Italy and Denmark. The naval expenses of England and France during the Crimean war amounted to $350,000,000, for a period of three years and five months.

SCRAPS FROM MY SCRAP-BOOK. 327

We are called upon to spend $40,000,000 more per annum than this."

Whether HALE will really make a thorough investigation, and lay bare the schemes to plunder the treasury and impoverish the people, or whether some of the men having mammoth contracts, and already gorged with greenbacks as the result of past rich plunderings, will quiet him with "a fee," remains to be seen.

Verily, we live in great times—great shoddy contracts—great pampered and rotten officials and great "fees" to propitiate the men of easy virtue who can, by nods and winks and favors, secure the ear of the corrupt dispensers of power and patronage under the present administration. Such wholesale, unblushing rascalities are unparalleled in the history of the world.

☞ Reader, the chapter of frauds is before you, compressed into the closest possible dimensions. We are not responsible for the facts, neither have we originated the testimony—it is all from Republican sources—the crime and the proof are theirs. Read then, and determine whether the country is safe in such hands.

CHAPTER XXXIX.

WARNINGS AND ADVICE OF AMERICAN STATESMEN, &c.

From Washington's Farewell Address...Jackson's Farewell Address...By Daniel Webster...By Henry Clay... By Patrick Henry...From Webster's Great Oration... Further from Jackson's Farewell Addresses...Madison on the Liberty of the Press...Mr. Seward on Free Speech ...Jefferson on the Plea of Necessity...John Adams on Arbitrary Power...Ex-President Filmore on the Negro Question...Gov. Seymour's Patriotic Letter...Senator Harris of New York, on the Despotism of Conscriptions ...Rob't J. Walker on State Suicide...Sen. Trumbull on the Tyrant's Plea...Gen. McClellan on Constitution and Christian Civilization...Sen. Crittenden on the cause of our Troubles...President Harrison on the Rights of the States...Montesquieu and Jefferson on Preservation of Liberty...James Madison on same...Gen. Harrison at Ft. Meigs...J. Q. Adams on the "Link of Union"...The Father of the Constitution on Confiscation...List of Members and Delegates in Congress, &c.

SOLEMN WARNINGS AND ADVICE OF AMERICAN STATESMEN, &c.

We are aware that the warnings of those great and illustrious men whose joint sacrifices secured to us the blessings of liberty, are now ignored by the pampered shoddyites; still, as there is yet a noble few who have not lost all regard for the teachings and wisdom of the past, we insert this last chapter, to stand as the "moral," or warning to that which proceeds it. Read, and reflect.

[From Washington's Farewell Address.]

"It is important that the habit of thinking in a free country should inspire caution in those intrusted with its administration, to confine ourselves within their respective constitutional spheres, avoiding, in the exercise of the powers of one department, to encroach upon another. The spirit of encroachment tends to consolidate the powers of all the departments in one, and thus create, whatever the form of government, a real despotism."

[From Jefferson's Works, by H. A. Washington, Vol. 7, pp. 223, 293.

"I see with the deepest affliction the rapid strides with which the federal branch of our government is advancing toward usurpation of all the rights reserved to the states, and the consolidation in itself of all power, foreign and domestic, and that, too, by constructions which, if legitimate, leave no limits to their power."

[From Jackson's Farewell Address, March 3, 1837.]

"Each state has the unquestionable right to regulate its own internal concerns according to its own pleasure; and while it does not interfere with the rights of the people of other States, or the rights of the Union, every state must be the sole judge of the measures proper to secure the safety of its citizens and promote their happiness; and all efforts on the part of the people of the state to cast odium on their institutions, and all measures calculated to disturb their rights of property, or to put in jeopardy their peace and internal tranquility, are in direct opposition to the spirit in which the Union was founded, and must endanger its safety. Motives of philanthropy may be assigned to their unwarrantable interference, and weak men may persuade themselves for a moment that they are laboring in the cause of humanity, and asserting the rights of the human race; but every one, upon sober reflection, will see that nothing but mischief can come from these improper assaults upon the feelings and rights of others. Rest assured that the men found busy in the work of discord are not worthy of confidence, and deserve the strongest reprobation."

[From Daniel Webster's Works, vol. 7, p. 134.]

"Through all the history of the contest for liberty, executive power has been considered a lion which must be caged. So far from being the object of enlightened popular trust—so far from being considered the natural protector of popular right—it has been dreaded as the great source of its danger."

[From the great Speech of Henry Clay against the insidious policy of Abolitionists.]

"Abolitionism! With Abolitionists the rights of property are nothing; the deficiency of the powers of the General Government is nothing; the acknowledged and incontestable powers of the states are nothing; a dissolution of the Union and the overthrow of a government in which are concentrated the hopes of the civilized world, are nothing; a single idea has taken possession of their minds, and onward they pursue it, overlooking all barriers, reckless and regardless of all consequences.

[From the great Speech of Patrick Henry on the Constitution.]

"Is the relinquishment of the trial by jury and the liberty of the press necessary for your liberty? Will the abandonment of the most sacred rights tend to the security of your liberty? Liberty, the greatest of all earthly blessings! Give us that precious jewel, and you may take everything else.

[From the great Oration of Daniel Webster on free speech in 1814.]

"Free speech is a home-bred right, a fireside privilege. It has ever been enjoyid in every house, cottage and cabin in the nation. It is not to be drawn into controversy. It is as undoubted as the right of breathing the air and walking on the earth. It is a right to be maintained in peace and in war. It is a right which cannot be invaded without destroying constitutional liberty. Hence this right should be guarded and protected by the freemen of this country with a jealous care unless they are prepared for chains and anarchy."

[From Jackson's Farewell Address, 1837.]

"The legitimate authority of the government is abundantly sufficient for all the purposes for which it was created; and its powers being expressly enumerated there can be no justification for claiming anything beyond them. Every attempt to exercise power beyond these limits should be promptly and firmly opposed; for one evil example will lead to other measures still more mischievous; and if the principle of constructive powers, or supposed advantages, or temporary circumstances, shall ever be permitted to justify the assumption of power not given by the Constitution, the General Government will, before long, absorb all the powers of legislation, and you will have, in effect, but one consolidated government."

MR. MADISON ON THE LIBERTY OF THE PRESS.

"The last remark will not be understood as claiming for the State Governments an immunity greater than they have heretofore enjoyed. Some degree of abuse is inseparable from a proper use of everything, and in no instance is this more true than that of the press. It has accordingly been decided by the practice of the states that it is better to leave a few of its noxious branches to their luxuriant growth, than by pruning them away, to injure the vigor of those yielding the proper fruits, and can the wisdom of this policy be doubted by any one who reflects, that to the press alone, chequered as it is with abuses, the world is indebted for all the triumphs which have been gained by reason and humanity over error and oppression; who reflects that to the same benificent source the United States owe much of the lights which conduct them to the rank of a free and independent nation! and which have improved their political system into a shape so auspicious to their oppressors! Had *sedition acts* forbidden every publication that might bring the constituted agents of the Government into contempt, or "DISREPUTE,' or that might excite the hatred of the people against the authors of unjust or pernicious measures been uniformly enforced against the press, might not the United States been languishing at this day under the infirmities of a sickly *confederation*—might they not possibly been miserable colonies, groaning under a foreign yoke.—*Elliott's Debates*, Vol. 4, p. 571.

MR. SEWARD ON FREE SPEECH.

On the 7th of August, 1856, Mr. SEWARD, in a speech in the U. S. Senate, used the following language :

"Where on earth is there a free government where the press is shackled and speech is strangled ?

"When the Republic of France was subverted by the First Consul, what else did he do but shackle the press and stifle speech ?

"When the second Napoleon restored the Empire on the ruins of the Republic of France what else did he do than to shackle the press and strangle debate?

"When Santa Anna seized the Government of Mexico, and converted it into a dictatorship, what more had he to do than to shackle the press and stifle political debate?"

JEFFERSON ON THE PLEA OF "NECESSITY."

"Those to whom power is *delegated* should be held to a strict accountability to their constitutional oath of office. The plea of *necessity* is no excuse for a violation of them."

JOHN ADAMS ON ARBITRARY POWER.

"Nip the shoots of arbitrary power in the bud, is the only maxim which can ever preserve the liberties of any people. *When the people give way, their deceivers, betrayers and destroyers press upon them so fast'that there is no resisting afterwards*. The nature of the encroachments is to grow every day more encroaching; like a cancer, it eats faster and faster every hour."

EX-PRESIDENT FILMORE ON THE NEGRO QUESTION.

"I am heart and soul with you in the object you have in view. Enough of treasure and blood have already been spent upon the negro question I am fully persuaded that the unwise and untimely agitation of this subject gives strength to the rebellion, and will cost millions of treasure and thousands of lives; and that there is no hope for anything else, but to restore the Union as it was, and the Constitution as it is. That all efforts for anything else must end in abortion, anarchy and dissolution."—*Letter to Connecticut meeting*, 1862.

SCRAPS FROM MY SCRAP-BOOK. 329

LETTER FROM GOV. SEYMOUR TO AN IMMENSE DEMOCRATIC MEETING IN ORANGE COUNTY, NEW YORK.

"EXECUTIVE DEPARTMENT,
ALBANY, June 29, 1863.

"GENTLEMEN: I regret that I cannot attend the meeting to be held at Middletown, Orange county, on the 2d of July; my engagements are such, that I cannot gratify myself by being present on that occasion.

"Our motto must be at this time, that we will do our duty and demand our rights, we will do every duty demanded by the constituted authorities acting within the limits of their jurisdiction, whether we like or dislike their policy. We will demand all our rights of such authorities, whether they like or dislike such demands.

"It is now apparent to all, that our country can only be saved by harmonious action among the people of the North. But it is equally clear that harmonious action can only be had upon one platform; and that platform is—the Union, the Constitution and respect for the laws. Harmony can never be made by threats, denunciations, or unconstitutional arrests of persons or seizure of property. It is easier for the Government to impose such illegal practices, than it is for a free people to submit to them.

"God grant that the afflictions of our country may teach our rulers this simple truth, and that these same afflictions may rouse in the hearts of our people the same patriotism and firmness in the defense of our liberty, which animated our fathers in the Revolutionary struggle.

"Yours truly, HORATIO SEYMOUR."

SENATOR HARRIS, OF NEW YORK, ON THE DESPOTISM OF CONSCRIPTIONS.

"England with her many wars, and often scarcity of men, never resorted to this despotic measure. It was a mode of raising armies only used by despots, but never by republican governments, and the principle, if adopted, would provide large standing armies, which almost inevitably lead to despotism. In a government of delegated power, and which rested upon the consent of the governed, it was inexpedient and unnecessary.

"Congress had not the power under the constitution, thus to destroy the militia of the states, which the constitution provided for as a reserved force of the Union. If this measure were adopted, there would be centralized power."—*Speech in Senate on Conscription Bill.*

ROBERT J. WALKER ON STATE SUICIDE.

"Will civil civil war preserve or restore the Union? * * Can a vanquished state, even if she can be vanquished, ever again become a member of the Federal Union? No, my countrymen; let us learn, ere it be too late, that this never can be a Union of victor and vanquished, of sovereign and subject states, but must be a Union of equals, which is the Union of the Constitution. It must be a cordial and fraternal Union, founded on interest, and cemented by affection. This was the Union founded by Washington and Franklin, and the patriots and statesmen of the Revolution; and that is the only Union that can be preserved and perpetuated. You might, perhaps, by superior force, drench in blood the fields of a sister state. You might, perhaps, wrap her villages in flames; but you could never afterwards restore such a state to the Union established by the Constitution. No, fellow citizens; WHEN THE STAR OF THE STATE IS EXTINGUISHED IN BLOOD, IT CAN NEVER BEAM AGAIN IN THE BANNER OF THE UNION, *for it will no longer be an equal, a sovereign, or a sister state.*"—*Speech in 1850.*

SENATOR TRUMBULL ON THE TYRANT'S PLEA.

"Necessity is the plea of tyrants, and if our Constitution ceases to operate the moment a person charged with its observance thinks there is a necessity to violate it, it is of little value. * * We are fighting to maintain the Constitution, and it especially becomes us in appeal to the people to come to its rescue, not to violate it ourselves. *How are we better than the rebels if both alike set at naught the Constitution.*—*Speech at Chicago, June*, 1863.

GEN. MC'CLELLAN ON CONSTITUTION AND CHRISTIAN CIVILIZATION.

"The General commanding takes this occasion to remind the officers and soldiers of the army that we are engaged in supporting the constitution and laws of the United States, and in suppressing rebellion against their authority; that we are not engaged in a war of rapine revenge or subjugation; that this is not a contest against populations, but a war against armed forces; that it is a struggle carried on within the State, and should be conducted by us upon the highest principles known to christian civilization."—*Address to the Army.*

SENATOR CRITTENDEN ON THE CAUSE OF OUR TROUBLES.

"What has brought this mighty change?—What has done it, Mr. Speaker? Do not we all know? Can there be any doubt on the subject? It has been our infidelity to the pledges made to the people. It has been because of the *reckless course of the dominant party.* * * * *

"If we want to get back the Union how must we do it? We must change our policy.

* * * * *

"Why do not the people have the same enthusiasm in the war, that they had at first?—Then they put a million of men in the field.—The country is still in peril, more than at first, and why is not our army of two million men now put into the fild? It is only *because of the bad policy by which you have established the dogmas of the abolitionists.*"—*From his last Speech.*

22

PRESIDENT HARRISON ON THE RIGHTS OF THE STATES.

"The citizens of each state unite in their persons all the privileges which that character confers, and all they may claim as citizens of the United States; but in no case can the same person act as citizen of two separate states, and he is therefore positively precluded from any interference with the reserved powers of any state but that of which he is for the time being a citizen.

"Our confederacy is perfectly illustrated by the terms and principles governing a copartnership. There is a fund of power is to be exercised under the direction of the joint counsels of the allied members, but that which has been reversed by the individual members is intangible by the common government or the individual members comprising it. Experience has abundantly taught us that the agitation by citizens of one part of the Union of a subject not confided to the general governmen is productive of no other consequences than bitterness, alienation, discord, and injury to the very cause which is intended to be advanced.—*See his Inaugural.*

"COPPERHEAD" SAYINGS.

"The enjoyment of liberty, and even its support and preservation, consists in every man's being allowed to speak his thoughts, and lay open his sentiments."—*Montesquieu.*

"The supremacy of the civil over the military authority; economy in the public expense, that labor may be lightly burthened; the honest payment of our debts, and sacred preservation of the public faith; the encouragement of agriculture and commerce as its handmaid; the diffusion of information and arrangement of all abuses at the bar of public reason.

"Freedom of religion; freedom of the press; freedom of the person under the protection of the *habeas corpus*; and trial by juries impartially selected. These principles form the bright constellation which has gone before us, and guided our steps through an age of revolution and reformation. The wisdom of our sages, and blood of our heroes have been devoted to their attainment; they should be the creed of our political faith, the text of civic instruction; the loadstone by which we try the services of those we trust, and should we wander from them in moments of error and alarm, let us hasten to retrace our steps, and to regain the road which alone leads to peace, liberty and safety."—*Thos. Jefferson.*

"To support the constitution which is the cement of the Union, as well in its limitations as in its authorities; to respect the rights and authorities reserved to the states, and to the people, as equally incorporated with, and essential to the success of the general system, to avoid the slightest interference with the rights of conscience, or the functions of religion, so wisely exempted from civil jurisdiction; to preserve in their full energy, the other salutary provisions in behalf of private and personal rights, and the freedom of the press."—*James Madison.*

GENERAL HARRISON ON ENCROACHMENTS OF POWER.

"The old-fashioned republican rule is to watch the government. See that the government does not acquire too much power.—Keep a check upon your rulers. Do this, and your liberty is safe. And if your efforts should result successfully, and I should be placed in the presidential chair, I shall invite a recurrence to the old republican rule, to watch the administration, and to condemn all its acts which are not in accordance with the strictest mode of republicanism. Our rulers, fellow-citizens, must be watched. Power is insinuating. Few men are satisfied with less power than they can obtain. If the ladies whom I see around me were near enough to hear me, and of sufficient age to give an experimental answer, they would tell you that no lover is satisfied with the first smile of his mistress.

"It is necessary, therefore, to watch, not the political opponents of an administration, but the administration itself, and to see that it keeps within the bounds of the Constitution and the laws of the land."—*Speech at Fort Meigs,* 1840.

JOHN Q. ADAMS ON THE "LINK OF UNION."

[Adams before the New York Historical Society, 1839.]

"But the indissoluble link of Union between the people of the several states of this confederated nation is, after all, not in the right, but in the heart. If the day should ever come (may heaven avert it) when the affections of the people of these states shall be alienated from each other, when the fraternal spirit shall give way to cold indifference, or collisions of interest shall fester into hatred, the bands of political association will not long hold together parties no longer attracted by the magnetism of conciliated interests and kindly sympathies; and far better will it be for the people of the disunited states to part in friendship from each other, than to be held together by constraint."

THE FATHER OF THE CONSTITUTION ON CONFISCATION.

"I was struck with surprise when I heard him (Mr Wythe) express himself alarmed with respect to the emancipation of slaves.— Let me ask, if they (the North) should even attempt it, if it will not be a *usurpation of power. There is no power to warrant it in that paper* (the Constitution.) If there be I know it not. But why should it be done?— Says the Honorable gentleman, for the general welfare: it will infuse strength into our system. Can any member of this Committee suppose that it (emancipation) will increase our strength? Can any one believe that the American Councils will come into a measure which will strip them of their *property*, and discourage and alienate the affections of five-thirteenths of the Union? Why was nothing of this sort arrived at before? I believe such an idea never entered into any American heart, nor do I believe it ever will enter into the heads of those gentlemen who substitute unsupported suspicions for reasons.—*Mr. Madison in the Convention—Elliott's Debates*, v 3, p. 621.

XXXVIIIth CONGRESS.

THE SENATE.

Politics.—R.—radical. C.—conservative. P.—peace.

CONNECTICUT.
Term Expires.
L. S. Foster............R 1867
James Dixon............C 1869

CALIFORNIA.
J. A. McDougal......C 1867
John Conness............C 1869

DELAWARE.
W. Saulsbury............C 1865
*Jas. A. Bayard......C 1869

INDIANA.
Henry S. Lane........R 1867
T. A. Hendricks......C 1869

ILLINOIS.
W. A. Richardson...C 1865
L. Trumbull............R 1867

IOWA.
Jas. W. Grimes......R 1865
Jas. Harlan............C 1867

KENTUCKY.
L. W. Powell............C 1865
Garrett Davis..........C 1867

KANSAS.
S. C. Pomeroy........R 1865
Jas. H. Lane..........R 1867

MARYLAND.
Thos. H. Hicks......C 1867
Reverdy Johnson.....C 1869

MAINE.
W. P. Fessenden....R 1865
L. M. Morrill..........R 1869

MASSACHUSETTS.
Henry Wilson........R 1865
Chas. Sumner........R 1869

MICHIGAN.
J. M. Howard........R 1865
Z. Chandler............R 1869

MINNESOTA.
B. S. Wilkinson....R 1867
Alex. Ramsay........R 1869

MISSOURI.
Term expires.
B. G. Brown............R 1867
J. B. Henderson......C 1869

NEW HAMPSHIRE.
John P. Hale..........R 1865
Daniel Clark............R 1867

NEW YORK.
Ira Harris..............R 1867
E. D. Morgan..........C 1869

NEW JERSEY.
J. C. Ten Eyck......C 1867
Wm. Wright............C 1869

OHIO.
Benj. F. Wade........R 1865
John Sherman........R 1867

OREGON.
Benj. F. Harding....C 1865
Jas. W. Nesmith....C 1867

PENNSYLVANIA.
Edgar Cowan..........C 1867
C. R. Buckalew......C 1869

RHODE ISLAND.
H. B. Anthony......R 1865
Wm. Sprague........R 1869

VERMONT.
Jacob Collamer......R 1867
Solomon Foot........R 1869

VIRGINIA.
J. S. Carlile..........C 1865
†L. J. Bowden........C 1869

WISCONSIN.
T. O. Howe............R 1867
J. R. Doolittle......R 1869

WEST VIRGINIA.
W. T. Willey........R 1865
P. G. Van Winkle..R 1869

Radical 29
Conservative 21

Total 50

HOUSE OF REPRESENTATIVES.

CONNECTICUT.
1 Henry C. Deming......R
2 James E. English......C
3 Aug. Brandegee........R
4 John H. Hubbard......C

CALIFORNIA.
(Elected at large.)
Thos. B. Shannon......R
Wm. Higby..................R
Cornelius Cole............*R

DELAWARE.
1 N. B. Smithers........R

ILLINOIS.
1 Isaac N. Arnold........R
2 John P. Farnsworth..R
3 Elihu B. Washburne..R
4 Chas. M. Harris........C
5 Owen Lovejoy............R
6 Jessie O. Norton......R
7 John R. Eden............C

*Resigned.

ILLINOIS—(concluded.)
8 John T. Stuart..........C
9 Lewis W. Ross..........C
10 Anthony L. Knapp....C
11 James C. Robinson....C
12 Wm. R. Morrison......C
13 Wm. J. Allen............C
Jas. C. Allen(at large)..C

INDIANA.
1 John Law..................C
2 James A. Cravens......C
3 H. W. Harrington......C
4 Wm. S. Holmes........C
5 George W. Julian......R
6 Ebenezer Dumont......R
7 Daniel W. Voorhees....C
8 Goodlove S. Orth......R
9 Schuyler Colfax........R
10 Joseph K. Edgerton..C
11 James F. McDowell....C

†Deceased.

IOWA.
1 James F. Wilson........R
2 Hiram Price..............R
3 William B. Allison......R
4 James B. Grinnell......R
5 John A. Kasson........R
6 A. W. Hubbard..........R

KENTUCKY.
1 Lucien Anderson........C
2 Geo. H. Yeaman........C
3 Henry Grider............C
4 Aaron Harding..........C
5 Robert Mallory..........C
6 Green Clay Smith......C
7 Brutus J. Clay..........C
8 Wm. H. Randall........C
9 Wm. H. Wadsworth...C

KANSAS.
1 A. C. Wilder............R

MAINE.
1 Lorenzo D. Sweat......C
2 Sidney Perham..........R
3 James G. Blaine........R
4 John H. Rice............R
4 Frederick A. Pike......R

MASSACHUSETTS.
1 Thomas D. Eliot........R
2 Oakes Ames..............R
3 Alexander H. Rice....R
4 Samuel Hooper..........R
5 John B. Alley............R
6 Dan'l W. Gooch........R
7 Geo. S. Boutwell......R
8 John D. Baldwin........R
9 Wm. B. Washburn....R
10 Henry L. Dawes......R

MARYLAND.
1 John A. J. Creswell....R
2 Edwin H. Webster......C
3 H. W. Davis..............R
4 Francis Thomas..........C
5 B. G. Harris..............P

MISSOURI.
1 F. P. Blair, jr............R
2 Henry T. Blow..........R
3 John G. Scott............C
4 J. W. McClerg..........R
5 S. H. Boyd................R
6 A. A. King................R
7 Benjamin Loan..........R
8 W. A. Hall................C
9 James S. Rollins........C

MICHIGAN.
1 F. C. Beaman............R
2 Charles Upson............R
3 J. W. Longyear..........R
4 F. W. Kellogg............R
5 A. C. Baldwin............C
6 John F. Driggs..........R

MINNESOTA.
1 William Windom........R
2 I. L. Donnelly............R

NEW YORK.
1 H. G. Stebbins..........R
2 M. Kalbfleisch............C
3 Moses F. Odell..........C
4 Benjamin Wood..........P
5 Fernando Wood..........P
6 Elijah Ward..............C
7 John W. Chandler......C
8 James Brooks............P
9 Anson Herrick............P
10 Wm. Radford............C
11 Chas. H. Winfield......C
12 Homar A. Nelson......C
13 John B. Steele..........C
14 J. L. V. Pruyn..........R..C
15 John A. Griswold......C
16 Orlando Kellogg........R
17 Calven T. Hulburd......C
18 James M. Marvin......C
19 Saml. F. Miller..........R
20 Ambrose W. Clark....R
21 Francis Kernan..........C
22 De W. C. Littlejohn....C
23 Thos. F. Davis..........R
24 Theo. M. Pomeroy......R

NEW YORK—continued
25 Daniel Morris............R
26 Giles M. Hotchkiss....R
27 R. B. Van Valkenburg..R
28 Freeman Clark..........R
29 Aug. Frank..............C
30 John Ganson............C
31 Ruben E. Fenton......R

NEW JERSEY.
1 John F. Starr............R
2 Geo. Middleton..........C
3 Wm. G. Steele..........C
4 Andrew J. Rogers......C
5 Nehemiah Perry........C

NEW HAMPSHIRE.
1 Daniel Marcey............C
2 Edward H. Rollins......R
3 Jas. W. Patterson......R

OHIO.
1 Geo. H. Pendleton......C
2 Alexander Long..........C
3 Robert C. Schenck......R
4 J. F. McKinney..........C
5 Frank C. LeBlond......C
6 Chilton A. White........C
7 Samuel S. Cox..........C
8 William Johnson........C
9 Warren P. Noble........C
10 James M. Ashley......R
11 Wells A. Hutchins....C
12 Wm. E. Fink............C
13 John O'Neill............C
14 George Bliss............C
15 James R. Morriss......C
16 Joseph W. White......C
17 Eph. R. Eckley........R
18 Ruf. P. Spaulding......R
19 John A. Garfield......R

OREGON
1 John B. McBride........C

PENNSYLVANIA
1 Samuel J. Randall......C
2 Charles O'Neill..........R
3 Leonard Myers..........R
4 Wm. D. Kelley..........R
5 M. Russell Thayer......R
6 John G. Stiles............C'
7 John M. Broomall......R
8 Syd'm E. Ancona........C
9 Thad. Stevens............R
10 Myer Strouse............C
11 Philip Johnson..........C
12 Charles Denison........C
13 Henry M. Tracy........R
14 Wm. H. Miller..........C
15 Joseph Bailey............C
16 A. H. Coffroth..........C
17 Archd. McAlister......C
18 James T. Hale..........R
19 G. W. Scofield..........R
20 Amos Myers..............R
21 John L. Dawson........C
22 J. K. Moorhead........R
23 Thos. Williams..........R
24 Jesse Lazear............C

RHODE ISLAND.
1 T. A. Jenkes............R
2 N. P. Dixon..............R

VERMONT.
1 F. E. Woodbridge......R
2 Justin S. Morrill........R
3 Portus Baxter............R

WISCONSIN.
1 James S. Brown........C
2 I. C. Sloan................C
3 Amasa Cobb..............C
4 C. A. Eldridge............C
5 Ezra Wheeler............C
6 W. D. McIndoe..........R

VIRGINIA.
1 L. H. Chandler..........C
†2 Joseph Segar............C
3 B. M. Kitchen............C

WEST VIRGINIA.
1 Wm. G. Brown..........R
2 Jacob B. Blair..........R
3 K. V. Whaley............C

Radical..92
Conservative.....................................69
Unconditional peace.......................... 5

Total...156

DELEGATES.

NEW MEXICO.
F. Perea

NEBRASKA.
Samuel G. Daily.

UTAH.
John F. Kenny.

WASHINGTON.
George E. Cole.

COLORADO.
Hiram P. Bennett.

IDAHO.
William H. Walace

The foregoing classification is not ours. It is in the main correct, but will bear sundry changes. It will do for refference.

THE IRREPRESSIBLE CONFLICT,

(BEGINNING OF THE END,)

OR,

THE RISE, PROGRESS AND DECLINE OF "ONE IDEA,"

INCLUDING THE PRINCIPAL ACTS IN THE LIFE OF ABRAHAM THE FIRST.

IN ELEVEN ACTS.

PROLOGUE.

The laugh comes in *here*—things now
Doth wear a weighty and a serious brow!
Sad, foul and bloody—full of crime and woe—
Such mournful scenes as cause the eye to flow,
I'll anon present. Those with hearts, may here,
If they feel that way inclined, let drop a tear!
My subject will deserve it. Such as give
Me money, out of hope that they may live
To see the end of war and tradgedy's alarm—
Rejoice in Peace—fearing naught of harm;
And read my "drama," how soon they'll see
That might and folly hunt in pairs for misery!
And if you can be "merry" then I fear,
A son may dance upon his mother's bier!

ACT I.

Scene—*In the Chicago Wigwam.*

[*Enter Politicians, Cormorants and others.*

1st Pol.—   Hoc considerationi tuæ est, my Lords,
We this day convene for most holy purpose,
To name a ruler that shall much improve
On the sorry ill-haps of King James, the Fourth.
    Our choice must be an hermafrodite;
Who hath a mealey mouth for utterance
Of sweet things, concerning sable Knights
Of yam, hoe cake and cruel cat-o'-nine-tails!
    The leader of our tribe must have no taint
Of ill omen, or Fuss and Feathers 'bout him!
With all the points of most honorable ignorance,
He must be fit for any point of compass—
And for treason, stratagem and spoils;
One that in town and ranche conservative,
May 'list the rabble, with no ill precedent
To 'pear in judgment 'gainst his sure success!
And who, in districts radical, at once,
May carry all before him, as the embodiment
Of the most rabid, redundant dogmas!
    We must the deepest current follow,
For that doth the proper channel indicate,
To the sea, where fishes do most school,
And where our nets, if cast within aright,
May, in fruition, become our *finished* hopes.
    We must our flaunting banners fitly garnish
With emblems and mottoes the public nerves to tickle,
Such as *Retrenchment, Freedom* and *Reform!*
These will careless eyes amuse, and then,
The public ear to charm, send out our Ciceroes,
To mount the rostrum, and this catch-vote trinity
Expound, and condemn with horror's holy unction,
The rascally counterparts that doth afflict us,
Under King James, the Fourth?
        Such, my Lords,
Is, in short, my plan, success to master;
What say you to't?

2d Pol.—   For one,
I'm most charmingly delighted, faith,
With all the noble Lord hath uttered!
My only fault-finding in this doth lie:—
That sundry details hath His Grace omitted

Which alone can vouchsafe success!
'Tis known to all, the Western Little Giant
Stands at this time, like a wall of fire
Betwixt us and our goal of hope.

*A Voice—(Interruptingly)—*We must dispatch him.

2d Pol.—(Continuing)—   Yea, that we must!
But how?   That's *the* most important question.
    [*Scratches his head, exclaiming:*
I have it, by Jupiter!—at last I have it.
The Democratic Sachems are in quarrel!
I would encourage their Charleston split
By a lever and entering wedge, at Baltimore.
The enemies of the famous Little Giant
Are bent on revolt—yea, secession,
And if we give but one grain of 'couragement
They will secede, and thus so weaken
The Democratic hosts, that we'll be sure
To win—not by our strength, but their weakness!
I've had a word with their great Benjamin,
The Senatorial Jew from Molasses town.
He hath a most ferocious speech agreed
To utter in the forum of the "Pantheon,"
Which, in return, did I stipulate,
To print and circulate two million copies,
As seed for Northern fallow fields.
Thus, may we use our foeman's stool
To conquer, though dragons follow after.

Office Seeker—   Bravo! bravo!!
The plan will office and the spoils secure us—
A most welcome dish to stomachs long in fast!
For, outside the crib so long we've anxious stood,
Like the fifth calf, our turn still waiting,
That any means to reach the pap, I welcome!
And mock all fear of consequences!

Compunction.—   Be cautious, friends, I chide,
There may in this tub lie concealed, a cat,
Or acid, that may cramp us with the bellyache!
Honesty may, e'en in politics be virtue;
And as Harry Clay did on occasion utter,
"I would rather be right than President!"
Therefore, mock I these villainous propositions.

Voices in the Pit.—   Hustle him out!
He's got a conscience, a quite conclusive fact,
That he to our tribe belongeth not!

*Voices from the Rostrum.—*Away with him!
    [*Exit Comp. in a shower of hisses.*

Delegate.—   Come, come my Lords, to business.
With the platform, and campaign *role* I'm pleas'd.
But who shall be the Patriarch to lead
Our forces thro' the gloomy valley 'fore us?
Our aching bones do need a goodly med'cine!
We hate the south, and the south hate us!
No shock of earth shall sunder our two hates!
The question is, who'll so lead us o'er Charybdis,
That we may 'scape dark, yawning Scilla?
        As a fit beginning, will I name
Abraham, the tall, and jocose Sucker Barrister;
Who, though a lion is a Western bar-room,
Will a juvenile sheep become—at court!
So docile, as to mould like Burgundy wax,
And as King Henry to Exeter remarked,

True, when the lion fawns upon the lamb,
The lamb will never cease to follow him.
Give me a flexible prince—mules I 'bominate.
New Yorker.—   Most noble Lords,
If I am permitted here my mouth to ope,
I will suggest the noble Duke of York,
Who hath too oft been shelv'd by expediency.
If we his claims now do overlook,
We dry the fount from which the sea of thought
Sucks its everlasting fill.
                Give us brains,
And less expediency, in alopathic doses—
A mind that greatness blends with actions—
An intellect above rail or hair-splitting quacks—
A something better than mere nose of wax.
Above all others, 'tis my oft expressed belief
That William, the Conquerer, is the man
To lead our conquering hosts.
Contractor.—I agree, in part, with the noble wight
Who hath regaled our ears with brains and sense,
And that so urgently the Duke of York doth press.
I, too like him, am a devotee of brains!
But I confess, my faith is somewhat shattered
In the insinuation that all the brains extant
Are by the Duke of York monopolized.
   All admit that where graces challenge grace
And brains oppress the skulls that hold them,
That our Simon hath no proud party peer!
Brains and money are his strongest holt!
These are graces, that when once combined
Will sweep the board, and let us into clover!
I therefore propose that Simon be
Our candidate and nominee!
He would lead us to the vast public larder,
Where, we'd fill our pich'd and billious stomachs!

New Yorker.—(Aside.)—   [Provided always,
That Simon himself, had *first* been gorged!]
            [*Laughter and hisses in the pit.*]
Sir Puke.—   Since thus your favorites are urg'd
I offer Edward, the nable Barron *von* St. Louis;
He will great Border strength conciliate,
And our platform fringe would soil the least.
I warn you, slight not his stronger claims.
Sucker.—   Talk not of Edward's "claims!"
Dear to the slaughter-house his mangled corse!
Away with such bloody-bones pretenders; for,
Honest Abraham shall, of our victorious tribe,
Become the Patriarch, *de jure*.
             I move the previous question!
Put out the lights—each one take care of self—
Clear the pit, and let the vote be quickly taken!
The motion's carried—now to honest ballot!
One—twice—yea to twenty rounds, at least—
All hail to honest Abe, our gallant chief!
       [*Exit omnes, after a short "collection"*]

ACT II.

SCENE....*After Election...Springfeld Hermitage.*

A MEDLEY:

DESCRIPTIVE...PATHETIC....POETIC....PROPHETIC AND NATURAL.

[*Enter numerous Cormorants.*]
1st Cor....   How now, my liege Lord,
The returns do indicate thou art chosen King.
Egad, I knew the Wide Awakes would save you!
'Twas *my* influence that carried things in our parts!
In fact, no one did e'er such forces muster!
At great expense, did I sweat and work for thee,
And of all the jokes thou hast e'er perpetrated,
The joke of thy success doth the climax cap,
And, as your Grace is mighty fond of jokes,
'Tis safe to guess you *this* do extra relish!
By the way, your Grace, how about the offices?
Is my sight good for the Tumbuctoo Charge?
I see you hesitate. I'll not o'erpress my suit
Now, since I fear the news hath o'ercome you.
What, your Grace, are you ill...displeased,...
Or, what's the matter? I ne'er did see you
Put on so solemn airs, 'pon honor...never!
Abraham...   Nay, away, good bore,
I'm neither ill nor sore displeased, withall.
'Tis only a modest fear that I may meet

With troubles worse than Liliput encountered!
I'm no Jackson, as the world will see anon!
Troubles are thick'ning in the southern zone,
Like unto steaming mush o'er the peasant's fire!
Our late allies who did assist to kill off "Dug,"
And thus to the Imperial Throne lift me,
Hath at my success sniff'd great offence
And now do threaten dissolution, which if it come,
Will force me to sue for Democratic succor!
For, our Wide Awakes, I fear, tho' good to burn
Their midnight *ile*, and to vocalize the streets
With nocturnal music, harsh to ears polite,
Will hardly prove efficient in the tug of war!

[*Enter the Dauphin (Bob) with the latest newspaper.*]
Dauphin...Good sire, from the post am I come, amain,
To signify that the rebels' backs are up,
Who, many loyal victims do put to sword:
Send succor quick, and stop the rage, betime,
Before the wounds do grow incurable,
For, being fresh, there is yet much hope of help.
Abraham...As I feared, this spark will prove a raging fire,
If wind and fuel be bro't to feed and fan it!
But, Dauphin, I'm neither King or Regent yet,
And if I were, I might well question
Whether I could roll back the flaming tide,
With more success than hath King James.
Tho' rather than jeopard all, as he hath,
Would I have lost my life betimes,
Than bring a burden of dishonor home,
For as Julius Cæsar, am I chivalric,
But, like the ostrich, that in Sahara's sands
Doth hide its head, and thinks nobody sees
Its form, because it sees nobody,
I must, from vulgar eyes conceal my purpose!
'Twill be time enough for secondary matters,
When I've toss'd to friends the bones of office.

2d Cor...   Most noble Sucker,
Thou dost wisdom almost divine betray!
The loaves and fishes! Ah, most gracious Sire!
Them's of our edifice the corner-stone...
The *alpha* and *omega* of our Chicago Platform!
I do most freely applaud your Grace's views,
And I trust your Grace will, in due time,
Heed my claims for the mission to St. Cloud!
Here's my papers, which my faith will prove,
In the irrepressible conflict, I love.

3d Cor...   Aye, yes, my friend hath fitly spoken;
Thou art the hero for these dreadful times!
I pray your Grace, *my* claims to also note.
But little do *I* care, your Grace, for pelf and place,
But then *my friends* do urge with grave concern
That as 'Charge to Quito I'm most fit to serve.
What says your Grace? Can I count upon
The gratification of my most urgent friends?
Abraham...   Most valued friends,
You presume much and do squeeze my honor,
As old Mrs. Battles said when being hugged
By the ungallant bear, in wanton mood!
I fain would to you all, serve pottage,
Yea, as ye have served myself, of late:
But, yet, 'tis meet young eagles should not feed
Outside the natal crib.
                Therefore, wait I pray,
Until my advent to the Fed'ral Mecca,
And when ensconced within the palace kitchen,
I may cogitate upon your several "claims,"
Until then, my friends...adieu!
         [*Exit Abraham and the Dauphin.*]

4th Cor...   Well, my waiting friends,
In the language of our old joker ice-gerent,
I think this devlish cool! Yes, and I may add,
The North Pole is a monster red-hot poker,
Compared with this frigid, gruff "Adieu!"
Why, his Grace dismissed us so curtly,
That my recommendations lie congealed
To the nether end of my untouch'd pocket!
The great altitude his Grace hath reached,
Reminds me of the monkey up the pole!

5th Cor...   Ha! ha! So! so!
Must we not take such as our betters give,
And ask no questions? Our Honest Abraham
Will soon become *the* Government...all-in-all,
And who that lispeth aught 'gainst *him*
Will against the *Government* inveigh...
That will be treason.

THE IRREPRESSIBLE CONFLICT.

6th Cor... True...it may be true,
But then what 'comes of the great corner-stone
Of our most solemn litany...*freedom!*
7th Cor... O, ye worse than geese,
To be thus hissing out complaints.
Let's return and wait events!
[*Exeunt Omnes, meeting at the door another swarm of Cormorants.*]

ACT III.

SCENE...*On the Road to Washington.*

[*Enter (the cars) Abraham, Q. Margaret, the Dauphin and Suit.*]
Abraham...(*in a soliloquizing and musing mood*)...[*Aside.*
[Ah, who'd have tho't some thirty years ago,
When on the turbid, roaring Wabash
I did a sea-worthy flat boat command,
Or, when among the Hoosiers, mauling rails,...
Or jokes in some country grocery cracking,
That I, alone, of all this mighty people,
Should thus have been found most worthy
To rule as monarch.
 Verily,
How little man doth know his mental powers,
Until by circumstance they luminate!
From small beginnings to lofty heights
Have I ascended by the ladder Douglas made,
Until I'm the observed of all observers!
And my name upon all tongues is hing'd.
I'm to that Mecca on my winding way,
Where politicians most do congregate!
With garlands hither my path is garnish'd,
And at each station will I meet acclaims
Of curiosity-seeking multitudes.
 Yet,
Alas! I fear, that in the sequel of that path,
There lies concealed, a bed of thorns,
And, envenomed dragon's teeth, by acres.]
The air feels chilly...the ague threatens!
Dauphin, pass the bottle!
[*Here the train arrives at I——s Station...Multitudes flock around and clamor for a speech.*]
Abraham— My generous friends,
I am rejoiced to see you, and should judge that you
Are right smart glad to welcome me.
[*Loud huzzas and cries of "Tell us what you're going to do."*]
Abraham—Well, my friends, my mood is none too amiable,
Yet, since you ask it, I've not the least objection
To 'quaint you that to yonder Mecca do I haste,
And what I there do, depends upon the fates,
And what the good Duke of York may urge.
The horizon with vast events o'erhangs,
And womanish minds with fear are wrung,
But, as "nobody's hurt," I'll pass—adieu!
[*Tremendous cheering—as the train starts.*]

SCENE 2D—*Hotel at Harrisburg—Midnight.*]

[*Enter Messenger in great haste.*]
Mess... How, now sir Boniface,
Is Father Abraham thy guest? I would see him.
I am son of the Duke of York, and
Have I business of the most pressing moment
With His Highness, our beloved Abraham.
I would see him instanter. The occasion presses.
Boniface... Abraham is now my honor'd guest;
Some two hours post did he and suit retire,
To woo Nature's sweet restorer, for
He's journy'd long, and needs repose.
He bad me to his slumbering presence
Admit no mortal wight.
 Thou must disturb him not,
For on his health depends the nation's life.
Mess... I must, and will disturb him,
For on his instant knowledge of my mission
Depends his own most precious life!
I ask an instant audience...yea, *demand* it,
With His Highness, for I possess a fearful secret,
Sent by the Duke of York, in lightning haste!
On which may'st depend our weal or woe.

Come, this instant, point out the way
To Abraham's apartments, or by St. George,
I'll grind your bones to fertilizing plaster,
Betwixt you ceiling and my sledge hammer fists.
Boniface...(*Aside*)... By hokey!
This fellow's either crazy, drunk or earnest.
There's something in his eye that tokens resolution
I'll to the chamber of my guest announce him,
But should he prove to be a fiendish regicide,
And should His Highness slay while he's my guest,
I'm busted as a Boniface, forever.]
Well, stranger, since your demand doth seem
So urgent, honest, and of so vast concern,
I will at once comply; but mind you, sir,
The least attempt at harm will 'rouse
All slumbering Harrisburg, and 'pon my word,
The Susquehanna fishes shall sate their greed,
And dine upon your carcass.
Come, sir, as I lead the way, follow thou,
With steps as light as unwrought cotton.
[*Boniface and Messenger depart for No. 1, bearin. each a flambeau.*]

SCENE...*They arrive at No. 1, and give heavy raps.*

Abraham (*within, half waking.*) What's up, my spouse?
Heard you not that racket? Strike a light!
The Dauphin out of bed hath fallen!
 [*The visitors rap again.*]
The Dauphin hath his neck quite broken—and
There goes the j——n. Fire! Thieves!
 [*More and louder rapping.*]
Who's at my chamber this late hour o' night?
Speak without, or my Derringer I'll level;
And wo be to him that my nocturnal sanctum
Doth invade at this unseasonable hour!
Boniface...(*without.*) Fear not, your Highness;
No enemy doth thee confront! 'Tis thy friends!
I am pressed by no common necessity
To thus arouse thee. 'Pon the sacred honor
Of thy most honored, loyal guest,
I do assure thee, it pains me sorely,
To thus disturb thy soothing slumber;
But a Messenger from the noble Duke of York
Doth await your Highness' instant pleasure.
He entreats thee, as thou life doth value,
To grant him instant audience.
Abraham...(*soto voce,*) [*Some office seeker,*
I dare say, who plays this clever ruse
To press his selfish suit. However,
As there may be danger of some fell garrote,
I'll grant him ingress, and probe the 'larum.]
 [*Unlocks the door.*]
 Walk in, knight errants,
And be quiet, while I the gas do luminate.
 [*Lights the gas.*]
Mess... I beg your Highness' gracious pardon,
For this most unseasonable interruption, but,
My noble sire, and thy friend, the Duke of York,
Having great concern for your Highness' life,
Hath me despatched to warn you of a plot,
The most diabolical, and...
Abraham...(*interrupting.*) What plot, pray?
Mean you to say some arch fiend is plotting
Harm against my person? Speak!
Mess... Yea, that do I, your Highness.
List, and ye shall learn the upshot on't.
My noble Sire, who awaits your Highness,
At the palace gate, hath, like a dashing rocket,
Sent me to warn you of the fatal danger;
That the vile Plugs of the Monumental City
Hath a hatching for your swift destruction.
A trusty friend, who had the secret gained,
Did, on the wings of extra pressure steam, fly
To 'quaint my father of the plot and plotters.
By the information, the story runneth thus:....
To-morrow, as the Programme's gazetted,
You are through seething Baltimore to pass,
The Rebels hath their machinations well arranged
To give yourself and suit a fitting welcome,
And as you the leading thoroughfare do pass,
The Plugs, in dissembling curiosity,
Will in vast array press upon you;

And, at the concerted signal from their chief,
A row and tumult will commence, amain,
And waxing hotter 'till it doth culminate
Into a riot of fearful motive power!
  Bowie knives, rifles and revolving shooters,
In that melee are all to play their purpose;
And, when the seed of this infernal plot be ripe,
A "chance shot"...perhaps a dozen...will pierce you.
And yet, no one aimed it...'twas random "accident,"
And *accidents*, you know, are seldom honored
By compunctions that at the death go weeping.
  Such, your Highness, is the full programme,
And such your danger, most imminent.
Here is a note from the Duke's own hand,
With particulars full. Read, and at once fly
Hence, by other routes, *incog.*
  [*Abraham takes letter and tremblingly reads.*]
Abraham...   But what, pray, can I do?
This note doth post me of your father's fears,
That on all the highways to the Palace
There may assassins lie concealed.
Mess...   For such contingency
Have we made provision, ample!
I have raised the *Curtin* from his couch,
The noble ruler of this Commonwealth,
Who hath arranged to cut the wires,
So they give no tongue that's contraband;
And thus announce, as *a la Mahomed*,
Your flight by night to Mecca.
The track is clear, and a special train
Awaits your Highness at the depot.
  [*Presents a large bundle to Abraham.*]
Take this Scotch cap and monkish cloak,
And, when disguised therein, you've naught to fear,
For, by my soul, you'll cut such grotesque figure,
That e'en your spouse won't know you.
Abraham...   Alas, I feel the pressure
Of your most kind regards. My inward fear
Doth move me your lead to follow;
But what of the morrow? What fresh excuse
Can our friends invent, to reconcile the crowd,
That will by thousands flock to see me?
What will say the press, when in the wind
Of such a dodge...so very ludicrous?
Will they not post me as an arrant coward,
When as brave as Cæsar I should appear?
I must summon counsel, e'er I start
On such a steeple chase, *incognito*.
Hail the Gov'nor and his trusty friends,
That I may with him and them divide
This vast responsibility.
              [*Rings the bell.*
     [*Enter Boniface in great concern.*]
Boniface...   I am your most obsequious servant...
What will'st your Highness?
Abraham...   I would you the Gov'nor summon.
I would confer with His Excellency, instantly.
Boniface...   Aye, your Highness!
His Excellency is e'en now in waiting, just below.
I will announce him at once.
     [*Enter Governor and friends.*]
Abraham...   Welcome to my perturbed chamber,
Most excellent Gov'nor. I did thee summon
For counsel in this perplexing throe of fear!
Hast thou learned the story? If yea, at once
Proffer me advice, most just and honorable.
Gov...   That I will, your Highness.
I know it all, and have contrived a mode
Which, though it will provoke much criticism,
Will save you, harmless as a suckling dove!
By all means, depart at once, in this disguise...
Yea, before your route with prying eyes
Shall be astir.
              I will explain
Your absence on the morrow; so now depart...
Yea, go at once, for time is precious.
Abraham...   As you will; but O,
That I were a god, to shoot forth thunder
Upon those Baltimorean, abject "Uglies!"
  Small things make base men proud. Those villains
Being captains of a gang, threaten more
Than Bargulns, the dread Illyrian Pirate!
But they shall yet pay interest on their folly!
Drones suck not eagles' blood, but rob bees!

It seems, indeed, impossible that I should die
By such dastard vassals as those Plug Uglies,
Whose vice move rage, but not remorse, in me;
I go, of message from the Duke of York, but
I charge ye, take me swiftly to the Palace!
  By vile Bezonians great men have died.
It was a Roman sworder and bandito slave
That great Tully murdered. Brutus' bastard hand
Stabbed Julius Cæsar,...savage Islanders
Pompey the Great, and Suffolk died by pirates...
But Abraham the First shall never fall
By Baltimore Plug assassins!
              So, don my guise
And hence I post, a monkish refugee.
  [*Exeunt omnes, in great haste and secrecy.*]

ACT IV.

SCENE...*4th of March.*

[*Abraham choseth his counsellors, consisting of the
Duke of York, Simon, the Leper, Gideon, the Fogy, Edward, the Barrister, Salmon, the Foxey, Caleb, of the
family of Smiths, and Montgomery, the paragon.
The time arrives for Abraham to doff the Scotch cap,&c.,
and put on the robes of power, and at 12 o'clock he, with
his counsellors and soothsayers, leads a dashing pageantry
for the Capitol to do some "tall swearing." The East portico, surrounded by thousands bayonets and civilians.*]

   [*Enter King James, sundry Lords, Nobles, &c.*]
Abraham...[*Holding up his right hand and fixing his
       eyes on the nude Statuary before him.*]
              I now before this vast array
Of soldiers and civilians, am about to swear
To protect and preserve the nation's *Magna Charta*.
Witness, O, people and my God, that solemn oath.
Judge Toney...   Most elevated Abraham!
Thou chosen ruler of the Jews and Gentiles
Of this great, disservered commonwealth!
Know thou that I am the distinguished author
Of that little-understood and misquoted tale, Dred
Scott,
And that by our great charter, am I empowered
To exact of thee, before God, an oath,
That thou, abjuring all other potentates,
Powers, platforms, creeds and principalities,
Will faithfully execute the statutes,
Uphold the Constitution as I expound it,
And place in trust or office, none except
The faithful of your creed and party,
So help you, Simon and the "Balance."
Abraham...   Most learn'd and ven'rable expounder
Of the law's delays and constitutional perplexities,
With profound delight have I heard thy speech,
And in the presence of thy August Self,
God and the people, do I offer solemn oath,
To abjure all other Potentates and Powers,
(Except Powers' Greek Slave and other Slaves,)
And that I will most faithfully execute the laws,
(And the rebels, if I can catch them,)
The Constitution in all things will I obey,
(Providing with my wish it interfereth not,)
And to office not a soul will I appoint,
Except the purely "loyal" of my own party,
So help me Simon and the "Balance."
Gen. Scott (as Nestor)   The deed is done,
Abraham is now monarch of all he surveys!
Soldiers, break ranks, and to your rations...
To your tents, O, Israel!
                 And thou, King James,
Farewell. As Dupe of Lancaster, do I 'point thee,
And may the evil of thy latter days
By no means survive thy issue!
King James...   Thank God!
I no longer bear upon my galled back,
The saddle of most perplexing office,
And that politicians, spurred and booted,
Shall no longer ride me legitimately,
By the grace of God!
                 Adieu, adieu,
My late terror-stricken subjects...Adieu.

   [*Exit King James, while Abraham seeks repose in
the Palace.*]

THE IRREPRESSIBLE CONFLICT.

ACT V.

Scene...*Cabinet meeting—War and Rumors if War.*

[*Enter Abraham, Simon, Duke of York, and the Balance.*]

Abraham... Well, my faithful Dukes,
To this solemn counsel I have you summoned,
That I may draw your opinions
Of our duty in this alarming crisis.
The Sesoshers have their ugly backs up,
And are bent on early mischief;
The Palmetto state hath taken leave,
And the Everglades are on the move;
Georgia, Alabama and Texas threaten...
The Mississippians are becoming huffy...
The Old Dominion wavers, and I fear
The whole caboodle will give us slip;
What shall be done, is now the question...
What *can* be done, is still a harder one.

Simon... I pray your Highness
Take little heed of these flying rumors.
Rest at ease 'till the offices be fill'd!
Our *friends* should be waited on
Before we pay attention to our foes!
Charity, your Highness, begins at home!

Gideon... Simon hath most fitly spoken.
'Tis clear that charity should *at home* begin:
And what greater charity than to give the spoils
To our most needy (yea, and seedy) friends,
Who hath swarmed around your Highness,
As a protecting armor, in your late peril,
And at the polls were most serviceable?

Salmon... From such a *role* I must dissent;
Our country first, and afterwards the spoils,
Would be my motto at such time as this.

Simon... "Country" be d—d!
I've too many friends awaiting army contracts,
To trifle 'bout the "country," yet awhile!

[*Enter Messenger.*]

Mess... Most mighty sovereign,
On our Eastern coast, the puissant rebels
Have attack'd and battered down Fort Sumter,
And they seem bent on more despr'ate mischief.
'Tis said that Beauregard commands them!
I assure your most Excellent Highness,
The very air is full of rumors.

[*Exit Messenger.*]

Abraham... Some light foot friend
Post to old Nester Scott, instanter.
Simon, thy self, or Catesby, where is he?

Caleb... Catesby? He's among the rebel galleys!

Simon... I prithee, be calm!
'Twill be but an hour's bubble, then all is quiet;
To-morrow will I post a platoon of Wide Awakes,
Who'll Charleston reduce to shreds...yea,
In six hours, by the watch!
Egad!
I'll make short work of these coward rebels!

Gideon... I pray your Highness, leave all to Simon,
He'll punish these recusant subjects!

[*Enter 2d Messenger, in haste.*]

Abraham... How, now, dolt!
What news? Why com'st thou in such haste?

2d Mess... Why, my Lord! The rebels are in arms!
Jeff. Davis is proclaimed vicegerent ruler
Of one half your Highness' realms!
He calls your Highness usurper, openly!
He vows to crown himself in Washington!
His army is a vast, ragged multitude
Of hinds and peasants, nude and merciless!
Old Hickory's death and your success
Hath given them heart and courage to proceed!
All Republicans, Abolitionists and gentlemen
They call false catterpillars, and intend their death!

Abraham... O, graceless Rebels!...
Fire-eating *serfs*...they know not what they do!

Nestor... My gracious Lord,
Retire to Chicago, 'till I a force do raise
To put them down.

Queen Margaret... Ah, were the Little Giant King,
These fiendish Rebels would be soon appeased!

[*Enter another Messenger.*]

3d Mess... Sad news, my Lords!
Stonewall's varlets hath near reached Long Bridge!
The citizens fly and forsake their homes!
The rascally people, thirsting after prey,
Join with the traitors, and they jointly swear
To spoil this city and your loyal court.
Our legions that did yesternight go forth
Into the Bull Run gorge to meet the Rebels,
Hath been repulsed in most disastrous slaughter,
and panic-struck, are flying hither;
And your highness,
Each soldiers wears a look of o'er-exhaustion;
While curses long and loud do rend the air!
All talk of treachery, and most affirm
That Patterson is a knave or fool!

Abraham... Merciful Heavens!
Is it come to this? My very palace gates
By a mob of ragged rebels threatened,
Whom we could beat by ballots, but not by swords!
I'll go the oysters, there's treachery in camp!

Simon...Then linger not, my Lord? Away! take horse!

Abraham...Come, my Queen, Scott and our platform
Will, in this trying hour, succor us.

Q. Mar....My hope is gone, now Douglas is deceased.

Abraham... Farewell, my Lords,
Beware the Kentish rebels. To my palace
Will I retire, and note events.

[*Exeunt omnes.*]

ACT VI.

Scene—*Cabinet Convention.*

Abraham... How now, my Lords,
Have you pondered well the fearful "situation?"
The ill mishaps on Manassas' gory plains
Have wrought my mind to most nervous pitch.
What think you of a change in commander
Of our grand Potomac Army?
There's Achilles,
The chivalrous West Virginia hero,
Who can from Stonewall bring those honors off,
Which alone can rid us of Jeff Davis,
The centrifugal Hector of the South!
What say you to Achilles, the young Napoleon?
Yet, in the trial, much opinion dwells—
For now, our party taste our dear repute,
With their finest palates. They trust to me,
And yet, *they* choose, and only ask my sanction—
Using me as a manikin, merely.
It is supposed,
That he who goes forth to meet the Southern Hector,
Issues from our own well studied choice,
And should disaster follow, we betide us.

Simon... Give pardon to my speech;
Therefore, 'tis meet that Achilles meet not Hector.
Let us, like merchants, show our foulest wares,
And think, perchance, they'll sell, if not
The luster of the better shall exceed,
By showing the baser lot at first!
Consent not that Achilles and Hector meet,
For both our honor and our party interest
Are dogg'd by two strange followers—
I mean the radical and conservative *pressure*.—
Achilles is a chieftain of Democratic stock,
He's valliant, and may win too many laurels!
We must to our party interest have an eye!

Abraham...In that light, I don't exactly see it.

Simon... What glory Achilles wins from Hector,
Were he of our party, we should all share,
But success would make his party insolent,
And we had better parch in Afric's sun,
Than in the pride of Achilles' glory!
No, let us make a lottery,
And by device, let blockhead Ajax draw
The man to fight with Hector. Among *ourselves*,
Give him allowance for the better man,
For that will physic most, the proud Democracy,
Who rail in loud applause, and make them fall
Their crests, that proeder than blue iris bends!
If the dull, brainless Ajax comes safe off,
We'll dress him up in voices! Should he fail,
Yet, go we under our good opinion still,
That we have *better* men. But, hit or miss,

Our plan one good shape of sense assumes--
Ajax employed, plucks down Achilles' plumes!
D. of Y.... My Lord Simon
Hath woven a most ingenious web, which
Might, and then it might not catch
The silly summer flies that buzz around
The purlieus of our royal palace. But I,
More foxey, would wob for gallinippers--
They do b.te and sting.
 No, we must not
Our brave Achilles jump by any noodle;
For should aught of ill betide our arms,
'Twill be to party scheming charged!
 The public is a tiger, which, when by degrees,
Tamed and docillated to one's own will,
Can by silken strings of sophistry be led:
But when fresh from jungles of the native herd,
'Tis no common plaything, and might, anon
Prove dangerous. We must be cautious!
 [*Enter Page.*]
Page... Please your Highness,
I am press'd by a seedy courtier, just arrived,
With pale and livered face, and greasy wardrobe,
To ask him audience with your Lordships.
Shall I announce him?
Abraham... Who is he, and what his purpose?
Page... Please your Highness,
I know him not, and can but from his exterior jib
Describe him.
Simon... Well, well, what looks he like?
Page... And, by the Powers that made me,
I should be puzzled to daguerreotype him,
He's crowned with a slouched hat, *a la Mose*--
Coat and jacket drab as pale charity--
Pants of the same fabric, closely pack'd
Inside his monstrous stogas,
 Such, your Lordship,
Are his quaint externals, which to other eyes,
More vulgar, 'pear as though once were clean,
Tho' now with grease and ink befuddled!
The sheepish looking stranger did flat refuse
To send his card, and I would you caution,
Scan him well, lest some cannibal spy
Shall for supper take your measure.
Abraham (aside.)... [Greely, by thunder!
There's no mistaking that quaint description.
Wonder what the cuss desires of me?
Perhaps some contract, or foreign mission--
Or, to bore me about the duties of my oath,
Or, in the contraband *role* impress me!
Well, a few sugar plums must quiet him.]
Admit the stranger, I know him well.
Page... Your Highness,
I haste to do your bidding.
 [*Aside.*]
[His Highness "knows him well," egad!
He seems familiar with all the greasy fellers!
However, I'll keep a vigil eye on the gold spoons
And silver plate, while that rustic stays.]
 [*Exeunt Page, and enter Gen. Greely.*]
Abraham... Welcome to our palace,
Thou most proficient mental engineer!
Wait, betimes, while I do call the lacquey,
To spunge thy dusty wardrobe.
Gen. Greely... O, trouble not, sweet Abraham,
About my wardrobe, for on July 4th,
One year ago, it was quite renovated.
But, good Abraham, I'm come not, I'll swear,
All the way from York, to shake my dust
Into your royal court. I am come, commission'd
To plead before your august Lordships,
The bleeding cause of contrabands, in general!
I do demand, that ignoring all other acts,
The Confiscation Act you follow, to the letter.
Issue the Proclamation, and "on to Richmond!"
Then, by St. Paul, the rebels soon must yield,
For I have nine hundred thousand warriors
That to arms will spring, the very moment
You sound the Proclamation trump.
D. of Y. (aside.)... [As I have oft prognosticated,
That Greely will yet ruin the House of Abraham.
I would he were ten leagues in Dixie.]
 Well, my honest friend,
It doth me honor to thus greet thee!

I pray thee be thou quite at home.
But, with aught valuable, meddle not -
Touch nothing here, and I'll give the "pass"
To enjoy the liberty of the palace yard!
Adieu, kind General--adieu!
Gen. Greely (aside.)... [Umph! Since these snobs
Are dressed in a little brief authority,
They put on airs, that cost the Bowery Thugs
Quite in the shade. Faith. I'll tickle 'em
With my trusty goose quill.]
 [*Exit Gen. Greely.*]
D. of Y.... Thank God for that good riddance!
 [*Enter Page.*]
Page... May it please your gracious Highness
A delegation in the anti-room doth wait
An audience with your Highness.
Abraham... Admit them not.
These interruptions doth spoil our purpose.
Salmon... Tell them we are not at home to-day.
Page... But, my Lords, they did me press
Most urgent, and besides, they are your allies,
Most potent in this crisis.
Gideon... Speak, rat,
What their wish? Come, make short tongue!
Page: My Lord, I can but say,
They're black as ace o' spades, and only talk
About "Freedom" and His Highness' "policy."
Simon... Ah! I smell the rat
These are our party *proteres*. I vow,
We must not these turn off in grief.
All voices... Admit them! Admit them!
 [*Enter Delegation of Contrabands.*]
Abraham... Welcome, welcome!
Most sable allies in freedom's cause!
D. of Y.... Welcome, thou motive power
Of the conflict, irrepressible.
Gideon... What can we do to serve thee?
1st Contraband... We hab come, Massa Abraham.
In behaf ob de gemmen ob de purest blood,
To enquire 'bout de collyzashuu question.
Abraham... Aye, aye, ye do flatter me,
To thus take notice o' that important point,
Which is the Alpha and Omega of my reign.
 [*Enter Messenger.*]
Simon... Why this interruption, bastard?
Mess... Pardon, your Lordships,
But Achilles; failing of ample reinforcements,
By Ajax, as he would, hath, by vast numbers,
Been quite repulsed, by Hector's Rebel Chiefs,
And hence, to Yorktown is retreating.
 Achilles did chide me,
As I lov'd our country, to fly with speed
That should distance the fleetest stag,
To reach the palace, and beg your Lordships
The send him succor, instantly, or
As he bad me say, all may be lost.
 [*Enter Edwin, Simon having withdrawn.*]
Edwin... Begone, ye lousey interloper,
And tell Achilles to give o'er Richmond—.
That Ajax to guard our royal palace
Hath been directed. Tell Achilles to flee
Or fight, for no succor shall he have from me.
Salmon... Avaunt! Avaunt!
We've more important business now!
Our colored cousins await our pleasure!
 [*Exit Messenger in grief.*]
1st Con... As I war sayin', Massa--
Abraham... O.--aye, I do remember,
Thou wouldst learn my arch device
To make you equals of the famed Aztecs.
2d Con... No, Massa, no,
You wou't 'mong dem alligators send us!
We am told you make dis war on our 'count--
Dat you promise to make us "free" and "equal,"
Just as de Declarashuu 'spresses it.
But, Massa, if you send us off from friends,
Agin our wish and our free inclinashuns,
What 'comes of de "freedom" and de "quality?!"
We ax you to carry out de one great principle,
Dat Massa Greely and Sumner 'splain so much!

Abraham... Ah, most illiterate ignoramuses!
Thou dost ill-comprehend our party teachings.
We by no means assert you free and equal
As ourselves, among our noble selves.
Such admission would most preposterous be.
2d Con...Well, Massa, den what you mean!
Abraham...We mean that you are "free" to emigrate,
And "equal" to my plan of gradual extradition,
If I but give your brethren all free passes,
And my subjects foot the bills, in "freedom's" name,
That's what we mean. We all do know
That you are much inferior to our noble race,
And so long as we all remain together,
The inferior must be slaves.
1st Con... Massa, dem's most 'culiar sent'ments.
You can't dose chiles fool by any such a stuff.
2d Con...We won't go to Quito or Liberia.
3d Con... No, dat we won't.
We'll wid de white folks be free and equal,
Just as you say Massa Jefferson foretold us.
4th Con... If de darkies all dis land do leab,
What will the bobolishioners do for votes?
5th Con... Da can't do widout us,
And, Massa Abraham, we all see you d--d
Afore we go wa to hunt up "freedom"!
Good da, Massa--good da.
[*Exeunt Contrabands.*]
Abraham (to the Duke of York)...I say, good Duke,
This contraband question is a double knot,
That more and more puzzles, as we make effort
To untie it. I'd rather beat the jungle,
And seize the hyena's snarling whelps,
In presence of their exasperated dam,
Than meddle with this contraband wolf.
D. of Y...I see the troubles thicken, and irrepressible
Are becoming.
Edwin... This was the fatal rock,
On which my late master, (or, rather, dupe,)
King James, did split. His affliction
Was of the Locompton type.
Gideon... We too late find it an *ignus fatuus*,
And our party its Frankenstien creator,
Deliver us from the monster of our own creation.
Caleb... And may we 'scape Acteon's fate,
Who by his own dogs was eaten up.
Montgomery... Long have I known
It was a phantom, which, for our classic party
'Twere death to hug, and no less fatal
To disembrace.
[*Enter Page.*]
Page... Please, your Highness,
The Lord Chancellor of the new Exchequer,
Doth urge your instant presence 'fore him.
Monster frauds have been discovered!
He fears that not less than five hundred millions
Hath thro' sundry agents taken wings!--
Parliament is all arage, and Van Wyck
Hath his portfolio filled with proofs!--
The press is loud--sedition stalks abroad?
The people are becoming restive!
Edwin...This sedition must be stopped.
Abraham...But how?
Edwin... Leave that to me.
If your Highness will sign a proclamation
Against "disloyal practices," egnd, I'll warrant
To gag these malcontent editors, who
Because our favorites may appropriate
A few paltry millions, do stir up sedition!
A few exampled victims in Ft. Lafayette
Will affright the rest to silence.
Abraham... I will do anything your Lordship urges,
Tho' Proclamations are not my best holt!
Caleb... Come, let's adjourn,
And con the matter o'er betimes.
[*Exeunt omnes.*]

ACT VII.

SCENE—*The Irrepressible Conflict—Storm in the Cabinet.*
Salmon... Good morrow, your Highness,
May I hope your health's par excellent?
You seldom 'pear in more rosy plight.
Abraham... Alas, your Lordship,
Appearances do oft, e'en the elect, deceive.
My physical, perhaps, wern't never better,
But in spirit am I most sorely troubled:
Yet, for that, good Lord, no matter!
I would enquire the state of our Exchequer.
The Wall St. barometer bodes storms, I fear!
The tempest swiftly comes, We must take in sail,
For by a private telegram it is announced
That our Legal Tenders wont stand the metal test,
And 'tis feared our plethoric batch of Green Backs
May sink to that old Continental standard,
When a solid cord of picture currency
Would hardly purchase one good brandy sling,
Such as I, for a levy, did once to Suckers sell!
Now, what can be done to save our credit?
Salmon... Good Father Abraham
I pray you on that score rest quite at ease,
For my ample "system" will ere long restore
The equilbrium 'twixt mint drops and our rags.
But that's neither here nor there--it's small concern,
Compared with that other matter pressing.
Abraham...What "other matter" mean your Lordship?
Salmon... Why, 'tis that peerless one,
Your counsellors have so often urged,
(Save Montgomery, Caleb and the Duke of York.)
I mean the *Proclamation*. It will at one fell swoop,
Crush the rebels and liberate the contrabands.
'Tis *cheaper* warfare than maintaining armies.
Abraham... No, no, I'll die,
E'er I'll so foul offense commit--
I cannot--will not listen to't--
So long as my spinal nerve holds out.
'Twould let loose a thousand vilest passions,
That breed in savage breasts, and loathing maggots
would prey upon the feted, decomposing stench,
Until a servile rising should in butchery end,
when our jealous neighbors across the sea,
Would seize the first occasion, as it ripened,
And add to rebel strength their own vast power!
And in such event, 'tis clear, we'd lose our throne,
And our contraband rabit i' the bargain.
We'd be like the greedy sow, seeing the moon's disc
Reflected in the well, her corn did drop,
To seize upon the new-made cheese,
And by her greed lost all her supper.

[*Enter Religious Delegation from Chicago.*]
1st Divine... We are come, your Highness,
To present from our great Western Synod,
A petition, urgent--that you will, at once
The Proclamation issue, and thus to Freedom
Lend the bent of your almighty power:
Say, shall we despond, or hope?
Abraham... If thou'lt convince me
That Ethlopes are of more due concernment
Than thirty millions of the Anglo Saxon race,
And that all our treasure, time and blood,
Should on black "extractions" be exhausted,
Then might I listen to your importunities.
But what can I do--of what avail
Would be my proclamation, in those parts
Where I have not the power to send an agent
To collect a shekel of our revenue?
Such a proclamation would do no more good,
Than the "Pope's Bull against the Comet :"
Or Crocket's swear against the earthquake.
[*Exeunt Delegation, in a huff.*]
D. of Y....Bravo! Bravo!
Edwin...I echo bravo, (in a horn.)
Salmon, (aside, to the balance.)...[My Lords, go steady
We must these foibles humor, yet awhile, untill
We can, by strategy, more *pressure* bring!
His Highness and the Duke of York doth fear
Too much the puissant Democracy,
And the conservatives of our own household.
But never mind--I've most cheering n

Of events, which, when ripe, will bring
His Highness down, as Scott did cooney.]
Gideon, (*aside, in reply.*)....Ah, indeed, my Lord,
And to what new *role* do you refer, I pray,
That e'en in hope looks cheering?]
Salmon (*aside--responsive.*)...   [I will explain:--
You must know that our most faithful friends,
The Royal Gov'nors of all New England,
Have convened at Providence, of late—
A plan of *moral coercion* to devise; and
By secret correspondence, am I advised,
That they, with sundry others, at Altoona,
Soon will meet, for more decisive action;
Then, we'll have their ultimatum--*no more troops!*
Unless the proclamation be forthcoming.
Thus you see, His Highness must succumb.]
       Pardon, your highness,
My *tete a tete* with Gideon. 'Tis only
A private affair of honor!
Abraham...   With all my heart, my Lord;
I observed you not.   No inconvenience.
                                        [*Aside.*]
[But I've heard enough to *settle* me
In the firm conviction that foul treachery
Doth in my very court go stalking!
I must probe this matter, and if 'tis thus,
I must yield per force of mad circumstance,
For I'll not abdicate--'twere too much
To yield up power--salary--glory--all.
Barely to show the mettle of my vertebræ,
                                        No, no;
I'll make the most on't, and before the vile traitors
Meet, will I the Proclamation issue,
Tho' it blow the realm to atoms.]
But come, my Lords, the clock's advancing;
'Tis time to sup. Full bellies stimulate good nature.
Page, draw the curtain.
D. of Y...And we the corks will draw.
                                        [*Exeunt omnes.*]

          ACT VIII.

SENE—*Altoona in the foreground.*
          [*Enter twelve Royal Governors.*]
Cardinal Andrew...Welcome to our conclave, noble
     Dukes!
This convocation is most opportune, indeed,
Since the main purpose on't is gained!
Read you not the Proclamation, just o'er the wires?
Egad! His Highness hath been bro't to milk!
Tho' I confess, he's fired 'twixt wind and water!
The Proclamation is as much a vain abortion,
As the choice we made of ruler at the polls!
However, we must *seem* to applaud it,
Or else the radical votes we lose.
Duke of Hampshire...   Thou hast spoken wisely,
Most gracious Cardinal. We must the potion swallow,
And fein convalescence, tho' the fell disease
In time becomes incurable!
Barron de Accident...Ich weis nicht was sie sagen wol-
     len
Hoffe es aber bald auszufinden.
Buckeye Pasha....   Away with all other questions,
And let us serve the notice on His Highness,
That unless Achilles be deposed, at once,
And Ajax raised to favor, no more troops
Shall o'er go forth by our commands.
What say you all?
Bishop Curtin...   To consent
To displacement of the brave Achilles,
Since he hath my Commonwealth defended,
With so much strategy and good omen,
Would most foul ingratitude betray,
And, besides, I know, the rebel Hector
Would glory in the change, since all else
Our Chieftains, Hector feareth not
More than the sportive winds.
Sucker...   Well, since of his removal
The valiant Bishop doth not agree
With the greatest number of us all,
Let us take our satchels and haste to meet
His Highness at the Central Palace,

That we may His Highness congratulate
On the great wisdom of his Proclamation,
And then we may such other measures urge
That will dismiss Achilles, and Ajax favor.
Come, the cars are waiting—All aboard.
          [*Exeunt twelve Royal Governors.*]

          ACT IX.

SCENE.—*In the Green Room.*
[*Enter Abraham, Councillors and Politicians, Nov.*]
Edwin...   Well, your Highness,
How think you the elections are decided? I fear
From the blue complexion of the October fashions,
That we may suffer still greater losses.
I e'en do fear New York deserting.
Salmon...   Poh! Impossible!
Edwin...I Sey-mour than perhaps you think I do,
And I begin to distrust, most seriously,
The policy of our *lettres de cachet*. That, I fear,
Hath played the d——l with our purpose.
The people, instead of being cowed, as 'twas intended,
Have been stung to madness. Look out,
I warn ye, for November gales!
Caleb...   If we are beaten, then the jig is up,
And we must the Dictatorship abandon.
Until the people, in more mellow mood,
Shall off their guard be napping.
Abraham...   Thy prognostications, my Lords.
Remind me of a story, about the jackass
And the kid, which I'll relate—
Edwin...(interrupting.)   O, d——m the stories.
I'm sick of stories, and besides, here comes the Page
With a telegram. Now look out for thunder!
                                        [*Enter Page.*]
Edwin...How, now--any news from York?
Page...   Aye, yes, my Lord, sad news, indeed.
Seymour, the "tory," and all his confederates,
Art chosen by most fearful odds,
And Wadsworth, alas, is *hors du combat!*
Salmon...   Great Moses! Can this be so!
Then I have lost the oysters!
D. of Y...   I knew it aforetime, and thus my wager
     sav'd ;
Your radical measures hath overturn'd our porridge.
As I have oft predicted.
Gideon...Well, Page, what news from other quarters?
Page...   Ah, your Lordships, most doleful.
The Badger State hath topsy-turvy turned,
And the Suckers—right at the very door sill
Of His Higness' hermitage, have "played h—ll,"
While the Wolverines, no more grateful,
Have nearly kicked the beam!
Abraham...   Alas, a fit response
To the bitter cup of my Proclamation.
O, foul conspirators! Thou hast ruined Rome,
Thou hast Cæsar stabbed. *Et tu Edwin!*
Et tu Salmon! O, Tempore! O, Mores!
Bring me no more news to night!
                                        [*Exeunt omnes.*]

          ACT X.

SCENE--*Cabinet Meeting.*
Abraham...   Alas, my Lords,
What an unkind hour is this to me!
For scarcely from delirious slumber did I wake,
On this bright, yet ill-boding morn,
E'er a courier, drunk with dread affright,
Did call me from my couch, to pour
Into my unwilling ears, results, astounding,
Of the Proclamation in Kentucky, where,
As his story runs, the exasperated masses
Do join the rebels by scores and grand divisions !
The Border States are said to be in uproar!
The Contrabands don't "rise" as first you urg'd !
But such as have no power or will to work,
Are pressing on our lines in such vast numbers,
That loyal men do stagger 'neath the weight
That's eating out their substance. I fear,

My Lords, that we've too well succeeded
In uniting the heretofore diverse feuds
That cooled and tempered Southern rage,
And that the loyal North we have divided!

While I did the middle course conserve,
While I did Ajax o'erthrow, and did "modify"
Simon, and brave Hunter, and while I did
Our Simon from my counsel banish,
All things went merry as a marriage bell!
The North was then a unit of power!
She did freely bleed her many millions;
And from her hill sides, plains and valleys,
Came forth her sturdy and brave legions—
Mighty and terrible as the hosts of Xerxes!
In the West—my own proud West—
The car of our triumphs was moving on!
Into our hands fell Henry and Donelson,
By the valor of troops that never quailed—
The prestige of my victorious army was felt
At Shiloh, Pea Ridge and Island Ten,
While Memphis and Mississippi's Queen,
Fell easy preys to my chivalrous legions!
And, no less mark'd were achievements
On our Eastern coast, where to attack,
Was victory, and victory us deserted not,
Until Parliament and Cabinet essayed
To load, and dictate plans beyond their ken,
Or power to execute. Politicians took the field—
Not in person—for they were chivalric bastards!
Instead of trusting to our war chieftains,
They chalk'd campaigns in the caucus room,
And did them execute in the civil forum!
Heroes they made of cornstalks, alas!
To be riven by the first ill-omened blast!
Military science they whistled down the wind,
And mock'd at "spades" and "strategy!"
They've press'd me night and day—"on to Richmond,"
By measures, routes, and geometric curves,
Of which they, themselves, as the unborn babe,
Were ignorant. Cause, they seldom study,
But jump at theories, to reach *effect!*
When our prosperity was at its highest flow,
Did they howl like packs of arrant wolves!
To stop enlistments, and to the Proclamation
Leave the job of crushing treason.
                        Well,
To please the malcontents, I the Bull did issue.
Behold what followed!—the forthwith call
For six hundred thousand victims, new hecatombs
To fill, and mines to blow up more treasure!
And behold disaster on disaster, since,
Without a parallel, excuse, or palliation:
And all to please the whim of party hucksters!
Thrice hath our Grand Army—Potomac's pride!
Been repulsed and flayed by Hector's ragged serfs,
And now I find me in that dread dilemma
Where, to "modify" my new *role*—under pressure chosen,
Would my reputation forever compromise,
And I be styled fool—dastard—nose of wax!
And yet, to perserve, on the chart ill drafted,
Would destroy my country, and dethrone my power.
So much for Buckingham!   [*Aside.*]
[O, fell disasters!—ripe fruits of giving o'er
To clamors of a rabble mob, insatiate.
O, Heaven's vengeance, swift as lightning's bolt,
Resign my Cabinet—make room for Holt!]

[*Faints, and subsides into an easy chair.*]

D. of Y.—   See, His Highness swoons!
His griefs do overcome him. Call the Page,
And summon quick the Knight of Physic.

*Edwin.—*Ho! there, without! Help!
                        [*Enter Citizen.*]

Cit. ..Pray, my Lord, what's the matter;

*Edwin...*O, nothing, save His Highness hath a fit;
That's what's the matter.

Abraham (*recovering*)...Cease for me, your pother,
For, in body am I quite well, indeed!
'Tis my country's cause that hath o'ercome
My agitated spirit...and *thou* the cause!

Edwin (*agitated*)—*Me* the cause!

Abraham...You—aye, and the whole pack of Radicals,
Who hath forc'd me to this unlucky blunder.
                        [*Enter Messenger.*]

Mess...   Your most worshipful Highness,
I am come, by order of your chief... Ambrose,
To 'quaint you of reverses diabolical.
That your Grand Army hath just befel,
At Fredericksburg, on the fatal Rappahannock;
Your faithful legions are badly cut to pieces,
And Ambrose hath across the stream retired,
Shorn of warriors, near fifteen thousand!
As brave as e'er did charge a bayonet!

*Abraham...*What needs Ambrose...succor?

Mess...   Nay, your Highness;
He did chide me, that of troops and ammunition
He had abundance, but, less rash orders
Would better suit his, and the nation's purpose!

Edwin...   That Ambrose is an arrant fool,
To thus cast suspicion on my orders!
I bad him take Fredericksburg at any cost,
And then "on to Richmond," by the shortest cut,
As pre-arranged in our party caucus;
And if he's failed, the blame be on his skirts!

Abraham...   Enough, enough!
My heart doth within me freeze to zero,
And more than ever am I now convinc'd
That party caucus can ne'er take Richmond!
The Proclamation have I uttered...fatal blunder!
And deposed Achilles...thrice fatal error!
                        Alas! I feel like one
Whom the vile intrigues of petty politicians
Have so incensed, that I am reckless
What I do to spite ill-fortune.
                        Alas, alas!
I am so weary of these sad disasters
That on any chance would I set my life
To mend it, or to be rid on't.
So cowards fight when they can fly no longer...
So doves do peck the falcon's piercing talons...
So desp'rate soldiers, hopeless of their lives,
Breathe out invectives 'gainst the officers!
Dreadful is the fate whom despair hath forced
To censure Fate...and pious hope forego!
All hope is lost...welcome any fate!
Save hope deferred, to be destroyed,
My court's dismissed; and to my sad pillow
Will I pour out my silent grief.
                        [*Exeunt omnes.*]

ACT XI.

SCENE...*Senatorial Caucus in the Capitol.*
                [*Enter thirty-one Senators.*]
Fessenden...   Most noble Senators,
We are to this solemn purpose call'd
To take action on the late disaster!
Unless something shall be quickly done,
To rescue our army, from oblivion,
The feast of fatal blunders, we might
As well all at once resign.

Wade...   But what can we do?
Will the noble Sen'tor some "Maine" end state
That we can by this caucus 'complish?

Fes...   We must revolutionize
The Cabinet. Abraham, we cannot stir,
But we must demand a change at once,
Among his effete counsellors.
                At least, the Duke of York
Must walk the plank! So should Edward,
In fact, the more the better, for then,
We all do stand a better chance!

*Trum...*That's what's the matter.

Fes...   I do affirm the Duke of York
To be the cause of our sad reverses.
He is the Jonah of the Cabinet, and then,
He doth denounce the proclamation
As an idle bagatelle.

Sumner...   He must go out, or else no peace
Will Abraham enjoy, Mark that.
I move that we His Highness do address
A firm, yet most decisive protest
Against the further party toleration
Of the imbecile clogs around him.
The motion's carried, and five of our number
Shall bear to Abraham our potent wishes.
Our purpose done, I declare this caucus
Dissolved till further orders.
                        [*Exeunt omnes.*]

SCENE 2D—*Cabinet Meeting.*

[*Enter Committee of five Senators.*]

Abraham... Good morrow, your honors;
What's now agog in Parliament?

Fes... We are come, your Highness,
As select men from last evening's caucus,
To favor your Highness with this Protest.

[*Hands out a paper, which Abraham reads.*]

Abraham... And is this your role?
My Court will understand the purpose:
Those doughty Senators do of me demand
A modification of my Cabinet, faith;
And the Duke of York, most faithful,
At least shall go. What say my Court?

D. of Y... I say, your Highness,
Here's my portfolio...take it back:
I can't be useful unless I'm wholly black.

Salmon... And here's my portfolio, full of checks;
Take it, and I'll run my chance for Senator.

Montgomery... And, your Highness,
I, too am ready for the slaughter.

Edwin... I'll see 'em d...d e'er I
Will yield an Inch. I'd rather die.

Abraham... Take back your folios, all;
We're all upon ill fortune's track,
And together we will sink or swim.
Go back, ye intermeddling solons,
Do your worst, but unless you're the stronger,
I'll stand *this* "pressure" a little longer.

[*Exeunt Committee, exasperated.*]

Edwin... A pretty bold attempt, your Highness
For little boys to *Wade* beyond their depths,
Without bladders 'neath their arms.

[*Enter Halleck.*]

Edwin... Here comes the fatal cause
Of all our most malicious ills.

Halleck... Such epithets address you sir, to me?
I'll not brook such contemptuous slurs.
Sir, you are a coward, and never fought for spurs.

Edwin... Me a coward...then you're a lying whelp,
And dare not resent, without procuring help.

Halleck...(Slaps his face.) Take that, paltroon, my legal tender,
And show how brave you play your own defender.

[*They clinch and have a savage set-to.*]

Abraham... My rabid Lords,
It grieves me sore to see this cruel sport,
Strewing blood and hair about my virtuous court.

D. of Y... Most vicious mastiffs,
I pray you both, preserve your strength;
You'll need it all on ropes, at length.

Chandler... Let them fight.
I admire the pluck they're now begetting;
It so pleaseth me to see blood-letting.
See the claret; good Lord, how Stanton reels,
And Halleck chucks him out...head, neck and heels.

[*Exeunt, actors, drama and all.*]

MORAL.

Sad is the moral...brother shouldn't war with brother,
Nor in the Cabinet sho'd they maul each other.
May God in future forbid such exhibitions,
And rid the country of *such* vile politicians,
Lest they our rights and liberties destroy,
Is the ardent prayer of the Carrier Boy.

INDEX.

A.

Arbitrary Arrests...Beecher on.................................. 236
  G. W. Jones vs. W. H. Seward............................ 237
  inion of Judge Clerke.................................... 237
  Case of Gov. Todd and others............................ 238
  "Liberated from the Bastile".............................. 239
  N. Y. Independent, on................................... 253
  Boston Advertiser, on.................................... 254
  Mr. Seward on ringing the bell........................... 116
  See Republican Confessions............................. 229
  Extracts from Milwaukee Sentinel, on.......... 230-31
  Washington Hunt, on.................................... 236
  Case of Gen, Stone...................................... 236
Arbitrary Power...Doolittle vs. Doolittle..................... 261
  Gen. Banks on Military Usurpations.............. 263-4
  See Declaration of Independence, revised......... 274
  Madison and Lincoln contrasted....................... 35
  Blackstone on, in England............................ 248
  Gen. Banks on... 190
  Ed. Livingston's Speech on Alien Bill................ 223
  Cause and Effect of--Banks on........................ 191
  Lincoln's Claim of--Order 38........................... 192
  Vallandigham's case.............................. 199-217
  Judge Duer on... 221
Atrocious Sentiments...Sen. Wilson on Shooting Copperheads... 240
Abolitionists...Selling Negroes for Cotton................. 263
  On Vallandigham Case................................. 219
  Anti-Slavery Standard on.............................. 219
  N. Y. Post and Tribune on............................. 219
  For Dissolution--Various Extracts on........... 54-63
  Reference to their Votes in Congress................. 90
  Where are They?--Pets of the Administration.. 106
  Republicans Mould Public Opinion for............. 122
Army, the...Adj't Gen. Thomas--Political use of....... 265
  And Politics--Case of Lt. Edgerly................... 267
  Weakened to carry Elections........................... 278
Army Voting...Borrowed from Cæsar and Napoleon.. 276
  To make a French Despot.............................. 276
  Dr. Lieber on... 277
  Tuttle and Vallandigham............................. 277
  Interference in Kentucky Elections.................. 280
Army Transportation...Van Wyck on........................ 318
Army of the Potomac...Too near Washington............ 293
Army Force...Number of men called for.................. 304
Anti-Copperhead Resolutions...How the Soldiers viewed them.. 265
Abolition Despotism...Schemes to Control Elections.. 276
Abolition Conspiracy...In New York,.................. 102-3
  In 1798.. 29
Abolition Roorbacks...To force Elections................. 287
Abolition War...Gov. Stone Admits........................ 161
Abolition...The Object of Negro Soldier Policy.......... 170
  Jefferson on (Mo. question)....................... 45-47
  Object of the War--Sundry Extracts................ 59
  Reference to Votes on, in Congress.................. 90
Abolitionists and Secessionists...Identical -- Blair's Speech... 176-183
Abolitionists and Republicans...All the Same........... 183
Amalgamation...Fred. Douglas on, &c.................. 119
Amnesty...President's Proclamation--N. Y. Round Table on.. 304
Arms...Frauds in purchase of.............................. 312
Andrew, Gov....His "Roads Swarm"--Letter......... 157
  What followed in Massachusetts Legislature... 157
Administration, the...N. Y. Times denounces........... 159
  Other Republican papers Denounce................. 160
  Radical Press "Disloyal" to,.................... 164-168
  N. Y. Times on "heavy load" of..................... 166
  Under Influence of Traitors............................ 166
  Phillips on the Rampage.............................. 172
  C. B. Smith pledges Policy of......................... 174

Atlantic Monthly Article...See Blair's Speech........... 176
Adams, John...In favor of a Monarchy................... 223
  On Arbitrary power.................................... 328
Alien Law...Livingston's Speech on....................... 223
Agitation...Of the Slavery Question...in Rome........ 9
  In France... 12 to 14
  Effects of in French West Indies.............. 13 to 14
  Effects of in British West Indies............. 15 to 18
  By Federals in 1815...................................... 29
  Sam. J. Tilden on, Slavery............................ 45
  Jackson, Clay and Harrison on...................... 48
  Sen. Wilson on.. 92
  Objects of in Congress...Thayer on.................. 123
Aid and Comfort—to the enemy...Blue Lights......... 34
American Flag...Greeley's "Flaunting Lie"............. 59
Ashley, J. M...On Emancipation............................ 91
Addison, H. M...Disunion or Abolition.................. 92
Autocratic Power...Ingersoll for........................... 94
American Anti-Slavery Society...Treason of.......... 101
Anti-Slavery...Wendell Phillips' "basis".............. 105
Altoona Meeting...Boston Courier on................... 115
  Midnight Session of.................................... 116
Adams, J. Q...Offers Petition for Dissolution........... 26
  On the Link of Union................................. 330
American Statesmen...Warnings of...................... 327

B.

Brown, John...His "solution"............................... 185
  His Harper Ferry Raid...Various Extracts, showing Republican endorsement of...Sermon of De Loss Love...Fort Atkinson Standard... La Cross Republican...Sermon of Rev. Mr. Wheelock...Milwaukee Sentinel...Elkhorn Independent...Telegrams...Winsted Herald...J. W. Phillips...Elder Spooner...Natick Resolution...Rockford Meeting...Firing Guns in Albany...Theo. Parker's Postula...Milwaukee Republicans...Rev. S. W. Bassett...More telegrams...Wendell Phillips...Milwaukee Free Democrat...Wisconsin State Journal...Rev. Mr. Staples...Milwaukee Sentinel...R. W. Emerson...Rev. M. P. Kinney...Menasha Conservator...Milwaukee Atlas...New York Tribune...Wood County Reporter...W. F. Yancey...Wisconsin Churches...New York Herald...J. W. Forney...Kansas Herald on Character of Brown........................... 64 to 72
  Seward and Hale toasted by Louisville Journal 64
Booth Case...Chronological history of............. 74 to 77
Blue Lights...Hoisted by Federals........................ 34
Blue Lights and Blue Laws...Early Puritans......... 108
Bingham, J. H....Radical views of........................ 90
Beecher, H. Ward...Constitution the "cause" of the War... 93
  Emancipation object of the war,................. 99, 100
  On God and the Negro................................. 118
  Declares the President the Government......... 121
  On the "Government"................................ 144
  On Vallandigham's case............................... 219
  On Arbitrary Arrests.................................. 253
  Glories in interference with elections.............. 290
Blair, P. M. General...Speech at Rockville.............. 176
  Speaks of Democrats on "gibbets".................. 267
Brougham, Lord...On coercion............................ 144
Burnside, General...Order 38...Spies..................... 192
  Approves of arrests for wearing badges........... 238
  Declares martial law in Kentucky................... 280
Bastile...Victims liberated from........................... 239
Blood-Thirsty Threats...Sen. Wilson in Maine........ 240
  Against copperheads............................... 286-7
Brinsmade, Mrs....Her arrest and remarks on.... 229-234
Bill of Rights...Massachusetts and Virginia............ 244

344 INDEX.

Blackstone, Sir Wm....On habeas corpus 248
Bad Actions...Spring from good beginnings............. 268
Bradford, Gov....Proclamation against military orders 282
Bribery...Money to carry elections........................... 287
   Athenians bribed by Philip of Macedon............. 287
Brough, John...Bullet vs. Ballot 258
Bertram, Col....Threats to hang Democrats............. 289
Breckinridge Leaders...In fat offices......................... 291
Burke...Maxim for "loyal" sneaks............................. 297
Banishing Females...Vicksburg discipline............... 305
Brokerage, Contract...Van Wyck's speech.............. 312
Banks, N. P...."Let the Union slide"......................... 94
   Predicts military government in 1856................. 122
Burlingame...For new bible, for new God, &c........... 94
Bellows, Rev. Dr....For subjugation and extermination.. 94
Balance of Power...Administration under ban of..... 105
Bigotry and Intolerance...Borrowed from the Pilgrims 148
Bayonets...To defy the People...Chicago Tribune.... 113
Book Swindle...By Reform Congress........................ 317

C.

Channing, Rev. Dr....Prophsies on Emancipation..... 18
Cuba and Jamaica...compared 20
Cause of the War...Is slavery the............................. 23
   Cause and effect illustrated................................ 23
   Beecher on the.. 23
   What is the... 26
   Rhett, Toombs, &c...Its date............................... 24
Constitution, the...The three parties in forming....... 24
   Early opposition to.. 25
   A covenant with death, &c................................. 58
   Greeley on suspending....................................... 92
   Thad. Stevens pronounces an absurdity........... 116
   Burnt by Garrison... 118
   Henkle "blows it away"....................................... 118
   Original plan of... 126
   Mr. Martin on, &c... 127-8
   Virginia and New Jersey plan of........................ 130
   Dr. Bellows cares not for.................................... 94
   As Beecher's Sheep skin parchment.................. 100
   The right to suspend claimed............................. 101
   Hale's bill to abolish.. 171
   Violation of...Cowan's speech............................. 182
   Doolittle on violating.. 261
   Violations of...see declaration revised............... 274
Corruptions...John P. Hale on................................... 314
Cameron, Simon...Eulogy on Volunteering............... 294
   Letter to McKinstry.. 321
Conscription...Cost of the.. 294
   Republican testimony on............................... 294-5
   Wickliffe's Amendment to Bill........................... 207
   New York Frauds in.. 284
   See Draft.. 291-296
Connecticut...Democracy of..................................... 300
Columbus, Ohio...Democracy of............................... 303
Compliments...By Stanton to Gov. Seymour............ 303
Cost of the War...Statistical.................................... 304
Clay, Henry...His Prophesy fulfilled.......................... 307
   On South Carolina Compromise..................... 131-2
   On Abolitionists.. 327
   On Missouri Compromise................................... 131
Clay, C. M....Opposed to Union as it Was................. 119
Cummings' Agency...$2,000,000............................. 310
Cattle Contract...Charter of the Cataline........... 310-11
   Brokerage of same... 312
Contracts...Horses--See Van Wyck's Speech........... 312
Correspondence...Between Democrats and Mr. Lincoln 199-217
   Resolutions and Address from Albany............. 199
   Mr. Lincoln's Reply... 200
   The Rejoinder... 204
   From Ohio Democracy--same............................ 209
   President's Reply... 212
   The Rejoinder... 214
   Between Conway and Mason........................ 96, 97
Crittenden, J. J....On Freedom of Speech................ 219
Crittenden Compromise...Object of the War............ 219
   Congress on... 154
   Complete History of..................................... 134-139
   Douglas and Pugh on.. 49
   Vote in Senate on.. 95
Congress...Members of the 38th.............................. 331
   How carried by radicals.................................... 268
   Reform...Mileage steal...................................... 319
   Censures--see Resolution.................................. 322

Civil Power and Courts...Judge Duer on.................. 221
Criticism...Gov. Hunt, on "Government"................... 226
Clerke, Judge...Opinion in Jones vs. Seward........... 227
Constable, Judge...Arrested on the Bench............... 239
"*Copperheads*"...Sen. Wilson on Shooting............... 240
   Abolition Threats--Halleck................................ 266
"*Copperhead*" *Breast Pins*...Arrests for wearing.... 273
Convention...In Kentucky--Broken up by Col. Gilbert 240
Civil Rights...In England...Blackstone, on................ 248
Civil War...Brough's threat of................................... 258
   Rev. O. Duvall prays for..................................... 94
Consistency...of Abolitionism...Vote on the Negro in Wisconsin and Illinois.. 262
Cotton Speculations...Selling Negroes for Cotton.... 263
Chase, S. P....Abolition, object of the War................ 267
   Union not worth fighting for.............................. 151
   An old Abolitionist... 151
   On State Rights... 120
   Petition for Dissolution....................................... 91
Compromise...Chicago Tribune opposed to.............. 95
   Edward Everett on... 143
   See Peace Congress................................... 144, 145
   General remarks on... 145
   See Crittenden resolution................................. 154
   Various efforts at...difficulties of....................... 125
   Of the Constitution.. 125
   Yates and Lansing withdraw from Convention ...Original plan of....................................... 125, 126
   Between Slavery and Navigation................. 128, 129
   Of 1850...the six points of.................................. 132
   Efforts at in 1861...Remarks, &c........................ 133
   Wisconsin Legislature on............................. 140-143
   Missouri Compromise, &c., &c............................ 131
   Douglas on...Peace Congress.............................. 49
   Chicago Tribune...Pugh...Chandler..................... 50
   A. G. Riddle against... 90
   General remarks on... 145
Comparison...America and French Reign of Terror.. 268
Contractors...Do their part in elections................... 280
   Gen. Wilcox on.. 320
Conway, M. D....To Rebel Mason........................ 95, 96
   Rather Defeat than Union, &c........................... 119
Conway, F. A....Treasonable Speech in Congress...96, 97
   Letter to N. Y. Tribune.. 90
   Would not vote another dollar........................... 91
Conway, Rev....Higher standard than Stars and Stripes 89
Conspiracy...Abolition in New York..................... 102-3
   The "Round Head".. 112
   The Fremont...Boston Courier............................ 114
   Soldier voting scheme...................................... 115
   Gov. Ramsey and Chicago Tribune on.............. 115
   The Altoona meeting... 114
   Northern, against the Union.............................. 29
   The Pelham, in 1798... 29
   Of New England, in 1814, &c............................... 32
   The great Northern...Douglas on........................ 53
   Sumner admits encouragement of..................... 64
   Of Wisconsin Republicans............................ 18 to 85
Conspirators...Against President, &c..................... 115
Coercion...Lord Brougham on................................. 144
Congress, Peace...Plan of Adjustment.................... 144
   Franklin's substitute.. 145
   N. Y. Post on tie, in.. 145
   Greeley Against.. 145
Chicago Platform...A Plank from--Lincoln........ 153-175
Conservative Policy...Pledged by C. B. Smith......... 17 *
Confiscation...Senator Cowan on............................ 182
   Doolittle on... 186
Cowan, Senator...See Confiscation......................... 182
Colonization, &c....Senator Doolittle on................... 184
Calhoun's Solution...Doolittle on............................ 185
Cause and Effect...Efforts to Divide the North........ 191
Conquest...Phillips' Barbarian................................. 105
Concessions...Greeley Opposes.............................. 111
Chandler, Z....On Compromise................................. 50
Cause...Of Agitation--Slavery the............................ 90
Cutler, W. P....On the "Cause"................................. 90
Currency, the New...Stand from under................... 325

D.

Dissolution...Radicals and Rebels agree.................. 291
   Republicans Clamor for..................................... 117
   Sen. Wade ready for...................................ce.... 120
   Seward's Justification of................................... 122
   No Terrors for J. P. Hale.................................... 123
   Republicans Stimulate...................................... 146
   Morrill Tariff to Aid.. 146

INDEX. 345

Dissolution...Sumner opens the Ball, 1860 153
  N. Y. Post and Wis. Journal on.......................... 153
  Wis. Journal--"No misfortune"........................ 81
  N. Y Tribune advocates.................................... 86
  Mr. Lincoln advocates, in 1848.......................... 87
  Vallandigham's Union Resolutions voted down 87-8
  Hale, Chase and Seward vote on Petitions for.... 91
  Boston Liberator on Petitions for........................ 92
  Lowell Republicans for..................................... 92
  Boston Free Soilers for..................................... 92
  Erie Free American on..................................... 92
  N. H. Gazette on Petitions for........................... 92
  R. S. Spaulding for... 92
  Abolition Petitions for...................................... 92
  Rev. Mr. Hodges for... 94
  Garrison on Growth of...................................... 93
  Banks "Let the Union Slide"............................. 94
  Oberlin Rescuers.. 103-4
  Phillips labors Nineteen Years for.................... 105
  Greeley for letting Cotton States go................. 111
  Phillips Appeal for.. 111
  J. Q. Adams--Petition for.................................. 26
  Giddings...petition for...................................... 26
  Factions of both sections desire........................ 26
  Know Nothingism to assist................................ 26
  Josiah Quincy proposes in 1811......................... 28
  Hartford convention...New England Conspiracy 28
  Gov. Strong on "board of war"......................... 28
  Spurned by Democrats in 1814........................... 29
  Paving way for...Public debt, &c........................ 45
  Object of forming Republican party.................... 45
  S. J. Tilden on Agitation, for.............................. 45
  Jefferson's prediction, of.............................. 46-7
  F. P. Blair's testimony..................................... 54
  Parson Brownlow on.. 54
  Thurlow Weed and Mr. Seward........................ 54
  Abolitionists in New York in 1859, for............... 55
  Republicans of Massachusetts in 1851 and 1856
    for... 55
  Ben Wade and Garrison................................... 55
  Republicans of Wisconsin................................ 55
  Burlingame...Wilmot...H. Mann........................ 55
  Phillips...Lowel Republicans............................. 55
  Boston Liberator...J. W. Webb.......................... 55
  Hampshire Gazette...Anti-Slavery society........ 55
  Redmond...P. Pillsbury...Stephen Foster...Chas.
    Sumner.. 56-7
  Of Northern growth...Boston Liberator...War
    brought on by North...Testimony of Wendell Phillips...The Kansas imbroglio, part of
    the scheme, &c.. 61
Draft, the...vs. volunteering................................ 291
  In Massachusetts and Rhode Island...A mysterious...Springfield Republican on................. 295
  Results of in Massachusetts and New York...
    Thurlow Weed on sneaks............................. 296
  In time of the Revolution.............................. 296
  Kept up for political purposes......................... 296
  See conscription bill...................................... 267
Democrats...Loyalty and patriotism of................ 297
  Of New York...Iowa...Ohio...Wisconsin...Kentucky....Minnesota...Pennsylvania...Connecticut...Indiana...of Columbus, Ohio...of Madison,
  Wis...The National Democracy...Gov. Seymour's
  Proclamation...His message of 1863...Gov. Perkin's proclamation...H. L. Palmer's views...*et
  tu* Vallandigham...Democrats rejoice at victories...testimony of their opponents...Mr. Seward and Judge Paine on...Stanton compliments
  Seymour... 298-303
  Threatened and punished for voting............. 286..7
  Hated by Republicans...Richmond Examiner
    and Mobile Register on............................. 290..1
  Of 1814 protest against disunion...................... 28
  Of New Jersey, spurn the treason..................... 29
Democratic Vote...In the loyal States................. 305
Defaulter...caught... 320
Debt...The public...cost of the war...is a public, a national blessing...................................... 304
  Our National, &c.. 324
Disgraceful Outrage...At Boscobel..................... 306
Discipline...At Vicksburg................................. 305
Despotism...Seeks semblance of legality...Solicitor
  Whiting misconstrues law.............................. 234
  Have we not a military................................... 263
  Adjutant Thomas punishing soldiers............... 265
  Avowed by Boston Commonwealth................ 268
  A leaf from French History............................. 268
  Message of Gov. Seymour, 1864, on............... 269

Despotism...Signs of approaching..................... 274
  Army voting to aid.................................... 276...
  Case of Lieut. Edgerly,................................. 267
  Capt. Sells punished for voting...................... 286
  Webster on grasp of power............................ 121
  Seward can ring a bell and arrest................... 116
  Confidence parent of...Jefferson...Webster on
    Free Speech.. 37
  Of Conscription...Sen. Harris on..................... 329
Dawes...Speech on Frauds................................. 314
  On Larcenies.. 320
Despotism Refined...A young lady fined for playing
  piano...Burnside arrests for wearing badges... 238
  Wilson on shooting Copperheads...Col. Gilbert
  breaks up Kentucky Convention...Janeaville
  Gazette on unlimited power......................... 240
Despotic Order...Gen. Rollin to Alexandria Gazette... 236
Despotism, petty...Arrests for wearing badges..... 273
Diabolical Sentiments...Halleck to New York meeting 266
  P. M. General Blair at same........................... 267
  Senator Wilson utters................................... 268
Doolittle, Sen...vs. Doolittle...on absolute power...... 261
  Speech on Colonization................................ 184
  Charges U. S. Senate with want of sympathy... 186
  Racine Journal on... 188
  On nullification and habeas corpus................. 85
District of Columbia...Military Governor...investigation suppressed................................ 262
Disloyal Republicans...List of, $500 reward........ 242
Disloyalty...Tables turned on charge of--Disloyalty of
  Radicals--Andrew Johnson on---Mr. Lincoln.. 148, 149
  Opposition to the "government"............. 158-162
  Of Radicals--Various Extracts.................. 164-166
  Testimony of Sen. Browning, &c.................... 165
  Revolutionary Spirit of Republicans................ 86
  And Treason--Various Extracts.................. 90-94
  Of Federals and Whigs.............................. 37-45
  Round Head Conspiracy............................... 112
  Hailing Extermination and Damnation........... 117
  Sumner's Revolutionary Spirit...................... 116
Declaration of Independence--Revised............. 274
Douglas, S. A...To S. S. Hayes, J. Taylor and Memphis Appeal.. 138
  On Cause of the War..................................... 24
  On Compromise.. 49
  On Northern Conspiracy................................ 53
Disunionists...The other class........................... 154
Duer, Judge...On Martial Law........................... 221
Discouraging Enlistments...Boston Liberator..... 90
Davis, Wm. M...Radical views............................ 90
Douglas, Fred...For Dissolution........................ 93
Douvall, Rev. Wm. O...Hopes for Civil War....... 94

E

Emancipation...Effects of, in St. Domingo......... 13,14
  Napoleon's Proclamation of............................. 13
  Agitation for, in England--Sudden--Paley's
    Opinion... 14
  Canning on... 14
  Effects of, in West Indies--In Hayti.................. 15
  Statistical effects compared--Barbarism, results of--Mr. Underhill's Testimony............ 16
  London, Missionary Herald on...Unfavorable to
    Jamaica...Comparisons before and after...
    Plantations abandoned................................ 17
  Abolition prophesies 30 years ago...London
    Times on...Trollop on, &c........................... 18
  Capt. Hamilton's statement...Editor New York
    Post on...Mr. Baird's opinion...Ex-Governor
    Wood's Experience...Kingston, a God-forsaken
    place...American Missionary on...American
    Anti-Slavery Society on...Effect on marriage
    relation... 19
  Loss of labor...Decay of estates...Only to free
    negroes from labor...Mr. Lincoln's testimony
    ...Mr. Underhill in Cuba...Cuba and Jamaica
    statistically compared...statistical comparison
    in the United States................................... 20
  And peonage in Mexico.................................. 21
  Proclamation...New York Tribune on............. 155
  Pope's bull against the comet...New York Tribune, Janesville Gazette, Waukesha Freeman,
    Boston Liberator...................................... 156
  Seward pronounces unconstitutional............. 158
  Lincoln's "greatest folly"............................. 168
  Springfield-Utica letter, on.......................... 168
  Wilberforce and English views on................ 171

Emancipation...Springfield Republican confesses a failure 173
Pledges of Caleb B. Smith 174
Mr. Madison on 174
Lord Dunmore in Revolution 174
Thurlow Weed's prediction...Gradual...Lincoln on...Chicago platform 175
Senator Doolittle on 184
Lincoln vs. Lincoln 262
Beecher on God responsible for 92
Mr. Seward in 1858 122
Beecher, God and the negro 118
J. M. Ashley on 91
Gov. Dennison on sudden 23
Elections...Military interference in Kentucky 281
Interference with in Maryland 282
Frauds in Pennsylvania and Ohio 285-6
Capt. Sells punished...&c 286
Case of Lieut. Edgerly 267
Bribery...use of money in 287
Discharge of disabled Democrats 287
New York Independent boasts of Administration interference in 290
Boston Commonwealth on 208
Anti-copperhead resolutions, &c 205
Electioneering...Expenses saddled on the people 278
Frauds, threats, &c 279
Contractors do their part 280
Burnside's martial law in Kentucky 280
Enlistments...Wilson and Fessenden on stopping 292
Thad. Stevens on ruinous expenses 203
See also 191
Exempts...See draft in Massachusetts, &c 296
Emerson, R. W....Radical extract 92
Extermination and Damnation...Wisconsin Republicans on 117
Executive power...Daniel Webster on 121
Everett, Edward...On compromise 143
Extremes...Political, compared 183
Excuses...By Administration organs for usurpations, &c 229-234
Edgerly, Lieut....Dismissed for voting democratic 267
Equality...Between races...McKenzie 22

F.

Frauds...Electioneering expenses saddled on the people 278
On the elective franchise 279-80
In New York quota 284
In Pennsylvania and Ohio election 285-6
Chapter on...poetical applications 307
Van Wyck's speech on 310-11
In Treasury department, &c 312
Geo. D. Morgan's operations 313
John P. Hale on corruptions 314
Dawes' spech on 314
Record of infamy...Ohio Journal 316
Stealing by Members of Congress...Senator Simmons $50,000...Honest Jack Hale...Middle men in Washington...Horse swindle...In Navy Yard...The book swindle, &c 317
In transports...Grimes committee...Vessel charters...Conclusions 318
Mileage steal...New York frauds 319
Swindle at Cairo...Defaulter caught...Gen. Wilcox on contractors...Larcenies ... Fremont's frauds...Beauties of Republican retrenchment 320
Millions upon millions wasted 320
McKinstry's developments 321
Old Abe, Cameron, and their pets 321
One of the coolest...Congress censures 322
Holy ministers and stolen libraries...Swindling soldiers...Hundreds of millions swindled...Impeachment of Republican officers for 323
Fremont...See frauds ....
The conspiracy...Boston Courier 114
Proclamation...Indianapolis Sentinel on 150
Festus...Paul and the Roman Law 253
Free Speech...Republicans mob Douglas 287
Green Co. (Wis.) mob 287
Abolished...Senator Howe on 273
Jefferson and Webster on 37
Federals, Whigs and Republicans...In juxtaposition 258
French History...A leaf from 208
Forney, On Union Leagues 288
Laws and safeguards, on 101
Proclamation test of loyalty 163

False Reports...To effect elections 287
Fessenden, Senator...On stopping enlistments 292
Also same 191
Free Negroes...Won't work in Africa 13
Character of...Sir M. Lighton...Capt. Hamilton on...Mr. Bigelow's views...Mr. Baird's opinion...Ex-Gov. Wood's experience...Sewell on Kingston...American Missionary Society on ...American Anti-Slavery Society on Licentiousness of...Marriage relations among, &c... 13
Federals...For dissolution in 1798 30
Caricature of the South by...Odious comparisons...Sectional prejudices aroused by...list of leading 31-35
For the government when in power...Federal Gazette, 1798...New York Federals, 1799... Sermon by Rev. Dr. Parish, 1799...Damn the Government in 1814...Rev. Dr. Parish in 1814 37
Various extracts from 39
Fugitive Law...Sumner on nullifying 57-58
Personal liberty bills, &c 158-9
Flaunting Lie...Greeley on the flag 58
Freedom of Speech...Daniel Webster on 218
Crittenden on 219
Frey, James D....Order on habeas corpus 234

G.

Government...Hamilton's strong 24
Is the President the? 100
Beecher on 121
This...Mason's prediction of fate of 130
Giddings, Joshua...Petition for dissolution 26
Choked down in Chicago convention...Reasons why 152
Gerrit Smith...For revolution in Kansas 63
Garrison, Lloyd...Constitution pro-slavery 78
Disunion and Republicanism grow together 93
No Union as it was 99
Nest egg of treason 100
Burns the constitution 118
Opinion of use of Republicans 122
Greeley, Horace...(New York Tribune.)...Advocates secession and peace 86-7
Superstition of the constitution 93
"Better that the Capitol should blaze," &c..... 93
Defiance to government 120
Opposes compromise 145
Advocates secession 145
Abuse of Administration 164
On Halleck and cabbages 167
On servile insurrection 173
On Vallandigham 220
On infallibility of government 274
On "Flaunting Lie" 58
Gilbert, Col....On Kentucky convention 240
Grimes committee...Gross frauds 318

II.

History...Logic and application of 9
Of slavery agitation in Rome, &c 9
A leaf from French 268
Hayti...History of Emancipation in 15
Hamilton, Alex....Strong government 24
Hartford convention...New England Confederacy... Democratic protest 28
A waif from 35
From address to 41
And Wisconsin Republicans compared 85
And conspiracies of '62 compared 113
Helper's...Impending crisis...Extracts from 62
Seward endorses 63
Habeas corpus...For negroes...Milwaukee Sentinel... 79
Senator Doolittle on 85
Act suspending, &c 109-10
Vote on same 110
Solicitor Whiting's "opinion" 234
Magna Charta...Reminisces 242-248
Suspension...General remarks on 245-6
Blackstone on, in England 248
What our fathers thought of it 248
Judge Geo. T. Curtis on 249
Proclamation suspending 254
Vote in Congress...Magna charta 255
Supreme Court of Wisconsin on 256
Hutchings, John...On the "cause" 91

INDEX. 347

Hale, John P...On Petitions for dissolution................ 61
   On dissolution, "let it come"........................... 123
   Honest Jacks...takes a "fee"............................ 316
Hopkins, Erastus...Will "make bullets effective"...... 92
Hodges, Rev. E...For dissolution.......................... 93
Howe, Sen. T. O..."Do in the name of God," &c....... 105
   On free speech... 273
Halleck...And cabbages...Greeley on..................... 107
   On "sneaking traitors"................................... 266
Hunt, Washington...On arbitrary arrests................. 236
Horse contracts...Van Wyck's speech..................... 312
Horse Swindle...A sample.................................. 317
Henry, Patrick...On liberty of the press................. 328

I.

Impending crisis...Helper's................................. 62
Ingersoll, E. C...For autocratic power.................... 94
Intolerance...Superstition and, of radicals.............. 107
Indemnity, Act of...Sedition law No. 2.................. 109
   Vote on politically classified............................ 110
Independent, N. Y...On conspiracy vs. Lincoln........ 112
Imbecility...Of the "government"...Radical proof...164-8
Insurrection, Servile...New York Tribune on........... 173
Illegal Arrests...See Vallandigham's case........199-217
   Mrs. Brinsmade and Mahony case.................229-234
Indictment of Administration...See Declaration Revised.. 274
Interference...By Administration in Kentucky Election... 280
   In Maryland election..................................... 282
   Also see... 290
Iowa...Democracy of, Patriotic............................ 208
Illinois...Democracy of, resolutions, &c................. 299
Indiana...Democracy of, resolutions, &c................ 300
Investigations...See record of infamy................... 316
Infamy...See investigations................................ 316
Irrepressible conflict...Shakesperean...Tragical...... 333

J.

Jamaica...Results of Emancipation in.................... 17
   Public debt of increasing............................... 18
   Condition of free negroes, in.......................... 18
   "Has become a desert!"................................ 19
Jefferson, Thos...On free speech and despotism....... 37
   On the Missouri question............................45-47
   Solution of the negro question........................ 185
   His solemn warning..................................... 327
   On plea of "necessity"................................. 328
Jackson, Andrew...Farewell Address.................327-8
   His spirit of compromise............................... 131
Julian, G. W...On conquered provinces.................. 91
Jacobin clubs...See Round Head conspiracy............ 114
Johnson, Andrew...On abolition treason................. 149
Jones, G. W...vs. W. H. Seward...Judge Clerke....... 237
Juxtaposition...Federals, Whigs and Republicans.... 258

K.

Know-Nothingism...Its object.............................. 26
   Cleveland Herald, Chicago Tribune, Illinois Republicans on...Federal Know Nothingism...
   Gen. Scott's views...Albany Advertiser...Col. Webb...Mayor Clark, on............................... 27
Kansas Imbroglio...Part of the Dissolution Scheme...
   Gerrit Smith, Reeder and Beecher on................ 63
Kidnapping...in New York...by Abolitionists.......... 235
Kentucky...Convention broken up........................ 240
   Burnside's Martial law.................................. 280
   War Eagle on voting "Union" ticket.................. 280
   Democracy of...their loyalty........................... 288

L.

Loyalty...Radical Editors...too good to fight........... 262
   Weed toasts Tilton and Opdyke....................... 296
   and Patriotism of Democrats...Remarks on........ 297
   of Democracy of New York...of Iowa...of Kentucky...of Ohio.. 298
   of Democracy of Wisconsin...of Minnesota...of Pennsylvania...of Illinois and Connecticut....... 299
   of Federals, when in power............................ 37
   See Boston Commonwealth and Liberator......... 115
   of Vallandigham compared with Republicans..... 241
   List of Disloyal Republicans........................... 242
   Judge Curtis on... 249
   Mr. Chase's opinion on................................. 252

Lincoln, President...Concerning negroes................. 20
   Opposes Mexican War................................... 43
   On Right of Secession.................................... 87
   His nest egg of treason.................................. 101
   His Abolition affinities.................................. 106
   "A firstrate second rate man"......................... 111
   New York Independent scores......................... 112
   No Government without consent..................... 122
   His Inaugural...no right to interfere with Slavery.. 143
   Message on same subject............................... 150
   Why nominated...G. W. Dawson on............... 151
   His letter accepting nomination, in juxtaposition with resolution of Chicago Convention... 153
   Emancipation Proclamation...his greatest folly 168
   Springfield-Utica letter................................. 168
   On sudden emancipation............................... 175
   His defense...New York World on................... 222
   Proclamation suspending writ........................ 254
   Lincoln vs. Lincoln...................................... 262
   His modification of Schenck........................... 283
   Proclamation of Amnesty...New York paper on 304
   Letter to Major McKinstry.............................. 321
   His Bull against the Comet............................. 156
Liberty, Personal...Paul and Agrippa.................... 253
   Magna Charta, &c....................................... 244
Leagues, Union...Machinery of............................ 288
   Secret, of New England................................. 32
Lieber, Dr...on Soldiers voting............................ 288
Law..."Positive Defiance" of.............................. 84
   Violations of...of the case............................. 287
Law of Suspected Persons...From Allison's History.. 246
Loyal States...Democratic vote in........................ 305
Larcenies...Dawes on Republican......................... 320
Laman, Marshal...Lincoln's Right Bower................ 321
Liberty of the Press...Patrick Henry on................. 328
   James Madison on....................................... 328
Liberty...overthrow of...............................68, 89
Lovejoy, Owen...Radical views............................. 90
Legal and Personal Rights...Webster on................. 218
Livingston, Edward...Great speech on Alien Bill, 1798.. 225
   Who was he?.. 229

M.

Montesquieu...on Free Speech............................ 330
Mexico...Emancipation and Peonage in................. 21
Mexican War...A. Lincoln and C. B. Smith oppose.... 43
   J. R. Giddings...Warren (O.) Chronicle...Xenia (O.) Torch Light...Lebanon (O.) Star...Cincinnati Gazette...Kennebeck (Me.) Journal...N. H. Statesman...Haverhill Gazette...Boston Sentinel...Boston Atlas...Boston Chronotype ...North American...Baltimore Patriot...Louisville Journal...Nashville Gazette...Mt. Carmel Register and Tom Corwin in opposition..44-5
Massachusetts...Treason of................................ 27
   Sets up for herself in 1814............................. 28
   For kicking Louisiana out the Union................. 29
   Treasonable resolutions in 1814....................... 29
   Various treasonsonable extracts, 1812-14........... 38
   Her treasonable Legislature in 1814.................. 42
   Stealing Negroes, &c..................................... 130
   Gov. Andrew for proclamation..."buts," "ifs," &c...Forced Conscription............................ 157
   Her Bill of Rights... 244
   Draft In... 296
Madison, James, and Lincoln...compared.............. 35
Madison, James...on Freedom............................ 330
   On Emancipation.. 330
   On Liberty of the Press................................. 328
Madison, Wis...Democracy of............................. 300
Mann, Horace...Disunion, Civil War, &c............... 91
Mason, J. M...Rebel...to M. D. Conway................ 96
   Disunion Letter to Jeff. Davis......................... 154
Military Government...Banks predicts, in 1856........ 122
"Modern Improvements"...Gen. Butler for............. 123
Martin, Luther...on Compromises of the Constitution...127 to 129
Mason, Geo...Predicts fate of the Government....... 130
Missouri Compromise...Clay and Jackson on......... 131
Mob Inciters...Weed on................................... 151
Military Necessity...Proclamation predicated on..... 155
Metaphors...Abolitionists and Republicans the same... 183
Manumission...National Intelligencer on.............. 184
Military Arrests...Arbitrary power, Banks on......... 190
   Republican confessions...Remarks on......229 to 234

INDEX.

Military Despotism...Have we not a............ 263
Military Interference...with election in Kentucky...... 251
  In Maryland, &c............................ 283
Martial Law...Judge Duer on............... 221
  Burnside declares in Kentucky........... 250
Monarchy...John Adams for................. 223
Mahoney...His case...Remarks on............229 to 234
Magna Charta...wrung from King John........... 246
  Judge Curtis on.......................... 251
  Vote in Congress on...................... 255
Mobbing Democrats, &c...Chapter on........... 256
  Schenck's order Suppressing Papers..Hascall
    to New York Express....................256-7
  Republicans Mob Douglas...Green County, Wisconsin, Mob......................... 257
  Disgraceful outrage...................... 306
Message...of Gov. Seymour on Rotten Boroughs........ 269
Maryland Election...Gov. Bradford's Proclamation.... 282
Milroy, Gen...on "Home Traitors"............. 288
Mobile Register...Agrees with Radicals............. 291
McClellan, Gen...Denial of troops to............... 293
Minnesota...Democracy of..................... 299
Miscellaneous...See chapter of.................. 303
Morgan, Geo. D...His Agency operations............ 313
Mileage Steal..."Reform" Congress............ 319
Millions...upon Millions wasted.................. 320
McKinstry, Maj...Trial of....................... 321
Mortgaged...We are all...Spaulding on...our National Debt............................... 324
McCulloch...on new Currency.................. 325

N.

Negroes, Free...Won't work in Africa............. 18
  Their character, by Lewis...Testimony of Sir H.
  Light....Capt. Hamilton's statement...Editor
  of N. Y. Post on...Robt. Baird's Opinion...Ex
  Gov. Wood's experience...Sewell on Kingston
  ...American Missionary on...American Anti-
  Slavery Society on...The Marriage Relation
  among, &c................................ 19
Negro, the, and God...Beecher's only hope............. 118
Negro Soldier Policy...Abolition the object, &c........... 170
Negro Rights...Republican consistency...vote in Illinois and Wisconsin.................... 262
Negro Nobility...Illustrations................ 304
Negro Question...Ex-President Filmore on............ 325
Negroes...sold by Abolitionists for Cotton........... 263
Northern Confederacy...N. E. clamors for........... 29
New England...Treason of...Various extracts in proof.. 38
  For the Slave Trade......................120-30
Nullification...Sumner pledges Republican party for... 57
  Of Wisconsin...Chapter on.................73 to 85
  Sumner in favor of........................ 92
  In Ohio...Wolcott on...................... 117
  Personal Liberty bills.................... 188
  The animus admitted....................... 189
Nest Eggs of Treason...By whom laid............100-1
National War Committee...Roundhead conspiracy..... 114
New York Riot...Weed one inciters of............. 151
New York Quota...Frauds in.................... 284
  Compared with other states................ 284
New York...Draft in 8th District............... 206
  Democracy of............................. 298
  Frauds in Quota.......................... 284
Newspapers Suppressed...Schenck and Hascall......256-7
Number of Men...called for by President............. 294
National Democracy...Their position in 1863........... 300
National Debt...a "Blessing," &c.................. 304
Necessity...Jefferson on plea of................ 328
Necessity...Tyrant's Plea...Sen. Trumbull on........... 329

O.

Opposing the Government...Numerous extracts from
  Federal Press, from.....................37 to 43
  By Mr. Lincoln and others during Mexican war   43
  Various similar extracts................43 to 45
Orton, Judge...His letter on precipitating the war....51-2
Oberlin Rescuers...Treasonable extracts..........103-4
Object of the War...Congress...Crit. Res........... 150
  Chase at New York meeting................ 267
Order 38...Real object of..................... 192
  Compared with Alien act..................223-4
Orthodoxy and Heterodoxy...The difference........ 268
Ohio and Iowa...Army vote compared............. 278
Opdyke, Mayor..."Weed on "Sneaks"............. 296
Opposition to Law...The issue in Wisconsin.......... 82

Ohio...Democracy of........................ 298
Outrage, Disgraceful...at Boscobel.............. 306
One Idea...Shaksperian and tragical illustration......... 333

P.

Proclamation...of Napoleon abolishing slavery......... 13
Fremont's...Indianapolis Sentinel on............ 150
Of Emancipation...Remarks...New York Tribune on.................................. 155
Predictions of good to follow................. 156
Of Emancipation...Unconstitutional...How the
  Radicals opposed the "Government" before
  the.....................................155 to 162
See false prophets............................161-2
In a nut shell...a test of Loyalty...Sen. Wilson's
  Address...Remarks on, &c................. 163
Lincoln admits "folly" of...................... 168
Lincoln's Utica-Springfield letter.............. 168
Views of Englishmen on........................ 171
Confessed a failure............................ 173
Lord Dunmore's, during the Revolution........... 174
Laws by, in England........................ 235
Lincoln vs. Lincoln.......................... 262
Thurlow Weed's predictions.................. 175
of Gov. Bradford...Maryland Election.......... 282
By Governors Seymour and Parker............300-1
of Amnesty...N. Y. Round Table on........... 304
Park, Mungo...on free negroes in Africa.......... 18
Parties...The three that formed the Constitution...... 24
Pelham...His conspiracy for a Northern Confederacy 29-30
Pugh, Senator...On compromise................ 42
Post, N. Y. Evening...on Reinforcing Sumter........ 52
Predictions...of speecy dispatch of Rebels......... 53
Phillips, Wendell...Republicans as a sectional party... 56
  On Republicans not a National party......... 91
  His nest egg of treason................... 100
  Don't believe in battles.................. 105
  Labored nineteen years to destroy the Union... 105
  Thanks God for defeat.................... 120
  On the "lickspittle" Administration......... 104
  On the rampage.......................... 104
Phillip of Macedon...How he bribed the Athenians... 287
Paine, Judge...Opinion on Fugitive Law........ 76-7
  His testimony favoring Democrats............ 302
Pillsbury, Parker...Treason of................. 87
  Discourages enlistments................... 148
Peace...Greely advocates with Rebels...Weed replies,
  &c...................................... 87
  Vote in Senate on Crittenden plan........... 95
  Chicago Tribune wouldn't yield an inch....... 95
  Republicans of Wisconsin reject all overtures
    for................................... 303
Peace Congress...Plan of Adjustment............ 144
Pike, F. A..."Tax, fight, and Emancipate"........ 90
Pibs, J. S...Nest egg of Treason............... 101
Partyism...Radicals prefer their principles to fifty Unions..................................... 89
Puritans...Chapter from the.................. 108
Protestants...Persecute the Quakers............ 103
Prophesies...Of Eli Thayer, fulfilled.......... 123
  Of Geo. Mason...fate of the Government...1787 130
  Of results, by Democrats................. 160
Platform, Chicago...Extract or plank from, &c..... 153
Patriotism...Money the foundation of, in Mass....... 157-8
  Greely on "grave doubts".................. 158
Policy of the War...Republican papers on........ 159-60
  Wisconsin Journal on..................... 164
Prophets, false...Wendell Phillips, N. Y. Speech...National Intelligencer, on &c.................161-2
Personal Liberty Acts...In the Northern States...... 188
Personal and Legal Rights...Daniel Webster on..... 218
  See Livingston's speech on the Alien Bill...... 223
Prisons...Opening of the doors of.............. 235
  Cincinnati Prison full.................... 240
Policy, Negro Soldier...Abolition the object....... 170
Provost Marshal...Powers of...Journal of Commerce
  on..................................... 239
Politics and the War...Col Gilbert breaks up a Convention................................ 240
Political use of the draft.................... 296
Discharge of Democratic disabled soldier...... 257
Threats of the Radicals...Boston Commonwealth
  endorses usurpations, &c................. 289
The Draft as a means....................... 296
Personal Liberty...Lord Campbell on........... 243
Of the Roman Law.......................... 253
Paul and the Apostles...On Personal Liberty........ 253

INDEX.   349

Practice vs. Preaching...Republican editors too good to fight.. 262
Platform...A flexible.. 273
Purse and Sword...Patrick Henry and Clay on......... 273
Proscription...Of Democrats...various proofs........... 279
Positive Defiance to Law...Wisconsin Radicals......... 64
Patriotism and Loyalty...Of Democrats............... 297-8
Pennsylvania...Democracy of................................... 299
Parker, Gov,...His Patriotic Proclamation.............. 301
Palmer, Hon. H. L....Patriotic speech of................ 301
Public Debt...Cost of the war, &c........................... 304
Plundering and Frauds...See chapter on................ 307
   See roll of thieves... 326
Policy of Administration...Sen. Crittenden on......... 329

Q.

Quakers...Whipped and branded.............................. 108
Quota...Greely's grave doubts.................................. 158
   Frauds in New York.. 284
   Compared with other States................................ 285

R.

Rome...Agitation of slavery in................................... 9
Rebellion...The four...Shay's...of 1832...the great Abolition...of 1861... 25
   Will the, Succeed?... 305
Revolution...Rebellion in Wisconsin...the four Rebellions... 73
   Complete chronological history of the Booth rebellion... 74-77
   U. S. Supreme Court on...Judge Paine............ 76-7
   Wisconsin Republicans...the Rescue fund...revolutionary resolves, &c.................................. 77
   Opposition to law a test...State Journal...Lloyd Garrison's opinion on constitutionality of the Fugitive Law... 78
   Habeas Corpus for negroes...opposition to Government a test.. 79
   Evidence of the conspiracy...Various extracts ...Judge Smith...T. O. Howe...the 7 Points..."Dissolution no Misfortune"........................ 61
   Elkhorn Independent...Republicans of Racine ...Judge Paine elected to oppose law...Gov't defied.. 82
   Republicans quote Southern Nullifiers...Gov'r Randall recommends resistance...Legislature responds... 83
   Legislature "positively defies" the government ...Votes down proposition to abide by the laws and judicial decisions...................................... 84
   Sen. Doolittle on Law and Habeas Corpus... Wis. Republicans and Hartford Conventionists compared...South Carolina quotes Judge Smith... 85
   In Kansas...Garrit Smith and others...Giddings for.. 63
   Redpath for, in Kansas...Greely on Nebraska Bill... 93
   Rev.W. O. Duvall for..Rev. Dr. Bellows for subjugation, &c.. 94
   E. C. Ingersoll for autocratic power................ 94
   Spirit of...Oberlin rescuers............................ 103-4
   Programme of...St. Louis Anzieger................ 114
   Conspirators against President........................ 115
   Spirit of taught by Chas. Sumner................... 116
   The Round Head Conspiracy........................... 112
   Startling Developments................................... 113
   C. M. Clay would hang Democrats................. 121
   Carl Schurz for.. 122
   Doolittle charges his party with...................... 261
   The Rotten Borough System........................... 269
   Threats of the Radicals.............................. 288-9
Republican party...Phillips declares Sectional....... 56
   List of Disloyal ones....................................... 242
   Thieves and Plunderers................................... 326
   Sectional..."national" struck out..................... 122
   Preaching vs. Practice.................................... 261
   Lincoln vs. Lincoln...Nigger vs. Nigger........... 262
Revolutionize the Government...Wis. Republicans..... 56
Republicans, Whigs and Federals...Linked together.. 86
   In juxtaposition... 258
Rebels...Greely pledged to aid................................. 90
   And rioters...Greely's Evangelists................ 103-4
   Their love for the Radicals........................... 290-1
   Mobile Register and Richmond Ex. agree with Radicals... 291

Riddle, A. G....No compromise................................. 90
Rice, John H....Radical views................................. 91
Riots...In New York...Abolition conspiracy........ 102-3
   Weed on, inciters.. 151
Ramsay, Gov....on "Legalized Treason".................. 115
Restoration...Boston Commonwealth declares a crime 117
Reconstruction...N. Y. Tribune, no wish for............ 118
   Ben Butler for "modern improvements"........... 123
   N. Y. Tribune and Abolition journals on......... 161
   P. M. Gen. Blair at Rockville............................. 176
Reign of Terror...French mode of Punishment........ 199
   Law of suspected persons................................. 246
Roman Law...Personal liberty...Paul and his Persecutors.. 253
Rotten Boroughs...Gov. Seymour on........................ 269
Roorbacks...Of Abolitionists, for effect.................. 287
Rhode Island...Draft in... 296
Record of Infamy...Ohio Journal on frauds............ 316
Rascality...Expositions of Grimes' Committee........ 318
Retrenchment, &c....Mileage steal........................... 319
   Dawes on Republican...................................... 320
Rights of the States...President Harrison on........... 330

S.

Slavery...Agitation in Rome...Its consequences, &c..... 9
   Effects of agitation...Remote periods of its existence...Bible references...No. of in time of Claudius...Roman law concerning...Agitation of by Gracchus, &c... 10
   Agitation of by Gracchus and others...Agitation, cause of downfall of Rome...Agitation in France...Destroyed Greece, &c...Statement of President Harrison...................................... 11
   Agitation in Constituent Assembly................... 12
   Effect of Agitation in St. Domingo...Various proofs from Allison's History........................... 13
   Agitation of, in England................................... 14
   Effect of Emancipation in West Indies............. 15
   Various statistical facts, extracts, &c........... 19, 20
   No defense of...General conclusions............ 22-3
   Is it the cause of the War?............................... 23
   Hartford Convention agitators......................... 29
   A pretext for dissolution in 1798..................... 30
   Tilden on the cause of the War........................ 45
   Gen. Jackson on agitation of...Clay, &c.......... 49
   New England for slave trade......................... 129
   Lincoln's Inaugural...No right to interfere with.. 149
   Message on same subject................................ 150
St. Domingo...Effect of slavery agitation in...... 12-14
   Statistical...Effects of Emancipation in........... 14
Scott, Gen. Winfield...On Know Nothingism............ 27
Strong, Gov....Of Mass., "Board of War"................ 28
Sectional Prejudices...Aroused by Federals...by Mil. Sentinel... 31
   Massachusetts arouses.................................... 35
   South not worth a copper................................ 118
Sectional Parties...Washington warns against........ 48
   Republicans, declared to be............................. 56
Sectional Agitation...Jackson, Harrison and Clay on.. 48
Sumter, Ft....Reinforcing...N. Y. Times, Tribune, Charleston Mercury, and Judge Orton on...
   Who begun the fight?..................................... 51
Sumner, Chas....For nullifying law........................ 57
   And again... 92
   Revolutionary spirit of................................... 116
   Opens ball of revolution in 1860...N. Y. Post and Wis. Journal on..................................... 153
   Toasted in Blair's speech at Rockville............. 178
Sedition Law...Objects and purposes of................... 36
   No. 2...(Indemnity Act.)................................ 109
Shanks, J. P. S....Radical views of........................ 91
Stevens, Thad....Set negroes to shooting their masters 91
   Declares Constitution an absurdity................ 116
   "Union as it was, God forbid"....................... 151
   No Union as it was.. 94
   On enormous expenses................................... 293
Seward, W. H....Vote on petition for dissolution...... 91
   Can arrest by ringing bell.............................. 116
   Declares Proclamation unconstitutional.......... 158
   Geo. W. Jones vs. Judge Clerke..................... 237
   Ask no question who shall govern us.............. 266
   His testimony for the Democracy................... 302
   On free speech... 328
   On emancipation and violence in 1858—his "last stage of conflict"—his justification for disunion... 122

Sedgwick, C. F....Irrepressible................................. 91
Strong Government...Federals for, sedition law, &c....35-6
Spaulding, Rufus P....For dissolution...................... 92
Spinner, Francis E....Nest egg of treason................ 101
Separation...Phillips would accept........................... 105
Superstition and Intolerance...Remarks on, &c......... 107
Soldiers Voting...See conspiracy.............................. 115
    Dr. Lieber on... 288
State Rights...S. P. Chase on................................. 120
Secession...Senator Wade for — Southern responses
    thereto.. 120
    Milwaukee *Sentinel* admits would not have oc-
    curred under Democratic success.................... 143
    Greeley advocates right of................................ 145
Slave Trade...New England for................................. 122
Schurz, Carl...For Revolution.................................. 122
    Telegram to "strengthen our side"..................... 143
"*Scatteration Policy*"...Milwaukee *Sentinel*, Pitts-
    burg *Chronicle*, &c., on.............................. 166-7
Servile Insurrection...Greeley on............................. 173
Smith, Caleb B....Pledges conservative policy............ 174
State Suicide...P. M. G. Blair's speech on............... 176
    Robt. J. Walker on... 329
Solutions of the Slavery Question...Jefferson's, Cal-
    houn's, and John Brown's, &c....................... 185
Spies...Sent out by Burnside................................... 192
Silence...A crime by Lincoln's code........................... 222
Star Chamber...Laws by Proclamation in England..... 235
Somers, Lord...See Star Chamber.............................. 235
Stone, Gen...His arbitrary arrest............................... 236
Suppressing Newspapers...Schenck's order—Hascall
    to New York *Express*.................................. 256-7
Selling Negroes...For cotton..................................... 263
Sallust...His motto, &c.. 269
Seymour, Gov. Horatio...On Rotten Boroughs........... 269
    Patriotic Proclamation...................................... 300
    Complimented by Stanton................................ 303
    His patriotic letter to meeting in Orange Co..... 320
Stanton, E. M....Boasts of electing Curtin................. 279
    Compliments Gov. Seymour............................. 303
Sells, Capt....Punished for voting Democratic ticket... 286
"*Sneaks*"...Thurlow Weed on..................................... 296
Shoddy and Fraud...See chapter on.......................... 307
Stealing...General mania for..................................... 311
    Holy ministers and Southern libraries................ 320
Swindling...Horse contracts...book swindle................ 317
    At Cairo...Post Master..................................... 320
    The soldiers.. 322
    Hundreds of millions....................................... 323
Statesmen...Solemn warnings of............................... 327

T.

Treason...Of the Federal clergy...Various extracts
    from, and Federal press, &c......................... 27-8
    Also later.. 33 to 43
    Various extracts in proof of......................... 54 to 57
    Abolitionism...Pamphlet Circular....................... 60
    Gerrit Smith and Reeder...Kansas..................... 63
    Various extracts relating to John Brown...64 to 72
    Racine Republicans, &c..................................... 82
    New York Tribune...Sundry extracts............... 86-7
    Rev. Conway on "higher standard"................... 89
    Boston Liberator discouraging enlistments......... 90
    Of various prominent Republicans.............. 90 to 94
    M. D. Conway to Mason (Rebel)..................... 95-6
    Speech of F. A. Conway in Congress.............. 96-7
    His letter to New York Tribune..................... 98-9
    Nest eggs of.. 100-1
    Oberlin Rescuers, &c................................... 103-4
    Chicago Tribune...Union as it *ought to be*...Bay-
    onets to defy the people................................ 113
    Garrison burns the Constitution....................... 118
    Phillips thanks God for defeat...N. Y. Tribune
    defies General Government............................ 120
    Chicago Tribune...Rather defeat than victory
    under McClellan.. 154
Terrorism...under Federals, 1814................................ 33
    Various proofs of... 34
Tyrants...Their first effort to seize power................ 121
Thayer, Eli...objects and consequences of agitation . 123
Tariff, Morrill...To stimulate Secession...N. Y. Times
    and Cincinnati Commercial on....................... 146
    N. Y. World and London Times on................ 147
    effects of a high tariff.................................... 306
Tod, Gov...Before Judge Van Trump........................ 238
Thomas, Adjutant General...Forces soldiers to hur-
    ra for Negro policy.. 265

Traitors, Home...Gen. Milroy on.............................. 288
Threats, Diabolical...Army Resolutions.................... 265
    Gen. Halleck on "sneaking traitors"................. 266
    Senator Wilson... 268
    To control elections, &c................................ 256-7
    John Brough...Bullet vs. Ballot...of Army Poli-
    ticians... 289
Tuttle, Gen...Army vote for, compared with that for
    Vallandigham... 277-8
Troops...No. called for.. 294
Tilton, Theo...Weed on sneaking.............................. 296
Testimony...of Republicans of Democratic loyalty..... 301
    Mr. Seward and Judge Paine.......................... 302
Taxes...Frauds, plundering...Chapter on.................. 307
Treasury, U. S...Van Wyck on frauds in................. 312
Thieves...Republican, and plunderers...N. Y. Tribune
    on.. 326
Trumbull, Sen...on Tyrant's plea............................. 329

U.

United States...Free and Slave...Statistics compared...20-1
Underhill...A British Abolitionist's opinion............16, 20
Union, the..."Nothing but a sentiment to lacquer 4th
    of July Orations".. 118
    No, with slave holders....................................... 60
    Vallandigham's resolutions voted down............... 87
    Abolition purpose to destroy........................... 124
    Mr. Chase...Not worth fighting for................... 181
    Do Radicals desire to preserve?....................... 293
Union as it was...Milwaukee *Sentinel* sneers at........ 32
    Thad. Stevens opposed to.................................. 94
    Garrison on "Bomba," &c.................................. 99
    Chicago Tribune...Old Abe on......................... 111
    "As it *ought to be*"....................................... 113
    Thad. Stevens...not with his consent................ 117
    Boston Commonwealth on...Bingham don't want 118
    "Hated by every Patriot"...C. M. Clay, better
    recognize Confederacy than have...M. D. Con-
    way against the.. 119
    "Spot it," says C. M. Clay............................. 122
    Thad. Stevens..."God forbid".......................... 151
    Chicago Tribune on... 165
Usurpation of Power...Judge Duer on....................... 261
    See Ed. Livingston's speech on the Alien Bill,
    1798.. 223
    Mrs. Brinsmade and Mahony's case.............. 229-234
    See vote in Congress...................................... 255
    Also vote on inquiry as to military Governor of
    Dist of Col.. 262
    To carry elections...Endorsed and justified,
    though admitted... 289
Unlimited Power...Janesville *Gazette* for................ 240
Union Leagues...Machinery of...Sentiments of in Cin. 288

V.

Victory of our Arms...Unbecoming a moral people
    to rejoice over... 29
Vallandigham...His Union resolutions voted down...... 87
    For law, Constitution, &c................................ 118
    Case of...Order 38... 192
    Charge and specifications................................ 193
    Trial of...Testimony.................................... 193-198
    Protest...Finding and sentence...Gen'l remarks
    on.. 198
    Albany resolutions and letter to Lincoln.......... 199
    See correspondence relative to.................... 199-217
    National Intelligencer on the law of the case... 217
    Mr. Crittendon on... 219
    Certain Abolition papers on....................... 219-220
    N. Y, World on Lincoln's defense................... 222
    See Livingston's speech on Alien Bill, 1798...... 223
    His acts compared with Republicans............... 241
    Army vote for him compared with that for Gen.
    Tuttle.. 277-8
    His letter to N. Y. Times...Views in Congress.. 301
Voting...In the Army...The Conspiracy..................... 115
    Capt. Sells punished for voting Democratic...... 286
    Dr. Lieber on soldier voting............................ 288
    Democratic vote in loyal States....................... 305
Volunteering...How the Proclamation aided in Massa-
    chusetts.. 157
    Fessenden and Wilson on............................... 191
    A success.. 292
    Cameron's Eulogy on..................................... 294
Vigorous Prosecution of the War...Beecher on...... 165-6
Van Trump, Judge...On case of Todd and others..... 238

Villainy...Defense of by Boston Commonwealth........ 268
Vicksburg...Discipline...Banishing females................ 305
Van Wyck...His testimony on Frauds.................... 313
Vessel Charter...Funds in.................................... 318

W.

War, the...Is slavery the cause of the...Beecher on... 23
  Douglas on the cause...A. H. Stevens on...Rebel Iverson on...Lincoln's election no cause...
  Benjamin and Toombs on cause...Dates back of Sumter 24
  Object of the...Col. Stone admits abolition war...M. B. Lowry on...Other extracts...Abolition the object... 50
  Who precipitated...Judge Orton's letter...........51-2
  National committee on...See Round Head conspiracy.. 114
  Congress declares object of...Crittenden resolution 150
  Vallandigham would vote to support................ 301
  Cost of the... 304
War with Mexico...Opposition to...Various extracts..43-45
War, Civil...Rev. W. O. Duvall prays for.............. 94
War Policy...Republican papers on..................150-60
War Power...Within the constitution...Doolittle on.. 261
Washington...From his Farewell Address................ 48
  See also 327
Wilmot, David...Blasphemous sentiments................ 91
Webb, Jas. Watson...On "Fire and Sword"............... 92

Webster, Daniel...On liberty and despotism.............. 37
  On grasp of executive power...................... 121
  On personal and legal rights..................... 218
  On executive power................................. 327
  From his great oration............................. 328
Wisconsin...Nullification...Chapter on 70
  Democracy of...Their loyalty, &c................. 299
  Republicans of, reject compromise................ 303
    do on compromise..................140-142
Weed, Thurlow...On Greeley............................... 87
  Predictions on the proclamation................... 175
  On "sneaks"... 296
Wade, Senator...No peace with slavery..............91-2
  No Union between North and South................ 93
  Pledges Republican party to dissolution......... 120
Wilson, Senator...On agitation........................... 92
  On proclamation..................................... 163
  On stopping enlistments........................... 191
  On shooting copperheads........................... 240
  Diabolical sentiments of........................... 208
Wilberforce...On Emancipation Proclamation............ 171
Whiting, Solicitor..."Opinion" on habeas corpus suspension... 234
Whigs, Federals and Republicans...In juxtaposition.. 258
Warnings, Solemn...Of great statesmen................. 327
Walker, Robt. J....On State suicide.................... 320

Y.

Yancey, W. L....Disunion letter to Slaughter.......... 154

www.ingramcontent.com/pod-product-compliance
Lightning Source LLC
Chambersburg PA
CBHW020246240426
43672CB00006B/654